LEADERS AND BATTLES

Cannon-balls may aid the truth,
 But thought's a weapon stronger;
We'll win our battles by its aid;—
 Wait a little longer.

—Charles Mackay

Daniel Morgan, portrait by Charles Willson Peale

LEADERS
AND
BATTLES
The Art of
Military Leadership

W. J. WOOD

PRESIDIO

For Barbara

Published by Presidio Press
31 Pamaron Way, Novato CA 94949

Distrubted in Great Britain by
Greenhill Books
Park House, 1 Russell Gardens
London NW11 9NN

Library of Congress Cataloging in Publication Data

Wood, W. J. (William J.), 1917–
    Leaders and battles.

    Bibliography: p.
    Includes index.
    1. Leadership—Addresses, essays, lectures.   2. Military
history—Addresses, essays, lectures.   I. Title.
U210.W66   1984   355.3'3041   84-6905
ISBN 0-89141-185-2

Printed in the United States of America

Contents

Introduction

HAVE YOU EVER read an account of a battle and wondered why the author seemed so incisive and the leaders so bumbling? I have, many times, and have found that it doesn't require military genius to find the answer. It takes simply an awareness that the indoor sport of Monday-morning quarterbacking can be played outdoors to allow the author to occupy what could be called an omniscient observation post. From his cozy O.P. the writer is able to see all and know all. Then, you may ask, what about the leaders who are under scrutiny? In fairness, they could not have seen everything, let alone have known everything, so why did they act as they did?

There are no pat answers to the question. Yet the reader is entitled to a clear answer, and that is why this book was written. The idea of a book which would show the general reader that leadership in battle is a practical art had been gnawing at my mind for years. Only recently has the idea been propelled into action by two persuasive prime movers. The first stimulus was James Fallows' illuminating book, *National Defense*,[1] particularly the passages pointing out the Army's growing need for team leaders of men who live, train, and fight as combat units. There is neither need nor space here to go into the details of requirements that Fallows treats so lucidly. It is sufficient to note that Fallows concludes his insights by suggesting "in broad terms, the efforts that should be made to impose more constructive patterns on national

1

defense." The recommendation that heads his list of proposed efforts: "To restore the military spirit."[2]

The second prime mover, a close ally of the first, was the growing awareness that a new Army is beginning to emerge from the troubles that plagued it during the 1970's, such as too many school dropouts, too few re-enlistments, the departure of officers and non-commissioned officers with essential skills, and rapidly deteriorating weapons and equipment. The new Army's emergence—really a rebirth—has been described in an article by Robert Dudney:

> The old battlefield doctrine of depending on massive firepower alone to crush foes is being scrapped in favor of a blend of maneuver, deception, and speed. The goal: Disorient an enemy that may be larger and more heavily armed. Known as "AirLand Battle", the concept emphasizes small, stripped-down units that can move swiftly. Battlefield commanders will have a rare degree of freedom to exploit enemy weaknesses, and their troops will be trained to fight for long periods without rest [and the Army Chief of Staff adds] . . . It's an awful lot for any organization to digest. It's going to take some of the greatest leadership we've ever had to get through this period.[3]

The aim of this book is to aid in restoring the military spirit by setting itself three goals. The first is to show Americans that battles can be won by the minds of leaders, those who are skilled in the art of leadership. The second is to demonstrate that the art of leadership is embodied in the man, not in some set of abstractions. The third is to establish that the art must be based on certain attributes which are found in leaders who have proved themselves in battle. When this book has attained those goals it can provide something else of value: It should point the way toward correcting the neglect of military history by showing how to sort out and use *real lessons* from the past.

Since this book is intended for the general reader, it should demonstrate that recognition of the art of leadership in battle represents a quantum stride toward appreciating the contribution that this art can make to the military spirit and hence to the national defense.

What then is meant by an *art* of leadership? Certainly the leader in combat is not exercising a set of aesthetic principles. Clearly his art is a practical one, a means of applying ideas that govern his craft. We are, therefore, concerned here with *an exceptional skill in conducting a human activity.*[4] Accordingly, my sights are set on examining the personal attributes of leaders whose thoughts and actions during critical battles can be deduced from the record.

When one's attention is fixed on such an examination, it is readily apparent that to include a discussion of war as a human institution would be irrelevant. Entanglement in an issue of morality would serve no purpose here and can be avoided by keeping a realistic eye on the book's aim. I have sought to do that by acknowledging the conclusions of two authorities whose backgrounds are as different as their views on the history of war are in agreement. The first, Gen. J. F. C. Fuller, the foremost twentieth century writer on the history and conduct of warfare, wrote: "Whether war is a necessary factor in the evolution of mankind may be disputed, but a fact which cannot be questioned is that, from the earliest records of man to the present age, war has been his dominant preoccupation. There has never been a period in human history altogether free from war, and seldom one or more of a generation which has not witnessed a major conflict: great wars flow and ebb almost as regularly as the tides."[5] The other source, Will and Ariel Durant, two humanists reviewing the lessons of history in the epilogue of their life work, *The Story of Civilization* (1968), wrote: "War is one of the constants of history, and has not diminished with civilization or democracy. In the last 3,421 years of recorded history only 268 have seen no war."[6]

When one descends from the mountain top view of war—from the omniscient observation post—one may scramble down the slopes toward the sound of battle, but not into battle—not yet. First, one should fix a perspective, and that means gaining the ability to look into the minds and natures of men who have led in battle. For we are going to see battle through *their* eyes and thoughts, to see how they think, act or react—without depending on hackneyed narratives or analyses.

Before we look into those minds and hearts we must recognize the forces that oppose and test the best qualities of the leader. These forces must be understood in order to appreciate their terrifying potential. I call them the Dynamics of Battle. After scanning more than 1,500 battles, from the earliest times (Megiddo, 1469 B.C.) to the present (don't we always have one going on somewhere "at present"?), I have observed six dynamics appearing with regularity and consistency.

The first—*danger*—should emerge as a surprise to no one.

It is scarcely necessary to tell anyone that the battlefield is a dangerous place. But in the context of the art of leadership, I do not refer to the personal, physical dangers that threaten the soldier, nor do I have in mind the dangers to a leader's person. What is under consideration throughout the battle scenes is a danger to the leader's command or a major part of it. As an example take the threat of encirclement, or an unexpected attack against a flank or the rear, or units taken by surprise and in danger of being overrun.

Chance, the second dynamic, is one that can upset the best-planned operation or present a leader with an unanticipated opportunity to strike his enemy a decisive blow. Clausewitz, the soldier-scholar-philosopher, tells us that "War is the province of chance . . . it increases the uncertainty of every circumstance, and deranges the course of events."[7] Chance should not be confused with luck in this context, for that will be considered later.

Exertion is the third force operating against the plans of the commander. It may affect the troops and the leader himself. It may run a gamut from the simple stress of climbing a hill under fire to the limits of human suffering such as the combined horrors of extreme thirst and Saracen arrow barrages at night which were suffered by the Crusaders at Hattin at the end of the Second Crusade.

Uncertainty may be defined as a lack of knowledge essential to the accomplishment of a mission. It can be a dearth of combat intelligence regarding a leader's units or those of his enemy. Uncertainty seems to infiltrate even operations that have been going according to plan. This demon is always lurking just behind the commander's shoulder, but is never visible when he looks around.

I have called the fifth dynamic *apprehension*, and find a dictionary definition fitting: "anticipation of adversity, dread or fear of coming evil."[8] A leader can himself feel apprehensive, but he must always be on guard against apprehension among his troops. It may further be regarded as the child of uncertainty and the father of fear; left to grow unchecked it may even become the grandsire of panic.

I have left the sixth dynamic, *frustration*, for last, because it is the hardest to portray to minds that have never experienced war. It was Clausewitz who first defined it and his definition remains the classic reference. He labelled it "friction", but I have elected to call it *frustration* because that term seems to mean more to the American reader. Terminology aside, here is the gist of what Clausewitz said in *On War*: "Everything is very simple in War, but the simplest thing is difficult. These difficulties accumulate and produce a friction which no man can imagine exactly who has not seen war. . . . This is one of the great chasms which separate conception from execution."[9]

Clausewitz goes on to use an analogy from civil life which concerns a traveler who, at the end of a trying day, finds his travel plans falling apart, with coach horses missing, and finally ending up at miserable accommodations. Clausewitz's parallel is apt enough in its nineteenth century manner, but too mild I think to show its meaning to modern readers. I prefer the story told by a friend in the good old days when automobiles were first coming out with automatic transmissions. He couldn't get his car started on a frosty winter morning until a neighbor pulled her car alongside his and asked if she could help. Delighted at the prospect of getting a push he was quick to accept the offer, then remembered to caution her that his Cadillac had an automatic transmission. He made it quite clear (in his version of the event) that the cars would have to reach a speed of thirty-five miles per hour before he could get his engine running. She nodded her understanding and proceeded to back up—almost the length of the block, as he recalled. After checking to see that his transmission lever was in the proper position, he looked in his rear-view mirror to see if the lady was bringing her car up to the rear of his. She was. To his horror he saw her bearing down on his rear—at thirty-five miles per hour!

That is frustration. It comes as close to its battlefield definition as I can imagine. In a broader sense frustration is the vast difference between plans and their execution, between expectation and reality. Oddly enough, the accumulation of difficulties mentioned in Clausewitz has been described graphically by a man who never saw a battle. Stephen Vincent Benét sketches such things lucidly as he recounts the opening of the Battle of Bull Run in *John Brown's Body*:

> If you take a flat map
> And move wooden blocks upon it strategically,*
> The thing looks well, the blocks behave as they should.
> The science* of war is moving live men like blocks,
> And getting the blocks into place at a fixed moment.

*Benét's terms, not mine. I would have used "tactically" instead of strategically and "art" instead of science, but then I am *un pauvre soldat* who has never been issued a poetic license. For a discussion of strategy and tactics see Appendix A.

But it takes time to mold your men into blocks
And flat maps turn into country where creeks and gullies
Hamper your wooden squares. They stick in the brush,
They are tired and rest, they straggle after ripe blackberries,
And you cannot lift them up in your hand and move them . . .
It is all so clear in the maps, so clear in the mind,
But the orders are slow, the men in the blocks are slow
To move, when they start they take too long on the way—
The general loses his stars and the block men die . . .
Because still used to being men, not block parts. . . ."[10]

I could never put it as engagingly as Benét, so simply bear in mind: Frustration=difference between plans and reality.

Fortunately for commanders in the past all six dynamics have rarely appeared in a *concerted combination* in a single battle. When such a rarity has occurred (like the notorious case of the collapse of the French Army at Waterloo) a leader has gone down, and one recalls the mournful truism that for every battle won, someone had to lose it.

In fact, when such a disastrous combination has arisen, it usually has been the fault of the leader who has allowed the dynamics to accumulate against him. Avoiding that accumulation is an essential element of the art of leadership. Avoidance, however, is only the secondary or negative theme of this writing. The main theme is positive in its nature, for its purpose is to bring out the *attributes of the leader*. These are the personal qualities without which there can be no base on which to build an art of leadership. These are the counterforces that have enabled the successful leader to overcome the dynamics of battle that oppose and threaten to destroy him. I call the personal counterforces *attributes*, not only because the word is more fitting than "characteristics," but also because the whole art of leadership can be attributed to them.

How to present attributes to the reader became the cause of more mental travail and just plain sweat than I have ever endured in a single project. To toss some kind of list in front of my reader would be an unthinkable affront, and a detailed discussion of abstract qualities at this point could result in something equally tedious. Yet negative aspects can sometimes provoke the mind into positive thought; that is what happened in my case. The positive side forced me to recall my promise to come up with answers by looking at leaders in action; not by probing into abstractions, but by looking at success in battle through the minds and eyes of leaders. This put me back on track, pointed toward realistic goals.

Along that track I came to think of the leader as a quarterback (certainly not the Monday morning type), as a *tactical leader on the field*. I was not concerned with leadership at the higher levels, since that should be left to the coaches and their staffs who represent the strategists. I soon found that the character of the quarterback/leader could be seen in a less complex and more understandable way by thinking of his attributes as the underpinning, the basis of his art. The whole of his art could then be seen as the sum of its parts. The idea of the whole being the sum of its parts is anything but new; however, what *is* new is that attributes can be brought to life when shown as parts of the art which have assured a leader of victory in battle.

Yet attributes cannot be displayed on isolated slides to be viewed under the microscope of the mind. They must be seen in the heat of action where they are forced to confront the dynamics of battle. In the Prologue that follows we will see a multi-faceted show of dynamic forces massing to overpower a leader.

Prologue: The Dynamics of Battle

Dan Morgan at the Battle of Cowpens, 1781

DAN MORGAN DISMOUNTED, swinging his six-foot frame from the saddle as lightly as he could without showing signs of the rheumatic twinges shooting down his legs. He managed it in the graceful motion that had always marked his movements, but now he had to act it out consciously to hide his pain from the others. Bad enough their commander having this cursed affliction in his first independent command without him having to put up with side glances and helpful gestures. He'd have none of that.

He snatched the map his aide-de-camp was handing to him, and glared down at it for the fifth time that afternoon. Kosciuszko, General Greene's engineer, had done a good job of charting rivers and creeks, but here, west of the Catawba River, he had barely sketched in the main roads. And it was no main road that Morgan's column was stumbling along now as it filed past him. In fact, calling it a road would be doing it proud—as they put it in the Carolinas—since it was no more than a cattle trail, scarcely visible through the bare branches of winter underbrush.

As the branches of laurel and dead briars were whipped back and forth by the passing infantrymen, Morgan looked up long enough to recognize the dark blue regimental coats with red facings as the uniform of a company of Howard's Maryland Continentals. They marched in open column keeping to their files as well as they could on the rough trail. Yet

8

who could care about drill ground formations here in this wilderness? They looked fit enough, though fatigue was showing in the faces of men who had been on forced march for over ten hours—and with half their breakfast rations left behind on the cooking fires. That was how quickly he had hurried them off on this march from Burr's Mill, after getting the reports that Tarleton was close on his trail.

His keen glance took in the column as far as the woods would allow. The Continentals showed all the marks of veteran infantry, from the muskets slung butt-up with their locks wrapped against the winter damp, to the way knapsacks were carried high behind the shoulders. Even the files were silent, with none of the jabbering that went on with a column of militia. The only sounds here were the clink of a bayonet scabbard or the rattle of twigs against a musket stock. He could almost hear their breathing, though that may have been an illusion caused by the sight of their wisps of breath on the wintry air.

His glance swung around, first toward Major Giles, then to portly Col. William Washington. He caught himself in time to stifle the grin that almost creased his rough face when he looked at Washington. *My God*, he thought, *how can the man be such a rare cavalry commander and stay so damned fat?* His mind turned back to business.

"Well, Colonel, how far are we from the Broad if we keep heading in this direction?" Morgan asked.

"We're on the watershed about midway between Thicketty Creek on our left and Gilkey Creek on our right. That'll put us about ten miles from the river, right about there," Washington jabbed a thick forefinger at the map.

"Any other word about the river?" Morgan asked.

"Same scouts' reports—she's still up to her banks and flowing fast."

"Can we still make it across the ford?"

"Yes, but we'll need plenty of time to rig the lines and get things set for the infantry and then the wagons."

"How much time is plenty?"

"Sir, we'll need at least two hours, and you know we can't do it at night," Washington said.

Morgan looked back at the map, and spoke half-aloud, so low that Washington and Giles had to strain to follow his words.

"Only four hours of daylight left. It'll take all of that just to reach the river, with no time left to cross. Then too, if Tarleton marches at night like he often does, tomorrow morning he'd be on us when we'd be trying to make it across. And can't you just see what Tarleton's dragoons could do to our militia—caught milling around with their asses to the river? Hell, those that didn't disappear in the swamps would be slaughtered like hogs at a county butcherin'."

He raised his voice, looking back at Washington. "Just two more questions, Colonel. Since we can't make a proper crossing today, what about that place you mentioned—the ground where the farmers let their cattle range?"

"That would be Hannah's Cowpens; open grazing land with a lot of trees. It would be about five miles from here, near the upper end of Thicketty Creek. But I must warn you, General, that whole area is cavalry country. Exactly the kind of ground Tarleton would love to have for maneuvering his dragoons," Washington said.

"I realize that. Now, how far do you reckon we're ahead of Bloody Benny?" Morgan asked.

"A half-hour ago my scouts spotted his van about four hours behind our rearguard, and that won't have changed much. But one more thing, Sir. Pickens' messenger has been waiting while I sent for Major McDowell." Washington pointed toward the two mountain men making their way through the underbrush.

"Why McDowell? What does he have to do with Pickens who isn't even here?"

"It's McDowell himself that's important right now. He and some of his North Carolinians were through this way three months ago on their way to whip Ferguson at Kings Mountain. The overmountain men used the Cowpens for an assembly area before heading east for Kings Mountain," Washington explained.

Morgan motioned a silent order to the two men in worn hunting shirts for them to stay in the saddle. Pickens' man made his report: his commander was on his way with 150 men to join General Morgan. Join him where? Colonel Pickens hadn't said, the messenger guessed he'd just catch up with the General.

Morgan shook his head, half in disgust, half in secret amusement. "The Old Wagoner," with five years of war behind him, knew so well what this mountaineer would never have considered—that one "where" unanswered could cost a commander a campaign. He turned to Major McDowell, a stocky Scotch-Irish frontiersman whose blue eyes met Morgan's without wavering.

"You know why you're here," Morgan said, "tell us about it."

McDowell described the Cowpens. The area consisted mostly of rolling or flat ground with scattered stands of hickory, pines, or red oaks. There was no underbrush, and the long grass made fine pasturing for the cattle that the Carolina farmers marked and turned loose to forage through the open forest. The center of the area, marked by the Green River Road, was about five miles from the Broad River and the same distance from Morgan's present location. At the mention of forage Morgan's eyes had lit up.

"By God, Washington, you know how bad we're needing that for the horses! Now, hold on just a minute, gentlemen. I won't keep you waiting long," Morgan said.

His head was bent over the map for silent seconds. Then, as he looked up, orders followed decision as one footstep follows another.

"We'll go to the Cowpens. You"—he looked at Pickens' messenger—"get back to Colonel Pickens and tell him to meet me at the Cowpens, as fast as he can make it.

"Colonel Washington, go ahead and scout out the area. I'll meet you there with my commanders. We'll ride on ahead of the column. When you pass the advance guard, have it bear left around the head of Thicketty Creek, toward the Cowpens.

"Major Giles, ride back down the column and round up the commanders, then rejoin me at the Cowpens.

"Come on, Major McDowell, let's get going."

Morgan and Washington met on the Green River Road in the fading light of the January day. The senior commanders, with the exception of Pickens who would not arrive until after nightfall, rode behind their general—Lieutenant Colonel Howard, commanding the Continentals, followed by the militia commanders. Morgan left them to wait and look over the near terrain while he and Washington reconnoitered the larger expanse of the area.

Looking to the northwest Morgan saw before him a wide and deep stretch of grassland studded with the trees McDowell had described. The ground in front of him sloped gently upward until it was topped by a low crest about four hundred yards away. Beyond that he could see a higher ridge, really two hills, and farther a glimpse of a low swale, and beyond, the highest hill of the area. It was all rolling terrain with gentle slopes, none of the high spots exceeding twenty-five yards above Morgan's position.

Washington guided him back and forth across the tract. As they rode Washington pointed out the key terrain features. Morgan listened and observed, yet his thoughts were racing throughout the conversation.

This will have to be it, he thought, *the ground I'll fight on . . . time is running out, Tarleton will be only four hours away . . . and what if he rolls his men out in the dark as he usually does? That means I've got to be ready to take on his advance guard at first light . . . Washington's reports are always reliable and they tell me that Bloody Ben has over a thousand men. I may have near that tonight if all my militia show up . . . But, my God, what a difference! His veteran regulars outnumber mine three to one, and except for Triplett's two-hundred Virginians my militia are an untrained, scraggly lot, as liable to disappear as to fight, though there are good riflemen among them . . . Tarleton's got three-hundred cavalrymen to Washington's eighty . . . and then there's this ground (will it be my last battlefield?) that I'll have to deploy on . . . the militia will know that the river is behind them, I'll see to that, and it will spark their "fighting spirit" because there'll be no swamps to disappear into . . . but that means that I'll have nothing to protect my flanks against Benny's dragoons; they'll be wide open . . . that's a chance I'll have to take, but it can be weighed against two things—Benny always comes up fast and hits as hard as he can straight on. He will only maneuver later if he's forced to. I'll keep Washington's cavalry as my fast-moving reserve to counterattack the flank or rear of any maneuvering force of Tarleton's . . . all of which means that I've got to deploy my force in depth. Well, the ground lends itself to that, so that's the way I'll fight . . . yet if I'm planning to fight a pitched battle, how will that fit into the meaning of my mission as I got it from Nathanael Greene? "This force—and such others as may join you—you will employ against the enemy on the west side of the Catawba River, either offensively or defensively, as your prudence and discretion may direct, acting with caution and avoiding surprises by every possible precaution . . . The object . . . is to give protection to that part of the country and spirit up the people, to annoy the enemy in that quarter."[1]*

Well, at this point how can I "spirit up the people" if I don't get Bloody Benny off their backs—and mine? So now my "prudence and discretion" are telling me to stop running and fight—either offensively or defensively—and I'll have to do that in reverse order, first on the defense then over to the offense. Damned if this isn't like an old, rheumatic hound being brought to bay by a feisty three-year-old, with all his sharp young teeth snappin' at the old one's arse.

His mind made up, he and Washington rode back to the others. He was no longer a cornered hound dog, but Brig.-Gen. Daniel Morgan, commanding the Southern Department's Army in the West. He waved his commanders to close in around him, keeping them on horseback as he spoke.

"I'm giving you the guts of my plan now while there's still light enough to see it on the ground. We'll talk over the details tonight, so now I'll take only questions about what I'm pointing out here.

"We'll post the infantry in three lines. The road we're standing on will mark the center of our deployment. All indications are that Tarleton will come at us from the east on this road, just as you came up it a while ago.

"The first line will be made up of picked riflemen. They will be the first to bring Benny's cavalry under fire when they advance to scout us out. Majors McDowell and Cunningham will each command half of this line, and it will be spread out along the lower slope—right across here.

"The second line will be a hundred and fifty yards farther back, midway up the slope—back there. It will contain the rest of the Carolina and Georgia militia. Colonel Pickens will be in overall command of the second line.

"The third line will consist of the Continentals as well as the Virginia militia and Beaty's South Carolinians, and it will be commanded by Lieutenant Colonel Howard. The line will be formed along the main crest and just down the slope with its center astride this road.

"Colonel Washington's cavalry will be in reserve, posted out of sight behind the second hill—back there. The whole idea is to lead Benny into a trap, so we can blast his cavalry and infantry as they come up these slopes. When they've been cut down to size by our fire, we'll attack *them*. All right, any questions?"

He looked around a ring of faces registering a gamut of reactions ranging from disbelief to delight. Major Triplett of Virginia spoke first.

"Sir, those militia out in front will run, sure as we're

standing here. They'll never face the bayonets of Tarleton's regulars."

"Don't you think I know that, Major? Hell, we're going to tell them to run—after they've gotten off at least two shots. Then the first line riflemen can run back and fall in with the second line's militia. On Pickens' command that whole bunch will get off at least two shots. Then Pickens' line will file off to the left and take position on the left of Howard's line. Remember this—if they're running on orders they won't panic. And we'll give 'em a little extra courage by reminding 'em the Broad River is still back there, five miles behind us, and if they run again they'll never get across it before Tarleton's dragoons catch up with 'em."[2]

That brought a laugh that ran around the circle of officers. They knew down-to-earth logic when they heard it, especially when it came from a man with Morgan's reputation as a fighter. As the laughter died Colonel Brannon of South Carolina spoke.

"We're with you, General, but what about our flanks?"

"We can bank on everyone's experience with Tarleton. When his dragoons find our position he'll go for us hell for leather, straight ahead, sure's you're born. He'll think he's got us far surpassed because he has some of the finest troops in the British Army, so it will never occur to him that he's taking a risk. I've thought this out, Colonel, and that's why Washington's cavalry will be hidden there in reserve. Then too, if Pickens and his officers can rally and reform the militia we'll be able to bring fire to bear on the flanks of Benny's formations at a time when they will be least expecting it."

As Morgan looked around for the final time he thought, *they may be tired, but they're spoiling for a fight—now that they know what to do and believe they can do it.*

"Very well then," Morgan's voice rose in its wagoner's bawl, "tonight as the men bed down, we'll get them educated too, so there'll be no confusion when they're posted in the morning."

Morgan was making his rounds an hour before first light, his rheumatism reminding him that it was very much with him. He kept his silence—trying though it was—until all was going as it should. He observed that the men were fed, the campfires stamped out, and the baggage loaded on the wagons. The militia companies were falling in, with all the jostle and noise that always marked their assembling. Howard's

Maryland and Delaware Continentals had already marched off silently to their positions on the rise. They were used to forming up and marching in the dark.

Morgan had kept silent for too long. He bellowed at the wagonmasters, his voice hoarse from the night's exertions, until the trains began to move out of sight through the trees, barely visible in the graying dawn.

After the last militia company had trudged away Morgan followed it as far as the Green River Road where he turned off to find his first line. Major McDowell's North Carolinians and Major Cunningham's Georgians had just finished filing off into their skirmishers' positions. Morgan joked with them as he rode past them, but there was deadly meaning in his "Aim for the epaulet men. Kill them first. Kill them and you've done a day's work.

"Remember to run straight back. Pickens' men will be leaving spaces for you in their line."

He rode back to the second line and met Pickens for a review of his Carolina and Georgia militia. Together they rode the full three hundred yards of the line, Pickens keeping his customary silence, Morgan joking and exhorting—

"Sit down, men. Ease your joints. No need to stand now, just keep in your places.

"You there, Georgia boy, no need to look so glum! We're going to have plenty of amusement mighty shortly.

"Remember, you owe me at least two fires, and when you take off, be sure it's to the left flank."

He left the taciturn Pickens at the end of his line and rode around the north side of the hill, far enough to see the long white coats of Washington's cavalrymen, standing alongside their horses in orderly lines in the swale behind the hill. He turned his horse and rode up the rear slope of the rise where Howard had taken post behind his four hundred Continentals and veteran militia. As he rode he could tell himself: *The men have been rested and fed well. They've been posted quietly, with no confusion. Now I can only hope that Tarleton's men will have been turned out hours ago, to march in the cold darkness across creeks, ravines, and rough trails, always stumbling over unknown terrain, watched all the time by my scouts. That ought to take the fighting edge off King George's mighty regulars. But if I don't get blessed by Tarleton's misfortune, I do have three blessings for sure in having Washington, Howard, and Pickens as senior commanders. I don't take kindly to Pickens when he's being preacher-like, but his militia will fight for him. Washington, in spite of being tubby, is the finest cavalry commander I could have found; he's all over the place and always in control. And John Howard, sitting his horse like a statue up there. He's maybe seventeen years younger than me, but just as cool in a fight, with five years of war and a half-dozen big battles behind him. He's a quiet man, never showing off his fine education, but he's mean as a cornered bear in battle. Yes, I'm lucky, though I'll need a lot of luck this morning.*

Morgan and Howard stood side by side on the crest of the hill. Behind them their horses were tethered amid a cluster of staff officers. Fifty yards below them on the forward slope the double-ranked line of Continentals had hunkered down on the hillside.

Another two hundred yards down the hill the line of Pickens' militia was harder to see; their brown hunting shirts and homespun had blended into the winter grass. The men had "eased their joints", lying or sitting half-hidden on the dun hillside.

Even Morgan's keen eye could not make out the skirmish line of McDowell's and Cunningham's riflemen, three-hundred and fifty yards away. The sharpshooters had taken cover be-

Continentals await the British attack at Cowpens
(a Bicentennial reenactment)

hind trees and in the long grass in their natural fashion, so it was not remarkable that their line remained out of sight.

A settled silence hung over the nine hundred men like their ghosts of breath in the frosty air of the rising dawn. Even Morgan had fallen silent, musing in the strange way that comes to men before battle.

Just as well, he thought, *that I can't see that line of skirmishers. If I can't, knowing where they are, then it's sure the British can't. What could be better? Well, it could be better, back there in Frederick County where I thought I'd gone into an earned retirement. Especially after that damned Congress had seen fit to pass over COLONEL Morgan. That is, until they had second thoughts about needing an old war horse, and pulling him out of his pasture. And thinking of pastures, I surely hope that Abigail isn't having trouble with those cattle getting loose again. That's no fit task for a woman, having to manage that farm by herself. Seems strange it could be Wednesday morning too, back there in Virginia, with everything quiet and—*

He was jarred back to reality by Howard's sudden movement. The infantry commander had brushed against Morgan's arm when he had raised his hands to frame his eyes.

"It's them all right, General, see them?" Howard was pointing toward the distant black treeline beyond the American skirmish line.

Morgan, staring, could see the tiny figures of mounted men in Lincoln-green jackets moving out of the woods. A thin scattered line emerged into the open and halted at the foot of the long slope. Their brass dragoon helmets began to reflect the growing light.

"Tarleton had come with the sun."[3]

As Morgan and Howard watched, scarlet jacketed cavalrymen appeared at the edge of the woods, followed by a green-jacketed officer. The little figure rode forward, its black helmet plume waving in the wind. It gestured to its front and the line of dragoons spurred forward. They must have seen several of the riflemen, for they broke from a walk into a trot. Morgan fancied he could hear the drumming of the hooves on the hard ground, but he knew that must be his imagination. It was not his imagination when he saw little puff balls of smoke blossom among the trees where the riflemen were lying. The rattle of rifle fire came on the clear air. Morgan saw saddles emptied as other horses were pulled up short when their riders wheeled them about and galloped for the rear.

"Now that's shooting!" Morgan boomed, exulting, "I count a dozen down. Right, Howard?"

"At least, Sir, maybe a half dozen more," Howard replied.

They saw the dragoon officer waving his saber in a futile effort to rally the fleeing cavalrymen, but they swept past him and disappeared into the woods.

"Well, by God, Benny should know for certain we're here now. What'll be the next act in his program?" Morgan said.

As if in reply, the panoply of Tarleton's army began to unfold from the forest, columns marching off to wheel into line where the Green River Road entered the Cowpens. A company of British dragoons led off to the British right, followed by the scarlet coats and white breeches of infantry companies wheeling into line with drill ground precision. A small blue-coated section followed the infantry, then there was a second column of infantry in green jackets. Behind it another scarlet and white column debouched from the forest and came up into precise line to the left of the green jackets. Another dark blue section moved up alongside the scarlet infantry, and finally another company of green dragoons took post on the British left flank. Sergeants dressed the ranks into rigid lines that became a brilliant array of scarlet, green, blue, and white. The colorful line was topped with a glittering line of bayonets as the British infantry shouldered arms, and the long line came marching forward, drums rolling and regimental colors rippling in the wind.

"Now you see Tarleton's order of battle," Morgan said. "He has posted British Legion dragoons on each flank. Then, going from his right to his left, there are companies of British infantry, then a grasshopper* where those blue coats are, then Legion infantry in the green jackets, another grasshopper, then more British infantry. And now I see his Highlanders, look at the kilts, moving into reserve behind his left flank, and it looks like at least two more companies of Legion dragoons going into reserve there with the Highlanders."

The British drums began to beat the long roll, and the line came on, battalions aligning on the colors. There were more puffs of smoke among the trees that sheltered the riflemen. Then they were jumping to their feet and running

---

*Soldier slang for a 3-pounder artillery piece carried on horseback for transport. It got its name from its recoil, which made it appear to jump when fired. The two guns at Cowpens were making a colorful history: captured from the British at Saratoga (October 1777), recaptured by the British at Camden (August 1780), taken back by Morgan's men at Cowpens, only to be lost to the British again at Guilford Courthouse two months later.[4]

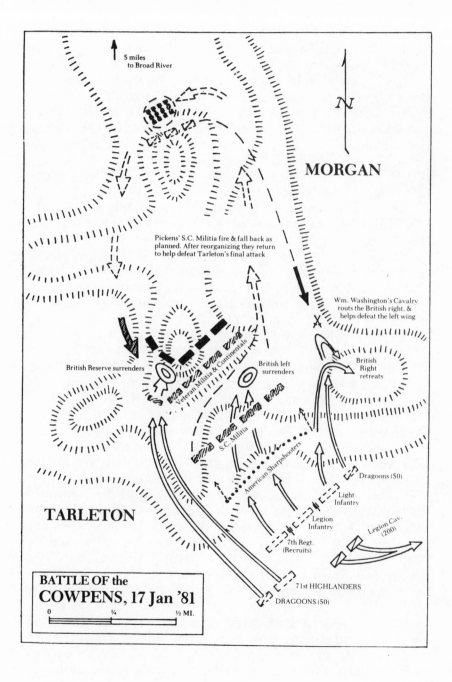

5 miles
to Broad River

N

MORGAN

Pickens' S.C. Militia fire & fall back as
planned. After reorganizing they return
to help defeat Tarleton's final attack

Wm. Washington's Cavalry
routs the British right, &
helps defeat the left wing

British Reserve surrenders

Veteran Militia & Continentals

British left
surrenders

British
Right
retreats

S.C. Militia

American Sharpshooters

Dragoons (50)

Light
Infantry

TARLETON

Legion
Infantry

Legion Cav.
(200)

7th Regt.
(Recruits)

BATTLE OF the
COWPENS, 17 Jan '81

71st HIGHLANDERS

DRAGOONS (50)

0   ¼   ½ MI.

back toward Pickens' line. Some were reloading and firing as they ran, a feat that always amused Morgan because it never failed to confound the British who were trained to load and fire only at a halt. Morgan looked at his watch and snapped its cover shut.

"I've got five minutes after seven," he said to Howard. "I'm going down to look again at Pickens' line."

He walked his horse through company intervals in the line of Continentals, then trotted forward to join Pickens. They watched the militia officers walking up and down behind the line, cautioning the men to hold their fire.

"Good, good," Morgan muttered to Pickens, "let 'em get within fifty paces before our first volley."

The British line swung up the slope, deadly in its grim beauty, muskets leveled at Charge Bayonet. Morgan saw the Carolina company officers glancing back over their shoulders at Pickens who was holding his right arm stiffly upright. Pickens dropped his arm, and the officers shouted "Fire!" The volley crashed into the British. The scarlet and green line could be seen reeling through the smoke, but it recovered, closing its ranks as it halted. British Army discipline ruled over shock, and a return volley was thrown at the Americans, though most of its effect ripped into the sod in front of Pickens' men.

There was a fatal pause as the British reloaded. This was the golden moment Pickens had been waiting for: catching the enemy standing stock still, within easy rifle range where even the muskets of his militia farmers could reap their toll of British casualties. Pickens' officers were shouting "Fire!" again, and another volley tore into the enemy ranks. Redcoats were going down, among them the lion's share of the "epaulet men" that Tarleton would lose that morning.

Incredibly the British were reforming, and their thinned but realigned line came on with leveled bayonets. This was the critical time that Morgan had dreaded. If Pickens' militia broke and ran, panicking, straight back toward Howard's Continentals, there would be chaos. Morgan peered through the drifting powder smoke, and almost cried out in relief. Yes, the militiamen were running, like the devil himself was on their heels, but the rush of men poured like a swift current off to the left flank, heading to pass around the slope where Howard's men stood like a dam before a flood.

Yet as Morgan stood in his stirrups, straining to see beyond the smoke, the next of his fears was materializing to his left front. He could see well enough now to make out Tarleton's right flank dragoons trotting off to their right oblique to pass around the British infantry, obviously maneuvering into position to launch a charge against the running American militia. Morgan's mind was racing, trying to put himself in Tarleton's thoughts. How would he be assessing the situation? Then he had to calculate how he should deal with Tarleton's cavalry:

Yes, Tarleton must have jumped to the conclusion that the running Americans were a horde of fugitives fleeing in panic as militia always had before a British bayonet assault. And so, Bloody Ben would be committing this cavalry to saber down the "routed" militia. He would try and use those dragoons to turn the rout into a flood that would pour over the Continentals' line, raising havoc to allow the British infantry to overwhelm Howard's men in the confusion. Well. The Old Wagoner was not going to let that happen. He must get word to Washington in time to have him smash Tarleton's dragoons on their right flank.

He bawled for Major Giles, unaware that his aide was at his left elbow, "Get back to Colonel Washington as fast as that nag will carry you. Tell him to attack around this hill and charge those dragoons on their flank, I want 'em wiped out or swept off this field."

Giles spurred his horse up the hill, his dark blue cloak

Colonel Washington's troopers (a Bicentennial reenactment)

streaming out behind him. Morgan rode up the hill at a walk. Aides could fly to the rear at a gallop, but the troops should not see their general move with anything but dignity, especially when he had turned his back to the enemy. Pickens rode beside him as they passed through an interval in Howard's line. When they had cleared the rear rank Morgan put his horse to a trot, and moved toward the left end of the line. They halted on the crest of the slope. Below them the Continentals and the veteran militia were standing at the ready. Farther down the slope Pickens' men were now a strung-out river flowing around the bottom of the east slope of the hill where Morgan stood. But they had not halted as he had directed! Instead they were heading toward the rearmost knoll that hid Washington's cavalry. Morgan sensed at once what had caused this failure to follow his orders.

I should have known, he thought, *that most of those militia have their horses picketed in the trees in rear of Washington's assembly area. And, by God, they're heading for those horses. Pickens and I will have to stop them and get them reformed. But right this minute my place is here, until I can make sure that Washington is coming up to counterattack. Damn, what a sorry plight I've gotten myself into . . . .*

He looked along Pickens pointing arm to see the white coats of Washington's dragoons coming over the rearward hill. The cavalry swept down across the swale, bearing left to avoid Pickens' men. In seconds that seemed hours to Morgan, stout Colonel Washington was drawing saber and shouting commands to his leading company. The company wheeled into line followed by another forming a second rank. Looking back to his left Morgan saw Tarleton's leading dragoons break formation to ride down the last of Pickens' militia.

It's going to be mighty rough on some of those men who'll feel those British sabers. But there's going to be reward in this, for Washington will be charging into a disorganized enemy and into their flank to boot.

He and Pickens watched long enough to see Washington's cavalry smash into Tarleton's horsemen. The British rear dissolved under the impact to become a flurry of fugitives fleeing to escape the American sabers. There was no time to stay and watch Washington's pursuit. Morgan and Pickens galloped back across the swale, all dignity forgotten, in their rush to get to the mass of fleeing militia.

Morgan would never forget the transformation of Pickens from a reticent iceberg of a man to a whirling dervish on horseback. The man was everywhere at once, shouting at one knot of men, grabbing at others to halt them and bring them to their senses. Between them, Pickens and Morgan got hold of officers, got the streaming flood halted and turned into a mass of milling men who at last could be rallied and formed back into companies and battalions.

There was no time for Morgan to remain here, either, to await an outcome. He paused long enough to hear a renewed rattle of musketry that was increasing to a rolling roar. He knew what was happening, the British infantry and the American third line had clashed and the intensity of the firing told Morgan they were slugging it out.

He left Pickens to reorganize his command, after directing him to send mounted messengers when his troops were ready to move out. He was off again at a gallop to rejoin Howard and resume command. When he reached the crest of the hill the battle was unfolding below him. The roar of the volleying had fallen away to scattered firing, and Morgan saw that the British line, center and wings together, had withdrawn halfway down the hill to reform a new line. The reason for their reorganizing was all too evident. The scarlet coats and green jackets of dead or wounded British littered the slope between the two forces. Morgan looked down to his right front and saw Howard trotting off toward his right flank, and in a flash he saw the cause of Howard's concern. Far beyond the right of Howard's line he could see Tarleton's battalion of Highlanders, the famed 71st or Fraser's Highlanders, marching in column and swinging wide to clear the British left flank. Tarleton was committing his only infantry reserve to envelope Howard's line and roll it up.

Well, no need for me to go rushing down there. Howard is one of the finest infantrymen I've ever known. He'll handle things, probably refuse that right flank* by pulling back a company or two. But God in heaven! What is he doing? What are they all doing?

To Morgan's horror Howard's right flank company, Wallace's Virginians, had faced about and was marching to the rear, backs to the enemy! And to make it more mystifying they appeared to be marching in perfect order. All down Howard's line other commanders, apparently believing that

---

*Refusing a flank means changing the front of a flank unit to face it toward the enemy threat thus protecting the force's flank.

a general withdrawal had been ordered, were facing their units about and marching them rearward, aligning on the Virginians. Morgan could see Howard riding back and forth in front of his marching line. He was giving orders as he rode, but he was too far away for Morgan to hear the commands.

He could certainly not afford to stay out of this. Such an appalling change coming at the critical moment in his battle could cost him the whole affair in minutes. He rode like the wind until he could rein up alongside Howard.

"What is this retreat?" Morgan demanded.

"I am trying to save my right flank. I had intended to wheel Wallace's company in order to refuse the flank, but there's been a misunderstanding, so I'm taking up a new position," Howard's words came rapidly but his voice was steady.

"Are you beaten?" Morgan asked.

"Do men who march like that look as though they were beaten?" Howard said, as coolly as if on parade. Morgan stifled a gasp of relief that might have been heard for yards.

"Right!" he said, "I'll choose you a second position. When you reach it, face about and fire."

He was off again down the reverse slope of Howard's hill and up the forward slope of the hill that had screened Washington's cavalry. As he mounted the slope two buckskin-clad horsemen rode over the hill to meet him. They were Pickens' messengers, the first to speak saying that Colonel Pickens wanted to know on what point to direct his march. Morgan pointed back toward Pickens' rallying ground, then swept his arm in a great arc that encompassed the American rear and Howard's right flank, and ended by pointing at the distant Highlanders.

"Tell Colonel Pickens that he has already gone halfway around the battle. I want him to complete the circuit by moving with all the speed he can muster and hit those Highlanders and any other British he comes across in their rear. Got it? Get going!"

He scanned the hillside for a suitable halting place for Howard. It appeared that any point midway up the hill would provide good ground. He looked back to see Howard's marching line coming toward him with the same steadiness that had marked it from the beginning. He turned his horse to go down the slope when Pickens' other man called out to him: "Another messenger comin', General."

It was one of Washington's officers on a black stallion whose sides were streaming with sweat.

"Sir, Colonel Washington sends his respects and—"

"Get on with it," Morgan snapped.

"He says to tell you those British infantry are coming on like a mob. Give them one fire and I'll charge them." The young lieutenant panted out the message, his eyes shining in his excitement.

"Tell Colonel Washington that is exactly what I want him to do. Tell him to move out around the hill so he can launch his attack when he sees Colonel Howard's men open fire."

The lieutenant was gone as quickly as he had come, and Morgan looked again at Howard's approaching line, then beyond it at the slope of the other hill. It was covered with scarlet coats of charging British infantry like masses of red leaves swirling over a brown field. Yes, Washington had called the shot. The enemy was coming on like a mob, no longer in ordered ranks, but like a shouting rabble, bayonets bobbing up and down in any direction.

"Like a damned dismounted foxhunt," snorted Morgan, "and this is one they'll never come back from."

He rode toward Howard, raising his right arm in the signal to halt. Howard waved his sword in acknowledgement, and gave his commands. His timing was perfect. The double ranks of Continentals and militia came to a parade-ground halt, faced about, and sent their volley crashing into the enemy. It was done so quickly that the Americans had fired from the hip, at a range of thirty yards, into the packed mass of howling British infantry. The shock that followed was a boxer's knockout blow. The enemy who were still standing reeled back in stunned confusion, and Howard, no longer the calm statue or the leader on parade, was shouting: "Give them the bayonet!"

The pent rage of men who had been retreating against their will needed no command to release it. They charged into the staggering redcoats, thrusting and slashing until those who could not escape were bellowing for quarter, some kneeling, others throwing themselves full length on the ground.

Morgan rode back far enough to survey the whole field, in time to watch Washington's dragoons in a thundering charge that swept around the hill to smash into Tarleton's right flank. The British Legion dragoons did not wheel to face the American charge, instead they scattered and fled. The American horsemen, unopposed now, rode down the British infantry, sabers rising and falling, until the light infantry and fusiliers broke and ran. Lieutenant Colonel McCall of Washington's command pursued the mass of fugitives (Morgan estimated it to number two hundred men), surrounded it, and made prisoners of them all.

The British center and right were collapsing before Morgan's eyes. Legion infantry and the 7th Fusiliers were dropping their muskets and throwing their crossbelts and side arms on the ground. But all was not over yet. Triplett's Virginians and South Carolinians, the right flank men who had fought like Continentals that day, were still engaged in a hot fight with the Highlanders. That battalion of Scots under their fighting commander, Major McArthur, was the only infantry unit of Tarleton's army that had not become casualties or prisoners. Yet their gallant fight was to prove hopeless. Pickens' men, reformed into their units, fell into firing line on the Highlanders' left rear. A rallied company of Tarleton's Legion cavalry rode toward the beleagured Scots in an attempt to prevent their encirclement, but they met a blast of fire from Pickens' riflemen. They broke and fled for the last time. In a matter of minutes the Highlanders were surrounded on three sides by Howard's and Pickens' men, and were being slaughtered under a hail of rifle and musket bullets. Pickens called on their commander to surrender, and Major McArthur had to tender his sword to Pickens to save his battalion from certain annihilation.

Now the only British soldiers left fighting were the Royal Artillery gun crews with the two grasshoppers. The blue-coated gunners continued to "serve their pieces" in the finest artillery tradition, but the full fury of Howard's nearest infantry was turned upon them. Howard ordered the guns taken. They were, as the gunners were cut down to a man.

Lieutenant Colonel McCall rode up to Morgan to make his report on the fate of Tarleton's cavalry. Evidently Tarleton had tried to lead his reserve of 250 Legion dragoons in a desperate attack to free the Highlanders and save the gunners. It was a final and futile gesture, for "the dragoons forsook their leader and rode off, bearing down any officer who opposed their flight."[5] And Washington himself had gone in pursuit of Tarleton, though there was yet no report of the outcome.

Morgan was for once speechless. He could not believe the extent of his victory. It is said that he was so exuberant that he picked up a nine-year-old drummer boy and kissed him on both cheeks. He had planned to lead Tarleton into a "fire trap" that would administer a stinging repulse to Tarleton's attack, severe enough to make him lick his wounds while Morgan got his army across the Broad. Instead he had wiped out Tarleton's army in a double envelopment that would sparkle as a tactical gem in anyone's military history. With his thousand men he had crushed Tarleton's army whose losses totaled 110 killed, 830 prisoners (including 200 wounded), 2 regimental colors, 2 artillery pieces, 800 muskets, 35 baggage wagons, 60 Negro slaves, 100 cavalry horses, large stores of ammunition, and all of the British "field musick." Morgan's losses were 12 killed and 61 wounded. The comparative losses in combat power: Tarleton's over 85 percent; Morgan's .7 percent. In another meaningful sense, Tarleton had lost 25 percent of Cornwallis' invasion army in one hour.

Before this prologue I said that we would see in this battle a show of the dynamics of battle massing to overpower a leader. Let us take a retrospective look at Cowpens in search of those dynamics.

Danger. There was danger aplenty. Morgan's little army had no logistical base and was all on its own with only the supplies it could carry. It was too far from any friendly force for even a prayer of support. Greene's other "half" of his army was 120 miles away, a week's march in those days, and Cornwallis' main army was between him and Morgan. Add to these dangers Tarleton's mobile task force, a more powerful force than Morgan's in terms of regular infantry and cavalry, capable of pursuing Morgan anywhere he could go and destroying him if he were trapped. And Morgan was, in a way, trapped between Tarleton and the Broad River.

Chance. Morgan had to take the calculated risk that Tarleton would attack with his usual impetuosity, straight ahead at whatever was in his way. Risk? Yes, because Tarleton would have the time and favorable terrain to feel out Morgan's flanks, then maneuver to strike a vulnerable area. But Morgan knew all about Tarleton's character and took the chance, just as Lee and Jackson would, eighty years later, against Union commanders whose characters they knew well.

Exertion. Morgan demanded the most of his men and

himself, though it is certain that no one was pushed to the verge of suffering. On the other hand, we have seen Morgan showing a strength of will just to keep on going with the physical exertion required of him. This was significant in his case because of his being plagued with the constant pain of rheumatism or sciatica (since there were no medical records we cannot know which an accurate diagnosis would have shown). In fact, he soon became so disabled by his ailment that he was unable to mount a horse, and less than three weeks after Cowpens he had to go into permanent retirement.

Uncertainty. There was uncertainty throughout and before the battle. How far was Tarleton behind Morgan at any time? Where or how fast could Tarleton move to corner or attack him? How could he cross the Broad and still hold on to his militia, with Tarleton poised to spring on him while he was in the act? Where was Pickens, and when and where would he join Morgan? Would the militia in the first and second battle lines heed his orders and move out as directed after firing two shots? Was Washington's cavalry, even with its augmentation of McCall's men, strong enough to accomplish the mission of counterattacking British threats to the flanks? Could Pickens' militia be rallied and recommitted to action in time to play a decisive role in the battle?

Apprehension. This dynamic Morgan had to deal with in handling militia. He knew their capabilities and limitations, and the major limitation was their fear of the measured advance of British infantry behind its hedge of leveled bayonets, if for no other reason than that the militia had neither bayonets nor training to counter the threat. Morgan counted on that fear to "inspire" the men after they had given him "his two fires." But that fear was on the verge of becoming panic until Morgan and Pickens had halted and rallied the fleeing militia.

Frustration. Robert Burns, certainly never a soldier, has put it neatly nevertheless: "The best laid schemes o' mice an' men/Gang aft agley," and Morgan's fortune with his "schemes" at Cowpens was neither better nor worse than any other successful commander's. This can be recognized in two events. The first occurred when Morgan discovered that Pickens' men—running after firing their two rounds—were not going into the designated "rallying ground," but, instead, heading for their horses picketed behind Washington's reserve area. If the flight had been allowed to continue, in all probability the militia would have mounted up and been long gone when Morgan needed them most. The second occasion, equally serious in its potential for disaster, was the sudden and unexpected withdrawal of Howard's line which could have been catastrophic. Howard, it will be remembered, had decided to refuse his right flank in order to cope with an impending envelopment by the Highlanders. Accordingly he gave orders that his right flank company, Wallace's Virginians, change its front ninety degrees. To execute Howard's order the company should have been given the command to face about, followed by the command to wheel to the left and halt. In actuality, the company faced about, but instead of wheeling to the left, marched straight ahead, i.e., to the rear. The error could easily have been corrected, but before that could have happened the error was compounded by other commanders in Howard's line who thought that Wallace was obeying an order for a general withdrawal. They proceeded to follow suit. But Howard, understanding what had happened, handled the situation with the coolness we have seen.

So much for the dynamics of battle; they have shown the dark side of Cowpens. What did Dan Morgan bring to the bright side?

First of all, *courage,* the indispensable attribute. He consistently showed physical courage at the most critical and dangerous turns in the battle. Equally evident was his moral courage, that other quality required to take the risks involved in making a bold plan and sticking to it to see it executed to the finish.

When one considers Morgan's *intellect* there is little doubt that he exhibited those qualities that go to make up that attribute: imagination, flexibility of mind, and sound judgment. He was able to seize the opportunity to innovate because of his knowledge of human nature in general and the frailties of militia in particular. This was demonstrated when he told Pickens' men to run, because he knew they would, in any event, once confronted with British bayonets. It was his way of controlling the uncontrollable, allowing the militia to run away and fight another day which, in effect, they did.

Flexibility of mind also contributed to the attribute of *intellect,* shown in the case of Howard's "retreat." "This was the climax of the battle and the crucial decision. If Morgan had panicked or not gone along quickly with Howard, the Cowpens would have had a different ending. As it was, the misunderstood order called for a lightning-like decision, an almost intuitive reaction. Daniel Morgan met the crisis superbly."[6] In taking the action he did at this critical turn of events he further showed his good judgment.

Then there are Morgan's qualities which add up to the attribute of *will*. It would be difficult indeed to find a finer example of a leader coping with that most unpredictable dynamic, frustration. Morgan was exposed to it time and again; the most critical events have been covered in the analysis of the dynamics of battle. The other contributing qualities of boldness and staunchness which were also the manifestation of Morgan's will can be seen in his reactions to situations wherein his best-laid plans could have blown up in his face. He had to have known that such frustrations can occur—and usually do.

Finally, the sum of Morgan's attributes shown at Cowpens—*courage, intellect,* and *will*—were welded together into a tactical art. The combination enabled him to achieve that most sought-after effect in battle, surprise.

Tarleton reacted exactly as Morgan calculated he would by attacking frontally without reconaissance or maneuver. Furthermore, Tarleton was taken in by the flight of Pickens' line which he thought was acting like militia always had when on the wrong end of British bayonets. This led him to continue his frontal attack, and let it get out of hand when the false sense of exhilaration spread through his infantry, causing it to rush forward in a disordered mass. No one could have been more astounded than Tarleton when he saw this miniature Cannae happening to *him*! In his own words, he and his men were the victims of ". . . some unforeseen event, which may throw terror into the most disciplined soldiers, or counteract the best-concerted designs."[7] Some of us who were not there might call it surprise.

The summing up of this inside look at Cowpens might be compared to an arrow of Robin Hood's in the contest at Nottingham. If the shaft were straight and the aim true, he had a bullseye. Our shaft has been Dan Morgan's character, and the aim to show that a leader's attributes are the substance of his art. In Cowpens we have watched three such attributes come to life. As I have recognized five in all, the following chapters will be devoted to the examination of a leader's attributes in the light of the contribution of each to the art of leadership.

Part One

COURAGE

Anthony Wayne at
Stony Point, 1779

Louis Nicolas Davout
at **Auerstadt,** 1806

COURAGE

"This marshal [referring to Davout after his victory at Auerstädt] displayed distinguished bravery and firmness of character, the first qualities of the warrior."
—Napoleon in a bulletin to the *Grande Armée*

"We know from experience that the valor of the troops consists solely in the valor of the officers—a brave colonel, a brave battalion."
—Frederick the Great, *Die Werke Friedrichs des Grossen*

"I have formed a picture of a general which is not chimerical. . . . The first of all qualities is courage."
—Marshal de Saxe, *Reveries on the Art of War*

"War is the province of danger, and therefore courage above all things is the first quality of a warrior."
—Clausewitz, *On War*

Is an array of four epigraphs necessary to demonstrate the importance of courage? In this case, yes, for the intent has not been to overwhelm the reader with quotations, instead to suggest that something more than coincidence has caused three great commanders and a renowned theorist to agree that courage is the first attribute of the leader.

When one examines the histories of successful commanders, one soon finds that each invariably manifested not just simple bravery but two kinds of courage—the physical and the moral. And when one looks deeper he will realize that the dichotomy is not a historical nicety; there are indeed wide differences between the two.

Physical courage in battle, as the adjective indicates, involves the exposure of the body to the threat of wounds or death. Moral courage belongs to the domain of the mind. Yet, as we shall see, the two are often employed together and in combination with other attributes. For our purposes, however, I will first consider each separately with a view toward bringing them into balance at the chapter's end.

Physical Courage

FACING UP TO FEAR, to danger, is the focus of our interest as we consider men and their fears in battle. At the outset let us dispose of an encumbrance, the "fearless man." We have all heard of such men or have seen them in the movies, but fortunately they are about as scarce as politicians on the battlefield. I say "fortunately" because I have known (and known of) such men, and I wouldn't want them around in combat, much less leading men whose lives were my responsibility.

Let us see how one great mind has dealt with the idea of courage as opposed to fearlessness. Plato in the *Laches* has Nicias present his view of the issue: "I do not call animals . . . which have no fear of dangers, because they are ignorant of them, courageous, but only fearless or senseless . . . There is a difference, to my way of thinking, between fearlessness and courage. I am of the opinion that thoughtful courage is a quality possessed by very few, but that rashness, and boldness, and fearlessness, which has no forethought, are very common qualities possessed by many men, many women, many children, many animals . . . my courageous actions are wise actions."[1]

Plato is seconded by Aristotle when he observes that "drunken men often behave fearlessly and we do not praise them for their courage." In the light of such observations it is apparent that defining courage in the leader must embrace the concept of "thoughtful courage," the ability to distinguish between the danger itself, and the necessity to get the job done in spite of it. For the leader to make decisions in battle he should be expected to act or react with thoughtful courage while being guided by his professional values.

Consequently we can disregard the "fearless man" and concentrate on the great majority of men, men who acknowledge fear while realizing they must act positively in spite of it. This lies at the core of the enigma that confronts the soldier in battle. Unfortunately he has neither the time nor the environment to study his problems and arrive at reasonable solutions, as we can do so calmly in these pages.

It is the soldier and his fears that demand attention before we can refocus on his leaders. My own experience tells me that it would take a lifetime of research to do justice to the combat soldier's travail. We are in luck, however, in being able to rely on the findings of two men who have delved deeply into the subject and whose writings are universally respected.

The first, Col. Ardant du Picq, was mortally wounded by a German artillery shell while leading his regiment into its baptism by fire at Longville-les-Metz in the Franco-Prussian War. A professional infantry officer in the French Army and a veteran of three campaigns, du Picq was the first nineteenth-century writer to investigate the behavior of men in battle. His early researches made him an unpopular fellow with his brother officers, for his original approach was based on a questionnaire which he circulated among them. According to John Keegan in *The Face of Battle:* "The questionnaire was not a success, most who received it finding its tone impertinent or its completion tedious. But his questions were intelligent and original and, when applied by du Picq (whose rebuff by his brother officers had not extinguished his curiosity) to documentary material, elicited fascinating answers."[2]

I can sympathize with du Picq, having made a similar attempt at the Army Command and General College a century later. My responses from some three hundred combat officers may have been more numerous than those received by du Picq but scarcely more rewarding. Therein lies a trace of irony: The veteran officer seems to be as cautious in expressing his opinions about men in battle as he is bold at leading them in combat. So cautious, in fact, as to supply inadequate answers on this less tangible aspect of behavior. In his small book, *Battle Studies*, du Picq found answers by recognizing clearly the nature of fear in battle and its effects on combat units. He came to two major conclusions, and one is still applicable to ground combat in our times. His first finding was that, in ancient times, organized masses of men approached each other with the apparent intention of coming into violent collision. The collision never really occurred except in a front rank. One side would hesitate, slow down, even halt on some occasions, then break and turn away. The first and foremost in flight were those soldiers in the rear who had not yet come face to face with the enemy. Then the forward ranks gave way and joined in the flight. After that came the wholesale slaughter of the defeated, so common in ancient warfare, because the fleeing men had exposed their backs to the enemy.

Du Picq's second conclusion—of far greater interest to modern readers—was that modern soldiers from civilized nations can be made to realize through reasoned discipline and realistic training, that the greater danger lies in flight, for safety, in some measure, can be found in maintaining the integrity of the soldier's unit. In this light several of du Picq's contributory findings are interesting:

> How many men before a lion, have the courage to look him in the face, to think of and put into practice measures of self-defense? In war when terror has seized you, as experience has shown it often does, you are as before a lion . . .

> Four brave men who do not know each other will not dare to attack a lion. Four less brave, but knowing each other well, sure of their reliability and consequently of mutual aid, will attack resolutely. There is the science of the organization of armies in a nutshell . . .

> To fight from a distance is distinctive in man. From the first day he has worked to this end, and he continues to do so. It was thought that with long range weapons close combat might return. On the contrary troops keep further off before its effects . . .

> The theory of strong battalions is a shameful theory. It does not reckon on courage but on the amount of human flesh. It is a reflection on the soul. Great and small orators, all of whom speak of military matters today, talk only of masses. War is waged by enormous masses, etc. In the masses, man as an individual

disappears, the number only is seen. *Quality is forgotten, and yet today as always, quality alone produces real effect**. . . .[3]

The other writer whose work is authoritative was the late Brig.-Gen. S. L. A. Marshall, who has deservedly been called the successor of du Picq. Slam Marshall (Samuel Lyman Atwood Marshall) succeeded where du Picq did not, for he lived to see his conclusions and chief recommendations bear fruit. He was able, in Keegan's words, "to persuade the American army that it was fighting its wars the wrong way."[4]

It became relatively easy for Marshall to draw the conclusions he did because his innovative methods produced the bases for the widely acclaimed campaign histories of the American army in World War II. Probably of greater importance was the quality and quantity of data about men in battle which now provides invaluable aid to historians and other analysts. It was Marshall who sold the high command in the European Theater his idea of debriefing, i.e., historical teams holding mass interviews with combat infantrymen *on the spot just as their companies came out of combat.* He developed techniques for getting the men talking—to an extent that unabashed and unembarrassed soldiers were sounding off freely—so that one man's recollections were reinforced and often amended by those of his comrades. In fact the stories, from memories fresh and uncluttered by subsequent events, poured out so freely and fast that the skills of the historical teams were often strained in trying to get down all the interrelated accounts. Yet they succeeded in an amazing tour de force.

Marshall's most disturbing discovery, at least to army officers and military analysts, was that

> a commander of infantry will be well advised to believe that when he engages the enemy not more than one quarter of his men will ever strike a real blow unless they are compelled by almost overpowering circumstance or unless all junior leaders constantly 'ride herd' on troops with the specific mission of increasing their fire. The 25 percent estimate stands even for well-trained and well-seasoned troops. I mean that 75 percent will not fire or will not persist in firing against the enemy and his works. They may face the danger, but they will not fight.[5]

In searching for a way out of this dilemma, Marshall had

*Italics added

found a key clue when he said: "Men who have been in battle know from first hand experience that when the chips are down, a man fights to help the man next to him, just as a company fights to keep pace with its flanks."[6]

Another contributor who helped find a key to controlling fear and behavior was none other than Charles Darwin. In his study of the development of intellectual and moral faculties in prehistoric man, he wrote:

> We may therefore conclude that primeval man, at a very remote period, was influenced by the praise and blame of his fellows. It is obvious, that the members of the same tribe would approve of conduct which appeared to them to be for the general good, and would reprobate that which appeared evil. To do good unto others—to do unto others as ye would that they should do unto you—is the foundation stone of morality. It is, therefore, hardly possible to exaggerate the importance during rude times of the love of praise and the dread of blame. A man who was not impelled by any deep, instinctive feeling, to sacrifice his life for the good of others, yet was aroused to such actions by a sense of glory, would by his example excite the same wish for glory in other men, and would strengthen by exercise the noble feeling of admiration.[7]

I believe that Marshall would have read this assertion of Darwin's with satisfaction, and I believe that he would agree with me when I sum up the gist of the solution in two key words—honor and companionship. These words are not meant to be used as guides in a crusade which would ennoble soldiers to a point where every company would contain a hundred Damons and an equal number of Pythiases. But Du Picq and Marshall have shown us the way. Marshall lived to see a major recommendation adopted by the Army dealing with the reorganization of fighting units at the lowest level, the infantry squad. This resulted in restructuring squads into small groups called fire teams. Marshall's concept included centering the fire teams on "natural fighters." Such a fighter might be exemplified by Stephen Crane's Henry Fleming in *The Red Badge of Courage*. Henry was the boy who ran from his first fire fight, then returned to become a man by leading a charge of his company and capturing the enemy's regimental color. This part of Marshall's proposal is difficult to implement in peacetime training, for it has only been in battle's natural process of selection that such fighters emerge.

Thus far we have focused on the problems of aiding the soldier to overcome "freezing" in combat. What about the leader? He cannot look to companionship for help in overcoming his fears. In fact the very nature of command makes the lot of the commander one of the loneliest conditions known to man. Since he cannot look outside for help he must look into himself for moral sustenance. That alone should remind us that du Picq was right when he spoke of quality as the only producer of "real effect." For nothing can exceed in importance the selection of officers and non-commissioned officers for positions of leadership. That selection should take heed of what William James termed the "heroic mind": "When a dreadful object is presented, or when life as a whole turns up its dark abysses to our view, then the worthless ones among us lose their hold on the situation altogether . . . But the heroic mind does differently . . . It can face them if necessary, without . . . losing its hold upon the rest of life. The world thus finds in the heroic man its worthy match and mate . . . [for] he can *stand* this universe."[8]

When one reflects on James's heroic mind would it not—once presented with a "dreadful object" or looking into one of "life's dark abysses"—resort to the kind of thoughtful courage propounded by Plato's Nicias? It would seem that any other kind of courage—such as so-called fearlessness—would not be consistent with such a mind.

If this is so, should we expect all our leaders to possess heroic minds? Not necessarily. I believe James's use of such a grand adjective as heroic was only a way of dramatizing what we commonly call a person with a "strong mind." For example, I would feel uneasy, if not downright embarrassed, telling someone that I thought that Harry Truman had a heroic mind. Strong, yes indeed; heroic, no.

In the event of a full scale mobilization we will not be afforded the luxury of a discriminating search for leaders with truly heroic minds. If we can find enough strong-minded men for leaders, experience has shown that courage can be expected to accompany their other qualities.

Honor should be considered concomitant with courage. It is the very heartbeat of the leader's role, for if his actions are not exemplary, what is he doing in that position? If he is doing his job, his presence among his men (where he belongs if he is really leading and not just operating some electronic device in a command post) places him under constant scrutiny. And the nature of that scrutiny rules out any kind of phoniness, for soldiers soon develop an uncanny sense for separating the counterfeit from the genuine. Any officer who has led in battle will tell you that such awareness is one of the first things acquired if one expects to succeed as a leader. It is a fact that has been around as long as warfare, and that is a long, long time.

Now it is time to show leaders in action, to observe battle through their eyes and minds. We have already witnessed one such action. This time the accent is on what Napoleon called "two o'clock in the morning courage," as we see Anthony Wayne and his light infantry leaders prepare for:

The Storming of Stony Point

The July night was still warm long after midnight. Its quiet had been unbroken until the baying of the running hound had brought the patrol to a halt. The four infantrymen sank down in their tracks and waited silently for their sergeant to come back down the trail. In seconds his broad bulk loomed alongside the first man in the file. The sergeant reached out in the darkness and tapped the two nearest men on the shoulder.

The two rose without a sound and disappeared, Indian-like, into the treeline that separated the trail from the clearing. The sergeant squatted beside the other two men, and all three listened intently. There was a low whistle and the sound of the dog lunging into the brush. The barking broke out again, this time rising in the ringing bay of the hound charging the intruder. The baying rose, then ended abruptly in a sharp yelping that broke off as quickly as it had begun.

The sergeant led the patrol forward on the trail to join the two men he had sent out. They fell in at the end of the file, the last man pausing long enough to wipe his bayonet on a handful of pine needles from the forest floor.

Washington rested his field glass on Anthony Wayne's right shoulder and turned his attention again to the abatis* encircling the outermost fieldworks of Stony Point. He shifted the focus of his glass slowly until he had taken in the lower artillery batteries, then repeated his surveillance of the inner

---

*Abatis—an obstacle formed by felling large trees so that the ends of their branches are pointing at possible enemy avenues of approach.

ring of abatis. Satisfied, he took another look at the British frigate anchored in the middle of the Hudson a mile and a half away. The reflection of the afternoon sun on the sparkling surface of the river was almost blinding, so much so that the commander-in-chief was quick to lower his glass.

"That's the *Vulture,* is it not?" Washington asked.

"You're correct, Sir. The British have kept her moored there ever since they took Stony Point on the first of June," Wayne replied.

"And so they have done all this fortifying in just five weeks. Busy work, and fast, for British soldiers," Washington said.

"But not too fast for our plans. You'll remember that part of Captain McClane's report about the incompleted wall on the west side of the citadel, a gap wide enough to march a platoon through in line abreast."

"That report is one of the chief reasons I'm on this reconnaissance with you. I believe that Major Lee* got McClane into the fort under a flag of truce where he made the observations in his report."

"Right again, Sir. McClane told me that the British commandant, Lieutenant Colonel Johnson, was so confident of the strength of Stony Point's fortifications that he did not have McClane blindfolded," Wayne said.

"McClane was in the fort just two days ago, and you made your own reconnaissance two days before that, on July 2. But before we say more about the fort, what is your latest estimate of the garrison's strength?" Washington asked.

"Hardly an estimate any longer, Sir, just cold fact. We've not only been watching the British with Lee's Legion, but we have all kinds of reports from civilians and the like. What the garrison amounts to is Colonel Johnson's 17th Regiment plus the grenadier company of the 71st Highlanders, a detachment of the Loyal Americans, and fifteen guns manned by Royal Artillery crews. In all, the total comes to a little over six hundred men."

Washington nodded his understanding as he seated himself on a boulder, motioning Wayne to do the same. The two generals had spent the past hour oblivious to everything except their observations and exchanges. Now the commander-in-chief relaxed, looking down the pine-clad slopes of the

*Light Horse Harry Lee, famed cavalryman and father of Robert E. Lee. Lee's Legion, made up of cavalry and infantry companies, was under Washington, with Lee reporting to Wayne.

View of Stony Point today

mountain toward distant Stony Point. The two were shielded from the warm July sun by the pines of the Buckberg and the rock outcropping they had used for cover. A hundred yards below them, just visible through the pines, they could see Light-Horse Harry Lee and Alexander Hamilton, Washington's senior aide, pacing impatiently back and forth as they waited for the generals to break off their reconnaissance and rejoin them. Wayne paid them no heed as he leaned forward to hand Washington the sketch that had been drafted by Colonel Putnam and added to by Wayne himself.

"I'm ready to talk about the details of my mission, if you are, Sir," Wayne said.

Washington took the sketch, pretending to examine it while his mind's eye was studying the man who had handed it to him.

I must have no doubts now, he thought, *that I've chosen the right man for this operation, for it seems all risk and with nothing but damaged reputations, even ruined careers, if it fails. I can't afford failure. I can't afford any more Long Islands or Germantowns, though we've come a long way in those three years since Long Island.*

Wayne has shown all the dash and daring needed for this work; now I need to know that he can plan it well, and carry out that plan. I must know that he will calculate as would I. Yet he must have the freedom of action he needs, for how else am I ever going to get generals fit for independent command, generals I can trust?

Washington looked up from the sketch that had been imprinted on his memory hours before this reconnaissance. His steady gaze fixed on Wayne's hazel eyes as he spoke.

"There are no more details to discuss here. I expect you to furnish enough of those in your finished plan to assure my approval. In the meantime I will confirm my ideas in writing, to reach you in at least four days, say by July 10. Now, since we're agreed on a general plan, let me summarize it. To begin, it must be a night attack, planned with the utmost secrecy, and made known only to senior officers who must be trusted with it. We are agreed, too, that the British outworks and the citadel itself must be taken by surprise. Yes, it must be stormed—"

An animated Wayne was on his feet, his hazel eyes lit with such excitement that he forgot he was interrupting his chief.

"General, if you give me permission, I'll storm Hell itself for you," Wayne said.

The briefest gleam flickered in Washington's eye.

"Perhaps you had better try Stony Point first," he said.

Wayne flushed as he became aware of his breach of military courtesy. He started to stammer an apology, but Washington's quiet smile and outstretched hand restrained him. The two wasted no time on formalities as they went back over Washington's guidelines to his chosen commander of the newly-formed Light Infantry Corps. Washington recounted each main point pausing only to answer Wayne's questions. The assault would be made by Wayne's light infantry alone. The thirteen-mile approach march, starting from Wayne's camp at Sandy Beach, must end under cover of darkness, observing the strictest security measures. Sole reliance must be placed on the bayonet, all muskets unloaded. When he got to that point Washington eyed Wayne, wondering if they both were thinking of the disastrous rout of Wayne's division by a British surprise attack at night, back in September of '77.

I know he still smarts at the memory of it, Washington thought. *Although he was fully acquitted by the court-martial he had demanded, Wayne will never get over it—nor should he. Surprised in the dead of night by the British general whose deed won him the title of "no-flint" Grey, Wayne's fifteen hundred men were overrun at Paoli where he lost a good tenth of his command in casualties and prisoners. It was a British victory won by careful planning, surprise, and reliance on the bayonet. I can see by his face he needs no more reminders: his appetite for revenge alone will assure that he has learned his lesson, one that he can turn to good account against the enemy at Stony Point.*

Washington went on to recall their agreement on the composition and direction of the main attack. The approach should be toward the south side of the peninsula that formed the base of Stony Point, across a sunken sandbar where the marsh surrounding the landward side of Stony Point ended. Wayne had already pointed out two critical factors that made the approach over the sandbar an invaluable aid to a *coup de main*. First, the British were unaware of the existence of the sandbar, for they had not set a night picket to cover that avenue of approach. Second, since the Hudson in the area was actually an estuary rather than a river, the marsh and the sandbar were flooded at high tide, but the bar could be crossed by wading at low tide.

Washington added that it was common practice for night attacks to be made a little before first light. Since the garrison should be well aware of that, however, and would keep a more vigilant watch at that time, it would be better to launch the assault near midnight on a moonless night. He went on to cover what he considered adequate forces for the main and secondary attacks: assault columns preceded by "forlorn hopes"* whose carefully selected leaders would make sure that paths would be cleared through the abatis while driving in the British outposts; advance parties to follow through the obstacles, composed of one to two hundred men; and, finally, the main bodies of the selected regiments which would assure enough weight of support to accomplish the mission.

Washington concluded by repeating his concern for the secrecy and security so essential to a successful surprise, even if it meant securing civilians who might observe the approach of Wayne's force. When Washington stood to indicate that the conference was at an end Wayne was on his feet with a final assurance.

"My plans already include such measures, for the farm-

---

*In today's journalese, suicide squads.

ers and their families, but I'm also going to be sure that not even a dog's barking will give away our approach march."

The fine July weather continued to grace the Hudson Highlands, and now on Thursday morning of the fifteenth Wayne's Light Infantry Corps stood in ranks for inspection in the sun beating down on the Sandy Beach camp. The four regiments were aligned, each in a two-battalion front, under Baron von Steuben's approving eye. Anthony Wayne's eye was not so approving. "Dandy"[9] Wayne winced inwardly as he looked down the ranks of the smartly-turned-out battalions. He knew he would never be happy with his corps on parade as long as the men had to wear the uniforms of the various regiments from which they had been drawn. To his mind, with its love of orderly display, these splendid men had been done an injustice in not being issued one distinctive uniform. The discordant array jarred his military sensibility. Here they were, handpicked men from six states, each still in the uniform of his own line. The overall cut of the uniforms was similar, but the color of the facings clashed, and there were the brown coats (obtained the previous year from France) worn by Continentals from Virginia, Pennsylvania, and Massachusetts alongside the blue of the North Carolina, Connecticut, and Maryland Line. Washington had given Wayne first priority on arms and equipment but he had flatly refused Wayne's request for a single uniform for the elite corps. Although the non-uniformity would continue to irk their commander the men in the ranks never gave it a passing thought. (One wonders: if the Light Infantry had contained a counterpart of an earlier Bill Mauldin in its eighteenth-century ranks, would he not at times have seen Dandy Wayne as the same pain-in-the-ass as the World War II G.I. cartoonist saw pistol-packing General Patton? Both generals loved color and dash, while sharing the same regard for discipline symbolized by a correctly turned-out uniform.)

Nevertheless, Wayne comforted himself as he gazed down the ruler-straight ranks, *I've still got the finest men in Washington's army, all 1,350 picked from the forty-six infantry battalions of the Continental Line. And the commander-in-chief had personally passed on every officer from ensign to colonel before he chose me for commander of the corps. What an irony lies behind that selection! It has been said that the choice was narrowed down to Dan Morgan and myself. Then, once Washington's decision had been made, I came*

*out of three months retirement, and Dan Morgan retired in disgust
to his farm in Virginia. So here I am only eighteen days in command
of the finest body of men in America—oh, the gleam in von Steuben's
eye when he watched the precision of their drill a half-hour ago—
and yet not a man jack aware that he is about to march off to take
part in the most dangerous operation ever attempted in this army.
Yes, only a little over twelve hours from now how many of those fine
men standing there will be blasted to earth by a British bullet or
grapeshot? Only the mighty Jehovah can answer that. Now here comes
my aide, Henry Archer, and I know he is going to tell me that the
Baron has declared the inspection complete and Brigade Major
McCormick can order the battalions to pass in review.*

As Wayne rode his horse at a walk to take post behind
the Brigade Major the commands began to ring out as he
approached the front of Colonel Febiger's 1st Regiment.

"Battalion! Present—Arms!"

The drums on the right wing began beating the salute
as Wayne returned the salutes of the officers. The drums on
the left of the regiment took up the roll as the commands
came from the battalion he had just passed.

"Shoulder—Firelocks!

"Rear rank! Close to the front—March!

"Rest!"

At the last command young Lt. George Knox in the 1st
Battalion, 1st Regiment relaxed and shifted his weight to the
espontoon* held upright in his right hand. The seven-foot
shaft of the pike was still awkward to his hand; the officers
had been issued the weapon only three days before and the
only practice in their handling had been the bayonet-like drill
which was clearly intended as combat training. Knox, formerly of the 9th Regiment of the Pennsylvania Line, was well
aware of Dandy Wayne's reputation for show, but the issue
of officers' espontoons and the practice that followed was
puzzling. If the weapons had been meant for show—as they
seemed to be in this parade—then why the battle drill?

*If any officer, Knox thought, can figure out Dandy Wayne's
plans he deserves to be a general himself. We've been marched and
drilled and inspected until the men are getting restless. We know by
now that we're bound for some special mission some day and that
we're as sharply-trained as men can get. Yet I hope the men don't go*

*Espontoon (or spontoon)—a pike with a wooden shaft from six to eight feet long. Wayne got
them for all his officers through a letter to Washington, and the weapons were issued to the
Light Infantry officers by July 12.

over that fine edge. This inspection was the strictest yet, by far. I've seen that every man in my platoon was "fresh shaved and well powdered" by brigade order, and I've checked every item of uniform from neck stocks to gaiters a dozen times per man. I've counted musket flints and inspected cartridge boxes, by brigade order, until I've been blue in the face. For what? Another march through the Highlands?

Knox's thoughts were cut short by a volley of commands from his battalion commander, Lieutenant Colonel Fleury.

"Battalion—Attention!

"Shoulder firelocks—

"Battalion—

"By platoons to the left—Wheel! March!"

All right then, fine. The men stepped out smartly in time with the marching beat of the drums. This was what they had been waiting for: the march past their general that would end this tedious day of inspection and parade. Soon they could fall out and relax in the shade of their tents, stretching out on the grass while the camp kettles were heated up for the noon meal.

Knox marched alongside his platoon with the swinging stride of the Light Infantry, which had already become accustomed to parading to the quick step. He cut his eyes to the right to locate the camp "street" where his battalion would be dismissed in front of its row of tents.

But what was happening? He could see the head of the battalion passing the end of their street. Fleury was not the kind of commander to allow a mistake like that, yet he could see Fleury's ramrod-straight back still aligned firmly to the front. Knox was marching at attention and could not turn his head, but he was sure they had passed their street. And in minutes they had left the camp behind. What was happening? The question was in every man's mind, and confusion was compounded by Fleury's next commands.

"Take care to break off by sections of four!

"Sections of four! Break off!"

The sections of the platoons were obliquing inward to form the column of fours required for a road march. Then the battalion *was* off on a march, this time headed south along the Hudson on the road to Fort Montgomery.

It had been straight-up noon when the whole of the Light Infantry—four regiments strong and all in one column for the first time—had left the camp at Sandy Beach. They had route-marched past the ruins of Fort Montgomery, turning

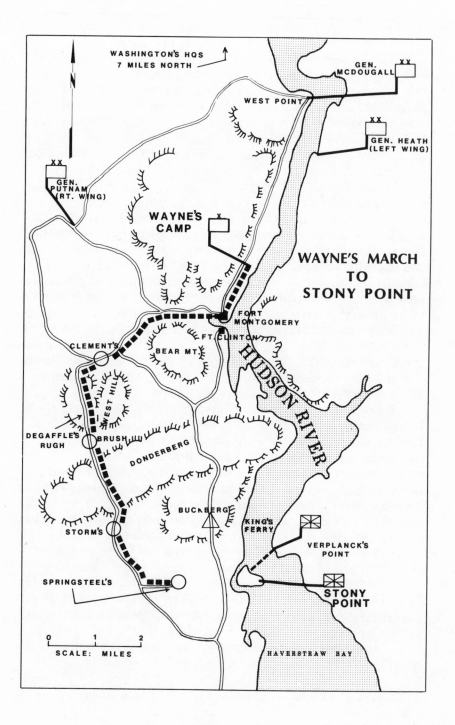

WASHINGTON'S HQS
7 MILES NORTH

N

GEN.
McDOUGALL   XX

WEST POINT

GEN. HEATH   XX
(LEFT WING)

GEN.   XX
PUTNAM
(RT. WING)

WAYNE'S
CAMP   X

WAYNE'S MARCH
TO
STONY POINT

FORT
MONTGOMERY

FT. CLINTON

CLEMENT'S

BEAR MT.

HUDSON RIVER

WEST HILL

DEGAFFLE'S
RUGH   BRUSH

DONDERBERG

BUCKBERG

KING'S
FERRY   VERPLANCK'S
POINT   ☒

STORM'S

STONY
POINT   ☒

SPRINGSTEEL'S

0   1   2

SCALE: MILES

HAVERSTRAW BAY

westward to pass between Torn Mountain and the mass of rugged Bear Mountain. They had forked left to the southwest and at two o'clock Wayne had ordered the first halt near the solitary house of a farmer named Clement.

While the corps fell out to rest along the roadside, the Brigade Major gave the assembled regimental and battalion commanders the orders for the rest of the march. Major McCormick finished by saying that the commander had directed that no soldier would leave the ranks, for any reason, except at a scheduled halt, and then only under the eyes of an officer. "Yes," the major said in reply to a query, "if it means a lieutenant has to take his platoon en masse off the road for a quick piss, that is exactly what he'll have to do."

The first half of the next leg proved to be the roughest part of the march. The rutted dirt road dwindled into a narrow, bouldered path as it crossed Degaffle's Rugh, until the column had to ascend and descend the tortuous way in single file; nothing new to these veterans, most of whom had seen years of war. The men sweated under their full field equipment, up and down steep ravines in the July heat, but none was allowed to slow the march, nor did any soldier want to. They picked their way through the pines down the Rugh, and then had to ascend painfully the steep slopes of the Donderberg.

By 6:00 P.M. the column was approaching Storm's farmhouse, and not a man had been lost to straggling. Wayne found Light Horse Harry Lee awaiting him, and the two went into the house for a final exchange of information.

The march continued through late afternoon into the July evening until, with dusk closing around them, the corps closed into its assembly area around David Springsteel's farm, a mile and a half directly west of Stony Point. Wayne had already dispatched Col. Richard Butler (commanding the 2nd Regiment), along with Maj. Tom Posey and Maj. Harry Lee, to a covered post where they could observe Stony Point and its garrison. Wayne left Springsteel's after he had issued his orders for the organization for combat, and went directly to join Butler. He took with him Col. "Old Denmark" Febiger* of the 1st Regiment, Col. Return Meigs of the 3rd, Maj. William Hull commanding the 4th, and their battalion commanders.

*So called because he had emigrated from Denmark to Virginia in 1774. He joined the colonists the following year, and in the army had proved himself a leader at Bunker Hill and Quebec.

In the failing light Wayne was still able to point out critical terrain features: the details of the fort's defenses, avenues of approach for the assault columns, and the objectives for each column. An elated Anthony Wayne then led the command group back to Springsteel's over the approach route the corps would take before it would split into two assault columns. Wayne had reason to be elated. He had closed his command in its assembly area with not a man lost, and more important, every security measure had been carried out so that he was able to say he had observed to the letter Washington's warning: "Knowledge of your intention ten minutes previously obtained can blast all your hopes."

When the command group had reassembled in the Springsteel house, Major McCormick spread out the enlarged sketch of Wayne's battle plan on David Springsteel's dining table and weighted its corners with candle holders. Before he spoke Wayne looked across the candlelight at the circle of faces above the battle plan. *This is the moment they've been waiting for,* he thought, *and with the exception of four of them, this will be their first exposure to my plan.*

"I'll be brief," he said, "and cover only the main points. Then Major McCormick will go over the written order in detail.* Later, you can give it to the troops. But first, a question—have the white patches for the hats been issued?"

"Every man has been given a square of white paper and the NCO's are making sure that each man fastens it to the front of his hat," Major McCormick said.

"Very well, here is the plan. As you see, there are two attacks—two assault columns—which will penetrate the British defenses and seize their joint objective, the citadel of the fort—here."

Wayne's forefinger rested on the highest, innermost point in the fort. His hazel eyes shone and his handsome, bold-nosed face showed its high color in the candles' glow as he continued.

"The main attack is on the right and I will lead it myself. It will come from the south following Route Number 1, crossing the marsh and the submerged sandbar which we should be wading over near midnight. This column will be preceded by a twenty-man forlorn hope under a selected officer, followed by the advance party led by Lieutenant Colonel Fleury—

*Appendix contains Wayne's order in full.

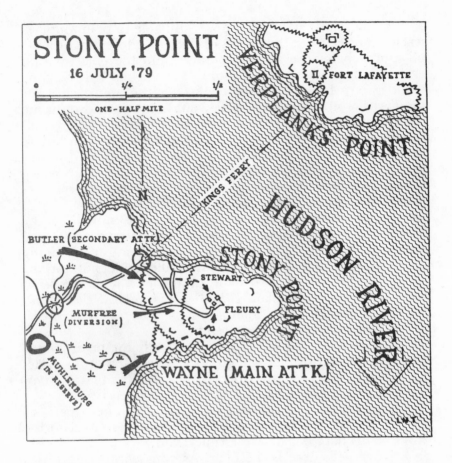

all from Colonel Febiger's regiment. The main body, following close on Colonel Fleury's 150 men, will consist of Colonel
Meigs' 3rd Regiment which will be followed by Major Hull
with the 1st Battalion of the 4th Regiment."

Wayne's finger traced the movements across the plan,
pointing to each unit as he referred to it.

"Colonel Butler will command the secondary attack on
the left, on the north over Route Number 2, and that attack
will be made in a similar fashion, that is, led by a forlorn
hope, followed by Major Stewart with 150 men of the 2nd
Battalion of Colonel Butler's regiment, that makes up the advance party. It will be followed by the remainder of Colonel
Butler's regiment.

"You can see the routes for the two attacks, but there is
a third element which has a mission just as important as the

two attacks. That is the diversionary force made up of Major Murfree's North Carolinians. He will lead his two companies, and his orders direct him to follow the rear of Colonel Butler's column until all are across the causeway over the marsh—here. At that time Major Murfree will break off with his men and advance toward the British center, prepared to conduct a diversion, commencing to fire as soon as the British pickets open fire on any element of our corps.

"Now note this, gentlemen. Major Murfree's command is the only one authorized to fire during the operation. All others will move to the assault with unloaded, shouldered muskets, so that their sole weapon will be the bayonet—and the officers' espontoons. Note also that I have included in my written order that any soldier who attempts to fire, unless so ordered by an officer, will be put to death by the nearest officer.[10] Finally, the matter of the watchword, 'The fort is ours', which will be shouted only when our men have broken into the inner walls of the fort. All clear then?"

Wayne answered the few questions from the group, then turned to his other aide, Major Fishbourne, who put the shaft of an espontoon into his general's outstretched hand.

"In case you are wondering, gentlemen, I'm not carrying this just to show it off to the troops. I trust you have the same intent in mind with your own. Our conference is dismissed. We will move out at 11:30, that gives you ample time to make your preparations," Wayne concluded.

Lt. Col. François Louis Teissedre de Fleury (plain Fleury to the Americans), scion of a French noble family of Provençal, commanding the 1st Battalion of the 1st Regiment, was a logical choice to lead the advance party of the main attack. Logical because of his outstanding record and reputation for gallantry, made as a volunteer in the American service in which he had enlisted three years before. In less than one year, starting in May of 1777, he had distinguished himself in a siege, a raid, and two major battles—Brandywine and Germantown. He had earned the thanks of Congress and the official gift of a horse for the first, then had the horse killed under him in the second, where he also took a wound in the leg. These actions and others had him promoted, in rapid succession, from captain to major to lieutenant colonel, all in the same year.[11]

Now that quick French mind was bent to the tasks of or-

ganizing his battalion for that most dreaded of operations, a
night attack. To Fleury's mind the first task was ensuring that
the officer who led the forlorn hope was thoroughly grounded
in his mission and all that it entailed. He took Lieutenant Knox
to one side while the advance party was being formed up.

"You are aware that you have been assigned the most
rewarding duty in all the corps," Fleury said, his face only
inches away from Knox's in the close darkness.

"Responsible, Sir—but rewarding?" Knox's voice carried
the surprise that Fleury was not able to see in his face.

"Ah yes, the glory. What else? What greater opportunity
will any lieutenant ever have? But you are ready, yes?"

"Well, if you mean me myself, I suppose so, Sir."

"Of course I mean you. You will have plenty of time to
inspect your men, their equipment, all that. But are you prepared in your mind—so you see each thing that must be done?"
Fleury asked, his tone almost fatherly in spite of his realization that, at the age of thirty, he could hardly have fathered
a lieutenant.

"I have much concern about my route. I've not had the
chance to see it but once in daylight, and since I will be in
the lead—"

Fleury's sudden interruption was eased by his reassuring
hand laid on Knox's shoulder.

"Two reasons for not worrying. I will be beside you even
though my post might be thought to be at your rear. Also we
will have as a guide one of Major Lee's best scouts, a sergeant
who has been reconnoitering the fort and its approaches for
a week, night and day. But now, do you have the plan of the
fort fixed in your head?" Fleury asked.

In his mind's eye Knox saw again the rocky promontory
rising 150 feet above the river and the marsh, a natural fortress now studded with outworks and gun emplacements and
guarded by a double ring of abatis, each extending all the
way around the rocky peninsula, the whole surmounted by
the citadel with its stone bastions. To Knox's young mind, it
was truly the Gibraltar of the West as the British had proclaimed it.

"Yes," Knox said, "I've had my turn at looking at the
map and the order, but I am concerned now about the approach to the first British picket."

"First you must remember that Stony Point is really an
island because of the salt marsh all around the landward side.

We will approach, first across the marsh, then over the sandbar which should be covered by only inches of water at midnight. The first picket will be to your left flank as we come out of the water on the beach of the Point—which we will follow for fifty paces to make sure that we have gotten around the south or water end of the first row of abatis. Then if the picket fires at us we will keep on going because he will draw the fire of Murfree's men, and that will keep the British occupied."

"And then?"

"And then comes the vital part of your mission, your double task."

"Double task? I don't follow you."

"Double because two things must be done at once if the whole attack is to succeed. Some of your men must take care of the nearest outpost while others, with axes and billhooks, must clear enough of the abatis to make a path for my advance party. Do you see?"

"I do now, Sir. Is that all?"

"Surely it is enough, is it not? Is it that I have found a fire-eater in this lieutenant? Yes, fire-eater, one final thing. You must not let the tales of this 'little Gibraltar' cause fear in you. It is far from being impregnable, and you must trust me when I say that surprise overcomes all. Now, back to your men. By this time they will have been issued their tools, and you must organize them for their work." The white outline of Fleury's face faded away in the dark.

At five minutes before midnight Knox and his men had forded the marsh, wading through marsh grass and ankle-deep saltwater. He halted, waiting for his men to close up, and tried to peer through the blackness. It seemed to Knox that the night had become a black curtain dropped across a darkened stage. The night sounds were reassuring though, the crickets and frogs making a background chorus over the subdued sloshing of the wading men. It was eerie here amid the clinging stink of the marsh air and all too quiet with hundreds of men yet to follow in their wake. *Yes, all going too well. Here they were stepping out to wade the sandbar only a few yards to their front, and still no sound from the British outposts.*

Knox felt the chill of the tidewater rising to his knees as he pressed forward, and then, incredibly, to his thighs and over his waist. Fleury too had felt the chilling surprise—"*Mon dieu,"* he muttered as he struggled forward. *My God, yes,* thought Knox, *if this is the ankle-deep sandbar, what in hell next?*

What-in-hell-next happened all too soon. The men behind Knox had slung their muskets in order to free their hands for carrying their axes. When the cold water became waist deep the soldiers started to unsling their muskets and hold them overhead with their axes. A swinging musket struck against the bayonet of the next infantryman with the unmistakable clang of steel against steel, and off to the left came the British picket's challenge—"Who goes there?"

Knox and his file leaders pushed on in silence, breasting the tide, their feet on the sand bottom giving them the foothold they needed. All of the forlorn hope was still in waist-deep water when the first British sentry fired. The flash and bang of the shot triggered off a ragged volley from other pickets, the bullets ricocheting off the water or whistling overhead. In seconds Murfree's companies opened up with a roar, and the night to the left and front of Knox's men was aflame with the answering fire of British muskets. Knox felt the water receding as he made his way onto the beach and felt his boots dig into dry sand. He heard the shouted commands of British sergeants as reinforcements charged down from the citadel and artillery gun crews ran to man their guns.

Knox and Fleury, side by side, were running along the beach, the forlorn hope on their heels when the first British cannon shot crashed out from the emplacement a hundred yards above them. The artillerymen had fired high and the whirring of the grapeshot ripped through the air overhead. Luckily for Knox, he was running with the point of his espontoon thrust forward when the blade glanced off a leveled tree branch. He was in the edge of the second row of abatis. He thrust the blade of his weapon into the ground and yelled his file leaders into their task of chopping and pulling aside the interlaced branches of the obstacle. No need for keeping silent now, the night had exploded into a red roar, with British muskets and artillery firing with such intensity that the slope in front of the Americans was lit by the discharges. No time for anything now but clawing and tearing at the abatis until bloodied hands were doing better work than axes. But British artillery had gotten the range and the rounds of grapeshot were rattling off the tree limbs and into the forlorn hope. Sergeant Baker, to Knox's left, took wounds in arm and leg but kept tearing his way forward.

We've got to get through here now, by God, Knox thought, trying to see an end to the tangle of branches, *or we will die here. I've got to get them forward, it's the only way they'll survive.*

He snatched up his espontoon and used its upper half like a club to batter his way through. He heard Fleury getting men to open another path. They were in the clear now, and the first files of Fleury's advance party were widening the gaps made by Knox's men. Fleury and Knox were running up the slope between the British gun emplacements.

Anthony Wayne and Old Denmark entered a gap in the abatis at the head of the main body, Wayne's once-fine uniform coat a mass of dripping mud—like those of his men—from the chest down. He grounded his espontoon and tried to shout above the crash of musketry to direct Major Posey and his men toward the gap.

"Over this way! Incline the column to the right—" Wayne's commands stopped short. He felt a searing stab on his forehead. There was a whirling rush of stabbing stars across his eyes. The ground rushed up at him, and he was down among the logs of the abatis.

Ben Fishbourne and Henry Archer, Wayne's aides, were on either side of their general and felt rather than saw him fall. Archer was the first to realize that Wayne had a head wound, and was probing in his commander's bloody hair when he regained consciousness. Wayne winced at feeling Archer's fingers touch the wound.

"Help me up to the fort. I must get to the head of the column." Wayne had gotten back his command voice.

"Let me get my handkerchief around your head and we'll get you moving," Fishbourne's tone was as firm as Wayne's.

The aides found that their general had taken a scalp wound, a bullet crease above the forehead, and in seconds had his head bandaged, and had him standing between them.

"All right, let's get moving," Wayne ordered, and the three moved alongside Febiger's column until they found an interval between companies. In minutes Wayne was back in command, directing elements of the main body forward and up to the citadel at the summit.

Fleury, outdistancing Knox by only yards, was the first to charge through the sallyport on the citadel's south side. He was followed by Knox, then Sergeant Baker of Virginia (now four times wounded), Sergeant Spencer of Virginia, and Sergeant Donlop of Pennsylvania, both twice wounded.[12] Fleury rushed to the flagstaff, shouting "the fort is ours!" He freed the halyards and hauled down the British flag. His men, pouring through the sallyport, took up the cry, but the watchword in itself could not assure that British resistance was finished.

For a quarter of an hour the inner walls and the works around it were bloody confusion as knots of British fought back with bayonets and swords. But it was soon evident the British cause was doomed. The head of Butler's column, led by Major Stewart, charged over the north side of the citadel where they were greeted by Maj. Tom Posey. While the mopping-up had gotten under way Fleury, Stewart, and Posey held a hurried conference, and they soon realized how the overall action had gone.

"Murfree's demonstration had achieved its purpose, and Colonel Johnson charged down the hill with half his garrison—six companies of the 17th—to meet what he thought was the main threat. He was cut off and captured by Febiger's Regiment when he tried to regain the fort. The others tried to hold out but were isolated into little packets where they vainly tried to resist the bayonets, swords, and spontoons— for about fifteen minutes the hilltop was the scene of a mad turmoil, and the British then began to throw down their arms and cry quarter. It is a further tribute to Wayne's discipline that Stony Point did not join the list of Revolutionary War 'massacres'." [13]

In less than an hour and a half after leaving Springsteel's farm the Light Infantry Corps had accomplished its mission. Anthony Wayne, wearing that archetype of heroic emblems, the bloody bandage around the head, sat down in the British colonel's quarters to pen his *veni, vidi, vici* to his Commander-in-Chief:

> Stony Point, 16th July, 1779
> 2 A.M.
>
> Dear Gen'l,—The fort & garrison with Col. Johnson are ours.
> Our officers and men behaved like men who are
> determined to be free.
> Yours most sincerely,
> Anth'y Wayne

He handed the dispatch to the waiting Major Fishbourne who took off in a hell-for-leather gallop for Washington's headquarters at New Windsor. Outside the commandant's quarters the American artillery detachment under Captains Pendleton and Barr was busily turning the British cannon to bear on the *Vulture* in mid-river as well as the enemy fortifications across the Hudson at Verplanck's Point. It was all over but the shouting.

In 1779 Stony Point was something to shout about. Anthony Wayne and the Light Infantry had delivered a stroke that fired the imagination and admiration of the Patriots. He and his men had done the impossible—taken the impregnable—and in the doing had given the Colonists' cause a badly needed "shot in the arm" while having the opposite effect on the British. From a historical perspective two factors should be recognized. The first and less significant factor was that Stony Point's capture gained no strategic advantage for the Colonists. In fact, Washington had to order the fort abandoned three days later. The second point, of real significance, was that the Continentals, properly led, could accomplish anything expected of the finest European troops.

And for once Congress acted with dispatch to reward proven merit. Wayne was voted official thanks and a gold medal. Silver medals went to Fleury and Stewart while Lieutenants Knox and Gibbons were given brevet promotions.

As for the dangers, frustrations, and uncertainties that confronted Wayne and his corps, it is evident that they were not only formidable but would have been overwhelming had they not been countered by something more formidable.

It was a rare combination of physical courage, discipline, and training that can provide a model for any army in any time or place. The Light Infantry Corps could have been brought to the Stony Point operation in the highest state of readiness, but it would not have succeeded in doing what it did without that cool courage shown at all levels. From Anthony Wayne to the three sergeants who charged into the citadel with Fleury and Knox, courageous leadership was the common denominator. And because we have seen the main attack through the eyes of key leaders in those scenes it would be unjust to overlook the same high standards of leadership in Colonel Butler's secondary attack. His men suffered heavier losses than did Wayne's column. For example, Lieutenant Gibbons, leading the other forlorn hope, lost seventeen men killed or wounded out of his twenty!

All that has been said about the physical courage that

made possible the victory at Stony Point is not to gainsay the importance of moral courage that must have contributed to the success of the American corps. That kind of courage is the subject of the next section. Stony Point deserves to be remembered because it highlights so brilliantly the physical aspects of courage.

Moral Courage

FIELD MARSHAL MONTGOMERY, writing in his *History of Warfare*, got at once to the heart of the subject when he said: "Many qualities go to make a leader, but two are vital— the ability to make the right decisions, *and the courage to act on the decisions. . . . Above all, he must have that moral courage, that resolution and that determination which will enable him to stand firm when the issue hangs in the balance. . . .* A battle is, in effect, a contest between two wills—his own and that of the enemy commander. If his heart begins to fail him when the issue hangs in the balance, his opponent will probably win."[14]

Because certain of those words bring out the essence of moral courage I have repeated them here in italics. They show us the other face of courage. We have seen the physical in action at Stony Point, now here is its counterpart and, in a sense, the other end of a spectrum.

In the opening of this chapter I stated that there were wide differences between the two kinds of courage. What are the essential differences?

In the first place physical courage is courage in action. It is *visible* bravery, usually exhibited at some critical point in time or place during battle: the youthful British lieutenant at the Somme in 1916 who stood on the parapet of the trench in full view of the enemy, pointing his swagger stick at the Germans, and saying "we had better be going now"; the twenty-six-year-old Bonaparte placing himself in front of his grenadiers to lead their column onto the fire-swept bridge at Lodi. Anyone who has known war or studied military history could add a dozen examples of this kind of courage under fire, all distinguished by visibility.

The moral sort is the quiet resolution and calm determination that Montgomery speaks of—the kind of courage seldom if ever observed by the troops. It exists and operates only in the mind—and heart, if you will. It strengthens the will against the uncertainties and frustrations that constantly beat upon the commander in every battle. It provides the strength that makes the strong-minded appear that way. It enables the commander to stand resolutely against anything his opponent can throw at him. There are times too when the same kind of firmness is demanded of him in knowing when to disregard the orders of his superiors. This, of course, requires judgment as well, but that judgment—once decision has been made—has to be supported by moral courage.

It would be shortsighted indeed if one were to associate moral courage solely with one quality such as resolution, for as the perception of the distance between the moral and the physical widens the more apparent becomes the idea of responsibility. This idea should not be confined to the dry terms of regulations (e.g., the commander is responsible for all that his command does or fails to do), rather it is the idea of the leader being responsible for the lives and welfare of those in his charge. It is the most sobering thought that can weigh upon a leader, one that causes lesser men to hesitate—"With this regard their thoughts turn awry,/ And lose the name of action." Thus is presented the enigma that so often confronts a leader—it takes moral courage to assume the responsibility for men's lives, yet moral courage is even more in demand when the situation calls for the commander to order men to take an action that clearly puts their lives at risk. Unhappily this is part of the loneliness of command, and there is nothing in anyone's writing (including The Regulations) that "teaches" a leader how to get through this traumatic experience. It is something that must be faced—alone; the decisions made—alone; the decision stuck to—alone. It is one of the high costs of command.

The final consideration to be borne in mind about any kind of courage, however essential an attribute courage may be, is that it cannot, *in itself*, foster a tactical art, an art of leadership; nor can any of the other attributes we will be examining. They must be linked together as appropriate, so that a balanced view may be sustained.

There is nothing novel about the idea of balancing courage with other qualities. Pericles in his great funeral oration, cited by Thucydides in *The History of the Peloponnesian War*, refers to such a balance.

> Again, in our [Athenian] enterprises we present the singular spectacle of daring and deliberation, each carried to its highest point, and both united in the same persons; although decision is usually the fruit of ignorance, hesitation of reflection. But the palm of courage will surely be adjudged most justly to those who best know the difference between hardship and pleasure and yet are never tempted to shrink from danger."[15]

And Napoleon, writing in his Maxims twenty-two centuries later, advises us that

> It is exceptional and difficult to find in one man all the qualities necessary for a great general. That which is most desirable, and which instantly sets a man apart, is that his intelligence or talent, are balanced by his character or courage. If his courage is the greater, a general heedlessly undertakes things beyond his ability. If on the contrary, his character or courage is less than his intelligence he does not dare carry out his plans."[16]

In the next battle scene we will see "a man of balance," a leader whose moral courage was great enough to match his superb tactical skill in the face of adverse odds.

Auerstadt—the Victory That Amazed an Emperor But Failed to Please Him

The two marshals were alone in the great dining hall of the schloss that had once housed the margraves who centuries before had made Naumburg their stronghold. Two Frenchmen more opposite would have been hard to conceive: Davout, short, stocky, balding, direct in manner to the point of bluntness; Bernadotte, the tall Gascon famous for his charm, whose ringlets of jet-black hair framed a handsome face with its beak of a hooked nose.

They stared at each other across the flicker of candles on the long table that separated them. Bernadotte was the first to look down at the map unrolled between the candelabra. The mass of thick hair fell over his forehead, shielding his eyes from Davout's searching glance.

"Then you will march on Apolda by way of Hassenhausen and Auerstadt?" Bernadotte asked without looking up.

"As you've seen in the Emperor's order of ten o'clock last night, that is the most direct route for me. And I have already alerted my division commanders to march at four this morning, hardly a half-hour from now," Davout said.

"So, your IIIrd Corps has its orders, and you've handed me mine for Ist Corps. It all seems clear enough to me, for both of us."

"Do you think that I, a Marshal of France, would come here as courier, just to hand you an operation order? For the last time I will point out the two things that change the intent—the spirit—of my orders and yours. First, I read to you the postscript of my orders, written in Marshal Berthier's own hand: 'If Marshal Bernadotte is with you, you may both march together, but the Emperor hopes that he will be in the position indicated at Dornburg.' My second point: I have personally questioned the Prussian cavalrymen made prisoner by my outposts near Hassenhausen only six hours ago. That interrogation, plus the reports of my patrols, confirms enough reliable intelligence to convince me that the Prussian main army, estimated at seventy thousand, is retreating from the threat of the Emperor's concentration near Jena. The Prussians are probably moving northward toward Halle or Leipzig. All of which means that you should follow Berthier's orders and move to support my IIIrd Corps as I march across the Saale toward Hassenhausen and block the Prussians' withdrawal," Davout's formal tone carried clearly the coolness between the two commanders.

"I read no spirit, as you call it, in either set of orders. Ist Corps will march this morning, when I am ready, for Dornburg via Camburg," Bernadotte said, raising his eyes from the map.

Davout didn't miss the sudden glint in the other's eyes, recalling how Frenchmen joked, only half in jest, about the combination of Gascon cunning and caution.

"Perhaps you don't choose to see, that by marching south, you will put two rivers—the Saale and the Ilm—between us. And that you will be obeying to the letter an order that has lost its validity, an order overtaken by events," Davout said.

"My dear Louis, you have your judgment. Be kind enough to leave me to mine. Now, if you have nothing further—"

"I do," Davout cut in, "to remind you that you will be turning your back on III Corps, with its strength of only twenty-six thousand to face an army of seventy thousand Prussians."

"Your estimate of seventy thousand—not mine. Now, have you finished?" Bernadotte asked, looking up again from the map. He found he was looking at Davout's back. The IIIrd Corps Commander was halfway to the hall door, the clack of his jackboot heels echoing between the stone floor and the vaulted ceiling.

Davout's staff and three division commanders were at his headquarters awaiting his return from the meeting with Bernadotte. As he entered the hotel foyer that served as a conference room the officers rose to their feet. Davout handed his hat and saber to an aide, and stood silent for a moment, his attention fixed on the corps operations map propped on its easel in front of the group. The map differed from Bernadotte's in the situation posted on it by the IIIrd Corps topographical officer. Davout studied the array of crayoned symbols—the enemy's units in blood red, the French in black—until he was satisfied with what he saw. He turned his attention to the waiting group.

"Listen carefully. We have little time. To sum up operations, the six corps of the Army debouched from the Thüringer Wald on October 9, five days ago. Since then the Army has moved northward in a *bataillon carré** to execute the Emperor's plan to bring the Prussian armies to battle on his terms.

"Two days ago, four corps of the *carré*—IVth, Vth, VIth, and VIIth—were turned westward toward Weimar and Erfurt where the Emperor has expected to pin down the main Prussian army. Meanwhile, our IIIrd Corps in conjunction with Marshal Bernadotte's Ist Corps was prepared to march to the southwest to strike the Prussians in flank or rear as the opportunity should arise.

"Now, as some of you know, I received orders from GQG**

Bataillon carré—Napoleon's flexible, wide-flung method of controlling the maneuver of the corps of the *Grande Armée*. See Appendix A for a detailed description of this "grand tactic."
**GQG—*Grand-Quartier-Général*, Napoleon's General Headquarters.

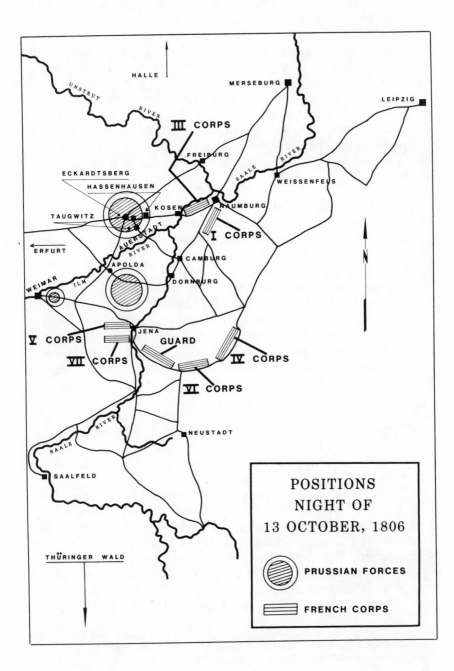

POSITIONS
NIGHT OF
13 OCTOBER, 1806

PRUSSIAN FORCES

FRENCH CORPS

at three o'clock this morning to march to Apolda—here—by the most direct route, that is via Kosen-Hassenhausen-Auerstadt. Our mission, as I have indicated, is to attack the Prussian army's flank or rear. However, the latest intelligence I have interpreted convinces me that the Prussian main army under the Duke of Brunswick has not been fixed and forced to fight by the four Corps now being concentrated under the Emperor's hand. Instead the Prussian army, which I estimate to number seventy thousand with over two hundred guns, is retiring northward headed for Halle or Leipzig—as you see here."

The Marshal paused long enough to scan the upturned faces of his staff and commanders. Some registered the surprise he had anticipated, others, such as the veteran Friant, remained impassive.

"I see some surprise, as well there might be, but save your questions until I have finished. Now, we will march as ordered, and as I conceive the situation to develop we will be prepared to strike the Prussian advance elements as soon as we find them. If our advance guard should be heavily outnumbered, it must be ready to assume the defense until it can be reinforced. What happens after that will depend upon my assessments and decisions.

"I have already directed General Gudin to dispatch a battalion, reinforced by a cavalry squadron, to secure the bridge over the Saale at Kosen. The corps strength in round numbers totals twenty-six thousand which includes forty-four guns and General Vialannes' Corps Cavalry Brigade with one thousand sabers. The Corps will march as soon as I dismiss this conference. The order of march will be with divisions moving out in reverse numerical order. That is, beginning with General Gudin's 3rd Division, eight thousand men. Following at one hour's march will be General Friant's 2nd Division, seven thousand men. Last, following as closely as time permits, General Morand's 1st Division, ten thousand men. My orders to the Corps Cavalry and Artillery will be given to their commanders by my staff after this conference. One final point: our outposts and patrols around Taugwitz—up here—report dense fog closing in over the whole area with visibility restricted to less than fifty meters. Now, gentlemen, I have but a short time for questions."

General of Division Friant spoke first.

"I don't question the Marshal's estimate of enemy strength,

but if we are forced on the defensive, what reinforcement can the Corps expect?"

"As you well know," Davout said, "the maneuver of the *bataillon carré* is based upon any corps being able to take on and hold against superior enemy numbers. How soon we'll be supported by another corps depends upon the Emperor— and God and the situation. At this time I can promise no one anything, except that we will support one another as I see the operation proceeding."

"Granted," Friant said, "but what about Ist Corps? Can't we expect them to support us, since its divisions are bivouacked along the road between Naumburg and Camburg?"

"Marshal Bernadotte is carrying out an order to march on Apolda via Dornburg. With Ist Corps moving in that direction, we can't expect it to help us at this time. What future developments might bring Ist Corps to our support will depend on factors I've already mentioned."

Thirty-five-year-old General Morand's face showed a puzzled smile, as he shook his head in seeming wonder. Davout looked at him with a trace of annoyance.

"I can see you are looking doubtful, Louis. If you have a question, let us hear it," Davout said.

"I don't know if I can put it in one question. What I mean is—if I understand what is happening—can it be possible that the Emperor with something over ninety thousand men has *not* brought to bay the Prussian main body, and because of that we must fight it?"

"That's true only in part," Davout replied. "We have no way of knowing the exact strength of any force the Prussian high command has positioned between the Emperor and the Prussian army moving in our direction. As I see it, I have no alternative but to maneuver against and fight that enemy force. Do I make that clear?"

Davout's grim glare was not directly solely at Morand, it took in the whole group. Heads nodded assent; the room became silent.

"Very well then, I and my key staff will march with General Gudin's advance guard. Messages will reach me there. This conference is dismissed." Davout turned, reaching for his hat and saber.

Davout and Gudin rode at the rear of Gudin's 25th Regiment as it cleared Hassenhausen village at seven in the morning. The fog had closed around them hours before, when they had crossed Kosen Bridge, and had continued to envelop the marching column for the three kilometers between the bridge and the village.

The last houses of the village were fading mistily away on Davout's right when Gudin brought the two staff groups to a halt to meet a cavalry courier riding out of the fog. It was young Captain Surcoupe who had been dispatched by the commander of the cavalry screen.

"Sir," the captain reported to Gudin, "Colonel Burke reports that we have run into an estimated four squadrons of Prussian cavalry, reinforced by an artillery battery, between Taugwitz and Poppel and—"

"Ah, so I was right when I thought I'd heard firing about a half-hour ago. Only pistol shots I suppose, Captain?"

"And carbines, Sir. They didn't have time to unlimber their artillery. There were no casualties, but we took three prisoners," Captain Surcoupe said.

Gudin's tone was that of a veteran infantry officer addressing a young cavalryman:

"So this bloody engagement *did* produce a result. And the prisoners confirm the Prussian units, right?"

"That's correct, General."

"Very well, get back to Colonel Burke and tell him I am deploying my two leading battalions to the north and south of this road. We will continue to advance. I want both flanks screened, as well as my front," Gudin ordered.

Leaving Gudin to give his next orders to the colonel of the 25th, Davout took the cart path to his right, trusting it would lead northward to the crest of the Ranzen-Hugel, the low ridge that paralleled the high road and overlooked Hassenhausen and Taugwitz.

As Davout and his staff officers walked their horses along the rutted path, the fields and their walls on either side began to emerge from the fog that had begun to drift away in thick patches. The path did ascend as Davout had hoped, and turned to bear to the northwest. In minutes they had reached the flat top of the ridge and Davout could see the rooftops of Hassenhausen and Taugwitz above the receding fog. He put on his special spectacles that he had had designed for wear in battle. They were ordinary eyeglasses, modified with double ear pieces, two of which were attached to a length of flexible ribbon that fastened in a catch at the back of his head,

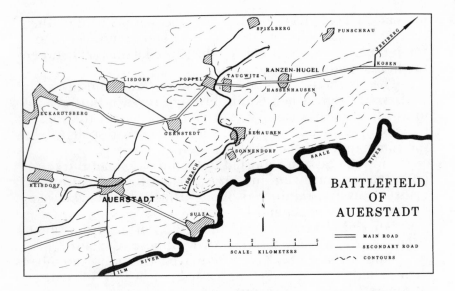

BATTLEFIELD
OF
AUERSTADT

=== MAIN ROAD
——— SECONDARY ROAD
〰〰〰 CONTOURS

SCALE: KILOMETERS

securing the glasses so that hard galloping could not budge them. Their commander's nearsightedness was common knowledge among IIIrd Corps staff, but when they saw their Marshal doff his cocked hat and slip his battle-spectacles over his balding head they knew that things were about to happen.

Things did begin to happen in the valley south of Davout's temporary observation post. As he looked to the south he could see Gudin's line of battle advancing westward toward Taugwitz. The 25th of the Line had deployed in the *ordre mixte,** its two flank battalions marching in massed battalion columns while the third in the center advanced in three-rank line. Davout looked toward Taugwitz and saw Prussian cavalry appear out of the mist less than a thousand meters from Gudin's advancing regiment. As he watched the French line, the battery of Gudin's divisional artillery unlimbered and went into action. The gunners opened up, ranging in with round shot on the Prussian cavalry. Horses and men went down as the eight-pound iron balls plowed bloody furrows through the ranks of the enemy squadrons. The artillerymen set to work with a will, shifting to ricochet fire so that every thirty seconds each of the battery's six guns was throwing a skipping round shot ripping through the cavalry.

Ordre mixte—a tactical formation wherein combinations of battalions in line and column moved into action, the column used for rapid cross-country movement and the line for immediate fire action.

The enemy cavalry's deployment into line ceased as suddenly as it had begun. The French artillery fire was more than horses and men could stand, and the double ranks dissolved into scattered horsemen fleeing to escape. Davout watched a moment longer before he turned with an order to the first officer in the line of aides at his left.

"To General Gudin—you may deploy the rest of your division, but do not advance farther than the Lissbach stream to your front. You will have to stand alone until I can bring up Friant and Morand to support you."

The hussar major was off at a gallop down the ridge toward the little cluster of mounted men behind the line of the 25th. Now Davout could focus his attention again on Gudin's infantry. The fog had broken up under the early morning sun, and he could see the dark blue blocks that were battalion columns fanning out across the gold and green of the fields. Gudin's other three regiments were moving up toward the flanks and rear of the 25th. The heads of the two battalion columns of the 25th seemed suddenly to explode as the tiny figures of the *tirailleurs** swarmed out to the front of the regiment.

Davout thought as he watched: *Those battalions all seem to march well enough, and at this distance it's impossible to tell that half of those men are conscripts going into their first battle. Still, they've been soldiering alongside veterans in every company, so the mixture should work as it has before.*

Davout watched the 25th's attack, noting that Gudin had had the good sense to halt its impetuous advance—for a far greater threat had materialized. Dense columns of Prussian infantry jammed the high road from Gernstedt to Poppel, and closer bodies of infantry were deploying in the fields on both sides of Taugwitz. Davout's experienced eye told him that at least a division of the enemy would soon be thrown against Gudin. Worse, his other observations showed that the menacing infantry attack was not the only threat.

Yes, there they are, he thought, *more cavalry massing around Spielberg, and they've learned to stay out of range of Gudin's artillery until they're ready to attack. There are at least a dozen squadrons, perhaps under old Blücher himself. At any rate that cavalry could turn Gudin's right flank, even attack his rear. And my corps cavalry*

Tirailleurs—skirmishers whose role was to attack and soften the defending force in order to assist the main attacking force.

*brigade still an hour away—as well as Friant's division and the corps
artillery. Gudin is not in position to see it all as I have. I'm wasting
time up here on this ridge.*

The aide who had returned from Gudin led the way to
the division commander's post at the northwest corner of
Hassenhausen.

Charles Étienne César Gudin, at thirty-eight, was two years
older than his corps commander, and he knew that chances
were that he had gone as far as he was destined in high command. Yet he was loyal to a fault—though Davout was never
a charismatic figure—as well as battle-hardened, full of grace
under pressure, and content to be one of the "three immortals" whose fame as Davout's division commanders had spread
through the *Grande Armée*. And he knew his chief well enough
to come right to the point. Davout never interfered with his
subordinates' operations, but he demanded concise reports
on them. Gudin's handsome face was lit by a grin as he took
off his gold-laced hat and took his sheaf of notes from it.

"As you see," he told Davout, "I'm pulling back the 85th
to base a defense on Hassenhausen and the walls and hedges
south of it. My other regiments will be positioned—the 21st
and 25th on line north of the village, the 12th in rear of the
last two as division reserve."

"I approve of your dispositions, but are you aware of the
cavalry threat to your right?" Davout said.

"Only those I took care of with my artillery a half-hour
ago."

"I estimate between two and three thousand sabers concentrating just now on this side of Spielberg," Davout said,
pausing to gauge Gudin's reaction.

He had no need to wait. Gudin was giving orders to two
aides.

"To brigade commanders—major Prussian cavalry attack
developing against our right. The 85th continues to defend
Hassenhausen. The 21st and 25th form battalion squares. The
12th forms in regimental square."

Davout and Gudin rode together toward the area where
the 21st and 25th Regiments would be redeploying. It was
8:20 A.M. and still no messages from Friant or Vialannes with
the corps cavalry. But Davout had no time to reflect on his
dire need for news from the rest of his corps. He could look
northward as he rode and see the long columns of enemy
cavalry crossing the skyline of the Ranzen-Hugel, not over a

kilometer away from the 25th Regiment on the division right. The regiment's three battalions were in the act of forming square, and there was no time to lose. Davout called over to Gudin:

"There are too many of us to get inside one square. Take your staff into the center battalion. I'll take post in the square this side of it."

Gudin waved a salute in acknowledgement, and spurred ahead, trailed by a half-dozen staff officers. Davout trotted his horse to the nearest corner of the square he had selected, coming to a walk as a company commander backed three files aside to let the horsemen enter. The *chef de bataillon* ran up to report to the Marshal, but Davout waved him back to his duties. Here there was nothing for a Marshal and his staff to do except cluster together in the center of the square and stay out of the way of battalion officers who were about to spend some of the busiest moments they might ever know in their trade.

Since a Marshal of France wouldn't be able to practice his trade for the next few minutes, Davout could turn his mind, with its accustomed precision, to matters like calculating the combat power of the Prussian cavalry vis-à-vis the firepower of the French square. Because of his cavalry background—he had been commissioned and trained in the Royal-Champagne Regiment of the old Royal Army—Davout was well aware of the futility of unsupported cavalry charges against steady infantry in square. He could recall such actions as the Battle of the Pyramids, eight years before, when he had witnessed six thousand splendid Mameluke horsemen battered to bloody bits by the fire of Bonaparte's squares.

His mind turned to calculation: *Now, counting files I can see that this 2nd Battalion of the 25th Regiment averages about 120 muskets per company, and the* chef de bataillon *has formed a square in a logical manner with a little over two companies making up each side. With all companies in three ranks that will average about 240 muskets for each side of the square. Then the most horsemen any cavalry unit can bring against each square side can be assumed to be 80, figuring the cavalry squadrons attacking in the usual two ranks, that is, with about 40 horses in each rank. Thus an attacking cavalry unit will be opposing 80 sabers against 240 muskets, and the infantry will be doing all the firing, since a charging cavalryman cannot be expected to fire anything, not even his pistol. But all this figuring is for naught if this is not steady infantry—infantry that*

*will act under strict fire discipline, delivering or reserving volley fire
on command. Now we'll see if months of training and a heavy leav-
ening of veterans will pay off.*

From his vantage point in the saddle Davout could see
over the ranks of the square and observe the other battalion
squares of the 25th and 21st. The tactical skill of the two regimental commanders showed clearly in the way the six squares
had been aligned to provide mutual support as well as clear
fields of fire for the "killing grounds" in front of each square's
face.

Davout turned to look over the side facing the advancing
cavalry. The squadrons had wheeled into double-ranked lines,
and were coming on at a walk three hundred meters away.
A hundred meters closer, leaders' sabers flashed overhead,
and the lines broke into a trot.

Fusilier Jean Daborde was on the side facing the oncoming cavalry. His company's deployment had placed him in the
center rank where his platoon stood at order arms except for
the front rank, which knelt with muskets grounded and slanted
forward to present a solid line of bayonets to the enemy. Jean's
youthful eye could not perceive the "line of squadron columns" as could his Marshal. To Jean, the front rank of cavalry was the leading wave in a sea of horsemen. As that wave
came out of a fold of ground a hundred meters distant he
saw the flash of sun on brass helmets and steel breastplates.
They were tall men on big horses, seeming to tower to awful
heights. Behind Jean, Sergeant Bruit was bellowing at the
platoon.

"They are cuirassiers in armor. Aim low—at the horses!"

The thunder of hooves grew until it drowned out every
other sound in the world. Jean couldn't look around him, but
he knew that every new *fantassin** must be clutching his musket, as he did, with whitened knuckles. This was not like facing the measured advance of infantry as they had a half-hour
ago. Now they were fixed in place, having to confront a
charging horde of monsters that would crash down upon them
and trample them into the ground. If only he could turn and—

"Present! Take aim!"

It was their captain shouting the commands. Jean looked
down the barrel of his musket and brought the muzzle down
until it was pointing at the chest of a charging horse.

"Fire!"

Fantassin—French soldier slang for an infantryman, a GI.

The kick of the musket's recoil turned Jean into an automaton that seemed to be going through the loading drill all by itself. When the platoon returned its muskets to the Order, Jean was astounded to see that the platoon on his right was still standing at the Present, a triple tier of bayoneted muskets. Why didn't they fire? Then Jean saw the answer. Forty meters in front of the square, wounded horses—their riders thrown clear—threshed and tossed on the ground, a few uttering high pitched screams that chilled the blood of the French conscripts. But what had happend to the sea of horsemen that had threatened to engulf them? The realization ran through the infantry like an electric shock: the following waves of cavalry had shied back from the slaughter in front of them and had veered off to either flank to pass around the square. But the veering off had only brought them into the killing grounds of the adjoining faces of the square, as another litter of dead and wounded horses and riders attested.

That shock of surprise was succeeded by elation that turned into backslapping and handshaking, sweeping through the companies that had fired. There was laughter, too, when a dismounted cuirassier, clumsy as a drunk in his heavy gear, took off on a waddling run to the rear, then turned and fired his pistol at the square. It was not a gallant act, it was simply a foolish gesture to the infantrymen.

Officers and sergeants were barking order back into the confusion, for fresh cavalry squadrons were forming to renew the attack. The next attack came on as had the first: columns of squadrons in line, starting from a walk, and, as the distance closed, going into a trot, then a canter, and finally a full gallop over the last fifty meters. Again the square's volleys were withheld until the cavalry's front rank reached the swath of dead and wounded horses forty meters from the square. Again the volleys crashed into them, and again the leading wave went down in slaughter while succeeding waves broke and flowed around the square, only to lose more dead and wounded to the fire from the other sides of the squares.

Incredibly, the Prussians reformed at a distance and repeated the attack. The result was the same, except that the swath of carcasses had grown to become a grisly barrier that brought the horses to a quivering standstill, resisting all efforts of their riders to spur them forward against the bristling rows of steel.

There were four charges in all, and all were disasters for

the Prussian cavalry. In the French squares the men were allowed to stand down, and a chorus of cheers ran from battalion to battalion. Even Davout's stern face had cracked into a smile, though he was heard to say to his nearest aide: "Let them cheer while they can. Poor devils. Their trials for this day have only begun."

After congratulating the *chef de bataillon* and his men, Davout rode out to join Gudin on the little hilltop halfway between Hassenhausen and Punschrau. Together they observed with growing anxiety the long lines of enemy infantry that now extended beyond either flank of Gudin's division. Since the Prussian cavalry had withdrawn in disorder toward Lisdorf, the infantry threat had become paramount. Davout and Gudin compared estimates and agreed that they were already faced with the elements of at least three divisions. Though it was not Davout's custom to express fears to subordinates it was essential that both commanders share freely their observations at their critical hour of 9:00 A.M.

"Still no word from Friant. It looks like you'll have to hold here. It appears that the enemy's next big effort will be directed again at your right flank. I believe they intend to keep their road open to Freiberg, and at the same time cut us off from Kosen and our reinforcement," Davout said.

"I'll extend as far as I can to the north and keep the 12th ready for counterattack in that direction. If our luck continues we'll hold until Friant makes it here," Gudin said.

"What luck continuing? What do you mean?"

"We've been twice lucky so far. First, not one of those cavalry attacks was supported by artillery. And now the Prussians seem to be taking their good time organizing their attack, so they are wasting minutes that are valuable to us."

"Right on both counts," Davout said, mounting his horse and looking toward the high road that disappeared over the crest of the hill east of Hassenhausen. A high, thin dust cloud was rising over the road, and Davout's spirits rose as he recognized the column of his corps cavalry followed by the guns of the corps artillery. He put spurs to his horse and galloped toward the head of the column.

By 9:15 he had sent Vialannes' squadrons trotting off to take position covering Gudin's right flank, and had sent an aide galloping ahead to select a firing position for the 12-pounders north of the village. Gudin would position the guns in single battery as Davout had directed, in order to cover his division's right and front with massed fires.

At 9:30 Friant arrived and Davout lost no time in having him deploy his division on the double on Gudin's right.

With Friant committed, as well as my cavalry and artillery, I can organize a stable defense, he thought, *until I can get Morand up. Yet, according to the latest report from him, he is still four kilometers away. It will take him another hour and a half to get here. It's 9:30 now, so he should be arriving at 11:00. The question is, what kind of a defense can I manage with my two divisions against the Prussians' five? There must be three divisions deployed against me now and two more to come. If the luck that Gudin spoke of holds, the worst I have to fear is a coordinated attack instead of the piecemeal efforts the Prussian command has been mounting.*

The worst of Davout's fears was only fifteen minutes in becoming a reality. At 9:45 the Prussian main attack began— and as Davout had estimated from reports and his own observations—with two divisions attacking frontally and a third appearing to divide its strength by sending a brigade to reinforce each flank of the Prussian attack. At 10:00 Davout's two divisions were in a critical situation. Friant on the north was taking a battering from the enemy's infantry and artillery while Gudin was just managing to hold firm in his center. There the Prussian preponderance in artillery had become all too evident as the French casualties were reported to Davout. He was certain now that his intelligence estimate of two hundred Prussian guns had been accurate. Two hundred guns against the forty-four in the whole of IIIrd Corps! Yet Gudin was still holding on to Hassenhausen, and here it was possible that luck was still looking over Davout's shoulder. The Prussian infantry of Schmettau's division (now a confirmed identity to Davout) was being handled ineptly in its attack on the village. The enemy battalions, lacking the experience of the French in fighting in built-up areas, were held in line, delivering ineffective volleys against the French, who were using the protective cover of houses, field walls, and hedges with skill in their defense.

Yet it was in the south, on Gudin's left flank, where Davout's worst fears were realized. The Prussian division attacking south of Hassenhausen was overpowering Gudin's 85th Regiment. The aide who brought that report was unable to inform Davout of Gudin's present location, only that he had ridden northward, presumably to coordinate operations with Friant. Davout saw that there was no time to search for Gudin. The situation called for immediate action and he was the one who must start it. He galloped off with an aide who knew the position of Gudin's 12th Regiment. He found Colonel Vergès with his staff and battalion commanders at the corner of the regimental square. Davout cut short the colonel's formal report with:

"Form your regiment for an immediate advance in line of battalion columns, and direct your center battalion to follow me. You will ride with me and I'll give you your mission as we march."

Behind Davout and the colonel the blue-white-red of the regimental tricolor streamed in the wind beneath its eagle. Drums were beating the quick march at the heads of the three battalions as they dressed their front ranks on the color. Davout had finished giving Colonel Vergès the mission of counterattacking to restore the situation on the corps left flank, south of Hassenhausen, and now the two rode side by side, guiding on a hedge corner south of the village. To their front the gravity of the situation was becoming all too clear. Groups of fugitives appeared in the open, first in twos and threes, then in large disordered bodies of fleeing men. Some were hatless, some few had even discarded their muskets and sidearms. The blue coats and white breeches of straggling infantry were showing more and more against the green of the farm fields. Davout motioned the colonel closer.

"You can't allow this mob to affect your men. Get your *tirailleurs* out now and clear the way," Davout growled at him.

The men of the *voltigeur* companies leapt into action, dashing through the intervals to fan out into a dense screen two hundred meters ahead of their battalions. Davout turned to the aide at his left.

"Major, take two officers from this regimental staff and set up a rallying point to collect those stragglers. We'll send any of their officers we can find back to you."

While he was turned in the saddle Davout glanced back at the regiment marching behind him. No soldier had to be told how to behave when he was being led into battle by a Marshal of France. The ranks were dressed in parade order, keeping their alignment in spite of the rough ground.

Davout turned the command back to the colonel as it became time for his battalions to deploy into line. He halted with three aides in a battalion interval until the rear ranks of the regiment had passed.

There it goes, he thought, *the last reserve of IIIrd Corps, and Morand must still be a half-hour away! If that 12th Regiment can only restore order on the left, there is nothing left to do in both my divisions but to fight these Prussians to a standstill.*

He gave his order to the nearest aide.

"I will take post over there," he pointed to the knoll on the ridge a half-kilometer southeast of Hassenhausen. "Ride to General Morand, tell him that the mission—yes, the survival—of the corps depends on the arrival of his division. He must push forward with all dispatch. Then direct General Morand to join me at my post."

From his post on the knoll Davout had an overall view of his battle. The irregular front of his two divisions stretched for four kilometers from Friant's right flank, at a point midway between Spielberg and Punschrau, through Gudin's division to its left where the 12th Regiment was restoring the line south of Hassenhausen. The fronts of the French regiments were now locked into their defensive positions. All the maneuver of large units was now the prerogative of the Prussians. Davout noted that their major efforts were being directed toward frontal assaults on Hassenhausen. If only the defenders of the village and the farms around it could hold, the whole of the corps line might hold. The battle for the village commanded his attention while the enemy threw no less than four assaults against it. Not one succeeded in penetrating the defenses; all were thrown back, leaving windrows of casaulties in the fields west of the village. The French infantry, firing from the cover of houses and field walls, supported by artillery firing canister, took such a toll that it was unnecessary to counterattack in order to hold their positions.

Davout felt something more than relief when he could break off his surveillance and greet Morand, who rode up at 10:45. The head of his division column was only fifteen minutes behind him as Davout pointed out the situation and assigned him his mission.

"You will deploy and advance to a line extending from the left of the 12th Regiment, directly south until your left flank reaches the Saale River. Prepare to attack to the west to seize Rehausen and Sonnendorf as initial objectives. You will note heavy concentrations of enemy cavalry apparently moving to attack our left, south of Hassenhausen," Davout said.

"Understood," Morand said. "I will deploy in line of battalion columns behind a screeening force made up of my light cavalry and the 13th Light Infantry."

"That is your affair, and you've no time to lose," Davout said.

In minutes Davout could watch Morand's cavalry, followed by the infantry skirmishers, moving past his post, advancing westward to clear the Prussian reconnaissance cavalry and infantry from the ridge running southwest from Hassenhausen. Behind Morand's screening force his battalions were deploying at the double, south of the Kosen road. Davout felt the huge burden of anxiety fall away as Morand's columns came up into line and moved westward in a coordinated advance. Another form of relief came with an aide-courier from Friant who reported that he had weighted the right of his line to attack Spielberg, and was moving west in spite of heavy losses from Prussian artillery.

Davout's relief was short-lived when he again turned attention to the situation in the south. The masses of enemy cavalry had increased in numbers far beyond those in the attacks on Gudin's squares. Those earlier attacks had employed around 2,500 sabers, while the masses moving against Morand must number five times more—as many as 12,000 to 15,000. It was obvious that Brunswick was mounting an all-out cavalry effort to overwhelm Morand. The latter's battalions were changing formation again, this time from column into firing line, and were engaged in fire fights with the Prussian infantry.

Morand can't withstand those masses of cavalry with his units in line, Davout thought, *but he knows as well as I that he will have to form squares. And he can see the situation even better than I, because he is closer to it. Yet, I've got to go down there, even if it's only to show myself to his troops.*

While Davout was riding to join Morand the battalions in the south were already redeploying into squares. Morand hurriedly briefed Davout on his plan to receive the cavalry attack. His battalions on the right would remain in line, they could easily fend off cavalry attacks since they had taken cover behind hedges and walls. Davout had scarcely voiced his approval when it was evident that he and Morand must seek cover in the squares just as he and Gudin had earlier.

The Prussian cavalry attacks were repeat performances of the morning's debacle, though on a massive scale never before experienced by Davout or his veterans. Yet Morand's *amalgame* of recruits and veterans—in much the same proportion as those in Gudin's units—behaved like solid formations of old hands, loading and firing at ranges as close as thirty meters. The bloody effects of their volleys were in direct proportion to the numbers of horsemen thrown against them. Yet squadrons were replaced or reformed and the waves of horsemen—cuirassiers, uhlans, dragoons—came on, were decimated as their waves broke around the rocks of the squares, came on again and were slaughtered until their squadrons were broken and scattered. The French repulsed with ease the succession of cavalry charges because the Prussian command failed to support the attacks with artillery.

Finally, the clouds of horsemen drifted off to the west, a beaten rabble. Davout left the square to reassume his post on the hill, leaving Morand to redeploy again and attack to the west to reach the Lissbach and take Rehausen and Sonnendorf.

Back on his hill Davout was amazed to see a development in the battle that was unforeseeable, but was to prove as favorable to him as it would be fatal to the Prussians. In their zeal to get around Haussenhausen—following the failure of their repeated assaults on the village—both Prussian flanks, north and south, had turned inward toward the village. It was a sudden opportunity for Davout, as golden as it was fleeting.

Battle of Auerstadt

Davout sent aides flying with orders to his three division commanders: Gudin to hold fast in order to provide a *point d'appui,* the base for a corps counterattack; Friant and Morand to push forward aggressively with their division artillery and use it to enfilade the Prussian lines.

While Davout's orders were on the way Morand's division was attacked by the elite of the enemy's infantry, the Prussian Guard. The attack was defeated by Morand's inspired infantry and artillery who resumed their advance. The interrogation of Prussian prisoners taken during this action revealed that the Duke of Brunswick had been seriously wounded as he had led forward a grenadier regiment in an attack on Hassenhausen. There were conflicting reports regarding Brunswick's successor in command; some said it was the chief of staff, Scharnhorst; others said the King himself had assumed command.

It was noon and at the zenith of the day there was a pause, a brief lull, while Davout's 1st and 2nd Divisions maneuvered to counterattack. Davout felt that surge of "second wind" that comes to a champion runner when he realizes that a final, vital effort will win. Now everything would depend on Friant's and Morand's skill and aggressiveness to exploit that second wind.

Davout knew that he need not worry about those qualities in his division commanders. Friant drove on, the axis of his advance aimed at Taugwitz and Poppel, while his artillery was pushed forward to positions from which it was pounding the Prussians with short range fires. In the south Morand's leading units reached the Lissbach after taking Rehausen and Sonnendorf. Morand had gotten his artillery into position on the Sonnenkuppe, the western end of the ridge above Sonnendorf. From there his guns were battering the flank and rear of the Prussian division on the south.

Caught in the murderous crossfire of Friant's and Morand's artillery, the Prussian flank units began to disintegrate. Davout watched fresh enemy infantry—he estimated them to be the major elements of a new division—thrown into the battle in desperate counterattacks, obviously meant to free the shattered flanks and restore the Prussian situation across their front. These attacks crumbled under the same deadly crossfire while Prussian units in the center were being hammered by Gudin's infantry. "Very soon a large number of Prussian troops were trapped in a narrow gully and a murderous close-quarter scrimmage ensued. Davout later paid tribute to his adversaries in his *Journal:* 'We were within pistol range, and the cannonade tore gaps in their ranks which immediately closed up. Each move of the [Prussian] 61st Regiment was indicated on the ground by the brave men they left there.' . . . By 12:30 the pride of the Prussian army was streaming away to the west and north. . . ."[17]

Davout's seizure of the initiative at the critical moment was paying off. While Morand was continuing his attack across the Lissbach, Friant had taken Spielberg, had gone on to take Poppel, lost it, retook it, and continued his attack toward Lisdorf.

Again Davout saw a critical phase open for him if he continued to take the initiative. He recognized it and made his decision. It was time to throw everything into a coordinated corps attack. He directed the axis of his corps attack on Gernstadt-Eckartsberg and ordered Gudin forward. Gudin stormed Taugwitz and drove on toward Gernstadt. "Davout's three divisions bore down on the Prussian army in a menacing crescent-shaped formation, horns pushed aggressively forward."[18]

A pattern was set which was to characterize the battle for the rest of the afternoon. Each time Prussian rear guards were deployed in the attempt to halt the triumphant French, Gudin would thrust forward frontally while Friant and Morand worked battalions and guns around the Prussian flanks and renewed their lethal crossfire.

As the enemy lines crumbled away before him Davout never ceased to wonder at the masses of Prussian reserves that he saw withdrawing, reserves that were never committed to battle. But he had little time to ponder over that observation. He was too deeply engaged in driving forward every element of infantry, cavalry, and artillery in his corps. His hat lost, the gold lace of his uniform as powder-blackened as his face, he continued to gallop from division to division, pushing to the last degree every element that could keep up the momentum of the advance. It was no longer an attack—it was a pursuit. He drove his exhausted units until those in the van collapsed on the crest of the Eckartsberg. Flesh and blood could endure no more, and with the greatest reluctance of his career, the Iron Marshal had to call a halt for his divisions. One can imagine this stern soldier as close to tears as such a man could come.

But he was not through. He ordered forward the only force he had left: three regiments of cavalry and a single infantry battalion. He flung them in pursuit, knowing that the tiny force—in terms of the numbers of Prussians they were chasing—could only harass, not destroy. Nevertheless he ordered them to drive as many Prussians as possible to the south and west in order to push the fugitives into the path of the other corps of the *Grande Armée*.

It was at 4:30 that Davout's divisions had been forced to halt, an hour before sundown on that October Tuesday. "The weary but triumphant soldiers of IIIrd Corps turned to the task of rounding up prisoners and caring for their wounded before taking a well-earned rest."[19] Then came the other unmistakable evidence of the exhaustion of Davout's combat power: the near tragic toll of French casualties. "Of the 26,000 men he had succeeded in bringing on the field, no less than 258 officers and 6,794 men, viz., $25^1/2$ percent, had fallen, and the 3rd Division, Gudin, with 41 percent, is perhaps the heaviest loss as borne by victorious troops in so large a unit as a division."[20] In comparison Davout had caused Prussian losses of 10,000 casualties, 3,000 prisoners, and 115 guns captured.

While IIIrd Corps soldiers were going about their grim afteraction tasks, Davout's courier, Colonel Falcon, was carrying the Marshal's report to Napoleon stating that he had defeated the Duke of Brunswick's army and driven it toward Weimar in a rout. The colonel arrived at Napoleon's headquarters at an inn in Jena where, as he awaited the Emperor, he watched aides decorating the walls with captured Prussian regimental colors. In time the Emperor arrived and allowed Falcon to deliver his report. Napoleon read it with growing scepticism and a certain lack of enthusiasm. Here, incredibly, it told him that: "Davout claimed to have fought and defeated the Prussian main body near Auerstadt, ten miles away. 'Your marshal must be seeing double,' he somewhat ungraciously snapped at the emissary. Little by little, however, he came to realize that in fact he—the Emperor with 96,000 men—had been engaging only the Prussian flank forces, jointly 55,000 strong, while Davout—the subordinate, a mere 26,000 troops under his command—had been locked in mortal conflict with Brunswick's main body. Napoleon found it hard to swallow the magnitude of the calculational error under which he had labored, but next day he awarded Davout the unstinted praise he richly deserved."[21]

There is another aspect of the vanity of emperors and the manner in which awards are disbursed by them. Davout was created Duke of Auerstadt, but it should be noted that an emperor who was capable of awarding a marshal's baton on the battlefield took two years to appoint Davout to that dukedom.

What then of Bernadotte's actions and their consequences? "When Napoleon demanded an explanation of his amazing conduct, Bernadotte tried to justify himself by describing the difficulties (largely imaginary) which he encountered along the road. The Emperor replied to this in no uncertain terms on October 23: 'According to a very precise order you ought to have been at Dornburg. . . . In case you had failed to execute these orders, I informed you during the night that if you were still at Naumburg when this order arrived you should march with Marshal Davout and support him. You were at Naumburg when this order arrived; it was communicated to you; this notwithstanding, you preferred to execute a false march in order to make for Dornburg, and in consequence you took no part in the battle and Marshal Davout bore the principal efforts of the enemy's army.' "[22]

If one studies Davout's life and military career it is not difficult to understand his display of moral courage at Auerstädt—courage that not only opposed the dynamics of battle, but overcame each as it arose.

Davout comes through as a stern, uncompromising figure, never a charismatic one to his soldiers or anyone else. He had the lasting reputation of being as incorruptible as he was exacting in enforcing discipline—two traits not common among Napoleon's marshals. He worshipped duty first and last, no doubt a quality inherited from his martial and aristocratic background. There was a saying in Burgundy that when a male Davout was born a sword was drawn from the scabbard. Hence it is not surprising that he became the most dependable of the marshals. "His troops were always the best trained, equipped, and disciplined in the *Grande Armée*, and usually got the hardest assignments."[23] Thus the Iron Marshal, who his soldiers also called "the just," was respected but not loved—except perhaps on one occasion, the evening after Auerstadt.

Part Two

WILL

Hernan Cortes at
Cempoalla, 1520

John R. M. Chard with Gonville
Bromhead at **Rorke's Drift**, 1879

WILL

Why is the will of the military commander deemed more decisive of success than the will of leadership in any other calling? Clearly it is because the inertia, frictions, and confusions of the forces of the battlefield make all positive action more difficult.

—S. L. A. Marshall, *Men Against Fire*

If Thucydides had interviewed the Athenian oarsmen and marine infantrymen as they were disembarking from their fighting ships following their victories over the Spartans at Naupactus, he might have been the first to profit from firsthand insight into the minds of men fresh from battle. We will never know whether the historian of the Peloponnesian War might have conceived such a system, but if he had he might well have been S. L. A. Marshall's historical harbinger. In any case we believe that Marshall stands alone in this regard, as the record shows.

Why then could Marshall have made the positive statement just quoted, and at the same time pull back with apparent skepticism saying, ". . . this whole subject of the will of the commander cries out for a modern resurvey and better understanding."[1] I imagine he saw the problem clearly enough, but realized in that small book of his—dedicated to finding clear-cut solutions to the problem of better command in future war—he could only point the way toward "better understanding" the influence of the leader's will. For he did light the way to understanding with two beacons that serve to keep us out of the byways and heading in the right direction.

Essentially he was able to open the heart of the matter and reveal a fundamental fact: in battle things don't get done simply because a leader wills, or wants to will an outcome. "They are done because they are doable," because a sensible leader sees what is possible and weighs that against the things that his men are capable of doing. In actuality Marshall had not uncovered anything startling. His was a simple way of pointing out what Napoleon had recognized, writing at St. Helena a century and a quarter earlier:

> The first thing for a commander to determine is what he is going to do, to see if he has the means to overcome the obstacles which the enemy can oppose to him and, when he has decided, do all he can to surmount them.[2]

86

To determine what he is going to do, to get things done because they are do-able—this means simply that if a leader wants to exercise his will, he first must know its limits in the situation in which he finds himself. Yet like most simple truths it continues to suffer obscurity because men hide it somewhere between wars. Un-oddly enough it has always been a truth as Thucydides learned 2,373 years before Marshall wrote his book; learned it the hard way by underestimating the capabilities of his opponent and, as a consequence, was not only relieved of his command but was exiled for twenty years.

Marshall's other way of shedding light on the development of the leader's will was to perceive another simple truth, namely that the concept of the strength of a commander's will has appeared, in the common and popular view, to be the peculiar property of generals; and the generals have done nothing to discourage the idea. Yet Marshall was to observe that "the good general is simply the good company commander in his post-graduate course." He pursued that truth until he found in the end that the ultimate test of the combat leader's will comes when he must be capable of making his men accomplish their mission in spite of their inherent human frailties—all this in what John Keegan has called "the face of battle." Marshall further concludes that a leader cannot *fully* know how to exercise his will until he has learned to do it in the crucible of "the small fight," that is, in combats where the leader develops his will through battle experience alongside the men he will lead later from higher levels of command. One—at least this one—finds that conclusion well-nigh impossible to deny.

Yet, though I find Marshall's conclusion an invaluable piece of guidance, it cannot be relied on as the single means of understanding the exercise of the leader's will in war. This might be seen as an unfortunate shortfall, but it also can be considered a blessing because it reminds one that one is seeking to examine a leader's attributes *without having to do it on the battlefield*. It will be recalled that a similar concept of Marshall's had to be held in abeyance because it could only be tested in battle. Accordingly, we may follow the path that Marshall's insights have lighted, though our main reliance continues to be on the lessons of history—and on trustworthy commentaries on them.

In extending the search for exemplary cases of the leader applying his will to win battles, I have re-scanned a number of battles to find a pattern emerging. The pattern took the form of a spectrum with two qualities outstanding at opposite ends. At one end there is *boldness* which, in its military sense, may be expressed as reflective intelligence undertaking a daring action; another way of saying it is that the will directs the effort to attain an intellectual aim.

At the other end of the spectrum one finds *tenacity* which, in this context, means that the will enables the leader—and hence his men—to hold out until the mission has been accomplished, no matter how adverse the odds or conditions. More about tenacity later.

Boldness

ONE QUOTE MOST frequently attributed to the wrong source is that made by poor old Georges Jacques Danton. I have seen his ringing words ascribed to sources ranging anywhere from Napoleon to Betsy Ross; therefore I'd like to give Danton credit for the conclusion of his stirring speech to the Legislative Assembly on the occasion of its facing the alliance threatening revolutionary France. He said: "Boldness, again boldness, and always boldness—and France is saved!"

There can be little doubt that Danton, the politician, delivered those words with flair, and boldness, employed by an intelligent military commander, has usually carried off victory with flair. Yet it is all too easy to get carried away with the idea of boldness as impetuous action. To reasonable men there is always an underlying awareness that boldness unrestrained by careful forethought equals rashness. The thought of the pratfall of boldness gone awry has been the chief deterrent to many a commander's action. The fear of failure has always haunted ordinary men, but the fear of ridiculous failure is more than haunting, it is damning to positive action. It is the same fear implicit in Hamlet's question as he tries to face whatever it is that ". . . puzzles the will,/ And makes us rather bear those ills we have/Than fly to others that we know not of?"

Hence there is a corollary question in the back of the reasoning leader's mind: When is the time for boldness and when the time for caution? If that leader is well-grounded in history he will recall that, with the rare exception of a commander like Charles XII of Sweden (who stuck his neck out once too often when he stretched it over a trench parapet in time to stop a Danish bullet), no successful leader has made a career of being consistently bold. This reminder was put nicely to our airmen in World War II in the adage: There are old pilots, and there are bold pilots; but there are no old, bold pilots.

With these admonitions in mind, how does the good leader go about deciding where and how to be bold? Let us see what great soldiers and thinkers have concluded in this regard. We have already heard what Napoleon had to say about a commander's first step in planning—to determine what needs to be done. He added to that another piece of advice that is ageless in applicability.

> The first quality for a commander is a cool head, which receives a correct impression of things. He should not allow himself to be confused by either good or bad news. The impressions which he receives in the course of a day should classify themselves in his mind in such a way as to occupy the place which they merit, for reason and judgment are the result of the comparison of impressions taken into just consideration.[3]

Which, in today's terms, says that the cool guy sorts out the facts before he acts.

Napoleon has been quoted as asking before appointing a general: "Is he lucky?" Now only the unthinking would conclude that the Emperor put his trust in commanders who seemed to come out well no matter how their battles were fought. David Chandler, the British military historian, saw what was really being asked: "Is he [the appointee] competent at taking calculated risks?"[4] Chandler went on to clinch his evaluation in another work in which he cites the British General Wavell, who had looked deeply into the matter: "Further qualities demanded of a good general by Wavell included boldness, which he stressed was what Napoleon really meant by luck: 'A bold general may be lucky, but no general can be lucky unless he is bold.' "[5]

The old *maitre* Clausewitz also thought boldness an important enough quality to devote a major chapter to it in his *On War*, but he is careful to place it following his remarks on foresight and prudence. Though he deems boldness an essential element—even "a creative power"—he points out repeatedly that "the higher the rank the more necessary it is that boldness should be accompanied by a reflective mind." He further observes, however, that boldness, in the light of history, becomes rarer as the commander attains higher levels of command.

To add proof to this latter point Clausewitz looks on the reverse of the coin to note that most of the generals in European history who have been rated mediocre in their performance in independent command were men renowned earlier in their careers (that is, while serving as subordinate commanders) for their boldness and power of decision. From this and other reflections he concluded:

> The higher we rise in a position of command, the more of the mind, understanding, and penetration predominate in activity, the more therefore is boldness, which is a property of the feelings, kept in subjection, and for that reason we find it so rarely in the highest positions, but then, so much the more should it be admired. *Boldness, directed by an overruling intelligence, is the stamp of the hero** . . . We think then that it is impossible to imagine a distinguished general without boldness, that is to say, that no man can become one who is not born with this power of the soul, and we therefore look upon it as the first requisite for such a career. . . .

Finally, one can scarcely overemphasize the thought that boldness, as an element of the will, must be developed from within before it can be exercised upon the leader's men. If he is made of the stuff that clearly sizes up the situation, sees what should *and can be done,* then gives his orders, his decisions and subsequent bold actions will lead to success in battle.

At this point it would be easy to turn to famous battles like Austerlitz or El Alamein for examples of contesting wills. It would be equally less rewarding to add to so much that has already been written. Instead, let us watch a bold leader stake his life, his army, and an empire on a night attack against a better-armed force which outnumbered his by three to one.

*Italics added.

Conquistadors, Cannon, and Cocuyos

"That which I have myself seen and the fighting. . . . And the
word came up there were ships hove-to in the offing:

And we knew well the governor's men had the wind of us . . ."
—Archibald MacLeish, "Conquistador"

Indeed fat Diego Velasquez, the Governor of Cuba, did "have
the wind" of Cortes' expedition, even though the scent was
more than a year old in this spring of 1520. And Velasquez had every reason, in his way of thinking, to follow that
scent. He had not forgotten a single detail of his public humiliation when Cortes had given his governor the slip by sailing
out of Santiago harbor in defiance of Velasquez's last-minute
attempt to countermand the expedition's sailing orders.

Cortes had had word of the governor's "secret" decision
to replace him as the captain-general of the expedition to
Mexico, and had weighed anchor with his half-prepared fleet
to slip out of the harbor. When the enraged Velasquez—half-
dressed in his haste to stop Cortes—had shouted from the
quay "Is this the way you part from me!" Cortes had replied
with something to the effect that "time presses, and there are
some things that must be done—has your Excellency any
commands?" The mortified governor, helpless and frus-
trated, could only watch Cortes' longboat pull away towards
his ship, quite unable to think of a proper command that would
bring back the expedition's commander, who was politely
waving his farewell.

Now the ships that had "hove-to in the offing" were truly
the fleet that carried the governor's punitive expedition. It
was commanded by the Castilian hidalgo, Pánfilo de Narvaez,
who had orders to displace Cortes and "establish the governor's jurisdiction over the conquered territories in Mexico."
Narvaez had landed on the same beaches at San Juan de Ulua
where Cortes and his tiny "army" had disembarked the year
before. The punitive expedition outnumbered Cortes' original force more than two to one, totaling nine hundred soldiers including eighty horsemen, eighty arquebusiers,* and
eighteen field cannon, and stores of ammunition with other

---

*The infantry armed with the unwieldly matchlock (arquebus) of sixteenth-century Spanish arm-
ies.

supplies to match. There were even one thousand Indians to do the menial chores.

This gallant armada anchored off San Juan de Ulua, on April 23, 1520, and began disembarking. Narvaez waded ashore and proclaimed his intention to march against Cortes in the name of the Governor of Cuba.

It was the news of this expedition that had been carried secretly to the Emperor Montezuma, the captive-guest of Hernan Cortes in Tenochtitlan, the Aztec capital. Montezuma had savored the intelligence for three days, tasting the sweetness of the surprise he would pull on Cortes and his conquistadors. Now it was time to receive his captor and his captains; they were being ushered down the halls toward his chambers in response to his invitation to an audience.

Montezuma heard the clink of armor and the sound of Spanish voices behind the green-plumed escort of Aztec noblemen before he caught sight of Cortes. When the ushers stepped aside he saw the familiar figure of his conqueror, wearing his three-quarter armor blackened against the tropical weather. Cortes was bare-headed, his casque carried by his page, Orteguilla. The Captain-General's face was pale as usual, in spite of much campaigning, a paleness seeming to belie the broad shoulders and deep chest that were the outstanding features of his muscular frame. Cortes bowed slightly, his dark eyes looking into Montezuma's.

Cortes saw a slight man of forty with shoulder-length black hair, staring back at him with Indian eyes under his miniature golden crown. Seated on his gold-mounted throne the Emperor seemed anything but a prisoner as he waved Cortes to the chair beside him. Montezuma waited until Doña Marina, Cortes' interpreter—and, as all knew, his mistress—took her place, standing behind Cortes' chair. When the three captains—Olid, Alvarado, and Marin—had ranked themselves to Cortes left, Montezuma spoke in carefully spaced passages so that Doña Marina had time to interpret between pauses.

"Malinche, we waste no time on formal things today. I have great news, received only moments ago, news that will change all your plans here in Tenochtitlan and at Villa Rica." Montezuma's guttural tones were as flat as his expressionless face.

Cortes' smile was quick, though his dark eyes were grave as he returned Montezuma's gaze. He nodded politely, almost carelessly, as though great news purporting to change his plans arrived every morning.

"I am grateful for your consideration, and I know that any news you have should be important," Cortes said.

Montezuma motioned to an aide whose gold lip plug showed him to rank high in the warrior caste. He knelt and extended a cotton-cloth roll to his emperor who took it and unrolled a series of picture writings which he began to read off to Cortes.

"Eighteen of your great high ships are landing an army on the beaches at the place you call San Juan De Ulua. They were men of your nation, numbering nine hundred, with eighty horses and eighteen cannon. Their leader is called Narvaez and he has said that he comes to march against you."

Cortes' eyes never shifted, and in his turn his face showed only polite interest.

"Surely you mean 'march to join me' not against me. And you must be aware that in the prophecies of your god Quetzalcoatl, there will come more men with white skin, bearded and in armor."

Montezuma continued to tick off the accounting of Narvaez's force to the last detail of men, equipment, and supplies as though he had not heard the Spanish leader's words.

His cursed couriers have outrun ours again, Cortes thought, *so I'll have to put my best face on the matter and get all I can out of this heathen bastard.*

"Your highness is well-informed as always," Cortes continued to smile, "so you must realize that my King has sent me reinforcements—as I had expected."

"Well then, Malinche, if these are indeed your reinforcements, you can stop building those ships at Villa Rica.* You now have plenty of ships to take you and your soldiers to your homeland. Am I not right?" Montezuma said, his face no longer expressionless, its stoniness replaced by a sly smile.

"You are right, highness, and that is why I am delighted to extend you the greatest honor that my King can bestow."

The three captains looked at one another in scarcely concealed and puzzled surprise as Doña Marina finished translating.

"I do not understand what you are saying—what is this

*Villa Rica de la Vera Cruz, Cortes' first settlement, near the modern port of Vera Cruz.

honor?" Montezuma's smile had faded as his gaze became a question.

"It is a thing as simple as it is great. You must come with us so that you will meet our ruler, our gracious King," Cortes said, rising to his feet while making a half-bow.

Doña Marina's words struck home like a bolt from a crossbow. "I? Come with *you*? I?"

"As I said—truly our greatest honor, both to extend and to be honored with your highness' presence—as my king's guest."

Montezuma's face was that of a man just sentenced to be executed. The hand that covered his lower face trembled before he lowered it.

That will teach the dog to play at trading intelligence with me. Now I'll leave him quickly so he can wrestle with the thought of being exhibited like a captive animal in a Spanish general's Roman triumph.

Cortes bowed again, and without waiting for the imperial gesture of dismissal, strode from the room, trailed by his staff.

Once inside the council chamber in his own compound Cortes was no longer the smiling courtier, but the Captain-General addressing his conquistadors.

"Already you've let the word slip to the troops. Diaz, be kind enough to stop at once those salute firings of the cannon. We'll have need of that powder before long," Cortes said.

Across the room the burly Alvarado's laugh died away. He had been describing the look on Montezuma's face to the other captains who had not been at the audience. The room became silent as Cortes looked around him.

"I am astonished at my senior officers. Haven't any of you bothered to reflect on the meaning of this so-called reinforcement? I thought not. Now listen to a little reasoning. In the first place, if those ships came directly from Spain, why did they not put in at Villa Rica, our headquarters on the coast, instead of San Juan de Ulua? And why was it not Narvaez's first action to send a messenger galloping to me here in Tenochtitlan—or to Sandoval at Villa Rica? No, my friends, those ships come from Cuba, not from Spain, and they carry anything but reinforcements."

The captains looked uneasily around the chamber; this was a Cortes few of them had ever seen. His jaw was set, his angry mouth a thin line.

"Now you can see what has happened if only you will

open your eyes. Something or someone has alarmed Velas-quez in Cuba. Maybe Puertocarrero or Montejo did land there in spite of my orders. Perhaps they were trapped and our gold seized. In any case, the bull is loose in the farmyard, and those eighteen ships are truly debarking nine hundred of the *governor's* men. God in heaven, here we've conquered an empire that could boast warriors in the tens of thou-sands—all this we did with less than half a thousand of our soldiers! And now we must face an expedition—brother Spaniards outnumbering us by three times—who come to dash all our hopes and all our conquests in the dust. How many are with me in this fight to come?"

Cortes unhooked his baldric, drew out his sheathed sword, and slammed it down on the table in front of him. Alvarado was the first to rise to his feet. He looked around the room, then faced the table.

"We have been with you all this way, Hernan, but what of this next fight, as you say?"

"What of it, indeed! Are you captains so dense that you cannot see the choice? Perhaps there are among you some who would join Panfilo de Narvaez on the coast. Surely that's the easy way to guard your gold. The hard way to keep it might be to stand behind me. But then how many of you still know how to soldier the hard way?"

That has got to do it, Cortes thought, *these conquistadors are all gamblers at heart, or they wouldn't be here.*

The reaction of the captains came as quickly as Cortes' thoughts, and they reacted as one man. Swords flashed out of scabbards and were laid in a line of steel, their hilts facing Cortes' sword on the long table.

"You see your answer, Hernan," Alvarado bellowed, "what say you now?"

Cortes picked up his sword, drew the blade from its scab-bard, and laid it down with its hilt alongside the others.

"Then, señores, we are for it. Pick up your blades and give me time to collect my thoughts. There is much that must be done—and now. Be ready to assemble on the terrace where I will join you in good time."

Cortes was left alone to agonize over his challenges and his scanty means of countering them—

Here, three score leagues from the coast, surrounded by potential armies of a hundred thousand Aztec warriors, what ways are open to me?

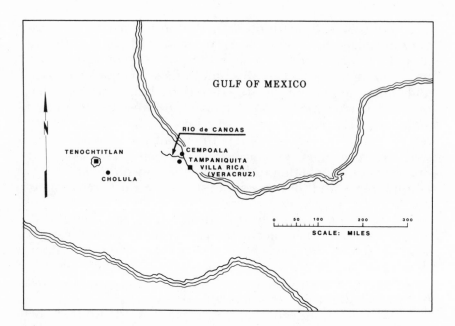

I see three. First, I can stay here, mobilize my Indian allies, and negotiate with Narvaez. I reject that, for it surrenders the initiative to Narvaez.

Second, I can take all of my force and some Indian allies, and march against Narvaez. But if I do that I abandon all that I have conquered and leave a hostile Montezuma in my rear as well, an emperor then free to assemble his warriors against me.

Or lastly, I can leave a garrison here that will keep Montezuma subdued. That would be a terrible risk—splitting my force—and that will be complicated by finding a way to attack Narvaez's army with all its horses, cannon, and muskets, outnumbering us with fearful odds.

Yet this third way is the one I must take. Risky and dangerous as it is, there will be two compensations. Velasquez de Leon and his 150 men can fall back and join my march at Cholula. I must take the chance on his remaining loyal, even though he is the Governor's kinsman. My other compensation may be the two thousand reliable warriors in Chinantla province. They are hostile to Montezuma, and may heed my summons—if they can be assembled in time!

Yes, this is the course I will follow, and I will need God's help to succeed.

His mind made up, Cortes called for his page to pass the order for assembling his captains.

From the terrace where they had assembled—it was actually a broad, flat roof surmounting the great temple-pyramid—Cortes and his officers could view the magnificent expanse of Tenochtitlan laid out before them on that sunny spring morning. The city with its teeming thousands, its myriad rooftops, wide avenues, and lines of canals extending to the great lake of Tezcuco, all seemed to sparkle in the sunlight that lit up flowered terraces and green gardens. It was all serene in its widespread beauty, encircled by its green environs and the deep blue of its surrounding lake. Yet each officer could never forget that the peaceful, charming scene was underlaid with the savage terror of the Aztec priesthood with its human sacrifices and bloody ceremonial feasts. There still remained the racks displaying thousands of human skulls outside the teocallis, the temple-pyramids, to remind the most careless cavalier.

Cortes, looking around before he spoke, sensed with his ever-present insight the feelings that dominated the group. He took advantage of the moment to make a sweeping gesture across the view.

"To think that a year ago we were struggling to survive beyond the beaches of San Juan de Ulua, facing a hostile land extending we knew not where. Yet look what we have done, four hundred of us conquering a vast empire that no white man dreamed existed."

He paused, knowing they would remember the body-racking marches, the fierce battles—victories and defeats—against incredible odds, the conquest of the Tlascalans and the alliance with them, the ascent of the towering mountain ranges, and finally the taking of Montezuma and the domination of his empire, which had accepted them as demigods. Neither was there need to remind them that there was a growing and seething restlessness throughout the capital, an unrest that could put these foreign god-warriors to the extreme test.

"Now all this," Cortes went on, "is going to be yours to rule, my friend, Pedro de Alvarado."

He ignored Alvarado's startled stare.

"I march, as soon as preparations permit, with 70 men. I'll give you the list of them by the end of day. I leave you all the artillery, all but 5 horses, and all but 8 arquebusiers. That gives you two-thirds of our force, 140 men. I will charge you with detailed, written orders to carry out your mission here, Pedro, as soon as time permits. For now, know that my command will march lightly-armed and with only the minimum of baggage."

Cortes' upraised hand silenced the murmurs of surprise and protest running through the group.

"The time for discussion has passed, *caballeros*. You will receive your assignments in my second set of orders. Return to your commands, and let your men know only that I await confirmation of the movements and destructions of the governor's force at San Juan de Ulua. Pedro, you and Cristobal de Olid will remain with me as well as my pages, Burguillos and Orteguilla. Cristobal, be kind enough to send also for Father Olmedo. All others are dismissed."

As Cortes led the four men back to his council chamber his mind was occupied with the writing of orders and letters. He had already decided that the letters must take first priority. There were things to be done with words and gold that his captains did not always understand. He looked at Alvarado and Olid as he took his seat at the table.

"I will detain you only enough to let you know about the letters I am going to write. First, those to Velasquez de Leon and Rangal to direct them to withdraw their detachments to Cholula and await my coming there. Also, to alert Sandoval at Villa Rica to march to meet me."

Cortes paused to allow Fray Bartolemé de Olmedo to take a seat on his left. As he watched the stout friar in his habit of the Order of Mercy take his place, the Captain-General's pale face took on the look of the fox, the look that never failed to set Alvarado and Olid on their guard.

"Now, Father," Cortes said, "we will draft a most conciliatory letter to friend Panfilo de Narvaez assuring him of our readiness to share the fruits of conquest. Oh, we will make him most welcome as our comrade-in-arms and make him know that our strength lies in the union of our forces. All this based, of course, on his producing the royal commission which will show us the requirement to submit to his authority—"

"But, my son," Olmedo broke in, "if Narvaez comes as an expedition from the Governor of Cuba he cannot be bearing a royal commission like that."

"Ah, Father, that must be the other key to Narvaez's understanding our situations—and that will throw him off balance," Cortes said, turning his courtier's smile on Olmedo.

"But the *other* key?" the friar asked.

"Certain articles of gold that you will carry, along with my letter. We will discuss later their distribution to Narvaez—and certain of his followers. This governor's cavalier will have to learn that campaigns are not always won with simple arms like swords and cannon."

On a mid-May morning the troops of Cortes and Alvarado were ranked, facing each other across the wide courtyard of Cortes' compound. In the open area between them Cortes was making his farewell to Montezuma. The emperor, seated in his gold-encrusted litter, embraced Cortes while Doña Marina interpreted their adieus.

When Cortes had mounted his horse, El Molinero, he reined up alongside Alvarado who was obviously ill at ease.

"Montezuma wants to accompany you to the great causeway. I don't think it wise to let him go that far—at least not fully attended," Alvarado said.

"You are seeing things as a master should, my old friend. Use your judgement as to the escort and the distance. We both know how far he can be trusted without our guards," Cortes tapped the hilt of his sword, "about the length of this blade."

Alvarado grinned and nodded his assent, while waving to his trumpeter to sound. The drums rolled, Cortes' troops wheeled into column, and the march began through the opening gates of the courtyard.

Outside Tampaniquita, the Indian town designated for the rendezvous, the barren volanic rock of the countryside begins to contrast with the fertile plain of the *tierra caliente* with its tall cottonwoods mingling with the lower stands of green bamboo and banana. Cortes had selected an open, rock-strewn field outside the town for the inspection of his army, if such an assemblage could be called an army. The Captain-General, while not a man subject to lingering doubts, did have mixed feelings about his force as he dismounted from El Molinero to make the review on foot. He had reason to feel relieved about the growing numbers of his force since he had left Tenochtitlan. At Cholula he had been joined by Velasquez de Leon with his detachment, and only yesterday Sandoval had arrived from Villa Rica with his sixty effectives. Today, after discounting the sick and others sent back to Alvarado, Cortes was ready to take stock of his 266 veterans. So while his total strength had increased about four-fold there was reason for despondency at what Cortes saw when he and his captains strolled down the ranks. They were looking at an infantry force, for only Cortes and 4 of his captains were mounted, hardly a cavalry to match against Narvaez's 80 horsemen! To make matters worse the comparison of fire-power with Narvaez's potential was almost laughable: Cortes' 15 arquebusiers against Narvaez's 80; Cortes' 14 crossbow-men against Narvaez's 150.

The armor of the infantrymen also might have raised laughter among Narvaez's men. With the exception of a handful of battered brigandines, the universal armor for pikemen, arquebusiers, and swordsmen was the tattered na-tive *escapuil*, the cotton quilted armor which could stop an Indian arrow but not a Spanish bullet. Months of campaign-ing in tropical heat had caused the infantrymen to barter off their steel armor and adopt the *escaupil*. Their heavy leather boots had also disappeared, worn out long ago and replaced by local hemp sandals. Yet they all hung on to their helmets, clearly as precious to the men as the heavy gold chains which the common soldier wore around his neck, his only way of securing his portable wealth.

When the men had been dismissed to march back to camp, Cortes faced a downcast half-circle of officers. It was evident to all that the inspection had done little to raise their hopes of defeating Narvaez in a pitched battle. Yet their confidence in Cortes had not diminished; he had pulled them through too many impossible situations for doubt to take hold now. As usual he was able to sense their feelings.

"A motley array of companies, yes. But did you look in the eyes of those men and note their bearing? These are vet-erans with confidence in us and themselves, veterans of the wars under the great Cordoba and here in Mexico. They have been unbeatable because they *know* they are unbeatable," Cortes said.

Gonzalo de Sandoval was quick to expand on that note.

"You could see too that their weapons are all in order, swords sharpened and bucklers shining," he said.

"Yes, but what good are the swords and bucklers against Narvaez's horsemen?" asked Diego de Ordas, who often played the part of the skeptic.

"It is fitting that you have asked, Captain Ordas, for that brings me to the next step in training these men to contend with Narvaez's cavalry—and infantry if need be. Father Olmedo is coming just now with Tobillos, the master pikeman, and you'll see for yourselves that we are going to become an army ready to take on Burgundians or Swiss, let alone Narvaez's men," Cortes said, pointing out the approaching friar and his companion, a helmeted infantryman who carried a twenty-foot spear over his shoulder.

Cortes had Tobillos demonstrate the employment of the weapon as a pike, after pointing out the deadly double head fashioned by Chinantec smiths out of native copper.

"Tobillos has brought three hundred of these from Chinantla," Cortes explained. "I had ordered them made in a letter written before we left Tenochtitlan. Now Master Pikeman Tobillos here, a veteran of the Italian wars and an expert at arms, will train a cadre who will, in turn, see that every foot soldier becomes proficient in the use of this pike, especially against cavalry. Are there other questions about dealing with Narvaez's cavalry?" Cortes said looking at Ordas.

Cortes let the silence sink in before leading the officers back toward the camp. Sandoval, anxious to channel conversation into other subjects, spoke up as the group started back across the rocky fields.

"I have heard talk while in Villa Rica of Father Olmedo's mission to Narvaez's headquarters, but all I have learned was that the father here was dispatched with a letter and some trinkets," Sandoval said.

"Far more than mere trinkets, Captain Sandoval. But Father Olmedo, why don't you tell him yourself about your mission and what you learned in Narvaez's camp," Cortes said.

The stout friar, living up to his notoriety for eloquence, was delighted to regale the captains—some for the third time—with the tale of his success as an emissary and intelligence agent. He told how Narvaez had moved his army to Cempoalla, which he now occupied. There Father Olmedo had delivered Cortes' letter to an enraged Narvaez whose first reaction was to clap the friar in irons, next to expel him from Cempoalla. He was easily dissuaded when he was presented with the gift of golden "trinkets." Olmedo had, however, held back similar presents which he later gave in secret to some of the more apparent malcontents in Narvaez's service.

Olmedo went on to describe Narvaez himself as a captain-general overawed by his own importance and, at the same time, one who was careless in his operations because of his overconfidence in the size of his force and the comparative weakness of Cortes' command. Narvaez, it seemed, was surrounded by captains who acted more like courtiers than officers. One, Salvatierra, a blusterer, had even declared his intention of slicing off Cortes' ears and having them broiled for his breakfast! Then too Olmedo had noted that many of the troops in Cempoalla held no love for their commander. Their loyalty was questionable at best, especially since these men had no stomach for fighting fellow soldiers. They had shown much interest in the stories about Cortes and his exploits, and their eyes had reflected gleams of gold when they saw some of the gold Olmedo had quietly distributed. Olmedo concluded with his final dismissal by Narvaez who gave him a letter, in reply to Cortes, ordering Cortes to submit to his authority and threatening him and his command with dire and deserved punishment. Thus, though Olmedo had been expelled, the poison of his intrigues was left behind to work on the least loyal of Narvaez's officers and soldiers.

When Olmedo had finished, the group had already entered the camp, and Cortes gave his orders for the next day.

"We march at the first hour, our destination a ford on the Rio de Canoas, a stream most of you have crossed before. We will make camp on this side of the river at this point about a league south of Cempoalla. From there I make a final reconnaissance, and after that I will give my final orders," Cortes said in dismissing the group.

The last stage of the march to the Rio de Canoas was the most wearing, not only because the men were tired, but also because the spells of torrential rain were at their worst as the afternoon lengthened. Late in the day the sun broke through, the clouds drifted off, and the heat plagued the marching men as much as had the rainstorms. When they reached the stream they found it had become a real river swollen from the rains. At the selected sites Cortes ordered the companies to fall out and rest before making camp for the night. After leaving orders that the camp should be made in quiet and without fires, Cortes, accompanied by Olid and Sandoval, rode off to reconnoiter the best place to ford the river. While they rode Cortes broke the news of his decision to carry out the operation that night.

"Nombre de Dios!" Sandoval could not restrain himself. "This may be madness, but it is the kind of madness that will catch Narvaez with his armor off. I like it."

"I know the men feel the effects of our last march, but they'll warm to their work once they understand fully what is happening," Cortes said.

"And how do you propose to let them know that?" Olid asked.

"As soon as we get back we'll dispense with the captains' assembly. I'll talk to one and all at this time," Cortes said.

Prescott said it well in his *Conquest of Mexico:* "Before disclosing his design, he [Cortes] addressed his men in one of those stirring, soldierly harangues, to which he had recourse in emergencies of great moment, as if to sound the depths of their hearts, and, where any faltered, to reanimate them, with his own heroic spirit. . . ." Bernal Diaz del Castillo, one of Cortes' captains, one not always animated with unrestrained admiration of his captain-general, says in *The Discovery and Conquest of Mexico* that Cortes ". . . began a speech in such charming style, with sentences so neatly turned, that I assuredly am unable to write the like, so delightful was it and so full of promise, in which he at once reminded us of all that had happened to us since we set out from the Island of Cuba . . ."

Delightful or not, honeyed words or not, Cortes did recapitulate the battles and campaigns, reminded them of the dangers and incredible odds they had overcome to attain victories, and, not the least, the wealth they had all gained. But now, they were about to lose it all to an adventurer who came in force *but with no commission from the Crown of Spain,* only a dispatch from a greedy governor who would *punish them* for their hard-won conquests. Their claims, based on their service to his majesty, were to be dishonored and they had already been branded as traitors by Diego Velasquez and Narvaez. "But now the time had come for vengeance and God would not desert his soldiers of the True Cross. And, if they should fail [in their coming attack on Narvaez], better to die like brave men on the field of battle, than, with fame and fortune cast away, to perish ignominiously like slaves on the gibbet. This last point he urged home upon his hearers; well knowing there was not one among them so dull as not be touched by it. . . ."

It is said they all "responded with hearty acclamations,"

Spanish light cannon

and when the shouting died two captains, Velasquez de Leon and De Lugo, spoke for all the rest, saying,

"We are ready to follow where you lead!"

Cortes looked around at them in the falling light of the day, knowing that it would no longer be necessary to raise their spirits; he needed only to guide them in the right direction.

"Gather closer now and hear my orders to your captains. The first objective I assign to Gonzalo de Sandoval who, as *alguacil mayor,* will seize Panfilo de Narvaez as prisoner. If he resists he will be killed. Captain Sandoval, you will have your chosen sixty men to accomplish this mission.

"Captain de Olid, as *maestro de campo,* you with sixty men must first capture and secure Narvaez's artillery. Then you will assist Sandoval by keeping any enemy from going to the aid of Narvaez.

"Captains Velasquez de Leon and De Ordas, with sixty

men each, will arrest the other officers of Narvaez that I shall designate, and prepare to assist my other captains on order.

"Lastly, I will keep under my own command the remaining twenty men to act as general reserve for our attack.

"A final word to all—I propose these awards from my war chest: To the soldier who first lays hands on Narvaez I will award three thousand gold pesos, to the second soldier, two thousand pesos, and to the third, one thousand.

"Our battle cry and watchword—because this is the eve of Whitsunday—will be *Espiritu Santo*. Captains, you may assemble your companies."

Cortes had marched with Sandoval at the head of the lead company in the column. It had started raining again as they had entered the ford and it had been rough going as officers and men had slipped time and again on the smooth stones of the river bed. Their twenty-foot pikes had turned out to be their mainstay as they used the long shafts to brace themselves and find their footing. Cortes had stood by on the far bank until the last dripping files had emerged from the river before he went up the halted column to rejoin Sandoval and give the order to continue the march. Already the night had become a vicious combination of torrential rain and buffeting wind.

"Hernan, this weather is no friend of ours," Sandoval said as they stumbled along in the howling darkness.

"You are wrong, Gonzalo. On the contrary, this storm has been sent by the Savior himself, for it will keep the enemy under cover in his stone quarters—no better aid for us in surprising him," Cortes said, his last words ending almost in a shout.

Sandoval's answering shrug was lost on Cortes in the dark, but his next movement was to reach out and place his gauntleted hand on the Captain-General's shoulder, bringing them both to a halt. As the files following them thumped into their backs Cortes realized that Sandoval had just encountered three of his scouts who were dragging a prisoner toward them. The two officers thrust their faces close to that of the soldier who led the scouts.

"Captain Sandoval, there were two of Narvaez's sentinels. We have here Gonzalo Carrasco, but his companion has escaped. Surely he has run to warn Narvaez," the scout reported.

"Did the other one see you or any other scouts?" Cortes asked.

"We think not. This prisoner says his companion ran when he heard us grabbing him."

"That much may be good. But here now, Carrasco, if you want to live, tell us of the locations of Narvaez and his artillery," Cortes said, shoving his face into the prisoner's.

The quick interrogation that followed ended in stubborn silence after the prisoner had confirmed that Narvaez occupied the great teocalli outside of which his artillery had been posted to cover the main avenues leading into the plaza. Carrasco would not—or could not—reveal more, and Cortes could waste no more time on him.

"Have him bound to a tree there, Gonzalo. We'll need these scouts out in front again. What the prisoner has told us confirms the intelligence of Olmedo and Duero who learned far more than this soldier seems to know. Come, we must be moving on. Every minute counts," Cortes said to Sandoval and the lead files.

Miraculously the rain slackened as the wind began to die down. For brief seconds the moon peered through a break in the clouds and was gone again. In that short spell of moonlight Cortes could make out the distant outline of the stone pyramids that marked the center of Cempoalla.

"Look, Hernan, see that light on one of the teocalli's towers?" Sandoval said.

"I see, I see. It's on the tallest one, and that has to be Narvaez's. That's our guiding beacon, Gonzalo," Cortes replied, and stepped up the pace.

In minutes the head of the column was passing the outlying Indian huts and in no time Cortes and the others began to feel the stone flagging of streets underfoot.

"For God's sake, Gonzalo, have your men split their column to both sides of the street. Have them stick close to the walls. If Narvaez's artillery should open up on us we don't want men slaughtered like cattle in a pen. Keep up the pace, I'm going to bring up my reserve to follow Olid's party as they go after the artillery," Cortes said, giving Sandoval a parting clap on the shoulder.

When Cortes had stepped aside to let Sandoval's men pass he had time to look around and orient himself. The rain had died away completely and the moon shone through the rapidly breaking cloud masses. Cortes stared in astonishment at the sight beyond the files of rushing men. Rising from the sodden fields, up between the huts and stone walls, all across his field of vision, Cortes watched the display of brilliant flashes winking on and off as hundreds of sparks seemed to rise from the earth. He was about to cross himself when he remembered his first night march, months before, when he had led another column through the *tierra caliente* in this same area. These winking lights were carried by the *cocuyos,* the huge firefly-beetles whose bodies emitted such an intense light that— so their Totonac guides had said—it was strong enough to enable one to make out picture writings by it.

God willing, Cortes thought, *this is an omen, a good sign sent by the True Cross.*

He stopped a passing pikeman long enough to find that Olid was only a few paces behind him.

"Follow me, Cristobal," he ordered Olid, "we're on the right street and now you can see your way to the plaza."

Olid had already followed Sandoval's example and deployed his men along the sides of the street as they began to dash forward. Cortes' order to Sandoval paid off within the next minute. The entire street was lit by the sudden flashes of cannon fire from the plaza. The crash of the artillery volley blasted their ears and downed three soldiers while sending other of Olid's men staggering against the walls. The air overhead was ripped with the passing balls and stones of langridge* some of which were ricocheting off the stone walls.

"In the name of God, get on, get on!" Cortes was shouting at the men who had stopped in their tracks. "Get on the gunners before they can reload—and we've got them and the guns!"

Olid had the coolness to direct a file of pikemen to take on a half-dozen horsemen who had loomed out of the night to the left of the artillery battery. He sent the next file to the right and in a flash the sword-and-buckler men were darting among a troop of cavalrymen who were still trying to mount their horses. The swordsmen were using their swords and daggers to slash the saddle girths before they turned their weapons on the cavalrymen.

In the same flash of time the rest of Olid's men were overrunning the gunners, doing deadly work, first with the

---

*Langridge—a kind of case-shot made up of irregular chunks of metal or, in some cases, stones; used for close-range fires against infantry or cavalry.

pike and then the sword. In the time it would have taken Olid to report it to Cortes the main battery was silenced, and Cortes had to order a halt to the slaughter.

"Stop them, Cristobal," Cortes shouted, "we'll have need of these guns and crews soon enough. We'll make these gunners part of us—as you can see they are crying out to do."

As Cortes started to leave and locate his captain of the reserve, Sandoval's messenger came dashing up to report.

"Captain-General, we fought Narvaez and his guards and have driven them up the great stairs of their teocalli. But they fight well and we are losing men to their arquebuses and crossbows."

"I will be taking my men to your captain's aid, but you go on—in that direction—and give Captain De Ordas my order to come to your captain's support as soon as he can," Cortes ordered.

Cortes found Olid reorganizing his company, having detached his swordsmen and their officers to supervise the gunners in preparing the guns for towing to a new position.

"A magnificent piece of work, Cristobal! Now send all the men you can spare to reinforce Sandoval. I'll see that the guns get in position to fire on all three of the main buildings," Cortes said.

He paused long enough to collect his thoughts, trying to picture the whole of the situation from his observations and the fragments of reports that were coming in.

We've got all the artillery but that is still only half the battle. I've got to have Narvaez, alive or dead, before we can get his officers—then his men—to lay down their arms. After all, if I can overcome Narvaez's army I want to take it as intact as possible. Dead and wounded men are of no use to my cause. Now, in case Olid does not find Sandoval at once, I'll send a messenger to tell him the guns are on the way. Then I can go on ahead while my men assist Olid's with the cannon.

He waited only long enough to send his page, Orteguilla, speeding off with the message to Sandoval. Then Cortes was off toward the great teocalli, after giving directions to his captain of the reserve for bringing up the artillery.

He found Sandoval and Olid at the foot of the great stairs amid a swirl of pikemen and swordsmen who were being reformed into their units while the wounded were being carried away.

"Hernan," Sandoval reported, "we've battled them up and

down these stairs, losing men to their bullets and crossbow bolts, but now we have driven them into the sanctuary at the top. So far, Narvaez and his men have been able to hold that narrow entrance against us."

"The artillery can batter our way in, but that's going to use up too much time because the guns are being pulled by hand. There's no other way in, other than that door?" Cortes asked.

"None, We've already checked that out," Sandoval said.

"And the roof—no way through that?"

"Wait—oh, mother of God, why haven't I seen it? Look, the roof," Sandoval was pointing at the top of the pyramid.

Cortes saw in a flash what was meant. He looked around him.

"Pass up the nearest arquebusier," he called out. In a moment a soldier was at his side.

"Let me see your match. Good, you've kept it burning," Cortes said, "now where is a man with a good right arm, a man who is a great thrower?".

A tall soldier pushed his way through the press of men; Olid recognized him.

"Martin Lopez, the shipbuilder, just your man. But what will you have of him?" Olid asked.

It was the work of seconds for Cortes to have the arquebusier set fire to an improvised torch. Lopez sprang up the stairs, stopped halfway, and threw the blazing torch onto a corner of the thatched roof of the sanctuary. As the blaze mounted, lighting up the sides and stairs of the teocalli, Cortes gave the order to Sandoval and Olid.

"They'll be popping out of there soon enough now. They're not going to stay in there and be roasted alive. As soon as they start to come out—up you go! Rush them, and remember the awards for the soldiers who capture Narvaez!" These last words were shouted at the waiting men, and grins broke out on faces gleaming with sweat in the light of the blazing thatch.

As if they had been prompted by Cortes' order the first of Narvaez's men came staggering out of the door onto the stairs. Sandoval and Olid led the dash up at them, pikemen and swordsmen at their heels. Cortes saw a figure in their midst, helmeted and clad in bright armor. As he watched he could see a tall, husky soldier drop his pike and grapple with the cavalier.

"It's Pedro Farfan, and he's got Narvaez. Look, it is him, Narvaez. He was wounded in the eye when we first rushed the stairs," Sandoval's aide was telling Cortes.

Two other soldiers had pinned Narvaez, dragging him to the ground and down the stairs where he was clapped into irons. Cortes was off again, leaving his two captains to take the surrender of the rest of Narvaez's headquarters men. The guns were being dragged up, and their new positions must be selected so that their fire would be directed on the other two teocallis which the remainder of Narvaez's force was defending against Cortes' units, now in the act of surrounding of the buildings.

Cortes stood in the interval between two batteries—his men had now brought up all eighteen guns—waiting for his messengers to return. He had dispatched them to deliver the summons of surrender to Narvaez's leaders, who were holding out in the two buildings. Both messengers returned with reports of arrogant refusals to surrender. Cortes turned to his captain acting as master of the ordnance.

"Very well, fire one volley over the roofs of the teocallis, and let us see what happens."

When the smoke from the volley drifted aside Cortes got his answer in the form of white cloths waving from pike staffs atop both pyramids.

"It would seem that the cannon are better at delivering proclamations than my messengers. Take your men, Velasquez de Leon, and seize the officers, then have their men come to the plaza with their arms," Cortes commanded.

In the full light of the morning Cortes, a richly embroidered orange robe draped over his shoulders and upper armor, was seated in the center of the plaza surrounded by the trappings of state—an awning under which his staff had placed his throne-like chair.

From his chair he had watched Narvaez's soldiers file by to stack their arms in the plaza, and he had made sure that four of his captains supervised a careful accounting so that the weapons could be returned to their owners after they had taken the oath to serve under Cortes' banner. After the mass swearing-in of Narvaez's men he had dismissed Narvaez himself, sending him off in chains to be taken to Villa Rica. The humiliation of the defeated commander had been carried out in true Spanish cavalier style. Narvaez, standing fettered in front of his conqueror, his ruined eye covered with a bloody bandage, had sought to depart gracefully with a knightly acknowledgement of Cortes' victory.

"Señor Cortes, you may hold high the good fortune you have had, and the great achievement of securing my person," Narvaez said.

Cortes smiled his courtier's smile as he looked down at his captive.

"Señor Narvaez, many deeds have I performed since coming to Mexico, but the least of them all has been to capture you."

After Narvaez had been led away, Cortes started to turn his attention to the matter of securing the ships of Narvaez's armada. He was distracted by loud laughter coming from a group of officers and soldiers in a corner of the plaza. They were grouped around Sandoval, who had always been a popular figure with the men. The tall, black-bearded captain had them guffawing at some tale he was spinning. Cortes motioned a page to his side.

"Ask Captain Sandoval to share his joke with us," he said.

Sandoval was brushing tears of laughter from his eyes as he approached Cortes.

"It's not one joke but two, Hernan," Sandoval said.

"So much the better. Let's hear them then."

"You saw them take away Salvatierra, the captain who was going to have your ears broiled for his breakfast. Well, it seems that he was standing under the roof of his teocalli when you had the artillery fire over that roof. His soldiers say that Salvatierra became suddenly ill, so violently ill in fact that he fell on the floor and cried that he could no longer stand to fight, his stomach was tied in such a knot."

"And that is the big joke?" Cortes asked.

"Not just that, Hernan. His soldiers said that they could not come to his aid. It seems that his stomach trouble had extended to his bowels, loosening them in a most explosive way so that no man would approach him."

"That can truly be said to be a sound reason for his solitude. But what of your other tale, how does it relate to Salvatierra?"

"It doesn't. It concerns the sentries Narvaez's captains had stationed in the towers, the ones who gave the alarm that tumbled Narvaez's men from their beds when we were first entering the streets in our attack. Do you recall then the cloud of *cocuyos* that rose from the fields and streets around us, just after the rain stopped?"

"Yes, for a moment I knew not what to think of it. Then, seeing what was happening, I remember counting it as heaven-sent."

"That *you* may have done, my general, but not Narvaez's sentries and the soldiers they aroused. One sentry, seeing the moving flashes of light, took them to be hundreds of arque-busier's matches, the matches of an advancing army. That one called out his fears and the word spread as though carried on the wind—to be taken up by the already confused troops who had just been shaken from their beds into the dark. But as you say, Hernan, it must have been our good fortune—yes, sent from heaven," Sandoval said.

"Not exactly, Gonzalo. One day when you are in high command, you will find that all good fortune does not come from heaven."

If Cempoalla were to be compared with other battles that led to the overthrow of empires—Arbela or Waterloo, for example—it would indeed seem a piddling affair: a night action lasting less than an hour and involving fewer than 1,200 men. Yet Cempoalla assured that Cortes' past and future conquests, subduing the mightiest empire in the New World, would open two continents to European colonization. When threatened by Narvaez's "counterinvasion" Cortes had stood to lose everything. Was it desperation then that made him bold? The question appears to be answerable in the affirmative, but less so when one looks into the character of Cortes. What sort of man was he really?

At first glance an obvious facet shows the daring conquistador, the brave warrior. Certainly he was that or he would not have been able to lead that rough crew of his for longer than a week under the best of conditions; the record shows him leading them under the worst. A second look reveals a scheming, plotting Machiavellian type to whom the end sought was worth any means to gain it. Let us remember that Machiavelli and Cortes *were* contemporaries, though worlds apart in certain senses.

A third observation of the man shows him to be the consummate politician, an actor of a higher order, and a persuader who could have run a night school for LBJ. A fourth and final aspect discloses the meticulous planner, the kind who never overlooks a critical detail.

Plainly Hernan Cortes was not made up of any *one* of these outward faces of character. He was a combination of them, showing only the face he wanted on the occasion he thought demanded it. He had all the courtly graces, employing them where needed. At other times he was the bluff, good-humored soldier, but never the hearty, backslapping kind, for he always maintained a cool reserve. Truly a complicated man, but a product of his times.

This attempt to look inside Cortes, brief as it has been, is enough to demonstrate that this was not a man forced to take the bold actions he did out of desperation. There are too many signs of an iron will guided by a subtle intellect throughout his operations. There was nothing of the impetuous in the planning and conduct of his campaign, from the time he first gained intelligence of Narvaez's expedition (later confirmed in several ways through his own reliable sources) until he led the night attack on Cempoalla.

There is enough evidence to permit one to view Cortes' actions from yet another viewpoint—from that of a reversed image, looking at them from the mirror provided by Narvaez himself. From beginning to end Narvaez never set himself a clear objective, one that he should have had to succeed in his mission. Hence he was never able to make a clear evaluation of his problems and come up with a workable plan. Conversely, Cortes saw from the outset what had to be done and how to muster the means to do it.

His critical shortcoming left Narvaez to be governed by events which he could not control. On the other hand, Cortes had set clearly-defined goals toward which he advanced with step-by-step actions. Lastly, Narvaez never got a clear conception of his opponent's character and, most important, his capabilities. Cortes employed every means available to assess the character of Narvaez and determine what his opponent could do with the means at his command—and to find the weakness of his enemy's seemingly powerful force.

Thus Cortes was able to direct that will of his in a way that allowed him to adopt bold measures, calculated measures that prepared him and his men to deal with the dynamic forces he knew would threaten his plans, and to capture intact a force three and a half times the size of his own.

Remembering the dynamics described in the introduction, one should have little trouble detecting their presence in the Cempoalla campaign. The danger to Cortes' command threatens at the very outset with the news of Narvaez's landing in Mexico. The other dynamics appear in the marches from Tenochtitlan to the coast, the approach march to Cempoalla, and in the night attack.

It may be argued that Cortes got two good breaks: in the weather and in the matter of the *cocuyos*. Yet Cortes had to be advancing to the attack or he would not have been able to turn either factor to his advantage. Finally, if the miracle of giant fireflies strains the credibility, there is some comfort in Byron's aphorism in *Don Juan*—

> "'Tis strange but true; for truth is always strange;
> Stranger than fiction; if it could be told."

Tenacity

At last the Persians, finding that all their efforts to gain the pass [of Thermopylae] availed nothing, and that, whether they attacked by divisions or in any other way, it was to no purpose, withdrew to their own quarters. During these assaults, it is said that Xerxes, who was watching the battle, thrice leaped from the throne on which he sat, in terror for his army.

Next day the combat was renewed, but with no better success on the part of the barbarians. The Greeks were so few that the barbarians hoped to find them disabled, by reason of their wounds, from offering any further resistance; and so once more attacked them. But the Greeks were drawn up in detachments according to their cities, and bore the brunt in turns. . . . So when the Persians found no difference between that day and the preceding, they again retired to their quarters.

—Herodotus, VII, 211–212.

The Persians had ample reason to "retire to their quarters." For three days running Leonidas and his Greeks held their ground against truly overwhelming odds (twenty-eight-to-one: two hundred thousand Persians against seven thousand Greeks) until the tragic end. Behind the story of one of the most heroic defensive actions in history stands the cold fact that Leonidas accomplished his mission of buying time for the Greek states. This in spite of the leader sacrificing himself and his three hundred Spartans in an epic rear-guard action. What made Leonidas do it?

He was a Spartan king and the well qualified leader of an allied force; however, do those facts supply the answer? Only in part. Was the famed Spartan discipline sufficient cause? Again, only in part because their discipline, while it enabled the Spartans to fight more effectively than their enemies, was not the underlying cause. The real reason was that Leonidas made the decision to hold out, to accomplish his mission as he saw it. He was able to make the decision and to see it carried out because of his sense of duty. A strong will guided by cool reasoning directed the course he would follow to fulfill his responsibility to the state. Leonidas' decision and its outcome speak for themselves in the famous epitaph on the tomb of the Spartan leader and his soldiers: "Go, stranger, and tell the Lacedaemonians that we lie here in obedience to their laws."

Before looking further into the idea of duty it will be remembered that, earlier in this chapter, we observed that *effective* boldness was an extension of the intellect; additionally that boldness when employed without reason becomes rashness. There is a parallel case here in linking the sense of duty to tenacity. A rational sense of duty provides a sound base for tenacious action; however, tenacity without basis in reason becomes mere obstinacy in its worst sense—commonly referred to as being bullheaded or "stubborn as a mule," hardly what we look for in a leader.

What is meant by a sense of duty as a mainstay of tenacity? It would be as easy as it would be unrewarding if one were to duck behind the idea of duty as something required by a regulation or as a quality learned in some academic setting. If our inquiry goes, as it should, beyond such patent cop-outs we will find eventually that duty is essentially a constitutent of morality. Marcus Aurelius, no mean leader by anyone's lights, said in *The Meditations:* "It is thy duty to order thy life well in every single act; and if every act does its duty, as far as is possible, be content. . . ." The Emperor went on to point out that man's only good will is a dutiful will—the sort of thinking that puts him on our side.

Coming down to a less lofty plane the whole thing can be reduced, for our purposes, to a straightforward progression:

> Reason governs a sound sense of duty.
> Duty provides a sound base for tenacious action.
> Tenacity becomes a function of the will.

Tenacity implies hanging on, sticking with it, but here a word of caution: time is not the only measure of tenacity, or else sieges would be our prime gauge for tenacious action. The intensity of combat can become a major—if not on occasion the chief—determinant of what tenacity can accomplish. It is with this thought in mind that we should watch this next action, one of the epic stands of all time.

Rorke's Drift

This is the story of not one leader but two, both lieutenants in Queen Victoria's army in South Africa in January 1879. Their story begins not with them, rather at the top of their chain of command.

Lt.-Gen. Sir Frederic Augustus Thesiger, Second Baron Chelmsford, KCB, Commander-in-Chief British Forces in South Africa, was not a soldier given to yielding to—or even expressing—his emotions. Yet this morning his stricken face showed every sign of the shock and horror that had overcome him. At first he had put up a front of cheerful incredulity; this had grown into grave disbelief as more reports had reached him, and now he was forced to believe his own eyes as he rode out in the rising mists of the African dawn.

He and his staff had ridden up to the foot of Isandhlwana Mountain at the head of the returning half of his center column, but it had been in pitch-black darkness and they had had to wait for daylight to ride over the rocky fields around the site of the massacre. Now he was seeing the ruin of his base camp for what it really was, no longer a battlefield but the scene of massacre. His horse, moving at a slow walk, picked his way cautiously to avoid the hundreds of bodies lying singly or in lines and heaps across the plain. Many of the slain soldiers had been stripped of their red jackets, but clothed or not most of the corpses were lying face up; many were horribly mutilated and all had been disemboweled by stabbing assegais, the heavy, broad-bladed thrusting spear of the Zulu warrior. Lord Chelmsford had heard his share of the stories about the slitting open of bellies of slain Zulu enemies, done, it was said, in accordance with Zulu belief, to prevent the bodies from becoming the abode of evil spirits.

Here, at a stroke—in less than three hours—the Commander-in-Chief had lost half of the center column that he

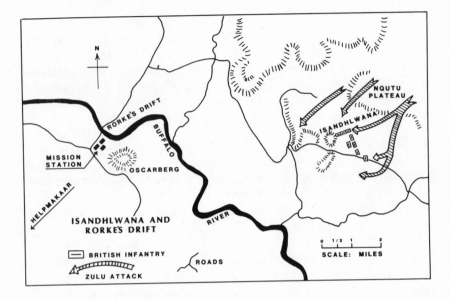

ISANDHLWANA AND
RORKE'S DRIFT

had led to invade Zululand only eleven days before. He was to learn, when all accounts were in and casualties counted, that out of the 1,774-man force he had left in the base camp at Isandhlwana 1,329 lay dead on the field—the Zulus took no prisoners. The dead British soldiers and the bodies of the native contingent soldiers were not alone on the rocky plain around Isandhlwana Mountain and Stoney Hill. Two thousand Zulu bodies were counted, these left by an army of 20,000 warriors. But that was of small consolation to Lord Chelmsford. No count of Zulu casualties could make up for the disaster that now confronted him.

He had ordered out half of his center column—the other two columns were several days march away to his north and south—to support the reconnaissance in force that he had sent out the day before. He had ridden with the center column's force to observe what he had hoped to be the first major encounter with Zulus in strength. Major Dartnell, the reconnaissance force commander, had called for support saying that the enemy was appearing in far greater numbers than he had anticipated. But Lord Chelmsford's supporting strike had fallen on empty air ten miles from Isandhlwana. The clouds of Zulu scouts and their supports had melted away before British attempts to engage them. Their retreat was to Chelmsford "nothing less than cowardly." Too late the Commander-in-Chief was to realize that his supporting force was chasing a decoy. There had been no Zulu impi* in front of him, instead a Zulu army of twenty thousand had been hiding five miles north of Isandhlwana screened by the Nqutu Plateau. And too late he had received the reports of the disastrous battle at his base camp, after the Zulu army had made its bloody counterstrike.

Back in his tent at Isandhlwana, Chelmsford was recalling lines from the letter he had written two weeks before to his commander in London, the Duke of Cambridge: "It is impossible to speculate what tactics the Zulus will pursue. . . . Our movements will all be made in the most deliberate manner. . . . Your Royal Highness, however, may rest assured that I shall do my best to bring it [the war in Zululand] to a speedy close, so that I may be enabled to send back to England some of the regiments now under my command."[6]

Never were words to come home to roost so woefully on a writer's shoulders! Yet they were not one of Chelmsford's immediate cares, for the Zulu victory had not only wiped out half his central column, it had also destroyed or captured all his supplies, including his command's reserve of ammunition. In a predominantly infantry force the only ammunition remaining was the seventy rounds each rifleman carried in his pouches.

No longer was the Commander-in-Chief forced to cope with the problem of deciding whether to advance, fight, or maneuver. Clearly his only recourse was to withdraw the remainder of his force back into Natal over the route by which it had advanced. That meant marching out, as soon as possible, over the ten miles of rough road back to Rorke's Drift where he could re-cross the Buffalo River. But even that inevitable course of action was overcast with a foreboding shadow. Scouting parties on the road back to Natal had sighted clouds of black smoke rising from behind the Oscarberg, the hill behind which lay the post of Rorke's Drift. Was that base lost too, gone up in flames from Zulu torches?

The afternoon of the same day that Lord Chelmsford's force had left Isandhlwana to support Major Dartnell's reconnaissance in force, a Lieutenant of Royal Engineers was supervising the securing of ferry cables at the drift, the ford named after the trader Jim Rorke. He was Lt. John Rouse

---

*Equivalent of a large regiment, an organized Zulu tactical unit.

Merriott Chard, R.E., and he was still concerned with the impression he had gotten that morning while visiting the base camp at Isandhlwana. He had ridden back to Rorke's Drift with the disturbing but unconfirmed news that a large Zulu force might have bypassed Lord Chelmsford's base camp on its north side and was still unaccounted for in the vast expanse of rugged country north and west of Isandhlwana.

Although Chard was temporarily in command of the post at Rorke's Drift, his official duties were limited to the completion of the ferry crossing, a task that he felt he could well have, by this time, left to Sergeant Milne and his work party of six natives. Chard's real interest—the one he wanted to get back to—was the laying out of earthworks at the former Swedish mission, now the military supply depot and hospital. He had already sketched out the work, now he was anxious to complete his plans in the hope that a company of Royal Engineers would arrive one day to do the work, though right now that remained only a hope. But there *was* the company of British infantry—Lieutenant Bromhead's B Company, 2nd Battalion, 24th Foot—now garrisoning the station, and Chard had work plans in mind for the company that would surely have failed to delight any of the infantrymen—from Bromhead to the latest-joined private.

Chard was a fine military figure standing there on the river bank. He was of medium height, his tanned face half-hidden by his dark beard and mustache under his white tropical helmet. He wore his scarlet uniform jacket, crossed by a leather shoulder belt, and instead of his sword he carried his sketch-case attached to his sword belt. He was thirty-two with eleven years of service before his recent arrival in Africa, and he had the good sense to listen to advice from Bromhead who had completed a tour of field service in South Africa. He had to smile under his mustache at the thought of his being "temporarily in command" and, as such, being Bromhead's commanding officer. Only an hour ago Major Spalding had left Rorkes's Drift after finishing his lunch and leaving Chard in command of the post. Spalding was officially the officer in command of two posts, Rorke's Drift and the depot at Helpmakaar ten miles to the southwest. The major had been annoyed enough to ride off to Helpmakaar for the purpose of personally seeing to it that a company of infantry from that garrison was moved up to reinforce Rorke's Drift. He had already sent orders for a company at Help-

Zulus rallying to renew an attack

makaar to move up, and now it was long overdue. Spalding's departure had been prompted by reports of large bodies of Zulus that had been sighted moving on Isandhlwana, the Spalding's two depots existed only to provide stations on the line of communications* for Lord Chelmsford's base camp and center column.

Chard had not been overwhelmed at the idea of his command responsibility since he expected Spalding to return in a few hours. Nor was he concerned over the odd command relationship between him and Bromhead. The infantry lieutenant, although two years older than Chard and with a year and a half more service, was actually the junior. The reason was the Queen's Regulations which allowed graduates of the Royal Military Academy like Chard to be commissioned directly as lieutenants** in the Royal Engineers or Royal Artillery. Bromhead, as an infantry officer, had to serve four years as a second lieutenant before his promotion to lieutenant. Fortunately for Chard and Bromhead, this state of affairs remained only a matter of the regulations. Their personal relationship was a cordial one with no professional jealousies or friction.

---

*For practical purposes this term denotes a major resupply route for a force in the field.
**The equivalent of first lieutenants in the U.S. Army.

Chard was making up his mind to ride back to the post when his thoughts were interrupted by the sound of galloping horses approaching the opposite bank of the river. He saw two horsemen ride down the slope to the ford and start swimming their horses across the hundred yard stretch of chest-deep, yellow-brown water. The one in the lead, evidently an officer, was shouting something but Chard could not make out the words. As they got closer Chard recognized the two as Lieutenants Adendorff and Vane of the Natal Native Contingent. Both their horses were streaming with sweat and river water. The officers wore the khaki slouch hats of the N.N.C., but the rest of their uniforms were in anything but parade order. Adendorff's jacket and shirt front flapped in the wind while Vane was in rolled shirtsleeves. Their faces were caked with dust that had been creased by rivulets of sweat. Adendorff had to catch his breath before he could pant out his news.

"The camp has been butchered to the last man. It's gone. Everything is lost—"

"Hold on now," Chard broke in, "I was up there earlier this morning and the only Zulus sighted were scouts—and they were two or three thousand yards away."

"Yes, but when did you start back from Isandhlwana?" Vane asked.

"I would say about midmorning. I was back here by noon," Chard said.

"There you are then. The whole affair started in late morning and it was all over by one o'clock," Adendorff said.

"We're wasting valuable time. Why don't you give him the rest of the news?" Vane said.

"You're right. What he means is that there's an impi—estimated to be four thousand strong—moving toward Rorke's Drift, and on your side of the river," Adendorff blurted out.

"My God, man, and we stand here talking. How far away are they?" Chard said.

"Might be only a matter of minutes. We can't be sure because we lost sight of them in getting away from them."

Chard didn't wait for Adendorff to finish. He was shouting for Sergeant Milne and his six men to report on the double. He had hardly got an acknowledging salute from his sergeant when he saw another galloper coming toward him, this one coming down the road from the post. Chard recognized him to be one of Bromhead's lance-corporals astride Bromhead's horse.

"Sir, Lieutenant Bromhead reports sightings of large numbers of Zulus coming from the east and northeast. He says to tell you that he has struck tents and is preparing to march or fight—whichever you will decide."

"Very well," Chard said, turning back to Adendorff and Vane, "both of you ride on to the post. Follow this lance-corporal. And Lieutenant Adendorff, inform Lieutenant Bromhead that I'll be close behind you. Then you can go on to Helpmakaar to alert the garrison there. I'll stay here only long enough to see that Sergeant Milne's men have secured the punts,* then I'll be there as fast as I can," Chard ordered.

After Chard had left at two o'clock to oversee the ferry construction, Bromhead was one of the two line officers left at the post. The other was Capt. George Stephenson, who commanded a hundred-man Natal Native Contingent which supplemented Bromhead's garrison. Since Stephenson was a colonial officer his captaincy did not outrank Chard's regular commission, so there was no question that Chard was in command.

A few minutes after the departure of Spalding and Chard, Lieutenant Bromhead was walking through the street of white conical tents that sheltered the eighty-five men of his company. He was not making an inspection though the thought had occurred to him to use that as a pretext for avoiding Stephenson. He held the colonial officer in the same low esteem as B Company's soldiers held Stephenson's natives—a scruffy, untrained lot as undisciplined as they were unreliable. But to Bromhead and Chard the native contingent could furnish an additional hundred badly-needed rifles for a defense.

As he strode down the company street he presented no less a military figure than Chard: good height, handsome features adorned with full muttonchop whiskers and a mustache that hid a small mouth. He also wore his scarlet jacket topped by his white tropical helmet. The only part of his dress that was not faultless were his leather riding boots, covered with the dust that layered the rocky ground of the area.

Twice since noon his sergeants had reported hearing cannon fire to the east, and each time Bromhead had had to accept the reports without question. This was not laxness on

---

*Flat-bottomed, iron ferry boats built to carry about eighty men. There were two in operation at the ferry.

his part; his deafness was common knowledge though no one of his company dared show that knowledge to his face. The reports had concerned him enough to consent to Surgeon-Major Reynolds' request to take the two clerics and ride to the crest of the Oscarberg, the hill called Itchiane by the natives, just to the east of the post. Bromhead's thoughts were on the three men on the Oscarberg as he turned back up the street, his boots scuffing up little whorls of dust in the hot African sun.

Four men were dismounting from their horses in front of the hospital verandah. Bromhead started to step up his pace, then saw that he need not have hurried. The four men, led by his colour-sergeant, were running to meet him. The sergeant brought them to a halt and saluted.

"Sir, these men come from the Isandhlwana Camp with a message and—"

The hatless corporal behind the sergeant interrupted before he could be stopped.

"Lieutenant, the base camp has been taken and all our men in it massacred. No power can stand against those thousands of Zulus," he gasped out.

Bromhead held up his hand to slow down the rush of the corporal's words. For a matter of seconds his gesture was useless. All four of the frightened men wanted to talk at once. Bromhead and his sergeant finally brought order out of the garbled reports. The corporal had calmed down enough to fumble in his shirt pocket and produce a pencilled message. He handed it to Bromhead who read snatches of it half-aloud.

"Captain Essex, 75th Foot, transport officer with center column . . . escaped on my horse . . . got to the drift four miles downstream from Rorke's Drift . . . hillsides black with trotting Zulus . . . some pursue fugitives across the drift, others heading north following the river . . . at least an impi made up of thousands . . ."

Bromhead stuffed the message in his jacket pocket. There was no sense in questioning these men further, he'd get only babble to add to the confusion. But he knew enough now to act without hesitating.

"Sergeant, let these men ride on to Helpmakaar. I don't want them alarming the native contingent and men in hospital. Then assemble the company—here, at once," Bromhead ordered.

Must get my kit from my tent, he thought, *I'll need my note-*

pads and case. After I've assigned company parties to tasks, there's that damned N.N.C. company of Stephenson's to put to work some-where . . . Good lord, what is Reynolds doing back here—in the devil's own hurry like everyone else all of a sudden.

The tall surgeon-major had dismounted and was leading his horse as he called out to Bromhead.

"I saw the four of them riding up. Thought I'd ride down and report," he said.

"Report what?" Bromhead stopped in his tracks.

"Good visibility toward Isandhlwana Mountain. Good enough to see clouds of natives coming around the mountain this way. Occasionally saw groups—large groups—poking into dongas* and Kraals for stragglers. What's the matter, Brom-head, why look at me like that? I'm only reporting what I saw."

"What you saw, Surgeon-Major, were natives all right—the tall kind that come from the north around Ulundi. And I don't have time to discuss their origin and intentions."

"Good heavens, man! You mean Zulus, do you?"

"Quite. Now please stay with me while I assign tasks to my NCO's. I'll be sending a party to help with what needs to be done at the hospital."

Bromhead hid a grin under his thick mustache. The Sur-geon-Major's face was a red study in amazement.

Chard met Bromhead and James Dalton on the veran-dah of the storehouse. Dalton, a retired sergeant-major living in Natal when the war broke out, was now serving as a vol-unteer at the drift in the capacity of Commissariat Officer. Both Chard and Bromhead valued his African service ex-perience and good common sense. Dalton's dust-brown ci-vilian jacket was in odd contrast to the scarlet of the two officers, but Dalton had never lost his sergeant-major's bear-ing, and it showed now as he stood listening to Chard, who was summing up his courses of action.

"And there's still time to get the wounded on the wagons, form column, and get across the drift and on the road to Helpmakaar," he concluded, looking at Dalton.

"Sir, since you're asking my opinion, I think that's the worst thing we could do. As far as we know the Zulus are

---

*Gullies or dry watercourses.

scouring the whole countryside, and I've known their warriors to trot as much as fifty miles in a day. We'd be tied down
to the pace of the wagon teams, then caught in the open to
be surrounded and slaughtered like that big force at Isandhlwana. What chance then of our hundred-odd men—we
know we can discount the natives here standing and fighting
in the open—against thousands of Zulus under those conditions?" Dalton said.

Chard and Bromhead looked at each other. The infantry
officer pointed to the orderly knots of red jackets grouped
along the road from the drift. His company, already assembled in work parties, was waiting.

"Dalton is right," Bromhead said, "and we know that we
do stand a chance here—if we'll just use all the materials we've
got. There are hundreds of mealie bags*, then the wooden
hundred-weight biscuit boxes, as well as the boxes of tinned
meat—all will serve to make barricades. We also have another
asset that will buy time for us."

"What asset?" Chard asked.

"Mr. Dalton, as you know, was qualified in laying out field
fortifications. He has already been marking out lines for barricades, and he can supervise the laying out of whatever other
walls you may direct."

"That settles it," Chard said, "we'll waste no more time
talking. We will make our stand here. Assign what NCO's
you think necessary to work under Mr. Dalton. After your
companies' work parties are started, see what you can do
to fortify the hospital. I'll be in the area sketching out the
perimeter walls. Mr. Dalton, you'd better start first by building a wall running from the northwest corner of the storehouse here to the nearest corner of the hospital. You can use
those two wagons there to form a section of the wall."

In seconds Chard found himself at the center of an ant-
hill of activity. Parties of soldiers, their jackets discarded,
sweated under the blazing African sun, dragging and lugging
mealie bags and crates from the storehouse out to lines where
sergeants and corporals were having them stacked into four-
foot high walls. Dust rose from the rocky ground, settling on
sweat-streaming faces, amid a din made by the scraping of
dragged boxes, grunts, and the rolling mutter of curses that
the British soldier always managed under stress. In spite of

---

*Sturdy bags of native corn weighing over one hundred pounds.

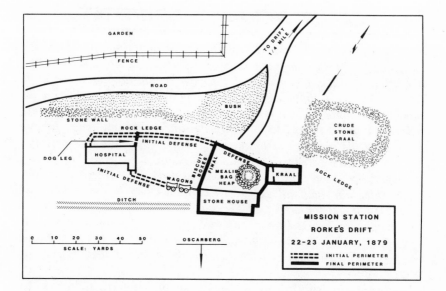

the heat and the noise there was order in the seemingly cha-
otic coming and going of the work parties.

For the moment Chard was the only stationary figure in
the bustling scene. He had taken post in the middle of the
forming compound, standing with his notebook in his right
hand, his left resting on the hilt of his sword.

Strange, he thought. *Don't remember at all picking up my sword
and the rest of my kit. Now that I've given my sketches to Dalton and
my list of priorities to Bromhead there is the problem of fields of fire
from these walls we're making. God save us, there couldn't be a worse
spot in all Africa less suited for building a fort than this place. Two
small buildings forty yards apart commanded by a hill rising five
hundred feet above them.*

He looked up at the crest of the Oscarberg, then at its
terraces sloping down to the rear of the storehouse and hospital.

*Any Zulus with guns taking cover up there can pot shot our
men defending the north wall that we're building from the front of
the hospital to the kraal adjoining the storehouse. But if what I've
heard is true only a few older warriors have guns—muzzle-loading
"Birmingham gas pipes" and maybe a few Sniders*—and they are
known to be very bad marksmen. What this fight will amount to surely*

---

*The former, old trade muskets as dangerous to the firer as to the enemy; the latter, the single-
shot, converted breech-loader that had been the standard British infantry rifle until replaced
by the Martini-Henry Model 1871.

will be the Zulus' light-throwing assegais and heavy-stabbing assegais against the Martini-Henry rifle and its bayonet. But Rorke's Drift being a supply point we will have plenty of ammunition, which reminds me to get some men opening those sealed crates of ammunition. Yet worst of all is the matter of the men in the hospital. I've been forced to include that building in the perimeter because there's no place to evacuate the sick—and everyone of those who can stand will have to handle a rifle. As soon as time—and the enemy—will permit I must get the men out of there and abandon that building and the whole perimeter between there and the storehouse. And there's the matter of the brush and the stone wall and the fruit trees, all on the north side. They will all give good close-in cover to the Zulus, but where will I get the men and the time to level all that cover? I see that Bromhead has had the good sense to strike his company tents. At least they won't be furnishing cover to screen an enemy advance and the tangle of guy ropes and tents will make a fine obstacle to a Zulu attack.

The whirl of thoughts that were making up Chard's dilemma came to a spinning halt when he heard shouting that sounded like cheers coming from Bromhead's men working on the north wall. Chard ran over to the half-completed barricade of mealie bags to see a sight that brought relief from his gloomy dilemma. It was Lieutenant Vause riding up the road at the head of his troop of Sikali Horse, a column of a hundred native horsemen equipped with Martini-Henry carbines. Chard leaned over the parapet.

"Are you coming in to join us?" he called down to Vause.

"Right you are, but let me ask two conditions," Vause shouted back as he reined in his horse and halted his troop.

"What are they? I've no time for discussions now."

"First, issue us rations—my men haven't eaten since last night. Then I ask you to use us on a cavalry mission; you don't want a hundred horses milling around in there."

"Send a party to Mr. Dalton and he'll see they get rations. Yes, I do need you to get your men deployed to screen the post—on the Oscarberg there, at the drift, and with vedettes posted between."

"Is that all?"

"No, of course not. You'll have to delay the main Zulu advance, and then fall back here to join the defense. You'll have to get going as soon as you've drawn your rations."

Chard didn't wait to return Vause's wave of a salute. He was on his way to give his news to Dalton and Bromhead, his elation bubbling up in him. Vause's troop would bring the total of defenders to over 350 men, which would allow—he calculated quickly—one modern rifle to about every six feet of the walls. This should give them the firepower they needed for a fighting chance to repel the Zulu assaults.

Many of the same thoughts had occurred to Bromhead as he made his rounds checking on dozens of tasks that had to be seen to. He saw that the loopholing had been completed in the storehouse, that ammunition had been issued all around, and that the necessary doors and windows in the hospital had been barricaded. The layout of the one-story hospital was a nightmarish crazyquilt of tiny rooms, and a centrally controlled defense was out of the question. Bromhead picked six of his men and assigned them, two to each of the three rooms with seriously ill patients, and sent runners to bring back haversacks full of cartridges. He also saw to it that the hospital defenders were issued pickaxes to loophole the walls.

As he came across the hospital verandah he caught sight of Dalton supervising the finishing of the mealie-bag wall in front of the building.

"Lieutenant, if you could spare the men I could start clearing some of those things to give us a better field of fire along here," Dalton said, pointing at Reverend Witt's old stone wall and the bush between the perimeter wall and the road.

"There's nothing I'd rather do, but I'll have to stand with Lieutenant Chard on the matter of not being able to spare a man until we've finished all work on the walls," Bromhead said.

The afternoon sun continued to beat down through the dust-filled air throwing a pale amber sheen over the toiling men. Bromhead could have prayed for a sudden shower to lay the dust and wash the stink of sweat from the air. He was too sensible a man to dwell on such wishful thinking, so he crossed the open area between the two buildings to encounter Chard and learn that his reply to Dalton had been a sound one.

"I know that your men need to rest and that there are a dozen other jobs to be finished, but I'm going to need a special work party, the strongest men you can find," Chard said.

Bromhead took off his helmet and mopped his forehead with a dirty grey handkerchief.

"What and where?"

"Here and now. We've got to have an inner defensive wall to run straight north—right across here—from that northwest corner of the storehouse, extending to the north wall. I've measured it—seventy feet," Chard said.

"More mealie bags?"

They grinned at each other, feeling that singular kinship born out of sharing danger.

"No, we'll be different this time. Use those hundred-weight biscuit boxes stacked in this end of the storehouse. Actually they're easier to handle than mealie bags," Chard said.

Bromhead started off to find his colour-sergeant, then turned back toward Chard as though he had overlooked something.

"I daresay we've hit on something of great import here," Bromhead said.

"And what is that?"

"You know, this is not the finest fort that was ever built by the British Army, but it does have one great distinction."

"Again—what?" Chard asked.

"I'm willing to wager that it will be the only edible one ever on record."

It was after four o'clock when the last biscuit box had been heaved in place, and Bromhead could start the posting of his riflemen around the walls. This task was complicated by the necessity to spread the rifles of Stephenson's native contingent in a way that would ensure control over their firing—or to make sure the native soldiery fired at all.

Bromhead solved this by first assigning each of his NCO's a section of wall, then giving each a share of B Company men and a share of natives armed with Martinis. When a post had been assigned to each man Bromhead, accompanied by Chard, repeated the round of the perimeter, checking each man's sector and field of fire. They also checked to see that each had a full water bottle, full ammunition pouches, and that an additional stack of cartridges was placed beside each man for his first firing. When that was done Bromhead made one final posting. He selected Pvt. Frederick Hitch from a handful of volunteers, and pointed to the roof of the hospital.

"All right, up with you to the ridge pole. I want a sharp lookout all around. Sing out when you sight Zulus in numbers," Bromhead ordered.

Hitch went scrambling up as fast as he could make it, feeling the stares of the grinning privates of B Company.

Bromhead gave his last formal command to his company.

"Fix bayonets!"

The steely ring of bayonets drawn from the scabbards was followed by the snapping of bayonet sockets on rifle muzzles. The garrison was ready.

Chard and Bromhead were still standing in the middle of the open area between the hospital and the storehouse when Hitch called out his first sighting.

"Mounted men coming down the Oscarberg and on the road."

The two officers dashed to the north wall and climbed up on the parapet for a better view. It was a wasted effort. The sight of the fleeing Sikali Horse could be observed from anywhere around the perimeter. Vause's horsemen were streaming down the flanks of the Oscarberg and flying down the road past the post in a disorderly rout. Following the last flurry of his fleeing troop was Lieutenant Vause, hatless, waving his saber, and shouting curses at the fast disappearing troopers. He reined in his horse opposite the wall long enough to shout.

"They've disobeyed my every order, but when they slow down I may be able to rally them."

"What about the enemy? What about a report?" Chard's rage carried clearly as he yelled at Vause.

"Maybe five thousand. Maybe more. They're approaching the Oscarberg from the east," Vause called back, and he was gone galloping after his men.

Chard jumped down and was joined by Bromhead. Chard was still trying to control his anger.

"In full sight of the garrison. What a show! And we've lost a hundred carbines just when we need them most," Chard almost snarled at Bromhead, but the other officer hadn't heard the rasp of Chard's voice. He was staring wide-eyed at the south wall and east end of the perimeter. It had started happening while the fleeing Sikali Horse were still galloping down the road.

The first of Stephenson's company to desert were his natives, armed only with assegais, who had huddled in the kraal near the storehouse. They were over the stone walls and gone before the men of B Company had noticed their flight. They were joined in seconds by the rest of the native contingent who simply vaulted over the north wall, dashed across the road, and ran through the garden and across the open fields. This part of the natives' desertion went on under the astonished eyes of B Company men stationed along the walls, but their astonishment had not checked their reaction. Someone shouted, "Come back here!" and before Chard and Bromhead could stop them infantrymen had opened up on the backs of the running blacks. Pent-up resentment exploded as men fired off a round before Bromhead's shouted "Cease fire!" could take effect. During the sudden affair—over as quickly as the natives had disappeared—it had not escaped Chard's notice that Captain Stephenson had joined in the flight of his company.

Chard and Bromhead faced each other, too stunned to really see one another. The shock of two mass defections in five minutes was too much for mere words. In the time it would take to relate it 60 percent of his garrison had vanished before Chard's eyes. There remained only 140 men of the 350 he had counted on, and over 30 of the 140 were incapacitated in one way or another. Bromhead's B Company, with 81 effectives, was now the garrison's only organized and reliable unit.

And with those 140 men, Chard thought, *we are supposed to defend nearly 300 yards of perimeter! Now the hospital has to be evacuated so that we can pull back and defend only the inner perimeter. Thank God we finished that last wall. But do we have time? Time, always time, nothing can buy it now with the enemy almost on us.*

There was no time. Before Chard could think more about the enemy, the alarm was sounded. Chaplain Smith and Reverend Witt had descended the Oscarberg at a run, and as they neared the south wall Smith could be heard yelling—

"Here they come, black as Hell and thick as grass!"

Private Hitch slid down the thatched roof of the hospital to hit the ground running to join his section at the wall. Bromhead took station near the middle of the south wall just in time to see the attack come on. A massive column of Zulus charged around the western end of the Oscarberg and broke into a dead run along the lower terraces, as if to parallel the south wall, then wheeled in a flash to charge the wall. The whole maneuver was being executed in silence and with precision.

Chard at his post behind the wall was seeing Zulu warriors for the first time. They were the tallest black men he had ever seen, seeming even taller under their nodding ostrich plumes, their glistening black heads bobbing up and down over the tops of their long cowhide shields with the gleaming assegai blades showing around the sides. There was no time to estimate, let alone count, the massed ranks coming toward Chard, but he knew they had to number in the hundreds. His impressions of the charge were blotted out by the first volley and the rapid fire taken up by the defenders. The trigger-guard levers of the Martinis were jerked up and down as the men ejected empty cartridge cases and reloaded the single-shot rifles.

Chard recalled the figures Bromhead had briefed him on regarding the rifle—a well-trained infantryman could get off twelve rounds a minute in aimed rapid fire and each heavy 480 grain bullet he was pumping out could knock a running man flat at 500 yards. Now he was seeing Bromhead's words coming to life. The flaming rapid fire of B Company's rifles was taking a fearsome toll of charging Zulus right before his eyes. It was more than even a Zulu regiment could stand. The mass swerved to its left leaving scores of warriors strewn so thickly in its wake that every move of the force could be traced by the bodies left behind. Some survivors jumped into the shelter of the ditch west of the storehouse, others took cover among the rocks and folds in the ground on the lower terraces of the Oscarberg. The roar of climactic rapid fire slackened down to an intermittent banging that was sufficient to pin down the Zulus who were still facing the wall.

Bromhead, watching the repulse of the first attack, saw the next stage taking shape. The bulk of the regiment making the initial attack was swerving around the west end of the hospital to link up with the main attack coming at the post from the north and northwest. Bromhead ran to a spot near the northeast corner of the hospital. The sight he watched from his new post would have alarmed the toughest veteran of colonial wars. To his front, extending from the rock ledge, over Witt's stone wall, through the bush and the garden beyond, surged black masses of the attacking impi. This was no silent attack, the hordes came on screaming, beating their assegais against their shields to keep up a rattling roar. The Zulu ranks poured forward until the earth seemed covered with a black flood that swept up the rock ledge and beat like breakers of surf against the barricade above. The leading wave hacked and stabbed at the soldiers manning the wall, then at the mealie bags of the barricade itself when they could not reach the defenders. There were knots of hand-to-hand combat when the soldiers were too rushed to reload. Zulus mounting the parapet were met with thrusts of the two-foot bayonets while other soldiers dropped back a pace or two to blast the Zulus off the barricade at point blank range. Such close combats came in spurts and the Zulus could not maintain the crest of their assault waves for long at the top of the barricade.

Bromhead saw this climax of the assault drop back, but this was by no means to mark the end of the attack. Hundreds of Zulus clung to the slopes of the rock ledge, springing upward from time to time to jump on the heaped bodies of their dead at the foot of the wall in desperate surges to mount the barricade and get at the defenders. When they could the soldiers didn't wait for the Zulus to climb the barricade and thus developed an on-the-spot tactic to thwart the constant rushes. A soldier would fire, reload and fire—leaning through the embrasures between bags—until the attackers were literally at bayonet point, then he would brace himself to lean forward and thrust his bayonet into face or neck of his enemy.

When the first series of surges began to subside, Bromhead saw a strange sequel to the leading assaults take form. Hundreds of warriors continued to swarm through the brush and the garden, and from these masses groups would suddenly detach themselves and charge furiously at the wall. Whether these separate charges were a Zulu tactical device or the effects of fanatical exhortations Bromhead had no way of knowing. Regardless of the cause, the uncoordinated assaults were to prove the salvation of the defenders during the later phases of the attack; this form of assault enabled the soldiers to concentrate their fire on a rushing group and repulse it after inflicting unendurable casualties. If the Zulu impi had continued to press its initial attacks en masse it might well have broken over the wall and overwhelmed the thinly spread garrison.

As it was, the battle for the north wall continued without let-up for over an hour, the Zulus constantly renewing fresh rushes of howling warriors. The Zulu mass attacks and rushes were not led by "suicide squads"—every man, every company, even the entire impi seemed to be inflamed with the same suicidal madness. The British soldiers had heard tales of it; now they were seeing it for fact. Yet the screaming warriors still had the presence of mind to find their own counter-tactic to oppose the defenders' point-blank firing and bayonet thrusts. The Zulus scrambling up the barricades snatched and clawed at the bayoneted rifles trying to wrest them away from the soldiers, even trying to wrench the bayonet from the rifle. The soldiers countered by stuffing a fresh cartridge in the chamber and blasting the Zulu with the muzzle shoved against his body. Often a soldier was rescued by his nearest comrade who did away with the attacker with clubbed rifle or bayonet thrust.

Bromhead, rifle in hand to assist in backing up the wall, watched an amazing performance by Cpl. Friederich Schiess, a Swiss who had enlisted in a native contingent and had chosen to stick with the garrison. The man was raging with a blood lust that would have done credit to a Zulu—in spite of a wound in the lower leg. He had sprung on top of a mealie bag to get at a Zulu below. The warrior, crouching against the bottom of the wall, rose and fired at Schiess, missing him so closely that the muzzle blast blew off the corporal's hat. Schiess bayoneted him, jumped back down and retrieved his hat, and put it back on his head just in time to shoot another Zulu who had scrambled up over his companion's body. Schiess had no time to reload when a third warrior's head and shoulders appeared on the parapet and Schiess sprang at him and killed him with his bayonet.

Chard had also picked up a rifle, dropped by young Byrne, Dalton's commissary assistant, who had been shot through the head. He stood back several paces from the south wall, firing at Zulus who showed themselves on the parapet. He kept his eye, however, on the fight as a whole, from time to time resuming his back-up firing. When he ran out of cartridges—he had no belt pouch to carry spares—he was resupplied by wounded Corporal Scammell, a hospital patient who crawled over to Chard and handed him his packets of ammunition. Even Chaplain Smith had entered into the fight as far as he thought his cloth allowed. The tall, red-bearded cleric kept up a constant patrol around the barricades replenishing the men's ammunition from the haversacks of cartridges slung from his big shoulders. When he ran out he refilled the sacks from the ammunition boxes that Chard had ordered opened and placed in front of the storehouse verandah.

When the mass attacks had slackened off into series of

uncoordinated assaults, Chard took time to confer with Bromhead.

"Two things must be done at once," Chard said; "you must take care of the first. I don't care how you do it, but you must clear the hospital, then the wall in front of it. That's got to be done so we can withdraw everyone into the inner perimeter."

"And the other thing?" Bromhead asked.

"Send me your colour-sergeant, so he can pick out a dozen of your best marksmen. I've got to stop that Zulu fire from the Oscarberg. They've already killed or wounded seven of those men along the south wall. The damned savages have got a clear field of fire to get at our men along that wall."

When Bromhead took stock of the situation at the front (north side) of the hospital he calculated the order of tasks to be done.

First, I've got to get a new barricade, a dogleg to run from the northeast corner of the hospital to join the barricade. When that's done I can start pulling away the eighteen men from the wall in front of the hospital. Next, I can repost those men in the perimeter, assigning six to posts behind the dogleg. Their fire must keep the Zulus who come over the abandoned wall away from the verandah and the front doors. Then we can get the men out of the hospital some way, even if we have to breach the walls.

The first two steps in Bromhead's plan were carried out without a hitch. With a corporal and four privates he hastily threw together the dogleg using mealie bags and boxes. He was able then to repost the men from the wall in front of the hospital. The latter step was by far the hardest since Bromhead had to lead two counterattacks, rifle in hand, to clear Zulus from the hospital front until rifle fire from the dogleg could take over.

But the evacuation of the hospital was a different story. It was not possible for the fire from the dogleg to keep the Zulus from assaulting the west and south sides of the hospital. Because Bromhead's duties kept him with his company, he was unable to learn until later—until the last survivor emerged through an east window of the hospital—of the heroic defense that had been made by the men assigned to defend and evacuate the patients. The battle inside the hospital became a nightmare of an epic defense in itself. That nightmarish defense posed a dilemma to the minds of both Bromhead and Chard. The former had to carry out his plans to accomplish the mission assigned him—as well as exercising the command of his company. The latter had to maintain overall control of all the post's defense. All of which meant that neither leader could become involved in the struggle within the hospital; in any case they could not have led anyone in that hand-to-hand, room-to-room battle through the rooms of the mud brick walled hospital.

Hundreds of Zulus stormed at doors and loopholes of the south and west sides of the building, snatching at rifle muzzles, battering in doors, while thrusting and throwing assegais at any opening. The six B Company soldiers assigned to the defense of the patients not only had to fight off scores of Zulus at every step but had to use their pickaxes to knock holes in the inner walls through which they had to pull the patients from room to room. The savagery of the Zulu attacks and the heroism of the defenders was acknowledged in the after-action awards: out of the eleven Victoria Crosses awarded to the defenders of Rorke's Drift, four went to soldiers who distinguished themselves in the defense and evacuation of the hospital. On the other side of the coin—the frightful side—was the fate of Joseph Williams, the Welshman who sacrificed himself in taking on the Zulus single-handed in order that his comrades could escape to the room behind him. The Zulus broke through and surrounded Joseph Williams, while his comrade, John Williams, "flat on the floor, peered through the opening and the horrified men in the room watched, [while] the Zulus spread-eagled Joseph Williams on his back, pulled away his belt and tore his tunic open. An assegai ripped down through his exposed belly, a dozen blades plunged into his body, and the maddened warriors quartered him and tore the corpse to bloody shreds."[7] Such was the ferocity typifying the room-to-room fight. Toward its end the Zulus had managed to set fire to the damp thatch of the hospital roof and pen the fourteen surviving defenders and patients in the center rear room. From there, after a series of struggles, the group managed to get through two more rooms and jump down into the perimeter from an east window.

As the savage fight raged within the hospital, Chard had started the general withdrawal to the final perimeter, the inner defensive area consisting of the storehouse and the walled enclosure attached to it. A step-at-a-time retreat was made by B Company and the other defenders, picking up each man along the north and south walls as they moved toward the

biscuit box wall by the storehouse. Now the thirty-yard gauntlet between the hospital and the storehouse had to be crossed
by the survivors who had escaped through the hospital east
window. Not all the surviving eleven patients made it safely;
one took a bullet wound in the leg as he was being carried,
another was not so fortunate. Trooper Hunter of the Natal
Mounted Police was too crippled to walk and as he was crawl-
ing across the yard a Zulu darted down and plunged an assegai into his back.

By now the hospital roof was fully ablaze. Darkness had
already fallen and the blazing roof became a godsend to the
garrison now lining the walls of the inner—and final—perimeter. The burning hospital lit up the entire area so that
Zulu attackers swarming over the abandoned walls became
easy targets for the defense. But the abandonment of the hospital and the original perimeter between it and the storehouse brought reinforcements to the Zulus. Scores came down
from the Oscarberg—no longer having exposed targets—while
the hundreds who had surrounded the hospital were released
to join others in encircling the last defensive perimeter.

Chard was well aware of these developments, but far too
occupied to give them his attention. He left the reorganization within the new enclosure to Bromhead while he looked
after other urgent demands. His engineer's mind turned to
them.

There are the wounded, he thought, *and I must see that Surgeon-Major Reynolds gets his aid station working on the verandah
of the storehouse. Then there's the matter of getting men on the roof
of the building to take the Zulus under fire when they're coming at
the enclosure from north and south; also one or two up there can
take care of the danger to the thatch of the roof. The devils have
already started to throw assegais with burning straw onto the roof.
With those things attended to I must get to my never-ending problem—that of constantly building up inner defenses. Even an innermost fort must have its citadel, its donjon-keep. And the means for
ours is here in front of my eyes—those two remaining piles of mealie
bags in front of the storehouse. I'll get a work party—that will be
easy now with the perimeter so reduced—and make the bags into one
great heap with the top hollowed out to form a breastwork. We can
put the worst of the wounded up there and still have room for fifteen
or twenty riflemen who will have an all-around field of fire at the
Zulus assaulting the walls and the storehouse.*

As Chard set about his tasks the Zulus' pressure was renewed around the new perimeter. This began with a series of night attacks, the strongest of which was concentrated on the stone kraal at the east end of the perimeter. The savage rushes began again, this time coming out of the dark shadows to emerge in the light cast by the burning hospital. Charge after charge was beaten back at the side and top of the stone walls. Supporting Zulu forces took shelter in the circle of boulders that made up a low kraal outside the permanent one linked to the storehouse. From there the charges were organized and launched again and again. Finally the roof of the hospital caved in and the firelight began to die out. The soldiers gave up the kraal, withdrawing step by step and leaving the bloody straw of the kraal floor covered with Zulu bodies. At last the kraal was abandoned and its western wall had now become the eastern barricade of the final enclosure. The Zulus poured into the kraal, and as they launched new rushes from there, new assaults came against the front wall up the rock ledge from the south, then from the west around the ruined hospital and across the open yard and along the abandoned walls.

By 10 P.M. Chard and Bromhead had to face each other for the last time that night. They were, like the rest of the garrison, beaten into bone-tiredness. Their once-scarlet tunics were patchworks of grimy powder stains, dust, and darker stains of blood. They had discarded their helmets, and, as they sank down to rest on the ammunition boxes by the storehouse, Chard managed a grin at Bromhead's powder-blackened features above his tangle of dirty side-whiskers. Bromhead stared back realizing what the other was thinking.

"You're not exactly a music-hall dandy yourself," Bromhead said.

"Never gave much thought to beauty lately. Do you realize that these men have been at this without rest for over six hours?" Chard said.

"There has been some slackening off by the Zulus in the last quarter hour. What do you say we try some sort of a stand-down?"

"We can try. Why not let every other man stand down— sort of sit down in place. God knows the men won't be able to sleep anyhow with this tension and din all around. Do give it a try."

"Very well," Bromhead said, "but there's the matter of inspecting the rifles. You've never seen such overheated barrels, hundreds of rounds fired through most, burnt hands from them and that's not the worst of it. Some of those barrels were hot enough to soften cartridge cases in the chambers, so that extractors have pulled the heads off cases—and that means the men had to dig out the empties with knives or whatever they could lay hands on. Hell of a state to be caught in during a Zulu charge."

"Quite right. So now while you're getting around the walls arranging the stand-down I'll get Dalton and a couple of your NCO's to work replacing the worst rifles with others we salvaged after the withdrawal. Get going like a good chap," Chard said.

After Chard had gotten the rifle inspection and exchange under way he had paused, halted in place by the moaning of the wounded outside the storehouse.

"Here," he said to the sergeant beside him, "pull six men off that mealie bag work and have them follow me—with loaded rifles and fixed bayonets."

When the party had followed him to the biscuit box wall Chard stopped and peered out into the semi-darkness lit now by sporadic showers of sparks thrown up by crumbling timbers in the hospital. He could see the bodies of Zulus all across the area, then he could make out the dim outline of the two-wheeled water cart halfway across the yard.

"All right, lads, over you go! Follow me and let's get that cart back here to the wall," Chard ordered.

The seven dashed across the fifteen yards of the open area, the men opening fire to right and left at Zulus along the walls. Two warriors who dared to rush them were bayoneted while four of the party got the cart moving. Pushing and tugging, they got it back to the outer side of the wall where they were covered by the fire of the garrison.

"There's no chance of getting the cart through the wall. Corporal, take that leather hose and lead it over the wall. Now, the rest of you, back over the wall!"

Chard turned on the valve on the cart end of the hose and scrambled back over the wall, almost deafened by the muzzle blast of Martinis two feet from his head. In a matter of seconds, water was running through the hose and the sergeant was having helmets filled and carried to the wounded.

Just after midnight the first relay of men who had stood down had just replaced the others when another series of all-around charges was launched out of the dark. The hand-to-hand combats across the barricades were renewed, neither side lacking in ferocity. Bromhead's head ached as though under a trip hammer, and he knew in his heart—though he would never say it aloud—that the exhausted men in his company had fought on beyond human endurance. Now they were existing in a dazed never-never land made up of ceaseless explosions, thrustings, stabbings, and blood—their own and the enemy's.

They can't go on. Yet they must. Even if relief were coming it couldn't come in the dark. And how does anyone know there is such a thing as a relief? You can't tell the men that and you can't let them think about it, let alone talk about it. Now I've got to see that the ammunition party gets around to this end. That, and the water bottles need to be collected and filled. . . .

He stumbled back to the storehouse, glad for once of his deafness. The firing party atop Chard's mealie-bag citadel had opened fire over his head as he passed beneath the mound.

It was almost 2:30 A.M. when the last of the Zulu attacks had subsided. The second relay of men was allowed to stand down and this time the stupefied men were allowed to fall asleep as they sank down. Their comrades, however, had to collapse across the barricades to strain reddened eyes into the darkness. They had lost all track of time, all count of the ceaseless charges against the walls. Even as they strained their eyes at the dark, they could still see in their minds the savage black faces that had lunged at them over the wall, before seeing them blasted out of sight.

By four o'clock the last of the Zulu sniping fire had died away, though the garrison knew that thousands of their enemies were hiding out there in the darkness waiting to gather strength for a new charge. The last sparks from the hospital's fires had gone out and the velvet black of the African darkness closed in on the men behind the walls. The reek of powder smoke was carried away on the night wind. Aching bodies relaxed and aching heads drooped, but the watch was maintained. Chard, who had taken the most strain of all, could not allow himself to relax. He marvelled at the working of his tired mind. How could it marshal all those thoughts that were staggering through it?

Thank God many of them have gotten some rest—if you can call that resting. What dangers still face us God alone knows. And our losses! It is well that only I count them now—fifteen dead and two dying, Dalton and seven others badly wounded, and of the eighty men who can fire a rifle half of them suffer burns and lesser wounds. I don't know if those eighty can beat off another mass attack like those this afternoon. Good God, eighty against how many? Even if we've given them five hundred casualties, there are still thousands of them squatting out there in the dark. And what about this post being relieved, where would such a column come from? I can't speak to those men about relief, and there'd be no sense in lying. They'd know better. We've got to go on fighting. Now I'll have to tell Bromhead how low our ammunition reserves are.

Dawn was slow in coming at first. The early morning breezes carried the stench of bloody bodies and burned thatch across the post. When it was light enough to see the crest of the Oscarberg, the grey light began to reveal the outlines of more distant hills. Chard and Bromhead realized with a start that the only sounds outside the walls were the quiet stirrings of the opening day. There were no other. At five o'clock the exhausted men on watch were straining to see the battlefield out in front of them. When the light came up suddenly, as it does once day breaks in Africa, the soldiers could see only the litter of battle—cowhide shields, assegais, and the heaps of dead. The only living things that moved were straggles of wounded warriors making their way around the distant east end of the Oscarberg. The Zulu regiments were gone.

Chard sent out cautious patrols after five o'clock to probe the dead and start collecting weapons. The rest of the men stood to at the walls covering the patrols in case Zulus sprang from the ground. But all the warriors who might have sprung to the attack had disappeared.

At seven a whole impi was sighted, this time loping slowly from behind the cover of the Oscarberg, headed down river. They were soon out of sight.

Chard sent a party out to clear the Zulu bodies from the cookhouse. It was time to heat up the water for tea.

An hour later Chard's lookouts sighted men moving from the hills across the river and down toward the drift. In minutes the men on the roof were shouting and waving a flag. There were mounted infantry—British troops—moving up the road toward the post. It was the advance party of Chelmsford's center column moving back into Natal.

Some have said that Rorke's Drift deserves a place of honor alongside Thermopylae and the Alamo. A later writer has asserted that the military significance of the herioc defense of Rorke's Drift was deliberately exaggerated by the British government in order to draw the public's attention away from its mismanagement of colonial affairs and army reform—as well as the disaster at Isandhlwana, the severest defeat ever inflicted on a modern army by untrained natives.

Our purpose in observing the things that happened at Rorke's Drift would not be served by taking sides on the question of whether the action was an epic or a political plum. The fact remains that 140 British soldiers successfully repulsed repeated attacks by an enemy who committed 4,000 highly motivated warriors to a twelve-hour battle. Since those are facts the question concerning us is: if the British soldier was so effective at Rorke's Drift, what enabled him to endure his twelve-hour ordeal and defeat his enemy?

Before evaluating moral factors, it might be wise to look first through the cold eye of the military-operations analyst at the comparison of the effectiveness of weapons systems in the kind of battle we have been examining. In so doing one should look at *both* Isandhlwana and Rorke's Drift. If one does not consider both, then the latter can be rejected out of hand as a simple victory of a modern rifle over spears. Such simplistic responses, however, usually lack substance on close scrutiny.

One of the most obvious measures of effectiveness is the number of casualties inflicted by the opposing weapons systems. This is a summary of such effects in the two engagements.

	Isandhlwana		Rorke's Drift	
	British	Zulu	British	Zulu
Total Casualties	1,320	2,000	25	470
Percent of Force	75%	10%	18%	8.5%
Caused by	Assegais and obsolete muskets/ rifles[1]	Martini-Henry Rifles[3]	Obsolete muskets/ rifles assegais[2]	Martini-Henry Rifles[3]

Notes: 1. Great majority caused by assegais.
        2. Majority caused by obsolete muskets/rifles.
        3. Includes casualties inflicted by the 24″ bayonet on the rifle, though the bayonet was a minor factor in causing casualties.

Note that there is a significant dissimilarity in the cause of the British casualties in the two engagements as indicated by Notes 1 and 2. That difference is a key factor in understanding what happened. The basic difference between the British (modern European) and Zulu (African natives) weapons and tactics lay in the ability of British firepower to hold at a distance the assegai-bearing warriors until the latter broke and withdrew; conversely, the Zulus to succeed had to bring a massive numerical superiority into close combat (hand-to-hand fighting) with their enemy so that their stabbing/thrusting assegais could attain their maximum effectiveness. A simpler way of saying it: it was a contest between two break points. If the British could keep on killing Zulus at a safe distance until the Zulus gave up, the British would win. On the other hand, if enough Zulus could crash through the hail of British bullets and use their assegais, they would win. That was the difference between the two battles.

Two things happened at Isandhlwana to bring on the British disaster. First, their rifle companies (the basic firepower units) were committed piecemeal and subsequently deployed in a manner to leave wide gaps between several companies, with the result that the Zulus could break through the gaps and exploit their success with their assegais. Second, when the British ammunition resupply faltered* causing a slackening in their firepower (an event quickly discerned by the Zulu leaders) the Zulu impis closed in and broke through the gaps and around the British flanks. The result we know.

At Rorke's Drift British infantry was protected by improvised barricades and blessed with an on-hand resupply of ammunition. Hence British firepower kept inflicting enough Zulu casualties to keep their *massive* force at a distance, though as we have seen, the rifle fire could never reach the intensity

---

*There was a plentiful supply of ammunition with the wagons in the camp behind the deployed British force. Two unfortunate factors made the resupply start to break down. The ammunition wagons were hundreds of yards from the fighting companies and there was no provision for moving a continuous resupply over those distances. Next, the ammunition wagons were under the direct control of battalion quartermasters (a set of bureaucratic supply officers with more rank than brains) who could not or would not see the tactical urgency for resupply. Finally, the heavy wooden ammunition boxes were sealed with copper bands, each held securely in place by nine large screws—and the only screwdrivers were in the hands of the quartermasters. All for want of a horseshoe nail!

needed to keep the defenders secure from hand-to-hand combat. In any case, rifle fire was the decisive *material* cause of the successful British stand.

Was firepower then sufficient cause for the British success? I think not. The soldiers of B Company, like the rest of their regiment and the other regular regiments in Africa, were disciplined and well trained. They were the rightful heirs of the tradition of the steadfastness of British infantry on the defensive: "As General Reille told Napoleon on the morning of Waterloo, 'British infantry in position are impregnable because of their quiet steadiness and their excellent fire discipline.' Napoleon had not believed him but Napoleon had been wrong."[8]

Given that the men of Rorke's Drift were sustained by their tradition and training, was that sustenance sufficient cause? Again I think not. From the beginning, it must be recognized that one company of infantry (the main source of defensive firepower at Rorke's Drift) could not have withstood 4,000 Zulus fighting in the open. The company would have been surrounded and overwhelmed on open ground in a matter of minutes *in spite of their firepower*. It was the protection of their improvised fort, and hence the assurance of an adequate resupply of ammunition, that made the difference. And those fortifications would never have been built had it not been for provident and active leadership by leaders who converted a highly vulnerable supply base into a defensible base for firepower.

Yet firepower, even with an adequate resupply of ammunition, was not self-sustaining. It took leadership of a high order not only to make the preparations for defense but to ensure that the defense held out until the enemy reached his break point—and the Zulu withdrawal was the uncontestable proof of that break point. Therefore, mere preparation was not enough. Leadership had to be maintained in order that the garrison put up a tenacious defense. In order to avoid misunderstanding or argument regarding the meaning of a tenacious defense I would rely on a respected semanticist, S. I. Hayakawa, when he says: "Tenacious has the implication of hanging on, refusing to let go no matter what the odds against eventual victory."[9]

Lastly, Chard and Bromhead could not have led a tenacious defense without a commonly shared and inbred sense of duty. It is fitting to point out here that Lieutenants Chard and Bromhead have been referred to in some accounts as "two young officers." This has been unfortunate because it leaves the reader to infer that perhaps the two "striplings" were leaders by the accident of their being there at the time and had probably been carried along by the discipline of the NCO's and soldiers. Nothing could be further from the truth. At the time of Rorke's Drift, Lieutenant Chard was thirty-two with eleven years of continuous service. Bromhead was thirty-three with over twelve years of service. Compare those ages and lengths of service with officers in today's American army and you would be talking about majors and lieutenant-colonels.

So, we have been looking at two mature leaders, winners of Britain's highest military award, the Victoria Cross. Leaders who had to contend with all the dynamic forces of battle and who overcame them through sheer force of will.

Part Three

INTELLECT

Scipio Africanus
at **Ilipa**, 206 B. C.

Henry Bouquet at
Bushy Run, 1763

George Custer at
Little Big Horn, 1876

INTELLECT

There are three classes of intellects: one which comprehends by itself; another which appreciates what others comprehend; and a third which neither comprehends by itself nor by the showing of others; the first is the most excellent, the second is good, the third is useless.

—Machiavelli, *The Prince* (XXII)

Since we are considering intellect in the light of its value as an attribute of the leader we can dismiss the third class out of hand and reject the second as not good enough. Concentration on the "most excellent," however, demands a definition of intellect that is centered on our purposes.

Without going into the processes of arriving at a definition, my best guideline seemed to be: keep it clear and straightforward. In trying to stick to that rule this is what I have found: *Intellect*, as used herein, *is the power of thought as the first cause of effective action.*

Armed with this intellectual probe I stirred through my historical specimens until I had uncovered three possibilities, staying always within the limits of the practicable. These fell into three areas each of which could be considered a quality that contributes to the attribute, intellect. They can be identified as *imagination, flexibility of mind,* and *judgment.* They may be thought of as making up a triangle, any side of which represents a practical application of intellect.

The diagram is not intended to suggest the dependency of its elements. Any single quality contributes to this attribute of leadership, and though the three might occur in combination in a leader, it can be said that any one by itself is enough to show intellect as a power to produce action.

Imagination

THIS QUALITY should be thought of as including innovation, for imagination operating in its own vacuum produces
nothing but images in the mind of their originator. Thus
imagination, unless it leads to innovation in a practical way,
is useless. "Leaps of the imagination" can produce innovative
and effective methods as long as the leaps are constrained by
reality.

Keeping within the bounds of reality, let us see what a
superior order of imaginative intellect could accomplish where
reliance on force of arms could have failed. The time: the
spring of a year two centuries before the birth of Christ. The
place: a hilltop overlooking the valley of the River Baetis (the
modern Quadalquivir) in southern Spain. The man: thirty-
year-old Publius Cornelius Scipio who holds the Roman supreme command in Spain and who in four years time will
defeat Hannibal, conquer Carthage, and gain a resounding
fourth name—Africanus. Now, however, Hannibal is still tying
up Roman armies in Italy while Scipio marches against another Carthaginian army that is spoiling for an all out fight,
and the prize that will go to the victor is no less than the
whole of Spain.

The Things That Happened at Ilipa

Here, even in the spring, one could see only brown hills backed by brown mountains—very different from the green hills and blue mountains of Italy. This was a hard land bearing a hard race of men who respected only two things: force and guile. Scipio's father and uncle had lost their last battles, and their lives, here in Spain because they had relied solely on force. Treachery and trickery had betrayed them. Scipio respected both Spanish toughness and trickery, and did not fear them.

From his hilltop Scipio watched the long column of his Roman and allied legions strung out in their march down the river valley road that ran southwestward toward Ilipa. There the army of his Carthaginian enemies was reported to be encamped, and if Scipio's intelligence was as reliable as it had been in his other Spanish campaigns, the odds had been set against him from the start. Against him, that is, if he were to base the odds on numbers alone: 70,000 Carthaginian infantry—Libyan and Spanish—4,000 African cavalry, and 32 elephants. To match that strength Scipio had been able to raise only 45,000 infantry and 3,000 cavalry.

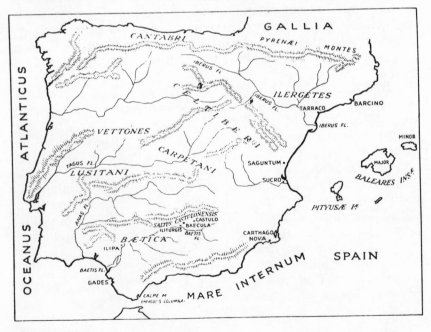

SPAIN 206 B.C.

Scipio was not the man to be dismayed by numbers. He had led those Roman legions through four years of the Spanish wars, and no one knew better the quality of those troops, infantry that could not be matched anywhere in the Mediterranean world. Behind them lay their victories—battles like Carthago Nova and Baecula—and he smiled as he thought of Baecula.

It was there that I gave the Carthaginians a sound thrashing, and that crowned my reputation for tactical genius. I handed those Carthaginians a rough leaf right out of Hannibal's book, pinning down their main body with my light troops, then smashing in their flanks with my heavy infantry. Yet now I will face this other Hasdrubal with my new and untried Spanish infantry, which means that the decisive stroke will have to be made by my Roman legions. I can make the show of force I need with my Spanish, but that tactical stroke I seek will only be disclosed to me when I see the enemy's array.

He mounted and rode down the rocky slope toward the marching columns. Days of marching lay ahead of the Roman army as it followed the north bank of the Baetis. Scipio's strategy called for placing his army between Hasdrubal's camp at Ilipa and the Carthaginian coastal base at Gades. Then if the Romans were victorious they would be in position to cut off any aid from Carthage. Following that course of action would then leave Scipio and his allies free to follow up the victory since there would be no other Carthaginian armies left in Spain.

At this point let Scipio take up his own story.

Seventy-two days have passed since I set out from Tarraco to launch this campaign. Seventy-two days of marching, all the while recruiting and training Spaniards as we marched. Now here in my destined spot I've made the last camp we will use before battle. This last one would have been finished and occupied a day earlier had it not been for Mago's "surprise" cavalry attack which I and Gaius agree was really a blessing in disguise. We were talking about it the following evening in my tent after we had led the legions and allies back into camp after their first—and uneventful—confrontation with Hasdrubal's whole army.

"There was an element of surprise in Mago's attack after all," I said.

"Surprise? If anyone were surprised it had to be Mago's Numidians—unless I'm not tracking your thought," Gaius said.

"I have been obscure, haven't I? No, I meant that I was surprised at Carthaginian aggressiveness so early in the game, though their whole approach to the action was rather clumsy, even a bit amateurish, right?"

"Right, I agree, especially when Mago must have thought a sudden cavalry strike against legionairies in the act of entrenching a camp would have caught them defenseless. Not very bright, considering that we're in our fifth year of operations in Spain," Gaius said.

"Granted, but he was taken in by failing to discover our cavalry that I'd posted out of sight behind that hill. Until they charged over the hill and smashed into his flank he had thought he was master of the situation."

"A truly smashing sight if you'll forgive the word, and a more than satisfying one when our lads were tumbling those African cavalrymen* off their horses, right and left. It was one of the finest calvary counter-attacks I've ever seen—and a successful one since not an enemy trooper ever reached the legionaries working on the ramparts."

"Yes, but remember that we did have to send out the *velites*** to follow up the cavalry and drive off Mago's supports before we had the situation in hand. But enough of Mago, it's Hasdrubal and his mind that is my first concern," I said.

"Your concern may be his mind, but it was the array of his army that impressed me this afternoon. Your army, fully deployed, has a frontage of six thousand yards, yet Hasdrubal's overlaps it on each flank by another thousand yards, and the phalanx of his veteran African infantry may have greater depth than our legions which oppose it," Gaius said.

I picked up the sketch that I had made that afternoon and unrolled it so that we could both examine it.

"Let's commit these deployments of ours and the enemy's to memory so that we can talk of them tomorrow, and later if necessary, without referring to the sketch again," I said.

"It's simple enough. Here our two camps on their ridge crests about three miles from each other. Down here is the

*The Numidian horsemen, though without peer in their world, rode with neither saddle nor bridle, controlling their horses with their legs and body movements; thus they could be unseated when taken by surprise.
**The lightly-armed, mobile infantry of the legions who fought usually as skirmishers, opening the battle before the commitment of the heavy infantry.

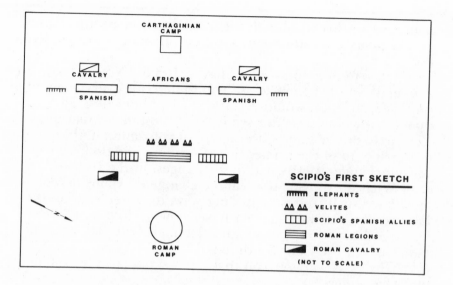

plain where we both deployed today, both armies in standard array, lined up almost a mile apart; it all looks as straightforward as it could be," Gaius said.

"Doesn't it though. Our legions—my only dependable troops—are opposed directly to Hasdrubal's Libyan infantry, his only tried veterans. And on the wings of each array the Spanish allied infantry, extending as you say in Hasdrubal's case, beyond our flanks, with his elephants extending protection to his allies and threatening ours. A rather formidable show on Hasdrubal's part, wouldn't you say?"

Gaius looked up from the sketch, his dark eyes clearly showing his concern.

"More alarming than I'd ever say outside this tent—in spite of the trust we both have in the legions' fighting abilities. Yet you've got to use all that fighting power to stop Hasdrubal's Libyan infantry, not to mention the elephants," he said.

"Gaius, you are repeating here just what your eyes told you this afternoon. Now you must see beyond that Carthaginian array there on the plain."

"How beyond it? There are times when you taunt me with mysteries. How can I see 'beyond' something that is no longer there?"

I rolled up the sketch and tossed it onto the red coals in the brazier standing between us and the tent wall. When the

papyrus had turned brown, then black as it burst into flame
I looked back at Gaius. He was still staring at me with puzzled
eyes.

"I don't taunt you—never have," I said. "Now if I know
you at all, and if I were to ask you to describe every element
on that sketch you would recount it all without hesitation or
doubt. Why? Because you see beyond those mere markings.
You could do the same with the eye of your mind in thinking
of the line-up of the armies this afternoon; and do it by conceiving changes, perhaps radical changes, in the future."

"What do you see that can be changed?" Gaius asked.

"I see such things as finding ways to better employ the
legions, but I cannot tell clearly yet how to do it. And we've
long ago learned how to handle elephants with our light infantry, given the right conditions."

"The gods will give you that inner sight, as every soldier
out there knows."

"They can believe that piffle, and well that they do. You've
known for years that I wouldn't expect it of you, so enough
of that. But I do see one great thing the gods have given us,
if we'll just use it," I said.

"Yes, what?"

"They gave me the foresight and the means to defeat
Mago's attack. But there was far more to that defeat than just
breaking up Mago's formations and driving them off with
heavy loss to them and little to ourselves. Did you notice this
afternoon that while our main force and Hasdrubal's stood
in rank confronting each other across the plain the cavalry
and light infantry skirmishes ended with a definite character
in our favor?"

"If you mean the reluctance of Hasdrubal's African and
Spanish cavalry to become engaged, yes I did," Gaius said.

"Well, that was clearly the result of our victory over Mago,
brief though that fight was. The enemy's cavalry not only
avoided decisive action, they were always the first to withdraw
to safety behind their infantry formations. Which means they've
got a bit of the wind up and Hasdrubal must see that as plainly
as we do," I said.

"Then why did Hasdrubal march out of his camp and
deploy on the plain before we did? And why was he first to
withdraw to his camp this evening at sundown?"

"I don't know—yet. Perhaps there's some bravado behind it, perhaps to convince his army that he will not avoid

battle, that he stands ready to fight. If so, he withdraws first to show his men that they've challenged Romans all day and they have not responded, so that makes him look the better for it."

"Do you intend to let him look better tomorrow if we deploy again?" Gaius asked.

"If he wants to consume time with these shows, we will make that time work in our favor. Let's see when and how he acts tomorrow. For now, let's take advantage of the time and get a good night's rest."

There are two reasons why I have made my escort ride back to our lines at a walk. First, when I had finished my reconnaissance we had to turn our backs on Hasdrubal's battle array, for it would be an unseemly action to ride away from the enemy in haste. Further, I will not have dust stirred up by our horses, dust that would blow in the faces of my legionaries. They have stood here in ranks, facing the Carthaginians across the plain, for a good six hours, and there's no need to add to their discomfort. Besides, my men have had to face to the southwest in order to oppose the enemy. Now, at an hour before sundown, the sun is in Roman eyes which tells me that I will not bring these men into battle in an afternoon. In fact the earlier in the morning the better.

This ride should end my last reconnaissance, for we are ending our third day of confrontation on this plain. I am ready to make my battle plan and I will start after the evening meal. These shows of force and challenges to battle for three days running have been wearing on all, but they have been rewarding to me. Hasdrubal and I have become unwitting—at least I believe unwitting on his part—partners in setting up a fixed pattern. For three mornings, always at a late hour, he has marched his army out of its camp and deployed it on the plain, always in the same order that I showed Gaius in my sketch—his veteran Libyan infantry in the center flanked on each wing by his Spanish infantry, with half his elephants extended on each flank. Each morning I have let him sally out first, then followed and arrayed my army in the same fixed deployment—my legions in the center, facing Hasdrubal's best troops, then my Spanish allies on the wings flanked by my cavalry. At the end of each day, near sundown, Hasdrubal has withdrawn his force back into his camp, and I have followed suit with mine, closing back into my camp at sunset.

Now the pattern has become such a matter of routine in both camps that it is no longer a subject of camp gossip. But of far greater importance, the whole procedure has become fixed in Hasdrubal's mind. And the seeds of that impression will give root to the groundwork of my plan. But first there is the matter of getting the army back to the camp, dispatching my aides with orders to the *legati** and the other commanders to march back in the usual formation.

I looked around the command group assembled that evening in my tent. I had restricted the group to the four *legati* as well as Gaius Laelius, Lucius Marcius, and Marcus Iunis Silanus. These key officers were the only ones to whom I would confide my battle plans, trusting them with its security until they would give their own orders to their troops tomorrow morning. I began by reminding them that the only troops on either side that had seen action so far had been the cavalry and a few light infantry.

"As you know," I said, "these petty skirmishes have shown no result except to exercise some cavalry and *velites*. Tomorrow's action will be another story. Know now that the whole army moves to attack Hasdrubal tomorrow at first light—no more shows of force or skirmishing. This will be the battle that we have been waiting for."

I caught Gaius's knowing eye and saw that he had managed to assume the same intent look that marked the faces of the others.

"I begin," I went on, "with the conclusions I have reached about our enemy and how we must act to destroy him. I have determined that, by now, Hasdrubal and his officers have fixed in their minds the habitual deployments of both armies. You must understand that that is the key to the four things we must accomplish tomorrow in order to gain the victory.

"First, we will defeat Hasdrubal by surprising him. I will come back in a moment to the means we will use.

"Next, we must use the legions to deliver the decisive stroke and that must be against Hasdrubal's weakest elements, his Spanish allies on the wings of his army.

"Third, we must 'fix'—pin down—the best of Hasdrubal's infantry, the Libyan phalanx that forms his center.

*Legion commanders.

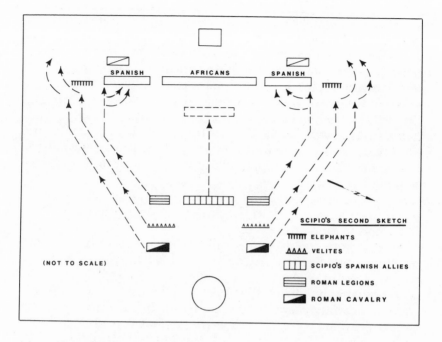

SCIPIO'S SECOND SKETCH

ⅢⅢ ELEPHANTS

▲▲▲▲ VELITES

▢▢▢ SCIPIO'S SPANISH ALLIES

▤▤ ROMAN LEGIONS

◼ ROMAN CAVALRY

(NOT TO SCALE)

"Lastly, we must destroy the Spanish on the enemy's wings before we can attack and defeat his center."

I could see that Marcius and Silanus were bursting with questions while struggling to make an outward show of stoic composure. The rest of the group were equally intense though various degrees of control were evident. Clearly there was no need to excite their interest further, so I launched into the matter of tactical surprise.

"We start by surprising Hasdrubal and his army in their camp in the morning. This means that our cavalry and the *velites* must move out to the attack at first light, and so they must be fed, armed, and the horses saddled before dawn."

Silanus could no longer control his old soldier's impatience with the idea of cavalry and light infantry attacking a fortified camp.

"I fail to see what is accomplished by this attack if it is unsupported," he said.

"It won't be—but must seem so to the enemy," I said. "While the light troops are throwing everything they can at the enemy's camp the rest of our units—under cover of that attack—will be falling in to move out as soon as the troops have been fed. But before we go into the advance of our army across the plain, let us see what we can accomplish by the light troops' attack.

"In the first place the alarms sounded in the Carthaginian camp will cause Hasdrubal to arouse his army in all haste and rush to deploy it on the plain, especially when it is light enough for them to see the rest of our army advancing to the attack. Now here comes the most important point. Hasdrubal has always moved his army out in late morning and has taken his own good time in deploying. But now what will happen to the Carthaginian army when it will have to be assembled so hastily?"

My question caught all but Gaius with their tunics showing. But of course he had the advantage over the rest of having some prior knowledge.

"It's quite clear," Gaius said, "that the enemy will have no choice but to form in the same order they've been using for the last three days."

The abrupt silence that followed Gaius's answer showed that its meaning was lost on the group. It was time for me to produce my new sketch and explain what it meant.

"Here is where Hasdrubal will get his second—and by far his greatest—surprise. Assuming that Gaius's answer is a sound one, and I believe it is, Hasdrubal will have his troops formed in his standard array expecting to find us opposing him with the same deployment we have confronted him with for the past three days. Instead, here is what he will see."

I unrolled the sketch and held it out for them to see.

"As you see," I went on, "our deployment will be reversed, with the Spanish in the center facing Hasdrubal's Libyans, and the legions will be on the wings. You will recall that I said that the decisive stroke must be made by the legions, and it must be against Hasdrubal's Spanish infantry on the wings. Here is how it will be done."

I paused to point out the movements of the legions.

"Each wing moves out obliquely at its fastest pace to move where it can outflank and strike the enemy wing. In the meanwhile our Spanish move at a slow pace to advance directly on the enemy center. Thus, so far, we will be accomplishing three of the four things I told you were essential—we surprise Hasdrubal as I've described, then deliver the decisive attack with the legions against the enemy's wings, and we will 'fix' Hasdrubal's center with our Spanish center. There

remains the fourth and final stage—the destruction of Hasdrubal's Spanish on the wings followed by attacks against the
flanks of his center."

The silence that followed must have been as profound
as the thoughts in the depths of their minds. Never in the
history of Roman wars had there been such a radical departure from the tactical norms built up through centuries of
warfare. Indeed, what I proposed to do must have seemed
more cataclysmic than radical to all but Gaius. When he put
his question I could sense the conflict between loyalty and
doubt going on within him.

"I see what you intend and how it should be done, but
I must say that I fear for the dependence upon our Spanish
allies against Hasdrubal's veteran Africans. What will happen
if Hasdrubal's center charges into our Spanish and shatters
their formations?" Gaius asked.

"Your fear is well founded. There is a risk in opposing
Hasdrubal's center with our Spanish, but the risk is lessened
by depending upon two things," I said.

"And they are?"

"Our center must be refused from time to time, avoiding
close engagement."

"And if the Libyans continue to advance?"

"That brings us to my second point. Hasdrubal's center
cannot advance too far without exposing its flanks to attack
by units of our legions. Furthermore, he will not allow his
center to break contact with his wings, thus leaving his allies
on his wings without the support of his veterans in the center.
If that were to happen, the same kind of attack by our legions
would be an unacceptable threat to his exposed flanks."

"The risk is still there, but I see no way of lessening it,
save as you say," Gaius said.

"I acknowledge the risk and accept it. In the morning we
will seek the omens from the augurs after the sacrifice before
battle, but I have no doubt of the outcome."

"Nor do I if you so believe. Also I see two other matters
affecting Hasdrubal when he is surprised by an early morning attack," Gaius said.

This was the sort of contribution that I had always en-
couraged from commanders and staff officers.

"Let us hear them," I said.

"Since we will advance directly toward his camp his army

will deploy with its front facing us and that will cause his soldiers to be looking into the sun all morning," Gaius said.

I gave him and myself mental slaps on the back.

"Excellent. And the other?"

"Because of the alarms and the hasty exit from their camp
Hasdrubal's men will miss breakfast, and they will have to
stand and face us feeling their hunger growing, and with no
chance of their being fed."

"Yes, and we will find ways to take advantage of that
sometime during the morning. Now, are there other questions or ideas?" I said.

"I have a question," Silanus said, "I understand the part
about the legions moving out in column from their wing positions so as to advance obliquely to attack Hasdrubal's flanks,
but how do you propose to maneuver the legions at that point?"

"Maneuver? *I* maneuver? What do you mean?" I said.

"If the heavy infantry and the light troops have to wheel
from column in opposite directions, won't the battle order of
some units be reversed?" Silanus asked.

I'd no doubt that Silanus would soon realize that he had
spoken without thinking first, and, what was worse, making
me look as though I had not anticipated critical events. I dismissed this as it deserved—a matter of detail properly left to
the *legati* and their tribunes and centurions.

"I don't propose to allow the mechanics of battle drill to
obscure *real* tactical problems. Now if certain stages of the
operation tomorrow call for changes in the execution of my
plan I will, as always, handle them on the spot. Are there
other questions?" I said.

This time the silence showed the relief of tension. It was
a settling back after problems had been cleared away and issues settled.

"Very well then," I said, "there remain two matters we
can deal with, and quickly, before you leave. First, Silanus
and Marcius will command on the left wing. I will command
the right wing seconded by Gaius Laelius. Until the legions
of both wings march away from the center, my battle station
will be in the interval between the center and the right wing.
Finally, a detail that you should see observed by your officers,
and the word passed among the troops when they fall in at
first light. When your tribunes report here in the morning
they will see displayed outside my tent one of my scarlet cloaks

tied to a spear* I have kept you long enough, I know you are anxious to get back to your commands. Know all of you that Jupiter and Hercules ride with us on the morrow.** Gaius, on your way out please pass the word that I wish to see the augurs within the half-hour."

The dawn mists were rising around us as we rode, making us draw our cloaks tighter against the chill plumes stirred up like surf by our horses' hooves. Gaius and I were followed by a double file of aides and behind them at a little distance rattled and clanked the column of my cavalry escort. The light troops had long ago disappeared into the mists of the plain toward which we were riding. The cavalry columns had moved past us at a walk to allow the files of loping *velites* to keep abreast of them. We could still hear from the camp the distant shouted commands of centurions that grew fainter as we rode down the gentle slopes to the plain. I gave the order to halt when we reached a spot where the rough path crossed a shallow ravine. The horses sniffed around like hounds at the smells rising from the damp earth. Gaius sniffed too and I laughed, thinking of how he sounded like my mare.

"You laugh," Gaius said, "it is a good sign, but I'm sure I don't know what it's about."

"You and the horses, are you related in this way?—how you test the air?" I said.

"No, but there is some of the beast in me—like anyone I suppose. Really though I was thinking of the boar hunts in the early morning on your estate at Liternum. I remember the horses sniffing like dogs when we'd assemble to follow the trackers."

"And so I remember too. But I didn't halt here to sample smells, I want to look, not to smell."

"By the gods, what is there to see here?"

"Don't you think it's time to appreciate a sunrise? Even if we have to look back toward our camp," I asked.

"The sun does appear to rise behind our camp and the crest of the hill is beginning to lighten. Is that an omen favorable to you?"

---

*The symbol-signal used by Roman army commanders to tell their soldiers that battle was imminent.
**Scipio was linked, in the minds of the people, with the gods, principally Jupiter and on occasion Hercules.

We had been talking in low voices, but when I answered I raised my voice so the escort could hear.

"Truly, as it was augured, Phoebus Apollo joins Jupiter and Hercules in crowning Roman arms with success this day."

As I spoke we began to hear the first sounds of battle from the direction of the Carthaginian camp.

"Come, let us ride," I ordered, "I must see the array of Hasdrubal's army as it begins to form."

At the second hour* the morning mists had been chased from the plain by the sun and we could see the whole front of the Carthaginian array as it stood fast in its ranks, just as it had in the past days. Our light troops had been driven back on the plain by the enemy's heavy infantry as it advanced to take up its battle positions, and now there were only infrequent clashes between opposing flurries of cavalry and light infantry. Fortunately for my reconnaissance there had been enough heavy dew left on the damp ground to prevent dust being raised by the horses and swarms of light infantry, so we had a clear look at the enemy army. Over Gaius's objections I led my escort within five hundred yards of the enemy's center before turning to ride toward his left wing.

"I'm in no danger here," I told Gaius, "we're hundreds of yards beyond the range of any archer and if any of their cavalry start to move this way in force we'll see them in plenty of time to get safely back to our lines."

He grumbled something I didn't bother to hear, but I did hear him charge the escort commander to be alert for the approach of groups of horse.

We rode at an easy canter, halting briefly now and again as I tried to get a closer look at Hasdrubal's men. After we had cleared the front of the enemy center I paused to get a glimpse of the Spanish auxiliaries who made up Hasdrubal's left wing. They too were formed in phalanx though not in as deep a formation as the center. They were easily distinguished from Hasdrubal's Libyan-Phoenician infantry even though both could be called heavy infantry. These *scutarii* were leaning on their long, flat, oval-ended shields with each man's pair of javelins, one light, one heavy, thrust into the ground at his right. They too wore a variety of headgear, though most

---

*The hours of the Roman day were counted from sunrise.

of them wore the sinew cap which protected the head and back of the neck but left the ears and face exposed. Most also wore belted white tunics edged in purple. Some had pieces of body armor such as flat breastplates, others had none. They were a tough looking lot but we Romans were well aware of their chief weakness as soldiery—they were fierce fighters as individuals but subject to sudden fits of mass panic making them unreliable in organized fighting formations.

When we were close enough to the left end of Hasdrubal's line I stopped long enough to count the elephants standing on the flank. There were sixteen, looming like distant miniature castles, the bulk of the huge beasts surmounted by their mahouts seated on their high-backed saddles. It was evident that Hasdrubal had, in his usual fashion, split his elephant force, placing half on each flank of his army.

"Fearsome beasts," Gaius said as though echoing my thought.

"Yes, until one's infantry learns their weaknesses, as ours has—sometimes the hard way. Though we may be past those trials," I said.

"I've been checking the training of the *velites* in that respect ever since we approached Ilipa. Just yesterday you'd have had to choke back a laugh as I did when I heard a *primus pilus** supervising *velites* in battle drill. After the centurions' usual summing up of the elephant's vulnerable spots**** he would break in with his version of the decisive stroke—'What's the best way to stampede an elephant? You slip up behind his tail and jam your javelin up his ass!' On the crude side, but effective wouldn't you say?"

"Of course I've heard of that tactic, but never heard it put so delicately. Excellent though. Now, I've seen enough, it's time we started back to our battle station," I said.

"Right, it's now past the fourth hour. Do you want to order the cavalry and the *velites* back to join their legions?" Gaius asked.

"Not yet, at least not all at once. You remember the point you made last night about the enemy having to charge out of his camp without breakfast? Well, I want that hunger to

---

*The highest ranking centurion of the legion, the position aspired to by every professional officer of the legion.
**Those vulnerable areas included not only the trunk (which could be slashed by spear or sword) but also the soles of the feet and the tender skin of their rumps.

go on working on Hasdrubal's men as long as we can prolong it to our advantage. But you can order the light troops to disengage and withdraw by detachments so that they will finish passing through their legions before the seventh hour. When they have completed their withdrawal I want them formed in rear of their legions, the *velites'* formations in front of the cavalry.

"By the seventh hour?"

"Yes, that will be the noon hour. By that time we will have played out this waiting game for all it's worth. Then I will signal a general advance."

Hasdrubal's Libyan infantry was drawn up in phalanx and I could make out the *speirai** that formed it. I was close enough to see their armor and weaponry—the long pikes, the round Greek-style shields, and a mixture of helmet types, Corinthian, Chalcidian, and even Roman. Gaius had noticed the Roman helmets and was cursing the wearers for their wearing the captured Roman body armor as well. Taken in all it was impressive array especially when one could imagine the long pikes, now rested upright, levelled in the fearsome hedge that would precede the advance of the phalanx.

At noon I rode forward alone from my station between the center and the right wing. I halted my horse at a hundred paces and turned to face about. By turning my head from left to right I could survey the whole order of my army. It was a splendid sight—forty-five thousand men aligned in their formations on a front, extending from flank to flank, of almost three miles. Every legionary, every Spaniard was at his appointed station. The last centurions and *optiones* had given their final commands, and the plain had fallen silent. As far as the eye could see the sun was reflected from crested helmets, steel cuirasses, and spear points. For the briefest moment I was seeing thousands upon thousands of steel statues arrayed as if they had stepped out of an immense frieze on some unearthly temple, then my mind snapped back to reality. These statues were living, breathing men who were on the verge of leaning forward, waiting for the command to step out in the advance against their enemy.

---

*It is believed that the Carthaginian African heavy infantry fought in a Macedonian-type phalanx made up of *speirai*, each *speira* could have been (if it were truly Macedonian in nature) formed in close order with a depth of sixteen men and a width of the same, i.e., a total of 256 men per *speira*.

The sun was directly overhead when I raised my right arm to give the signal. I dropped my arm, my *tubicen* sounded his trumpet, my *signifer* dipped his standard, and the horns of the legions' *cornicens* blared out, blast after blast, and the long line began the advance.

I beckoned Gaius to my side and we rode forward together in the interval between the center and the right wing. The sun had long since dried the hard ground, and now dust from thousands of marching feet rose in thin brown clouds over the helmets of the legions and the Spanish cohorts. Yet from my vantage point on horseback I had a clear view of both armies. The Carthaginian line was standing fast, an immobile wall of armed men awaiting the onslaught. I set the pace for the advance, a battle-drill pace so even the Spaniards could maintain their alignment.

We crossed a half mile of plain moving directly toward the enemy until I estimated that we were nearing a point eight hundred yards from his line. I gave the orders, and aides went flying to Silanus and Marcius on the left and the senior prefect leading the Spanish allies in the center—the left wing to break off from the center and begin the maneuvers that would become mirror images of what my right-wing legions would execute; the prefects in the center would take up the slow march so that the Spanish would be moving forward at a slackened pace, less than half that at which the legions would be marching.

At the eight-hundred-yard point I signalled a general halt and nodded to Gaius. He gave the commands to face the legions to the right, then rode off to lead the legionary columns as they began their march taking them away from the center at an oblique angle of 45 degrees. Following Gaius's orders, the legions were marching at the quick step, moving in the four columns that would wheel into line of battle when the command was given. I rode across the rear of the columns to make sure that all was in order. From left to right the columns were composed of the *hastati* whose maniples would form the first line of battle. To their right were the *principes* of the second line, next to the right were the old veterans, the *triarii* who would form the third line of battle.* The rightmost column was made up of the bodies of *velites* and cavalry which

---

*Appendix E contains a summary of the legion's tactical formation and manipular tactics.

would wheel outwards—to their right—on my command in order to start the maneuver which would outflank Hasdrubal's elephants and his left wing.

Satisfied with the formations and their order of march I trotted up the right side of the column of *velites* and cavalry, checking as I rode on the condition of the men and their marching pace. It was a cheering sight. The dust-covered, sweating soldiers were swinging along, hard-muscled men in the top of condition and eager for action after days of standing uselessly—at least in their minds—in ranks facing an enemy with whom it seemed they could never come to blows. Now they were spoiling for a fight, anxious to get the day's dirty business behind them. Nothing would have suited me better, and I was going to see that they all got a full measure of fighting.

When I reached the head of the rightmost column Gaius trotted over from his station at the head of the infantry columns.

"I'm getting a sore neck from trying to look back at these legions' columns and keep an eye on the enemy's flank, all at the same time," he said.

He was grinning like a boy beating his opponents at trigon,* whether at his idea of a joke or at the prospects of getting the legions into action I couldn't tell.

"We'll both get a little more neck exercise in trying to follow what's happening to our Spanish in the center," I said.

We both turned in the saddle to look back over our left shoulders at the now distant center which we were leaving farther behind with every step.

"They're moving slow enough all right. I see a gap of at least a couple of hundred yards between them and Hasdrubal's center," Gaius said.

"So thus far all is well there, for you can see that the Libyans haven't moved a foot. That means that Hasdrubal will keep them on the defensive, at least for now, and we couldn't ask for more. Every minute that passes in this way gives me more assurance that Hasdrubal's center will continue to be fixed in place," I said.

We rode together, each judging the width of the narrowing gap between the heads of our columns and the flank

*A game with three players who try to make an opponent miss catching the ball.

of Hasdrubal's Spanish infantry. There was no time now for checking on the march of our center or even our columns following at our heels. When I saw that I was opposite the last enemy file and three hundred yards from it I turned to Gaius.

"This is the moment we've waited four years for. May the gods ride with you," I said.

His only reply was to raise his hand to his helmet, and he and his tribunes were gone. Our next moves were prearranged, leaving me no time to watch what was happening with the rest of the army. Gaius's duties lay with the redeployment of the legions' heavy infantry which now had to wheel to the left, going from column into their lines. My part was to oversee the wheeling outward—to the right—of the light troops so they could come up into line and advance to attack the elephants and the flanks of the enemy infantry. I sent an aide galloping with word to the tribune commanding the light troops to begin his maneuver.

That done I was free to take station with my staff on a low knoll which allowed an overview of the action. I watched the next moves of the legions, fascinated at the drill-ground precision with which they came into line to attack Hasdrubal's Spanish. Gaius had halted the four columns, faced them left into line, then each line—following in turn—wheeled through 45 degrees to come into line facing the Spanish. When the maneuver had been completed Gaius gave the order and the legions were launched into the attack. Even at my distance from the battle the din was deafening. The trumpets were blaring as the first maniples shouted their war cry and dashed forward to get within javelin range of their enemy. At the same time the second and third lines were clashing their javelins against their shields and shouting themselves hoarse as they cheered on the *hastati*. The front line halted long enough to volley their javelins—first the thin one, then the thicker— into the ranks of their enemy. As the two volleys crashed into the enemy the *hastati* had already drawn their swords and were charging full tilt into the shaken Spanish. The young Roman legionaries threw the full weight of their bodies against the flat shields of the Spanish, raising a clamor that could be heard all across the plain. They were trying to knock their enemies off balance while thrusting at them with their swords. In individual encounters where a Roman had not overthrown his enemy he would rest the bottom end of his shield on the ground, put all his weight behind his left shoulder and his shield, and continue his sword-thrusting attack.

In the meantime the deployed maniples of the second line, the *principes*, were followed by the third line of the *triarii* as they advanced within supporting distance of the now-committed first line. The second line, made up of the finest fighting men of the legion, were waiting their turn at the enemy in case the first line's attack failed to shatter the enemy formation. As I watched I could see that the Spanish were fighting back furiously in spite of the terrible losses in their front ranks. It was time for committing the second line, and I could hear the first trumpet blasts that were signalling the recall of the first line. This was carried out with precision despite the heavily engaged front ranks. The forward centuries disengaged, moving back under the protection of the other centuries, then withdrew through the gaps between the maniples of the second line. After the *hastati* had passed through, the rear centuries of the second line moved up to close the gaps, forming a solid phalanx. On the next trumpet blasts the *principes* volleyed their *pila* into the enemy, just as the *hastati* had done, and charged. The worn down and dismayed Spanish could not withstand the attack of this fresh, battle-tried infantry. As the first ranks of *principes* smashed into their enemy I witnessed the sight that never ceased to surprise me during these clashes of heavy infantry when a beaten formation begins to break up. The foremost ranks of Spanish infantry continued to resist, individual soldiers standing and fighting back, fearing to turn their bodies to enemies who were within sword's length. But it was the rearmost ranks who turned and fled, followed by their companions who had been ranked between them and the engaged front. It was that ever-strange phenomenon of a phalanx beginning to disintegrate from the rear instead of from its front, which could not disengage.

Despite my fascination with the infantry combat my attention had to be directed next to the attack of the light troops against the elephants and the rest of Hasdrubal's left flank. The *velites* and cavalry had wheeled into line at right angles to the enemy flank behind which a detachment of his cavalry had formed. The line of light troops was made up of alternated bodies of *velites* and cavalry. Following my orders the *velites* ran forward out of the line while the cavalry stood in place. There were good reasons for this—while the *velites* went for the elephants the cavalry waited to support them or, if necessary, take on the enemy's cavalry if it interfered. Our cavalry would have been more hindrance than support to the *velites* at this stage, for the horses feared the elephants, even their smell frightened them.

Each advancing body of *velites* broke into two groups as the running men charged around the line of elephants, one element going for the enemy's light infantry in the intervals, the other for the elephants. As they ran they raised enough racket to alarm men as well as animals, clashing swords or javelins against their shields, every man shouting at the top of his voice.

What followed was over in no time, an action as swift as it was involved. As swarms of *velites* poured through the intervals and battled hand-to-hand with the Carthaginian light infantry, their comrades attacked the sides and rear of the elephants, slashing at trunks, thrusting javelins into their rumps, and spearing the mahouts or leaping up to pull them from their saddles. The uproar that rose out of this milling mass of men and animals would easily have drowned the clamor that the *velites* had started. Clouds of choking dust rose from the melee obscuring the men and at times even the elephants. The shrill trumpeting of the maddened beasts made my hair rise as I tried to imagine what it was like to be caught up in that deadly game.

That part was over in seconds. The violent action was spread in all directions by the panicked elephants, like rushing waters thrown from the vortex of a whirlpool. All control of the great beasts had been lost at the height of the *velites'* attack, and now the elephants—trunks upraised and great ears spread wide in terror—broke and ran in all directions, trampling friend and foe alike, anyone who was unlucky enough to get in their path. Some even reached the withdrawing Spanish heavy infantry, while two other beasts tore through the closed ranks of the nearest legion leaving a welter of dead and maimed in their wake.

Then occurred an event that I can ascribe only to the intervention of Jupiter himself. A half-dozen of the panic-stricken elephants had whirled about and plunged through the ranks of the enemy cavalry which had been formed up to support Hasdrubal's left wing. The Spanish horsemen, their white tunics flying in the wind, broke and scattered, all organization lost in their flight. After the elephants had passed on to disappear in the distance I could see officers trying to rally knots of Spanish cavalrymen, and several had succeeded in forming a semblance of order among a half-dozen troops. It was what our cavalry had been waiting for—there had been no point in committing them into the violent melee that had just broken up—and the prefect commanding the cavalry had seen the opportunity as soon as I had. He launched all his squadrons with one trumpet blast and they swept across the field in a knee to knee charge that sent the rallied remnants of the Carthaginian cavalry flying, never to be reassembled.

While I was watching our cavalry complete the defeat of Hasdrubal's left wing, one of Silanus' aides galloped up with the best news I would receive that afternoon: Silanus and Marcius had smashed Hasdrubal's right wing in an attack that had gone almost like a duplicate of our victory over the left. But the battle as a whole could never be won until we could crush Hasdrubal's center. I sent an aide with an order to Silanus and Marcius to attack the right flank of the Libyan phalanx as soon as possible while I would take immediate steps to launch my legions against the left of the Libyans.

There was no time to lose in my sphere of command. I could see that my Spanish allies, while trying to withdraw from the grip of the Libyans, were getting seriously entangled in combat. Also *speirai* of the Spanish infantry that my legions had just broken were being rallied and regrouped in an obvious effort to protect the center's left flank. The Spanish enemy were being formed up to face toward my reorganized legions. I sent two aides galloping—one to Gaius directing him to advance directly against the enemy's Spanish infantry, destroy it and continue the attack to smash the left flank of the Libyans; the other courier carried orders to my cavalry to re-form on the right of the legions prepared to exploit the destruction of the enemy infantry.

When the legions signaled their readiness I had my trumpeter and *signifer* give the signal for a general advance. I started to ride forward when another messenger arrived, this one from Gaius. He also brought welcome news—while my attention had been riveted on the engagement of the light troops and the subsequent destruction of the enemy cavalry, I had missed seeing more widespread effects of the elephant stampede. A number had charged through the Libyan infantry spreading destruction and confusion and now was the time to strike and reap the harvest of my enemy's troubles.

Since Gaius's legions were already launching their renewed attack, all the necessary orders had been given, and I
found a low rise behind the legions where I could observe
the action. It was obvious that Gaius must finish off Hasdrubal's rallying Spanish infantry before the legions could get at
the Libyans, and that began to happen under my eyes.

The *hastati* repeated their earlier attack against the Spanish who were only partially re-formed and scarcely the threat
they had been in the beginning. Again the *hastati* threw their
pila and dashed into the disorderly array of spears that were
lowered against the attackers. The ragged spear hedge proved
to be no obstacle to the leading rank of *hastati*. They either
thrust aside or battered down the spears, and then were among
the spearmen, thrusting and slashing. And again the rearmost ranks broke and fled leaving the foremost of their comrades to their fate. It was a fate that came as suddenly as the
throwing of the javelins into the Spanish. There was no need
for the legions to commit the *principes*. The job was done. The
Spanish phalanx disintegrated into a horde of fugitives who
were dashing to either flank and some even sought refuge
among the Libyans who, of course, were facing to their front
against my center. Libyan officers coolly faced their two outer
files to the left to present a bristling line of pikes to the fleeing
Spanish. However, the greater mass of fugitives was running
toward what had been the Spanish left—the right of the
legions—in the direction of their camp. Now if I could
drive that mass into the rear of the Libyans that might create
confusion on that quarter. I sent an aide to my cavalry commander who led off at once in a cavalry charge that thun-
dered down into the broken Spanish and scattered them across
the plain. There was no discernible damage to the rear of the
Libyan phalanx, so I sent another message to the cavalry
commander to reassemble in his last position to the right of
the legions.

There was no need for an order to Gaius to continue the
attack to strike the Libyan left flank. The *hastati* had again
withdrawn through the gap left by the *principes*, and now the
elite of the legions dashed forward against the Libyans. This
threat had long been an obvious one to the Libyans' leaders,
who faced more files to the left to counter the legions' attack.
If the Libyan phalanx had had only to take on the attack of
Gaius' legions, they might have succeeded in beating it off.
But the plight of Hasdrubal's center—the only fighting force

left in his army—was truly a prelude to disaster. Silanus and Marcius were attacking the Libyan right in concert with Gaius's attack, and the prefects commanding my Spanish allies seized their opportunity to switch from skirmishing tactics to an all-out frontal attack on the Libyans. In addition to all these troubles, I recalled that these veterans of Hasdrubal's had been fighting—or the majority just standing in ranks—since early morning, over eight hours without breakfast and with no hope of getting food or water. Now, since they were surrounded on three sides, with my cavalry threatening their rear, their leaders had no choice but to try to withdraw to the security of their camp a good half-mile to their rear. Their retreat began in an orderly manner, step by step, keeping their ranks as veterans should. However, by this time every Roman and allied soldier could see that victory was in sight if only every man would put forward his best, and they did.

Later I heard that Hasdrubal, after taking personal command of his center, had sought to encourage his men by shouting, "the hills in the rear will afford a safe refuge, if you will but retreat without hurry." I will never know if that desperate cry marked the beginning of the end, but in any event something happened within the Libyan phalanx as it tried to make a final stand at the foot of the ridge on which they had built their camp. Just when the Libyans had halted and renewed the fight, panic struck in their rear, and the rear ranks turned tail and bolted. The phalanx crumbled like a sand castle in the surf as more rearward ranks broke and joined in the flight. In minutes what had been a steadily moving fortress became a disorderly mob running for its life—and its camp. My light troops were nipping at the heels of the fleeing rabble while the legions and allies were closing ranks to assault the camp when it happened.

If the gods had chosen to aid our cause throughout the battle they must have decided at this point to call it a day and return to Mount Olympus. The hot skies were suddenly darkened with thick thunder clouds and before my legions could ascend the slope rain fell in sheets that turned the dust to mud. The slippery mud soon became ankle deep under thousands of churning feet. If it had been a passing shower, I would have ordered the attack renewed. But the downpour showed no signs of slackening, and with the greatest reluctance I had to order the withdrawal to our camp. I left behind enough light troops with legionary infantry reliefs to screen Hasdrubal's camp, and we marched back in the rain.

While we marched I sent orders to see that the men got fed and assured of a good night's rest because I knew they would need it at first light on the morrow. I knew also that my plans must be completed and the orders given before I could sleep, for this victory would be meaningless if I did not destroy the remainder of Hasdrubal's army.

The finish of Scipio's story is the story of the finish of Carthaginian aspirations in Spain. At daybreak the morning after Ilipa, Scipio's light troops reported that Hasdrubal's army had evacuated its camp and was trying to escape on the road to Gades. Scipio immediately launched a pursuit, one that turned into a strategic pursuit scarcely matched in history and never surpassed until Napoleon's destruction of Prussian armies after Jena twenty centuries later.

The Roman cavalry and light infantry caught up with Hasdrubal's rear guards—in spite of losing their way in attempting to cut the Carthaginian line of retreat—and kept up such a series of flank and rear attacks against Hasdrubal's columns that forced frequent halts, allowing the legion infantry to catch up. What followed, in Livy's words, "was not a fight, but a carnage of cattle." This relentless slaughter and the pressure on the fugitives were kept up until Hasdrubal, with only 6,000 out of his original 74,000, escaped into the hills and fortified a camp on the highest hill. That night Hasdrubal deserted his men, reached the coast, and took a ship to Gades, followed by Mago. It remained only for Scipio to leave Silanus with enough troops to take the surrender of the doomed camp while he marched back to Tarraco, now the undisputed master of Spain.

In regard to the conduct of the battle of Ilipa, it is only fair that the reader be aware of the controversy among some commentators concerning the complexity of Scipio's maneuver of the legion infantry and cavalry in their attack on the enemy's wings. There has been some "quibbling over the minutiae," over the wheeling inward (by legion infantry) and outward (by the cavalry and *velites*) resulting in some cases in reversed order from "normal" formations just as the troops moved to the attack. I have dealt with that problem exactly as I believe Scipio would by leaving the mechanics of the maneuver to subordinate commanders. I likewise believe that if the commentators paid less attention to Polybius's remarks on the complexity of Roman battle drills at Ilipa, and gave more heed to his comment on generalship (Book XI, 23) the controversy might yet die a natural death. Polybius, the innocent perpetrator of all the fuss, went on to vindicate himself (to anyone who would listen): "But the general [Scipio] regarding this [all the wheeling] as of small importance, devoted his attention to the really important object—outflanking the enemy—and he estimated rightly, for a general should, of course, know the actual course of events, but employ those movements which are suited to an emergency." Amen—to another case for learning about leadership from leaders.

Leaving those small potatoes to wither in their jackets, two salient points in Scipio's planning and conduct of Ilipa demand recognition. His study of his enemy and his exercise of imagination were the bases of an innovation which remains a tactical masterpiece, in its conception as well as in the simplicity of its execution. The other factor was Scipio's step-by-step course from perception to deduction to action, making Ilipa more than a victory; it was a triumph of practical reasoning.

Once Scipio had proceeded from deduction to action, it is the nature of his action that sets his genius apart. Before he resorted to physical action—battle itself—his operations were being carried out on an intellectual plane: he was working on the mind of his opponent before any major forces came in contact. In today's terms, Scipio "conned" Hasdrubal into a comfortable mode of thought. The fixed pattern set up in Hasdrubal's mind was designed to lure him into two nasty surprises. He got the first one in the early morning because he had fallen into the rut of a daily sequence he himself had established—moving his army out of camp first, then, after offering battle all day, withdrawing first to his camp at sundown. Hence Scipio's attack at first light tumbled Hasdrubal and his men out onto the plain sans breakfast and sans choice of deployment since they were given no time for "falling in" in any order other than their standard one.

And the second surprise: "indeed it followed hard upon" the first. This was caused by Scipio's reversal of his order of battle which resulted in his best troops attacking his enemy's worst, while Hasdrubal's best troops, in his center, were pinned down during the critical phases that followed.

Flexibility

THERE REMAINS IMBEDDED in our American mores the obligation to quote Mark Twain at least once in a lifetime. It is my turn to sin. In *Life on the Mississippi* there is a passage that puts to shame any other writer's attempts to dramatize flexibility.

> This . . . brought back to me the St. Louis riots of about thirty years ago. I spent a week there, at that time, in a boarding house, and had this young fellow for a neighbor across the hall. We saw some of the fightings and killings; and by and by we went one night to an armory where two hundred young men had met, upon call, to be armed up and go forth against the rioters, under command of a military man. We drilled till about ten o'clock at night; then news came that the mob were in great force in the lower end of the town, and were sweeping everything before them. Our column moved at once. It was a very hot night, and my musket was very heavy. We marched and marched, and the nearer we approached the seat of war, the hotter I grew and the thirstier I got. I was behind my friend; so finally, I asked him to hold my musket while I dropped out and got a drink. Then I branched off and went home. I was not feeling any solicitude about *him* of course, because I knew he was so well armed now that he could take care of himself without any trouble. If I had had any doubts about that, I would have borrowed another musket for him. . . .

I am not, of course, foolhardy enough to imply that Mark Twain's "branching off" was an exemplary act. I view his con-

175

duct with fascination when it comes to flexibility, but after that one has to draw a line.

On the other side of that line there is a manifest responsibility—within the bounds of this book—of defining flexibility as a quality contributing to intellect. Such a definition should take into account the certainty that the leader will have to exercise his flexibility in the face of such battlefield dynamics as danger, uncertainty, and frustration. With that in mind flexibility can be seen as *the ability to shift mental gears under pressure without confusion of purpose.* The key conditions are clear: there will be pressure and the leader's decisions must be taken without losing sight of the overriding consideration—his mission.

In the next example we will see a leader under a host of pressures that threaten not only his mission but the very survival of his command. First, however, we should recognize the two elements that must be appreciated in following the action: the man and the conditions he had to master before he could hope to win his battles.

Henry Bouquet has been called a soldier of fortune serving in the Army of King George III. Lest he be tarred with the same brush as the mercenaries of our times, Bouquet should be seen for what he was—a professional soldier, born of a good Swiss family, who was following the custom of his day by seeking combat experience as a commissioned officer in European armies. Born in Canton Vaud in 1719, he entered the service of the States General of Holland at age seventeen as a cadet, and two years later was commissioned a lieutenant. In the War of the Austrian Succession (1740–1748) he served in the Sardinian Army, where he showed such coolness and tactical skill in action that the Prince of Orange engaged him, promoted him to lieutenant-colonel, and made him captain-commandant in his regiment of Swiss Guards. After the war he traveled through Europe with Lord Middleton, from whom he began to learn the English which he eventually mastered to a high degree of fluency in speech and "grace and precision" in writing. This association also laid the foundation for a lifelong and amicable relationship with the British military. Their recognition of his abilities led to an offer of the lieutenant-colonelcy of the yet-to-be-formed 1st Battalion of the 60th Royal American Regiment (later, after the Revolutionary War, to be re-titled the King's Royal Rifle Corps) which he would have to assist in organizing and recruiting. He accepted, and in 1756, the third year of the French and Indian War, found himself recruiting among the Germans of Pennsylvania. He liked the Americans and they liked him, a great deal due, no doubt, to his patience, intelligence, and friendly manner. He is said to have been both handsome and ordinary in appearance (if that was an inconsistency it has not been explained), with a tendency to portliness. However that may have been, it is the composition of Bouquet's

Colonel Henry Bouquet

upstairs that should concern us more than the configuration of his downstairs, for he was an exact opposite of the British officer Churchill described a century and half later as being so stupid that even his brother officers had begun to notice it.

Bouquet had a love for mathematics and scientific inquiry that formed a natural base for the working of his inquisitive and analytical mind. He had none of the make-up of the British professional soldier who despised the colonials and who showed a closed mind to their problems and the conditions under which they had to fight the French-supported Indians on their frontiers. The Swiss colonel was not too proud to seek the best advice and instruction available in order to learn the ways of frontier rangers and their Indian enemies. His inquiries led him to concentrate on developing tactics for employing regular troops against Indians. To his inquiring mind this meant finding ways of adapting the advantages and disadvantages of European-type discipline to the conditions of wilderness warfare. When his ideas had crystallized, he began to train his Royal Americans as mobile light infantry in methods that would make them effective in the fluid kind of fighting that characterized Indian warfare. By the time he could put his ideas into practice Bouquet had come to know something that no other British commander knew—his enemy.

Bouquet knew too that provincial soldiers—like his Pennsylvania Germans—could be molded into elite units if properly led, disciplined, trained and equipped. He made his Royal Americans a model light infantry, armed with light fusil instead of the heavy musket, with hunting knives and tomahawks instead of clumsy swords, and with a light pack designed for forest warfare. And instead of close-order drills and firing by volleys, his men were trained to fight as skirmishers in open order so that they could fire and maneuver more effectively than large bodies of Indians. One observer of this training wrote in 1758 (the year Bouquet was promoted to full colonel): "Every afternoon Colonel Bouquet exercises his men in the woods and bushes in a particular manner of his own invention which will be of great service in an engagement with the Indians." In the years that followed this proved to be of great service indeed in the minor actions that the battalion fought against the Indians on frontier outposts. When the war ended in 1763 it would have seemed that the need for Bouquet's men and his tactical skill had finally ended. This turned out not to be the case, in fact the greatest challenge Bouquet and his light infantry would ever face was in the making.

The victorious British commander in North America, Lord Jeffrey Amherst, may have been a fine administrator but he was contemptuous of the Indians and the means the French had used to secure their alliances. The Indians, in turn, resented their new masters and saw them not as new allies but as a mounting threat to their lands and peoples. Their resentment was abetted by the French who wanted the Indians to rebel and so spread rumors that the French would renew the war by sending an expedition to recapture Montreal and Quebec. A remarkable Indian leader arose in the midst of this situation: Pontiac, an Ottawa chief with amazing political and military abilities. In April, 1763, Pontiac exhorted a council of chiefs to unite in a great confederacy that would join all the tribes from the Great Lakes to the Gulf to fall upon the British settlers and drive them from Indian lands. Pontiac's grandest schemes never worked out, but what did follow—known variously as Pontiac's War, Rebellion, or Conspiracy—was a series of bloody, concerted Indian attacks of an intensity that the colonists had never experienced, even when the Indians had been led by the French. The onslaught was cleverly planned and carried out under cover of the In-

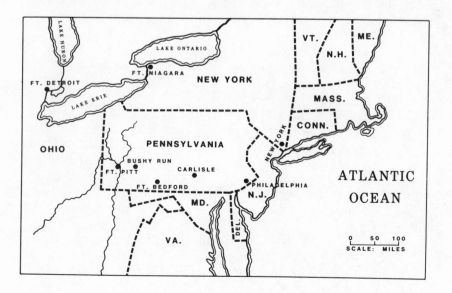

dian gatherings during the trading season, quiet assemblages that had become customary over the years. At a given signal war-painted warriors sprang from hiding, burst into stockades and slaughtered the British settlers. Panic-stricken settlers who escaped fled to frontier outpost forts. By the end of June the terror had flamed across the whole frontier, and in the end only two westernmost posts still held out: Fort Detroit and Fort Pitt.

Finally Amherst became convinced that the Indian attacks were not mere sporadic outbreaks and that full-scale Indian warfare threatened the provinces that would become the states of New York, Ohio, Michigan, and Pennsylvania. Correspondence between Amherst and Bouquet resulted in the latter hurrying to Carlisle in Pennsylvania to assemble a relief column which he would lead westward to save Fort Pitt.

Bouquet's "army" when assembled totaled 460 regulars—his battalion of the Royal Americans, 214 men of the 42nd Highlanders (later the "Black Watch"), 133 of the 77th (Montgomery Highlanders), and a small detachment of rangers. Welcome as the reinforcements were to Bouquet, there were, as he saw it, two serious shortcomings in the build-up of his force. Now his Royal Americans, the trained forest fighters, would be in the minority, and the Highlanders were worn down from their recent service in the West Indies. There were, however, some comforting thoughts: the Scots were well-disciplined, with good morale, and all born fighters. Bouquet consoled himself by determining to make Indian fighters out of the whole force if it meant on-the-job training.

He was ready to march by the end of June, but was held up until July 18 because of the difficulty in getting volunteers from the terrified settlers to serve as wagoners for the wagon train—a logistical liability even Bouquet could not dispense with. A week after his departure Bouquet reached Fort Bedford, where he was delayed for another three days. On August 2 he had gotten to Fort Ligonier when he learned from Lieutenant Archibald Blane that Fort Ligonier had had no word from Captain Ecuyer at Fort Pitt since May 30—no communication for sixty-four days! This lack of intelligence could only mean that Fort Pitt was under siege, if it had not already fallen.

Bouquet acted with his usual alacrity. He stripped his command down to the bare essentials, his only unavoidable burden being the supplies for Fort Pitt. He had the flour barrels emptied into sacks, and rid himself of the wagons by transferring the flour and ammunition to 350 pack horses. He led the vanguard of his force out of Fort Ligonier in the early morning of August 4. He still had learned nothing of the situation at Fort Pitt, and was of course unaware that Captain Ecuyer, staring out of a blockhouse loophole while nursing an arrow wound in his leg, had come to realize that the Indians had lifted the siege and had disappeared into the woods, heading eastward. Simeon Ecuyer, a Swiss professional like Bouquet, knew that they were going to ambush a relief column. Would its commander and his men meet the same fate as had Braddock's force in the same wilderness eight years before?

Bushy Run: Indians, Highlanders, and Light Infantry Mix it Up

Bouquet rested his right foot on a stump, plunked his gold-laced hat down on his knee, and wiped back his sweat-streaked hair with his linen handkerchief. He could see all kinds of low stumps that offered inviting seats, but he was not going to rest while his men were still marching. As far as he could see to his front, the double files of his Royal Americans shared Forbes Road with companies of the 42nd Highlanders from the main body of the column. It was a road in name only, really a track hacked out by General Forbes' axmen five years before and now walled in by dense stands of timber and matted thickets. Some of the tall oaks had since grown canopies whose tops almost joined over the wilderness trail. The forest with its towering trees and thick underbrush held in the August heat, and although it shaded the plodding files from the noon-high sun, the scarlet jackets of Highlanders and provincials showed dark sweat patches under the arms and down the open fronts. Most of the light infantry and the Scots marched bare-headed, their caps or bonnets tucked under the tops of their packs, but Bouquet could see an occasional bearskin-tufted, blue bonnet topping a stubborn Scottish head.

This is the eighteenth day, he thought, *since we marched out of Carlisle. We've crossed the Alleghenies—easier done than I'd have believed—then the high Laurel Hills, and now Chestnut Ridge is behind us. We've made something like seventeen miles today and we should be approaching the site of the abandoned blockhouse near Bushy*

Run. If I'm not mistaken I see that Byerly has dropped back from the advance party to report something.

Andrew Byerly's battered cocked hat and stained brown homespun marked him clearly for the wilderness farmer he was. Bouquet had been delighted to recruit Byerly's services as a guide for this stage of the march since he had only recently been driven from his farm near Bushy Run Creek and knew the local terrain better than any scout. And Bouquet had heeded his suggestion that the column make an afternoon halt at the old blockhouse. After that Bouquet planned to make a night crossing of Turtle Creek, thus avoiding a daytime march through the steep defiles along that creek, an ideal spot for an ambush.

Byerly raised a knuckle to his hat, a gesture that amused Bouquet, as he acknowledged the "salute." The blond young farmer used the back of his saluting hand to wipe the sweat from his forehead.

"Colonel, your advance men are coming up on Edge Hill just off the right of the road. That puts them about a half-mile from Bushy Run," Byerly said.

"Good, but you needn't have brought the word yourself. Now you're going to have to run to catch up with the advance party," Bouquet said.

"I know a path that cuts across the long bend in the road, so I'll be back with them in no time."

"Very well, but is that all? Have the rangers seen any signs at all?"

"Not a thing that we know of. It has been a quiet morning's march, not a sound from the woods on either side."

"Just too quiet, I'd think. Well, be off with you, and next time let one of the soldiers carry back any message."

Byerly knuckled his crude salute and trotted off, slipping through the left file of light infantry and vanishing into a gap between two thickets. He was scarcely out of Bouquet's sight and mind when the first firing began. Up ahead and far out of sight there was a scattered banging of muskets followed by the sharper crack of rifles. In seconds the musketry grew in volume until it sounded to Bouquet like a series of ragged volleys. But he knew it for what it was—not volley fire but the uncontrolled firing of scores of Indian muskets, perhaps hundreds. He put on his hat and looked around into the wide-eyed stare of the young lieutenant at his side. No better time to teach this youngster how an officer should behave at the prospect of action; he fetched out his watch, looked down at it, and carefully put it back in a pocket of his waistcoat.

"Hardly on one o'clock. It seems that lunch will be delayed somewhat this afternoon. Would you mind going forward and telling Major Campbell with the advance guard to be prepared to send his companies to the support of the advance party? Messengers will find me at the head of the main body," Bouquet said.

The lieutenant's stare was still awe-filled, but he had the presence of mind to salute before he took off at a run up the column.

In a matter of minutes Major Campbell's return message convinced Bouquet that his first fears had been well founded.

If my ears and Campbell's messenger tell me the same thing this is no mere harassment of my column. No, they're in numbers strong enough to make an ambush. But why have they attacked only the advance party? I've gotten no reports from the rangers covering each flank. Perhaps the Indian chiefs haven't coordinated their movements yet; that has happened more than once in their attacks. And if that's the case a quickly mounted counterattack, in force, could wreck their schemes for an ambush.

Bouquet's orders to the assembled company commanders and the officers with the convoy were, as always in an action, brief and to the point.

"We will deploy the forward companies on line in advance of the convoy for a frontal attack to pass through the advance guard. We'll rely on the bayonet after the men have fired their first shot. When the advance guard has been passed through, it will re-form as the reserve.

"I want the pack horses assembled off the left side of the road on that hill slope back there.

"The rear guard will close up and form to protect the assembly of the convoy. That is all; we move out at once."

Bouquet went forward to take post in an interval between his Royal Americans, deploying on the left of the road, and the companies of the 42nd, coming into line on the right. He took advantage of a felled oak log to stand and observe the deployment. Bouquet's provincials, accustomed to moving in open order, came into line long before the Scots. Seeing that they were under the eye of their commander, the Royal Americans, their scarlet jackets and blue facings flashing through the trees and thickets, darted into line and waited derisively for the Highlanders to come up even with them.

Bouquet watched the colorful 42nd line forming deliberately, marching with shouldered arms, bright red jackets contrasting with the *feilidh beag,* the small kilt with the dark green background of the Campbell tartan. For a moment Bouquet felt himself the victim of an illusion, for the Highlanders' lower legs were hidden in the undergrowth while the dark green tartan of their kilts had blended so naturally with the shaded green of the forest that their scarlet jackets seemed to float by themselves through the underbrush.

He had no time to muse about illusions. The company commanders were signalling their readiness to advance, the Scots with an upward flash of their claymores,* the Royal American officers with their hats raised overhead. Bouquet dropped his arm to the front and the double-ranked line went forward as shouldered muskets came down to Charge Bayonet to present a gleaming hedge of steel to the enemy. Drums were beating the long roll and high above the steady drumbeat came the high-pitched skirl of the 42nd's bagpipes. This was no shoulder-to-shoulder drill-ground maneuver since the companies had to move in open order to make their way around thickets and through the trees. Yet Bouquet was noting with approval that the overall formation remained intact so that a line was maintained in spite of the rugged terrain.

As the attack swept forward, the skirl of pipes and the roll of the drums began to fade under the crashes of musketry in the woods ahead. When Bouquet's line came up to the rear of the advance guard's line, he saw that Major Campbell had deployed his companies in extended order with the men taking cover behind trees and logs, firing back individually at their enemy. Bouquet's spirits lifted at the sight.

Mon dieu, it may be that these Scots can learn after all. So my instructions to their officers and sergeants at Carlisle and on the march haven't been wasted. I must find Campbell before I can follow the attack.

Bouquet found that Campbell was waiting for him. The red-faced, perspiring major had discarded his scarlet, gold-laced coat and hung it on a stump along with his sword belt and scabbard. His white waistcoat showed grey patches of sweatstains, but it was clear that it was not simply the steaming heat of the forest that was sending rivers of sweat down his chest and back. He was the picture of the clansman rel-

---

*The Scottish basket-hilted broadsword.

ishing the heat and smell of battle as he paced back and forth, bared claymore in hand, meeting messengers and dispatching them back to their companies with new orders. When he caught sight of Bouquet he saluted and made his report.

"Twelve of the eighteen rangers with the advance party fell in the surprise attack on them. I carried through with a bayonet attack but the Indians just kept melting away before us. They'd stand and fire until the bayonets bore down on them, then they'd simply disappear in the woods. So after I got the word of your general advance I formed up here, as you see. I've no count of killed and wounded yet, but that will be in soon. I'm ready to reassemble my companies as soon as your line has passed through."

"You've done well and that won't be forgotten," Bouquet said. "When you speak of the count of killed or wounded, remember that the tactics you've used here will cut that accounting to a fraction of what it would have been if your men had tried to stand and fire in close order. Now I've got to catch up with the advance. One thing you must do when your companies have re-formed—be prepared to deploy a company to each flank to act as flank guards in case I must withdraw this attacking force back to the convoy." Bouquet was gone without waiting for Campbell's acknowledgement.

There was a lull in the Indians' firing as they became aware of the advance of the British main body. The lull died to silence before the steady advance of the long line of bayonets, and the braves faded away into the dense forest just as they had when Campbell's men had made their bayonet attack. The elation Bouquet had felt on seeing Campbell's firing line faded away too as he realized what was coming. In another hundred yards the silence was shattered by a fusilade from the forest to front and flanks. The only signs of the new ambuscade were the muzzle flashes of the Indian muskets and the puffs of white smoke that followed; nothing else was revealed, not a feather or scalp-lock, so cleverly concealed were the Indian warriors among the trees and underbrush.

Following Bouquet's orders, the British infantry had withheld their fire until this moment. The line halted long enough to deliver a crashing volley and dashed forward with lowered bayonets. A new sound arose to replace the banging of musketry. All through the woods resounded the war whoops and shrill yells of the Indians as they darted back to new cover.

As he had feared, Bouquet's attack was having the effect

of a sword thrust piercing thin air, and that was only the prelude to a new predicament. Hardly had the bayonet assault been launched when a buckskin-clad rifleman arrived with a message from Lieutenant Randall, commanding the rangers. The Indians had started to mass on the flanks of the British advance in such swarms that the ranger flank-guards had had to fall back in haste to avoid being overrun. There was nothing to do but order a withdrawal, and Bouquet wasted no time in sending aides scurrying to the companies with the order. His last message went to Major Campbell.

"Tell the major to deploy a company to each flank as I had directed him. He must see my flanks secured so that my main body can make an orderly withdrawal," Bouquet ordered, as he turned his attention back to his companies.

To his great relief the troops were retiring in good order, in steady lines with no confusion showing anywhere. Off to either flank the growing rattle of musketry told all too well of the new threat of the extending Indian attack.

Moving just as they did on Braddock, Bouquet thought, *to encircle the whole force. But these are not Braddock's troops, and I'm not Braddock. We're going to do this right and we're going to join up with the rear guard to form a perimeter around the convoy. That hill where I had the pack horses drawn up will make a good defensive position, and my next concern is to get the position organized—as soon as I can get the companies directed to their positions.*

Now the war crys and firing of the Indians were concentrating on the flanks, though the retreating British main line was still getting a harassing fire from muskets and arrows. But Campbell's Highlanders were keeping the flanks secure, and Bouquet used the brief breathing spell to get new orders to his company commanders.

When the last company had reached the lower slopes of the hill and contact had been established all around, Bouquet sent new orders to assemble his commanders on the hilltop. He had hoped for a respite in order to get in reports and make the inspections to assure that the dozens of details for the defense were attended to: carrying in the wounded to a central point, directing ammunition parties to the supply point, and a host of others. But his enemies were not going to slow down their assaults, and a fresh disaster was looming that could destroy the convoy.

As war whoops rose around the perimeter, new assaults were launched time and again against each part of the circle.

Each party of painted, screaming braves was repulsed with aimed fire and then the bayonet when the Indians charged up to a section of the defensive ring. The Indian chiefs were quick to seize on a new opportunity that would threaten the British from an unexpected quarter. They pressed new attacks with arrows and muskets against the circle of pack horses. Whinnying horses—mad with fright—broke loose, plunging and rearing, to break out of the cordon and into the woods. There was no use in trying to restrain or capture the horses, for their civilian drivers and teamsters had sought cover in the thickets at the first sign of attack.

After a counterattack by a company of Royal Americans had driven off the threat against the convoy, Bouquet was able to take stock of the situation. He called his commanders to a hurried conference on the hilltop. The grave faces of his officers reminded him that it was going to take leadership of the highest order to keep the morale of the men at a fighting pitch, and it was only from him that the officers could catch that spirit. He began by looking at Major Campbell who returned his look with a fighter's grin.

"Well," Bouquet began, "they have got us surrounded— the poor devils!"

A quick glance around the half-circle of faces revealed eyes bright with surprise and a sense of relieved tension. This was the Bouquet whose name was known to every soldier and ranger across the frontiers, the strange foreigner who knew more about Indian fighting than the Indians themselves. If he stood confident in this situation, then things couldn't be hopeless. Bouquet went on quickly to seize the advantage of his pause.

"The rangers report at least five tribes' warriors out there—Shawnees, Mingoes, Delawares, Hurons, and Ottawas—and there may be others. They may outnumber us, but we don't know that to be a fact. What we do know is this: it's got to be our fight all the way because there'll be no column coming to relieve us. But remember this, we've got plenty of food and ammunition, and we have the best men with us because all the sickly and weak were dropped off to garrison Forts Bedford and Ligonier. Every man is a fighter, and all they need is you to keep their spirits up. But above all remember this—those whooping devils out there are, sooner or later, going to make a mistake. They always have because they have no organization and no discipline to act as a controlled force, and their chiefs have no overall control of this hodgepodge of tribesmen. Finally, if there are any signs of faint hearts—though I don't anticipate any signs of such—a gentle reminder will suffice to restore the fight in a man; if we were to give up and surrender, the same fate would await every man. There won't be any lucky ones to die by the tomahawk; to be roasted alive is the least to expect. Now, to the business of organizing our defenses."

Bouquet went on with the details: closing gaps between companies, the exercise of fire discipline, ammunition resupply, followed by a quick dismissal of the officers to their units.

The lull that followed Bouquet's counterattack was short-lived. No sooner had he overseen order restored in the convoy area than the Indians' attacks were renewed all around the beleaguered perimeter. But Bouquet was quick to sense the lack of concerted control by the tribal chiefs. Although the succession of stinging attacks was battering the defenders unmercifully, the assaults were repulsed with bullet and bayonet because each effort, no matter how fiercely mounted, was a local effort. Bouquet had the satisfaction of knowing that his officers were realizing the truth of the counsel he had just given them. Still, Bouquet knew, the enemy's leaders were well aware of the great advantage that now lay with their cause. The British were surrounded, cut off from any conceivable relief, and without access to water. Thus time was on their side and their local attacks, even if they subsided to occasional sniping, would make the battle one of attrition.

Yet, as the afternoon wore on, the Indians continued their ferocious attacks at different sections of Bouquet's defenses, seemingly careless of casualties. A group would deliver a heavy fire from concealed positions then spring to the attack with yells and war whoops intended to terrify the defenders as the painted braves drove to break through the cordon. Each time the assault was met with a controlled volley followed by platoon-strength bayonet charges. And each time the Indians, leaping from cover to cover, vanished like smoke in the forest.

Bouquet, observing the pattern of these local attacks and counterattacks, carried his admonishing word in person and by messenger to his commanders:

"Stop making counterattacks with the bayonet. They do no good and the Indians know they're wearing us down when they run to cover. Instead, make the men lie flat, even though it's hard to load a musket in that position. Then pair off your men for loading and firing, so that one man's musket is always loaded and can cover his partner while he is reloading."

Nom de nom, am I the only one who seems to remember what happened at Braddock's ambush? Bouquet asked himself. *How he raged at the Virginia militia when they took cover on the ground, and how he ordered them to stand up and re-form in ranks—so that instead of killing Indians with aimed fire they could stand in formation and be slaughtered like his British regulars! Well, with God's help I've stopped that nonsense. Now there is the matter of getting the wounded under cover and tended to.*

By three o'clock Bouquet's wounded totaled thirty-five, all of whom had to be carried up to the open hilltop and laid out in an area where they could be cared for. Even in that location they were not safe from enemy fire, since every point within the circular defense could be reached by an Indian bullet. Bouquet listened to the suggestions made by his convoy commander and ordered a work party formed from teamsters and drivers to haul flour bags up the hill. At the top Bouquet's adjutant directed the construction of a circular wall of bags to protect the wounded.

That matter attended to, Bouquet resumed the point-to-point round of his units over the protests of the company commanders, who appeared to be far more concerned for his safety than he was. He did yield to Capt. Tom Basset's persuasion that he shed his scarlet uniform coat and hand it to a sergeant, who hung it over a tree limb. The wisdom of the captain's suggestion was shown to Bouquet on a later visit to the position when Basset pointed out fourteen bullets imbedded in the tree where the coat had hung.

Moving on in white breeches and waistcoat Bouquet used his calm presence and resolute bearing to steady his men and maintain their confidence in him and in themselves. With his sure insight he could feel that confidence had bred confidence, and his eyes told him that his system of fire control was showing its worth all around the perimeter. His tactical methods continued to pay off as the Indians found that their rushes to break through the cordon were proving too costly in casualties and were no longer effective in drawing the British from their covered positions to waste their strength in futile bayonet charges.

Yet, in spite of Bouquet's show of optimism and his soldiers' trust in him, time was on the side of his enemy. The chiefs knew as well as Bouquet that any attempt on his part to advance or retire with his whole force would expose his command to disaster. They knew too that the encircled British were running out of water with no hope of getting any even by digging. What they did not know was that their enemy had long since emptied every water bottle and there was none left even for the wounded whose sufferings were being redoubled by thirst.

By late afternoon the Indians had resorted to sniping and shooting arrows while constantly moving from one hidden cover to another. But they showed no intention of letting up on the harassment of the British, and their change in tactics was causing casualties and tying down the defenders as much as had their earlier rushes.

This kind of action continued to wear down the British until nightfall. The exhausted men had been fighting for seven hours, from the initial ambuscade at one o'clock until eight when the blessed darkness closed in. And that seven hours of fighting had followed seventeen miles of marching over rugged terrain in the worst of the summer's heat. One consolation alone could comfort Bouquet's men: the Indians feared to attack an unbeaten enemy at night. Yet that knowledge was to be offset by sporadic sniping and shouted taunts coming out of the darkness. Even so, rest could be taken in relays so that each would get his turn. Each except the commander.

Major Campbell had to take off his hat and stoop to enter the candlelit shelter where Bouquet sat writing his after-action report. The tiny cubicle, walled with flour bags and roofed with a stretched tent, was so cramped that the only other seat was Bouquet's cot. The Colonel motioned for Campbell take his seat on it, laid aside his pen, and stared for a moment into the Major's blue eyes.

"That cot was not intended for a chair, so feel free to stretch your legs out there," Bouquet said.

Campbell, glad to take a rest, did as his commander suggested and stretched his booted legs toward the entrance.

"You're here to report on security measures, I know, so get on with it," Bouquet said.

"Yes, but first, Sir, the confirmed dead and wounded, if you don't mind," Campbell said.

"Of course, Allan, I didn't know you'd made another count."

"Late returns, Sir. There are twenty-five dead out there and—"

"You don't have to say it," Bouquet broke in, "we have no way to recover them after the withdrawal to this hill, and those bodies will, by now, have been under the scalping knife. Go on."

"Thank you for saving me that. The wounded total thirty-five, some uncertain of recovery, and there's no water for them."

"Or for anyone, I know. Have you finished your check with company commanders on security measures for the perimeter?" Bouquet asked.

"I have, Colonel. No fires anywhere and no pipes to be lit by officer or soldier—"

"Standards good for any forest bivouac, but I think the business about tobacco a bit *de trop*. Is there a man out there whose throat is not drier than his tobacco pouch?"

The tough Campbell face cracked enough to allow a dour smile. He had long since given up trying to anticipate what this incredible colonel would say next.

"Every company has double sentries at least fifty yards advanced from the perimeter and these are backed up by outposts. Reliefs have been assigned at short intervals so that there's no danger of men tired as these falling asleep on post," Campbell said.

"Excellent, now one more thing. Have arrangements been made for the men not on guard to lie down in their formations?"

"The men are sleeping—if you can call it that—under arms, each where he can take up the firing position he'd been in at nightfall."

"Thank you, Allan. Now why don't you see if you can get some sort of rest. I don't have to tell you that those painted fiends will be after us again at first light."

Left with his thoughts Bouquet picked up his pen, then laid it down.

Mon Dieu, what did I do to deserve such rotten luck? My frontal attack took us within a half-mile of the creek, but of course I had to withdraw to save the convoy and to set up the defense back here. So now every man has to suffer from thirst and with no promise of relief. And to think of young Byerly volunteering to make his way through the Indian lines to fetch water for the wounded! If he could have carried a hundred water bottles like I'd carry my hat, he wouldn't have gotten two hundred yards before those devils got him—then what would have happened to him? No, I was right in keeping him here.

I've read that Cortés and his army had their noche triste *when they were driven out of Tenochtitlan, but at least he could share that with his men. Henry Bouquet has to spend his "sad night" alone, at least where it comes to sharing the anguish of the mind. But no one made me take this command, and this must be a part of it.*

There is no use in my wasting time tonight in making plans that will never come to fruition. I must wait until those Indians present me with even the slightest opportunity, one mistake of theirs, one chance that I can seize on. Something to make them stand and fight, something that will allow my troops to get at them with the bayonet as well as the bullet. But there I go, enough of wishful thinking, it is simply that I must be ready to seize my opening.

If there is no victory for me tomorrow, then there is no hope— no hope for this command, for Fort Pitt, and for all the Northwest Territory. With my force gone the last settler will be driven from his land or he and his family massacred.

I must get on with this letter to Amherst. If we fail tomorrow there may be a chance for a mounted and escorted courier to escape with this. But I am not going to fail tomorrow.

He picked up his pen again and went on with his next paragraph:

"Whatever our fate may be, I thought it necessary to give your excellency this information, so that you may, at all events, take such measures as you will think proper with the provinces for their own safety and the effectual relief of Fort Pitt. In case of another engagement I fear insurmountable difficulties in protecting and transporting our provisions, being already so weakened by the losses of this day, in men and horses; and there is the additional necessity of carrying the wounded, whose situation is truly deplorable."

The sentry outside the commander's tent paused in his pacing to listen to a renewed burst of Indian war-whooping and a ragged salvo of musket shots. As he turned back to his duty he could see his colonel's shadow silhouetted like an outline of a bust in the candlelight. His head was bent to his writing and he didn't look up.

The restless night wore on into early morning with the men catching a few winks in relays in spite of the sniping and howling from the dark forest. Most were exhausted enough to at least rest their bodies even if sleep would not come.

Promptly at first light the Indians launched a new series

of attacks much as Bouquet had anticipated. Although the British were as prepared as men could be under the conditions, casualties continued to mount. The greater part of the encircled cordon was suffering under a hail of bullets and arrows fired by an unseen foe who was taking every advantage of the plentiful natural cover. As the August sun rose higher and grew hotter, renewed torments of thirst began to plague the men until—as Bouquet would say in his next report—they were "distressed to the last Degree by a total want of Water, much more intolerable than the Enemy's Fire."

The weakening condition of the troops was not lost on the Indian chiefs who led their braves to come in even closer, becoming more brazen with every effort. There were taunts in broken English, and Bouquet caught a glimpse of a Delaware chief whom he recognized as Keelyushung, a bold leader whose English was better than most.

"You have thirst now, Englishmen, but wait until we roast you as soon as the sun is high," he shouted from behind a thick tree.

Bouquet resumed his rounds of the companies, continually encouraging the men to reserve their fire for clearly exposed targets and not to waste breath in shouting replies to the insults thrown at them from the woods.

"Better one good shot for revenge than all the hollering in the world," he told a section of Highlanders on the north side of the circle.

At the end of the fifth hour—the renewed Indian attack had begun at five o'clock—Bouquet's spirits had reached their nadir, though he could still conceal that from the officers and men. He had to shake his head to clear away the numbness brought on by physical and mental exhaustion.

These men have performed wonders for the past twenty hours, but they can't endure much longer. And if we all weaken to the point of collapse, all about the same time, the Indians will discover it and overrun us, especially if they can manage some kind of final concerted effort.

He leaned against the trunk of a great oak on the eastern slope of the hill and tried to look out over the companies farther down the slope. He strained his reddened eyes trying to detect the movement of any enemy in the distant trees, but he could make out nothing. It certainly was quiet in those woods in front of this sector. There the realization struck him like the blow of a fist.

Those companies down there are as alert as could be expected, but they're not firing a shot! And there's no fire coming from the woods in front of them! Can it be? Can it be what I am thinking?

He ran as fast as his stiff legs could carry him back to his tiny command post.

"Lieutenant Dow," he shouted, "send for Major Campbell, Captain Basset, and their company officers. Run, man, and tell them to get up here at a run!"

In minutes he was issuing orders to the assembled officers in a flow that threatened to inundate their weary minds, yet all were following him intently.

"Listen now and carefully, for I've got no time for questions and answers. By God, they have done it! The Indians have finally given us the chance to strike them where we can beat them on our terms.

"Their circle around us is no longer complete. They have thinned out to nothing for at least two hundred yards on each

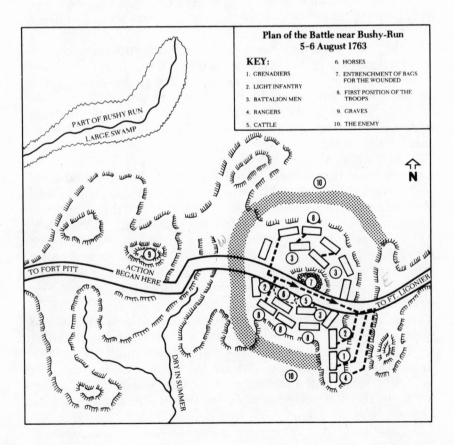

Plan of the Battle near Bushy-Run
5-6 August 1763

KEY:

1. GRENADIERS
2. LIGHT INFANTRY
3. BATTALION MEN
4. RANGERS
5. CATTLE
6. HORSES
7. ENTRENCHMENT OF BAGS FOR THE WOUNDED
8. FIRST POSITION OF THE TROOPS
9. GRAVES
10. THE ENEMY

PART OF BUSHY RUN

LARGE SWAMP

TO FORT PITT

ACTION BEGAN HERE

DRY IN SUMMER

TO FT. LIGONIER

N

side of the road back toward Fort Ligonier, on the eastern face of our perimeter. They have left two flanks open, and they don't yet realize it. Now see that spur that extends southward from the lower slope of this hill. Note that the spur begins just about where the Ligonier road starts to ascend our hill.

"We are going to use that spur to hide our counterattacking force. Major Campbell, you will lead the attack and you will have two companies, the 3rd Light Infantry Company and the Grenadiers of your 42nd. Your left flank will be covered by a detachment of rangers. You will form your line under cover on the east side of the spur, prepared to attack, on my signal, to the west against the Indians' south flank. Major Campbell's force will be supported by two companies of the 60th under Captain Basset. All four companies—Major Campbell's plus Captain Basset's—will be withdrawn from the west side of the perimeter."

Bouquet's orders continued to pour out in a torrent as the details of his battle plan fell into place, and every officer involved in its maneuvers knew his role in executing the plan. When Bouquet had finished, he dismissed his officers with this charge:

"Every man in this command has been aching to thrust a bayonet into one of those red devils, and here is his opportunity. I want to see every Indian we get in the open slaughtered or driven, like the mad beasts they are, from this ground. Now, to your stations."

He took post on the western slope of the hill just below the flour bag fort. From there he could watch the withdrawal of Campbell's and Basset's four companies. As the men of those companies rose from cover and assembled into ranks, he could see other companies on either flank extending their fronts to cover the gap that would be left by the four withdrawing companies. The men who were closing the gap passed just below him as their officers directed them to new positions, tightening the circle into a greatly shrunken perimeter. While the extending files were taking cover on the hillside, Bouquet saw the red jackets and green kilts of Campbell's Highlanders moving to form column on the road below him. Their commander was losing no time in moving his companies out. As the last files came out of the trees and onto the road, Campbell was ordering them into a double-time march that moved his two companies as fast as the stumps and ruts

of the road would allow. While the Highlanders and the light
infantry company were double-timing to the east, Basset's two
companies had completed their withdrawal and were following on the heels of Campbell's men.

When he was satisfied that the gap had been closed and
the new west side of the perimeter tightened in, Bouquet
moved to the east end of the flour-bagged enclosure where
he could get a panoramic view of the south half of the perimeter and the ground sloping outward from it. Peering
through the trees he watched the scarlet flow of Campbell's
column come to a halt and face into line. At Campbell's next
command the companies wheeled to their right to disappear
into the forest on the east side of the spur. He waved an ac-
knowledgment to the courier Campbell had posted on the
roadside to await Bouquet's signal to launch the attack.

He turned his attention to Basset's companies who had
halted on the road just short of Campbell's courier. The late
morning sun was reflected in flashes from the bayonets of
the light infantry as they filed southward to positions at the
bottom of the hill below the cattle corral. Then they too disappeared as they sought cover for their new firing line.

A renewed roar of musketry and wild whooping told
Bouquet that the Indians were closing in on the west side of
the perimeter.

This will be the boldest attack the chiefs can launch, he thought.
*They think we've been beaten into a retreat and they will be going
all out to overrun us from the west and take this hill and all the
"victims" on it. Now if they will only mass on the west and south to
make that final attack, we will have them where we want them.*

Bouquet's thoughts became reality as the whooping and
firing reached a new crescendo. Painted warriors burst into
the open, dashing forward against the British circle from the
west and south. The braves were recklessly exposing themselves as they came running out of the thickets. He watched,
fascinated by the naked bodies flashing through the trees,
shaven heads and scalplocks shining and bobbing, as the Indians came on at a dead run. Most of them had discarded
their muskets and ran with tomahawk in hand, ready to close
in for the kill.

He saw that the officers were carrying out his orders to
withhold the fire of the companies until every shot would tell.
When the foremost warriors were within fifty paces the volley
crashed out from the defenders. The volley smoke had not

cleared as the infantrymen stood up and rapidly reloaded their muskets. A second volley rang out as Bouquet saw a scattering of Indians burst through the smoke to be met by the bayonets of the soldiers. As the smoke cleared he saw the ground littered with Indian dead and wounded, but beyond them new waves of warriors were massing among the trees two hundred yards beyond the littered ground.

This was the moment. To wait any longer would risk the rupture of the British cordon and certain destruction of the command. Bouquet picked up his fusil and held it overhead at arm's length, then dropped his arms bringing the light musket to the level of his knees. He saw Campbell's courier repeat his signal before he darted into the forest toward his commander. In seconds Bouquet witnessed the most pleasant sight of his career.

The long line of Campbell's Highlanders and light infantry emerged from the forest at the foot of the western slope of the spur. The scarlet line, topped by a crest of gleaming bayonets, swept forward toward the exposed flank of the Indians who were renewing their attack on the south perimeter. Bouquet heard the distant ring of Campbell's command, and the British line snapped to a halt. A hundred muskets came down as one at the next command, all levelled at the mob of yelling savages. He saw Campbell's claymore flash downward and heard his shouted—"Fire!"

The volley crashed into the crowd of warriors at a distance of thirty yards, leaving scores of dead and wounded heaped in front of the advancing British line. Campbell had not allowed time for his companies to reload. The Scots and the Royal Americans charged into the mass of Indians with lowered bayonets. A number of intrepid braves stood and fired back, but the greatest number stood for a second or two, stunned by the surprise volley and the sight most dreaded by Indian warriors—the line of cold steel charging at their naked bodies. The mass then turned and fled westward, but their troubles had only begun. Their headlong retreat led them straight across the front of Basset's waiting companies. A beautifully-directed volley laid low another swath of braves before Basset's light infantry broke from cover. They fell into line on the right flank of their Highland comrades and joined in the bayonet assault. There arose a combined chorus of ferocious Highland yells and American cheers as the pent-up fury of the long-suffering infantry was unleashed on their

The Black Watch at Bushy Run by C. W. Jeffries

hated enemy. Now the bayonet came into its own as the charging British infantry thrust away at the backs of the fleeing Indians. The Scots and the Royal Americans left a mounting trail of Indian bodies in their wake. The four united companies continued their attack to the west, then on command wheeled and fell on the now-exposed flank and rear of the mass of warriors who had been attacking the perimeter from the west.

This body of Indians, seeing destruction bearing down on them, became a pack of fugitives which Campbell's and Basset's companies pursued, leaving a new trail of Indian corpses behind them. Bouquet watched the Scots and Royal Americans vanish into the woods still in chase of bloody retribution. Bouquet was to learn later from Campbell that the pursuit had been a complete success; the Indians had dispersed in hopeless confusion, never to reunite.

For a matter of minutes, while Campbell's and Basset's men were driving off Indians from the south and west of the circle, the rest of the Indians broke off their attacks. Then, seeing the fate of their comrades, they turned and joined in their flight.

Quiet had settled over the bloody hill and the corpse-littered forest to its south and west before Bouquet had time to sag down to a seat on the flour-bag wall to collect his thoughts. The stillness, after twenty-two hours of battle, had so stunned his senses that he sat motionless for a space of time. Finally, he could turn to his officers and give his orders for reassembling his command and marching it on toward Bushy Run and life-restoring water.

Bouquet's victory did not come without cost. His little force, fewer than 500 strong before battle, lost 50 killed, 60 wounded, and 5 missing, a total of 115, almost a fourth of the command. Yet damaging as the losses were to Bouquet, the effects of Bushy Run were indeed as far-reaching as they were rewarding to the British settlements in America. The most immediate effect was the relief of Fort Pitt, but that was only the beginning. Bushy Run had a powerfully negative effect on the Indian tribes. Not only had they been soundly whipped, they had been beaten at their own game of ambush. Additionally, Bushy Run was a decisive action, in spite of the small numbers engaged, because it proved to be a turning point in Pontiac's War. From there on, the Indians were no longer on the offensive, and eventually Pontiac's grand vision of driving the English into the sea led only to surrender. In 1764, a year after Bushy Run, Bouquet led an expedition of 1,500 men into the depths of Shawnee and Delaware country. In a display of force—not a shot was fired—he recovered over 300 white captives from the Indian tribes and made peace while laying the groundwork for the treaties that followed. In all, Bouquet proved himself an able statesman as well as a soldier honored by the frontier peoples, white and Indian.

In regard to the battle itself and the decisive moments in it, one aspect deserves examination. It seems to be fashionable to refer to Bouquet's decisive maneuver as an act of "desperation." The precedent may have been set by Sir John Fortescue (*History of the British Army*, 1911, III, 17) when he referred to Bouquet's action as "a last desperate resource." The adjectives are at best misleading. While there can be little doubt that Bouquet conceived and executed a plan in a dangerous situation, one should evaluate the man and his methods before accepting an implication that he acted in desperation at Bushy Run.

Although I have sketched Bouquet's background and represented dramatically his actions in the battle, a closer look

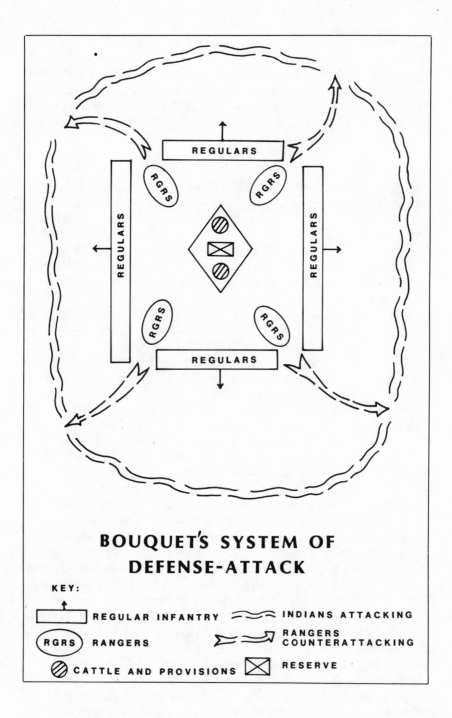

BOUQUET'S SYSTEM OF DEFENSE-ATTACK

KEY:

REGULAR INFANTRY   INDIANS ATTACKING

RGRS RANGERS   RANGERS COUNTERATTACKING

CATTLE AND PROVISIONS   RESERVE

at his tactical analyses and concepts will shed more light on the reasons and reasoning for his perception and decisions at Bushy Run. These brief extracts from Bouquet's writings will illustrate the man's insight and methods. He summed up Indian tactics this way:

> "The first, that their general maxim is to surround their enemy.
>
> "The second, that they fight scattered, and never in a compact body.
>
> "The third, that they never stand their ground when attacked, but immediately give way to return to the charge."

Bouquet went on to develop, in detail, conceptual models as guides for dealing tactically with Indian methods of forest fighting. The sketch is a simplified diagram of his system of shifting from the defensive to the offensive against an Indian force which has encircled a British force composed of regular troops and rangers. The essence of this tactical method lies in the counterattack (charges covered by fire from the defensive circle) that breaks the Indian encirclement into segments, thus creating artificial flanks which can be attacked in turn. In the final steps the regulars and rangers unite in rolling up the exposed flanks, demoralizing the Indians with cold steel charges (bayonet and tomahawk) followed by a relentless pursuit until the enemy is destroyed or dispersed.

These illustrative examples, taken from his extensive studies and correspondence, are positive indicators that Bouquet's experience and study led to the formulation of principles that were firmly set in his mind. What he exercised at Bushy Run was no more than an imaginative adaptation of his own ideas. He didn't need to be pushed to desperation in order to react effectively. All he needed was an opportunity to use his limited resources in a manner that would ensure success. His cool courage enabled him to wait until his keen perception could sense that opportunity, then his flexible mind came up with a practicable solution.

Judgment

> In the next place I experienced in myself a certain capacity for judging which I have doubtless received from God, like all the other things I possess; and as He could not desire to deceive me, it is clear that He has not given me a faculty that will lead me to err if I use it aright.
>
> —Descartes, *Meditations* (IV)

If we can accept Descartes' statement as he intended—that is, not applying solely to him as an individual but to all rational men—we have a base for observing judgment in a practical way. If we can further accept that base as being a sound one (what other kind would we want?), it should be enlarged by one assumption: that all rational men possess the faculty of judgment, *but in varying degree*. Looking again at Descartes' declaration, the last five words, "if I use it aright," point toward that difference in the quality of judgment as we observe it in different men. There is no need to pursue this thought with the idea of proving, through abstract reasoning, that judgment varies from person to person. All that anyone need do is search his memory to find examples of good and bad judgment in private life or in public. Remember the time your neighbor got fleeced by the con artists who were going to resurface his driveway? Or the time your congressman finally did something right and voted against that tax bill—as you had urged?

If we are going to observe the practical application of judgment, we should not overlook that twin quality that led Voltaire to point out: "common sense is not so common." We all use the term in daily life, but just what is common sense? The Oxford English Dictionary tells us that it is: "The endowment of natural intelligence possessed by rational beings; ordinary, normal or average understanding; the plain wisdom which is every man's inheritance . . . More emphatically: Good sound practical sense . . . general sagacity."

Then if we agree (as Voltaire would not) that we are generally sagacious, our next step would be to define judgment as it should be exercised by a leader in warfare. I would propose: *The ability to make a sound assessment of what he knows of the enemy and his own command, decide upon a practicable course of action, and act upon it.*

In the next case we will watch the actions of a leader that have caused his judgment to be questioned by some and defended by others.

The Battle of the Little Bighorn

> Thus we see how all the judgements that are founded upon external appearances, are marvelously uncertain and doubtful; and that there is no so certain testimony as every one is to himself.
>
> Montaigne, *The Essays* (II, 16)

Many Americans, old or young, might think of the Battle of the Little Bighorn as a contest between dance-band trumpeters, but if one calls it "Custer's Last Stand" everyone recognizes this minor military disaster that has been turned into a legend of almost epic proportions. Why such recognition?

In the most matter-of-fact terms it is the most written-about battle in American history, but that simple answer poses another "why." In over a hundred years no other event in our frontier history has so stirred the imagination of Americans. It was—is—a tragedy wrapped in a mystery with a bright side lit by heroic action and a dark side shadowed by the unknown. Its leader gained for himself glory in death and defeat that has far exceeded his grasp for it during his adventurous life. That glory and the legend that grew up around it have kindled a controversy that continues to be fanned by a succession of such a curious assortment of stokers as historians, dime novelists, responsible and irresponsible journalists, poets, military "experts," and movie scriptwriters. Out of all this has evolved an accumulated store of "Custeriana" which is continually being probed by Custerphiles and Custerphobes. The former maintain that the only orders known to exist gave full rein to Custer's aggressiveness, and had his subordinates Reno and Benteen given their full measure of duty things would have been different. The Custerphobes say that Custer disobeyed orders, began his battle prematurely, and risked the lives of his whole command in a reckless attack designed to restore the prestige which the "American Murat" had lost in the public eye.

Things have gotten so hot in a critical sense over the years that a friend of mine who had become interested in the battle essayed to enter the lists but quickly withdrew when his opening statement was challenged. When I asked him why on earth did he back out if only his first assertion had been disputed, he replied, yes, it was his only statement, but it had been that the twenty-fifth of June, 1876, was a Sunday.

There are things, however, that we do know. Foremost is the knowledge that when Lieutenant-Colonel Custer, formerly Major-General of Volunteers, led five companies of his 7th Cavalry down into Medicine Tail Coulee that Sunday afternoon, not a man was ever seen alive again by white men. There are other ascertainable facts that will be outlined in a moment in bare-bones form, but first the reader should be alert to a change in the way of presenting the leader in this battle.

In each of the seven cases we have examined, from Cowpens to Bushy Run, it has been possible to reconstruct the leader's thoughts and personal actions in a way that is both graphic and historically accurate. This has been possible because enough records were accessible for research and analysis to assure validity. However, when one approaches the quality of a leader's *judgment* one is stepping from firm ground onto quicksand. There are too many intangibles, even with the best of records, to portray the man's judgmental processes in a fair manner. Consequently, *just this once*, I will show in a narrated history what happened, in this case to Custer and his 7th Cavalry.

But, you may ask, why Custer and the Little Bighorn? I would reply that this case never fails to create an irresistible incitement to investigate the question of military judgment. Note that I am not saying that Custer's judgment was questionable. I *am* saying that the question will have to be resolved by each of us in his own way.

On a related point that cannot be questioned: to enter into this enigma can be a hazardous adventure in itself. So, if you are game, you will be ready to Stand to Horse and Prepare to Mount, for though we ride in company each man listens for his own bugle call.

The most important parts of the background are the figures of the chief players. First, without question, is George Armstrong Custer. Marshall has referred to him in *Crimsoned Prairie*, somewhat obliquely, as being cast in a stellar role as "the indispensable man," at the opening of his last campaign. With a greater show of sympathy the staid *Dictionary of American Biography* likens Custer's last days to those of "the central figure in a Greek tragedy, hemmed in by a closing net of adverse circumstances, while his every movement to extricate himself served only to hasten the inevitable end." Hardly an analogy likely to win the hearts of latter-day professionals, but there you have him—Custer the enduring enigma.

He comes on strong in this final act, still the dashing figure of the Indian fighter despite a put-down by President Grant that cost Custer the command of the expedition (which then went to General Terry) and almost the command of his regiment at the start of the campaign. Rescued by Terry and General Sherman, who were the chief instruments in getting Grant's grudging reprieve ("if you want General Custer along he withdraws his objections"), we see the star of the show, booted and spurred, wearing his buckskin battle jacket, ready to mount up and lead out his regiment—with the regimental band at parade ground's edge playing "Garry Owen."

How did he get to this stage entrance? Purely and simply by being the flesh and blood incarnation of the image he had fought to project throughout his military life. Never curbed by discipline (ninety-seven demerits his last half-year at West Point, three short of dismissal) he needed only battlefields and cavalry charges to blaze his name with *la gloire*. A second lieutenant at the first Bull Run, two years later he was the youngest brigadier-general ever appointed in the United States Army. The "boy general" went on to become Phil Sheridan's most trusted cavalry commander. Brevetted a major-general of volunteers in 1864, in the following year he wound up a meteoric career by throwing his cavalry division across the front of Lee's Army of Northern Virginia (in all fairness, by then the dying shadow of a once-great fighting machine) to block its final movement and cause its commander to meet Grant at Appomattox Court House.

In the cutbacks of the postwar years he was reduced to his permanent grade of lieutenant-colonel and began to have his ups and downs on frontier service. One of his downs was being found guilty by a court-martial in 1867 and sentenced to a year's suspension from the army. He may have been the scapegoat for the failure of General Hancock's campaign of that year—the major charge was deliberate absence from duty—but by the fall of 1868 he was recalled to command of his regiment by none other than General Sheridan, who had succeeded Hancock. That winter, on November 27, Custer redeemed his name by leading his 7th Cavalry in a surprise attack against Black Kettle's Cheyennes at the Washita River, where he gained a brilliant victory.

What is he like, now as we see him boarding Terry's steamboat, the *Far West,* for the final command conference? At thirty-six he is still as slender as he was at Appomattox, tall, with the rangy muscularity of the superb horseman. He looks through us with steady blue eyes, and we see that one of his most distinguishing features, his flowing golden locks, has been trimmed short for this campaign. He still wears his full mustache, which shows tawny gold against his sunburned face. He is in splendid physical condition, and his voice can be just as strong on the occasions he wishes it so, sharp and brusque; on others, earnest and appealing. He uses neither tobacco nor alcohol and in these later years has become a dedicated student of military science as well as a working and published writer. His courage is unquestioned and he has a high sense of integrity. He has a following of devoted relatives and friends (going with him on campaign are his younger brother, Capt. Tom Custer, his brother-in-law, Lt. James Calhoun, his nephew, "Autie" Reed, and his youngest brother, Boston Custer), but he has also accumulated a string of vindictive enemies. He can be positive to the point of brusqueness, but is also noted for the Custer charm. To his superiors—an acknowledged few—he seems obsessed with ambition and lust for glory; he can be erratic and impulsive, yet a hard driver and a ruthless fighter—a Peck's-Bad-Boy and the spirited earner of that other title, "the American Murat."

There is, of course, a succession of other dramatis personae, but we need concern ourselves with a look at only three. Alfred Howe Terry was a Yale man, a lawyer turned professional soldier after finishing his Civil War service as a corps commander. He is now the commanding general of the Department of Dakota and commands the column which includes Custer's 7th Cavalry. A kind and generous man, twelve years older than Custer, he has the full respect of both superiors and subordinates. His kindness was showing, as the story goes, when Custer implored him, on his knees and with tears in his eyes, to intercede on his behalf and get President Grant to relent and restore Custer to command of his regiment. That he did so intercede is proof of Terry's good heart and intentions, though some have not been so praiseful of his judgment in the matter.

Waiting in the wings are the two other officers with whom we cannot help becoming involved. Maj. Marcus A. Reno is the senior, ranking next under Custer in the 7th Cavalry. A West Pointer who graduated four years before Custer entered the academy, he attained the rank of brigadier-general of volunteers in the Civil War and earned two citations for gallantry. Older than Custer and used to his own command, he is anything but an admirer of his regimental commander. He is a darkly handsome man, stocky, looking back from his photographs with bland countenance and dark eyes. He will become the senior survivor of the battle and the one who will suffer most from that survival. He will be acquitted, in 1877, of misconduct in the battle by a court of inquiry, but will go on downhill until he will be dismissed from the army for drunkness and being a main contender in a tavern brawl. He is physically courageous and perhaps never should have arrived at the storm center of the recriminations and muckslinging that followed the American people's fascination with the "massacre."

Then there is Frederick W. Benteen, the senior captain of the regiment and from an altogether different kettle of fish than Custer or Reno. Born to an aristocratic Virginia family he chose to serve in the Union army despite the fact that his brothers served the Confederacy and his father had dismissed him as a disloyal son. He rose to the rank of colonel and after the war remained in the army, one of those few who were of independent means and who stayed in the ser-

Custer in dress uniform

vice simply because of love of the life. He is a year older than
Reno and six years older than Custer. He is an uneasy ally
of Reno's in the anti-Custer faction of the regiment—their
only common ground being the dislike of Custer—and he is

Major Marcus Reno   Captain Frederick Benteen

no doubt the stronger personality. His dislike of Custer had swelled to hatred after the Battle of the Washita. Benteen could never forgive Custer for what he considered the abandonment of Major Elliott and sixteen troopers. He had an unsigned letter published in the *St. Louis Democrat* wherein he took Custer to task for the alleged abandonment. When Custer read it he was enraged, summoned his officers to his tent, and, slapping his boot with his whip, said he was going to horsewhip the letter's writer. One of the officers present stated that Benteen calmly spoke up: "All right, General, start your horsewhipping now. I wrote it." Custer stared at him in astonishment, and turned and left the tent. Benteen hates Custer, but it is well to remember that Benteen dislikes almost everybody.

Our method of viewing the coming events may be compared to a photographer's coverage. First, things are seen in broad panoramic view as through a wide-angle lens. Next, we switch to a zoom lens to come closer to the action. Finally, we see things happening in a series of close-ups.

First then, are the column headings from the *Bismarck* [Dakota Territory] *Tribune's* extra of July 6, 1876:

MASSACRED

___

GEN. CUSTER AND 261 MEN THE VICTIMS

___

NO OFFICER OR MAN OF 5 COMPANIES LEFT TO TELL THE TALE

___

3 DAYS DESPERATE FIGHTING BY MAJ. RENO AND THE REMAINDER OF THE SEVENTH

___

FULL DETAILS OF THE BATTLE

___

LIST OF KILLED AND WOUNDED

___

THE BISMARCK TRIBUNE'S SPECIAL CORRESPONDENT SLAIN

___

SQUAWS MUTILATE AND ROB THE DEAD

___

VICTIMS CAPTURED ALIVE TORTURED IN A MOST FIENDISH MANNER

___

WHAT WILL CONGRESS DO ABOUT IT?

___

SHALL THIS BE THE BEGINNING OF THE END?

___

In less lurid terms these are the bare-bones facts of the campaign and battle.

The Sioux nation and its allies took to the warpath in 1875 when a railroad and a gold rush threatened their territory. When the Sioux and allied tribes gathered in the Powder River country of southern Montana for the Teton

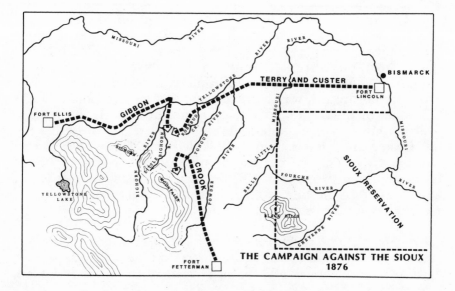

THE CAMPAIGN AGAINST THE SIOUX
1876

Council, the United States Army planned a three-pronged advance to move on the assembly and capture it. A column from the southeast under Brig.-Gen. George Crook would move first. Another would move east from Montana under Col. John Gibbon. The third, under General Terry (which included the superseded Custer and the 7th Cavalry), would move westward from Fort Lincoln, pick up the Yellowstone River and follow it to the mouth of Rosebud Creek before it moved southwest to meet the other two columns.

General Crook's column was checked at the Battle of the Rosebud (June 17, 1876), and withdrew back to Fort Fetterman. Meanwhile, General Terry and Colonel Gibbon planned to link up on the Little Bighorn River on June 26. Terry dispatched Custer with the 7th Cavalry (no attachments other than its pack train) on a reconnaissance in force. After a forced march, Custer reached the Little Bighorn on June 25. At noon he divided his regiment (less than six-hundred strong) into three battalion groupings. Major Reno with three companies (troops) moved across the river and upstream with orders to attack the Indian village from the south. Out to Reno's left, Captain Benteen with another three companies was sent on a scout to cover the left flank and "to pitch into" any Indians encountered. Custer took five companies to advance downstream on the east side of the river, leaving one company to guard the pack train. On the west side of the river, Reno ran head on into a superior force of Indians and was driven back across the river where he set up a defensive perimeter. Reno was joined by Benteen later in the day and their combined units held out through June 25–26, suffering over one hundred casualties. In the meantime Custer, continuing his advance northward, was attacked from several directions when the bulk of his command was opposite the east flank of the village. His force was subsequently encircled. In an hour or so Custer and all his men were killed in the famous "Last Stand" or "massacre," depending on a point of view: "When the white man wins, it is a battle; if the Indian wins, it is a massacre."[1] In the final event, on June 27, Terry and Gibbon arrived in time to save Reno and Benteen.

Note: Starting at this point italics are used, not to show a leader's thoughts (as in preceding cases), but to represent comments on critical matters or events which bear on the outcome of the Battle of Little Bighorn.

If one is to see clearly the impact of decisions and events leading up to the battle, it will be wise to get an overview of those events from June 19 to June 25, the day of battle. General Terry, the commander of the Department of Dakota, was now commanding two columns: his own (including Custer) and that of Colonel Gibbon moving eastward from Montana. Terry's mission, by June 21, was unchanged: to bring the Sioux Nation to battle on his terms and either force it to capitulate (meaning going back to the control of Indian agencies) or face annihilation. There is no doubt that Terry would not hesitate to attack if he could catch the Indians between his two converging columns. To do this it is obvious that he had to have a continuing flow of timely intelligence of the location and movements of the Sioux tribes, wary and highly mobile forces who carried their logistical support with them in the form of their portable villages.

By June 19 Terry had gotten word that Major Reno had returned from a reconnaissance with six companies of the 7th Cavalry and made contact with Colonel Gibbon's column now encamped on the north bank of the Yellowstone at a point opposite the confluence of Rosebud Creek with the river. Terry's reaction to Reno's report was twofold. He sent an order to Reno to remain where he was and Terry's column would move to rendezvous with him. The general's other reaction was extreme irritation. Reno had exceeded his orders and instead of going up the Powder River and descending the Tongue River to the Yellowstone he had gone on west and scouted up the Rosebud, a clear violation of his orders. Custer, hearing the news of Reno's reconnaissance, had an even more violent reaction. He was angry in the extreme, but for a different reason. He thought that Reno should have followed the great Indian trail discovered going up the Rosebud and, if at all possible, fallen on the Indians and smashed them. That the latter action would have been a further violation of Reno's orders seems not to have occurred to Custer.

Regardless of Terry's and Custer's reaction to Reno's scout, two things were evident, the first factual, the second a logical deduction. Fact: Reno's scouts had found a huge Indian trail a half-mile wide, made by thousands of lodgepoles, and an abandoned village of 360 lodges, indicating the presence of at least 800 warriors. Deduction: from this and other intelligence the Sioux and allies were moving toward an assembly in the valley of the Little Bighorn. Terry's deductions and intentions are clear in the extract from this telegram he sent his boss, General Sheridan, on June 21:

> No Indians have been met with as yet; but traces of a large and recent camp have been discovered twenty or thirty miles up the Rosebud. Gibbon's column will move this morning on the north side of the Yellowstone for the mouth of the Bighorn . . . Custer will go up the Rosebud tomorrow with his whole regiment and thence to the headwaters and thence down the Little Horn . . . I only hope that one of the two columns will find the Indians.

That last sentence is important for it contains the essence of the conviction of Terry and his commanders that each major force could handle the situation on its own or at least for the time it would take for the approaching force to link up. *The difficulties of conducting convergent operations against a mobile enemy over vast and rugged expanses of terrain without timely communication seems, incredibly, to have gone unappreciated at the highest levels of command: Sheridan's (in far-off Chicago), Terry's, or Gibbon's.*

In the afternoon of that same day, June 21, Terry held his final command conference before Custer's departure with the 7th. We will never know the details of just what was said in this meeting aboard the *Far West*, for Custer would soon be silent forever and the accounts by participants who did survive are contradictory and marred by attempts to justify actions that followed. In any case we can be sure that the following items were critical to the conference:

1. Terry's strategy was reviewed: his aim was to get the Indians between his two detachments and bring them to bay.
2. If the Indians were allowed to escape into the Big Horn Mountains, the Army's plans would be foiled and operations would have to start all over again.
3. Custer should move up the Rosebud until he found which way the great trail led. If that trail turned west (over the divide between the Rosebud and the Little Bighorn) Custer should not follow it, instead he should proceed south for about twenty miles—maintaining a vigilant reconnaissance to his left (east)—then turn west and move up the Little Bighorn valley (northward) toward Gibbon.
4. It appears that Terry failed to provide for coordinating the general movement of the link-up forces (Terry's and Gibbon's columns), thus leaving that undefined requirement to Custer whose mission was actually a reconnaissance in force.
5. Despite the insistence of reliable Indian scouts that the hostile warriors could not number less than 5,000 the general consensus of the officers was that there were not more than 1,000 to 1,500 warriors. It is believed that only Custer put the latter estimate that high.[2]
6. The strength and capability of Custer's regiment to go out on such a mission without reinforcement was questioned. Accordingly it seems that Terry wanted to explore the possibility of attaching Major Brisbin's battalion of the 2nd Cavalry to Custer's command, but that was declined by Custer who said that his regiment could handle any Indians they might encounter and the extra battalion (whose companies could have increased Custer's force by a third) would then not be needed. To the proposal of attaching the platoon of Gatling guns to the 7th, Custer again declined on the grounds that the guns could not keep up with his horsemen in the rugged terrain they must cover and hence would not be an asset but a liability.

The conference ended apparently without anyone questioning the details of just how all this would result in the army's "catching" the Indians. *The only reliable evidence of the discussion of details points to Custer's rejection of the two reinforce-*

ments. In the case of the Gatlings he must have been justified. The Gatling attached to Reno's reconnaissance had failed to keep up; the guns were drawn by "condemned horses," ones unsuitable for cavalry mounts. As for Custer's refusal of Brisbin's battalion, that is another story: there is little doubt that his real reason was making sure that any upcoming battle with the Indians was going to be a 7th Cavalry show.

However, the conference was not without tangible results. On the morning of the day after the conference—that is June 22, the day of Custer's departure with his regiment— Terry sent this written order to Custer. It is reproduced in full because of its significance to what followed in the next three days:

> Camp at Mouth of Rosebud River,
> Montana Territory,
> June 22d, 1876
>
> Lieutenant-Colonel Custer,
> 7th Cavalry.

Colonel:

The Brigadier-General Commanding directs that, as soon as your regiment can be made ready for the march, you will proceed up the Rosebud in pursuit of the Indians whose trail was discovered by Major Reno a few days since. It is, of course, impossible to give you any definite instructions in regard to this movement, and were it not impossible to do so the Department Commander places too much confidence in your zeal, energy, and ability to wish to impose upon you precise orders which might hamper your action when nearly in contact with the enemy. He will, however, indicate to you his own views of what your action should be, and he desires that you should conform to them unless you shall see sufficient reasons for departing from them. He thinks that you should proceed up the Rosebud until you ascertain definitely the direction in which the trail above spoken of leads. Should it be found (as it appears almost certain that it will be found) to turn towards the Little Horn, he thinks that you should still proceed southward, perhaps as far as the headwaters of the Tongue, and then turn towards the Little Horn, feeling constantly, however, to your left, so as to preclude the possibility of the escape of the Indians to the south or southeast by passing around your left flank. The column of Colonel Gibbon is now in motion for the mouth of the Big Horn. As soon as it reaches that point it will cross the Yellowstone and move up at least as far as the forks of the Big and Little Horns. Of course its future movements must be con-

trolled by circumstances as they arise, but it is hoped that the
Indians, if upon the Little Horn, may be so nearly inclosed by
the two columns that their escape will be impossible.

The Department Commander desires that on your way up
the Rosebud you should thoroughly examine the upper part
of Tulloch's Creek, and that you should endeavor to send a
scout through to Colonel Gibbon's column, with information of
the result of your examination. The lower part of this creek
will be examined by a detachment from Colonel Gibbon's command. The supply steamer will be pushed up the Big Horn as
far as the forks if the river is found to be navigable for that
distance, and the Department Commander, who will accompany the column of Colonel Gibbon, desires you to report to
him there no later than the expiration of the time for which
your troops are rationed, unless in the meantime you receive
further orders.

> Very respectfully, your obedient servant,
> E. W. Smith
> Captain 18th Infantry
> Acting Assistant Adjutant General

Much discussion—scholarly or otherwise—has arisen from
interpretations of this order. Custerphobes say it was a set of
orders which was subsequently disobeyed. Custerphiles maintain that the document was a "letter of instructions" and, as
such, left much open to Custer's discretion. I see nothing to
be gained by traipsing through this vale of disputation in the
company of learned men who never had to write, receive, or
execute an order in the field. *It seems to me that since Custer
himself referred to the communication as an order,[3] that it was delivered to him over the signature of Terry's adjutant, and that the
recipient knew it to be genuine, how could he have regarded it as
anything but an order confirming in writing what had been gone
over verbally at the conference the day before?* Perhaps I wallow
in ignorance, but I have never heard of a commander who
had his adjutant or adjutant-general draw up a set of billets-
doux, kindly hints, gentle suggestions, or persuasions to a
subordinate commander who was getting set to carry out a
combat mission just assigned.

At noon on the day that he pocketed Terry's order, Custer stood with Terry and Gibbon as the 7th passed in review.
Men and officers were in high spirits and it showed as the
long ranks swept by while the band played "Garry Owen."
After the twelve companies had cleared the parade ground

and wheeled into a column of fours Custer turned to shake hands with the others before mounting up. As he rode off to take his place at the head of the column, Terry called after him, "God bless you!" Gibbon added his shout, "Now, Custer, don't be greedy! Wait for us!"

Custer turned in the saddle and answered over his shoulder, "No, I will not!", and rode away. Which of Gibbon's exhortations Custer was answering we will never know, but it is fascinating to conjecture what he had in mind if he had been answering the latter.

If officers and troopers had been in high spirits at the review, they were soon to find that they would have need of them in the forced march coming up. As it turned out, the first leg of the march was the easiest, but things were going to get tough and tougher as time and dusty miles would tell. Custer led the regiment up Rosebud Creek preceded by two groups of Arikara scouts who scouted each side of the creek far in advance of the command. Ahead of those scouts rode Mitch Bouyer and six Crows who knew the area. Bouyer was a half-breed with a deserved reputation for being one of the best in his business.

The regiment was halted at 4:00 P.M. after covering some sixteen miles, an easy half-day's march. The early halt was largely caused by the necessity to close up the pack train, whose mules were straggling into camp as late as sunset. At that time Custer held an officers' call, the accounts of which have aroused a great deal of speculation because of its unusual nature and the fact it was called at all. Custer normally kept counsel to himself and gave orders only when he felt it necessary. Now he was to take his officers into his confidence while making an obvious effort to win theirs—both uncharacteristic actions of their dashing and self-confident leader. After covering such details as march stages—he said easy ones of twenty-five to thirty-five miles a day—he surprised the gathering with a detailed rationalization of his rejections of the offered Gatling guns and Major Brisbin's battalion. It soon became obvious that this confiding in his officers—so unlike him—was intended, at least in part, to indicate that he was looking for a quick and brilliant victory, an action whose success would wipe out the cloud that had hovered over him after the temporary loss of his regimental command when Grant replaced him with Terry as expedition commander. Custer ended with an appeal for cooperation and loyalty, for he intended to track down the Indians if it meant following them as far as their agencies in Nebraska or on the Missouri River, distances far in excess of the time for which the regiment was rationed. After the council broke up and officers were returning to their duties, Lieutenants McIntosh, Wallace, and Godfrey were walking toward their bivouacs, in silence for some time. Then Wallace spoke out.

"Godfrey, I believe General Custer is going to be killed."

"Why, Wallace," Godfrey said, "what makes you think so?"

"Because I have never heard Custer talk in that way before."

Later Godfrey went on his rounds before turning in and came across Mitch Bouyer, who at the request of Half Yellow Face, asked Godfrey if he had fought the Sioux and how many hostiles the regiment expected to catch up with. Godfrey replied that he had fought Sioux and that he guessed the Indians could number as many as a thousand to fifteen hundred.

"Can the regiment handle that many?" Bouyer asked.

"Oh yes, I guess so," Godfrey replied.

After interpreting the lieutenant's answer in sign language, Bouyer turned back to Godfrey.

"Well," Bouyer said, "I can tell you we are going to have a damned big fight."

Before we leave the regiment bedded down in bivouac, one statement made by Custer at his officers' call deserves attention: "I intend to follow the trail until we get the Indians even if it takes us to the Missouri River or Nebraska agencies." This statement should be compared with the last sentence of General Terry's order: . . . "and the Department Commander, who will accompany the column of Colonel Gibbon, desires *you report to him there no later than the expiration of the time for which your troops are rationed,** unless in the meantime you receive further orders."

If Custer told his officers—as the accounts show—that they could be out after the Indians for a great deal longer time than that for which they were rationed, is that obeying the letter or the spirit of Terry's orders?

The next morning at five o'clock (June 23) Custer mounted up and led the regiment out, his old dashing self, trailed by two color-sergeants, one carrying the regimental

*Italics added.

standard, the other bearing the same headquarters flag that had been Major-General Custer's when commanding his cavalry division during the Civil War. This vain display might have gotten by on a parade ground but was a little out of place for a march or campaign, especially when Lieutenant-Colonel Custer no longer rated a major-general's personal flag. But unlike his conduct at the previous evening's officers' call this was all part of the man's make-up and, as such, accepted by the cavalrymen as matter-of-factly as the morning's sunrise. The column pushed on up the Rosebud where the bluffs rose higher and steeper and where the trail crossed the stream as often, in one leg of the march, as five times in three miles. Five miles out of bivouac the scouts picked up Reno's old trail and, in another three miles, the signs of the large Indian camp reported by Reno.

Three times during the day the column passed old Indian camp grounds and halts were made at each. There were all sorts of speculation about the signs and how old they were, but it appears that none of the Indian scouts was called in to pass on these important matters. As the column wound its way past the bluffs and around ravines, the Indian trail that Custer was following became more heavily marked, out to a width of about 300 yards. The scouts interpreted this one trail as being made by 1,500 lodges indicating a population supporting at least 3,000 warriors. Custer apparently was not impressed with this widening trail because he persisted in believing that it had been made by the same tribal village making successive camps rather than a growing number of groups funneling into a march toward an assembly area.

In all, the regiment made a good thirty-three miles on its second day's march and went into camp around four-thirty in the afternoon.

The following morning (June 24) Custer again led the regiment out at five o'clock, and an hour later the Crow scouts, who had been out for several hours, reported fresh signs of movements by the Sioux. At the time of the report the column was passing through the site of a great Indian village with sure signs that the camps had been arranged in circles. In spite of the fact that these were obviously camps of a number of tribes and the signs all of the same age the cavalry officers were not impressed. In fact, there was such a puzzling naivete among those experienced officers that the great number of wickiups (bushes stuck in the ground with the tops bent in to support covers made by blankets) were taken to be shelters for dogs. Any scout could have told them that they were shelters for transients and not for dogs, which Indians traditionally left to fend for themselves. But it seems that the scouts were not consulted, and as far as Indian numbers were concerned the officers clung to their belief in the earlier estimates that they would not encounter over eight hundred warriors.

That afternoon the regiment ran across another large trail coming up from the south to join the one being followed. The joined trails showed every indication that even a recruit could have read—hoof and travois marks scratching deep runs in the softer ground and scads of pony droppings. All signs were clear: the 7th was catching up to the hostiles who could not be many miles ahead. About the time this evidence had become clear the white scout, George Herendeen, requested permission to ride back to Terry and make a report as had been directed (see the opening sentence of the last paragraph of Terry's order), but Custer did not grant the permission.

It should be noted that in the same sentence the order specified that "you [Custer] should thoroughly examine the upper part of Tulloch's Creek." By this time the command had passed the upper reaches of Tulloch's Creek *without any effort at making a reconnaissance of that area. Thus, in one afternoon, Custer had disregarded two specifications of Terry's order: no scout was sent to report as directed and no "examination" of Tulloch's Creek had been made.*

Yet before this day and the night that followed were over we will observe another departure from Terry's order that will make the two preceding deviations seem like mere "tut-tuts." After packing in another thirty miles the regiment went into camp about 8:00 P.M. In all, the 7th had now covered some seventy-five miles in fifty-six hours and its commander was well ahead of the schedule discussed in the conference on the *Far West.* Custer was re-earning an old sobriquet among the troopers, the "horse killer," but the worst was still to come. Custer had dispatched the Crow scouts to seek out the continuing direction of the great Indian trail. They reported back at 9:00 P.M. to state definitely that the trail had turned right (to the west) and crossed the divide which separates the valley of Rosebud Creek from the valley of the Little Bighorn. Custer was electrified and at once ordered a night march to begin in two hours, at 11:00 P.M. Then, having heard of the Crow's

Nest (a high, rounded hilltop on the crest of the divide from which an observer could see for miles up and down the Little Bighorn valley), he directed Lieutenant Varnum, the officer in charge of scouts, to take Bouyer and Charlie Reynolds, along with several Crow and Arikara scouts, to see if they could locate the Indian village by its campfires that night or by other sightings in the morning.

Having made those decisions and given the orders to carry them out, we see the stark evidence of the third—and by far the most fateful—disobedience of Terry's order which specified: "Should it [the Indian trail] be found . . . to turn towards the Little Horn, he [Terry] thinks that you should still proceed southward, perhaps as far as the headwaters of the Tongue, and then turn towards the Little Horn . . ."

At this juncture it has been conjectured (it remains conjecture) that since Custer had been aching for the opportunity to gain a glorious victory over the Sioux with the glory going to him and the 7th alone, he knew that to delay action would mean having to share the credit with Terry and Gibbon. Additionally, it has been suggested that if he continued on to the south he might encounter General Crook and be absorbed into his command to become a mere subordinate commander who would not get the credit for the larger force's victory (Custer, as well as Terry and Gibbon, did not know of Crook's check and retreat after the Battle of the Rosebud on June 17).

Whatever his motives, Custer's plan went into execution late that night. The night march, with fatigued horses and riders, made excruciatingly slow headway up a little tributary of the Rosebud. It was pitch dark, so black that the troopers had to maintain contact in file by clanging messkits or banging tin cups on their saddles. Needless to say, the resulting uproar would have sounded to a hostile scout like the advance of an army. After about six miles had been crossed in this Laurel-and-Hardy fashion the command was halted at about 2:00 A.M. While the regiment got an uneasy rest for a couple of hours, Custer was able to check out more details with some scouts regarding the hostile strength. Fred Girard, a white scout, told him that the consensus of the scouts was that the number of warriors somewhere in the Little Bighorn valley would total at least 2,500.

At dawn the scouts on the Crow's Nest saw what was to them conclusive evidence of an immense Indian village. Although details could not be seen at the estimated distance of fifteen miles, two things were cited as proof: the smoky haze from innumerable campfires and the movements of a pony herd, described by Charlie Reynolds as "the biggest pony herd any man ever saw." He was seconded by Mitch Bouyer who added, "Biggest village. A heap too big." Lieutenant Varnum's tired eyes could not make out the sightings, but he knew his experienced scouts and trusted them enough to send a messenger to Custer with the news.

At 8:45 on Sunday morning, June 25, Custer again led the regiment forward. After about four miles he halted it and rode on to the Crow's Nest. He spent some time observing the area, but stated flatly that he could not see the scouts' signs of the village. It has been pointed out by Dr. Hofling in *Custer and the Little Big Horn* that it *was* possible that Custer did not see the indications "for conditions had changed. The scouts had made their observations in the early morning, when the earth was not warmed by the sun. Now, at 10:30 or so, there was a shimmering haze over the valley. [But] Bouyer assured him that the village was the largest ever seen on the plains."[4]

There were other reports when Custer returned to the regiment. Two small war parties, sighted at some distance, had seen the regiment and ridden away toward the village. Herendeen reported seeing a warrior only hundreds of yards away who was obviously scouting the regiment. Then a sergeant from F Company and two men had ridden back to search for missing provisions and had found a warrior helping himself to hardtack. The hostile brave mounted up and took off when he sighted the soldiers. By now it should have been clear to the officers as well as the scouts that the Indian village would soon know of the regiment's location and its approach march.

At an officers' call following his return from the Crow's Nest, Custer told the assembly that the regiment must attack now or the Indians would escape. This was not a piece of advice, it was a tactical decision followed by orders. Custer's decision to move at once into an attack has been criticized— not without reason—as the error from which all that followed that day could be traced. From a purely tactical viewpoint, the criticism seems justified. The time for the 7th to exploit surprise had passed, hence an all out attack held no promise of overrunning the Indian camp as the 7th had done in the Battle of the Washita. Thus, sound tactical sense would have held that the regiment be kept under tight central control until the enemy strength and dispositions were clarified and, if indicated, a new course of action could be adopted.

There is the reverse side of the coin: what was known to Custer at the time and what were the influences operating on him? First, he knew that he had lost the chance of surprise, but he also knew—in his sublime confidence in his regiment and himself—that no body of Indians could stand up to a charge of the 7th Cavalry. Further, in spite of his intelligence of the Indian trail signs and scout reports, he knew that a large Indian encampment could be scattered as easily as a small one. That is probably why he sent his scouts on ahead to stampede the pony herds. Without their horses the warriors would be easy prey for cavalry attacks on the village. Thus, Custer could have discounted large numbers of Indians due to overconfidence. Finally, Custer might well have been a man whose mind was not functioning clearly because of the strain he was under. His military career had been under a cloud ever since he had incurred the President's wrath, and now was perhaps his last chance to redeem himself with a resounding victory. On the other hand, if he let the Sioux escape, that failure would end his military career, and he knew of no other future for him.

Sound or not, the decision was made to attack and that decision was to form the base for all the actions that followed.

After ordering the scouts to attack the pony herds Custer took measures to assure the security of the pack train. Captain McDougall's B Company was assigned the task and it was reinforced by seven men from each of the other companies. Altogether the pack train guard totaled 130 men, a fifth of the regiment's strength.

At noon on June 25 Custer led the regiment over the divide and descended into the valley of the Little Bighorn. After moving less than a mile toward the mouth of Sundance Creek (now Reno Creek), Custer halted and gave the orders which divided the command into three battalions. Reno was given command of three companies (A, G, and M), and three others (H, D, and K) were placed under Benteen. The five remaining companies (C, E, F, I, and L) were retained under Custer's control.

Benteen was then detached with orders to move out to the left to cover the left flank (after crossing the Little

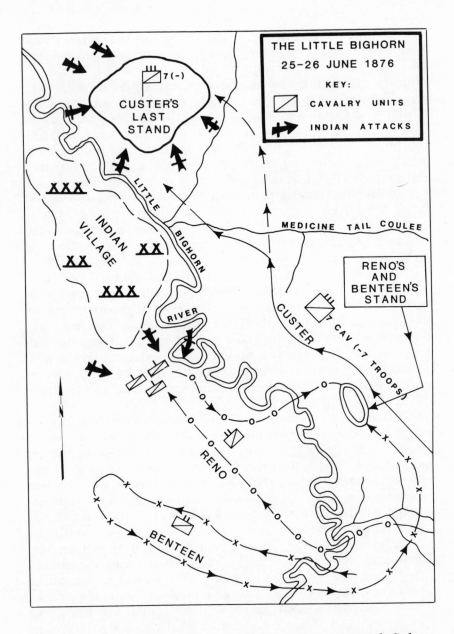

THE LITTLE BIGHORN
25–26 JUNE 1876

KEY:

CAVALRY UNITS

INDIAN ATTACKS

CUSTER'S LAST STAND

7 (-)

XXX

INDIAN VILLAGE

XX

XX

XXX

LITTLE BIGHORN

RIVER

MEDICINE TAIL COULEE

RENO'S AND BENTEEN'S STAND

7 CAV (-7 TROOPS)

CUSTER

RENO

BENTEEN

N

Bighorn) and to "pitch into" any Indians encountered. Subsequently orders were sent to Benteen by courier to reconnoiter as far as the second line of bluffs (to the west), and if no Indians were found "to go into the valley."

Meanwhile Reno's command was to remain with the regiment and, as it developed, Reno would receive further orders.

The division of the command into four parts, including the pack train, was, of course, the first result of the decision to attack. From this point on, all maneuver of the regiment would have to depend on this organization for combat—right or wrong, sound or unsound. In this kind of fluid situation there could be no "point of return."

By 12:15 Benteen's battalion was out of sight of the main column, which continued to march roughly northward and parallel to the river. When the valley widened Reno crossed to the west side of the stream and his column moved parallel with Custer's and abreast of it. The two columns continued to move in this manner until Custer motioned Reno to cross back and move on alongside his column.

They made a temporary halt at a point which has been known as the Lone Warrior Tepee. Custer and Reno could now see several miles into the valley, though the great village was still obscured by hills and tree lines. About this time Fred Girard rode up and shouted, "There go your Indians, running like devils!" What he was reporting was his sighting of a group of about forty warriors riding away to the north on the near (east) side of the river. Whether this sighting was confused with a dust cloud that had been raised in the direction which Custer and Reno had been observing (up the west side of the river where the Indian village was supposed to be) is not clear. In any event Custer's officers, apparently infused with Custer's *idée fixe* of preventing the escape of the village, were enthusiastic at the prospect of action. Custer evidently decided to speed up his attack even if the rest of his command had not come up.

His first order was that the scouts pursue the hostiles in the direction of the dust cloud. They refused to go, apparently convinced of the vast numbers of the Sioux. Custer derided them for cowardice, "If any man of you is not brave, I will take away his weapons and make a woman of him." There were replies in sign language but no movement, so Custer decided to send Reno to attack with his battalion in the direction of the dust cloud and, it was hoped, the village. There was disagreement over the wording of the verbal order and how it was delivered—by Custer or by Lieutenant Cooke, his adjutant—but Reno was ordered, in effect, to "pursue and charge the Indians where you find them, *and you will be supported by the whole outfit.*"*

This order was given about 2:15 and Reno moved across the river at a ford, accompanied by about twenty scouts. He trotted forward about three miles until what had begun as a kind of fox hunt turned into a real fight.

Reno, spurring forward into what he thought was the pursuit of warriors retreating toward their village, was accompanied for a short while by Capt. Myles Keogh, one of Custer's company commanders, and Lieutenant Cooke. They had neither the authority nor sound reason for attaching themselves to Reno's command and, as it has been pointed out, it would have been better for Custer and all concerned if they had stayed with Custer the whole time. The two watched Reno's spirited advance long enough to see that all was going well, then rode back to Custer to report that "fact," a perfectly true report for what little they had seen. But they had not stuck around long enough to see what really happened, a common enough occurrence in anyone's war. With that message reinforcing his made-up mind, Custer cantered his column on northward, following the river's course but out of sight of it at times due to the line of bluffs fronting the river.

Reno had meanwhile sent a trooper with a message to Custer that he had the enemy in front of them in great strength. In continuing his advance Reno deployed his three companies with two in line followed by the third in reserve. Soon he found that he was not pursuing a dust cloud, and that, if anything, the cloud was coming at his pounding troopers. Then everything seemed to happen at once. Reno's scouts disappeared from his left flank (it has been said they left to carry out their role of stampeding the enemy's horses) leaving it unprotected. Then hordes of hostiles began to appear on his left flank and rear. Reno lost the initiative. Although no losses had been suffered and his men were within a few hundred yards of the village, Reno dismounted his men into a skirmish line and sent the horse-holders, each with his four, to a wooded bend in the river to the right rear. In about twenty minutes the dismounted line began to disintegrate and Reno let it withdraw to the "shelter" of the wooded bend. At this time, unbelievable as it seems, Reno's command had lost only two or three men killed in spite of the exchange of fire

*Italics added.

between the two sides. As the line fell back the swarms of Indians were reinforced from the village until an estimated five hundred warriors were circling around the dismounted cavalrymen. The Indian tactics, to say the least, were more adapted to the situation than Reno's. They circled at a trot or gallop outside and inside carbine range seeking their chance to pounce. When that chance came, its effects were incredible.

Reno's command, properly organized and with good fire discipline, could have held out for hours. But the fire control and organization of the position never developed. The uncontrolled expenditure of ammunition began to tell while the Indians were beginning to close in from several directions, finally to infiltrate the woods from the east bank of the river. Reno, seeing that his right could be turned and the men cut off from their horses, considered a retreat. He decided on it and gave the order to mount. There was no bugle call and some troopers got the word only when they saw others running for their horses. A great deal of what has been called "disorder" ensued, and the situation increasingly resembled that well-known maneuver known as "getting the hell out of there." Reno has been called a coward for this action, but there are a good many things to be said on each side of the charge. One thing, however, is certain: what may have begun as an orderly withdrawal turned into a mounted rout. While the troops were starting to form to mount up, a party of Sioux broke into the timber and poured a volley into the cavalrymen at point-blank range. Troopers were hit, and the scout Bloody Knife was struck by a bullet between the eyes, splattering blood and brains in Reno's face. This may have unnerved Reno, who led the mounted troops out of the woods in a beeline for the ford on the east side, leaving behind two lieutenants and about fifteen unwounded men. As the troops started out in a column of fours the Indians fell back in surprise, thinking they were being counterattacked. They quickly recovered and began pouring their fire into the flanks of the column. This became an ordeal by fire as the troopers became fugitives trying to gallop away from the screaming warriors, who soon made a gauntlet out of the rout. Here Reno's command suffered its real losses, a common occurrence in rout and pursuit. Reno had not made any attempt to cover the withdrawal which became a desperate run for the ford. The bulk of the panicked cavalrymen made it across the ford and up the steep bluff beyond to the heights now known as Reno Hill. The Sioux, for reasons not known, did not pursue across the river, and Reno's exhausted troopers were allowed to collapse on the hilltop at about 4:00 P.M.

There may be argument, pro and con, ad nauseam, about the alleged incompetent employment of Reno's command and his "panicking" at critical turns in his battle, *but what deserves consideration is Custer's failure to support Reno in some manner or to withdraw him to the east side of the river before he (Reno) got too involved.* Instead of consigning Reno's command to an indeterminate future, why didn't Custer at least establish observation posts with couriers to keep him informed about Reno's attack? And the story about Custer appearing on a height across the river and waving his hat at Reno to signal him forward in his attack can be dismissed as pure drivel. For a commander to wave his hat, from a bluff a mile or more away, at a battalion commander who is in the act of leading a cavalry attack which is kicking up clouds of dust, is—to put it mildly—stretching one's imagination. *The question remains unanswered: why did not Custer support Reno as he had promised?*

While Reno was fighting his battle and leading his disastrous retreat, Custer was leading his five companies into epic and legend. There are so many unknowns, so many variables, about the route he took and the orders he may or may not have given that it is purely daunting to try to reconstruct the details of Custer's advance and subsequent actions. It can be worse than daunting; it may be so far off target as to be criminally misleading. Let us, then, stick to the *events that had to have happened.*

Custer and his five companies covered about twelve miles, after splitting away from Reno, before coming opposite the Indian village across the river. What followed has been put succinctly by Marshall: "What we know for certain is that Custer charged deliberately into a neatly rigged trap, though it is likely that the trap came about empirically rather than through preconceived design, there being no centralized Indian leadership."[5] What is not so certain is Marshall's assumption that Custer ran into an ambush in the shape of an inverted L and that the Indians set up a blocking force to prevent him entering the lower (northern) end of the village.

It would appear that Custer's strung-out force was stopped by fire from the front and quickly attacked from west, north, and east until the five companies were nearly encircled. Then a band of Sioux charged the rear companies, already dismounted, and completed the encirclement. The Indian strength has been estimated at anywhere from 1,800 to 9,000, but 3,000 seems to be a reasonable figure in the lower range. If that is so, Custer's force was fighting against 13-to-1 odds, giving the Indians somewhat of an edge.

The return fire from the troopers of the rearward companies was heavy enough at first to check the Sioux attack from the south. There was a rush from the cavalrymen down the ravines toward the river, which was then checked in its turn by fire from dismounted Indians. The soldiers then withdrew, backing up the hill. Jack Red Cloud, son of Chief Red Cloud, has given a typical Indian account of that action and the final phase of Custer's stand: "The Sioux kept circling around Custer and as his men came down the ridge we shot them. Then the rest dismounted and gathered in a bunch, kneeling down and shooting from behind their horses."[6] The "bunch" was probably the true Last Stand, the site now marked by the enclosed headstones at Custer Battlefield National Monument.

The duration of the action, measured from the encirclement until its tragic end, has been estimated variously at from forty minutes to two hours. If the latter period is accepted, the fight was over by 5:30, which would have been before Reno started to move toward the scene. Whenever the end came, the Sioux overran the field, killing every soldier who showed signs of life. Then the bodies were stripped and the uniforms thrown into a pile which was set afire while the Sioux did a war dance around the flames. About 225 soldiers and a few civilians died. One must say "about" 225 because of the army's sloppy record-keeping.

Custer's body was stripped but unmarred, unlike the others which were scalped or mutilated in other ways. He could have died from either of two bullet wounds, one in the left breast, the other in the head. It has been said that the Sioux did not mutilate Custer's body because they respected his qualities as a warrior. That assertion has been contradicted by the claim that the Indians would not have recognized Custer because "Yellow Hair," as they called him, had his long locks cut short early in the campaign.

This brief venture into the Custer myth and its attendant controversy has been far from a joyful task, and I wish to step outside the circle of controversy when I say that I am convinced that Custer died a hero's death. If I could leave my own version of an epitaph it would be to use these two lines of Shakespeare's:

> Nothing in his life
> Became him like the leaving it

It may seem anticlimatical to add the account of Reno and Benteen, but it should be briefly told so that one can try to keep the whole picture in perspective.

First Benteen. His reconnaissance produced only negative intelligence; not an Indian had been encountered. Some time after he had come back to the main trail (about 2:20 P.M.) Benteen met a galloping courier, Sgt. Daniel Kanipe, bearing a verbal message to McDougall, the commander of the pack train. Kanipe wanted to give his message to Benteen, a not-unnatural tendency of couriers in battle situations, but Benteen sent him on to McDougall to deliver the word to "rush the train forward."

In less than a quarter of an hour, when his column had reached a spot about a mile south of Reno Hill, Benteen was met by Trumpeter John Martin who handed the captain the scrawled (now famous) message:

> Benteen—
> Come on. Big village. Be quick
> bring packs.
> P.S. Bring pacs

Benteen read it and asked Martin, "Where's the general?" Martin answered that Custer had run across Indians in a ravine leading to the river. When queried about the Indians, Martin replied he thought they were "skedaddling." After consulting Captain Weir, commander of D Company, who had no comment, Benteen did not act on the order. Benteen may well have been puzzled by the message which must have referred to ammunition packs. He could see the pack train coming on, at its regular slow pace, about a mile behind him. He chose to ride on into the Little Bighorn valley where he could see to the north.

The first thing he saw was the small group of Reno's abandoned troopers on the opposite (west) side of the river, fighting a dismounted action against a mass of Indians. He next saw several Arikara scouts leading some captured horses. They informed Benteen that the bulk of Reno's command was on a hill to the right. Benteen led his column up the hill to meet a distraught Reno.

"For God's sake, Benteen, halt your command and help me. I've lost half my men." By actual count he had lost 3 officers and 40 men, and had with him about 105 effectives. Benteen asked where Custer was, and Reno told him that Custer had gone northward (downstream) with five companies and he had had no word from him.

Benteen had his men divide their ammunition with Reno's, so that every soldier ended up with more than half his regular load. In looking around for the enemy, all that could be seen were a few scattered warriors over a thousand yards away. The united commands were now in no immediate danger, so what followed is difficult to understand. There were reports of firing downstream, yet neither moved to take any action. *Benteen's failure to act is the more remarkable for three reasons.* He was the dominant, unshaken personality. His command was intact and his horses recently watered. And, most important, he had Custer's written order to come forward. *What he did do was to place himself under Major Reno's command.* The latter, though scared and shaken, still had two-thirds of his command, now reinforced by Benteen's battalion. He had fought through the Civil War and had seen heavy fighting. *Yet he too stayed put.*

Two hours before, Captain Weir had asked Reno's permission to move forward, but he was refused. Sometime short of 5:00 P.M. Weir repeated his request, and was again refused. Weir decided to have a look for himself and rode northward. He was followed by his company (D) which was temporarily under command of Lieutenant Edgerly, who mistakenly thought that Weir had been given permission to move the company. They moved about a mile and a half to a promontory (now Weir's Point) where there was a view of the battlefield about two miles to the north. A heavy cloud of dust and smoke cut off most of Weir's vision but he could see Indians riding around and shooting into the ground. At about 5:30, Weir's company closed on the hilltop and, at about the same time, the pack train started arriving on Reno Hill.

Reno delayed his advance until a little after 6:00 P.M., then moved the command to join Weir's company. No sooner had the command closed around Weir Point than masses of

Indians were seen advancing toward them. By now all sounds of firing from the north had ceased, but the air in the battlefield area was still filled with dust and smoke. After a hasty consultation, Reno and Benteen decided that Reno Hill was, for several reasons, the more defensible position, so the command withdrew to that hill and set up its defensive perimeter.

The saucer-shaped top of the hill afforded a central area in which the wounded and the pack mules and their burdens could be placed. The Indians began an all-around series of attacks that lasted for three hours until dark. The command held out against ferocious attacks by Sioux who were burning with their triumphs over Custer and over Reno in his first battle. In this period, eighteen soldiers were killed and forty-six wounded. With nightfall came blessed relief. Most of the Sioux withdrew to their village to celebrate with feasting and dancing. But rest was denied the soldiers on the hill until rifle pits were started—there were few tools and many had to resort to messkits, spoons, and knives—redeployments made, and pickets posted.

At dawn the returning Indians renewed their attacks, but the command held its own until mid-afternoon when the hostiles started withdrawing. Later in the afternoon, the whole Indian village could be seen moving up the valley. Not until the command was relieved on the morning of June 27 by Terry and Gibbon was it learned that the Sioux had moved southward toward the Bighorn Mountains because of the advance of the Terry-Gibbon columns.

Let us review our goals. First, we stand to lose perspective if we proceed down the narrow alley of: "what did Custer do wrong and what should he have done?" Instead, our goals are to see where the leaders' (Custer, Reno, Benteen) judgment can be evaluated *and* what may be learned from it.

Secondly, it would also be beneficial to rid ourselves of another fallacy—that the Little Bighorn stands out as a series of glaring errors. The same thing may be said of the battle as J. F. C. Fuller said of Waterloo: "It has been so thoroughly investigated and criticized that the errors committed in it are apt to appear exceptional and glaring."[7]

If we peer through the fog of war—which has only partially cleared—we can find a number of key questions that should lead to useful answers. That number, however, can be reduced from a baker's dozen to four main "judgment points."

Why did Custer decide to attack when surprise was lost and the size of the Indian village was apparently not clear to him?

Why did Custer divide his regiment into four groupings in order to execute his attack?

Why did not Custer keep his "promise" to Reno?

Why did Reno and Benteen fail to move to Custer's support?

Regarding Custer's decision to attack, it has been pointed out that the decision formed the basis of all that followed. Tactically it seems to have been unsound, but extenuating circumstances, mostly bad for Custer, must have influenced his thinking and judging of the situation. As for his judging the size of the village (and the number of warriors it would support), if Custer chose not to accept at face value the scouts' estimates he may be said to have been making his own intelligence estimate of the situation. And when he spent a reasonable amount of time at the Crow's Nest trying to confirm—it has been said that he used his field glasses—the scouts' sightings of an immense village and pony herds, he probably did not see anything. Whether this was due to atmospheric conditions, we may never know. Then too, it should be remembered that Lieutenant Varnum also failed to see anything, and he was looking (through tired eyes?) at the same time the scouts were making their observations.

The question of dividing his command has occasioned more criticism than any other action Custer took before and during the battle. It is easy to say, because it *is* a valid criticism, that Custer should have kept the regiment grouped under his centralized control until the valley of the Little Bighorn had been adequately reconnoitered. Granted; but may he have been thinking that he was doing that initially when he kept Reno's battalion with the rest of the regiment? It will be recalled that Custer kept Reno's command moving parallel to his own for quite some time, and, in the meantime, he detached Benteen (with roughly a fourth of his command) to make a reconnaissance to the west while simultaneously protecting the regiment's left flank. Only when Custer ordered Reno to split away and attack northward did he make the final, fatal division of the regiment. When that commitment had been made, the clearest course of action was to follow and support Reno, which brings us to the question of Custer's promise "that the rest of the outfit will support you."

Everything hinges on the words "promise" and "support." There has been much fuzzy thinking in regard to the meaning of the latter at this point in the action—regrettably even among military critics who should know better. Support does not necessarily mean that one part of a command will come to the aid of another by physically placing itself alongside or behind the supported unit. It can mean that a supporting unit will maneuver or engage the enemy in a manner that will relieve enemy pressure on the supported unit so that it can accomplish its mission. Custer may well have believed that if he could maneuver so as to attack the Indian village from the east or north he would not only destroy the village and the Indian force in it but also would, by so doing, come to Reno's support. Consequently, as it has been observed, it is possible that Custer rode to his death thinking that he was on his way to keeping his promise.

Lastly, there is the matter of the failure of both Reno and Benteen to move northward in support of Custer after Reno had retreated to his hill and had been united with Benteen. It has been noted that Reno's command, following its disastrous retreat through the woods and across the river, collapsed on the hilltop exhausted and ineffective for further combat. This was no doubt true, but the question arises: How long would it have taken to get Reno's shaken command reorganized and back into shape as a fighting force? Reno and Benteen were united some time around 4:00 P.M., but it was not until after 6:00 P.M. that the two battalions, now nominally under Reno's command, moved out toward Weir Point. That allows two hours during which there was more than enough time to reorganize, reissue ammunition—which was done—and prepare to move out northward. Yet, as we have seen, Reno and Benteen did nothing about moving out. Reno had six companies in the united command (before the pack train's reinforced company arrived between 5:30 and 6:00 P.M.), or half the regiment, which was a force numerically stronger than Custer's, yet both leaders chose to remain inactive.

If one acknowledges that Reno was a badly shaken man whose combat effectiveness was questionable after his disaster, then what about Benteen? The latter has been described as cool and courageous throughout the day as well as being the dominant personality in the united command, so this leads to other questions about his judgment. Benteen was handed Lieutenant Cooke's message (actually an order from Custer over his adjutant's signature) by Trumpeter Martin about 3:00 P.M. (Benteen's time as given at Reno's court of inquiry), and had it in his possession for the rest of the time. So one may wonder why Benteen did not take one of two courses of action. He could have shown the order to Reno to emphasize a recommendation that Reno lead the command forward. Or, if it is accepted that Reno's original command was so exhausted that it could not be restored to combat effectiveness, why could not Benteen have taken it on himself to move out with his three companies? This would not have been an act of insubordination in the sense of leaving Reno even without his permission, for Benteen had his regimental commander's written order to "come on—be quick," which was still in effect.

Despite all the investigations, inquiries, and analyses, these three figures, Custer, Reno, and Benteen, seem to remain enigmatic at this distance of over a hundred years. Are there really critical points where their respective judgments can be questioned? What do you think?

Part Four

PRESENCE

Lannes at
Ratisbon, 1809

Brazenose at
Lungtungpen, 1899

PRESENCE

You know we French stormed Ratisbon
   A mile or so away
On a little mound, Napoleon
   Stood on our storming-day;
      . . . . . .
      My plans
   That soar, to earth may fall,
Let once my army-leader Lannes
   Waver at yonder wall,—
          —Browning, *Incident of the French Camp*

In April, 1967, an action officer in the Office of the Chief of Staff of the Army was handed the four volumes that were the final product of the *ARC Study: Art and Requirements of Command*. Although the study raised no great waves of action or reaction at the time, it did in its quiet way represent a leap of the imagination in exploiting a wide and deep reservoir of leadership experience. For the first time in our military history an incisive effort had been made to learn firsthand from the commanders themselves the lessons they had learned the hard way in the hard ways of war. The study was launched "on the premise that high-level tactical command . . . is a highly personalized art as well as a clearly defined professional discipline." And though its immediate goals were "directed toward identifying and analyzing the command-control support requirements of senior commanders,"[1] it affords a once-in-a-lifetime opportunity for us, as observers of the leader's art, to gain unobscured insight into the attribute of presence.

Volume II of the study—"Generalship"—represents the firsthand findings from experience that are its major and most valuable product. The basis for this effort was a detailed questionnaire which was returned by more than eighty respondents. The number seems of no significance when considered by itself, but what is remarkable is the fact that every one of those queried had held long and high-level tactical command in World War II; high-level meaning command of an army, corps, division, or regiment. Question 4.5 is of particular interest, not only for its subject, but for the consensus of the responses: "In this step [the following-up by the commander of his own orders], how important was face-to-face contact with subordinates?"[2]

238

To Rally

THE CONSENSUS WAS "all-important." But of particular value are these typical comments:

"Most important especially when [a] unit had been having tough going."

"I regard it as vital."

"Absolutely, Number 1."

"The most important factor of all."

"Most important. Spreads confidence."

"Invaluable."

"Essential to highest morale and confidence."[3]

Since these combat commanders were all of one mind in regard to the matter of physical presence, just why did they consider that an indispensable attribute? The answer, in terms of common sense as well as the findings of the study, is that *presence* was the only wholly reliable way that the commander could assure himself that his orders were being carried out in an effective and timely manner.

In fairness to the reader I should point out that the responding leaders considered the use of presence as a matter of routine, as well as a means of handling "emergencies."

We are concerned in this book with emergencies and not with matters of routine. Upon examination, in the former there are two ways in which the leader's use of presence can bring events under his control: to rally and to inspire. What does

239

the term "to rally" mean in this context? Simply defined it means *that the leader uses personal example and force of character to bring order out of potential chaos during a critical turn of events;* further, he uses them *as a means of assuring that the rallied unit will go on to accomplish its mission.* Admittedly, defining "rallying" is a simple matter, but doing it under the stress of battle is not so simple a thing.

In our next case we will see a leader in the act of rallying units whose morale was on the verge of being shattered; had that morale collapsed the mission of an army would have been jeopardized.

There are two major characters in the action, and events will unfold through their eyes. First, Marshal Jean Lannes, Napoleon's great advance guard leader whose skill and dash assured French victories in such campaigns as Marengo, Jena, and Friedland. The other, Marcellin de Marbot, at the time a captain of cavalry and veteran aide-de-camp to Lannes.

In great part we are indebted to Marbot's *Memoirs* for their wealth of detail and quality of "you-are-thereness." I go to the trouble of mentioning Marbot not only because of my debt to him, but also because he has been, on occasion, the butt of commentators who tend to dwell on his Gallic enthusiasm for embellishing exploits in which he played a part. However that may be, Marbot is a delight to read, and the incident which makes up the climax of the upcoming action is by no means Marbot's imagination at work. The story of the storming of Ratisbon—and our focus of interest on it—can be found in any authoritative source which goes into detail in the account of Napoleonic battles. Then too, Marbot's participation in the incident calls for a final caveat. If his actions appear to be excessive for those of an aide, one should realize that the duties of an aide to Napoleonic generals demanded much more than would be the case today. These handpicked officers were anything but glorified body-servants or brilliantly uniformed couriers. They were expected to carry their commander's orders—often verbal in the heat of battle—and once they were delivered, the aide would often remain to observe the orders being put into execution. He was further expected to return not only with the subordinate commander's reply but also with a detailed situation report for his chief. On occasion he could be directed to guide units into action or even lead them if the situation called for it. All this under extreme pressure and in constant danger.

Over the Wall and Through the Gate

In the dusk of the April day they had watched the leading
infantry battalions of Gudin's division halt in place to allow
the heavy cavalry of Nansouty's and St. Sulpice's brigades make
their passage of lines. The grateful infantry, exhausted after
hours of forced marches and a half-day slugging match with
the Austrians, sank to the ground where they had taken their
last steps, too tired even to curse the cuirassiers for raising
the dust as they passed, too tired to exchange the usual insults that were bantered back and forth whenever French
cavalry rode past French infantry. The big men on the tall
horses were tired, too, as were their mounts, and the squadrons moved at a walk even though they would be deploying
in minutes to attack the Austrian cavalry which had come forward to cover the retreat of their beaten infantry. In the fading twilight the steel cuirasses and helmets no longer flashed
as they had in the late afternoon sun, for their glitter had
been dulled by the dust which had settled over the once-
colorful columns. The dark blue sleeves of their under-
jackets now seemed a dull black, and the scarlet epaulets and
shoulder linings had turned a dusty maroon. The only
uniform fittings that had kept their luster were the long
black horsehair plumes of their steel helmets.

The weary infantrymen would not have looked up long
enough to share Captain Marbot's biased interest in the soldiers of his own arm, nor would his commander, Marshal
Lannes, spare the passing cavalry a glance. The commander
of the Provisional Corps had thirty thousand men of his own
who were his chief concern now as he strained his eyes to
study his map in the failing light. The marshal and his aide
had dismounted at the roadside long enough to spread the
map on the top of the rock wall that separated the orchard
from the dusty road, and Marbot's momentary distraction with
the cavalrymen had caused the marshal to look up at him
with one of his penetrating glances, this time one of irritation.

"Look here, Marbot, since you have given so greatly of
your attention to studying this map, be so kind as to inform
me of the distance from our location to the walls of Ratisbon," Lannes said.

Marbot did not need the Marshal's keen stare to tell him
he had put himself on the spot by being caught like a school-
boy staring out a classroom window. He had served on Lannes'

staff in Spain in enough campaigns to know how the quick-tempered "Roland of the French Army" could punish a wool-gathering aide. But Marbot's hussar's luck was working for him, and two things combined to save him. His quick memory told him that it was about fourteen kilometers from Alt Eg-glofsheim to the city, and the marshal had inadvertently kept the tip of his forefinger on the road junction a stone's throw from the orchard.

"I make it to be fifteen kilometers, *Monsieur le Maréchal*," Marbot answered without hesitation.

Lannes grunted, made a crumpled roll of the map, and thrust it into Marbot's hands.

"Here," he said, "have the staff mount up. We'll go forward far enough to get a look at what happens when these *grosse-bottes** meet their enemy."

"Yes Sir, but I thought you intended to go into Alt Eg-glofsheim to meet the Emperor," Marbot said.

"He'll not be there yet, and besides, how could I recommend continuing to advance my infantry until I know what happens to the Austrian cavalry who are covering the withdrawal of their infantry?"

Marbot started to suggest posting couriers to watch the cavalry action, but quickly closed his mouth with the realization that he was about to say a foolish thing. Would the finest advance guard commander in the *Grande Armée*—or in all Europe—be contented with receiving messages when he could be assessing the outcome of a combat for himself? He ran through the trees toward his horse, calling out to the others to mount up and follow.

The wall in front of the Bavarian farmhouse made an improvised gallery for Lannes and his staff to observe the deployment of the heavy cavalry. Junior aides and orderlies perched on the far reaches of the wall like farm boys at a fair, while the marshal and senior officers stood behind it and braced their elbows on the top ledge. Lannes handed his field glass back to Marbot, it was getting too dark to focus on any distant object. Already the twilight was being reinforced by the light of the rising moon, so that the deployed lines of horsemen could be seen as dark masses on the flat plain that stretched all the way to Ratisbon and the banks of the Danube. The green shoots of the young wheat and barley, now

---

*Literally "big boots," soldier slang for the heavy cavalry of the Guard or the cuirassiers.

only visible as a lighter-shadowed background, would soon be ground to a damp pulp under thousands of hooves.

"I see that our light cavalry has withdrawn to the flanks just in time. Safer there for hussars and chasseurs I suppose," Lannes said with a side glance at Marbot.

The aide had been through this chaffing too many times to take it in any way other than it was intended—the marshal's bluff way of showing his gentler side to his veteran staff officers. And when it was Marbot's turn it always took the form of an old infantryman bantering with a young cavalryman; it was an old game and the aide always played well his side of the court.

"Of course the marshal realizes that the flanks of our 'heavies' must be protected. As you see, the enemy's light cavalry is doing the same, so they must be countered," Marbot replied.

"Oh, of course, of course. But look now, don't I see the Austrian cuirassiers moving forward?" The marshal's tone was serious now, all business, as Marbot recognized.

"Yes, and General Nansouty's squadrons advance to meet them. St. Sulpice follows in support, his Bavarians on the right and Würtembergers on the left. What a sight it should have been, had we only some daylight left."

"But, my God, so slowly! Is this what Nansouty calls a cavalry charge?"

"Sir, the horses are too worn to work them up from a walk to a trot, then to a gallop. Unless I'm mistaken, Nansouty will be able to charge only at the trot."

Marbot was not mistaken. The shadowy massed lines of the French cuirassiers broke into a trot and smashed into their oncoming Austrian counterparts. The melee that followed was as eerie as it was majestic, as thousands of armored horsemen crashed into each other. The shouts of the cavalrymen were almost drowned by the ringing blows of sabers against steel helmets and cuirasses. The night was actually lighted at times by sparks flying from the clash of steel against steel. It soon became impossible for the observers to distinguish friend from foe as more lines of opposing squadrons charged into the fray. Now the plain seemed filled with rearing, whirling horsemen—demons' shadows in the dim half-light of the moon. But Lannes and the others could see that the rearmost squadrons of the French cavalry had come to a halt, standing fast, short of the melee.

"St. Sulpice is playing his game well. No need for him to

commit any of his brigade into that brawl, and he knows that some must be held back to pursue if Nansouty can win his battle," Lannes said.

"That must be it, Sir, and Nansouty's men have a double advantage over the Austrians in that action," Marbot said.

"Oh, and what do you find those to be?"

"Our heavies are better swordsmen and they have double cuirasses, front and back, while the Austrians are protected only in front."

"So you are saying that, in that hand-to-hand fighting, the advantage goes to him who can strike at the rear of his opponent when his back is exposed."

"Exactly, Sir. In that sort of a melee everyone is circling about trying to get in a killing stroke, and our troopers need not worry when their backs are exposed."

"Thank you, Marbot. It won't take long to see if you have sized up the situation accurately."

Marbot's words were proven sound for the second time that evening. Such a violent combat could be sustained for only a matter of minutes. In that short time French swordsmanship and complete armor did end the fight. The Austrians, realizing the heavy losses they were taking, pulled out of the battle, wheeled and tried to flee the field. Marbot's words about exposed Austrian backs came true with a vengeance, as he tells it in his *Memoirs*: "When they [the Austrians] had wheeled about, they understood still better what a disadvantage it is not to have a cuirass behind as well as in front. The flight became a butchery as our cuirassiers pursued the enemy, and for the space of half a league [a mile and a half] the ground was piled with killed and wounded cuirassiers."

The marshal stayed long enough to see St. Sulpice launch his brigade in pursuit of the broken Austrian cavalry, then, satisfied, he gave the order to his staff to mount up and follow him back to Alt Egglofsheim. As the group started to find its way down the moonlit road, Lannes summed it up as they rode.

"What we have seen is an omen, if not a beacon. If there are any unbroken Austrian battalions between us and Ratisbon they could be overrun in no time. If only the Emperor can be convinced of that we can have the Archduke Charles's army in our pocket."

His were words that could make up prophecies, yet it must be noted that his statements contained two significant "ifs."

Lannes was accompanied by Marbot and one other aide, the young De Viry, when he made his way toward the *Maison,* at the center of Imperial Headquarters. The three had left their horses with orderlies at the edge of the great encampment, and followed on foot after their guide, one of the senior aides-de-camp. They passed the circle of tents that housed Marshal Berthier's army staff, past sentries who snapped to Present Arms when they caught sight of the crossed batons on Lannes' gold-fringed epaulets, on to the huge tent with the green drapes that was the heart of the *Maison,* the Emperor's secretarial cabinet and personal staff.

Lannes quickened his step when he saw Marshal Masséna standing outside the front entrance to the anteroom. The two marshals greeted each other warmly, Masséna's dark eyes sparkling in his Italian face. He grasped both of Lannes' hands in his and gave a smiling nod to the two aides.

"Well, IVth Corps seems to be following you as usual, *mon cher* Jean, you who seem to make a profession of leading advance guards," Masséna said.

"I do as I'm told, like the rest of you, that's all," Lannes said with the quick grin that lighted his scarred face.

"And here comes our 'teller of what to do'—no less than the Prince of Neuchâtel himself," Masséna said as he turned toward the brilliantly uniformed figure coming out of the entrance. This was Louis Alexandre Berthier, Marshal of the Empire, Prince of Neuchâtel, and Chief of the Army Staff. He was hatless, his thick curly hair tousled as always. He was resplendent in full-dress foot uniform with his dark blue, knee-length coat glittering with gold braid and crossed by a broad scarlet shoulder sash. He was frowning and biting the nails of his left hand, and with his right he was waving a dismissal to a green-coated valet.

"That'll be all for now, Constant, His majesty won't need you until this conference is over," Berthier said.

When he became aware of Lannes' and Masséna's glances the frown disappeared, and a jolly, joking Berthier emerged. He was all smiles as he greeted the other two marshals.

"Why are you two looking so serious? You've got everything going your way, haven't you?" Without giving either a chance to reply, he went on as though he had not already spoken.

"The Emperor is with Bacler d'Albe at the map table. He'll see us in just a moment."

As he spoke, a small dark man with a handsome, smooth-

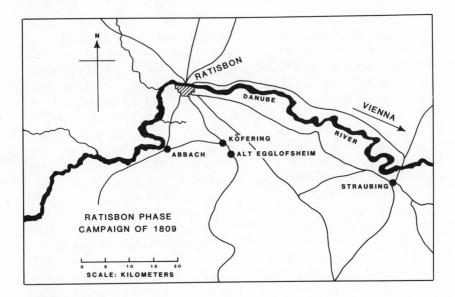

RATISBON PHASE
CAMPAIGN OF 1809

shaven face emerged from the inner room and passed silently behind Berthier, giving a pleasant nod to the group as he passed.

"So, d'Albe has finished the evening situation map-posting. I'll see if we can—"

He was interrupted by a sharp voice from within the tent, one that crackled with command.

"Berthier, Berthier, get in here, and bring the others with you. We haven't got the rest of the night to dawdle over greetings and the like!"

The Prince of Neuchâtel spun on his heel like a sergeant-major, his short, stocky body muscling to attention, and marched through the anteroom into the "sanctuary of genius." Lannes and Masséna followed, trailed by their aides who quickly aligned themselves against a tent wall.

Napoleon, still clasping a pair of compasses in his right hand, turned from the map on the table at room's center, and faced the marshals. The five-foot-six figure in the dull green uniform coat of a colonel of chasseurs was half in shadow from the light of the table lamps, but the face was in full light. Marbot had seen his Emperor at a distance in the field and less often close up on occasions such as this, and he never ceased to wonder at the piercing glare of the great grey eyes which seemed to hypnotize anyone on whom they were focused. Their glance swept around the room, and as it passed over Marbot's face an icy tingle ran down his spine. Suddenly the Emperor's facial muscles flexed, and a quick smile enveloped them all, so that they seemed to relax in its warmth.

"Let us to it, gentlemen. As you see here we have reached this line stretching from Abbach on the north to the east of this village of Alt Egglofsheim. The Austrians are beaten at all points, and the latest reports indicate no organized, large-scale capability of resistance. And I've just had the word of the heavy cavalry's battle. Do you take it to be as successful as Nansouty's courier would have us believe, Lannes?"

"I witnessed it myself, your majesty, a complete victory in every sense. I stayed long enough to see St. Sulpice's thirty-four squadrons launched in pursuit. And, if you will permit, that fact brings me to my point: I believe that we can destroy the Austrian army between this present line and the Danube, but only if we keep moving," Lannes said.

The grey eyes turned expressionless as they looked into those of Lannes. Then they were turned on Masséna and Berthier.

"What say you two, can we continue with a night advance?"

Masséna's alert face was a portrait of mixed dismay and anger.

"Since you ask, Sire, every infantryman in every corps is drunk with exhaustion. When their formations are halted, they drop to the ground, senseless with sleep. We can't pursue with an army of corpses," Masséna said.

"He is right, your majesty, every report that has come in within the last two hours would confirm that," Berthier added.

"Is that it then, Masséna?" Napoleon asked.

"No, Sire, that is not the whole picture. We are still far from Ratisbon and the Danube, with neither time nor means to prepare a night attack. I don't have to tell you what confusion could ensue—with mixed-up units and intermingled commands and all that goes with it. And an enemy who has fought us as stubbornly as this today, might still be capable of a fight. That is the rest of the picture," Masséna said.

The Emperor started to speak to Lannes when an aide of Berthier's stepped through the anteroom and slipped a rolled paper into his chief's hand.

"Excuse it, Sire, but General Mouton has admitted this aide with an urgent dispatch," Berthier broke in.

"Go ahead, Alexandre, if it bears on our council here."

"General St. Sulpice reports sweeping everything in front of his advance as far as Köfering. In that area he overran two Austrian grenadier battalions which he says were the last organized resistance he found. And there is a postscript which tops off the whole affair."

"Well, go on, go on," Napoleon said.

"St. Sulpice says that he came within a hair's breadth of capturing the Archduke Charles himself."

"If you're telling me that my cavalry leader *almost* captured the enemy army's commander, that is pure dramatics, and not a military report," Napoleon's tone was scornful.

"Your majesty is correct, of course, but the incident does show the extent of the cavalry pursuit," Berthier said.

Napoleon looked at Lannes who seemed about to burst out of his marshal's coat.

"Sire, is this talk of exhaustion, of puny distances, of confusion in night attacks—is this the spirit of Lodi, of Arcola, of Friedland? Thou* can see for thyself what the heavy cavalry—*exhausted* heavy cavalry—can accomplish with drive and leadership. Wouldst thou listen to this drivel about sleepy men? True, my men are tired, they've gone farther than any other infantry, but I can make them go on. Why can't the others?"

Napoleon's swift glance caught Masséna's Italian temper bristling, and the once-jovial Berthier was showing signs of temper.

"You have the esprit, I know, Jean. But cool that Gascon temper, and face reality with me. Masséna and Berthier are right, I must admit. And I *could* order a continuation of the attack, but I will not."

Lannes gave a shrug that spoke sentences of resignation. Napoleon went on for a tense quarter of an hour, the stream of orders pouring out until the marshals were wearied just listening as the secretaries took it all down. The Emperor paced back and forth, hands clasped behind his back, as he glanced from the map to a perspiring Berthier. Then he was done. Lannes and Masséna knew from long experience that there would be no formal dismissal, so motioning their aides to follow, they slipped quietly out of the tent.

"There you are, Jean, and no bad feelings, I hope." Masséna said with his head cocked to the left in the gesture that he used to show interest or sympathy.

---

*Lannes was the only marshal who dared use the familiar "tu" in addressing Napoleon.

"Of course not, Andre, it's all quite simple in spite of all that detail that Berthier has to master. You swing your IVth Corps eastward toward Straubing and capture the bridges near there and intercept any Austrians who try to escape down either side of the Danube," Lannes said.

"And you and Davout and Lefebvre continue to advance on Ratisbon."

"That's it, and as usual, at first light. With any luck we'll be joining forces again and soon," Lannes said.

"What do you mean, 'with luck.' " Doesn't our Emperor say that all his generals must be lucky? I'll see you in Vienna, my friend."

He left Lannes staring after him for a space of seconds before he started for the dismounting point.

Three of Lannes' aides-de-camp—Marbot, de Viry, and Labédoyère—had dismounted and were observing the walls of Ratisbon from a point where the Straubing road ascends a slope southeast of the town. Labédoyère handed his field glass back to Marbot.

"From even two kilometers I can see that those old medieval walls could never withstand the fire of siege cannon for long, don't you agree, Marcellin?" Labédoyère asked.

"Agreed, but hardly the point," Marbot said.

"How do you mean?"

"We've ridden within musket shot of those walls and have drawn enough fire to know that those walls are still defended in strength by infantry and artillery, enough to make it really rough on any assaulting force."

"Then you still think we'll assault the town rather than besiege it?"

"I'll wager that that's the subject being discussed by our marshal and the Emperor right now," Marbot said, gesturing toward the knot of horsemen on a low hillock a hundred meters to his right.

"That's hardly a betting matter. How about your two louis against mine that there'll be no assault?" Labédoyère challenged.

"Done, if I'm saying that there will be a storming—no siege," Marbot said.

"Done then. Will you hold the money, de Viry?" Labédoyère asked. "And now are we agreed on the report to the marshal of the results of our little reconnaissance, Marcellin?"

"I see little to report other than an estimate of the Austrian garrison's strength. As for the rest, anyone with a field glass can see for himself," Marbot said and made a sweep of his arm that took in the town walls as far as the eye could see.

The noon sun beat down bringing to the spring day the promise of a hot afternoon. The crumbling walls of the town, decaying after centuries of standing guard, shimmered under heat rays reflected from the old ramparts. An occasional glint was reflected from a bayonet or musket barrel, showing the presence of watchful Austrian infantry manning the walls. Yet despite their dilapidated condition the walls rose to a height of ten meters above the dry ditch that had served as a moat in medieval times. The ditch itself was as deep as the walls were high, its outer side almost cliff-like in its steep slope. Marbot's fascination with the rich greenness of the wide ditch bottom had been quickly quashed by young de Viry, whose eye had been quicker than the older aide's. "Those are really vegetable gardens, kept by the town folk living just inside the walls," de Viry said, laughing at Marbot's embarrassment. The approaches to the ditch from the French side would have to be made across the wide promenade that encircled the town and bordered the dry ditch for its entire length. From their position on the forward slope the aides could see the battalions of Morand's division moving up in dense columns to positions short of the promenade, just out of range of Austrian muskets. Labédoyère exclaimed and pointed to the artillery guns being towed at a walk through the wide intervals between the dark blue masses of the infantry columns.

"There go the twelve-pounders forward, they're foot artillery from our corps. That doesn't make my money look any too safe," he said.

"We'll see soon enough," de Viry said. "Look, they're going into position now."

As the aides watched, the gun teams pulled ahead of the halted infantry and swung from column into line, each eight-man team preparing for action as it arrived at its designated place. When all eight guns of the battery had signalled readiness, the first ranging rounds began booming out.

"Ranging in on that house there, that one that extends from the walls halfway across the ditch," Marbot said.

"Unlucky people to have built in that place," de Viry said, "but why that house as the target? Why not breach the wall itself at some point?"

Labédoyère's reply carried the lofty tone of the veteran condescending to correct an errant recruit.

"In the first place those walls are far too thick to be breached by field guns. Now, if you'll watch, you'll see that the walls of that house, even though they are made of stone, will soon crumble. See, right there, those rounds striking at the base of the house!"

Powdery grey blossoms of smoke marked the strikes of the round shot against the lower wall of the house. Round after round battered the ditch side of the house until its wall began to fall apart and its debris began tumbling into the ditch. De Viry's embarrassed nod showed he had heard but had still not understood the senior aide's meaning.

"Now, see here," Labédoyère went on, "those broken stones and mortar will soon pile up enough to fill part of the ditch and form an incline that could make a base for a storming party's assault."

"Ah," Marbot broke in, "so you do admit then that there will be a storming—and no siege! Hand over my money, de Viry."

"Oh no you don't," Labédoyère put himself between Marbot and the younger aide, "I'll admit nothing until we hear our marshal himself announce the orders."

"Very well then, let's back to business. I was going to submit an estimate of at least five Austrian battalions holding the town that I got in great part from General Gudin's senior aide. After all, that division learned the hard way this morning after having made a half-dozen attacks and failing to penetrate the walls in each."

"Agreed," Labédoyère said, "and we'd better be getting over there within voice range of the marshal. He may call on us any time now. Have you anything to add, de Viry?"

"Well, no, but it occurs to me that if the Emperor had heeded Marshal Lannes' recommendation last night all of this bloody work would never have to be. We'd be inside those walls instead of an Austrian rear guard."

"Would you listen to our little general now," Labédoyère said, "and while you're wishing why didn't you wish that Colonel Coutard with his 65th of the Line had never surrendered the town to the Austrians three days ago! What about that, my young crystal-gazer?"

Marbot sighed, then set the example as he swung into the saddle.

"All right, you two. What's to be gained by all this child's gabble? If you'd open your eyes instead of your mouths, you'd see that we're being summoned."

The Emperor's eyes were sparkling as he watched the battery's salvos taking their effect on the rapidly crumbling walls of the house. While he was enrapt in his artillery observations—the old gunner back again behind the Toulon batteries or overseeing Marmount's guns at Marengo—none dared attempt to distract his attention. None until Lannes, chafing to get away to his task, spoke up with the familiarity that never failed to shock the household staff.

"If thou hast naught else to say, I ask confirmation of my mission."

Napoleon spoke without taking his eye from his field glass.

"I know I should have listened to you at last night's council, but now that's water under the bridge—Ratisbon's bridge that has carried Archduke Charles' escaping army. And we've been over all the rest of the matter this morning. To sit down here in front of these walls and dig in siege works, batteries, mines and all that would be fatal to my purpose, so near the end of this campaign."

The Emperor handed his field glass to an aide, and directed his attention to Lannes who knew it would only delay attaining his object if he were to make Napoleon's monologue a discussion.

"Yet," Napoleon went on, "you know as well as I that I cannot turn away from an Austrian-held Ratisbon and march down the Danube to take Vienna. If I did, Charles could recross the river by Ratisbon bridge and cut my lines of communications. On the other hand, if I am checked here by a siege or any other kind of delay, Prussia and those other German states could join actively in Austria's cause."

He shifted his seat in the saddle, and looked back again at the artillery battery and its target. His irritation showed in his indecision about whether to continue his ponderings or simply to refocus his attention on the artillery fires. After a few seconds he turned his eyes on Lannes.

"It's a good thing you're on horseback, you know," Napoleon said.

"Why, Sire, I don't understand," Lannes said.

"If you were standing, it would be on one foot and then the other. Very well, you will have the orders you've been waiting for. I put the whole matter in your hands. You take Ratisbon, however you will, and now!"

"I thank your majesty, and have I leave to go and make preparations?"

"To make preparations, indeed. Do you think your Emperor is blind? I see that you have ordered up Morand's division, and right under my eyes. Yes, go, and report when you are ready to—"

Napoleon's face contorted, and his unfinished sentence was cut short with his muffled cry of pain.

"I'm hit, Jean," he managed to gasp under his breath, "don't alarm the others."

Napoleon was leaning forward, supporting his right shoulder against his horse's neck. Lannes was off his horse in a flash, running to the Emperor's side. He freed his chief's boot from the stirrup, got his arms around him, and lowered him to the ground, where he held Napoleon erect by pulling his right arm around his shoulders.

"Where, Sire, where?" Lannes asked.

"My right foot—the ankle."

Before the words were out, Napoleon and Lannes were surrounded by Berthier, General Mouton, and a dozen aides and staff officers. Lannes had gotten the Emperor to sit on the ground and stretch out his legs. The marshal looked up at the circle of stricken faces, and snapped his orders at them.

"Mouton, get the others back from here, and send for Doctor Larrey. Alexandre, help his majesty sit up while I get his boot off. Duroc, get some cloaks or blankets together and make a cot to put him on," Lannes ordered.

Lannes grasped the heel and toe of the Emperor's right boot, and pulled firmly and as gently as he could. Napoleon's face was as expressionless as he could manage, but Lannes saw that he was biting his lower lip to stifle an outcry. When the foot of the boot was free of the ankle the boot slid off smoothly. Lannes and Berthier saw the oozing of blood just forward of the ankle bone. When the silk stocking had been peeled off, the two could see that the bullet had spent its force when it had penetrated the boot. While they were uncovering the wound, Larrey, the surgeon-general, arrived and quickly finished his examination.

"Well, Dominique, what is it? What do you say about it?" Napoleon demanded.

"Sire, it is only a scratch of a flesh wound. The bullet was spent, and no wonder, at this distance. It must have been one of those Austrian Tyrolese sharpshooters taking an off-chance that his rifle shot could reach the command group here. I will dress it, and you must stay off your feet. There will be a lot of muscular pain, that's all," Larrey said.

"Well, get on with it. Mouton, I must get mounted at once. Have Marengo brought back," Napoleon said.

The word of the Emperor's wounding had spread like wildfire through the army, and already soldiers were running up to the imperial cavalry demanding news of the Emperor's condition. The hillock threatened to become smothered under masses of excited soldiers, alarmed by confusion and rumor. When his grey Arabian was ready, Napoleon was assisted into the saddle and was on his way to show himself to his troops. As he left he called back to Lannes.

"Get on with it, Jean. Don't wait to make a report, go when you're ready. Everything will be all right as soon as the troops see me riding."

Lannes was already in the saddle, needing no further word to start him on his mission.

When the marshal and his three aides dismounted behind the long storage building at the near edge of the promenade they found that Lannes' preparatory orders had been carried out to the last detail. The first storming party was organized and ready; fifty hand-picked volunteers from grenadier companies were stretched on the ground in the shelter of the stone building, their scaling ladders lying between the leading files. Other ladders were being unloaded from carts rounded up from the surrounding farm villages. Morand was at Lannes' side as he dismounted, and made his report.

"Excellent, Louis," Lannes said, his grin showing his pleasure, "let's get them on their feet and ready to move out."

When the storming column had fallen in, Lannes faced the file leaders at its head, and raised his voice so that even the supporting companies behind the grenadiers could hear him.

"You know you've got to move fast to get across that hundred and fifty meters of open ground before you get to the ditch. Remember that you will need ladders to get down into the ditch and more ladders to get up the walls. You must find footing for them in the rubble that the artillery made of that house. No cheering, now, there'll be time for that later. Be off with you, lads, and God go with you!"

Lannes and Marbot watched from the corner of the building as the closely packed column swung into the open and started across the promenade. The last files had scarcely cleared the building when the column was met by volleys of musketry and a storm of grapeshot. The leading files carrying the ladders broke into a run, the rest of the party following on their heels. Men began to drop until the storming column's path was marked by a trail of dead and wounded. Lannes watched a handful of leaders, fewer than twenty in all, disappear over the side of the ditch and saw the ramparts obscured by clouds of powder smoke. He thrust aside the field glass Marbot had held out to him. He needed no glass to see the ramp of rubble that was the storming party's first goal. In the seconds that followed, the first of the walking wounded made their way back to the shelter of the stone building, bloodstained and beaten men. Even worse, in Lannes' sight, was that the inclined pile of rubble had been undisturbed by the feet of any French soldier; not a man had made it across the ditch, for all had been mowed down by nearly point-blank fire from the Austrian infantry on the ramparts.

Morand knew as well as Lannes that no time should be wasted in dispatching a second storming column. The sight of the wounded and the tales of Austrian firepower that would follow would wreak havoc on the morale of the supporting infantry. Morand and Colonel Valterre of the 30th of the Line had the next group poised, ready to charge forward. Lannes made no address to the men, they had already heard his sendoff to their predecessors. He simply waved them on with his blessing. Again he watched from the corner of the building as the next fifty volunteers dashed across the promenade. And again he saw the slaughter as the wreckage of the column made it into the ditch, never to reappear on the rubble against the far wall. This time even fewer wounded returned with their stories of the hail of bullets and cannon shot that had almost annihilated their column.

Morand's third call for volunteers—"from any company"—was met with a gloomy silence. Lannes' attempt to support Morand with his own call met with the same silence.

My God, Lannes thought, *here we still stand, in full view of the Emperor and the whole army, an utter failure with not a single Frenchman reaching that wall, let alone scaling it.*

His racing thoughts were interrupted by Morand's plea.

"Sir, these battalions of Colonel Valterre's 30th stand ready to charge if you will only give the order." Morand's desperation showed in every line of his livid face. Here was a renowned soldier, one of the "three immortals," ready to go down before Austrian bullets rather than face the disgrace of failure in the eyes of the army and the Emperor. Lannes knew that as well as he knew he drew breath. That was why his voice was almost gentle in his answer.

"I know I could give that order, Louis, but you know I will not. You know only too well the difference between *élan*

Marshal Lannes at Ratisbon, from a drawing by John W. Thomason, Jr.

and simple obedience. We will go next with volunteers or we will not go at all. Now, I'll try once more with them," Lannes said.

He turned to face the columns drawn up in the rear of the building, and put his innermost thoughts into his shouted words.

"Do I have to tell you men that your Emperor and the rest of the army are watching you? No, you know that as well as I. Then, will it be said by them that the soldiers of this division refused to volunteer because they had seen their comrades fail?"

Lannes paused, waiting to hear the shouts of men pressing forward to take their places in the next storming party. Instead he was met with the same stubborn silence. The men in the front ranks were staring at the ground to avoid the blazing eyes of their marshal. Lannes felt the silence that had fallen across the massed battalions and over the whole plain and the army behind it. Even the Austrian ramparts were silent, as though the infantry there would share the scene with their enemy. The silence lasted for seconds that seemed to stretch into hours. Suddenly it was shattered by Lannes.

"*Eh bien,* I will let you see that I was a grenadier before I was a marshal, and still am one!" He snatched a ladder from an astonished grenadier, and heaving it to his shoulder, marched around the corner of the building toward the corpse-littered promenade.

An astounded Marbot and de Viry dashed after him. When they caught up to him, Marbot grabbed at the front end of the ladder while de Viry tried to seize the other end. Lannes swung the ladder away from them and raged at them:

"Let be! If you will follow, do so, but I am carrying this ladder."

Marbot dared to place himself two paces ahead of his chief before he spoke.

"*Monsieur le Maréchal,* do you want us disgraced, and that we will be if you were to get the slightest wound while carrying that ladder—and as long as one of your aides was left alive."

Lannes marched stubbornly on, as if he had not heard a word. Marbot and de Viry, seeing that the time for words had passed, grabbed for the ladder again. This time the younger men succeeded in wrenching the ladder from their marshal's grasp, even though he continued to resist. As the three men came to a halt they realized that the plain was re-sounding with the cheers of Morand's division. At the sight of a marshal of France, struggling with his aides-de-camp over the leading of an assault, Morand's battalions had begun to voice their esprit and the shouts of aroused men had run through the whole division.

When the three got back to the building they were almost overwhelmed with officers and soldiers who had rushed for-ward to seize ladders and join in the next assault. Morand and his senior officers restored order, and as the men re-turned to their ranks, they began their selection of the next fifty. It was not a simple task, for every man was now a vol-unteer, but in moments the best officers and the tallest gren-adiers had been chosen and formed into a new column. While this was being done, Lannes had time for a calmer exchange with Marbot and de Viry.

"So now, fire-eaters, the cork has been drawn, and the wine must be drunk, bitter though it may be," Lannes said.

"Sir, we have earned the right to lead this next storming party, and we would continue to deserve disgrace if we were thought to have put on a show just to turn the job over to someone else," Marbot said.

The marshal took off his great cocked hat with its white fringe, red cockade, and gold loop, and wiped his brow be-fore fixing both aides with a stare.

"Very well then, Marbot, you may lead, accompanied by de Viry and Labédoyère. I suppose I should also send all my staff, so that I alone will be my own headquarters after all have been lost. And, Marbot, you had better have a plan after what we've seen this afternoon," Lannes said.

"Sir, I already have a plan based on what we've seen hap-pen to those other two assaults. They failed because they were storming columns, not parties. They presented a mass, a tar-get to the Austrians that couldn't be missed. What's more, the ladder men were all in front, getting tangled up with each other and slowing up those behind them." Marbot almost stuttered in his haste to get out his lessons from the situation.

"But how do you propose to remedy all that?" Lannes asked.

"If General Morand will designate a staff officer to dis-patch my groups that will follow, de Viry and I will take off with the first ladder. The other ladders should follow at twenty-pace intervals, everyone moving at a run," Marbot said.

"And after that, what? How do you intend to get at the walls?"

"When we reach the ditch all the ladders should be placed against the near side of the ditch, two paces apart. After the leading files have descended they will take every other ladder, climb the pile of rubble, and place those ladders against the ramparts a half-meter apart."

The marshal gave his approval and saw that Morand's officers and men understood Marbot's plan. Finally, the details were settled and Lannes sent them out by saying,

"Off with you, lads, and Ratisbon is taken!"

At those words, Marbot and de Viry led out, darting around the building, and crossing the promenade at a dead run. They slung their ladder down the rear wall of the ditch and slid rather than climbed down it. The Austrians, bewildered by the sight of running pairs of men who presented only small fleeting targets, loosed off renewed volleys. But the musket is not an accurate weapon even against men standing in ranks beyond fifty paces, and now its ineffectiveness showed immediately. All of Marbot's officers and the fifty grenadiers reached and crossed the ditch without the loss of a man. The rearmost grenadiers acted as *tirailleurs*, blazing away at the Austrians on the ramparts.

Marbot and de Viry, now carrying separate ladders, ran stumblingly up the heaped rubble and got their ladders seated and leaned against the wall. Marbot was the first to ascend his ladder up the wall, double a man's height from the top of the rubble to the ramparts. Labédoyère was climbing the ladder next to Marbot's, only a forearm's length away, when he felt his ladder's bottom end begin to slide out from the wall.

"Marcellin, give me your hand. My ladder is slipping!" Labédoyère shouted.

Marbot heard his cry in spite of the muskets banging away overhead. He grasped the aide's left hand in his right, and together they reached the rampart. For a second or two they were standing there in full view of the Emperor and the army. Even at a distance of hundreds of meters they could hear across the plain the cheers coming from scores of thousands. One cannot doubt the sincerity of Marbot's words when he says in his *Memoirs*: "It was one of the finest days of my life."

In a moment the two were joined by the other officers and the fifty grenadiers. The Austrian infantry had disappeared into the streets below, and Marbot could look back over the wall and see the columns of supporting battalions swarming into the ditch and placing more ladders against the walls. The impossible had been made possible, and the French were in Ratisbon, but Marbot and his storming party had still to carry out the rest of Marshal Lannes' orders: "Get to the Straubing gate and open it to the marshal who will be leading the battalions which have been designated to penetrate the town and seize the bridge before the Austrians can destroy it." The gate was scarcely more than a hundred meters distant from the point where Marbot and his men had scaled the wall. But what enemy force was there between them and the gate?

As soon as Marbot and his little group were down in the street nearest the wall, he divided the fifty grenadiers into two sections and assigned officers to each. His orders were brief:

"Each section to a side of the street, keeping in double file and hugging the houses. I will lead the right section, and both sections will guide on me."

Their advance was cautious but steady, and as they moved down the street and around the first corner they found no signs of Austrian soldiers. The streets and even the houses, as far as Marbot could tell, were deserted; no doubt the townfolk living near the walls had fled at the sounds of heavy firing. Marbot was leading them down the closest street that paralleled the wall. It was a narrow thoroughfare, and Marbot could see it curving to the left, out of his sight for the next thirty meters. He covered that distance at a quick pace until he was able to see around the curve into the tiny *platz* where the streets met under a wide archway. What he saw across the little square brought him to an abrupt halt. Marbot had seen more than his share of strange sights this day, but what confronted him now made him freeze in place.

Under the arch that extended to the Straubing gate and in front of the gate itself an Austrian infantry battalion, a thousand strong, was massed in close order facing the gate. Every man in the formation was facing the gate, obviously deployed there to counterattack any French assault on the gate. Even the battalion commander who had posted himself near the center of the rear rank was facing in the same direction. Marbot was quick to note another incredible detail— no sentries had been posted over the gate or on top of the wall!

Marbot silently signalled his two sections to halt and form into double rank across the street they had just come up. The rattle of the grenadiers' arms and the sound of boots on the cobblestones must have alarmed the Austrian commander, who faced around toward the French with a startled oath. His sharp cry, in turn, alerted his officers who faced the rear ranks about and had them level their muskets. Labédoyère gave a similar command to the French grenadiers, and Marbot found himself facing the Austrian major at a distance of three paces, each commander looking into ranks of levelled muskets, cocked and ready to fire.

Sacrebleu! Marbot cursed to himself. *What a hell of a thing to happen after all we've been through today. This is indeed a situation calling for "military tact." One thing is certain—this Austrian can see only the front rank of my party, and he doesn't know what is behind it. This leaves but one thing to do.*

He had been carrying his unsheathed hussar's saber; he snapped to attention and saluted the Austrian with it. The major's eyes grew even rounder at the amazing sight of a brilliantly uniformed French cavalry officer saluting him in front of two ranks of grenadiers with levelled muskets. His right hand came slowly to the salute as though it was being raised by an unseen force.

"The major speaks French?" Marbot asked.

He did.

"Then I must ask that your men lay down their arms. I lead the advance guard of Marshal Lannes' corps of thirty thousand men, and the town is in our hands. The corps of Marshals Davout and Lefebvre have already reached the bridge and captured it. You have no choice but to accept the terms of an honorable surrender," Marbot said.

The Austrian's face was a study in dismay and disbelief. As he struggled with his conscience and a sense of the inevitable, Marbot's quick eye took in another fact—the white-coated Austrian infantrymen's uniforms were as clean as if on parade, and the major's glistening, gold-topped boots showed no traces of dust. Clearly this was a battalion that had not yet been committed to action, and as such must have no knowledge of the tactical situation. This was confirmed when the major decided that Marbot had indeed summed up the situation with accuracy. He gave the command to ground arms, and then in a torrent of German explained the situation to his men.

His words were heeded by the companies in front—those

which had been the rearmost before the confrontation—who passed forward their muskets to be grounded by the front rank. But three companies, now in the rear and nearest the gate, began shouting refusals to surrender. The Austrian commander sent officers to subdue the commotion and restore order when a new disaster threatened to wreck Marbot's "tactful" victory.

The fiery Labédoyère had jumped to the conclusion that Marbot had let things get out of hand and that the Austrians were going to resort to a last-ditch fight. He sprang at the Austrian major and grabbed him by the throat. When the Austrian pushed him back in order to defend himself, Labédoyère threatened to run him through with his drawn saber. Marbot knocked the blade aside with a swing of his saber while de Viry put his arms around Labédoyère from behind, pinioning him until he could be calmed down.

Order restored, the surrender went on without further incident until all the Austrian muskets had been piled and the battalion had marched away under its own officers, guided by a French officer with a file of grenadiers.

Hardly had the Austrians cleared the square when Marbot and the others were treated to the sound of French axes battering at the outer side of the gate.

"It sounds like our marshal has a rude way of announcing his entry. But things would go smoother if we were to open the gate ourselves, don't you think?" de Viry asked Marbot.

When Marbot could make himself heard, the battering on the other side stopped, and the grenadiers were able to unchain the great bars and slide them aside until the gates swung inward. Marshal Lannes, sword in hand, stood facing his aides while double files of infantry swirled past him through the gateway. Marbot ran forward to make his report, and Lannes motioned him to the far side of the square in order to get out of the way of the columns of infantry pouring through the square. Lannes listened with his usual intentness until Marbot had finished the story of his bluff and the Austrian surrender. The marshal's face lit up with a grin at the thought of a thousand Austrians being duped into surrender by a storming party one-twentieth of their strength.

"So now, Marbot, you have no twinges of conscience after telling such tall tales—you with three army corps behind you, indeed. *Merveilleux!*"

"None, Sir, especially when one remembers that you and Marshal Murat took the Spitz bridge five years ago from the Austrians without a shot fired—and with some of the same kind of persuasion."

"*Bien touché,* we will not pursue that point further, at least not now. But now I want you to find Major Saint-Mars and have him bring his guides along. He can find me, I'm taking that street over there that should lead to the town center. You can catch up with me, along with Saint-Mars. I'll take the other aides with me, for now," Lannes said, taking off across the square with his swift stride.

Labédoyère and de Viry started to follow the marshal when Marbot stepped in front of them.

"Just one moment, old friends, but we have a small matter to settle before you join the marshal. Monsieur de Viry, I believe you are carrying four gold louis which belong to me," Marbot said.

"Ah yes, I believe I am," de Viry said, reaching inside his pelisse for his purse, "if, of course, Monsieur Labédoyère has no questions about the total coming to four louis."

"I think not, de Viry. Even a man who confuses sieges with assaults can add two and two," Marbot said. "Is that not true, Labédoyère?"

Marbot never got his answer. Labédoyère was already halfway across the square, hastening to catch up with his marshal.

Inspiration

ONE OF THE MOST widely known admonitions of World
War II was not given by a superior officer to a subordinate.
Yet the reversed warning made a great deal of sense: "General, do you have to draw fire while you are inspiring us?"
This, an obvious misuse of *presence*, often fetched results that
were as undersirable as they were opposite to the intent.

In its most pragmatic sense *inspiration* must, to be effective, produce the results the leader sought before he arrived
on the spot where he thought his presence would turn the
trick. And perhaps "turning the trick" is the key to finding
a criterion, a simple definition: *The leader's presence should be
used only when it can be seen as a requisite for moving men to actions
that are essential to accomplishing the mission.* In more soldierly
terms, don't do it unless you are sure that you are the one
who is needed on the spot to get the job done. If the latter
terms seem to imply something short of the heroic, just recall
that the leader has no more immunity to enemy action than
has the newest replacement; and the dead or seriously
wounded leader is of no more use to his command than a
dead replacement.

Thus, calculation ought to govern a leader's use of inspiration rather than impulse, no matter how heroic the aim.
The exposure of the self to physical danger should, to produce the desired end, be resorted to only when there is a
reasonable probability of success.

In our next example the leader has chosen to expose himself in two ways, as we shall see. For me it is a dramatic instance that shows the use of presence as inspiration. I have not been able to find an equal to it.

The Taking of Lungtungpen*
by
Rudyard Kipling

My friend Private Mulvaney told me this, sitting on the parapet of the road to Dagshai, when we were hunting butterflies together. He had theories about the Army, and colored clay pipes perfectly. He said that the young soldier is the best to work with, "on account of the surpassing innocence of the child."

"Now, listen!" said Mulvaney, throwing himself full length on the wall in the sun. "I'm a born scutt of the barrack room! The Army's meat an' drink to me, because I'm one of the few that can't quit it. I've put in seventeen years, an' the pipeclay's in the marrow of me. If I could have kept out of one big drink a month, I would have been an honorary lieutenant by this time—a nuisance to my betters, a laughin' stock to my equals, and a curse to meself. Bein' what I am, I'm Private Mulvaney, with no good-conduct pay and a devourin' thirst. Always barrin' my little friend Bobs Bahadur,** I know as much about the Army as most men."

I said something here.

"Wolseley be shot! Between you an' me an' that butterfly net, he's a ramblin', incoherent sort of a devil with one eye on the Queen and the Court, an' the other on his blessed self—everlastin'ly playing Caesar and Alexander rolled into a lump. Now Bobs is a sensible little man. With Bobs and a few three-year-olds, I'd sweep any army off the earth into a towel, and throw it away afterward. Faith, I'm not jokin'! 'Tis the boys—the raw boys—that don't know what a bullet means, and wouldn't care if they did—that do the work. They're crammed with bull-meat till they fairly romps with good livin'; and then, if they don't fight, they blow each other's heads off.

---

*Reprinted from *Soldiers Three* by permission of Doubleday & Co.
**Bobs Bahadur—Field Marshal Lord Roberts, this five-foot-three idol was known by his soldier nickname "Bobs," and was the most popular of Victorian generals; the Bahadur was a title of respect, traceable to the ancient Asiatic title of knight or lord.

'Tis the truth I'm tellin' you. They should be kept on water and rice in the hot weather; but there'd be a mutiny if 'twas done.

"Did you ever hear how Private Mulvaney took the town of Lungtungpen? I thought not! 'Twas the Lieutenant got the credit; but 'twas me planned the scheme. A little before I was invalided from Burma, me and four-an'-twenty young ones under a Lieutenant Brazenose, was ruining our digestions trying to catch dacoits.* And such double-ended devils I never knew! 'Tis only a dah** and a Snider*** that makes a dacoit. Without them, he's a peaceful cultivator, and felony for to shoot. We hunted, and we hunted, and took fever and elephants now and again; but no dacoits. Eventually, we puckarowed one man. 'Treat him tenderly,' says the Lieutenant. So I took him away into the jungle, with the Burmese interpreter and my cleaning-rod. Says I to the man, 'My peaceful squireen," says I, 'you squat on your hunkers and demonstrate to my friend here, where your friends are when they're at home?' With that I introduced him to the cleaning-rod, and he commenced to jabber; the interpreter interpreting in betweens, and me helpin' the Intelligence Department with my cleaning-rod when the man misremembered.

"Presently, I learn that, across the river, about nine miles away, was a town just drippin' with dahs, and bows and arrows, and dacoits, and elephants, and jingles.**** 'Good!' says I; 'this office will now close!'

"That night, I went to the Lieutenant and communicates my information. I never thought much of Lieutenant Brazenose till that night. He was stiff with books and theories, and all manner of trimming's of no manner of use. 'Town did you say?' says he. 'According to the theories of War, we should wait for reinforcements.'—'Faith!' thinks I, 'we'd better dig our graves then;' for the nearest troops was up to their stocks in the marshes out Mimbu way. 'But,' says the Lieutenant, 'since it's a special case, I'll make an exception. We'll visit this Lungtungpen tonight.'

"The boys were fairly wild with delight when I told 'em; and, by this and that, they went through the jungle like buckrabbits. About midnight we come to the stream which I had

---

*Dacoit—Burmese or Indian robbers, killers, thieves.
**Dah—a machete-like knife used for slashing vegetation or fighting.
***Snider—at the time the obsolete British Army rifle musket converted to a breech-loader.
****Jingle—the jingal, a bell-mouthed, heavy musket fired from a support.

clean forgot to mention to my officer. I was on ahead with four boys, and I thought that the Lieutenant might want to theorize. 'Stop boys,' says I. 'Strip to the buff, and swim in where glory waits!'—'But I can't swim,' says two of them. 'To think I should live to hear that from a boy with a board-school education!' says I. 'Take a lump of timber, and me and Conolly here will ferry you over, you young ladies!'

"We got an old tree-trunk, and pushed off with the kits and the rifles on it. The night was chokin' dark, and just as we was fairly embarked, I heard the Lieutenant behind me callin' out. 'There's a bit of a nullah here, sir,' says I, 'But I can feel the bottom already.' So I could, for I was not a yard from the bank.

" 'Bit of a nullah! Bit of an estuary!' says the Lieutenant. 'Go on, you mad Irishman! Strip boys,' I heard him laugh; and the boys began strippin' and rolling a log into the water to put their kits on. So me and Conolly struck out through the warm water with our log, and the rest came on behind.

"That stream was miles wide! Ortheris, on the rear-rank log, whispers we had got into the Thames below Sheerness by mistake. 'Keep on swimmin' you little blackguard,' says I, 'an Irriwaddy.'—'Silence, men!' sings out the Lieutenant. So we swam on into the black dark, with our chests on the logs, trustin' in the Saints and the luck of the British Army.

"Eventually, we hit ground—a bit of sand—and a man. I put my heel on the back of him. He skreeched and ran.

" 'Now we've done it!' says Lieutenant Brazenose. 'Where the devil is Lungtungpen?' There was about a minute and a half to wait. The boys laid a hold of their rifles and some tried to put their belts on; we was marching with fixed bayonets of course. Then we knew where Lungtungpen was; for we had hit the river-wall of it in the dark, and the whole town blazed with them messin' jingles and Sniders like a cat's back on a frosty night. They was firin' all ways at once; but over our heads into the stream.

" 'Have you got your rifles?' says Brazenose. 'Got 'em!' says Ortheris. 'I've got that thief Mulvaney's for all my back-pay, an' she'll kick my heart sick with that blunderin' long stock of hers.'—'Go on!' yells Brazenose, whippin' his sword out. 'Go on and take the town! And the Lord have mercy on our souls!'

"Then the boys gave one devastatin' howl, and pranced into the dark, feelin' for the town, and blindin' and' stiffin' like Cavalry Riding Masters when the grass pricked their bare legs. I hammered with the butt at some bamboo-thing that felt weak, and the rest came and hammered contagious, while the jingles was jingling, and ferocious yells from inside was splittin' our ears. We was too close under the wall for them to hurt us.

"Eventually, the thing, whatever it was, broke; and the six-an'-twenty of us tumbled, one after the other, naked as we was born, into the town of Lungtungpen. There was a melee of sumptuous kind for a while; but whether they took us, all white and wet, for a new breed of devil, or a new kind of dacoit, I don't know. They ran as though we was both, and we went into them, bayonet and butt, shriekin' with laughin'. There was torches in the streets, and I saw little Ortheris rubbin' his shoulder every time he loosed my long-stock Martini; and Brazenose walkin' into the gang with his sword, like Diomedes of the Golden Collar—barring he hadn't a stitch of clothin' on him. We discovered elephants with dacoits under their bellies, and, what with one thing and other, we was busy till mornin' takin' possession of the town of Lungtungpen.

"Then we halted and formed up, the women howlin' in the houses and the Lieutenant blushin' pink in the light of the mornin' sun. 'Twas the most indecent parade I ever took a hand in. Five-an'-twenty privates and an officer of the Line in review order, and not as much as would dust a fife between 'em all in the way of clothin'! Eight of us had their belts and pouches on; but the rest had gone in with a handful of cartridges and the skin God gave them. They was as naked as Venus.

" 'Number off from the right!' says the Lieutenant. 'Odd numbers fall out to dress; even numbers patrol the town till relieved by the dressing party.' Let me tell you, patrollin' a town with nothin' on is an experience. I patrolled for ten minutes, and begad, before 'twas over, I blushed. The women laughed so. I never blushed before or since; but I blushed all over my carcass then. Ortheris didn't patrol. He says only, 'Portsmouth Barracks and the Hard of a Sunday.' Then he lay down and rolled any ways with laughin'.

"When we was all dressed, we counted the dead—seventy-five dacoits besides the wounded. We took five elephants, a hundred and seventy Sniders, two hundred dahs, and a lot of other burglarious truck. Not a man of us was

Private Mulvaney

hurt—except maybe the Lieutenant, and he from the shock of his decency.

"The Headman of Lungtungpen, who surrendered him- self asked the interpreter—'If the English fight like that with their clothes off, what in the world do they do with their clothes on?' Ortheris began rollin' his eyes and crackin' his fingers and dancin' a step-dance for to impress the Headman. He ran to his house; an' we spent the rest of the day carryin' the Lieutenant on our shoulders round the town, and playin' with the Burmese babies—fat, little, brown little devils, as pretty as pictures.

"When I was invalided for the dysentery to India, I says to the Lieutenant, 'Sir,' says I, 'you've the makin' in you of a great man; but if you'll let an old soldier speak, you're too fond of theorizing.' He shook hands with me and says, "Hit high, hit low, there's no pleasing you, Mulvaney. You've seen me waltzing through Lungtungpen like a Red Indian without the warpaint, and you say I'm too fond of theorizing?'—'Sir,' says I, for I loved the boy; 'I would waltz with you in that condition through Hell, and so would the rest of the men!' Then I went downstream in the flat and left him my blessin'. May the Saints carry him where he should go, for he was a fine upstandin' young officer."

So saying, Mulvaney took up his butterfly-net, and re- turned to the barracks.

Part Five

ENERGY

**von Lettow-Vorbeck
at Tanga, 1914**

ENERGY

Beware of rashness, but with energy and sleepless vigilance
go forward and give us victories.
—Lincoln, *Letter to Major-General Hooker*

A review of the attributes of courage, will, intellect, and presence shows
that each must be supported by a vigorous physique which can produce
and sustain the energy the leader needs for forceful action. When General
Grant was asked what he thought were the qualities that most sustained
him throughout his Civil War campaigns, he replied that health and energy
should head the list. In his words, they gave him "the power to endure
anything."

In that light it appears sound to consider energy as the "life support"
for the other four attributes. It then becomes evident that energy per se
has no value until it is coupled with a desirable quality. This has been illustrated fittingly in the advice (apochryphal, but useful) supposedly given
to officers of the German General Staff concerning the selection and assignment of army officers:

"Observe first that sort of officer, the brilliant and the lazy. There is
command material there that must not be overlooked.

"Next, consider the brilliant and energetic. These combined qualities
make for an excellent chief of staff, chief of the operations section or intelligence section.

"Thirdly, one may encounter the stupid and the lazy. This sort may
be retained as line officers, for they will not rise to positions of great responsibility, and they can perform all kinds of dull duties.

"Finally, one may discover the combination of the stupid and the energetic. When this kind is discovered, get rid of him immediately. There
can be no greater danger to the armies of our Fatherland!"

Or anyone else's fatherland. Since we are fortunate in our survey in
not having to consider stupidity (with the possible exception of its popping
up as an element of the dynamic frustration), we may now observe an uncommon combination of the leader's attributes in action all being supported by the leader's energy. In this case there should be but a wee challenge to the reader's perception in identifying all six battlefield dynamics
being countered by the five attributes.

Energy

The Junker, the Governor, the British, and the Killer Bees

IT WAS THE evening of August 3, 1914 when the Governor of German East Africa began to feel his world falling apart. The realization came suddenly and in a most ungentle way while he was trying to steel himself to face down the arrogant junker who was the commandant of the colony's crack *Schutztruppe*. The Prussian's artful gesture of defiance—placing his monocle in the eye wounded during the Herero uprising—had made things no easier for Governor Schnee. He had handed the commandant the Reuters dispatch that confirmed the state of war between Germany, France and Russia, and stated that England's declaration of war on the Central Powers was expected momentarily. It was when the Commandant laid aside the dispatch that the confrontation came to a head. The soldier's reaction showed a thorough lack of understanding of the role he was expected to play under the Governor's policies.

"Good," Lieutenant-Colonel von Lettow-Vorbeck said, "I shall alert the *Schutztruppe* to stand by for my next directive."

"What sort of directive?" the Governor asked.

"I have already sent you my strategic estimate, Excellency, so that you realize how we can assist the Fatherland in a war with the British, and that is by tying up all the British

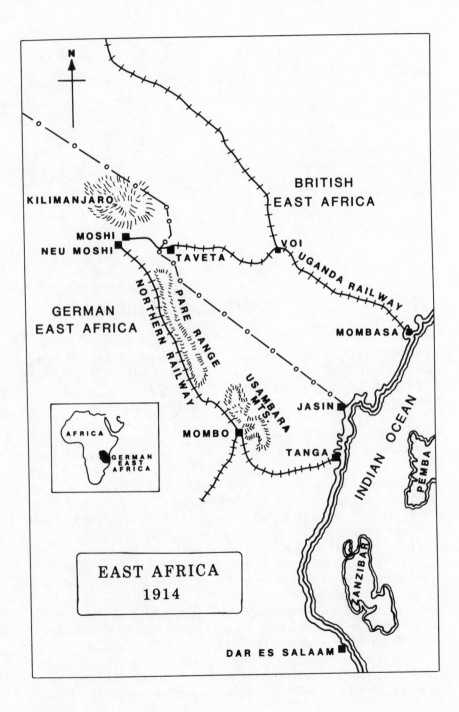

EAST AFRICA
1914

forces we can in Africa. That effort can only be launched effectively against the enemy by striking where it will be felt the most."

"You mean that it is actually your intention to attack the British?" the Governor stammered out his amazement at this affront to his avowed policy of neutrality.

"But of course, Doctor Schnee. And, as I have pointed out, the area where we must strike is through the great gap between Mount Kilimanjaro and the Pare Range, that is via Moshi and Taveta, in order to cut the Uganda Railway that forms British East Africa's vital link from the port of Mombasa to the interior. When we have done that we shall have seized the initiative, thus forcing the British to react, and that reaction will have to come through British forces that otherwise could be employed in Europe."

Halfway through Lettow-Vorbeck's curt military summation, the Governor was out of his chair and pacing behind his desk, his face sweating from more than the African heat.

"I think, Colonel, that it is time that you are oriented in regard to this government's positions on African questions. To put it in words that you will understand, I did not send for you to hear military estimates or plans. You are here to listen to *my* orders and for no other reason."

"With all respect, Your Excellency, it is no longer a case of colonial government giving orders to its commandant. My channel of command runs through the commander of colonial troops in Berlin, and through him to the High Command."

"Aren't you forgetting, Colonel, that I, as Governor of this colony, am also the commander-in-chief of its military forces? I have had my staff draw up plans which will ensure that German East Africa will maintain a neutral status. Accordingly, in order to guarantee the security of the capital, I order you to evacuate Dar es Salaam by noon tomorrow and move your troops to the interior."

"I don't see what good purpose that would serve. You and that staff can't possibly believe that German citizens would be guaranteed their safety by removing the only means of protecting them. So, Excellency, I must ask what objectives you seek by acting in this manner?"

The Governor's effort at self-control was becoming more obvious with each pace. He did not look around at Lettow-Vorbeck as he took up the challenge.

"Look, I, as Governor, have no obligation to answer that. Now, if I have to, I am capable of relieving you of command of the *Schutztruppe* and placing you under arrest. I trust I make that clear."

Lettow-Vorbeck's rugged face was expressionless as he fixed the Governor with his good eye.

"I must ask—what do you intend to do to secure the capital and the other ports?"

"I'll answer that with my question. Are you the military servant of this government or not?"

"Very well, Excellency, if I evacuate Dar es Salaam, and if I must move my troops from here and to the other coastal garrisons, I require concurrence in concentrating them at New Moshi in the Kilimanjaro area."

The Governor smiled, but it was a taut, humorless smile.

"You know that I know New Moshi is too close to the frontier of British East Africa, too close in the sense of making the sort of provocation that I've been trying to avoid. Now, for once and for all, you will move your troops to the interior—and far from the frontier. Is that order clear enough for you, Colonel?"

"Quite, Excellency."

The click of the commandant's heels came precisely as his saluting hand touched his forehead.

"But hold on, Lettow-Vorbeck. We are gentlemen, you and I, and we shall not part without a drink to settle this in a seemly fashion. In all things I hope you'll understand that what I have said here this evening has been in the interests of our colony."

"While I, Excellency, have spoken in the interests of the Fatherland."

Who was this upstart commander who had taken it upon himself to set aims for German strategy in East Africa? And what were the military forces he could count on to carry out those aims?

Lt.-Col. Paul Emil von Lettow-Vorbeck has been characterized as the archetype of the Prussian junker. That sort of characterization might serve to describe Lettow (for that is what we may call him) at a passing glance—blond hair cropped close to the skull in the Prussian fashion, steely blue eyes set beneath rugged brows, a fierce beak of a nose and a narrow mustache over a thin-lipped mouth—yet that glance would

General von Lettow-Vorbeck

miss the real man within. The incisive mind that went straight
to the core of a problem was wedded to a Spartan self-dis-
cipline that enabled his lean body to endure all the hardships
that would have to be faced in the four years of fighting his
enemies in some of the roughest terrain in the world.

At the age of forty-four, in 1914, Lettow had come to
his post in Africa with twenty-five years of service that provided unmatched credentials for command of the colony's

military. After graduation from the military school at Kassel and postings to regimental duties, he served alongside the British in Peking during the Boxer Rebellion, where he gained an impression of "the clumsiness with which English troops were moved and led in battle"—a prophetic insight into the battle where we will see Lettow in action against them. His first experience with operations in Africa came while on detached service with pre-Boer War forces in South Africa under the famed commando leader Louis Botha. Lettow's introduction to African bush fighting followed in 1904 when he was assigned in South West Africa as adjutant to General von Trotha. In the German service of that time and area of operations, the adjutant was not a paper shuffler; he was a chief of personal staff who was required to serve as the occasion demanded as a line officer. It was during the latter kind of duty that Lettow was wounded in the eye and chest while fighting the Hereros. During that campaign, the Hereros had combined with their allies, the Hottentots, to give white colonials their greatest headache since the Zulu Wars.

Initially the Germans learned the hard way, for they found themselves pitted against skillful bush fighters whose operations were masterminded by cunning tacticians. These uncharted and desolate wastes, which varied from savannas to rockbound hills to endless miles of dense thorn growths, the *nyika* or the *bundu,* formed the bitter background in which the young Lettow saw at firsthand something his brother officers failed to appreciate—that small groups of highly motivated men, inured to and familiar with the terrain, could tie up much larger European-trained and organized forces. The Africans could survive and fight where European troop movements became "walking hospitals." Moreover, the native guerrilla fighters could find water in deserts where white men dropped from thirst, and they could move more swiftly through the brush than their enemies could follow on horseback.

There were lessons to be learned in that hard school, and Lettow went on to learn them from the enemy. Like Henry Bouquet a century and a half earlier, Lettow was not too proud to learn from either unfriendly or friendly natives. He soon picked up the basics of bush fighting: how not to be led by a "fleeing" enemy into an ambush; how to meet night attacks with the bayonet instead of with wild firing; to realize that organized units were most vulnerable when in the act of breaking camp; and to develop a healthy respect for the crude weapons of the bush fighter—be they muzzle-loading muskets, spears, or poisoned arrows. When Lettow came back for a tour of duty in Germany he was beyond doubt the Kaiser's most skilled officer in conducting guerrilla warfare in African terrain.

When Lettow returned to take command of the defense forces in German East Africa (later Tanganyika, then Tanzania) he had no sooner reported to the Governor than he was off into the up-country on his first inspection of his *Schutztruppe* companies. He went north from Dar es Salaam by ship to the port of Tanga, then overland to the Usambara Mountains where he met Capt. Tom von Prince, the famed *"Bwana Sakarani,"* the Man Who Is Drunk With Fighting. This walking legend had been a classmate of Lettow's at Kassel. He had been born an Englishman, Thomas Prince, had been refused a commission in the British Army, and had turned to the Prussian service. After years of savage fighting against the rebellious Hehes, Prince had been awarded the teutonic "Von," and had settled down as a retired farmer in the up-country. He would prove an invaluable subordinate in the coming days when the chips were down.

Lettow's survey of troops and terrain took over half a year, during which he had ample time to think of his upcoming role; his busy mind was fully aware of the war threatening in Europe. By the time he returned to the capital his strategy had been clearly formed. He had no illusions about the strategic capabilities of his fourteen companies (totaling 216 officers and 2,450 askaris) in the vastness of German East Africa, a territory three times the size of the Fatherland. So he sat down and thought it out. As soon as war would be declared, the Royal Navy would cut off any reinforcement from Germany, while the British and Belgians would be able, at will, to build up forces and supplies until their numerical superiority would be unquestioned. *But there was the key—that numerical superiority.* Why should not he, Lettow, see that those numbers grew and grew? Obviously he would be outnumbered at the start by at least two or three to one. Why not employ the *Schutztruppe* (augmented by porters, native police, rifle clubs, and what have you) tactically in a guerrilla war to force the British to a buildup that would require at least ten to one odds just to stand off Lettow's raids? And ten (or more) to one odds would mean tying up British men and guns away from the European theater where they would have greatly increased the threat to German arms. It was clear to Lettow that he should take the offensive, using guerrilla tactics, so that he could "grip the enemy by the throat and force him to employ his forces for self-defense."

The question of where that jugular would be most vulnerable was the factor that had brought Lettow into his confrontation with Governor Schnee. The answer was as clear to Lettow as it was repulsive to Schnee: it was the "Taveta Gap," south of Kilimanjaro. A British force coming from Voi (at the critical junction of the Uganda Railway and the Voi-Moshi Line) would have the best chance of invading German East Africa through that pass in order to strike at the German Northern Railway and into the interior in conjunction with other forces invading through coastal ports like Tanga or Jasin. Now, if Lettow could win guerrilla-type victories over such invading, European-type forces ("victories" that could be won by bogging down or harassing organized forces would be just as effective as winning pitched battles), he could also mount a series of raids to cut that vital artery, the Uganda Railway. We have seen the Governor's reaction to that strategy, but Lettow plunged ahead in the fall of 1914 to win out eventually over the Governor and to concentrate his companies at New Moshi and along the Northern Railway. What were these companies that made up the *Schutztruppe*?

In the first place they were the finest bush fighting force, native or European, in East Africa. Clearly the askaris (native soldiers) of the *Schutztruppe* were not trained into an elite overnight. The Germans, having learned from their wars subjugating the hostile tribes, began to hand-pick the officer cadres that would lead the askaris. Selection boards took only the best qualified, and their African service counted for double when computing pensions. Leadership counted first, followed by intelligence and character, and the medical exam was the toughest in the German Army. In the end, a colonial officer corps without parallel led the companies which had been recruited from selected bush fighters. The recruits were selected from tribes with great martial traditions, and the pay, privileges, and attendant prestige allowed the German recruiters to pick and choose. As an example of the incentives, the pay scales were twice what the British had set for their askaris.

The end products were combat units with native mobility, trained and equipped to fight in either European-style or bush warfare. The basic unit was the company, a small independent command of seven or eight German officers and NCOs and 150 to 200 askaris. The company had two machine gun teams, and could be reinforced with porters and *ruga-ruga*, tribal irregulars. The company was not bound into a rigid battalion or regimental structure—there were no such administrative or tactical headquarters—instead, when necessary, a provisional *abteilung* could direct two or more companies. There were no supply links or lines, each company being self-sufficient and able to operate indefinitely on its own. In short, the *Schutztruppe* company was a mobile combat team ideally adaptable to guerrilla warfare. There were, however, in Lettow's eyes, two serious shortcomings in some companies: the low level of rifle marksmanship and the obsolete rifle with which German colonial infantry had been armed. The first Lettow could strive to overcome with higher standards of training. The second was, for the time being, an incurable headache. The single-shot, Model 71, .450-caliber Mausers were dubbed an enemy "secret weapon" by Lettow because their clouds of black powder smoke were an instant giveaway of the firer's position. Eventually Lettow was able to get six companies armed with modern magazine rifles (many through the courtesy of the British Army), but at war's opening in 1914, eight companies had to fight under this serious handicap.

Although the African sun was beating down on the galvanized iron of the verandah roof, the light upland breeze kept things pleasantly cool for Lettow and his bearded companion. Lettow eased back in his straight-backed chair and handed the sheaf of telegrams to von Prince.

"There you are," Lettow said, "all in order by date, so help yourself to a light bit of history."

"Why do you say 'light,' Colonel?" von Prince asked.

"Light in the sense of comic opera, if you will. But read on, we don't have all afternoon, and I have troop trains to dispatch, as you know. Go ahead and read them aloud, that will be a good review for both of us."

Von Prince's white teeth gleamed in his black beard as he picked up the telegram on top.

"This one, dated the twenty-fifth of October, is from your pal, the Governor. Can you imagine that fool in his dream world? The war has been going on for three months in Europe, and he still dashes about mouthing neutrality. Well—"

"Well, get on with it, or you'll be sitting here in New Moshi by yourself," Lettow said.

"His Excellency says—'Stop military occupation of Tanga, town and harbor, because not defensible. Send telegraphic information about such new circumstances as make in your opinion the occupation of Tanga necessary.' That sounds direct enough. Then this one is your answer, correct?" von Prince said.

"Of course, sent the next day."

"I like this part—'Use of Tanga lodgings seemed advisable in view of healthy climate. Dar es Salaam was until now used for accommodating First Rifles. Please wire whether despite this Tanga should be evacuated.' So—Tanga lodgings indeed!"

"I thought you'd appreciate that part about the healthy climate. The next one you have there should be the Governor's reply, of the twenty-seventh of October."

"So it is—'Stationing in Tanga approved with proviso that forces must be evacuated inconspicuously immediately when warships appear. Executive power remains with district commissioner.' And so that was what prompted you to go to Tanga and talk with District Commissioner Auracher, right?"

"Correct. I had to go in person in order to remind Auracher that he was still a lieutenant in the reserve and, further, that his responsibility to the Army in time of war superseded his civil administrative duties," Lettow said.

"Was that enough to bring him around?"

"Yes, but it remained for me to order him to start helping to prepare the defenses of Tanga, and under no circumstances was he to hand the town over to the enemy—unless he wanted to face a court-martial. Oh, he came around all right, especially when I assured him that I would take full responsibility for his actions."

Von Prince started to unfold the next telegram when a German unteroffizier ran up the verandah steps, banged to a halt, and saluted Lettow.

"Herr Oberst-leutnant, Captain von Hammerstein's train from Tanga will be at the station in fifteen minutes. Shall I say that you wish him and the other officers to report to you here?"

"Thank you, Baumer, tell them instead to meet me at the station-master's office. And tell the adjutant to have my operations map set up there," Lettow ordered.

The Commandant was on his feet, as lithe and quick as a cat. He showed one of his rare, thin-lipped smiles to von Prince.

"Come on, Tom. What I've got to say to these officers will bring you up to date faster and better than reading telegrams."

All of the nine *Schutztruppe* officers on the station platform were well acquainted with von Prince, so Lettow wasted no time on formalities. There were no such luxuries as chairs in the tiny shack that represented the New Moshi terminus of the Northern Railway, so the group stood in a half-circle around Lettow with the map propped on the easel.

"A couple of you know most of my plans, others only fragments, which means that I will bring us all into the picture in order that we carry on the operation from here on a common ground.

"First, our intelligence picture. I have confirmation which shows that the British expeditionary force from India—what they call 'Force B'—reached Mombasa, then sailed from there on 1 November en route to Tanga, obviously the first British objective. We don't know their whole order of battle, but we do know that there are two brigades comprising as many as eight to ten battalions—a force I estimate to number at least six thousand infantry.

"There can be no doubt that the enemy seeks to seize Tanga, then advance up our Northern Railway toward New Moshi. If they can reach this point, Force B would link up with other Indian Army units moving up the Uganda Railway through Voi and Taveta toward Moshi. Yes, von Hammerstein, what is it?"

"Colonel, is it possible that the other British force is already on the way up the Uganda Railway?" the captain asked.

"No such intelligence has been confirmed. What we do know—and what is critical to understand here and now—is that the 17th Field Company in Tanga succeeded in beating back the first enemy landing force this morning. Next, you all know that I started troop trains moving the *Schutztruppe* companies down this railway to Tanga, beginning the day before yesterday after I received District Commissioner—I should say, Lieutenant—Auracher's telegram that the captain of the British cruiser *Fox* had entered Tanga harbor and demanded the surrender of the town. Auracher stalled him off, and when he got back to Tanga from the cruiser, hauled down the white flag the Governor had ordered flown, and replaced it with the Imperial colors. Then, I'm told, he went home, put on his uniform, and went to join the 17th Company.

"But enough of that. Know that within eighteen hours we can have all thousand of our men in Tanga, that is, by four tomorrow morning. I will stay here until I see the last train loaded, and I will come into Tanga on that. I see you smiling, Captain von Prince. What have I done to make you so cheerful?"

Von Prince returned Lettow's piercing stare without losing his broad smile.

"Sir, I have cause to be glad to be going into this fight with you, but I was thinking now about this toy railway with its eight engines pulling those little coaches 190 miles with askaris bulging out every window—and every man wearing a grin you could see in the dark," von Prince said.

"A trip on a train is the delight of their lives even though they know it means going into battle. Since you've mentioned it, you all should know that we are working every official and man of the Northern Railway right around the clock. Now, no more interruptions, gentlemen. Time is precious, and I want to end this conference by bringing you up to date on what has happened to the 17th and its reinforcements in Tanga.

"Early this morning a British force had completed disembarking on the east side of Ras Kasone and sent what has been estimated to be two battalions against Tanga. Our 17th Company was dug in in prepared positions east of the railway yard. The company, reinforced with reservists and police, numbered about two hundred and twenty men with four machine guns. They waited until the enemy had struggled through the bush and the plantations to within a hundred yards, then they opened fire. Even their old Model 71s were effective, and I must add that the marksmanship records of the 17th, one of the best in the *Schutztruppe*, paid off handsomely. The enemy attack was halted, then cut to pieces. The Indian soldiers panicked and fell back, and at least a dozen of their officers were killed while trying to rally them. The two enemy battalions—identified later as the 13th Rajputs and the 61st Pioneers—broke and ran when our 17th counterattacked. Their estimated losses were over three hundred killed and wounded, and the rest ran like stampeded cattle back to their landing beach near the Red House.

"I want the word passed through all your companies about the splendid conduct of the men of the 17th. It will be the best reward they can have to know that the *Schutztruppe* can take on and defeat with ease any number of these Indian and British insects. Yes—*Wahindi ni wadudu!**

"Now, to your companies. I'll see you tomorrow morning in Tanga."

Lettow swung off the engine cab step, and felt his boots scrape solid ground. He ignored the outstretched helping hand of the railway official, and called for his bicycle. It was already being handed out the door of the first coach by two askaris. Lettow reached up and took the bicycle, grunting his thanks in Swahili. In the bright African moonlight he could not miss the astounded looks on both black soldiers' faces. Then he remembered his blackened face, a precaution he had taken after boarding the train. What had gone through those askaris' minds when they saw their *Schutztruppe* Commandant revealed as a black man there in the moonlight would one day make a wonderful story to relate to the officers' mess, but there was no time for such thoughts now. He wheeled his bicycle down the crushed rock of the railway shoulder and swung into the seat just as he heard Major Kraut, his second-in-command, and his assistant crunch down the embankment to halt beside him.

"I've stopped the train at the three-mile marker, we'll have to make it into Tanga from here on our own. What time do you make it?" Lettow said.

"I have four minutes past three," Major Kraut said, "we should meet Captain Baumstark on our way, if he's on time."

"You won't have to worry about him. That's probably him coming now," Lettow said.

The captain's stocky figure emerged from the shadow of the palms at the edge of a clearing. He put down his bicycle and reported to Lettow.

"I've pulled the 17th back to the west side of town. Didn't

*"The Indians are insects"—"insect" representing one of the vilest insults in Swahili.

have enough strength to hold the whole place, not knowing where and in what strength the enemy could be coming at us next."

"A sound move, Captain," Lettow said. "What security measures have you taken around the town?"

"I have outposted the east side of Tanga, mostly along the railway, and there are patrols operating between outposts. And the last thing I did before coming to meet you was to put the 6th Field Company—they had just arrived— in a forward position near the railway station to cover the south flank and to man the post at the railway embankment," Baumstark said.

"Excellent, but we don't know anything of the enemy beyond our outposts, do we? I'm going to have a look for myself. In the meantime, Captain Baumstark, there could be no better guide than you to lead the troops from this train into their assembly areas on this side of town. See that their company officers start unloading the train now. I'll see you later at your command post," Lettow ordered.

"Sir," Major Kraut was quick to speak because Lettow was already back on his bicycle, "I must make two recommendations. Anything might happen to you at night in the town. Let me and a patrol go ahead on reconnaissance. You should stay here and get some rest. You have not had a wink of sleep for at least thirty hours."

"Since when, Major, have I had my officers do my reconnoitering for me? As for sleeping, this is hardly the time for it, with an enemy who outnumbers us at least six-to-one and who are getting set to launch a new attack. No, you and your adjutant come with me. We're wasting the one resource that can never be replaced—time."

The major knew better than to argue with the Prussian disciplinarian. He and the adjutant mounted up in silence.

Tanga was deserted. The silent streets bordered by the European houses—stark white under the African moon in contrast to the black shadows of gardens and their borders of trees—echoed only to the soft swish of their bicycle tires. The three rode on in silent file through the town, turning northward until they came to the harbor. Lettow paused long enough to watch the glare of lights around the British transports where the din of activity was loud enough to carry across the harbor to Lettow and his companions a half-mile away.

He spoke in a lowered voice to Kraut, his teeth gleaming in his blackened face.

"God, I suppose they can afford to be noisy. The fools had already given Baumstark a good twenty-four hours notice before their first attack. What I wouldn't give for those two old 1873 field guns! Even those could raise a bit of hell with that unloading going on out there. Any word on those guns yet?"

"Only that they had to hold them in New Moshi until all the troop trains had been dispatched," Kraut said.

Lettow only grunted, but that spoke a world of disgust. He mounted, and they turned eastward on the Hospital Road that led out to Ras Kasone. They parked their bicycles at the dark Government Hospital, and continued eastward on foot along the beach. They plodded along in silence, pausing now and then for Lettow to stare out toward the cruiser *Fox* and the lighters milling around the transports. After a half-mile of such patrolling, Lettow turned back toward the hospital. In all their reconnaissance, through and around Tanga as well as along the beach, they had not come across a single enemy soldier. In a matter of minutes, Lettow was to learn they had been inside enemy lines even before they had left the hospital.

They retrieved their bicycles and were riding back toward town. As before, they moved in silence. When Lettow rounded a bend to head westward, he skidded to a halt at a sharp challenge from the shadows. The voice sounded military, but the language was strange. Lettow's reaction was instantaneous.

"*Stambuli!*" He bellowed in his loudest parade-ground manner, using the *Schutztruppe* countersign.

The only reply was a crashing through the brush as the Indian sentry fled into the blackness. Lettow picked up his bicycle, shrugged, and they rode on toward the railway station and Baumstark's command post.

It was growing light when Lettow laid aside the Governor's telegram. Lieutenant Auracher had given it to him an hour before, but he had thrust it into a pocket of his jacket, too busy at the time giving final deployment orders to company commanders. Now, he found himself mid-way between dismay and righteous indignation.

"You are forbidden," it read, "to subject Tanga, and the

defenseless subjects of the town, to the rigors of war. Even should the enemy land in force, there must be no resistance. Tanga must be saved from bombardment . . ."

My God, Lettow thought, *the "defenseless subjects" are long gone, and "the rigors of war" are here. Does Schnee think that I'm going to let the British walk into Tanga, and then move, as they please, up the Northern Railway or into the interior?*

Later, he was to voice his thoughts in somber detail when he wrote in *My Reminiscences of East Africa:* "Already my method of waging active war had met with disapproval. If on top of that we were to suffer a severe defeat the confidence of the troops would probably be gone, and it was certain that my superiors would place insuperable difficulties in the way of my exercising command [less formally—the Governor would fire him, and that would be an end to military operations] . . . But there was nothing [else] for it; to gain all we must risk all."

He repocketed the telegram, and went back to the operations map that had been set up in the railway station waiting room. Major Kraut, a box of map pins in his left hand, was marking the company positions with blue pins and what was known of the enemy with red.

"Are you ready to give this a final going over before you disappear again?" the major's question was posed in a familiar tone that no one else dared use with Lettow.

"You sound like a mother hen. Really, did you ever fail to know my whereabouts?" Lettow asked with a straight face.

"I know better than to try and answer that. Well, to make a recapitulation, here is where you had the 6th Field Company move—on about an eight hundred meter front along the railway cutting to cover the east side of the town."

"I know they're stretched thin, but they've got the Gewehr 98 Mausers, and so with the best of magazine rifles and their good marksmanship scores, the 6th will hold that position," Lettow said.

"Baumstark's *abteilung,*" Kraut went on, "made up of the 16th and 17th Companies, will cover the front to the right of the 6th, as well as our right flank, using the railway embankments wherever possible."

"And that leaves us with only the 13th Company and von Prince's units as force reserve?" Lettow asked.

"Yes, and since the 13th and von Prince's 7th and 8th

Schutzen Companies* are our only troops who have traded shots with the British, before yesterday, you should find them a reliable reserve."

"I'd feel more comfortable if I knew when we could expect the 4th and 9th Companies to arrive. And what about the two field guns?"

"All we know," Kraut said, "is that the two companies, and the guns, are somewhere en route."

"*Wunderbar*," Lettow growled, "and you realize that even with the 4th and the 9th we will still be able to face the British with only a thousand rifles. That against what we now estimate to be over six thousand Indians and British."

"True, but why don't you count our other firepower?" Kraut asked.

"Yes, of course, the machine guns. You're right to count them in. We've got our best men on the machine-gun teams, and it remains for us to see how hard training will pay off. Any more word on the British?"

"Our observers see many more units unloading than yesterday. They probably used only two battalions in that initial attack, but now by dependable count the battalions unloading indicate that Aitken may be going to employ his whole force. And that appears to indicate that your estimate of six thousand may have been too low," Kraut said.

"I'll worry about that when we see them coming. I'm off now. I'll be out there checking on the 6th, the 16th, the 17th, and then the reserves, in that order."

"Things are quiet, a good time for you to catch a nap. There's plenty of time."

"Not while we're still organizing our defense. I'll be keeping in touch by telephone."

By midmorning the boiling humidity of the coastal plain had begun to build up. Most of the *Schutztruppe* companies had relaxed for three months in the mountain breezes of the up-country along the Northern Railway, and now the officers and askaris were paying for it as they tried to get used to the tropical heat. Here, five degrees south of the equator, it was eternal summer with one of the most humid atmospheres in the world.

---

*Sharpshooter companies made up of colonial German volunteers, many from rifle clubs.

Lettow ignored the searing sun, or made a good pretense of it, as he made his way from platoon to platoon and to the machine gun teams. There were fields of fire to be verified for the riflemen, traverse limits and overlapping fires for the machine guns. There were company ammunition reserves and resupply measures to be checked. Lettow had to be shown all the essentials, even using the field telephone to call back to his command post—not always to talk with Major Kraut, but to verify that wire communications were in order.

At last, satisfied, he returned to his command post at noon for a final prebattle conference with his commanders. He had traded his tropical helmet for the slouch hat with the upturned side brim that was to become a distinguishing mark for the war years. His face was still caked with blacking that had begun to crack and peel. Two bandoliers crossed his chest over his dusty uniform jacket, and he had rested his rifle in a corner of the room before he had opened the conference. Now, he was concluding his summation before he sent them back to their units.

"See that your men get all the rest in the shade that they can. They're going to have a long wait. The enemy may have started his advance about ten this morning, but they still don't realize what kind of a hell they have to move through. They will be hours struggling through the bush, the undergrowth of the rubber plantations, and the sisal crops, and don't forget the dense thorn-brush.

"Remember that we know how to fight in the bush. They don't. We know how to maneuver here on our ground, and they don't. Our troops are fighting on their kind of land, and the enemy is not. Now, back to your commands, and remind your men that God is with us."

Lettow yielded at last to Kraut's insistent appeals and stretched out on a field cot for a catnap. It seemed to Kraut that he had scarcely gotten back to his map and messages before Lettow walked back in, looking at his wristwatch.

"I have ten minutes after one. Same with you?" Lettow asked.

"You know it is. We synchronized our watches when you started that last conference," Kraut said.

"Now, *I'm* being the old woman. Any reports of importance?"

"Not any particular one, but there is a sameness to what the observers are reporting. The Indians and the British keep trying to maintain a general line as they advance, but the bush is too much for them. They are trying to use some kind of open order, but they don't know how to control squads and platoons in the mangrove swamps, the plantations, or the thorn scrub. What's more, squads of sepoys are collapsing from heat exhaustion."

"Poor devils. All this after weeks of rolling in their own puke, jammed aboard those transports for 2,500 miles in the heat of the Indian Ocean. But all the evil things that have happened to those Indians make it easier for our men."

Lettow had to wait for over two hours, pacing the rooms of his command post and chain-smoking in the way that was to become his habit before battle. The smoking was the only sign of his restlessness. His face and bearing showed an otherwise outward calm. One-thirty passed, then two o'clock, and still no word of forces in contact. At two-thirty the rattle of intermittent rifle firing could be heard, and Lettow soon realized that *Schutztruppe* snipers, firing from skillfully concealed positions in the baobab trees and coco palms, were picking off enemy officers and NCOs.

Three o'clock had passed when Lettow could tell it in his own words, "an askari reported to me in his simple, smart way: '*Adui tayari.*' (The enemy is ready.) Those two short words I shall never forget."

As the reports of the enemy's coming within rifle range increased, Lettow could no longer keep the lid on his boiling impatience. He hurried down to the 6th Company where he could see things at firsthand. After settling down to share the company commander's observation post, the situation in front of the 6th gave him cause for renewing his confidence in his troops. The dit-a-dit-dit of the 6th's Maxims took up a measured rhythm as the machine gunners showed off their training in firing carefully controlled bursts. They were joined by the rifles of the platoons, firing first in volleys, then in fire-at-will as the platoon leaders gave their commands for taking up individual, aimed fire. All across the front of the 6th the results were uniformly disastrous for the sepoys of the 63rd Palmacottah Light Infantry, the Indian battalion that had been unlucky enough to be advancing in the center of the 6th Company's sector. Those Indian soldiers who were left standing after the first German volleys and machine-gun rakings turned and took to flight in a body back toward their landing beach, many throwing down their rifles as they ran.

Lettow turned his attention toward the left center of the 6th's sector where the Indian 13th Rajputs and 61st Pioneers were repeating their performance of the day before in their first engagement against the 17th Company. The two battalions were panicking and joining in wild flight to the rear, in parallel fashion with the 63rd Palmacottah Light Infantry. For a flash of time all that could be seen to the front of the 6th were glimpses of the khaki turbans and cutaway jackets of the fleeing Indians. The cry passed from squad to squad as the askaris took up the shout—"*Wahindi ni wadudu!*"

Lettow was leaving to observe the defenses on the right flank when a phone call from Kraut caught up with him before he got away from the 6th Company's command O.P.

"Things may be going well in front of the 6th," Kraut said, "but you had better get back here. You can't be at the center and on both flanks at once, and you're needed here because I see the need for command decisions coming up soon."

"Things not going as well on the flanks then. Is that it?" Lettow asked.

"Not well at all, and there is too much to tell you over the phone. You will have to see the situation on the map to follow it all."

"I'm on my way."

Major Kraut's tense face had told Lettow, more than mere words could, that his attention was badly needed at the map.

"So they have gotten around the 6th's left flank and into the town. They must be a different kind of soldier than what I saw in front of the 6th," Lettow said, grinding out his cigarette and fixing his monocle in his left eye.

"That's right, these are Gurkhas of the Kashmir Rifles, and they've already sliced up a few of our men with their *kukris*. But what's more important, the Gurkhas have gotten around the Customs House and reached the Hotel Deutscher Kaiser where they've hauled down our flag and run up the Union Jack," Kraut said.

"And on our force right flank—what is happening there?"

"The British battalion, the L.N.L., you know, the Loyal North Lancashires, have broken through across the railway cutting, and some elements have managed to link up with the Gurkhas, and they seemed to be able to adapt to street fighting."

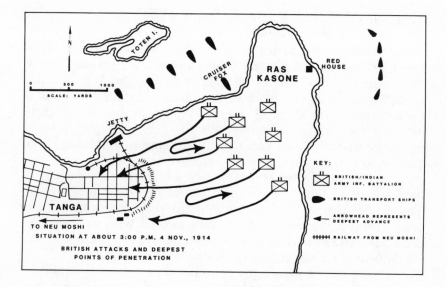

RAS
KASONE

RED
HOUSE

CRUISER
FOX

TOTEN I.

JETTY

TANGA

TO NEU MOSHI

SITUATION AT ABOUT 3:00 P.M. 4 NOV., 1914

BRITISH ATTACKS AND DEEPEST
POINTS OF PENETRATION

SCALE: YARDS

KEY:

BRITISH/INDIAN
ARMY INF. BATTALION

BRITISH TRANSPORT SHIPS

ARROWHEAD REPRESENTS
DEEPEST ADVANCE

RAILWAY FROM NEU MOSHI

"My, aren't we bursting with good tidings! If that is all of the situation report, give me one piece of good news—I hope that our phone line to von Prince is still working."

Kraut took the field phone from an *unteroffizier,* gave its crank a turn, and handed the handset to Lettow who got his good news in the form of von Prince answering in person.

"Quickly," Lettow said, "how much do you know of the situation in our center—in the town itself."

Von Prince's voice carried the calm tone of the veteran bush fighter.

"I've had a few pot shots myself at Gurkhas and British near that little square this side of the office buildings. They are trying to make up enough assault teams to get through the center of town. But I've moved up my machine guns and am getting ready to deploy my—"

"If you're ready, go ahead and do it," Lettow cut in, "commit everything you have. It's up to you to restore the center and kick those bastards out of Tanga."

"If you hadn't said that, I'd have thought I was on the wrong line. We are moving out, Herr Oberst-Leutnant."

Tense moments passed before Lettow got the first of welcome reports from flank units and von Prince's command post. The 7th and 8th *Schutzen* Companies tore into the town with blazing machine guns and rifles. The German volunteers had been chafing at being held back in reserve, and now they sprang into action with a vengeance. Firing from roof-tops, windows, and down alleys and streets, they over-whelmed the enemy assault teams before they could renew their attack. They drove the Gurkhas and the L.N.L. back toward the railway cutting, and though they had not yet turned the situation around, von Prince's riflemen and machine-gun-ners had saved the German center.

Now that his line in and east of Tanga was holding, Let-tow could turn his attention to his right flank—and none too soon. Baumstark's two companies had been forced back by a new penetration of the railway cutting on the south side of Tanga. Baumstark had committed his reserve platoons in a counterattack, but some of the new askaris who were seeing their first action had begun to falter and were taking cover. In minutes Lettow had raced to the scene.

It took only a glance for him to see that if positive action was not taken on the spot the young askaris would panic and that contagion could spread throughout both companies; the result could mean only disaster for the force's flank.

Lettow marched through the coco palms to the clearing where he would be in full view of his askaris—and the en-emy. Turning his back to the British, Lettow faced the cowed men gaping at him from behind the palms, and began to mock them.

"Are these the great warriors of the Wahehe and the Angoni? And are there other little children here from the Wanyamezi and the Wagogo? What would the chiefs of those warrior tribes say of these little men who hide behind trees in fear of their enemies?" Lettow's derisive voice reverberated through the trees, and for seconds there was silence.

The tension was broken by Captain von Hammerstein who was striding toward Lettow. An askari near the captain's right got up and took a step toward the rear. Von Hammer-stein reached in his map case, fetched out a half-empty wine bottle, and hurled it at the soldier. The bottle caught him alongside the head, and sent him reeling. There were bursts of laughter as askaris got sheepishly to their feet, picked up their rifles, and began to form into skirmish line under their squad leaders. The bizarre episode, coming at the moment of Lettow's shaming them, was all it took to restore order and get the counterattack moving.

It was near 4:30 when Lettow got back to his C.P. for an update on the overall situation. This time the intelligence reports lacked the note of pending disaster to Lettow's force, but things remained in a precarious state when he reviewed the whole picture in his mind.

The British, he thought, *attacked initially on about a thousand-meter front with something like ten battalions. We have routed at least four and have caused severe casualties in at least three others. But they almost took the town from me, and only now has my reserve under von Prince restored the center. That center seems to be holding, but—and there is the greatest "but"—that leaves me no force reserve, no reserves at all. The 4th and 9th Companies have still not shown up, and the only maneuverable unit that I can possibly use is the 13th Company.*

He looked back at the map, this time focusing his attention on Kraut's red map pins marking the enemy's battalions in his center and left flank.

"Look here," he said to Kraut," the British have never been able to plug the gap the Palmacottah Light Infantry left when we routed them. Am I correct, and are those pins still showing our latest intelligence on the L.N.L. and the 101st Bombay Grenadiers?"

"You are right in both cases."

"Then that 101st has been trying, as I see it, to shift to its right in an effort to close the gap left by the Palmacottahs. That leaves the 101st's left flank, and the whole British force's left flank, extended and wide open."

"My God, you're right. I see what you mean."

"Well, then take this down."

Lettow's orders directed the immediate move of the 13th to swing wide around the British left and cut in on it with enfilading fire from the flank. He reinforced it with two machine guns in the expectation that the four guns would be sufficient to wreak havoc with the 101st Grenadiers.

His expectation was realized beyond anything he had dared imagine. The four machine guns were rushed into their new positions, and within minutes their interlaced fires were slaughtering the Indians. These sepoys were made of better stuff than those who had turned and run in midafternoon. These Indians stood and fought, and within the next quarter-hour it became evident that those brave men had fought back for nothing. It might have been better—certainly less of a bloody debacle—if they had run. Within minutes the methodical German gunners had reduced the battalion to company strength, and the 101st as an effective fighting unit could be wiped from the map.

While the 13th Company was throwing everything it had in straining to keep up the momentum of its counterattack, the gods of war began to smile on Lettow. The overdue 4th Company arrived, and Lettow had it brought forward at the double and thrown in on the left of the 13th. The two companies swung forward together, and the new impetus to the German counterattack doomed the forces on the British left. Lettow watched the collapse of the British flank units, and when he could see those battalions fold and stream away to their rear he was able to ascertain without doubt the beginning of a general withdrawal by the whole enemy force.

He grabbed the nearest field phone and got an excited Major Kraut on the other end.

"My God, the reports coming in!" Kraut was shouting so loudly that Lettow had to hold the handset away from his ear. "They're beaten! They're falling back everywhere!"

"If you'll stop shouting, Georg, you would find out that I'm aware of all that, and that I'm calling to give an order, not to listen to dramatics." Lettow's voice was sharp but calm. The chastened major answered that he was ready to acknowledge.

"Order a general advance—a bayonet attack all across the front. I will be at this observation post if you need to reach me."

In the minutes that followed the transmission of Lettow's order, the rattling din of rifle and machine gun fire gave way to a pandemonium made up of whistle blasts, tribal war cries, and bugle calls as the *Schutztruppe* companies swept forward to get at their enemy with the bayonet. The British retirement that had begun as an attempt at orderly disengagement began to dissolve into a rout. Then something happened to deliver the coup de grâce to an already ruined British cause.

It was the native custom to hang their beehives on tree limbs, and a number of hives had been struck by random bullets. The infuriated bees poured forth to launch an attack of their own against the unfortunate Indians and British. Charles Miller in *Battle for the Bundu** makes the comparison

*Macmillan, 1974.

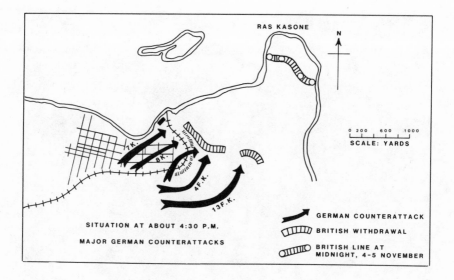

RAS KASONE

N

SITUATION AT ABOUT 4:30 P.M.

MAJOR GERMAN COUNTERATTACKS

0   200   600   1000
SCALE: YARDS

GERMAN COUNTERATTACK

BRITISH WITHDRAWAL

BRITISH LINE AT
MIDNIGHT, 4–5 NOVEMBER

that African bees "were to European bees what a leopard is to a tabby cat." Whatever their comparative ferocity, it is certain that each bee wielded his own bayonet, and in no time sepoys and British Tommies were seen dancing wildly about, throwing rifles aside to roll and writhe on the ground, or were leaping up to dash away in an effort to outrun their assailants. It was anything but funny to the participants; many faces, arms, and legs were swollen to twice their normal size. A British signalman managed to take down a message while under attack by the bees, and had to have over three hundred stings removed from his head; he was awarded the Distinguished Conduct Medal, no doubt an award that must have set a record for uniqueness in the history of the British Army. But the bees, however neutral their status before having their homes shot from beneath them, showed a savage impartiality in their assaults. The four machine guns of the 13th were out of action while the crews made frantic displacements to new positions. Lettow gained an unwanted notoriety that persisted for years among the British survivors: the bee attack had been a diabolical contrivance, master-minded by the German commander, that released the bee attack through trip wires that sprang open the lids of the hives. The myth was entirely unfounded, as Lettow never ceased to maintain.

When things had finally buzzed to an uneasy quiet in the bee zone, Lettow could survey the battlefield, bees and ter-

Native wild beehives at Tanga

rain permitting, to find that his victory was complete. Force B's rout had ended only at the water's edge, and by sundown the British were taking cover behind a defensive perimeter around the beachhead. There was no need for Lettow to try an assault on the beachhead, which he could not have managed in any event. It became clear on the following morning (November 5) that the whole thrust of Force B's activity was now directed toward evacuating all the unwounded to the safety of the transports, following which the force would steam back to Mombasa, a battered monument to—in the words of one historian—"a fruitful lesson on how not to start a colonial campaign."

Major-General Aitken, commanding Force B, left behind at Ras Kasone more than his wrecked career. In their haste to reembark the British abandoned on the beaches sixteen machine guns, enough rifles to rearm three of Lettow's companies, 600,000 rounds of ammunition, all their field telephones, and enough clothing and blankets to last the

Schutztruppe for the rest of the war. In addition, the British losses in casualties were shocking: 800 dead, 500 wounded, and an indeterminate toll of missing. On the other hand, Lettow's triumph had not come without its costs: 15 Europeans and 54 askaris; and worst of all, von Prince was killed in a Tanga street while leading his men, an incalculable personal loss to Lettow.

Yet this tremendous bag of captured materiel and supplies was nothing compared to, in Lettow's words, "the enemy's loss in *moral* [sic]; after being so soundly thrashed by a force one-eighth their own strength, the British and Indians almost began to believe in spirits and spooks."

All true, but Tanga was to establish three things that were beyond measures such as materiel and military morale. These factors can be considered in their ascending order of significance. Lettow had become a colonial hero, and Governor Schnee had to swallow the bitter medicine that would change his policy of neutrality as well as his plans for influencing Lettow's operations. Secondly, even the neutralists in a hitherto-divided colony were caught up in the patriotic spirit that swept across German East Africa, putting the colony squarely behind Lettow's cause for resisting invasion and providing him with volunteers and lasting material support. Lastly, Tanga gave Lettow the resounding send-off that he needed to launch and carry on a grueling four-year war of attrition and guerrilla operations; the war wherein he accomplished his deduced mission of tying up (keeping troops away from the war in Europe) over 130,000 Allied troops, mostly British and Indian Army, from November, 1914, to November, 1918.

General von Lettow-Vorbeck surrendered to the British on November 25, 1918, but only after he had been convinced that Germany had acknowledged defeat in the armistice of November 11, 1918, and the surrender of his forces had become obligatory. As Charles Miller has so aptly described the surrender: it was a "capitulation of an army that had not lost to an army that had not won."

Only in the last two decades has Lettow received belated recognition as the father of twentieth-century guerrilla warfare involving large-scale operations (no apologies to T. E. Lawrence). Lettow's right to such a title is being substantiated in a growing bibliography of no mean quality.

This chapter was designed to demonstrate the essentiality of personal energy as a force required to give life to one or more attributes of a leader. When one follows Lettow's actions, beginning with his supervision of troop movements (190 miles from Tanga) until the end of the battle three days later, one witnesses an incredible output of energy that enabled this leader to win his battle under a host of pressures. However, Tanga was not selected as a means of focusing on energy per se; it was selected because the leader's energy can be seen providing continual support to all the other attributes.

Yet Lettow should not be elevated to the status of a "better" leader simply because he appears to embody elements of five attributes. Such leaders appear once in an era and become stamped as "great captains" (Napoleon, Caesar, and Alexander are examples) and there are neither better leaders nor great captains in this book. There are only men whose actions have epitomized an attribute of leadership.

Lettow and his battle were chosen because they were representative of the leaders and battles in this study. By now the reader will have observed also that "decisive battles" do not appear in these pages. The omission has been deliberate so that the reader's insight would not be diverted by generations of writers who have concentrated on household words and great events. If this omission has helped the reader's vision, that alone should be reward for this work.

Epilogue

> Whereas there are for all men two ways of improvement, to wit
> by one's own disasters or those of others, the former is the more
> vivid, the latter is the less harmful.
>
> —Polybius

Bismarck is alleged to have stated the idea in blunter form:
"Fools say they learn by experience; I would learn from the
experience of others." In any event, no reasonable man wants
to learn the hard way, and that is what this journey through
time has been about: *ideas illuminated by the experience of others.*
The "others" have been men who used certain attributes to
develop, each in his own way, an art of leadership. The journey we have taken to look at that art in its formative stages
has reached four continents and covered a span of almost
twenty-two centuries. Any yet there have been only eleven
stops en route, and one of those in a fictional setting. The
matter of a limited number of stops—case histories—may
arouse some criticism.

   The more perceptive critics (those, of course, who think
as I do) might think that a sampling of ten factual cases is
not sufficient to convey the impact of the art over a period
of 2,200 years. There are two responses to that criticism. First,
when confronted with the task of scanning 1,500 battles for
examples of an art in practice, one soon finds that one must
adopt an eclectic method. Second, common sense will reveal

that a protracted parade of examples, no matter how color-ful, will in time tire the reader and "lose the name of action."

Yet the argument for examining a more extensive "spread" of leaders and battles is most persuasive, especially if the reader can be shown more leaders in a variety of situations across a broad range of history. However, before we venture further afield it would be helpful if we could get an over-the-shoul-der glance at where we have been and what we have seen. Table 1 enables us to take that look. The left and center col-umns are listings of leaders and battles in the order in which they have appeared in the text. The right-hand columns rep-resent the leader's attributes as they can be deduced from the depiction of the battle. The quality (or qualities) that went to make up an attribute are italicized and listed in the order of their contribution. For example, Scipio's *moral* courage was shown in his plan to attack a numerically superior enemy and in the execution of his plan; his *boldness* in conceiving and making his attack was a manifestation of his will; and his *imagination* enabled him to innovate—a clear demonstration of his intellectual powers. There may be cases where a reader disagrees with my conclusions regarding either an attribute or a contributing quality. If so, he has become an ally, for he has shown the readiness and the ability to make his own eval-uation.

Missing from the table is Kipling's Lungtungpen since, as a fictional case, it may have doubtful validity in an analysis of our observations. Also, *energy* is not shown as an attribute because, at this stage, it is evident that it is *essential as a main-stay of the others* and, as such, may be assumed to exist across the board. We will return to Table 1 when we can make a final evaluation of our findings. Table 2 presents an ex-tended range of leaders and battles. There are two additions to this table as an extension of Table 1: a column with dates and another with brief descriptions of the battles. These ad-ditions are aids for identifying a battle's place in history and its nature. The right side represents this writer's conclusions regarding the leader's attributes and qualities. One's accep-tance of these conclusions must, at this point, be based on faith if we are to complete an evaluation of this book's claim for finding the bases of an art of leadership. I say "based on faith" for two reasons: it would take another book merely to show the reasoning behind the selection and analyses of the lead-er's actions in each of the twenty-six battles in the table; fur-

Table 1
Conclusions Deducible From the Text

LEADER	BATTLE	ATTRIBUTES/QUALITIES			
		COURAGE	WILL	INTELLECT	PRESENCE
Morgan	Cowpens	*Moral* *Physical*	*Boldness*	*Imagination* *Flexibility* *Judgment*	
Wayne et al	Stony Point	*Physical*	*Boldness*	*Flexibility*	
Davout	Auerstadt	*Moral*	*Boldness* *Tenacity*	*Flexibility*	*Inspire*
Cortes	Cempoala	*Moral*	*Boldness*	*Judgment*	
Chard & Brom-head	Rorke's Drift	*Moral* *Physical*	*Tenacity*	*Flexibility*	*Inspire*
Scipio	Ilipa	*Moral*	*Boldness*	*Imagination*	
Bouquet	Bushy Run	*Moral* *Physical*	*Tenacity*	*Flexibility*	*Inspire*
Custer	Little Big Horn	*Physical*			*Inspire*
Lannes	Ratisbon	*Moral* *Physical*	*Boldness*	*Flexibility*	*Rally*
Lettow-Vorbeck	Tanga	*Moral* *Physical*	*Boldness* *Tenacity*	*Imagination* *Flexibility*	*Rally* *Inspire*

303

Table 2

Conclusions Deducible from an Extended Range of Leaders and Battles

Leader(s)	Battle	Date	Description	Attributes and Contributing Qualities
Epaminondas	Leuctra	371 B.C.	Tactical masterpiece defeats Spartans	Courage—Will—Intellect/Moral/Boldness/Imagination
Philip II of Macedon	Chaeronea	338 B.C.	Macedonian system conquers Greece	Courage—Will—Intellect/Moral/Tenacity/Flexibility
Alexander the Great	Arbela	331 B.C.	Alexander conquers Persian Empire	Courage—Will—Intellect—Presence/Moral-physical/Boldness/Flexibility/Inspire
Hannibal	Cannae	216 B.C.	Classical masterpiece of annihilation	Courage—Will—Intellect/Moral/Boldness/Imagination-innovation
Julius Caesar	Ilerda	49 B.C.	Bloodless tactical triumph over the Pompeians	Courage—Intellect/Moral/Imagination-judgment-flexibility
Narses the Eunuch	Taginae	552 A.D.	Justinian's general conquering Italy	Courage—Intellect/Moral/Imagination-flexibility
William the Conqueror	Hastings	1066	Norman conquest of England	Courage—Will—Intellect/Moral-physical/Boldness/Flexibility
Richard the Lion-Hearted	Arsouf	1191	Third Crusade victory over Saracens	Courage—Will—Presence/Moral-physical/Tenacity/Inspire
Sabuti & Batu	Sajo (or Mohi)	1241	Mongol invasion of Central Europe	Courage—Will—Intellect/Moral/Boldness/Imagination-flexibility
Henry V of England	Agincourt	1415	English archers/men-at-arms defeat French chivalry	Courage—Will/Moral-physical/Boldness-tenacity

Gonzalo de Cordoba	Garigliano	1503	Spanish surprise attack on the French	Courage—Will—Intellect—Presence/Moral/Boldness/Imagination/Inspire
Gustavus Adolphus	Breitenfeld	1631	Protestant victory over Catholics, Thirty Years War	Courage—Will—Intellect/Moral/Tenacity/Flexibility
Johan Baner	Wittstock	1636	Swedish victory over Saxon-Imperial Army	Courage—Will—Intellect/Moral/Boldness-tenacity/Imagination
Frederick the Great	Rossbach	1757	Prussian victory over French, Seven Years War	Courage—Will—Intellect/Moral/Boldness/Judgment-flexibility
Napoleon	Lodi	1796	Charge to seize bridge held by Austrians	Courage—Will—Presence/Moral-physical/Boldness/Rally-inspire
Napoleon	Castiglione	1796	Swift maneuver defeats Austrian strategic thrusts	Courage—Will—Intellect/Moral/Boldness/Judgment-flexibility
Napoleon	Austerlitz	1805	Tactical gem—defeats Austrians & Russians	Courage—Will—Intellect/Moral/Boldness/Imagination-flexibility
Wellington	Salamanca	1812	Outmaneuvers French to gain surprise	Courage—Will—Intellect/Moral/Boldness-tenacity/Judgment-flexibility
Stonewall Jackson	Valley Campaign	1862	Strategic/tactical masterpiece of maneuver	Courage—Will—Intellect/Moral/Boldness/Imagination-judgment-flexibility
Lee & Jackson	Chancellorsville	1863	Masters of maneuver gain surprise	Courage—Will—Intellect/Moral/Boldness/Imagination-judgment
Grant	Vicksburg Campaign	1863	Swift maneuver and rapid strikes separate the Confederacy	Courage—Will—Intellect/Moral/Boldness/Imagination-flexibility

Table 2 (continued)

Conclusions Deducible from an Extended Range of Leaders and Battles

Leader(s)	Battle	Date	Description	Attributes and Contributing Qualities
Hindenburg & Ludendorff	Tannenberg	1914	Masterful maneuver and surprise defeats Russians	Courage—Will—Intellect/Moral/ *Boldness/Imagination-flexibility*
von Below & Hutier	Caporetto	1917	Tactical surprise and exploitation	Intellect/*Imagination-flexibility* (adaptation of a new tactical system)
Byng & J. F. C. Fuller	Cambrai	1917	Tactical surprise, first use of massed tanks	Will—Intellect/*Boldness/ Imagination-innovation*
Rommel	Mersa Matruh	1942	Bold stroke in following up Gazala victory	Courage—Will—Intellect/*Moral/ Boldness/Flexibility*
Vo Nguyen Giap	Dienbienphu	1954	Vietminh exploit French strategical blunder	Courage—Intellect/*Moral/ Judgment-flexibility*

ther, if a skeptical and undaunted reader wishes to make his own evaluations (or selections) there are annotated sources in the last section of the bibliography which will aid in charting one's own course.

For those faithful who will follow the course of this evaluation, we should consider Tables 1 and 2 as superimposed to form a common ground on which we may move toward further inquiries. Table 3 shows the results of such an inquiry. These numbers are based on a count of the occurrence of certain attributes when all thirty-six cases (Table 1 plus Table 2) have been examined. While the resultant percentages may be interesting, let us lay them aside for a moment as we go on to look at Table 4. Here attributes have been scrutinized with these objectives in mind: to find what combinations have been demonstrated in the thirty-six cases; and to determine the percentage of occurrence of each combination when considering all the case histories.

When we place Tables 3 and 4 side by side we find two related and significant factors emerging. Table 3 shows courage, will, and intellect occurring respectively 94 percent, 86 percent, and 89 percent of the time. Turning to Table 4, we find the combination of the same three attributes occurring in 58 percent of the cases.

Then what is the significance of these findings? In answering this critical question it should be fair to reader and writer alike to review what has been accomplished and also to assess the means of discerning attributes in the leaders of today and tomorrow.

Table 3
Data on Single Attributes as Derived from Tables 1 and 2

Attribute	Number of Times Occurring[a]	Percentage of Occurrence[a]
Courage	34	94%
Will	31	86%
Intellect	32	89%
Presence	10	28%
Energy (assumed in all cases)		100%

a = Out of a total of 36 cases (Table 1 plus Table 2).

Table 4
Combinations of Attributes as Derived from Tables 1 and 2

Combinations	Number of Times Occurring[a]	Percentage of Occurrence[a]
Will—Intellect	1	3%
Courage—Will	1	3%
Courage—Intellect	3	8%
Courage—Presence	1	3%
Courage—Will—Intellect	21	58%
Courage—Will—Presence	2	6%
Courage—Will—Intellect—Presence	7	19%

a = Out of a total of 36 cases (Table 1 plus Table 2).

In the Introduction three goals were set: to show that battles could be won by the minds of leaders who were skilled in their art; to demonstrate that the art of leadership is embodied in the man himself; and to establish the fact that the art is based on certain attributes found in leaders who have proved themselves in battle. The reader was able to see skilled leaders practicing their art and sharpen his insight by seeing actions (and reactions) revealed through the minds and hearts of the leaders.

Moreover, attributes have been defined and the contributing qualities isolated to enable the reader to visualize each as a building-block in the creation of a leader's art. By no means, however, need the scope of historical examples be limited to those depicted in the book. Following the definitions of attributes, any number of selections and evaluations can be made.

It is a less simple task to determine the significance of the related findings from Tables 3 and 4. When one takes a second look at Table 4 one cannot avoid focusing on the triad: courage—will—intellect. It is remarkable enough that it occurs in 58 percent of the cases, but another look reveals that it recurs in the last-listed combination: courage—will—intellect—presence. Thus if we were to "combine the combinations" we would find the triad appearing in 77 percent (58 percent + 19 percent) of the cases—something of a revelation!

Surely such a combination, even if our sampling of case histories seems limited, points the way toward discerning and evaluating desirable attributes in military leaders. When that direction has been made clear, this book will have served yet another purpose: showing a better way of profiting from the experience of others. The better way has been established in these pages; its essence lies in the act of showing rather than telling. The lessons of military history can be stimulating as well as instructive if they are not reeled off as narratives told from an omniscient viewpoint.

When leaders and battles are presented by *showing*, the leader-to-be will learn to examine each historical case through his mind's eye, and ask the following questions:

What and where were the dynamics of battle that confronted the leader?

What attributes of the leader's art did he employ in overcoming his problems?

How should I have acted in the same situation?

Appendixes

Appendix A
Levels of The Conduct of War

This brief review is intended to serve only the theme and aims of this book. If it were not so restricted it would blunder into the crossfire that historians and analysts have raised in their sniping at one another's definitions for a half-dozen generations. That is why only three levels are defined (a fourth is considered but not retained) and exemplified; and then only in the descending order of their relevance to this writing.

TACTICS *is the art of fighting battles*—regardless of the size and extent of the operations of opposing forces. Prior to the First World War, tactics could be seen in action because the commander had a personal view of his battle. As the size of engaged forces increased in hitherto inconceivable proportions, the historians and analysts began to struggle with their definitions of battle and tactics. This was unnecessary. Despite the apparent disproportionate numbers in troops, space, and time the above definition retains its meaning.

Dan Morgan's Battle of Cowpens was over an hour after the first shots were fired. The total forces engaged numbered a little over 2,000 men, roughly the equivalent of two modern U.S. infantry battalions. The whole affair was consummated in an area less than a mile and half deep by three-quarters of a mile wide.

Thirty-four years later Waterloo was fought almost entirely on a Sunday afternoon, and the opposing forces totaled 140,000. The battle raged over a relatively small area about a mile and a half deep by two miles in width.

Almost a century after Waterloo (1815 to 1914), Tannenberg lasted five days and involved 600,000 men. The maneuver of the German and Russian armies took place in an arena 120 miles deep and 90 miles wide. Yet Hindenburg and the enemy army commanders at Tannenberg were fighting a *battle* no less than had Morgan and Tarleton at Cowpens. Thus, opposing commanders in all the cases examined in this book—as well as in over 1,500 battles dating from 1479 B.C. to the present—were attempting to employ their *tactics* to defeat their enemies.

It has been said, with a good deal of soundness, that tactics and its big brother, strategy, may seem to look alike on occasion, but in actual practice they are anything but twins. It may be helpful to see the two as did Sun Tzu in 500 B.C. when he told his audience "all men can see these tactics whereby I conquer, but what none can see is the strategy out of which victory is evolved."

MILITARY STRATEGY, or simply strategy, *is the disposition of military power within a theater of operations in a manner designed to increase the probability of victory.* In other terms, the high command moves its forces to bring enemy forces into situations most favorable for capture or destruction.

The German strategy in the 1941 invasion of Russia wisely foresaw the overwhelming advantages of employing rapidly moving armored forces to bag hundreds of thousands of prisoners vis-à-vis slugging it out in battles with the Russians.

Grant's Vicksburg campaign in 1863 was the implementation of a bold strategy which included Grant abandoning his lines of communication in order to defeat his enemies in five successive battles before he could invest and take Vicksburg. When all that had been accomplished, Grant succeeded in carrying out the ultimate aims of the North's grand strategy: to cut the Confederacy in two, invade the Southern states east of the Mississippi, and destroy its armies or its people's will to carry on the war.

GRAND STRATEGY represents *the highest level at which national (or allied) policies are established and the resources of the nation (or alliance) are mustered and allocated in a manner assured to maximize their potential for achieving the ends of policy, military or political.*

Napoleon's Continental System is an example of grand strategy whereby he attempted to close the ports of Europe to England as a means of bringing her to his terms of non-interference with his imperial aims.

A case in recent times was the joint decision of Roosevelt and Churchill to assign first priority to the American war effort in supporting plans for the Allied invason of Europe.

GRAND TACTICS which took its place between military strategy and battlefield tactics in Napoleon's art of war is mentioned only because his *bataillon carré* system was an important part of that art. We saw Marshal Davout's operations at Auerstadt as an extension of the *bataillon carré's* functioning. The term grand tactics has been favored by some historians for general use, but it is not used by military planners and field commanders in modern armies.

Appendix B
Anthony Wayne's Nicknames

Because Anthony Wayne deservedly won his reputation as an outstanding leader, his two military nicknames require exposition lest they be taken in a disparaging sense. Neither should be seen in a bad light.

Wayne was a leader who believed in setting a personal example in dress as well as on-the-ground leadership in battle. He was a stickler for discipline and training, and to him the uniform symbolized the martial spirit. He wanted his men to look like soldiers and spared no effort or expense in trying to keep them properly clothed and equipped. That he did not consistently succeed was not to his detriment in an army where even the commander-in-chief's constant efforts didn't always spell success in providing for the men.

It was only natural for Wayne to set the example for immaculate dress wherever he commanded. Yet he did not affect show for show's sake. He wanted to look the general, and he succeeded. Hence the sobriquet "Dandy" which followed him from his earlier days in command. But it should be recognized that the soldiers who bandied the name about would volunteer to follow him into the hottest action and the most dangerous assignments.

While Wayne eventually outlived "Dandy," he seems to

have gotten stuck with "Mad Anthony," and there is little that can be done about that except to explain that the "mad" is entirely undeserved if it is interpreted as a badge of rashness. One of Wayne's biographers, Harry Emerson Wildes,* cites the originator of the nickname as a disgruntled chronic deserter, one Jeremy the Rover, who proclaimed Wayne to be "Mad Anthony" when the general did not act to get him released from jail: "He must be mad, or he would help me. Mad Anthony that's what he is!"

Somehow the name took with the soldiers and became indelibly stamped on Wayne. Then, years later, as both Wildes and Stillé affirm it, "Washington Irving, wholly misunderstanding the nickname, jumped to the false conclusion that it was given Wayne because of rashness, recklessness, and unbridled daring, and by so doing not only smirched Wayne's military reputation as a cautious, careful strategist who never took unnecessary chances, but in addition gave him a stigma of mental unbalance which many of Irving's uncritical readers accepted."

Fortunately, in our day Wayne comes through without the stigma, and the nickname now reflects only an appreciation of his "bridled" daring.

Appendix C
Wayne's Order for The
Storming of Stony Point

The order is quoted verbatim from Henry P. Johnston's *The Storming of Stony Point* (James T. White & Co., New York, 1900).

> The troops will march at ——O'clock and move by the Right making a short halt at the Creek or run next on this side Clements's. Every Officer and non-commissioned Officer must remain with and be answerable for every man, in their platoons; no soldier will be permitted to quit his ranks on any pretext whatever until a general Halt is made and then to be attended by one of the officers of the Platoon.
>
> When the Head of the Troops arrive in the rear of the Hill Z Fuger [Febiger] will form his Regiment into a Solid Col-

---

Anthony Wayne: Trouble Shooter of the Revolution, Harcourt, Brace and Co., New York, 1941, p. 236.

umn of a half Platoon in front as fast as they come up. Colo. Meggs will form next in Febiger's rear and Major Hull in the rear of Megg's which will form the right column.

Colo. Butler will form a Column on the left of Febiger and Major Murphrey in his Rear.

Every Officer and Soldier are then to fix a piece of white paper in the most conspicuous part of his Hat or Cap as an Insignea to be distinguished from the Enemy.

At the word March Colo. Flury will take charge of One Hundred and fifty determened and picked men, properly Officered, with their Arms unloaded, placing their whole Dependence on the Bay[onet] who will move about twenty paces in front of the Right Column by the Rout 1 and enter the Sally port b. He is to detach an officer and twenty men a little in front whose business will be to secure the sentries and Remove the Abattis and obstruction for the Column to pass through. The Column will follow close in the Rear with sholder'd muskets led by Colo. Febiger and Genl. Wayne in person. When the works are forced—and not before, the Victorious troops as they enter will give the Watch word ["The fort's our own"] with a repeated and loud voice to drive the Enemy from their Works and Guns which will favor the pass of the whole troops. Shou'd the Enemy refuse to Surrender and attempt to make their escape by water or otherwise, effectual means must be used to effect the former and to prevent the Latter.

Colo. Butler will move by the route 2, preceded by One Hundred chosen men with fixed Bayonets, properly officer'd, and Unloaded [muskets] under the command of ———, at the distance of about 20 yards in front of the Column, which will follow under Colo. Butler with shouldered Muskets and enter the Sally port E or d occationally; these Hundred will also detach a proper Officer and twenty men a little in front to Remove the obstruction. As soon as they gain the Works they are also to give and continue the Watch Word which will prevent confusion and mistakes.

Major Murphey will follow Colo. Butler to the first figure 3 when he will divide a little to the Right and left and wait the Attack on the Right which will be his Signal to begin and keep up a perpetual and gauling fire and endeavour to enter between and possess the Work aa.

If any Soldier presumes to take his Musket from his sholder or Attempt to fire or begin the Battle until ordered by his proper Officer, he shall be instantly put to Death by the Officer next him, for the misconduct of one man is not to put the whole Troops in danger or disorder and be suffered to pass with life.

After the troops begin to advance to the Works the strictest Silence must be observed and the closest attention paid to the commands of the Officers.

The General has the fullest Confidence in the bravery and fortitude of the Corps that he has the Happiness to command. The distinguished Honor conferred on every Officer and Soldier who has been drafted into this Corps by His Excellency, Genl. Washington, the Credit of the States they respectively belong to, and their own Reputation will be such powerful motives for each man to distinguish himself that the General cannot have the least doubt of a Glorious Victory; and he hereby most Solemnly engages to Reward the first man who enters the works with Five Hundred Dollars, and will represent the conduct of every Officer and Soldier who distinguishes himself on this occasion in the most favorable point of view to His Excellency, whose greatest pleasure is in rewarding merit.

But shou'd there be any soldier so lost to every feeling of Honor, as to attempt to Retreat one single foot or Skulk in the face of danger, the Officer next to him is immediately to put him to Death,—that he may no longer disgrace the Name of a Soldier or the Corps or State he belongs to.

As General Wayne is determined to share the danger of the Night—so he wishes to participate of the glory of the day in common with his fellow Soldiers.

Appendix D
Napoleon's Bataillon Carré System

The system was apparently conceived early in Napoleon's career as an army commander, and the first evidence of its use showed in his first Italian campaign during the maneuver that resulted in the French victories at Lonato and Castiglione in 1796. The system which later became the bridge between the Emperor's strategy and battlefield tactics was further developed in the first Italian campaign when General Bonaparte used it to parry and defeat the Austrian strategic thrusts into northern Italy (1796–1797).

Then clearly the *bataillon carré* system, for Napoleon's purposes, tied the strategic plan and the strategic advance to his grand tactics by climaxing the campaign with a decisive concentration against his ultimate objective, the enemy main army. There can be no confusing the use of the *bataillon carré* with minor tactics, since the need for the system had ended when

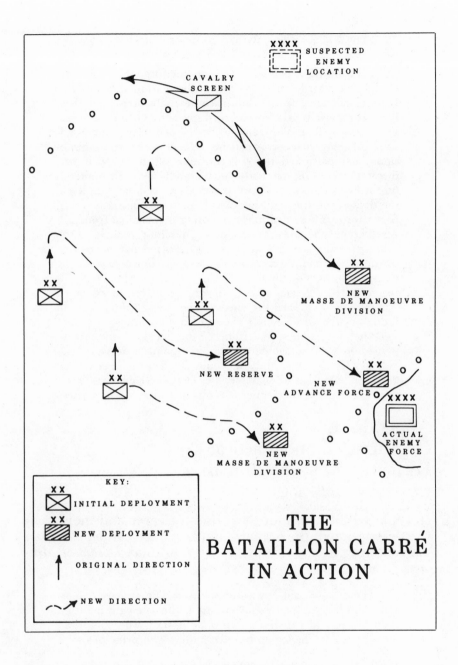

THE
BATAILLON CARRÉ
IN ACTION

Napoleon's major elements had concentrated on or near the battlefield.

How did Napoleon, after Castiglione, forge this grand tactic into the sword which was to cut down army after army of France's enemies? In the first place he was acutely aware that Bourcet's magic words "controlled dispersion" provided the real key to the system. This came to be the carefully planned advance of divisions over a road net in a time and space disposition that permitted the concentration of the army in any direction. Thus if the hostile main body were encountered (normally by units of the cavalry screen) on, say, the right flank, the division on the right became the new advance guard and fixing force. Those divisions composing the original front and rear became the *masse de manoeuvre*, marching directly to the support of the advance division. Usually, the new maneuver divisions now had the mission of enveloping one or both of the enemy's flanks. The division marching on the original left now reconstituted the army reserve, having, in effect, to execute a "column right" toward the enemy. The over-all effect was, in Liddell Hart's words, like "a widespread net whose corners are weighted with stones; when one of the enemy's columns impinged on it the net closed in round the point of pressure [Napoleon's fixing force] and the stones crashed together on the intruder." Later, as we shall see, the *bataillon carré* became magnified in scale, as the Emperor replaced divisions with corps.*

Appendix E
Organization and Tactical
Formations of The Roman
Legion, c. 220 B.C.

It would be difficult indeed to find a clearer and more concise description of the organization and basic battle drills than the following excerpt from the Dupuys' *Encyclopedia of Military History***:

> There were four classes of soldiers. The youngest, most agile, and least trained men were the **velites,** or light infantry. Next in age and experience came the **hastati,** who comprised the first line of the legion heavy infantry. The **principes** were

*"Forgotten Sword," William J. Wood in *Military Affairs*, Vol. XXXIV, No. 3, Oct. 1970, 77–79 with permission. Copyright 1970 by the American Military Institute. No additional copies may be made without the express permission of the author and of the editor of *Military Affairs*.
**Pages 72–74 from *The Encyclopedia of Military History*. Copyright 1970 by R. Ernest Dupuy and Trevor N. Dupuy. Reprinted by permission of Harper & Row, Publishers, Inc.

veterans, averaging about 30 years of age; the backbone of the army, mature, tough, and experienced, they made up the second line of the legion. The oldest group, the **triarii,** who contributed steadiness to offset the vigor of the more youthful classifications, comprised the third line of heavy infantry.

The basic tactical organization was the **maniple,** roughly the equivalent of a modern company. Each maniple was composed of two **centuries,** or platoons, of 60–80 men each, except that the maniple of the **triarii** was one century only. The **cohort,** comparable to a modern battalion, consisted of 450–570 men (120–160 **velites,** the same number of **hastati** and **principes**, 60–80 **triarii,** and a **turma** of 30 cavalrymen). The cavalry component of the cohort rarely fought with it; the horsemen were usually gathered together in larger cavalry formations.

The legion itself—the equivalent of a modern division—comprised some 4,500–5,000 men, including 300 cavalrymen. For each Roman legion, there was one allied legion, organized identically, except that its cavalry component was usually 600 men. (Some authorities suggest that allied contingents were not organized in this formal manner, but that it was merely Roman policy to support each legion with an approximately equal number of allied troops, whose largest formal organization was the cohort.)

A Roman legion, with its allied counterpart, was the equivalent of a modern army corps, a force of some 9,000–10,000 men, of whom about 900 were cavalry. Two Roman and two allied legions comprised a field army, known as a consular army, commanded by one of Rome's two consuls.

A consular army was usually 18,000–20,000 men, with a combat front of about one and a half miles. Often the two regular consular armies would be joined together, in which case the consuls would alternate in command, usually on a 24-hour basis. In times of war or great danger, however, Rome might have more than the 8 standard legions (4 Roman, 4 allied) under arms. In such cases, if a dictator had been appointed, he would directly command the largest field force, exercising overall control over the others as best he could under the circumstances. Whether or not there was a dictator, additional armies were usually commanded by proconsuls (former consuls), appointed by the Senate, or praetors, elected officials.

Since consuls were elected executive officials, both military and political power lay in their hands; rarely were Roman commanders harassed by directives from home. On the other hand, this system often resulted in mediocre top military leadership. Another drawback to this system was that consuls changed each year; yet in a long-drawn-out war, such as against Hannibal, Roman generals had to keep the field for years on end.

Under the consul or proconsul was a staff of senior officers or quaestors, who took care of administrative and planning tasks delegated by the army commander. The senior officers of the legion were the 6 tribunes—2 for each combat line. In a peculiar arrangement, the 6 tribunes rotated in command of the legion, though later a legate was frequently appointed over the tribunes as legion commander. Below the tribunes were 60 centurions, 2 for each maniple.

The flexibility of the legion lay in the tactical relationship of the maniples within each line, and between the lines of heavy infantry. Each maniple was like a tiny phalanx, with a front of about 20 men, 6 deep, but with the space between men somewhat greater than in the phalanx. Each man occupied space 5 feet square. Between the maniples in each line were intervals of the same frontage as that of a maniple, about 20 yards. The maniples in each line were staggered, with those of the second and third lines each covering intervals in the line to their front. There were approximately 100 yards between each line of heavy infantry.

This cellular, checkerboard type formation had a number of inherent advantages over the phalanx: it could maneuver more easily in rough country, without fear of losing alignment, and without need for concern about gaps appearing in the line— the gaps were built in. If desired, the first line could withdraw through the second, or the second could advance through the first. With its triarii line, the legion had an organic reserve, whether or not the commander consciously used it as such. The intervals were, of course, a potential source of danger, but one that was kept limited by the stationing of other troops immediately behind those of the first two lines. In battle it appears that the lines would close up to form a virtual phalanx, but these could quickly resume their flexible relationship when maneuver became necessary once more.

The hastati and principes were each armed with two sturdy javelins, about 7 feet long, and with a broad-bladed short sword, about 2 feet long. The javelins were usually thrown at the enemy just before contact, with the sword (**gladius**) being wielded at close quarters. The tactical concept would be comparable to modern bayonet attacks preceded by rifle fire. The triarii each carried a 12-foot pike, as well as the gladius. The velites were armed with javelins and darts. To obtain greater diversity in range and effective missile weapons, the Romans sometimes employed foreign mercenaries, such as Balearic slingers and Aegean bowmen.

Notes

Introduction

1. Random House, 1981.
2. Fallows, *National Defense,* p. 171.
3. Robert S. Dudney, "The New Army With New Punch," *U.S. News & World Report* (September 20, 1982), pp. 59–62.
4. *The Random House Dictionary of the English Language* (New York: Random House, 1981), p. 84: definition 9 of art.
5. J. F. C. Fuller, *A Military History of the Western World* (New York: Funk & Wagnalls Company, 1955), I, p. xi.
6. Will and Ariel Durant, *The Lessons of History,* as the Epilogue to the work, *The Story of Civilization* (New York: Simon & Schuster, 1968), p. 81.
7. Carl von Clausewitz, *On War* (London: Routledge and Kegan Paul, 1966), I, p. 49.
8. *Random House Dictionary,* p. 73, def. of apprehension.
9. Clausewitz, op. cit., p. 77.
10. Stephen Vincent Benét, *John Brown's Body* (New York: Heritage Press, 1948), pp. 112–113.

Prologue

1. Kenneth Roberts, *The Battle of Cowpens* (Eastern Acorn Press, Eastern National Park & Monument Association, reprinted 1981), pp. 48–49.
2. Ibid., pp. 72–73.
3. North Callahan, *Daniel Morgan: Ranger of the Revolution* (New York: Holt, Rinehart and Winston, 1961), p. 213. This one sentence is so brilliantly

apt that I found I could not improve on it, so those five words must be credited to Callahan.

4. Mark M. Boatner III, *Encyclopedia of the American Revolution* (New York: David McKay Company, 1976), p. 445.
5. Banastre Tarleton, *A History of the Campaigns of 1780 and 1781 in the Southern Provinces of North America* (Dublin, 1787), pp. 217–218.
6. Edwin C. Bearss, *The Battle of Cowpens: A Documented Narrative and Troop Movement Maps* (Washington, D.C.: National Park Service, 1967), p. 38.
7. Tarleton, op. cit., p. 221.

Part One

1. *Great Books of the Western World (GBWW)* (Chicago: Encyclopaedia Britannica, 1952), 7, p. 35.
2. John Keegan, *The Face of Battle* (New York: The Viking Press, 1976), p. 70.
3. Ardant du Picq, *Battle Studies* (Harrisburg, PA: The Military Service Publishing Company, 1958), pp. 112–131.
4. Keegan, op. cit., p. 74.
5. S. L. A. Marshall, *Men Against Fire* (New York: William Morrow & Co., 1947), p. 50.
6. Ibid., p. 161.
7. *GBWW*, 9, p. 322.
8. *GBWW*, 2, pp. 253–254.
9. See Appendix B for sobriquets of "Mad Anthony Wayne" and "Dandy Wayne."
10. Boatner, op. cit., p. 1065. Also, Charles J. Stillé, *Major General Anthony Wayne and the Pennsylvania Line* (Port Washington, N.Y.: Kennikat Press, 1983), p. 190 and n.
11. Boatner, op. cit., pp. 1092–1093.
12. Ibid., p. 1066; Stillé, op. cit., p. 403.
13. Boatner, op. cit., p. 1066.
14. Bernard Law Montgomery, *A History of Warfare* (New York: World Publishing Company, 1968), pp. 15–16.
15. *GBWW*, 6, p. 397.
16. Conrad H. Lanza, *Napoleon and Modern War: His Military Maxims* (Harrisburg, PA: The Military Service Publishing Company, 1949), p. 81.
17. David G. Chandler, *The Campaigns of Napoleon* (New York: The Macmillan Company, 1966), p. 494.
18. Ibid., p. 494.
19. John G. Gallaher, *The Iron Marshal: A Biography of Louis N. Davout* (Carbondale and Edwardsville, Illinois; Southern Illinois University Press, 1976), p. 130.
20. Frederick N. Maude, *The Jena Campaign, 1806* (London, New York: The Macmillan Company, 1909), p. 172.
21. Chandler, op. cit., p. 488.
22. Ibid., p. 496.

23. V. J. Esposito and J. R. Elting, *A Military History and Atlas of the Napoleonic Wars* (New York: Frederick A. Praeger, 1964), Chapter: "Sketches."

Part Two

1. S. L. A. Marshall, op. cit., pp. 174–175.
2. Lanza, op. cit., p. 103.
3. Ibid., p. 96.
4. David G. Chandler, *The Art of Warfare on Land* (London, New York: The Hamlyn Publishing Group, 1974), p. 7.
5. David G. Chandler, *Atlas of Military Strategy* (New York: Macmillan Publishing Company, 1980), p. 11.
6. Rupert Furneaux, *The Zulu War: Isandhlwana and Rorke's Drift* (Philadelphia and New York: J. B. Lippincott Company, 1963), pp. 43–44.
7. Donald R. Morris, *The Washing of the Spears* (New York: Simon & Schuster, 1965), pp. 408–409.
8. Michael Glover, *Rorke's Drift: A Victorian Epic* (London: Leo Cooper, 1975), p. 97.
9. S. I. Hayakawa, *Use the Right Word* (Pleasantville, N.Y.: The Reader's Digest Association, 1968), p. 689.

Part Three

1. Edgar I. Stewart, *Custer's Luck* (Norman, Okla.: University of Oklahoma Press, 1955), p. ix.
2. Ibid., pp. 242–243.
3. Charles K. Hofling, *Custer and the Little Big Horn: A Psychobiographical Inquiry* (Detroit: Wayne State University Press, 1981), p. 26.
4. Ibid., p. 33.
5. S. L. A. Marshall, *Crimsoned Prairie* (New York: Charles Scribner's Sons, 1972), p. 148.
6. Ibid., p. 155.
7. J. F. C. Fuller, *A Military History of the Western World* (New York: Funk & Wagnalls Company, 1955), II, p. 492.

Part Four

1. Technical Report 1-191, *Art and Requirements of Command (ARC)* by Joel N. Bloom, Adele M. Farber, et al (prepared by the Franklin Institute Research Laboratories for the Office of the Director of Special Studies, Office of the Chief of Staff, Department of the Army, Contract No. DA 49-092-ARO-154, April 1967), I, p. vii.
2. Ibid., II, p. 74.
3. Ibid., pp. 74–75.

Bibliography

These listings include the works I have used in writing this book as well as other writings suggested for further reading. The last section of this bibliography, under *Epilogue*, contains recommended sources for the reader who wishes to pursue his own researches in the field of leadership in war.

Introduction

Benét, Stephen Vincent. *John Brown's Body*. New York: The Heritage Press, 1948.

Clausewitz, Carl von. *On War* (3 Vols.). London: Routledge and Kegan Paul, 1966.

Dudney, Robert S. "The New Army With New Punch," *U.S. News & World Report*, September 20, 1982.

Dupuy, R. E. and T. N. *The Encyclopedia of Military History*. New York: Harper & Row, 1970.

Durant, Will and Ariel. *The Lessons of History* as epilogue to the work, *The Story of Civilization*. New York: Simon & Schuster, 1968.

Fallows, James. *National Defense*. New York: Random House, 1981.

Fuller, J. F. C. *A Military History of the Western World* (3 Vols.). New York: Funk & Wagnals, 1954.

Prologue

Bass, Robert D. *The Green Dragoon: The Lives of Banastre Tarleton and Mary Robinson*. Columbia, S.C.: Sandlapper Press, 1973.

Bearss, Edwin C. *The Battle of Cowpens: A Documented Narrative and Troop Movement Maps.* Washington, D.C.: National Park Service, 1967.

Boatner, Mark M. III. *Encyclopedia of the American Revolution.* New York: David McKay Company, 1976.

Callahan, North. *Daniel Morgan: Ranger of the Revolution.* New York: Holt, Rinehart and Winston, 1961.

Davis, Burke. *The Cowpens—Guilford Court House Campaign.* New York: J. B. Lippincott, 1962.

Graham, James. *The Life of General Daniel Morgan of the Virginia Line of the Army of the United States.* New York, 1859.

Higginbotham, Don. *Daniel Morgan: Revolutionary Rifleman.* Chapel Hill, N.C.: University of North Carolina Press, 1961.

Lee, Henry. *The Campaign of 1781 in the Carolinas.* Spartanburg, S.C.: The Reprint Company, 1975.

Roberts, Kenneth. *The Battle of Cowpens.* New York: Doubleday and Company, 1958.

Sawyer, Winthrop S. *Firearms in American History.* Boston: published by author, 1910.

Tarleton, Banastre. *A History of the Campaigns of 1780 and 1781 in the Southern Provinces of North America.* Dublin, 1787.

Windrow, Martin and Embleton, Gerry. *Military Dress of North America, 1665–1970.* New York: Charles Scribner's Sons, 1973.

Part One

Billias, George Allen (ed.). *George Washington's Generals.* New York, 1964.

Boatner, Mark M. III. *Encyclopedia of the American Revolution.* New York: David McKay Company, 1976.

Boyd, Thomas. *Mad Anthony Wayne.* New York: Charles Scribner's Sons, 1929.

Chandler, David G. *The Campaigns of Napoleon.* New York: The Macmillan Company, 1966.

————. *Dictionary of the Napoleonic Wars.* New York: The Macmillan Company, 1979.

Copeland, Peter F. *Uniforms of the American Revolution.* New York: Dover Publications, 1974.

Davout, Louis N. *Operations du 3ème Corps, 1806–1807: Rapport du Maréchal Davout, Duc d'Auerstädt.* Paris: Calmann Levy, 1896.

Delderfield, R. F. *Napoleon's Marshals.* Philadelphia-New York: Chilton Books, 1962.

Dunn-Pattison, R. P. *Napoleon's Marshals.* London: EP Publishing Limited, 1977.

Esposito, V. J. and Elting, J. R. *A Military History and Atlas of the Napoleonic Wars.* New York: Frederick A. Praeger, 1964.

Freeman, Douglas Southall. *George Washington* (7 Vols.), Vol 5. New York, 1948–1957.

Fuller, J. F. C. *A Military History of the Western World* (3 Vols.). New York: Funk & Wagnalls, 1955.

Gallaher, John G. *The Iron Marshal: A Biography of Louis N. Davout*. Carbondale and Edwardsville, Ill.: Southern Illinois University Press, 1976.

Johnston, Henry P. *The Storming of Stony Point*. New York: James T. White and Company, 1900.

Katcher, Philip. *Armies of the American Wars, 1753–1815*. New York: Hastings House, Publishers, 1975.

Keegan, John. *The Face of Battle*. New York: Viking Press, 1976.

Klinger, R. L. and Wilder, R. A. *Sketch Book '76: The American Soldier 1775–1781*. Union City, Tenn.: Pioneer Press, 1967.

Lanza, Conrad H. *Napoleon and Modern War: His Military Maxims*. Harrisburg, Pa.: Military Service Publishing Company, 1949.

Liddell Hart, B. H. *Strategy*. New York: Frederick A. Praeger, 1957.

Lossing, Benson J. *The Pictorial Field Book of the Revolution*. New York, 1851.

Marshall, S. L. A. *Men Against Fire*. New York: William Morrow & Company, 1947.

Maude, Frederick N. *The Jena Campaign, 1806*. London & New York: The Macmillan Company, 1909.

Montgomery, Bernard Law. *A History of Warfare*. New York & Cleveland: The World Publishing Company, 1968.

Du Picq, Ardant. *Battle Studies*. Harrisburg, Pa.: Military Service Publishing Company, 1958.

Schultz, A. N. (ed.). *Illustrated Drill Manual and Regulations for the American Soldier of the Revolutionary War* (Collector's Edition). Charlotte, N.C.: Sugarcreek Publishing Company, 1976.

Smith, Page. *A New Age Now Begins* (2 Vols.). New York: McGraw-Hill Book Company, 1976.

Stember, Sol. *The Bicentennial Guide to the American Revolution* (3 Vols.). New York: E. P. Dutton, 1974.

Stillé, Charles J. *Major General Anthony Wayne and the Pennsylvania Line in the Continental Army*. Philadelphia, 1893 (re-issued by Kennikat Press, Port Washington, N.Y., 1968).

Ward, Christopher. *The War of the Revolution* (2 Vols.). New York: The Macmillan Company, 1952.

Wildes, H. E. *Anthony Wayne: Trouble Shooter of the Revolution*. New York: Harcourt, Brace and Company, 1941.

Wood, William J. "Forgotten Sword," *Military Affairs*, Vol. XXXIV. No. 3, Oct 1970, pp. 77–82.

Part Two

Bancroft, Hubert Howe. *History of Mexico* (5 Vols.), *Vol I, 1516–1521*. San Francisco: The History Company, Publishers, 1886.

Bernal Diaz del Castillo. *The Discovery and Conquest of Mexico, 1517–1521*. New York: Farrar, Straus and Giroux, 1956.

Blacker, Irwin R. *Cortes and the Aztec Conquest*. New York: Harper & Row, 1965.

—— and Rosen, Harry M. (eds.). *Conquest: Dispatches of Cortes From the New World*. New York: Grosset and Dunlap, 1962.

Colenso, Frances E. *History of the Zulu War and Its Origin*. London: Chapman and Hall, 1880.

Coupland, Reginald. *Zulu Battle Piece—Isandhlwana*. London, 1948.

Furneaux, Rupert. *The Zulu War: Isandhlwana and Rorke's Drift*. Philadelphia and New York: J. B. Lippincott Company, 1963.

Glover, Michael. *Rorke's Drift: A Victorian Epic*. Leo Cooper, 1975.

Harford, Henry. *The Zulu War Journal of Colonel Henry Harford, C. B.* (ed. Daphne Child) Hamden, Conn.: The Shoe String Press, 1980.

Helps, Arthur. *The Life of Hernando Cortes* (2 Vols.). London: Bell and Daldy, 1871.

Laband, J. P. C. and Thompson, P. S. *A Field Guide to the War in Zululand 1879*. Pietermaritzburg, So. Africa: University of Natal Press, 1979.

MacLeish, Archibald. "Conquistador" from *Collected Poems, 1917–1952*. Boston: Houghton Mifflin Company, 1952.

MacNutt, Francis Augustus. *Fernando Cortes and the Conquest of Mexico*. New York and London: G. P. Putnam's Sons, 1909.

Morris, Donald R. *The Washing of the Spears*. New York: Simon and Schuster, 1965.

Prescott, William H. *Conquest of Mexico*. New York: The Book League of America, 1934.

Sedgewick, Henry Dwight. *Cortes the Conqueror*. Indianapolis: The Bobbs Merrill Company, 1927.

Simpson, Lesley Bird (transl. & ed.). *Cortes: The Life of the Conqueror by His Secretary*. Berkeley and Los Angeles: University of California Press, 1965.

Tarassuk, Leonid and Blair, Claude (eds.). *The Complete Encyclopedia of Arms and Weapons*. New York: Simon & Schuster, 1982.

Wise, Terence. *The Conquistadores*. London: Osprey Publishing, 1980.

Part Three

Ambrose, Stephen E. *Crazy Horse and Custer: The Parallel Lives of Two American Warriors*. Garden City, N.Y.: Doubleday and Company, 1975.

Anderson, Niles. *The Battle of Bushy Run*. Harrisburg, Pa.: Pennsylvania Historical and Museum Commission, 1975.

——. "Bushy Run: Decisive Battle in the Wilderness," *The Western Pennsylvania Historical Magazine*, Vol. 46, No. 3, July 1963.

Asprey, Robert B. *War in the Shadows* (2 Vols.). Garden City, N.Y.: Doubleday and Company, 1975.

Balsdon, J. P. V. D. *Romans and Aliens*. Chapel Hill, N.C.: University of North Carolina Press, 1979.

Boatner, Mark M. III. *Encyclopedia of the American Revolution*. New York: David McKay Company, 1976.

Bomberger, C. M. *The Battle of Bushy Run*. Jeanette, Pa.: Jeanette Publishing Company, 1928.

Boucher, John H. "Old and New Westmoreland," *American Historical Society*. New York, 1918.

Bouquet, Henry. *An Historical Account of the Expedition Against the Ohio Indians in the Year MDCCLXIV Under the Command of Henry Bouquet, Esqre. 1766.*

Caven, Brian. *The Punic Wars*. New York: St. Martin's Press, 1980.

Connolly, Peter. *Greece and Rome at War*. Englewood Cliffs, N.J.: Prentice-Hall, 1981.

————. *The Roman Army*. London: MacDonald and Company, 1982.

Coughlan, T. M. "The Battle of the Little Big Horn: A Tactical Study," *Cavalry Journal*, No. 34, Jan–Feb 1934.

Dictionary of American Biography (21 Vols.), Vol. I. New York, 1943

Dupuy, R. E. and Dupuy, T. N. *The Encyclopedia of Military History*. New York: Harper and Row, 1970.

Dupuy, T. N. *Evolution of Weapons and Warfare*. New York: Bobbs-Merrill Company, 1980.

Encyclopaedia Britannica, 1946 edition, Vol. 12 (Ilipa) and Vol. 20 (Scipio Africanus, Publius Cornelius).

Fortescue, Sir John W. *A History of the British Army* (13 Vols.), Vol. III, 1763–1793. London: Macmillan and Company, 1911.

Frost, Lawrence A. *The Custer Album*. Seattle: Superior Publishing Company, 1964.

Fuller, J. F. C. *British Light Infantry in the Eighteenth Century*. London: Hutchinson and Company, 1925.

Godfrey, Edward S. "Custer's Last Battle," *Century Illustrated Monthly Magazine*, Vol. XLIII, No. 3, Jan 1892.

Graham, W. A. *The Custer Myth: A Source Book of Custeriana*. New York: Bonanza Books, 1953.

Grant, Michael. *History of Rome*. New York: Charles Scribner's Sons, 1978.

Grimal, Pierre. *The Civilization of Rome*. New York: Simon & Schuster, 1963.

Hofling, Charles K. *Custer and the Little Big Horn: A Psychobiographical Inquiry*. Detroit: Wayne State University Press, 1981.

Johnston, Harold W. *The Private Life of the Romans*. New York: Scott, Foresman and Company, 1932.

Jones, Douglas C. *The Court-Martial of George Armstrong Custer*. New York: Charles Scribner's Sons, 1976.

Kinsley, D. A. *Favor the Bold, Custer: The Indian Figher*. New York: Holt, Rinehart and Winston, 1968.

Kuhlman, Charles. *Legend Into History: The Custer Mystery*. Harrisburg, Pa.: The Telegraph Press, 1951.

Kurtz, Henry I. "The Relief of Fort Pitt," *History Today*, XIII, Nov 1963.

Lazenby, J. F. *Hannibal's War: A History of the Second Punic War*. Warminster, England: Aris and Phillips, 1978.

Liddell Hart, B. H. *A Greater Than Napoleon: Scipio Africanus*. Boston: Little, Brown and Company, 1927.

Livy (Titus Livius) (transl. Baker, George). *The History of Rome*. Book XXVIII. London: Jones and Company, 1830.

McDonald, A. H. *Republican Rome*. New York: Frederick A. Praeger, 1966.

Marshall, S. L. A. *Crimsoned Prairie*. New York: Charles Scribner's Sons, 1972.

Monaghan, Jay. *Custer: The Life of General George Armstrong Custer*. Boston: Little, Brown and Company, 1959.

Morison, Samuel Eliot (ed.). *The Parkman Reader*. Boston, 1955.

Parker, H. M. D. *The Roman Legions*. New York: Barnes & Noble, 1928.

Parkman, Francis. *The Conspiracy of Pontiac* (2 Vols.). Boston: Little, Brown and Company, 1903.

Peckham, Howard H. *Pontiac and the Indian Uprising*. New York: Russell and Russell, 1947.

Polybius (transl. W. R. Paton). *The Histories*. Books X-XI. Cambridge, Mass.: Harvard University Press, 1960.

Reeve, J. C. "Henry Bouquet and His Indian Campaigns," *Ohio Archeological and Historical Quarterly*, XXVI, 1943.

Scullard, H. H. *Scipio Africanus: Soldier and Politician*. Ithaca, N.Y.: Cornell University Press, 1970.

Sheridan, Philip H. *Record of Engagements with Hostile Indians Within the Military Division of the Missouri, 1868 to 1882*. Washington, D.C.: Government Printing Office, 1882.

Stewart, Edgar I. *Custer's Luck*. Norman, Okla.: University of Oklahoma Press, 1955.

Utley, Robert M. *Custer and the Great Controversy: The Origin and Development of a Legend*. Los Angeles: Westernlore Press, 1962.

Van De Water, Frederic. *Glory-Hunter: A Life of General Custer*. New York: Bobbs-Merrill Company, 1934.

Walkinshaw, Lewis C. *Annals of South Western Pennsylvania*. Chapters XXI-XXII. New York: Lewis Historical Publishing Co., 1939.

Warry, John. *Warfare in the Classical World*. New York: St. Martin's Press, 1980.

Watson, G. R. *The Roman Soldier*. Ithaca, N.Y.: Cornell University Press, 1969.

Windrow, Martin and Embleton, Gerry. *Military Dress of North America 1665–1970*. New York: Charles Scribner's Sons, 1973.

Part Four

ARC: Art and Requirements of Command (4 Vols.). Philadelphia: Franklin Institute Research Laboratories (Prepared for the Office of the Director of Special Studies, Office of the Chief of Staff, Department of the Army), 1967.

Chandler, David G. *The Campaigns of Napoleon*. New York: The Macmillan Company, 1966.

————. *Dictionary of the Napoleonic Wars*. New York: The Macmillan Publishing Company, 1979.

Delderfield, R. F. *Napoleon's Marshals*. Philadelphia and New York: Chilton Books, 1966.

Dunn-Pattison, R. P. *Napoleon's Marshals*. London: Methuen and Co., 1909 (Republished by E. P. Publishing, Ltd., Easy Ardsley, West Yorkshire, 1977).

Esposito, Vincent J. and Elting, John Robert. *A Military History and Atlas of the Napoleonic Wars*. New York: Frederick A. Praeger, 1964.

de Marbot, Marcellin. *The Memoirs of Baron de Marbot: Late Lieutenant-General in the French Army* (transl. Butler, Arthur John). London: Longmans, Green and Company, 1892.

Thomason, John W., Jr. *Adventures of General Marbot*. New York: Charles Scribner's Sons, 1935.

Warner, Richard. *Napoleon's Enemies*. London: Osprey Publishing Co., 1977.

Part Five

Asprey, Robert B. *War in the Shadows: The Guerrilla in History* (2 Vols.). Garden City, N.Y.: Doubleday and Co., 1975.

Chandler, David G. *The Art of Warfare on Land*. London: The Hamlyn Publishing Group, 1974.

Dolbey, Robert V. *Sketches of the East Africa Campaign*. London: John Murray, 1918.

Encyclopaedia Britannica. Edition of 1946. Vol. 7 (East Africa, Operations in).

Gardner, Brian. *German East: The Story of the First World War in East Africa*. London: Cassell and Co., 1963.

Hordern, Charles (compiler). *Military Operations East Africa, Vol. I, August 1914-September 1916*. London: His Majesty's Stationery Office, 1941.

Hoyt, Edwin P. *Guerilla: Colonel von Lettow-Vorbeck and Germany's East African Empire*. New York: Macmillan Publishing Co., 1981.

von Lettow-Vorbeck, Paul Emil. *Heia Safari!: Deutschlands Kampf in Ostafrika*. Leipzig: R. F. Koehler, 1920.

————. *East African Campaigns*. New York: Robert Speller & Sons, Publishers, 1957.

Meinertzhagen, Richard. *Army Diary 1899–1926*. Edinburgh and London: Oliver and Boyd, 1960.

Miller, Charles. *Battle for the Bundu: The First World War in East Africa*. New York: Macmillan Publishing Co., 1974.

Mosley, Leonard. *Duel for Kilimanjaro: An Account of the East African Campaign 1914–1918*. London: Weidenfeld and Nicolson, 1963.

Young, Peter. *A Dictionary of Battles, 1816–1976*. New York: Mayflower Books, 1977.

Epilogue

This selected bibliography is intended for the reader who wishes to: one, gain an appreciation of the scope of military history and the battles considered in seeking examples of leadership—good or bad; two, consider works that reveal vistas looking into broader fields of the art of war.

The sources marked with an asterisk are actually encyclopedic collections of abstracts of battles or leaders. They represent good starting points for appreciating the scope just mentioned. Of particular value in considering world history are the indices in the Dupuy's *Encyclopedia of Military History*.

The anthology *Men at War* heads the list because it contains so many keen insights into the hearts and minds of men in battle. The ten suggested readings are most in keeping with the ideas developed in this book. The reader, however, may take my suggestions as biased samplings—which indeed they are.

*Boatner, Mark Mayo III. *The Civil War Dictionary*. New York: David McKay Company, 1959.

*———. *Encyclopedia of the American Revolution*. New York: David McKay Company, 1976.

*Calvert, Michael with Young, Peter. *A Dictionary of Battles 1715–1815*. New York: Mayflower Books, 1979.

Chandler, David G. *The Art of Warfare on Land*. London: The Hamlyn Publishing Group, 1974.

———. *Atlas of Military Strategy*. New York: Macmillan Publishing Co., 1980.

*Dupuy, R. E. and T. N. *The Encyclopedia of Military History*. New York: Harper & Row, 1970.

Dupuy, Trevor N. *The Evolution of Weapons and Warfare*. New York: The Bobbs-Merrill Co., 1980.

*Eggenberger, David. *A Dictionary of Battles*. New York: Thomas Y. Crowell Co., 1967.

Esposito, V. J. and Elting, J. R. *A Military History and Atlas of the Napoleonic Wars*. New York: Frederick A. Praeger, 1964.

———. *The West Point Atlas of American Wars* (2 Vols.). New York: Frederick A. Praeger, 1959.

Falls, Cyril. *The Art of War: From the Age of Napoleon to the Present Day*. New York: Oxford University Press, 1962.

Freeman, Douglas Southhall. *Lee's Lieutenants* (3 Vols). New York: Charles Scribner's Sons, 1942.

Fuller, J. F. C. *The Conduct of War 1789–1961*. New Brunswick, N.J.: Rutgers University Press, 1961.

———. *Generalship: Its Diseases and Their Cure*. Harrisburg, Pa.: Military Service Publishing Co., 1936.

Goodenough, Simon and Deighton, Len. *Tactical Genius in Battle*. London: Phaidon Press, 1979.

Hemingway, Ernest (ed). *Men at War*. New York: Bramhall House, 1942: SUGGESTED READING:
The Battle of Arsouf, Charles Oman;
The Red Badge of Courage, Stephen Crane;
The Pass of Thermopylae, Charlotte Yonge;
Custer, Frederic van de Water;
Blowing Up a Train, T. E. Lawrence;
Lisette at Eylau, General Marbot;
Gallipoli, J. F. C. Fuller;
The Stars in Their Courses, John W. Thomason, Jr.;
Borodino, Leo Tolstoy;
Oriskany, 1777, Walter D. Edmonds.

*Keegan, John and Wheatcroft, Andrew. *Who's Who in Military History: From 1453 to the Present Day*. New York: William Morrow & Co., 1976.

Liddell Hart, B. H. *The Ghost of Napoleon*. New Haven: Yale University Press, 1934.

————. *Strategy*. New York: Frederick A. Praeger, 1957. (Special Attention is invited to the "Index of Deductions.")

Machiavelli, Nicolo (transl. W. K. Marriott). *The Prince*. Chicago: Encyclopaedia Britannica, Inc., *Great Books of the Western World*, Vol. 23, 1952. Chapters 12–15 and 19.

Marshall, S. L. A. *Men Against Fire*. New York: William Morrow & Co., 1947.

Montgomery, Bernard Law. *A History of Warfare*. New York: The World Publishing Co., 1968. (Special Attention is invited to Chapters 1–2).

Montross, Lynn. *War Through the Ages*. New York: Harper & Brothers, 1946.

Napoleon's Military Maxims (ed. Conrad H. Lanza). *Napoleon and Modern War*. Harrisburgh, Pa.: Military Service Publishing Co., 1949.

Preston, Richard A. and Wise, Sydney F. *Men in Arms: A History of Warfare and Its Interrelationships with Western Society*. New York: Praeger Publishers, 1970.

Sun Tzu. *The Art of War* (transl. Samuel B. Griffith). New York and Oxford: Oxford University Press, 1963.

*Young, Peter. *A Dictionary of Battles 1816–1976*. New York: Mayflower Books, 1977.

Index

FLAG

ALSO BY MARC LEEPSON

*Saving Monticello: The Levy Family's Epic Quest to Rescue
the House that Jefferson Built*

*Webster's New World Dictionary of the
Vietnam War* (editor)

FLAG

An American Biography

MARC LEEPSON

THOMAS DUNNE BOOKS

ST. MARTIN'S PRESS ❧ NEW YORK

THOMAS DUNNE BOOKS.
An Imprint of St. Martin's Press.

www.stmartins.com

Design by Phil Mazzone

Library of Congress Cataloging-in-Publication Data

Leepson, Marc, 1945–
    Flag : an American biography / Marc Leepson.
       p. cm.
    ISBN 0-312-32308-5
    EAN 978-0-312-32308-0
    1. Flags—United States—History.

    CR113 .L44 2005
    929.9'2'0973—dc22
                         2004065920

First Edition: June 2005

10 9 8 7 6 5 4 3 2 1

In memory of my grandparents:

Pauline Tarnovsky Leepson
Morris Leepson
Rose Friedenberg Levin
Herman Levin

Our flag carries American ideas, American history and American feelings. It is not a painted rag. It is a whole national history. It is the Constitution. It is the Government. It is the emblem of the sovereignty of the people. It is the NATION.

—Henry Ward Beecher, 1861

Your flag decal won't get you into heaven anymore.

—John Prine, 1969

Contents

CONTENTS

Foreword

A BIOGRAPHY, according to most dictionaries, is an account of a person's life, written or told by another.

But here, Marc Leepson has expanded the meaning of the word and written a biography of an inanimate object: the American flag. And what a great job he has done.

Mr. Leepson begins at the beginning with the birth of the flag in 1777 during the American Revolution, and proceeds through the flag's infancy during the War of 1812, its childhood during the Civil War, its adolescence during the Spanish-American War, and its coming-of-age during the world wars.

And then there was the Vietnam War, when the flag, always venerated until then, became a symbol of the divisiveness that split the nation. The chapters that deal with the Vietnam period, at home and overseas, are worth the price of the book.

On a personal note, I served in Vietnam and during my year there, I rarely saw an American flag displayed at military installations or in combat operations. In fact, my photographs taken in Vietnam verify that memory. Mr. Leepson in his book writes:

> In Vietnam, some American troops flew the flag as their fathers did
> in Korea and in Europe and Japan during World War II and as their

grandfathers did in the trenches in World War I. The flag flew over American bases, remote outposts, and landing zones. Some troops carried small flags into battle, especially during the war's early years before it became controversial at home.

The key words there are "especially during the war's early years before it became controversial at home." By the time I got to Vietnam in November 1967, what was happening at home was starting to affect how newly arriving troops viewed the war, and thus conspicuous displays of patriotism, such as flying or carrying the American flag, were waning. This was in stark contrast to the Viet Cong and North Vietnamese troops as well as our South Vietnamese allies, who often carried flags into battle, and rallied around their flags, and also raised them in defiance of the enemy. I saw little of that on the American side during my tour of duty, and one might say that this period was the absolute low point of the American flag.

By the time of the first Gulf War, however, the flag had again become a unifying symbol, at least to most of the nation. And on September 11, 2001, the American flag flying over the ruins of the World Trade Center sprouted tens of thousands of new American flags across this country, Europe, and the world.

Many countries have more than one national symbol or emblem, some of which are religious, cultural, or pertain to royalty. In America, however, there are only two national symbols — the bald eagle, not known by everyone in other nations, and the American flag — known to the entire world. Marc Leepson explores the close identification of America and Americans with their flag and their country. A quote from Henry Ward Beecher in 1861 on the eve of the Civil War sums up this feeling:

> Our flag carries American ideas, American history and American feelings. It is not a painted rag. It is a whole national history. It is the Constitution. It is the Government. It is the emblem of sovereignty of the people. It is the NATION.

Mr. Leepson also discusses "the cult of the flag," which swept the nation following the Civil War and led to the incorporation of the flag motif into many aspects of American life, art, home decoration, and public displays — a phenomenon that continues to this day and one that is rarely seen in other countries.

Flag: An American Biography is not a book with an agenda, or a subjective point of view; it is an objective history of the American flag, well researched, well presented, easy to read and understand, and very informative and entertaining.

One of the most entertaining aspects of *Flag* is its focus on personalities. For instance, Francis Hopkinson, a signer of the Declaration of Independence, is probably the designer of the American flag—not Betsy Ross. There are other such tidbits in the book, which keep us turning the pages, and probably causing us to read out loud to anyone nearby.

This is one of those books that seem as though someone should have written it years ago—but better late than never. *Flag: An American Biography* is a must read for scholars, history buffs, patriotic organizations, flag wavers, flag burners, anyone who owns an American flag or has seen a flag in the last forty-eight hours.

This iconic symbol of the nation, which is so ubiquitous in our lives, needs a history, and this is the definitive history of the Flag of the United States of America. Marc Leepson has done a wonderful job of making this inanimate object come alive and speak to us.

—Nelson DeMille

Acknowledgments

THE IDEA FOR THIS BOOK came from a series of conversations with my friend, literary agent, and fellow Vietnam veteran, Joseph Brendan Vallely. This book simply would not have come to pass without Joe's inspiration, encouragement, and advice. My undying gratitude goes to him.

Thanks, too, to my excellent editor at Thomas Dunne Books, Peter Wolverton, the associate publisher, who saw the merit in this book and steadfastly and expertly shepherded it through to publication. My appreciation for invaluable publishing assistance also goes to Thomas Dunne Books associate editor John Parsley, editorial assistant Katie Gilligan, to the copyeditor, Marcy VL Hargan, and David Stanford Burr, the production editor. Special thanks to Nelson DeMille for graciously agreeing to write the book's preface.

Several flag experts took time to answer my questions and provide insights into the history of, and the changing meaning of, the American flag. Thanks to Whitney Smith, the director of the Flag Research Center in Massachusetts, the world's No. 1 vexillologist; to Scot Guenter, the Coordinator of the American Studies Program at San Jose State University and the leading expert on the changing meaning of the American flag; to Henry Moeller, who has done pioneering research on the origins of the flag; and to

John W. Baer, the leading student of the history of the Pledge of Allegiance.

Thanks also to the following flag authorities who consented to interviews: Dr. Jeffery Kenneth Kohn, American flag collector and appraiser; Bob Heft, the designer of the fifty-star flag; Sally Johnston, the executive director, and Eric Voboril, the curator, at the The Star-Spangled Banner House in Baltimore; and Scott Sheads, park ranger/historian, and Anna von Lunz, cultural resources manager, at the National Park Service's Ft. McHenry National Monument and Historic Shrine in Baltimore. Thanks also to the artist Dread Scott, the creator of "What is the Proper Way to Display the American Flag?"

I owe a great deal to Marilyn Zoidis, the curator of the Star-Spangled Banner Project at the Smithsonian Institution's National Museum of American History who generously shared her knowledge about that flag and about the early history of the American flag, and to Suzanne Thomassen-Krauss, the project's chief conservator. Special thanks to Marilyn Zoidis for kindly agreeing to read and critique the chapter on The Star-Spangled Banner.

I have long been an ardent admirer of librarians and archivists. Many librarians and archivists helped me with invaluable research assistance. Thanks to: Sheila Whetzel, Tia Maggio, Tina Thomas, Mary Beth Morton, Heather Eickmeyer, Jeanine Raghunathan and Karen Warner at the Middleburg Library in Middleburg, Virginia; Mary Lou Demeo, Linda Holtslander, Robert Boley, and Michael Avera at the Loudoun County (Virginia) Public Library; Library Director Peggy Stillman at the Chesapeake Public Library in Chesapeake, Virginia; and to Steve Matthews and Alex Northrop at the Currier Library at Foxcroft School in Middleburg.

Also: Sam Anthony, director of lecture programs; Milton Gustafson, archivist, NWCTC; Rodney Ross, archivist, Center for Legislative Archives; and Darlene McClurkin at Museum Programs at the National Archives in Washington; Conley Edwards, the State Archivist; Tom Camden, director of Special Collections; Nolan Yelich, the Librarian of Virginia; Mary Dessypris, Government Reference Services & Outreach coordinator; Audrey C. Johnson, Picture Collection manager; and David Feinberg, reference librarian, at the Library of Virginia in Richmond; and my friends at the Library of Virginia Foundation: Mary Beth McIntire, Kathy Holmes, Heather Krajewski, and Richard Golembeski.

Also: My old friend and colleague Michael Koempel and his staff at the Library of Congress's Congressional Research Service Government

Division, and Patrick Kerwin, Manuscript Reference Librarian, at the Library of Congress's Manuscript Division; James W. Cheevers, associate director of the U.S. Naval Academy Museum in Annapolis; Carol Ganz, reference librarian at the Connecticut State Library; Rosemary Switzer, special collections assistant at Princeton University's Seeley G. Mudd Manuscript Library; my friend Bill Hammond, chief of the General Histories Branch at the U.S. Army Center of Military History; and Lynda L. Crist, editor of *The Papers of Jefferson Davis* at Rice University.

Also: Jane Ehrenhart, supervisor of Reference and Technical Services at the Illinois State Historical Library; Dr. Mark Benbow, resident historian at the Woodrow Wilson House in Washington, D.C.; Lisa Moulder, collections manager at the Betsy Ross House in Philadelphia; Howard M. Pollman, community relations officer at the State Museum of Pennsylvania in Harrisburg; and Andrea Ashby Leraris at the Independence National Historical Park Library in Philadelphia.

Also: Tom Sherlock, the historian at Arlington National Cemetery; Clare M. Sheridan, the librarian at the American Textile History Museum in Lowell, Massachusetts; Martha Mayo, director of the Center of Lowell History at the University of Massachusetts-Lowell; Rob Schoeberlein, director of Special Collections at the Maryland State Archives in Annapolis; Jon N. Austin, director of the Museum of Funeral Customs in Springfield, Illinois; Janie C. Morris, research services librarian at the Rare Book, Manuscript, and Special Collections Library at Duke University; Susan Pittman, press officer at the U.S. State Department; Bob Matthias, museum coordinator at the Grand Army of the Republic Museum in Lynn, Massachusetts; Tom Duclos, associate curator at the New York State Military Museum in Saratoga Springs; and Michael Moss, the director of the West Point Museum at the United States Military Academy.

I received much-appreciated support during the researching and writing of this book from a wonderful group of friends, family, and colleagues, especially Jay Adams, Xande Anderer, Tim Ashwell, Bernie and Linda Brien, Quentin Butcher, Bob Carolla, Chad Conway, Larry Cushman, John Czaplewski, Marianne and Tommy Dodson, Russell Duncan, Dale Dye, Bernie Edelman, Gloria Emerson, Carol Engle, Bill Fogarty, John Gardiner, Reno Harnish, John Hoffecker, Michael Kazin, Mike Keating, Liz Keenan, Michael ("M-60") Kelley, Evan Leepson, Peter and Ellen Leepson, Glenn Maravetz, Ashley Matthews, Kevin McCorry, Gregory McNamee, Dave Miller, Pete Nardi, Andre T. and Gayle Parraway, Angus Paul, Margaret Peters, Mokie Pratt Porter, Avrom Posner, Susan and Gray

Price, Dan and Margie Radovsky, Barbara and Pat Rhodes, Kathy Jo Shea, Margo Lee Sherman, Sally Sherman, Jaclyn Tamaroff, Angus Theurmer, Pam Turner, and Jim Wagner. Special thanks to all my valued colleagues at Vietnam Veterans of America's national office.

For help with understanding flag customs in other nations I would like to thank Caroline Toplis of New Zealand's Ministry for Culture and Heritage, Corinne Lyon Kunzle of the Swiss Embassy in Washington, D.C., and Joana Cavalcanti of the Brazilian Embassy's Cultural and Public Affairs Office. Thanks, too, to Johan Bonink and Peter Hans van den Muijzenberg, Holland; Roberto Toselli, Italy; Xavier Llobet, Spain; Conde Cargadito, Venezuela; Michael Adams and Bart Connolly, Ireland; Victor M. Martinez, Mexico; Tamer Olui, Egypt; Dan Palm and Jouni Maho, Sweden; Jukka Aho and Hiski Haapoja, Finland; Albert Reingewirtz, Israel; Steve Hayes and Moira de Swardt, South Africa; John Anderson, Germany; Greg Goss, J. R. Pelland and Rich Wales, Canada; Anthony Desportes and Eric Savary, France; Ammar A. Samandar, Syria; and Mark Terzano, Peru.

My wife, Janna, and our children, Devin and Cara, put up with me spending inordinately long periods of time researching and writing this book. I thank them for their patience, love, and support.

Introduction

AMERICANS HAVE a unique and special feeling for our flag. And that's putting it mildly. This is not to diminish the respect and pride people in other nations feel for their national emblems. However, no country in the world can match the intensity of the American citizenry's attachment to the fifty-star, thirteen-stripe Stars and Stripes, which is as familiar an American icon as any that has existed in the nation's history.

Nowhere on earth do citizens fly their national flags, as Americans do, everywhere they live and everywhere they go, from our front porches to our pickup trucks. The flag is a fixture in our nation's schools, in our mass media, and in our advertising. The flag flies in front of our government buildings and business establishments of all types, including countless automobile dealer showrooms throughout the land that specialize in flying extra large Stars and Stripes.

Nor does any nation turn to its flag as an emotional, political, and patriotic symbol in good times and bad the way Americans do. We display the red-white-and-blue American flag at festive cultural and social events to celebrate and, at times of national tragedy, to grieve and show our resolve.

No nation displays its national flag as ubiquitously or as proudly as Americans do at sporting events, from local Little League fields to the Super Bowl.

And no nation can match the widespread use of the American flag as a decorative part of countless items of apparel and accessories, from headbands to designer jewelry.

We Americans, alone among the nations of the world, have our schoolchildren pledge their allegiance to the flag, and we have done so for more than a century. Our National Anthem is a hymn of praise to our flag. Our largest veterans' service organization, the American Legion, has had an Americanism division since it was founded in 1919. It promotes the display of, and dispenses advice about, the proper use of the American flag. The second largest veterans' group, the Veterans of Foreign Wars, similarly promotes the flag through its own Americanism program.

The proper use of the flag itself is detailed in a one-of-a-kind document, the official U.S. Flag Code, a long, detailed set of rules that was developed at the instigation of the newly formed American Legion in the early 1920s. The code has been a federal statute since 1942.

No other country can boast of well-organized, well-funded nonprofit nationwide organizations, such as the National Flag Foundation, the National Flag Day Foundation, and the Citizens Flag Alliance, which work full-time to promote respect for the nation's flag. The latter organization lobbies exclusively for congressional passage of a constitutional amendment to protect the flag from desecration. Legislation calling for the Flag Desecration Amendment, which would be the twenty-eighth amendment to the Constitution, has fallen short by just a handful of votes in recent years in Congress.

★   ★   ★

The flag's image has figured prominently in the national iconography since the War of 1812. Examples include the 1776 "Betsy Ross" thirteen-star flag, which has been memorialized in countless books and paintings and other widely disseminated images since 1870; the Star-Spangled Banner itself, which survived "the rockets' red glare" and "the bombs bursting in air" in 1814 at Fort McHenry; the hoisting of the red, white, and blue by six marines atop Mount Suribachi on Iwo Jima during World War II; and Neil Armstrong's proud planting of the flag on the Moon in 1969.

In recent years we have seen a damaged but intact American flag pulled from the debris of the World Trade Center following the September 11, 2001, terrorist attack; the huge American flag unfurled by firefighters from the roof of the Pentagon on September 12; and the widely disseminated media moment of the Iraq War in 2003 when a U.S. marine briefly placed a small American flag atop the face of a tumbling statue of Saddam Hussein in Baghdad.

Artists in every media have featured the American flag in their work, from folk artists to internationally renowned painters such as Jasper Johns and Childe Hassam. The flag also has been lionized in countless songs, including George M. Cohan's "You're a Grand Old Flag" and the nation's official national march, John Philip Sousa's "The Stars and Stripes Forever," as well as in poems, from the prosaic to the patriotic to the literary.

Tens of millions of Americans have served in the armed forces, and hundreds of thousands have given their lives in battle for the flag. In the wake of the events of September 11, 2001, the flag became an instant and widely used symbol of a nation united against terrorism as millions of Americans proudly and defiantly unfurled American flags in every corner of the country.

★   ★   ★

This unalloyed and unique feeling that Americans have for their flag is even more remarkable given the fact that the American flag's origins are murky and that Americans labor under several widespread misunderstandings about our national emblem. We do not know for certain, for example, who designed the first flag. Nor is it known who made the first flag—the Betsy Ross story notwithstanding. There is no document setting out the meaning of the flag's colors, even though pundits have promulgated their ideas about what the red, white, and blue stand for since the 1780s. We know why the first flag had thirteen stars and thirteen stripes—to represent the original colonies. But no document exists explaining why the flag's designers chose the stars and the stripes or why they picked red, white, and blue as symbols for those colonies.

The current feelings of near religious reverence many Americans have for the flag, which some have dubbed the "cult of the flag," date not from the Revolutionary War as is widely believed, but from 1861 and the start of the Civil War. Before the Civil War—for the first three quarters of this nation's history in fact—it was not customary for private individuals to fly the American flag. Until 1861, the flag was flown almost exclusively at federal facilities and by the American military, primarily on U.S. Navy ships. Contrary to images promulgated well after the fact, the Continental Army did not fight under the Stars and Stripes against the British; George Washington's troops displayed regimental flags.

It was not until the fall of Fort Sumter in 1861 that the American flag began to take on something approaching its current meaning to the American public. Soon after that fort fell to the Confederates, Northerners began displaying the flag ubiquitously as a symbol of the fight to keep the Union intact.

Another largely unknown factor in this equation is that the federal and state governments have not been the instigators in implementing the important milestones in the American flag's evolution. By and large it has been individual American businessmen, teachers, journalists, politicians, and private organizations—primarily but not exclusively veterans' groups and patriotic organizations—that have developed and pushed for many of the important changes in the evolution of the flag's cultural importance.

Those milestones include:

- The push to make "The Star-Spangled Banner," which was written in 1814, the official National Anthem, something that did not occur until 1931.

- The adoption of the Pledge of Allegiance, which was written by Francis Bellamy in 1892, but was not recognized by the federal government until 1942.

- The development of the Flag Code, which was put together primarily by the American Legion in 1923 and 1924 and not made into law by the government until 1942.

- The national June 14th Flag Day commemoration, which was the brainchild of a Wisconsin schoolteacher in 1885, was pushed by the American Flag Day Association in 1895 but did not receive presidential sanction until 1949.

What is not widely known today as well is that from the time the Continental Congress passed legislation establishing the flag's elements on June 14 (Flag Day) 1777, until June 24, 1912, there was no law setting out the exact order of the stars or the actual proportions of the flag. American flags during those 135 years often had different arrangements of the stars and differing proportions. Although most American flags had straight rows of stars and proportions similar to the official flag that was codified in 1912, the designs were left to the creative talents—and whims—of individual flag makers. And it wasn't uncommon for people to stitch all manner of symbols and slogans onto flags.

★   ★   ★

The question of why the American flag looms so large in the social, political, and emotional hearts and minds of millions of Americans has several answers. The flag, of course, stands for everything that is admirable in America's political history, especially our democratic form of government and the many freedoms Americans have enjoyed since 1776. It also has served as a unifying symbol for a relatively young nation made up predominantly of immigrants. And, it has been argued, the near religious fervor many accord to the flag derives from the fact that this nation has neither a state religion nor a royal family.

Alexis de Tocqueville, the acutely perceptive French aristocrat who visited these shores in 1831–32 and many of whose observations about this country ring true today, pointed to American democracy itself as the main force behind what he called Americans' tendency to "feel extreme pleasure in exhibiting" our "recently acquired advantages." People "living in democracies," de Tocqueville said of an era when the American flag was rarely exhibited by individuals, "love their country just as they love themselves, and they transfer the habits of their private vanity to their vanity as a nation."

Be it vanity, quiet pride, or boastful patriotism, there is little doubt that Americans have a special feeling for the red, white, and blue. This book looks at what's behind that special feeling by tracing the complete history of the American flag—it's biography, so to speak. It examines the many changes in the American flag and the evolution of its cultural importance beginning in the Revolutionary War and ending with the flag's prominent role as a symbol of American resolve in today's war against terrorism. It also traces the look of the actual flags themselves, which—like the meanings attached to the flag—changed over time.

The American flag is an unwavering part of life for untold tens of millions of Americans. My hope is that what follows will shine an informing light on what has become the object of veneration for so many Americans and the very visible symbol of this amazing nation.

CHAPTER ONE

Antecedents

★   ★   ★

The flag of today represents many centuries of development. Probably no other inanimate object has excited so great an influence over
the actions of the human race. It has existed in some form among all
peoples and from the earliest times.

—Frederic J. Haskin, 1941

HISTORY DOES NOT record the first time a human being attached pieces of cloth to a staff to use as a symbol. But wooden, metal, and
cloth flaglike objects—statues, standards, banners, guidons, ensigns, pen-
nons, and streamers—date from the ancient Egyptians who flew carved
elephants and other symbols mounted on poles on boats and perhaps in
front of their temples more than five thousand years ago.

Other early prehistoric cultures also placed carvings or animal skins
atop poles, sometimes accompanied by streamers or feathers. Among the
oldest is an ancient Persian metal flagpole that had a metal eagle perched at
its top. There also are recorded uses of flag predecessors—nearly always as
communications or identification devices on the field of battle or to signify
religious affiliations—among the Assyrians, Phoenicians, Saracens, Indians,
Aztecs, and Mongolians.

It is believed that the ancient Chinese first used cloth banners in the second century BC. The founder of the Chou dynasty (ca. 1027 BC), for example, is thought to have displayed a white flag to announce his presence.
The main use of flags by the Chinese, though, was as a military communications device. "Because they could not hear each other, they made gongs
and drums. Because they could not see each other they made pennants and

flags," the ancient Chinese military general and philosopher Sun Tzu wrote in his classic *The Art of War*: "Gongs, drums, pennants and flags are the means to unify the men's ears and eyes."

That was the case in China in the fourth century BC, according to Sun Pin, the military strategist and Sun Tzu descendant. "Commands should be carried out by using various colored banners," he advised. "Affix pennants to the chariots to distinguish grade and status. Differentiate among troops that can easily be mistaken for each other by using banners and standards."

The ancient Roman legions carried banners called vexilla. These were small square ensigns, most often red in color, that were attached to crossbars at the end of lances. They often were adorned with animal figures, such as horses, eagles, wolves, or boars. Flags in ancient India typically were carried on chariots and elephants. They were usually red or green triangularly shaped banners that had figures embroidered upon them and were surrounded by gold fringe.

The Vikings flew several types of flags, primarily on their famed sailing ships in the tenth and eleventh centuries AD. The most common was the Raven flag, in the shape of a triangle with two straight sides and a curved side. Historians believe that that emblem flew from the masts of Danish Viking ships and probably from the Norwegian Viking ships that landed in Newfoundland a thousand years ago. If so, the Viking Raven banner has the distinction of being the first flag to fly in North America.

The idea of flags as symbols of the rulers of nation states began to evolve in Europe in the Middle Ages and the Renaissance. One of the banners that Christopher Columbus displayed when he reached the West Indies in 1492, for example, bore the Spanish royal standard: two lions and two castles representing the arms of Castile and Leon. Columbus also carried a special white expeditionary flag with a green cross. It consisted of the letters F and Y for Ferdinand (Fernando) and Isabella (Ysabel), each of which was topped by a crown.

The English flag of the period, the red cross of St. George, the nation's patron saint, set on a white banner, dates from the Crusades and was considered a type of national emblem as early as 1277. It was not, however, considered a national flag as we know the concept today. The St. George's Cross rather was a royal banner—the symbol of the king's authority. It was flown on English ships and emblazoned on soldiers' shields. English ships also flew several types of rank-identifying pennants called ensigns, including the all-red, all-white and all-blue English naval ensigns. The word *ensign* itself derives from the British military rank of the same name; the "ensign" was the officer in charge of carrying the colors into battle.

Historical evidence about the use of flags in the fifteenth, sixteenth, and seventeenth centuries is scant and sketchy. Because flags did not have anything close to the meaning they took on as symbols of nations beginning in the late eighteenth century, primary documents rarely contain descriptions of flags. Much of our knowledge about flags during those centuries, therefore, is based on fragmentary evidence and historic supposition.

Historians believe that the first St. George's Cross to make its way to North America was brought by the Italian navigator and explorer Giovanni Caboto (known by his adopted English name, John Cabot), who sailed under the aegis of King Henry VII. The best historical evidence indicates that Cabot's small ship, the *Matthew*, reached Newfoundland in May 1497. When Cabot took possession of the land for England, he unfurled the St. George's Cross along with the Venetian flag of St. Mark.

The first explorers from the other nations who came to North America also sailed under various types of banners and ensigns, most often representing their countries' monarchs. That included the blue royal French flag adorned with three fleurs-de-lis likely carried by Giovanni da Verrazzano, the Italian-born navigator and explorer who sailed under the French king Francis I (François). Verrazzano made landfall off present-day Cape Fear, North Carolina, in March 1524 and sailed on to what is now New York harbor and New England. Jacques Cartier, who explored the Saint Lawrence River for Francis I in 1534, also is believed to have brought his monarch's banner to these shores.

Several types of French merchant flags—typically a white cross on a blue field with the royal arms at its center—were flown by the other pioneering French navigators who came to explore the New World: Samuel de Champlain in 1604; René-Robert Cavelier, Sieur de La Salle, and Jacques Marquette in 1666; and Louis Joliet in 1669.

The English navigator and explorer Henry Hudson, sailing for the Dutch, took his ship, the *Half Moon*, into what is now New York harbor on September 3, 1609. Hudson did so most likely flying the orange, white, and blue horizontally striped flag of the Dutch United East India Company. Hudson also probably carried the Amsterdam Chamber flag, a red, white, and black horizontal tricolor affair. Both flags also contained initials in the center white stripe.

The British Union Jack was created by King James I three years after he succeeded Queen Elizabeth I. James came to England to take the throne in 1603 after serving as James VI of Scotland, where the monarch's flag since the time of the Crusades had been the St. Andrew's Cross, a diagonal white cross on a blue background. On April 12, 1606, James decreed that all English and Scottish ships should fly the new red, white, and blue union flag on their main masts. That flag was known as the Union Jack and also as the "king's colors." It consisted of an amalgam of the crosses and colors of St. George and St. Andrew. The ships were directed also to fly either the banner of St. George or of St. Andrew on their foremasts.

It is believed that the *Mayflower* flew the red cross of St. George when it landed at Plymouth Rock on December 21, 1620, and it is possible that the ship also displayed the Union Jack. And it also is likely that one or both of those flags was flown by the members of the Virginia Company whose three ships—the *Susan Constant, Godspeed,* and *Discovery*—had landed on Jamestown Island in Virginia, on May 14, 1607, and began the first permanent British settlement in North America.

There is concrete evidence that the Union Jack flew in the Massachusetts Bay Colony as early as 1634. Court records show that John Endicott, a local government official who had previously served as governor, that year ordered the cross cut out of a Union Jack. This was not a protest against British rule however. Endicott, acting probably at the behest of the nonconformist pastor Roger Williams (who later founded the colony of Rhode Island), did so to spotlight his Puritan belief that the cross was an idolatrous and pagan symbol. Endicott was tried in a local court for the offense and censured.

The official Union Jack changed several times during the often-chaotic seventeenth century when England underwent two revolutions and a civil war. In 1707, when the turbulence ended under Queen Anne, the new Parliament of the United Kingdom of England, Scotland, and Wales officially adopted James I's Union Jack. "The ensigns armorial of our kingdom of Great Britain," Parliament decreed on January 16, 1707, shall be "the crosses of St. George and St. Andrew conjoined to be used on all flags, banners, standards, and ensigns both at sea and land." This flag, which was used exclusively on ships and on government buildings and military fortifications, came to be known as the "Union Flag."

★   ★   ★

English colonial governors and local military commanders in America, most often small militia companies, began designing and displaying their own flags not long after the establishment of the first settlements in Jamestown in 1607 and in Plymouth in 1620. Nearly all of the colors and symbols used in the earliest colonial flags were borrowed from the Union Jack and the various types of flags carried by British infantry units.

Not all were red, white, and blue, however, and not all used crosses. That is the case with one of the oldest flags of colonial America that still exists, the banner of the English troops based in the counties of Essex, Suffolk, and Middlesex, Massachusetts, known as the Bedford flag. Dating from about 1705, the Bedford flag was crimson in color and featured an arm reaching through a cloud, holding a sword. The arm, cloud, and sword were silver, gold, and black. The colors of Capt. Thomas Noyes's company of troops in 1684 in Newbury, Massachusetts, consisted of a solid green field. The upper left-hand corner (known most often as the canton or the union) contained a red cross on a white background.

Many other colonial flags of the seventeenth and eighteenth centuries contained a canton. That includes the Massachusetts Red Ensign, a red flag with a plain white canton, which flew from about 1636–1686. That flag, it is believed, was the first flown in America that contained the canton-and-field design combination.

The Saybrook, Connecticut, military company flag in 1675 was red with a white cross in the canton, augmented with a blue ball, most likely in a red field representing a bullet. The Newbury, Massachusetts, militia flag, as noted above, was green with a red cross in its white canton.

The flag with the canton that most resembled what would become the first American flag, though, was not directly associated with the British colonial government. It was the flag of the East India Company, which was formed on December 31, 1600, by Queen Elizabeth I following the 1588 defeat of the Spanish Armada. The East India Company was designed to be the official English entrant into the lucrative spice trade in East and Southeast Asia and India. But the company soon became much more than a commercial venture. It expanded into other commodities, including cotton and silk, and into other areas of the globe, including the Persian Gulf. In addition to its monopoly on trade in the East, the East India Company was given the authority to assume military and political power in the countries where it established itself.

The first reference to an East India Company flag was in 1616 when Japanese authorities complained about the cross on a flag flying from a company vessel. That cross likely was the St. George's Cross. Evidence indicates that in 1670 and in the 1680s the company's ships flew a flag with red and white horizontal stripes and the red St. George's Cross in a white canton. A book published in 1701 shows the East India Company flag with seven red and white horizontal stripes and the red cross of St. George in a white canton. Sometime after 1707, when the Union Jack was created, the company substituted it in the canton for the St. George's Cross. By 1732, the flag's number of stripes had grown from seven to thirteen.

★   ★   ★

By that time many in the thirteen American colonies were chafing under the heavy-handed British rule. As sentiment against King George grew and colonists banded together to protest against colonial rule, they adopted a variety of mostly anti-British flags as emblems of their rebelliousness. These flags featured three main images: the snake, variations on the theme of the word "liberty," and the pine tree. The idea for the "Don't Tread on Me" coiled snake flag came from the pen of Benjamin Franklin. In 1751 in his *Pennsylvania Gazette* Franklin wrote satirically that Americans should send rattlesnakes to England to thank the British for sending convicts to these shores.

On May 9, 1754, Franklin again used the snake in his newspaper, this time to induce the colonies to unite during the French and Indian War (1754–63), during which the English and French battled for control of colonial North America. Franklin, in what is believed to be the first political cartoon to appear in an American newspaper, drew a cartoon depicting a snake cut into eight sections, representing the colonies in a shape suggesting the Atlantic coast with New England as the head and South Carolina as the tail. The cartoon's caption read: "Join, or Die."

In the decades that followed, as discontent with British colonial rule intensified, Franklin's snake image became an expression of revolution. Christopher Gadsden, a patriotic South Carolinian who was a colonel in the Continental army, likely designed one of the first snake flags while serving in 1775 as a member of the Marine Committee of the Continental Congress. Gadsden appointed Esek Hopkins of Rhode Island to lead the first Continental Navy fleet in December of 1775. Hopkins, the first commodore of the U.S. Navy, took command of his five-ship fleet with a personal flag, which Gadsden likely had designed and given to him. That flag had a yellow field with a rattlesnake coiled in the middle and the words "Don't Tread on Me!" underneath.

Aside from what became known as "the Gadsden flag," the rattlesnake appeared on many other American colonial banners, including several flown by military units during the Revolutionary War. A flag used by the minutemen of Culpeper County, Virginia, for example, included the rattlesnake, the "Don't Tread on Me" motto, and the famous words of Virginia's Patrick Henry, "Liberty or Death."

Another similar banner was the 1775 flag of Col. John Proctor's Independent Battalion in Westmoreland County, Pennsylvania. That flag (more than six feet long and nearly six feet wide) consisted of a coiled rattlesnake and Gadsden's words painted directly on top of a solid red field with the British Union Jack in the canton. The snake's menacing tongue is pointed at the symbol of the British crown. Above the snake are the letters "J.P." and "I.B.W.C.P.," which stand for "John Proctor, Independent Battalion, Westmoreland County, Pennsylvania."

The flag of the Train of Artillery company in Provincetown, Rhode Island, also had Gadsden's words emblazoned under a coiled rattlesnake, as did the banner displayed by Major General John Sullivan's Life Guard in Rhode Island, also known as the Rhode Island Militia. That flag, which was used in 1778–79, had nine blue and white alternating stripes and a white canton with a coiled snake.

Although it did not have a snake, the Forster flag of 1775 is believed to have been the first flag with red and white stripes used to represent the colonial cause. Family lore has it that Maj. Israel Forster and the Minutemen captured a flag from the British at the Battle of Lexington on April 19, 1775. The patriots then replaced the Union Jack canton with six white stripes, spacing them over the red background to represent the thirteen colonies, and displayed the flag that day at that battle and the ensuing fighting at Concord.

★   ★   ★

Another popular theme that made its way onto anti-British flags during the years prior to the American Revolution was the word "liberty." Most often liberty flags were solid colored, usually white, with the word "liberty" spelled out in large capital letters. They date from the summer of 1765 and the secret revolutionary radical group the Sons of Liberty, which grew up that year throughout the colonies to protest the infamous British Stamp Act. The group took its name from a February 1765 Parliamentary speech in which rebellious Americans were mockingly referred to as "sons of liberty."

Sons of Liberty groups first met under "liberty trees," where they stirred up support for colonial resistance. When the colonial authorities cut down those trees, the rebels took to meeting under liberty poles, which often featured protest banners, such as one that contained the words "Liberty and Property." A flag displayed at Taunton, Massachusetts, featured the words "Liberty and Union" across a red field with the Union Jack in the canton. Another had the image of a tree, with the words "Liberty Tree" on top and "An Appeal to God" below. Another early liberty flag in New York contained the words "Liberty, Property and No Stamps."

Historians believe that one Sons of Liberty flag that flew from Boston's Liberty Tree contained nine red and white stripes in honor of the representatives of the nine colonies who attended the October 19, 1765, Stamp Act Congress. Those stripes likely were displayed horizontally. If so, that flag is the first recorded on the continent with alternating red and white stripes and could be the progenitor of the stripe design in the American flag. Thirteen horizontal stripes, in blue and silver, also appeared in the canton of the yellow silk regimental flag of Capt. Abraham Markoe's Philadelphia Light Horse Troop that accompanied George Washington to New York in the summer of 1775.

The third widely used symbol on anti-British colonial flags, primarily in New England, was the pine tree. The pine tree symbol in New England dates from the 1629 seal of the Massachusetts Bay Colony, which featured the images of an Indian and pine trees. The red 1686 New England flag contained a canton with the English St. George's Cross in it and a small green pine tree displayed in one corner of the cross. That banner was flown by Col. William Prescott, who commanded some one thousand American militiamen against a force of more than twice that number of British army regulars at the pivotal June 17, 1775, Battle of Bunker Hill, fought at Breed's Hill above Charlestown, Massachusetts.

The most popular image of that Revolutionary War battle—the 1786 painting *The Death of Warren* by John Trumbull—contains an image of the colonial troops flying a red flag with a green pine tree on a white background in the canton. But that image of the flag, minus the cross of St. George, is inaccurate. "Certainly Trumbull, like many artists of the Revolutionary War period, allowed his imagination free rein in the matter of depicting details in battle scenes," Whitney Smith, the nation's foremost vexillologist (flag expert), said of the Trumbull's artistic flag license in that painting.

Trumbull may have been influenced by the fact that not long after the Battle of Bunker Hill, pine tree flags began to be displayed on American Revolutionary War vessels. The first was in September 1775 when two heavily armed scows, called "floating batteries," flying the pine tree ensign adorned with the words AN APPEAL TO HEAVEN opened fire from the Charles River onto British houses in Boston.

The first six schooners commissioned by the Continental Congress to intercept British ships sailing into Boston in October 1775—the *Hancock*, *Lee*, *Franklin*, *Harrison*, *Lynch*, and *Warren*—flew the pine tree flag. An order dated October 20, 1775, from George Washington's secretary Col. Joseph Reed, proposed that the ships show a flag "by which our vessels may know one another," a flag with "a white ground and a tree in the middle, and the motto, 'An Appeal to Heaven.'" By January 1776 the *Franklin* was flying that pine tree flag. On April 29 the Massachusetts Council passed a resolution ordering its naval officers to wear green and white uniforms and that "the colors be a white flag with a green pine-tree and the inscription, 'An appeal to Heaven.'"

⋆   ⋆   ⋆

But it was not the rattlesnake, the pine tree, nor the word "liberty" that appeared on what is now considered the first American flag, although at the time it was not officially recognized as such. This is the flag that George Washington ordered hoisted on January 1, 1776, to recognize the birth of the Continental Army on Prospect Hill in Charlestown outside of his camp near Boston. The Second Continental Congress had named Washington commander in chief in June following the battles of Lexington and Concord.

On New Year's Day, Washington unfurled the improvised Continental Colors, also known as the Grand Union flag, the Continental flag, the Cambridge flag, the Somerville flag, the Union Flag, and the Great Union—the first flag that came into general use throughout the colonies. Washington, who referred to it as the "Union Flag in Compliment to the United Colonies," had the banner hoisted on a towering seventy-six-foot-high liberty pole so that it could be seen as far away as Boston. The flag had thirteen alternating red and white stripes. In the canton of the Continental Colors was the British Union Jack with its interwoven crosses of St. George and St. Andrew. Washington's flag was almost a carbon copy of the flag the East India Company had been flying since the 1670s.

⋆   ⋆   ⋆

The generally accepted explanation of the origins of the Continental Colors is that the thirteen stripes represented the colonies and the Union Jack the rebellious colonists' loyalty to the British crown, if not its Parliaments' policies. That sentiment held in general for most American rebels, at least during this stage of the revolt, six months before the signing of the Declaration of Independence.

Still, the origins of the Continental Colors are not clear. Historians do not believe that it was based on the strikingly similar East India Company flag for two reasons. First, few colonists were familiar with the East India Company flag because there is no evidence it ever flew in American waters. Second, it seems highly unlikely that rebellious colonists would purposely choose an emblem that stood for an organ of the British crown.

It also is not clear exactly who designed the Continental Colors. It may have been the work of Benjamin Franklin, Benjamin Harrison, and Thomas Lynch, who were appointed by the Continental Congress in the summer of 1775 to advise Washington in forming his new army. The first respected American flag historian, retired admiral George Henry Preble, writing in the late-nineteenth century, ascribed to that theory. Franklin, et al., "were appointed to consider the subject" of "a common national flag," Preble wrote. They "assembled at [Washington's] camp in Cambridge." The "result" of that meeting, he said, was the design for the Continental Colors. However, no mention was made of the flag in the Franklin committee's detailed report to Congress on November 2, nor have historians been able to find other concrete evidence to support Preble's proposition.

★   ★   ★

Esek Hopkins's small armada—the *Alfred, Columbus, Cabot,* and *Andrew Doria*—the first regular American fleet, set sail from Philadelphia on January 4, 1776, flying several flags. One was his personal "Don't Tread on Me" rattlesnake flag. Another was what Hopkins called "the strip'd jack" or "striped flag," most likely a simple red and white striped flag used for identification. Also flying on the ships was the Continental Colors.

Before his fleet departed on December 3, 1775, the Continental Colors was raised for the first time on an American fighting vessel, the fleet's flagship, the *Alfred*, under the command of Capt. Dudley Saltonstall. This was about a month before Washington unfurled that flag in Charlestown. Just who raised the *Alfred*'s flag is not completely certain. But the senior lieutenant on the *Alfred*, the renowned naval hero John Paul Jones, took credit for it. "I hoisted with my own Hands the Flag of Freedom the First time that it was displayed on board the Alfred on the Delaware," Jones wrote in 1779.

Historians disagree about Jones's claim. Some believe that Jones raised the "Don't Tread on Me" rattlesnake flag, not the Continental Colors. Others believe Jones may have raised the Continental Colors on the *Alfred*, but that he was not the first American to do so. John Adams, among others, claimed that the "first American flag as hoisted," as he put it an 1813 letter, was the work of Capt. John Manly, who commanded the schooner *Lee* and the frigates *Hancock* and *Hague*. John Adams's after-the-fact claim notwithstanding, historians believe that in all likelihood the *Lee* flew the pine tree flag, not the Continental Colors.

Hopkins's fleet claimed other flag firsts. When Hopkins's small armada captured Forts Montagu and Nassau on the eastern end of New Providence in the British-owned Bahamas on March 17, 1776, it marked the first overseas victory for an American flag–flying navy ship. When Capt. John Barry's *Lexington* fought and defeated the British brig *Edward* on the seas off the Virginia coast on April 17, it marked the first time an American flag vessel captured a foreign flagged ship.

The American brig *Andrew* (sometimes called *Andrea*) *Doria* sailed into port on the small Dutch-owned West Indies island of Saint Eustatius (Sint Eustatius) on November 16, 1776, on a mission to obtain clothing, cannons, gunpowder, and other war supplies. The ship, under Capt. Isaiah Robinson, dropped anchor in the port city of Orangetown in front of Fort Orange. An English ship in the harbor reported that the Dutch flag at Fort Orange was lowered in welcome, and then the *Andrew Doria* lowered its sails and fired an eleven-gun salute. The fort's commander then sought advice about the efficacy of returning the salute from the Dutch governor. It was decided to return the salute with an eleven-gun reply. This marked the first foreign salute to an American flag.

The honor of presenting the Continental Colors to Europe for the first time went to the sixteen-gun brig, *Reprisal*, the first Continental navy vessel to reach European waters. Under the command of Capt. Lambert Wickes, the *Reprisal* set sail from Philadelphia on October 24, 1776, carrying Benjamin Franklin to assume his duties as the American Commissioner to France.

By the end of the year 1776, the Maritime Committee of the Continental Congress considered the Continental Colors as the de facto official flag of the American naval forces. The committee let all its commanders know early in 1777, for example, that "it is expected that you contend warmly All necessary occasions for the honor of the American flag."

Incorporating the Union Jack in the Continental Colors, Washington soon discovered, may have been a mistake. When British troops saw it, they took the Union Jack as a sign that the colonials were surrendering. "It was received in Boston as . . . a signal of submission," Washington wrote three days later.

Still the Continental Colors, although it was never formally adopted by Congress, remained the unofficial flag of the rebellious colonies until June 14, 1777. In the eighteen months following Washington's unveiling of that flag, it was used as a symbol of the rebellious colonies' unity—primarily, but not exclusively, on Continental navy ships.

The first Stars and Stripes—of whatever arrangement—to be raised in victory over a foreign force flew from the twenty-eight-gun frigate *Providence* on January 27, 1778, under command of Capt. John Peck Rathburne (sometimes spelled Rathbun). The *Providence,* sailing from North Carolina, captured the British Fort Nassau in the Bahamas, seized ammunition, and freed more than two dozen American prisoners. The ship also captured a British ship and reclaimed five other American vessels that had fallen into British hands.

Military units on land displayed the Continental Colors as well as a wide variety of other types of regimental flags. Many had single-color fields with emblems and cantons with various designs. The Second Rhode Island Regiment's flag, for example, had thirteen stars in its canton. The all-black Massachusetts unit, the Bucks of America, flew a flag with thirteen white or gold stars in a blue canton. The field featured a pine tree and an antlered buck. Troops of the Third Continental Infantry under Col. Ebenezer Learned, on the other hand, displayed the Continental Colors in Boston as they drove Gen. William Howe, the commander in chief of the British army, and his troops from that city in March 1776.

In his January 1776 report on the publication of Tom Paine's landmark pamphlet *Common Sense,* which passionately made the case for independence from England, the British spy Gilbert Barkley noted that armed colonial ships in Philadelphia flew "what they call the American flag," a banner that almost certainly was the Continental Colors. The ships commanded by Gen. Benedict Arnold flew a version of the Continental Colors at the ill-fated Battle of Valcour Island on Lake Champlain on October 11–13, 1776.

Joseph Hewes, a Continental Congress delegate from North Carolina, purchased a large Continental Colors from the Philadelphia flag maker Margaret Manny, who worked with the Wharton Ship Yard in Philadelphia, in February 1776. That flag subsequently flew in his hometown of Edenton. In April 1776 the Continental Colors was depicted on the North Carolina seven-and-a-half dollar bill. And it was flown in Williamsburg, the colonial capital of Virginia, on May 15, 1776. The occasion was the sendoff of Virginia's delegates to the Continental Congress in Philadelphia. The "union flag of the American states" flew from the colonial Capitol Building that day, according to one eyewitness. That "union flag" was the Continental Colors.

CHAPTER TWO

The Birth of a Symbol

★　★　★

Resolved, That the flag of the United States be thirteen stripes, alternate red and white: that the union be thirteen stars, white in a blue
field representing a new constellation.

— Resolution adopted by the Second Continental Congress,
June 14, 1777

ON JULY 2, 1776, the Second Continental Congress approved a
resolution declaring that the colonies "are, and of right ought to be, free
and independent States." Late in the afternoon on July 4, the body approved the Declaration of Independence. Church bells chimed in celebration in Philadelphia, and copies of that seminal document made their way
throughout the colonies to be read publicly. When the news hit Boston on
July 18, the Union Jack and every other emblem of King George in the
city were taken down and burned by the populace.

Despite the spirited celebrations, the Continental Congress took no immediate action to adopt a flag to represent the self-declared newly independent states. And no action would be taken on that front for nearly a year.

In the meantime the Continental Colors continued to serve as the de
facto symbol of the newly created United States of America. Congress's
Marine Committee certainly considered that to be the case. On September
27, 1776, the committee reported to Congress that it had given permission
to a Francis Guillot to "equip and arm" a privateer (a private ship refitted
to attack British ships) "under the colours of the United States."

During this time flag makers, including several in Philadelphia, continued to produce the Continental Colors, primarily for naval ship providers.

One of the earliest recorded flag makers was a Philadelphia seamstress, twenty-five-year-old Elizabeth Griscom Ross, who sold "ship's colours &c." to Capt. William Richards's store for fourteen pounds, twelve shillings in May 1777.

On July 4, 1777, celebrations took place throughout the United States to mark the young nation's first birthday. In Philadelphia all the naval ships in the harbor gathered together at one o'clock in the afternoon, and each one of them fired thirteen cannon to honor the thirteen states. The ships were festooned with streamers as well as the Continental Colors. Those colors also were proudly raised that day at all the forts, batteries, and ships in the harbor at Charleston, South Carolina.

Three weeks earlier, on Saturday, June 14, 1777, the Continental Congress had opened a short session in Philadelphia dealing with fiscal matters, including advancing several hundred dollars each to three Continental Army militia captains "for the use of their respective independent companies." After that came a Marine Committee matter: granting that panel permission to command Continental Navy ships in the Delaware River.

The next order of business was a brief resolution that read in its entirety: "Resolved, That the flag of the United States be thirteen stripes, alternate red and white: that the union be thirteen stars, white in a blue field, representing a new constellation."

Congress did not set the dimensions, the proportions, the size of the canton or field (the main body where the stripes are) or even the shape of the flag. Nor did the resolution say anything about the shape of the stars or the pattern for the stars in the constellation. The record does not show which member of Congress introduced the resolution or if a committee did so. The official record simply notes that the resolution was adopted without any debate, comments, or explanations.

Why did the Continental Congress seemingly pay such little attention to the Flag Resolution? Historians who have looked deeply into the matter have not discovered why Congress took so little time and expended such little energy with the piece of legislation that created our national flag. Nor has it been determined exactly what prompted Congress to act on June 14, 1777. There is speculation that navy officers were not happy with the Continental Colors because it contained the Union Jack, the sentiment that George Washington had expressed early in 1776. And flag suppliers, hearing those complaints, may have been pressing Congress to come up with a new all-American flag. William Richards, the Philadelphia ship outfitter, for example, had written to the Pennsylvania Committee of Safety, the state's governing body for military matters at the time, in August and in October of 1776, asking when a new design would be forthcoming.

Another theory holds that a petition to Congress by an American Indian may have precipitated the First Flag Resolution. On June 3, 1777, the Congress had received a petition from William Green, complete with "three strings of wampum." Green's request: "that a flag of the United States might be delivered to him to take to the chiefs of the nation, to be used by them for their security and protection." There is no record of the response Green received, although the wampum and the letter may have spurred Congress to act eleven days later.

The main reason the Flag Resolution was so little noted in the Congress or by the citizenry at large most likely has to do with the fact that in 1777 the flag was not looked upon as the archetypal symbol it would become a century later. It would be a stretch, in fact, to say that in 1777 Americans even recognized the Stars and Stripes as the national emblem or symbol.

"The American flag as a sovereign flag did not occur until 1782," says Henry Moeller, a marine biologist who has specialized in studying the usage of the flag during the Revolutionary War. "In the 1777 period, the flag was not a device that was used by the average citizen," according to Moeller. "It was used for communication," he said. Most historians concur with that assessment. But Moeller goes further, contending that the reason the Flag Resolution was enacted on June 14, 1777, was because the Continental Congress "needed a signal flag to communicate alarm" on the Delaware River.

"That flag that was being talked about on the floor of Congress was being discussed as some form of American identification to be used by the Navy or by the Army," he said. "They were getting ready for a threat in Philadelphia with British naval forces. They needed that device. They could distinguish the Continental Navy from the Pennsylvania State Navy and any other entity that was on the river or the bay. So there was a need for a flag that could be used to communicate. It wasn't until the end of the Revolutionary War when sovereignty was about to be obtained that they really got down to such things as the Great Seal and the formal flag of sovereignty."

★   ★   ★

Most of the summer elapsed before news of the passage of the Flag Resolution was reported in the nation's newspapers. The first newspaper to mention it, Benjamin Towne's *Pennsylvania Evening Post*, a triweekly, ran a brief item on August 30. The *Pennsylvania Packet,* or the *General Advertiser,* published by the printer John Dunlap (best known for printing the first copies of the Declaration of Independence), mentioned the resolution on September 2 in a column listing the proceedings of the Continental Congress. The news appeared in the *Boston Gazette,* that city's first newspaper, on September 1, and in the noted newspaper editor Isaiah Thomas's *Massachusetts Spy* three days later.

In one of history's intriguing coincidences, the Continental Congress's next order of business on June 14 after passing the Flag Resolution was to dismiss John Roach, the captain of the warship *Ranger,* because he was "a person of doubtful character." Congress immediately replaced Roach with an up-and-coming young navy officer, Capt. John Paul Jones. The Scottish-born Jones, who went on to become the top American naval hero of the Revolution, also claimed several flag firsts in his career, including two as captain of the *Ranger.*

He had been the first person to unfurl the Continental Colors on a naval vessel in December of 1775. On February 14, 1778, Jones arranged for the *Ranger* to exchange salutes with French Admiral of the Fleet La Motte Piquet in France's Quiberon Bay, marking the first time a foreign nation saluted the Stars and Stripes. On April 24, 1778, Jones captured the British sloop *Drake* off the Irish coast—the first victory at sea for a U.S. Navy ship flying the Stars and Stripes.

On September 23, 1779, in one of the most famous battles in U.S. naval history, Jones was in command of the frigate *Bonhomme Richard,* when the British frigate *Serapis* shot down his Stars and Stripes during a vicious four-hour battle in the North Sea. Jones's vaunted courage under fire eventually won the day, and he forced the *Serapis* to surrender. The *Bonhomme Richard* was so damaged in the battle that Jones abandoned it and sailed the captured English warship to port in Holland under the American flag, although that banner likely was not the one shot down during the battle. This was the battle during which John Paul Jones reportedly uttered the words: "I have not yet begun to fight."

★   ★   ★

A handful of militia units may have flown the Stars and Stripes during the Revolutionary War. But the flag never was officially supplied to George Washington's Continental Army. And apocryphal accounts and fanciful paintings notwithstanding, there is no evidence that Washington's troops flew the Stars and Stripes at the victorious Battles of Trenton and Princeton on December 26, 1776, and January 3, 1777, respectively, which took place before the Flag Resolution was passed.

The most famous artistic historic misrepresentation of the Stars and Stripes is German-born Emanuel Gottlieb Leutze's iconic 1851 painting *George Washington Crossing the Delaware*. In that much reproduced, twelve-foot-high, twenty-one-foot-long painting, Leutze depicts the flag being heroically clutched by Lt. James Monroe, the future president, standing behind a resolute George Washington on a small, wind-tossed boat.

Washington Crossing the Delaware, now in the Metropolitan Museum of Art in New York, does depict a real event, Washington's daring Delaware River crossing from Pennsylvania to New Jersey that took place on Christmas night, December 25, 1776, more than six months before Congress enacted the Flag Resolution. The truth is that Washington did not display the Stars and Stripes on that fateful journey. If he were carrying a flag on the Delaware crossing, historians believe, it would have been his personal headquarters flag, a blue field dotted with thirteen stars.

It is all but certain, moreover, that Washington and his commanders did not fly the Stars and Stripes at any of the big post–June 14, 1777, Revolutionary War engagements: the Battles of Saratoga on October 17, 1777, and Monmouth on June 28, 1778; the February–May 1780 siege at Charleston; and Corwallis's surrender at Yorktown on October 19, 1781. John Trumbull's famous oil paintings of Saratoga and Yorktown—*Surrender of General Burgoyne at Saratoga* and *Surrender of Lord Cornwallis at Yorktown*—which hang in the U.S. Capitol Rotunda, include prominently placed American flags. Trumbull, whose other heroic Revolutionary War paintings include *The Death of Warren* and *The Battle of Princeton* (which also contains the Stars and Stripes), painted the Saratoga and Yorktown oils long after the war was over, in 1817 and 1820 respectively. He admitted that he put his desire to commemorate those events heroically and patriotically over historical accuracy.

Trumbull received a commission from Congress in February 1817 to create the Saratoga and Yorktown paintings, as well as paintings of the signing of the Declaration of Independence and Washington resigning his military commission. Trumbull all but admitted that he used fanciful elements, such as including the Stars and Stripes, in these paintings in a June 11, 1789, letter to Thomas Jefferson. "The most powerful motive," Trumbull told Jefferson, "I had or have for engaging in or for continuing my pursuit of painting has been the wish of commemorating the great events of our country's Revolution."

There is evidence that some militia units fought in the Revolutionary War under flags that contained thirteen stars and thirteen stripes—although not the red, white, and blue stars and stripes. Two flags with thirteen stars have been associated with the August 16, 1777, Battle of Bennington in Vermont. In that engagement New Hampshire militia troops—including the famed Green Mountain Boys—under Brig. Gen. John Stark, a veteran of Bunker Hill and Trenton, and Vermont militiamen under Seth Warner defeated the British under Hessian mercenary Lt. Col. Friedrich Baum.

The Bennington flag, which is displayed today in the Bennington Museum, has seven white and six red horizontal stripes and a canton containing the number 76, above which are eleven stars in a semicircle and two additional stars above them. Each star has seven points. Some historians believe the Green Mountain Boys flew that flag—which is also known as the Fillmore flag after its original owner Nathaniel Fillmore, a veteran of that engagement—at the 1777 battle. Others say that the flag, which was handed down through three generations of the Fillmore family before it was donated to the Bennington Museum in 1926, was made in the nineteenth century. The consensus of opinion is that the latter argument in closer to the truth, and that the Bennington flag likely dates from the War of 1812 or to the celebration of the nation's jubilee in 1826.

There is another thirteen-starred flag, however, that historians do believe flew at the Battle of Bennington. It is the Stark flag, a green silk banner with a blue canton in which thirteen white or gold five-pointed stars are painted. That flag, too, came down through the family of a man who fought at the battle—in this case, Gen. John Stark. It was made public in 1877 by one of his granddaughters who testified that he owned the banner and that it had flown during the fighting at Bennington. It is not the Stars and Stripes, however, and is considered a militia flag.

A flag reputedly flown at the Battle of Brandywine on September 11, 1777, also has sometimes been referred to as the first Stars and Stripes used in battle. That flag—which is red with a small red-and-white-striped canton with thirteen red stars—supposedly was flying while some thirty thousand British and American troops under Washington and Howe faced off along the rolling hills near the Brandywine River in the hamlet of Chadds Ford, Pennsylvania. In one of the largest and bloodiest battles of the American Revolutionary War, the British outlasted the Continentals and forced Washington to retreat. Stories also have circulated that the flag flew at the September 3 Battle of Cooch's Bridge in Delaware, which took place just before Brandywine.

The Brandywine flag was, in fact, one of the first American flags with

A militia flag reputedly flown by the 7th Pennsylvania Regiment's Company at the Battle of Brandywine on September 11, 1777, is red with a small red-and-white-striped canton containing thirteen red stars. It is displayed today in Philadelphia's Independence National Historical Park. *Independence National Historical Park*

stars and stripes, but it was not an official flag of Washington's army. Historians believe that the Brandywine flag, which is displayed today in Philadelphia's Independence National Historical Park, was a militia color carried by Capt. Robert Wilson's seventh Pennsylvania Regiment's Company, which likely went on to carry the banner at the Pennsylvania Battles of Paoli on September 21 and Germantown on October 4.

Another early red, white, and blue flag made up of stars and stripes is the Easton flag—a silk banner with thirteen red and white stripes in the canton and thirteen white eight-pointed stars in its blue field arranged in a circle of twelve with one star in the center. That flag, which is displayed today at the Easton, Pennsylvania, Public Library, east of Allentown, at one time was thought to have been made for the July 8, 1776, reading of the Declaration of Independence in Easton. Historians believe, though, that it dates from the War of 1812 when Easton's citizens presented it to the city's First Company's First Regiment of Volunteers.

A red, white, and blue, thirteen-star, thirteen-striped flag with twelve stars arranged in a circle and one in the center of the canton was thought to have been carried at the January 17, 1781, Battle of Cowpens in the up-country of South Carolina. That flag, which today is housed in the Maryland State House in Annapolis, was said to have been carried by William Batchelor, the color bearer of the Third Maryland Regiment. In that crucial battle, Brig. Gen. Daniel Morgan led a force of some three hundred Continentals to victory against a British army force under Lt. Col. Banastre Tarleton in an area well known for pasturing cattle. Nine months later came the surrender of Cornwallis at Yorktown.

The flag was handed down in the Batchelor family, donated to the Society of the War of 1812 in 1894 and presented to the state of Maryland in 1907. However, an investigation of the flag by Maryland State archivists and by a Smithsonian Institution textile expert in the early 1970s concluded that the flag dated from the nineteenth century.

"The problem with Maryland's 'Cowpens flag' is that, first, there was no Third Maryland Regiment in the field at the Battle of Cowpens," Gregory A. Stiverson, Maryland's Assistant State Archivist, reported. "Second, despite repeated requests, there is no indication that General Washington ever received U.S. flags for the use of the army. Units of the army carried regimental, or state, colors." Stiverson went on to say that while Maryland regiments carried their own and state colors into battle during the Revolutionary War, the first Stars and Stripes made by the Maryland government "was not constructed until 1782, long after the Battle of Cowpens."

Because of those facts, as well as an examination of the thread and textiles used in the flag, he said, "we have concluded that Maryland's 'Cowpen's Flag' is in fact of nineteenth-century origin."

★　　★　　★

More evidence that the Stars and Stripes was not displayed at Bennington or Cowpens—or, in fact, used at all by Washington's army—is the fact that despite the June 14, 1777, resolution, the Continental Congress's Board of War never embraced the flag as the nation's emblem. "As for the Colours," Richard Peters, the Board's secretary, wrote to General Washington on May 10, 1799, "we have refused them."

Peters went on to explain that each Continental Army regiment "should have two Colours, one the standard of the United States which should be the same throughout the Army and [the] other a Regimental Colour which should vary according to the facings of the Regiment." There was one problem, though, with the "standard," he reported: "it is not yet settled what is the Standard of the U. States." Peters requested Washington's opinion so the board could ask Congress to "establish a Standard" and order enough made "sufficient for the Army."

Washington replied to the board four days later with a one-sentence answer at the end of a four-page letter. "The arrangement respecting Colours," Washington said, "is not [yet] made." The board and Washington never did come to an arrangement on the army's use of the colors before the final British troops left American soil in November 1783.

★   ★   ★

Two even bigger unanswered questions surround the June 14, 1777, Flag Resolution: Who came up with the thirteen-star, thirteen-stripe design? And why exactly did Congress choose the stars and stripes and the red, white, and blue color scheme? Historians have found no definitive answers to the latter question mainly because records either were not kept, were destroyed, or have not survived.

However a significant clue as to who designed the Stars and Stripes may be found by taking a look at the development of the Great Seal of the United States, the federal government's official emblem. Official seals were first used by monarchs in the seventh century. King John of England employed the first Great Seal during his reign in the early thirteenth century to differentiate his emblem from the privy seal used by his king's chamber. In this country the Great Seal (there are no lesser seals) is used by an officer in the U.S. State Department to seal documents. The Great Seal is impressed upon treaties and various presidentially signed documents, such as the appointments of ambassadors, cabinet officers, and Foreign Service officers. The Great Seal also is affixed on the outside of envelopes containing letters accrediting U.S. ambassadors and ceremonial presidential communications to the heads of other nations. The Great Seal has been depicted on the reverse of the dollar bill since 1935.

Almost immediately after adopting the Declaration of Independence, Congress took action on devising an official seal for the new nation. Late in the afternoon of July 4, 1776, Congress appointed a prestigious three-man committee—John Adams, Benjamin Franklin, and Thomas Jefferson—to come up with the nation's seal.

Franklin, Adams, and Jefferson had many gifts, but heraldry was not one of them. Congress did not accept the design their committee drew up with the help of the Swiss-born painter Pierre Eugène Du Simitière on August 20. It featured a shield with the emblems of England, Scotland, Ireland, France, Germany, and Belgium and the Goddess of Justice.

Congress set up a second Great Seal committee on March 25, 1780, consisting of James Lovell of Massachusetts, John Morin Scott of New York, and William Churchill Houston of New Jersey. That committee received significant help from its consultant Francis Hopkinson, a New Jersey lawyer and a signer of the Declaration of Independence, who also was an artist, and who was then serving as treasurer of the Continental Loan Office. Hopkinson's design, delivered to Congress on May 10, 1781, contained a blue shield with thirteen red and white diagonal stripes carried by a male figure holding a sword and a female figure holding an olive branch. The seal's crest, the device above the shield, contained thirteen six-pointed stars.

Historians believe that Francis Hopkinson (1737–1791), a signer of the Declaration of Independence, designed the American flag. Hopkinson also created the official seal of the State of New Jersey, and contributed to the design of the Great Seal of the United States. *Independence National Historical Park*

Francis Hopkinson's 1781 design for The Great Seal of the United States contained a blue shield with thirteen red and white diagonal stripes. The seal's crest has thirteen six-pointed stars. *National Archives and Records Administration,* Records of the Continental and Confederation Congresses and the Constitutional Convention

The Continental Congress turned down the second design, and on May 4, 1782, set up a third committee. It was made up of Arthur Middleton and John Rutledge of South Carolina and Elias Boudinot of New Jersey. Arthur Lee of Virginia replaced Rutledge and the committee received significant design input from Charles Thomson, the Congress's secretary, and from heraldry expert William Barton of Philadelphia. Congress accepted that committee's design—which has served since then as the nation's official seal—on June 20, 1782.

That familiar seal—a red, white, and blue eagle clutching thirteen arrows in one claw and an olive branch with thirteen leaves in the other, with thirteen stars arranged over its head—was primarily the work of Thomson. An ardent patriot and Philadelphia merchant, Thomson was born in county Derry in Ireland in 1729 and came to America as a young boy. He served for fifteen years, 1774–89, as the Continental Congress's secretary.

What is significant about the design process of the Great Seal vis-à-vis the design of the Stars and Stripes is the work of Francis Hopkinson, one

of colonial America's most accomplished citizens. A friend of and correspondent with many of the Founding Fathers, including George Washington, Thomas Jefferson, and Benjamin Franklin, his mentor, Hopkinson
was a lawyer, a member of the Continental Congress, and a signer of the
Declaration of Independence. He also was a poet, artist, essayist, inventor,
and musician. An accomplished harpsichord player, Hopkinson composed
many religious and secular songs. Because he began writing sentimental
love songs as early as 1759, some consider him to be the first American
composer. He created what is believed to be the first American opera, *The
Temple of Minerva,* in 1781. Hopkinson's "My Days Have Been So Won-
drous," which he wrote in 1759, is thought to be the first secular song composed by a native-born American.

Francis Hopkinson was born in Philadelphia on October 2, 1737, the
son of an English immigrant, a lawyer who was a friend of Benjamin
Franklin and who died when Hopkinson was thirteen. Franklin took young
Hopkinson under his wing after his father's death and shepherded him
through the College of Philadelphia, which later became the University of
Pennsylvania. Hopkinson became that institution's first graduate in 1757,
and then studied law.

In 1766, when he was twenty-nine, Hopkinson visited his father's
homeland and later in life used connections he made there to find good jobs
in the colonies, first as collector of customs in Salem, New Jersey, and later
in New Castle, Delaware. He married into colonial aristocracy, to Ann
Borden of the New Jersey Bordens. The Hopkinsons lived in Bordentown,
New Jersey, where Hopkinson plied his legal trade and then became active
politically.

Hopkinson in 1774 was appointed to the New Jersey Governor's Council. Two years later he represented that state in the Continental Congress.
Among his committee assignments in that body: the Marine Committee and
the Secret Committee. After signing the Declaration of Independence,
Hopkinson held several positions in the rebellious American government.
In the fall of 1777, he became a commissioner on the three-member Continental Navy Board, which Congress had created on November 6, 1776,
consisting of "three persons well skilled in maritime affairs" to "execute the
business of the Navy under the direction of the Marine Committee." The
other members were shipping merchant John Nixon and Philadelphia
shipyard owner John Wharton. Hopkinson later served as the committee's
chairman. He went on to become treasurer of the Continental Loan Office
and Judge of the Pennsylvania Admiralty Court. From 1789 until his death

two years later, Francis Hopkinson served as U.S. District Court judge for eastern Pennsylvania.

In addition to all his legal, governmental, and musical accomplishments, Hopkinson was a prolific and adept artist who had an affinity for designing seals and emblems. Among his designs: the seals of the American Philosophical Society, the state of New Jersey, and the College of Philadelphia. He also wrote many essays, anti-British satires during the Revolution, and works of fiction. His *A Pretty Story Written in the Year of Our Lord 2774*, which was published in 1774, is among the first works of fiction by an American writer.

Hopkinson habitually sent his writings and songs to Washington, Jefferson, and Franklin. Thomas Jefferson, for one, a man with well-known good taste, was impressed with the quality of Hopkinson's work—as were his daughters. The author of the Declaration of Independence thanked Hopkinson for sending him a packet of papers, pamphlets, and songs in 1789 while Jefferson was serving as U.S. Minister to France in Paris.

"Accept my thanks for the papers and pamphlets which accompanied them, and mine & my daughter's for the book of songs," Jefferson wrote from Paris on March 13. "I will not tell you how much they have pleased us, nor how well the last of them merits praise for its pathos, but relate a fact only, which is that while my elder daughter was playing it on the harpsichord, I happened to look towards the fire & saw the younger one all in tears. I asked her if she was sick? She said 'no; but the tune was so mournful.'"

★   ★   ★

"Francis Hopkinson," Whitney Smith said, "designed the flag." Smith's statement reflects the consensus of opinion of nearly all historians and flag experts who have studied and weighed the scant evidence that exists dealing directly with the Stars and Stripes' design.

On May 25, 1780, two weeks after the Second Great Seal Committee submitted his proposal to Congress, Hopkinson wrote a letter to the Continental Board of Admiralty containing his thanks that the seal he designed had been approved—something that later turned out not to be the case. He went on to mention his other patriotic designs, which he had completed during the previous three years. One was the Board of Admiralty seal, which contained a red and white–striped shield on a blue field. Others included the Treasury Board seal, "7 devices for the Continental Currency," and "the Flag of the United States of America."

In the letter Hopkinson noted that he hadn't asked for any compensation for the designs but was now looking for a reward: "a Quarter Cask of the public Wine." The wine would, he said, "be a proper & reasonable Reward for these Labours of Fancy and a suitable Encouragement to future Exertions of a like Nature."

The board sent that letter on to Congress. On June 6, Hopkinson forwarded a second, more detailed, bill to the Board of Treasury, dropping his bid for wine and asking, instead, for twenty-seven hundred pounds. Hopkinson submitted another bill on June 24 for his "drawings and devices." The first item on the list was "The Naval Flag of the United States." The price listed was nine pounds.

The Treasury Board turned down the request in an October 27, 1780, report to Congress. The board cited several reasons for its action, including the fact that Hopkinson "was not the only person consulted on those exhibitions of Fancy, and therefore cannot claim the sole merit of them and not entitled to the full sum charged."

However, the only design on his list that Hopkinson did not work on alone was the Great Seal, and it is likely that the final design was completely his work. The board cited no evidence—nor has any come to light since then—that Hopkinson's flag design was a collaborative effort. Hopkinson's itemized bill, moreover, is the only contemporary claim that exists for creating the American flag.

Why did Congress choose the colors and the stars and stripes to represent the states? One common theory, which has been discredited by historians and flag experts, is that the stars and stripes came from the Washington family coat of arms, which contains two horizontal stripes or bars on a white field topped by three red five-pointed stars.

The design came from George Washington's English descendants who lived in Northamptonshire. The coat of arms came to this country in the seventeenth century when Washington's great grandfather immigrated to Virginia. Washington displayed a wood carving of the family symbol above the mantel in the front parlor at Mount Vernon, his home in Alexandria, Virginia. He also used the coat of arms on the panels of his coach, on his personal bookplate, and on his silver.

Speculation that the Stars and Stripes is based on Washington's coat of arms appears to be an apocryphal attempt to add to Washington's patriotic legend. Historians can find no mention of the connection between the two symbols until 1876. The lack of contemporary evidence, the fact that the design of the Washington coat of arms is very different than the Stars and

Stripes, and Washington's well-known disdain for these kinds of trappings lead clearly to the conclusion that the two are not related.

As for stars, they have been used as a heraldic device since ancient times to symbolize humankind's strong desire to achieve greatness. Among the earliest use of the star symbol in the American colonies was the 1680 seal of Providence, Rhode Island, which contained a group of six-pointed stars. It is possible that the iconography of the secret fraternal order of Freemasonry influenced the choice of stars. The practice of Masonry, based on the guilds of stonemasons who built the Gothic cathedrals, abbeys, and castles of medieval Europe, was very common in eighteenth-century America. George Washington, eight signers of the Declaration of Independence, including Benjamin Franklin and John Hancock, as well as John Paul Jones, Robert Livingston, and Paul Revere, among many other influential early Americans, were Masons.

Stars are a prominent feature in Masonic iconography, as are arches, compasses, pyramids, and the "all-seeing eye." The Order of the Eastern Star, a charitable arm of Freemasonry for women, dates from the mid-nineteenth century. Historians believe that the stars in the Bennington flag of 1777 may have been inspired by Masonry, and there is no reason to doubt that the stars in the Stars and Stripes were as well.

As for the stripes, historians trace their American lineage to a 1765 Sons of Liberty flag that flew in Boston. That flag contained nine red and white stripes. Another early flag that used stripes was the 1775 flag containing thirteen horizontal blue and silver stripes flown by Capt. Abraham Markoe's Philadelphia Light Horse Troop. With the lack of any contemporary evidence to the contrary, it is most likely that whoever drew up the Flag Resolution's call for "thirteen stripes, alternate red and white" was influenced by those two flags.

As for the colors, no law, resolution, or executive order exists providing an official reason for the choice of red, white, and blue. The closest thing to an explanation consists of the personal views of Charles Thomson, the secretary of the Continental Congress who was instrumental in the design of the Great Seal. Thomson's report to Congress on June 20, 1782, the day the seal was approved, contained a detailed explanation of the seal's elements, including his ideas on the meaning of the its colors.

"The colours," Thomson said, "are those used in the flag of the United States of America. White signifies purity and innocence. Red hardiness and valour and Blue . . . signifies vigilance, perseverance and justice."

Variations of Thomson's "meaning of the colors" have been expounded ever since 1782. Most often the explanation is stated as though it is official government policy. In a May 12, 1986, proclamation honoring the Year of the Flag, for example, Pres. Ronald Reagan said, "The colors of our flag signify the qualities of the human spirit we Americans cherish: red for courage and readiness to sacrifice; white for pure intentions and high ideals; and blue for vigilance and justice."

But the red, white, and blue do not have—nor have they ever had—any official imprimatur. What historians believe is the explanation of the derivation of red, white, and blue in the Stars and Stripes is the simple fact that those colors were used in the first American flag, the Continental Colors. And there is little doubt where the red, white, and blue of the Continental Colors came from: the Union Jack of England, the mother country.

CHAPTER THREE

Mother of Invention

★　★　★

Betsy Ross sewed the first American flag

— **The Independence Hall Association, 2003**

There is no substantiation for the legend that Betsy Ross was responsible for the Stars and Stripes.

— **Milo M. Quaife, et al.,** *The History of the United States Flag,*
1961

WHY THE FOUNDING FATHERS chose stars, stripes, and
the red, white, and blue colors for the American flag remains an open question. So, too, does the question of who made the first American flag. It is all
but universally assumed today that Betsy Ross stitched together the first
Stars and Stripes in her seamstress shop in Philadelphia. Betsy Ross was,
indeed, a Philadelphia seamstress who made flags. But a careful reading of
the facts reveals that the story that Betsy Ross—born Elizabeth Griscom
on New Year's Day 1752 in the City of Brotherly Love—sewed the first
flag is a myth.

Elizabeth Griscom was the eighth of seventeen children of Samuel, a
builder, and Rebecca James Griscom. Elizabeth's great grandfather, Andrew Griscom, had immigrated to the United States from England in 1680.
He was a member of the Society of Friends, a Quaker, who came to this
country seeking freedom to practice his religion. Elizabeth Griscom likely
attended the Friends elementary school on South Fourth Street in Philadelphia and then became an apprentice to an upholsterer, William Webster.

Two months before her twenty-second birthday, on November 4, 1773,
Elizabeth Griscom ran off to Gloucester, New Jersey, where she married
John Ross in Hugg's Tavern. The son of an Episcopalian minister from New
Castle, Delaware, John Ross also worked as an upholsterer's apprentice at

Webster's. Six months later Elizabeth Ross was disowned by the Society of Friends for marrying outside the faith. She became an Episcopalian and worshipped with her husband at Christ Church in Philadelphia.

By March of 1775 John and Elizabeth Ross had opened a small shop on Arch Street in the commercial district of Philadelphia, close to Independence Hall, several blocks from the bustling wharves along the Delaware River. The young couple lived and worked in the house on Arch Street, which they rented. Upholsterers of the day performed tasks other than making and repairing chairs and other furniture, including seamstress work, which Elizabeth Ross, known as Betsy, performed.

John and Betsy Ross's life together was cut short when John Ross was killed on January 21, 1776, soon after he had joined a local militia company. He was on patrol near a wharf when a stockpile of gunpowder blew up, injuring him fatally. Betsy Ross continued to work as a seamstress and upholsterer after her husband's death. She married colonial war privateer Joseph Ashburn on June 15, 1777, the day after the Continental Congress enacted the Flag Resolution. Betsy and John Ashburn had two daughters in 1779 and 1781, after which John Ashburn shipped out as first mate on the armed merchant marine brigantine *Patty*. That ship was captured by the British and the crew imprisoned in the Old Mill Prison in Plymouth, where Ashburn died on March 3, 1782.

One of John Ashburn's fellow prisoners, John Claypoole, an old friend of the Ross family, was released in a prisoner exchange and returned to Philadelphia in June. Claypoole relayed the news of Joseph Ashburn's death to his widow and her family. A Continental Army veteran of the Battles of Brandywine and Germantown, John Claypoole had been wounded at the latter battle and forced out of the army. He signed on to work on an American cargo ship, which the British captured on its way back from France.

Betsy Griscom Ross Ashburn married John Claypoole on May 8, 1783. After the marriage, she continued to work as an upholsterer and seamstress in the house on Arch Street. He worked for a time at the U.S. Customs House in Philadelphia, then joined his wife in the family business. Contemporary business directories refer to the firm of "John Claypoole, upholsterer," although it is likely that Betsy Claypoole did the lion's share of the work because of John Claypoole's war wounds, which grew worse as the years passed.

Two years after they married, the Claypooles joined the newly formed Society of Free Quakers, a breakaway Society of Friends group. Sometimes referred to as the "Fighting Quakers," that group was made up of people who were "read out of meeting" by the pacifist main Quaker community for taking part in the American Revolution.

Elizabeth and John Claypoole had five daughters. John Claypoole died on August 3, 1817. After his death, until she retired at age seventy-five in 1827, Betsy Claypoole, working with her daughters, granddaughters, and nieces, continued to run her upholstery business and produce flags. After her retirement she lived with her daughter Susanna Satterthwaite in Abington, Pennsylvania, but moved back to Philadelphia in 1835 to stay with another daughter, Jane Canby. Betsy Ross died there on January 30, 1836, at the age of eighty-four.

★   ★   ★

Virtually every historian who has studied the issue believes that Betsy Ross did not sew the first American flag. Yet a significant number of others who have looked into the matter, such as the Independence Hall Association, the Philadelphia nonprofit group that supports that city's Independence National Historical Park, believes that Betsy Ross did, indeed, stitch the first American flag. That flag, widely known as "the Betsy Ross flag," contains thirteen stars arranged in a circle in the canton.

If you go to the Amazon.com Web site—or to any other online bookseller or bookstore for that matter—and type in the words "Betsy Ross" in the search field, you will discover many titles, nearly all for children, and nearly all carrying the same message: that Betsy Ross made the first American flag. While most qualify the claim by saying the story comes from oral tradition, nearly all of the children's books contain fanciful images of Betsy Ross sewing a flag with the thirteen stars in a circle in the canton, often with George Washington looking on approvingly. Some books also promote the message that Betsy Ross designed the Stars and Stripes. That is the case, for example, in Ann Weil's 1986 book aimed at children aged nine to twelve, *Betsy Ross: Designer of Our Flag*, which fancifully recreates Betsy Ross's childhood.

The message that Betsy Ross sewed or even designed the first American flag has generally been accepted among the American public for more than a century. And the name "Betsy Ross" has become an ingrained part of the national fabric. A popular playwright, Henry A. Du Souchet, produced a play on Betsy Ross's life in 1901 and went on to write the script for "Betsy Ross," a silent movie starring Alice Brady as the colonial seamstress, which appeared in September of 1917.

Another early Hollywood movie, starring the silent film stars Francis X. Bushman as George Washington and Enid Bennett as Betsy Ross, appeared in theaters in 1927. The twenty-minute Technicolor short—called *The Flag: A Story Inspired by the Tradition of Betsy Ross*—includes a scene in which George Washington asks Betsy Ross to design and make the first Stars and Stripes. Its last scene, a flash forward to a World War I battle, shows the American, British, and French flags flying side by side. That film regularly appears on television in the twenty-first century—most recently on July 4, 2004, on the cable channel, Turner Classic Movies (TCM).

In 1952 a three-cent U.S. postage stamp was issued marking the two hundredth anniversary of Betsy Ross's birth. The stamp shows Betsy Ross holding the American flag in her parlor. A heavily used bridge spanning the Delaware River between Philadelphia and New Jersey was renamed the Betsy Ross Bridge in 1973. There's a colonial-style hotel in the Art Deco National Historic District of Miami's South Beach named the Betsy Ross Hotel. And Timberland, the big footwear company, offers a women's no-nonsense black Betsy Ross shoe.

Bugs Bunny, the wise-cracking cartoon rabbit, added his special brand of humor to the Betsy Ross story. In the 1954 Warner Bros. cartoon "Yankee Doodle Bugs" and again in "Bugs Bunny: All American Hero" (1980) Bugs gives his nephew Clyde an American history lesson replete with tales of the important roles played by rabbits. In one scene Betsy Ross has just sewed a flag containing red, white, and blue stripes. Bugs steps into the picture and tells Betsy Ross that something else is needed to improve the banner. Whereupon he steps on a rake, which smacks him in the head. Bugs, of course, sees stars, and recommends that Betsy Ross add them to the flag.

When college students were asked in a study done in the 1970s and 1980s to name the first ten people they thought of in the category of "American history from its beginning through the end of the Civil War," excluding presidents, generals, and statesmen, Betsy Ross came out on top in seven of the eight surveys. She placed second in the eighth to Benjamin Franklin. In doing so Betsy Ross topped John Smith, Daniel Boone, George Washington Carver, Christopher Columbus, Lewis and Clark, Harriet Tubman, Eli Whitney, and Pocahontas, among others.

The name "Betsy Ross," however, was virtually unknown outside her circle of family and friends until 1870 when her last surviving grandson, William J. Canby, read his paper, "The History of the Flag of the United States," before the Historical Society of Pennsylvania in Philadelphia in

March of that year. Canby, who was a member of the society, announced that day that his maternal grandmother made the first Stars and Stripes at George Washington's behest and, moreover, that she helped come up with the flag's design. Canby based his paper on stories he had heard from family members since his childhood, along with his own memories of his grandmother's tales of her involvement in making flags. Betsy Ross had died when William Canby was eleven years old.

Canby reported that day that he had searched congressional and other records dealing with the June 14, 1777, Flag Resolution and could find nothing indicating the origins of the Stars and Stripes. "The next and last resort then of the historian (the printed and the written record being silent)," he wrote, "is tradition." That tradition turned out to be stories told by Betsy Ross to his mother and her sisters, to two of his aunts, and to one of Betsy Ross's nieces.

"According to a well sustained tradition in the family of Elizabeth Claypoole (the Elizabeth Ross), this lady is the one to whom belongs the honor of having made with her own hands the first flag," Canby said. His mother and her sisters learned this fact, he said, "from the recollection of their mother's often repeated narration and from hearing it told by others who were cognizant of the facts."

Canby reported that his grandmother made the flag after George Washington visited her "with her girls around her" in her shop on Arch Street in Philadelphia in June 1776. Washington was there with two other members of a congressional committee—Col. George Ross, Betsy's late husband's uncle, and Robert Morris, the merchant and Philadelphia banker and powerful member of Congress who played a pivotal role in financing the war effort. The three, Canby said, were charged by the Continental Congress to come up with the design of a flag for the new nation.

Canby said that George Washington had been a frequent visitor to Betsy Ross's shop. He "had visited her shop both professionally and socially many times," Canby said, "a friendship caused by her connection with the Ross family." Betsy "embroidered his shirt ruffles, and did many other things for him."

Canby's paper contended that Washington, Ross, and Morris told Betsy Ross that they were the members of a congressional committee appointed to "prepare a flag" and asked her if she could make one. She replied, Canby said, "with her usual modesty and self reliance, that she did not know but she could try; she had never made one but if the pattern were shown to her, she had no doubt of her ability to do it."

At that point the group adjourned to the shop's back room, a parlor, where Colonel Ross "produced a drawing, roughly made, of the proposed flag," Canby said. Betsy found that sketch "defective" and "unsymetrical" and "offered suggestions which Washington and the committee readily approved." Her exact suggestions, Canby said, "we cannot determine," but his grandmother's input caused Washington to redraw the design "in pencil, in her back parlor." As he was doing the new sketch, Betsy Ross interrupted and said that the stars in the flag should be five pointed rather than six pointed, as Washington had sketched them.

Could Betsy Ross make the more difficult five-star flag, the committee asked. "'Nothing easier' was her prompt reply, and folding a piece of paper in the proper manner, with one clip of her ready scissors she quickly displayed to their astonished vision the five pointed star," Canby said, "which accordingly took its place in the national standard."

After he read the paper, Canby produced affidavits to back up his claims. They came from his first cousin Sophia B. Hildebrant, the daughter of Clarissa Claypoole Wilson; from Margaret Donaldson Boggs, a niece of Betsy Ross; and from Canby's aunt Rachel Fletcher, Betsy Ross and John Claypoole's then eighty-one-year-old daughter.

"I remember to have heard my grandmother, Elizabeth Claypoole, frequently narrate the circumstance of her having made the first Star Spangled Banner," Hildebrant said in her affidavit, which was taken on May 27, 1870. "It was a specimen flag made to the order of the committee of Congress, acting in conjunction with General Washington, who called upon her personally at her store in Arch Street, below Third Street, Philadelphia, shortly before the Declaration of Independence."

According to Hildebrant, Colonel Ross was so pleased with the flag that he gave Betsy Ross the congressional flag-making concession. "To my knowledge," Hildebrant said, "she continued to manufacture the government flags for about fifty years, when my mother succeeded her in the business, in which I assisted."

Margaret Donaldson Boggs, the daughter of Betsy Ross's sister Sarah, echoed that testimony in her affidavit, which she gave on June 3, 1870. "I have heard my aunt, Elizabeth Claypoole, say many times that she made the first Star Spangled Banner that ever was made with her own hands," Boggs said. "I was for many years a member of her family, and aided her in the business. I believe the facts stated in the foregoing article which has now been read to me are all strictly true."

Rachel Fletcher corroborated the entire story in her affidavit, which she gave on July 31, 1871. The first flag, her mother said, "was run up to the peak of one of the vessels belonging to one of the committee then lying at the wharf, and was received with shouts of applause by the few bystanders who happened to be looking on." Later that day, Betsy Ross reported, Washington's committee "carried the flag into the Congress sitting in the State House, and made a report presenting the flag and the drawing and . . . Congress unanimously approved and accepted the report."

★ ★ ★

The family version of the Betsy Ross story was made public when the nation was recovering economically, socially, and emotionally from the Civil War. It struck a chord among many individual Americans, and among the many patriotic and veterans groups that were formed in the last half of the nineteenth century. Another factor that influenced the Betsy Ross story's acceptance was the emergence of the American feminist movement.

It is possible to make a case that Betsy Ross's story—a strong-willed woman, twice widowed, running her own successful business out of her home while caring for her children—is a profeminist one. But in the latter half of the nineteenth century the story was regarded primarily as a rebuke to the emerging American feminist movement, which largely focused on women's suffrage beginning in the late 1860s.

The domesticity of the Betsy Ross story served as a sort of counterbalance to the message promulgated by organizations such as Elizabeth Cady Stanton and Susan B. Anthony's all-female National Woman Suffrage Association. That organization was founded in 1869 and considered by some to be too radical and dangerous and a threat to the future of the American family. The picture presented of Betsy Ross—doing a traditional woman's job of sewing at home, surrounded by her family, and doing the work for her country—contained the opposite message presented by the women who were outspokenly bold as they worked for the vote.

Betsy Ross "became America's founding mother to complement the Founding Fathers," said Morris Vogel, a Temple University history professor. "It was the immaculate conception: George Washington comes to visit and the flag literally issues forth from Betsy's lap."

The story was helped along also by several female descendants who, beginning in the 1870s, produced small "Betsy Ross" flags, known to collectors as flaglets. "The flaglets were made by her granddaughters or great granddaughters from the 1870s, and, as late as 1900–02," said Jeffrey

Kohn, a prominent Pennsylvania flag collector and dealer. "They sold as souvenirs for five dollars in 1890s. Now they go for between one and two thousand dollars, depending on condition."

The Betsy Ross story gained new momentum and took hold strongly across the nation in the 1890s, a period that marked the beginning of an era of widespread feelings of nativism and nationalism in reaction to large numbers of newly arrived emigrants from Europe. The backlash against the imigrant influx included a surge of nationalism and patriotism surrounding the American flag. Flag Day was born in 1885; the Pledge of Allegiance was written in 1892; a movement grew up during that time to require all public schools to fly the flag, and the Betsy Ross first flag story was memorialized and popularized in prominent magazine and newspaper articles and in books.

In "National Standards and Emblems," a long, detailed article on the history of flags that appeared in the July 1873 issue of *Harper's New Monthly Magazine*, for example, H. K. W. Wilcox relates the Betsy Ross story much as Canby told it. The "construction of the first national standard of the United States," Wilcox wrote, "took place under the personal direction of General Washington, aided by a committee of Congress." Wilcox repeated the story of Washington and the committee going to Betsy Ross's "little shop," putting the date "probably between the 23rd of May and the 7th of June, 1777," a year later than the time Canby reported.

Wilcox, echoing Canby, said that Betsy Ross suggested changing George Washington's choice of six-pointed stars to five-pointed ones because "the stars would be more symmetrical and pleasing to the eye if made with five points." She then demonstrated to the committee how easily it was to make five-pointed stars. After Washington approved the change, Wilcox wrote, Betsy Ross "at once proceeded to make the flag, which was finished the next day."

Betsy Ross, Wilcox reported, was then "given the position of manufacturer of flags for the government," something Canby never claimed, "and for some years she was engaged in that occupation."

The most influential book that dealt with the Betsy Ross story as fact is *The Evolution of the American Flag*, first published in 1909 by William Canby's brother George and his nephew Lloyd Balderson. The book was based on William Canby's first flag research, which ended when he died in 1907. It greatly expanded on Canby's 1870 paper and contained information about the American Flag House and Betsy Ross Memorial Association, which had been incorporated on, appropriately enough, June 14, 1898, to raise funds to purchase and start a Betsy Ross house museum on Arch Street in Philadelphia.

That group was founded by Charles H. Weisgerber of Philadelphia, who in 1893 had created the much-reproduced, life-size painting *Birth of Our Nation's Flag*, in which Betsy Ross is seated in her parlor, sunbeams pouring down on her, in the company of George Washington, George Ross, and Robert Morris. She is holding the thirteen-star Betsy Ross flag, which is draped across the floor and her lap and is meeting the admiring gaze of General Washington. The flag's stars are arranged in a circle in the canton, one of the first depictions of that arrangement. That painting "is the primary reason that the circle of stars has been identified with Betsy Ross," according to flag expert Edward W. Richardson.

Weisgerber's nine-by-twelve-foot work was reproduced on the three-cent stamp in 1952. Because no portrait of Betsy Ross existed, Weisgerber based his Betsy Ross on miniatures of her two daughters dating from around 1806. Those paintings have been attributed to Rembrandt Peale, the noted neoclassical artist and son of the American master Charles Wilson Peale (1741–1827), the preeminent painter of his generation.

Weisgerber's inspiration for the Betsy Ross painting, according to family lore, was a one-thousand-dollar prize offered by the city of Philadelphia in 1892 for the best artistic rendition of a local historical event. Weisgerber decided to enter the contest as he walked by the house on Arch Street. Outside was a sign that read: "Home of Betsy Ross: seamstress, upholsterer and maker of the first American flag." After consulting with William Canby, Weisgerber completed the painting, which won the prize.

Birth of Our Nation's Flag caused a minor sensation when Weisgerber exhibited the painting shortly after it was completed at the Columbian Exposition in Chicago in 1893. The attention the painting received generated a great deal of national interest in the Betsy Ross story. It was also at that large and well-publicized exhibition that the Pledge of Allegiance was introduced.

Weisgerber headed a group that in December 1898 purchased the house at 239 Arch Street where Betsy Ross lived from 1773–86, and where the scene in the painting supposedly took place. The price for the dilapidated brick row house was twenty-five thousand dollars. The plan was to turn the circa 1740 building—which most recently had been used as a combination general store and crude Betsy Ross museum by its previous owner, Charles P. Mund—into a shrine to Betsy Ross under the auspices of Weisgerber's American Flag House and Betsy Ross Memorial Association.

The building's future had been in doubt before Weisgerber's group acquired it. In December of 1895, The *Philadelphia Ledger* reported that the city's two councils had "declined to appropriate money for its purchase," and there were concerns that the building would "fall before the march of public improvements." Those concerns were temporarily allayed when the Schuylkill Council of the Junior Order of American Mechanics started a movement to purchase the house. When that effort did not materialize, Weisgerber's group stepped in.

Weisgerber's association's objectives, as his promotional literature put it, were "to purchase and preserve the historic building, situated at No. 239 Arch Street, Philadelphia, Pa., in which the *first flag* of the *United States of America* was made by Betsy Ross and subsequently adopted by Congress, June 14th, 1777, and to erect a national memorial in honor of this illustrious woman."

The main money raiser came from the sale of souvenir certificates of membership in the association—a way, the association said, "to have all Americans, *of every shade of religions and political opinion, affiliate alike*," become "the preservers of the birthplace of the 'Stars and Stripes.'" The eight-by-fourteen-inch certificates contained a color reproduction of Weisgerber's painting, flanked by black-and-white drawings of the house on Arch Street "in which the first American flag was made," the certificate said, and of Betsy Ross's grave in Philadelphia's Mount Moriah Cemetery. The cost of a certificate was ten cents. Those who formed a "club" with thirty members received a larger, twenty-two- by twenty-eight-inch reproduction of the painting. More than two million of the certificates were sold, mainly to schoolchildren.

Weisgerber moved into the Betsy Ross House with his wife and brother around the turn of the century. When his son was born in 1902, Weisgerber named him "Vexil Domus" (Latin for "flag house") Weisgerber. The *New York Times* in 1908 called six-year-old Vexil Weisgerber "one of the most interesting of the house's attractions." On "state occasions," the paper said, "attired in a diminutive 'Uncle Sam' suit . . . he is lifted to the counter in the shoplike front room, and from that stage recites, with juvenile gestures, but a with flair quicker than that of the average child, what Nathan Hale said about the flag: 'My only regret is,' &c." and other famous patriotic and flag quotations.

Despite his big plans, within three years after gaining control of the house, Weisgerber tried to sell it to the federal government. A measure that would have made the house a government-run shrine to Betsy Ross was turned down by the House Committee on Public Buildings and Grounds in

The house on Arch Street in Philadelphia where Betsy Ross, then known as Elizabeth Claypoole, lived and earned her living as a seamstress. *American Flag House and Betsy Ross Memorial*

1905. In 1907, Weisgerber tried, again without success, to give the house to the City of Philadelphia.

Weisgerber died in 1932 and his association went out of business three years later. During the three decades of Weisgerber's ownership, the Betsy Ross house had fallen into serious decay. Weisgerber's association had raised and spent thousands of dollars purchasing the property and preserving it, but funds to maintain the building proved to be scarce. "Plaster is falling from the walls, exposing old hand-split laths," the *New York Times* reported on February 14, 1937. "The roof is leaking, the cellar kitchen where Betsy Ross cooked is damp and cluttered with waste material, and the treads of the stairs have been worn away with the use of two centuries." The savior of the house was A. Atwater Kent, who led a fund-raising effort to restore the building, which he donated to the city of Philadelphia in 1937.

"When I first learned of the condition of the Betsy Ross House through a newspaper story," Kent, who had made a fortune manufacturing automobile ignition systems and radios in the 1920s, said in 1937, "I thought it was a shame that so historic a shrine should be permitted to fall into decay. I felt that the house in its present dilapidated condition gave a very bad impression to the many thousands of visitors who come to visit it each year."

Today the house is known as the Betsy Ross House and American Flag Memorial. It is owned by the city of Philadelphia and managed by the non-profit group Historic Philadelphia, Inc. The house is one of the city's most visited historic sites, attracting more than 250,000 visitors a year. Only the Liberty Bell and Independence Hall draw more visitors.

Charles Weisgerber's "Birth of Our Nation's Flag" is not displayed in the Betsy Ross House. After the painting was vandalized while on exhibit in the old Pennsylvania State Museum in Harrisburg in the 1950s, it was placed in storage for more than four decades in a Delaware County, Pennsylvania, barn and later in a dye-making shop in southern New Jersey. The artist's descendants offered the painting to the city, but Philadelphia officials declined to exhibit it in the city's museums or other public buildings. After undergoing a forty-thousand-dollar restoration in 2000—during which the painting was cleaned, restretched, remounted, and retouched—the family donated the painting to the State Museum of Pennsylvania in Harrisburg, where it is on exhibit today. "We wanted it to be in a place that would guarantee accessibility to the public and give it the protection it needs for the long term," said the artist's grandson, Charles Weisgerber II.

"Birth of Our Nation's Flag," is "important not necessarily from an aesthetic point, but from an historic point," said Lee Stevens, the state museum's senior curator for art collections. "No other paintings quite inspired the rise of American patriotism at the time."

Visitors to the Betsy Ross House in Philadelphia may not actually be visiting the house where Betsy Ross lived. The evidence showing the exact house on Arch Street where Betsy Ross lived is unclear. That is due to the fact that Betsy Ross and her husbands rented; they never owned the property. One document indicates that Elizabeth and John Claypoole lived at 335 Arch Street. But because Philadelphia's street-numbering system changed several times in the nineteenth century, the best that can be said with certainty is that Betsy Ross lived either at the present day 239 Arch Street or next door at 241.

★   ★   ★

What is all but certain, however, is that Betsy Ross did not sew or help George Washington design the first American flag. George Canby's version of his grandmother's role as the nation's first flag maker was almost universally accepted for nearly forty years. Then, in 1908, William J. Campbell, the chairman of Philadelphia's Historic Sites Committee, published a report titled "The Betsy Ross House: Where Betsy Ross Did Not Design the American Flag," in which he called Canby's Betsy Ross story "a fake of the first water."

Campbell's committee had investigated the authenticity of many of Philadelphia's historic sites in preparation for a Founder's Day celebration in October 1908. "The story is nothing but a foolish tradition," the report said. "Betsy Ross never had any interview with George Washington, nor did she plan a five [pointed] star flag as the school books would have it." Betsy Ross, the report claimed, "was nothing more than an ordinary seamstress, and no doubt was glad to get a day's work sewing on any flag, five-starred or otherwise. She had absolutely nothing to do with the designing or planning of the flag."

That report was met with scorn by Weisgerber's association. "I have in my possession bills which show how much Betsy Ross received for making the flags, for she continued to make them and her daughters and granddaughters after her, down to 1856," said Col. John Quincy Adams, a member of the association's board who claimed to be a descendant of a cousin of Pres. John Adams. "And how do I know that Washington went to her house? Because she told George Canby, her grandson so, and he told me." Betsy Ross, Adams said, "did not die until 1836 and her story of the making of the flag was never doubted by her contemporaries."

Today some continue to claim that Canby's story is historical fact. That includes the message given to visitors at the Betsy Ross House in Philadelphia. Signs throughout that house museum are written as though the flag maker herself is telling her story. "So, of course, she's saying, 'I made the flag and I was visited by the flag committee,'" said Lisa Moulder, the Betsy Ross House collections manager. "But our brochure mentions that there is some controversy behind the story."

The brochure notes that "no official records exist to authenticate the story of Betsy Ross and the making of the flag." The "image of Betsy Ross sewing the first American flag has been imprinted in the minds of Americans since the late 1880s," the brochure says, "when the legend of Ross making the flag was first taught as a true historic event. The Stars and Stripes [is] one of our nation's most prominent symbols of national unity and common purpose, and the desire to know—with certainty—who made the first flag continues to this day."

The consensus among historians is that Betsy Ross undoubtedly made flags, but the earliest evidence shows that she did so in May 1777, when she was paid fourteen pounds, twelve shillings by a merchant for "ship's colours, &c," which, most likely, was the Continental Colors.

No evidence exists backing up the Ross descendants' claims that the Continental Congress set up any kind of committee to design a national flag in the spring of 1776. And if there were such a congressional committee it would have been extremely unlikely that George Washington would have been on it because he was commander in chief of the Continental Army, not a member of the Continental Congress, as Ross and Morris were.

Washington visited Philadelphia from May 22 to June 5, 1776. But he was there to consult with Congress on war matters. There is no evidence that he came to the Ross upholstery shop on Arch Street. There are no mentions of any discussions or debates or meetings about a national flag in the Journals of the Continental Congress in 1776, nor at any other time, except for the Flag Resolution of June 14, 1777. Nor is there any mention of national flag matters in any newspaper articles of the day or in any diaries or letters that have surfaced written by Washington, Robert Morris, Colonel Ross, or any other member of Congress.

Betsy Ross was known as an excellent businesswoman who kept detailed records of her transactions. Yet no invoice or other documents have surfaced linking her flag making to the Continental Congress or to George Washington. Betsy Ross is not mentioned in any shipping merchants' account books in 1776. And, notwithstanding the Betsy Ross descendants' oral history, historians have been unable to document the fact that Betsy Ross and George Washington knew each other.

The noted colonial era flag expert Edward W. Richardson, among others, studied the issue exhaustively and concluded that the story is not true. "There are elements of the Betsy Ross story which simply are not supported by recorded history," Richardson said. The "Betsy Ross family tradition probably became clouded with a number of embellishments and inaccuracies, which is a typical problem with most unrecorded and with some recorded history dependent on human memory and interpretation."

Whitney Smith, among others, believes that Betsy Ross "may have made some of the first Stars and Stripes just prior" to June 14, 1777. On the other hand, Smith said, "the popular image of the young girl in her shop showing Washington how to cut five-pointed stars in one snip undoubtedly began in the faulty recollections of an elderly lady and the impressionable mind of her young grandson."

Henry Moeller has a similar assessment. "Where there's smoke, there's fire," he said. "I think that Betsy Ross in her own way contributed to the actual manufacture of the flag, but how much she contributed to the actual design is a second question."

The question remains, then: Who did sew the first American flag? Historians and others who have researched the records cannot find any indication of the name of the first flag maker. More than a few other Philadelphia flag makers, both men and women, may have done so. Searches of the records of Philadelphia shipping supply merchants of the time, including an exhaustive study undertaken by Henry Moeller, show that at least seventeen upholsters and flag makers (including John Claypoole and Elizabeth Ross) worked in Philadelphia from 1775 to 1777. Most of them produced ensigns for ships.

The list includes:

- William Barrett, a flag painter;

- Cornelia Bridges, who appears to have made naval ensigns as early as December 22, 1775;

- Plunkett Fleeson, who set up his upholstery shop on January 18, 1775;

- Anne King, who was paid twelve pounds, thirteen shillings, eleven pence for 32 and 5/8th yards of "bunting for colors for the fleet" by the Navy Board of Pennsylvania on September 10, 1777;

- Rebecca Young, who made flags for the Quartermaster Department of the Continental army during the Revolution;

- Margaret Manny, who began making jacks and ensigns in December of 1774. A year after that, the records show, Manny made the Continental Colors for the *Alfred*—the first flag raised on an American fighting vessel by John Paul Jones on December 3, 1775.

Some historians, including the well-respected Barbara Tuchman, have bestowed the mantle of America's first flag maker on Margaret Manny. "Everyone knows about Betsy Ross, why do we know nothing about Margaret Manny?" Tuchman wrote in *The First Salute*. "Probably for no better reason than that she had fewer articulate friends and relatives to build a story around her."

A strong case can be made that Margaret Manny did make the first flag—although it was the Continental Colors, not the Stars and Stripes.

Pres. Woodrow Wilson, who presided over the first official national

Flag Day on June 14, 1916, may have best summed up the feelings of many Americans on the subject. Stories have circulated for years that when asked his thoughts on the Betsy Ross story, Wilson replied, "Would that it were true." Historians, though, have been unable to determine when, or even if, Wilson made that statement—which, ironically, mostly likely is another myth involving Betsy Ross and the making of the first American flag.

CHAPTER FOUR

First Additions

*   *   *

Be it enacted . . . that . . . the flag of the United States be fifteen
stripes alternate red and white. The Union be fifteen stars, white in a
blue field.

—The Second Flag Act, January 13, 1794

THE UNITED STATES OF AMERICA took a giant step in
its political evolution following the end of the Revolutionary War in 1783.
The weak federal authority created by the colonial Articles of Confederation gave way in 1787 to a new Constitution, which became the law of the
land the following year. The U.S. Constitution created a republican, federalist system of government with many powers shifted from the states to the
federal government. Two years later George Washington was elected the
new nation's first president and became the nation's leader for the next
eight years. During that time the American flag flew mainly on navy ships,
commercial sailing vessels, and American military installations on land.
And not all ships during the Revolution displayed the Continental Colors
or the Stars and Stripes.

"At this time we had no national colors, and every ship had the right to,
or took it, to wear what kind of fancy flag the captain pleased," Capt. John
Manly, then serving on the privateer *Cumberland,* wrote early in 1779.

Since the June 14, 1777, Flag Resolution did not specify the shapes of
the stars or their arrangements in the canton, and since all flags were made
by hand, there were many variations. Most stars on the flags had five or six
points, but others had four or eight points. Some stars were arranged in

a circle, some in horizontal rows of varying numbers, the most popular being four, five and four, and three, two, three, two, and three. But others had the stars arranged in the shape of a cross, a straight line, or a square with one star in the center.

Although most of the flags' stripes followed the wording of the Flag Resolution and were white and red, some had red, white, and blue stripes. A letter dated October 9, 1778, from Benjamin Franklin and John Adams, who were in Paris lobbying for French support for the Revolution, to the king of Two Sicilies, provides the best documentation of that fact. The "flag of the United States of America," Franklin and Adams wrote, "consists of thirteen stripes, alternately red, white, and blue." A "small square in the upper angle, next the flagstaff," they explained, "is a blue field, with thirteen white stars, denoting a new constellation."

Some flags had emblems sewn into them. Among the most popular was an eagle, often nestled in the canton below the stars. One of the busiest Stars and Stripes of the post–Revolutionary War years was a flag flown at the celebration of the end of the war on the public green in New Haven, Connecticut, on April 24, 1783. It was a "continental flag," a "grand silk flag," made by several local women, according to an eyewitness, Ezra Stiles, the president of Yale College. Stiles described the flag as having thirteen red and white stripes "with an azure blue field in the upper part charged with 13 stars."

The "upper part" also was crowded with words and symbols, Stiles said. Nestled below the stars were the words "Virtue, Liberty, Independence," Pennsylvania's motto (then and now), and among the stars were "a ship, a plough, and 3 sheaves of wheat," along with an eagle and two white horses.

That same motto was written on a flag flown at the Fourth of July celebration in 1783 in Princeton, New Jersey. "A flag was displayed, on a pole in the street before the college gate," Charles Thomson, the secretary of the Continental Congress, reported in a letter to his daughter Hannah the next day, "emblazoned with stars & stripes & with a motto, Virtue liberty & independence."

$$\star \quad \star \quad \star$$

A twenty-four-year-old American, Elkanah Watson, on a business trip to London, claims to have hoisted the first American flag in England. The date was December 5, 1782, the day that King George III opened Parliament with a speech in which he formally recognized the victory of the American forces in the War of Independence. Watson, according to his journal, was having his portrait painted in the London studio of John Singleton Copley, the renowned Boston-born painter who had immigrated to England in 1775. Copley had painted his portrait, including the background that Watson requested, a ship flying "the stripes of the union." But the artist was not willing to paint the flag on the ship until the war was officially over because "the royal family and nobility" often came to his studio.

After King George's concession speech, Watson, who was in attendance at the House of Lords to hear it, hurried to Copley's studio. He made his case that the time was right for the flag to be added to his portrait. Through "my ardent solicitation," Watson said, Copley "mounted the American stripes on a large painting in his gallery—the first which ever waved in triumph in England."

Less than two months later the first American ship carrying the Stars and Stripes sailed into English waters. It was a commercial vessel, the *Bedford* of Nantucket, and it carried a huge cargo of whale oil. The *Bedford*, under Capt. William Mooers, sailed up the Thames on February 3, 1783, arriving at the customs house in London on February 6. It was "the first vessel which has displayed the thirteen rebellious stripes of America in any British port," a London periodical put it.

The first Stars and Stripes carried around the world was a banner that flew on two ships during the pioneering 1787–90 circumnavigation of the globe by the ships *Lady Washington* and *Columbia* under the command of Capt. Robert Gray and Capt. John Kendrick. A veteran of the Continental navy during the Revolutionary War, Gray was born in Rhode Island in 1755. He was working for a Massachusetts trading company in 1787 when he set sail from Boston with a cargo of buttons, beads, cloth, and other items. He reached the Oregon coast ten months later, then sailed across the Pacific to Asia before returning to his home port in August 1790. On a second trip in 1792, Gray explored what is now Gray's Harbor in the state of Washington and the Columbia River, which he named for his ship.

On March 4, 1791, Vermont joined the thirteen original colonies and became the fourteenth state. The fifteenth state, Kentucky, entered the Union on June 1, 1792. It was not until the end of 1793, however, that Congress set about changing the makeup of the American flag to reflect the newly added states. The fact that Congress took so long to get to the matter is another indication that the American people, as represented by their senators and congressmen, did not in general have strong feelings about their national flag.

On December 23, 1793, Vermont senator Stephen Row Bradley, who was elected to the Senate when his state was admitted to the Union, announced his intention to introduce a bill "making an alteration in the flag of the United States." The legislation called for a flag with "fifteen stripes, alternate red and white," with a union of "fifteen stars, white in a blue field." It would go into effect on May 1, 1795. The proposed measure was read for the first time in the Senate on December 26 and passed on December 30 without debate.

The House of Representatives took up the nation's second piece of flag legislation on January 7. A lively debate took place in the House that day. Congressman Benjamin Goodhue, a Massachusetts Federalist, opened the proceedings by ridiculing the idea of changing the flag. Goodhue called the proposed law "a trifling business which ought not to engross the attention of the House" because it had "matters of infinitely greater consequences" to attend to. He went on to say that he believed the thirteen-star, thirteen-stripe flag "ought to be permanent," and warned that if new stars and stripes were added every time new states entered the Union "we may go on adding and altering at this rate for one hundred years to come."

Israel Smith, a Vermont Republican, agreed with Goodhue, basing his opposition on fiscal grounds. "This alteration would cost [me] five hundred dollars," Smith said, "and every vessel in the Union sixty." Smith denounced the Senate for passing the bill, something he said was done "for want of something better to do." Nevertheless, Smith recommended the House endorse the measure, with one caveat. "Let us have no more alterations of this sort," he said. "Let the Flag be permanent."

William Lyman, a Republican from Massachusetts and a former major in the Continental army, spoke in favor of altering the flag. His main argument was that if Congress failed to do so, it would "offend the new states." That view was seconded by Congressman Christopher Greenup, a Republican from Kentucky who served in the war as an infantry colonel. Greenup said he considered adding two stars and two stripes in honor of his state and of Vermont "of very great consequence to inform the world that we had now two additional states."

Nathaniel Niles of Vermont also saw the matter as a trifling affair, "neither worth the trouble of adopting or rejecting." In order to get back to important congressional business though, Niles argued that the House should "pass it as soon as possible."

James Madison of Virginia, the nation's future fourth president, weighed in in favor of passage without elaborating on his reasons for doing so. Virginia Republican William Branch Giles argued for the bill as well, saying he "thought it very proper that the idea should be preserved of the number of our States and the number of stripes corresponding."

The debate continued the next day, January 8. After defeating a motion by Federalist Party congressman Benjamin Bourne of Rhode Island to refer the matter back to committee and a move by John Watts of New York to enact another bill calling for no future alterations of the flag, the matter was put to a vote. It passed 50–42. Pres. George Washington signed the bill into law on January 13, making it the first piece of legislation enacted by the Third Congress of the United States.

The fifteen-star, fifteen-stripe flag would be the nation's official emblem for the next twenty-three years. It flew on the ships of America's reconstituted navy beginning in the mid-1790s. That included the *Constitution,* one of six frigates authorized by Congress on March 27, 1794. The *Constitution* gained the nickname "Old Ironsides" during the War of 1812 for its extraordinary durability under battle conditions. One of the most celebrated warships in U.S. naval history, it was launched flying the fifteen-star, fifteen-stripe flag on October 21, 1797. Today the restored and preserved *Constitution,* the world's oldest commissioned floating warship, resides in the Boston's Charlestown Navy Yard.

The new flag made its way around the world in the 1790s. When future president James Monroe went to Paris as U.S. Ambassador to France during the French Revolution in August 1794, he presented the flag with great ceremony to the French National Convention, the assembly that governed the nascent French Republic during the most critical period of the French Revolution. The flag, according to Admiral Preble, was first displayed in Japan in 1797 by the American merchant ship *Eliza.* The frigate *George Washington* flew the Stars and Stripes for the first time in Turkey in 1800.

The fifteen-star, fifteen-stripe flag was the first American flag to be flown over a captured fortress outside the United States. The event occurred in the heavily fortified city of Derna (sometimes spelled Derne), the easternmost province of Tripoli (present-day Libya) on April 27, 1805, during the Tripolitan War. That undeclared war, sometimes called the Barbary War, was the first conflict waged by the new nation on foreign soil. It pitted American marines and naval forces against the Barbary pirates on Africa's Mediterranean Coast. The victory at Derna that day become legendary in the history of the U.S. Marine Corps.

The fight was waged by a heavily outnumbered force of American marines, working with European mercenaries and local forces, and supported by three U.S. Navy ships, the *Argus,* the *Hornet,* and the *Nautilus.* The contingent of marines and mercenaries was led by Gen. William Eaton. He commanded about sixty troops, plus cannon support from the ships at sea, as he faced a heavily defended city with a force that outnumbered Eaton's men by about ten to one.

Soon after the fighting began, Eaton was wounded. Marine Lt. Presley N. O'Bannon took command of the American troops and led a frontal assault that involved hand-to-hand combat. The marines won the day. When they lowered the ensign of the city and replaced it with the Stars and Stripes, the marines and sailors cheered lustily. The engagement turned O'Bannon into the Marine Corps's first hero. The marines' actions that day are honored with the words "to the shores of Tripoli" in "The Marine's Hymn."

It was during the post–Revolutionary War period, too, that images of the flag began to appear on consumer items for the first time. Among the first was inexpensive china from England and China. Most often the flags that appeared on the china made for the American market flew from the masts of sailing ships. There is evidence, too, of the flag motif showing up in wallpaper. As far as textiles, such as kerchiefs and bandannas, the flag images that were used were in nearly all cases part of depictions of sailing ships.

Still, in the post–Revolutionary War era, the flag, as a symbol of the nation, played a minor role. Other images of the nascent nation were used much more widely. They included sculptures, paintings, and engravings of George Washington, the universally revered "Father of Our Country," and images such as the eagle and the female figures of Liberty and Columbia.

CHAPTER FIVE

Our Flag Was Still There

★   ★   ★

O say, does that star-spangled banner yet wave
O'er the land of the free and the home of the brave?

— Francis Scott Key, 1814

As Secretary of the Smithsonian Institution, I am often asked which of our more than 140 million objects is our greatest treasure, our most valued possession. Of all the questions asked of me, this is the easiest to answer: our greatest treasure is, of course, the Star-Spangled Banner.

— I. Michael Heyman, 1998

THE MOST FAMOUS fifteen-star, fifteen-stripe American flag — in fact, the most famous American flag and the banner that gave the American flag its most famous nickname — gained its place in American iconography during the War of 1812. Important milestones in the history of the American flag very often have been associated with armed conflict. That was the case with the Revolutionary War and the origins of the flag. And it was true with the War of 1812 and the American flag that gave this nation its National Anthem, "The Star-Spangled Banner."

The short but bloody War of 1812 pitted the young nation against its former colonial ruler in land battles in this country and in Canada and in sea battles along the Canadian-American border, in the Atlantic, and in the Gulf of Mexico. On June 12, 1812, Pres. James Madison signed a declaration of war against Great Britain in response to years of accumulating disputes over Britain's refusal to respect American sovereignty on the high seas, including the impressment of American sailors, as well as border disputes involving the Northwest Territories and Canada.

The war began in the summer of 1812 with the unsuccessful American invasion of Canada and ended in the early months of 1815 with the successful American defense of the city of New Orleans. Although the war generally was perceived in this country as a victory for the United States, it ended inconclusively, with losses and victories on both sides.

The events leading to the dramatic Star-Spangled Banner story began in the spring of 1814 when the War of 1812 took on a new complexion after Napoleon's defeat in Europe. That situation freed up large numbers of British troops to cross the Atlantic and do battle with the Americans. Their numbers included Maj. Gen. Robert Ross and his five thousand battle-hardened British army regulars and Royal Marines. Ross's men landed in this country on August 1, 1814, in Benedict, Maryland, near Washington, D.C. The British force also included a fleet of warships under Vice Adm. Sir Alexander Cochrane. That small armada entered the Chesapeake Bay on August 16.

Three days later Ross began a march toward the nation's capital. Just outside Washington, in the small town of Bladensburg, Maryland, on August 24, 4,000 of Ross's men faced off against some 6,000 American troops under the command of U.S. Army brigadier general William Winder. All but 350 of the American troops were inexperienced militiamen. The British routed the Americans in a four-hour battle. Ross's men then entered the city of Washington.

During most of the next two days, the British troops burned the Executive mansion (later known as the White House), the Capitol, the Library of Congress, and many other public buildings. The purpose of the destruction, the British said, was revenge against American troops' burning of government buildings in the city of York (now Toronto) in Canada in April 1813. President Madison and other American officials had fled before the British troops entered the city. They returned after Ross and his men left the capital during the night of August 25.

Meanwhile, some thirty-five miles north of Washington, in Baltimore, American forces under Maj. Gen. Samuel Smith made ready to defend that city. Smith had some 9,000 militiamen, which he massed on the city's eastern end. That included about 250 artillerymen and some 750 infantry regulars, sailors, and militiamen under U.S. Army major George Armistead in place at Fort McHenry.

That fort, named after former secretary of war James McHenry, stands on a narrow peninsula known as Whetstone Point on the Patapsco River, guarding the Baltimore harbor. Fort McHenry was built in 1798 on the site of the former Revolutionary War earthen mound fortress called Fort Whetstone.

After they left Washington, the British naval and ground troops repaired to Tangier Island in the Chesapeake Bay, where, on September 8, Admiral Cochrane and General Ross made their final plans to attack Baltimore, the nation's third largest city.

While the Americans prepared to defend Baltimore, a force of some six thousand British troops, including a naval brigade, under the overall command of Admiral Cochrane, landed at North Point, Maryland, some fourteen miles south of the city, in the early morning hours of September 12. At noon, Ross's troops encountered a small American force of Maryland militiamen. During the ensuing skirmish, Ross was shot and killed. Lt. Col. Arthur Brooke took over command of the British army after Ross's death and the Battle of North Point continued into the early afternoon. Dozens were killed and wounded on both sides in the fighting, which ended when the British broke off contact and made camp for the night in the nearby woods.

That evening, three British frigates, five British bomb vessels, and one rocket ship under the command of Admiral Cochrane sailed up the Patapsco and paused about two miles from Fort McHenry, just out of range of the fort's guns. At 6:30 the next morning, September 13, the ships began bombarding the fort with mortars and cannon. The relentless assault lasted throughout that entire day and into the night. When some of the British ships moved in closer, the guns at Fort McHenry opened fire and scored several hits. The Fort McHenry defenders also purposely sank some American vessels to block the British naval advance. The British ships retreated out of range of the fort's cannon. But they kept up the bombing, raining a nearly constant stream of shells onto the fort.

In the early afternoon of September 13, as the bombardment continued, the British ground troops circled into the city and came within sight of Fort McHenry. Brooke planned an assault on the American defensive lines. He held back, though, for three reasons: weather conditions—it was raining heavily; because Cochrane could not provide naval support; and because the army did not have the resources to carry off captured materiel if he had taken the city.

The bombing continued unabated into the night. The nearly constant stream of bomb, mortar, and rocket shells from the British Fleet was punctuated with loud thunderclaps as the rainstorm lashed the area. A two-hour diversionary attack by some twelve hundred British marines and sailors early in the morning of September 14 was repulsed by Fort McHenry's guns and by the artillery at two of the fort's nearby batteries. The British bombing recommenced after the attack at around 2:00 a.m. It continued relentlessly for several more hours until Cochrane called a halt to the onslaught at around 7:00. When the guns went quiet, the British war fleet turned away from the city and sailed back down the Patapsco, heading eventually for the island of Jamaica.

As the British ships retreated, the Americans at Fort McHenry "hoisted a splendid and superb ensign on their battery," a British sailor wrote, "and at the same time fired a gun of defiance." That ensign came to be known as the Star-Spangled Banner.

★   ★   ★

The man who named that flag, Francis Scott Key, witnessed the Battle of Baltimore aboard a sixty-foot sloop in the harbor. How Key found himself in the harbor while the battle raged is an intriguing and not widely known story.

Francis Scott Key was born on August 1, 1779, at his affluent family's estate called Terra Rubra in Frederick County in western Maryland. His great grandfather, Philip Key, had come to Maryland from England in the early 1720s. When he was ten years old, Key went to Annapolis to attend St. John's College. He graduated from that prestigious small liberal arts institution in 1796, then studied law under Judge J. T. Chase in Annapolis.

Francis Scott Key began practicing law in 1801 in Frederick, Maryland. His partner was Roger B. Taney, who married Key's sister Anne in 1806. Taney went on in 1836 to become the fifth chief justice of the U.S. Supreme Court. Shortly after Key married Mary Tayloe Lloyd in Annapolis 1802, he moved to the Georgetown section of Washington, D.C., to practice law with his uncle, Philip Barton Key. Francis Scott Key became one of the city's most prominent attorneys, eventually serving as U.S. Attorney for the District of Columbia, and arguing many cases before the U.S. Supreme Court. An amateur poet, Key also was a very religious man who was active in the Episcopal Church. He died in Baltimore on January 11, 1843.

The circumstance that led to Key's ringside seat at the Battle of Baltimore took place in the immediate aftermath of the British sacking of Washington. Before all of the British troops made their way aboard ships bound for Baltimore, a group of them raided several farms in Maryland outside

Washington. Dr. William Beanes, a prominent Upper Marlboro physician and a friend of Key, organized opposition to the renegade British troops. After Beanes's men captured some of the pillaging British troops, he and several other Americans were arrested and taken prisoner by the British.

A prisoner exchange followed, and everyone but Dr. Beanes was released. He was taken away in the *Tonnant,* Admiral Cochrane's flagship, as the British sailed toward Baltimore. Intermediaries contacted Key to ask him to arrange for Dr. Beanes's release. Key secured permission to negotiate the release from President Madison and Gen. John Mason, who was in charge of matters relating to military prisoners during the War of 1812. Key's orders were to go to Baltimore and rendezvous with U.S. Army colonel John S. Skinner, who had dealt with British rear admiral George Cockburn on prisoner exchanges and other issues in that city.

Key and Skinner met in Baltimore on September 4. The next day they sailed on a sixty-foot sloop carrying a truce flag in search of the British Fleet. They met up with the *Tonnant* and were welcomed aboard by General Ross and Admiral Cochrane. Key convinced the British commanders that Dr. Beanes was a civilian noncombatant. After what has been described as a cordial dinner on board the ship, the British agreed to Dr. Beanes's release. But there was a condition. Key, Skinner, and Beanes were not permitted to return to Washington until after the British attack on Baltimore.

The three men were first escorted to a British frigate, which towed their sloop toward Baltimore. On September 10, Key, Skinner, and Beanes were allowed to return to their vessel, accompanied by British marine guards. They set anchor in Baltimore harbor, about eight miles from Fort McHenry, and spent the next four days there, witnessing the fighting, including the relentless barrage during the stormy night of September 13–14. It was an emotion-laden experience. Key expressed his high feelings as the British Fleet sailed away from Fort McHenry by writing a poem, which he began to compose on the back of a letter he had in his pocket.

Key finished the four verses of the poem either while sailing back to shore or at a hotel—accounts differ—on September 16. The next day he presented the verses to his brother in law, Judge Joseph Hopper Nicholson, the chief justice of the Baltimore District of the Maryland Court of Appeals. Hopper had commanded the Maryland Volunteer Artillery's First Regiment, known as the "Baltimore Fencibles," at Fort McHenry during the Battle of Baltimore. Either Nicholson, his wife, Key, or Skinner took the poem to a printer, most likely Benjamin Edes, who also was a

veteran of that battle, having commanded a Maryland militia company at
the Battle of North Point. Edes owned and operated a print shop on the
corner of Baltimore and Gay Street, from which copies of Key's poem,
bearing the title "Defence of Fort M'Henry," were printed on handbills or
broadsheets and distributed throughout the city. The text appeared in the
daily afternoon newspaper, the *Baltimore Patriot,* and the *Evening Advertiser*
on September 20.

The newspaper and broadsheets included a short introduction, probably written by Judge Nicholson. "The following beautiful and animating
effusion, which is destined long to outlast the occasion, and outlive the impulse, which produced it, had already been extensively circulated," the introduction said. "In our first renewal of publication we rejoice in an
opportunity to enliven the sketch of an exploit so illustrious, with strains
which so fitly celebrate it."

The broadsheet and the newspaper went on to describe the "circumstances" under which the "song was composed." Key, who was described
only as a "gentleman" and was not named, "was compelled to witness the
bombardment of Fort M'Henry, which the Admiral [Cochrane] had
boasted that he would carry in a few hours, and that the city must fall." Key
"watched the flag at the Fort through the whole day with an anxiety that
can better be felt than described, until the night prevented him from seeing
it. In the night he watched the Bomb-Shells, and at the early dawn his eye
was again greeted by the proudly-waving flag of his country."

The article indicated that the song was meant to be sung to the tune of
"To Anacreon in Heaven," an English song, popular in pubs, that was
composed by John Stafford Smith around 1775 and was well known in
the United States. The tune was the theme song of the Anacreontic Society of London, a gentlemen's club that met periodically to listen to musical performances, dine, and sing songs. It was named after Anacreon, the
ancient Greek poet known primarily for his verses in praise of love, wine,
and revelry. Several similar organizations were formed in the United
States, including the Columbian Anacreontic Society in New York, which
had begun in 1795, and the Anacreontic Society of Baltimore, which
would start in 1820.

On September 21, 1814, the *Baltimore American* published the song, and
it soon became known, if not popular, throughout the nation. It was first
performed publicly on October 19, 1814, in Baltimore at the Holliday
Street Theatre, popularly known as "Old Drury," after the performance of
a play. The song became known as "The Star-Spangled Banner" after it was

published for the first time in sheet music form by Carr's Music Store in Baltimore in November. The title on the sheet music reads, "THE STAR SPANGLED BANNER," below which are the words "A PATRIOTIC SONG" and "Air, Anacreon in Heaven." The song was subsequently reproduced widely in newspapers and magazines and soon appeared in sheet music and in songbooks throughout the nation.

Fifty-seven years later "The Star-Spangled Banner" became the unofficial National Anthem of the North soon after the start of the Civil War. The widespread use of the song beginning in 1861 marked the first time that the nation widely and significantly embraced the flag as a symbol of American patriotism. In the decades following the war the song grew in popularity nationwide.

Although it remained popular from the time Key wrote the song in 1814—as evidenced by the cover of this 1861 sheet music—"The Star-Spangled Banner" did not become the official National Anthem until 1931. *The Library of Congress, Prints and Photographs Division*

The United States Naval Academy adopted "The Star-Spangled Ban-ner" as its anthem in 1889, the same year in which navy bases and ships started playing it when the flag was raised each day at morning colors. The U.S. Marine Band began playing "The Star-Spangled Banner" at its public performances in 1890. The U.S. Army adopted the song for retiring the colors in 1895, and the U.S. Military Academy at West Point took the song as its official anthem in 1903. During the Spanish-American War in 1898, the American public for the first time began standing during the playing of "The Star-Spangled Banner." In 1916, just prior to America's entry into World War I, Pres. Woodrow Wilson issued an executive order calling for the song to be played at military and naval occasions. In 1917 the army and navy officially named "The Star-Spangled Banner" as "the National An-them of the United States" for all military ceremonies.

There is anecdotal evidence that "The Star-Spangled Banner" was played at various sporting events, primarily baseball games, in the late nineteenth and early twentieth centuries. The first documented perfor-mance of the song being performed at a sporting event came during World War I at Comiskey Park in Chicago. The date was September 5, 1918; the occasion, the first game of the World Series between the Chicago Cubs and the Boston Red Sox. The Cubs were using Comiskey Park, the home of the White Sox, because their home, Wrigley Field (then called Weeghman Park), was deemed too small.

The historic event took place during the seventh-inning stretch. As the Cubs band played "The Star-Spangled Banner," the players and the nineteen-thousand-plus spectators stood, took off their hats, and sang along—much as they do today at professional and collegiate sporting con-tests. At Boston's Fenway Park on September 9 in the fourth game of the Series, the National Anthem was played before the first pitch. The Red Sox, led by pitching star Babe Ruth, prevailed in that post-season contest—and did not win another World Series until 2004.

"The Star-Spangled Banner" was played before the opening-day game and each World Series game the following season, 1919, but not at regular season games. That didn't take place until 1942, during World War II. Since then the National Anthem has been played before virtually every professional—and many collegiate and high school—baseball, football, basketball, hockey, and soccer contests in this country.

Members of Congress started introducing legislation to proclaim "The Star-Spangled Banner" the National Anthem of the United States around 1910. More than forty bills and resolutions were considered in Congress over the next two decades. On January 30, 1913, for example, Rep. Jefferson Levy, a New York Democrat, and the owner of Thomas Jefferson's Monticello, introduced such a joint resolution in the House. That measure, as was the case with dozens of other pieces of similar legislation, went nowhere.

The legislation did not succeed for several reasons. First, some believed that it was inappropriate for the nation to adopt as its National Anthem a song derived from an English drinking tune—especially after January 19, 1920, when Prohibition went into effect. Others objected to "The Star-Spangled Banner" because the music was not written by an American. Another objection had to do with the difficulty of singing the tune, which has a very wide range of notes. There also were arguments that Key's words were directed at a military enemy, Great Britain, that had become a close American ally. And some believed that the song was only appropriate as a martial air and not in times of peace.

" 'The Star-Spangled Banner' suggests that patriotism is associated with killing and being killed, with great noise and clamor, with intense hatreds and fury and violence," Clyde R. Miller, an administrator at Columbia University's Teachers College, said in 1930. "Patriotism may on very rare occasions involve all of these, but not everyday life."

There also was sentiment to designate other patriotic songs as the National Anthem. A popular favorite was "America the Beautiful," which Katharine Lee Bates, an instructor at Wellesley College in Massachusetts, wrote after climbing Pikes Peak, Colorado, in 1893. The words to that song were first published as a poem in 1895. The lyrics were revised twice, in 1904 and in 1913. Until 1910 the poem was sung to many different tunes, including "Auld Lang Syne." In 1910 Bates's words were put together with the tune we know today, "Materna," which was composed by Samuel A. Ward in 1882. The other song most frequently suggested for the National Anthem was the traditional folk tune "Yankee Doodle," which was written in the late 1760s.

A long lobbying effort by patriotic and veterans groups led by the American Legion and the Veterans of Foreign Wars won the day on behalf of Key's song. The VWF had been on record as early as 1917 favoring the "The Star-Spangled Banner" as the National Anthem. In December 1926 the group launched a lobbying campaign in support of a "Star-Spangled Banner" National Anthem bill pending in the House of Representatives. "There is a powerful and well-financed propaganda emanating from pacifist sources to replace Francis Scott Key's inspiring words with something more flowery and meaningless," said Herman R. La Tourette, patriotic instructor for the VWF's Department of New York, following a meeting in which the group asked the public to write to members of Congress urging them to support the bill.

That bill died in Congress, but the VFW continuing lobbying for subsequent similar legislation during the next four years. Representatives of more than sixty veterans and patriotic groups held a conference in Washington on January 30, 1930, to make a big push for another "Star-Spangled Banner" bill that had been introduced by Rep. J. Charles Linthicum, a Maryland Democrat who represented the congressional district in Baltimore that included Fort McHenry.

The following day the Veterans of Foreign Wars presented the House Judiciary Committee with a petition—which VWF commander in chief Walter I. Joyce called "fifty miles of names"—containing some five million signatures urging the adoption of "The Star-Spangled Banner" as the National Anthem. Sopranos Elsie Jorss-Reilley of Washington and Grace Evelyn Boudlin of Baltimore, backed by the U.S. Navy Band, performed the song for the committee that day "to refute," the *New York Times* said, "the argument that it is pitched too high for popular singing." The hearing room was packed with members of women's patriotic organizations decked out in what the *Times,* in a front-page article, described as "broad bands of red, white and blue."

The House approved the bill on April 21, 1930. The Senate voted for it unanimously on March 3, 1931, and on that same day Pres. Herbert Hoover signed into law a measure officially designating "The Star-Spangled Banner" as the National Anthem of the United States.

★   ★   ★

No flag sewn by Betsy Ross is known to exist today. But the flag that inspired the National Anthem, the flag known as the Star-Spangled Banner, today resides in the Smithsonian Institution's National Museum of American History in Washington. There is, moreover, indisputable evidence showing that Mary Young Pickersgill of Baltimore was the creator of that enormous and enormously influential, thirty-by forty-two-foot, fifteen-star, fifteen-stripe flag.

"She sewed the Star-Spangled Banner flag," said Sally Johnston, executive director of The Star-Spangled Banner Flag House in Baltimore. "We have the original receipt for the flag in our collection."

Mary Young Pickersgill (1776–1857), a Baltimore seamstress and flag maker, made the Star-Spangled Banner, the flag that flew over Ft. McHenry and inspired Francis Scott Key to write the National Anthem. *The Flag House and Star-Spangled Banner Museum*

That receipt, dated October 27, 1813, was given to Mary Pickersgill and her niece Eliza Young by the U.S. Army for making "1 American Ensign, 30 by 42 feet, first quality Bunting" and for another flag "17 by 25 feet." The army paid $405.90 for the larger flag, the Star-Spangled Banner, and $168.54 for the smaller one, which also flew at Fort McHenry.

Mary Pickersgill's home at 844 East Pratt Street in Baltimore, where she sewed the Star-Spangled Banner, opened in 1927 as the Star-Spangled Banner Flag House Museum. It became a National Historic Landmark in 1969. *The Flag House and Star-Spangled Banner Museum*

Mary Pickersgill was born on February 12, 1776, in Philadelphia. Following the death of her father two years later, Mary's mother, Rebecca Flower Young, supported the family by making flags in Philadelphia at her shop on Walnut Street and, later, in Baltimore. She made several dozen ensigns, garrison flags, and Continental Colors for the Continental Army and for the Pennsylvania navy. "All kinds of colours, for the Army and Navy, made and sold on the most reasonable Terms, By Rebecca Young," read her advertisement in the *Pennsylvania Packet* in 1781.

Shortly after Mary Young, who was nineteen years old, married John Pickersgill, a merchant, on October 2, 1795, the couple moved back to Philadelphia and had four children, only one of whom survived infancy. Two years after John Pickersgill died in 1805, his widow moved to what today is known is known as "The Star-Spangled Banner Flag House" at the corner of Albemarle and Pratt Streets in downtown Baltimore. It was in that house near the Baltimore waterfront that Mary Pickersgill lived with her daughter Caroline and her seventy-four-year-old widowed mother.

Mary Pickersgill supported her family by working as a seamstress and flag maker. She designed, sewed, and sold what a city directory of the time listed as "Ships Colours, Signals, etc." That included ensigns and other flags that she sold to the army, the navy, and to privately owned merchant ships.

Pickersgill was commissioned during the summer of 1813 by the army's Commissary Office in Baltimore to produce two large banners, a standard-sized garrison flag and a storm flag, for Fort McHenry. The fort's commanding officer, Maj. George Armistead, ordered the large flags primarily for identification purposes. He wanted anyone approaching the fort from the water to be able to see that the fort was flying the colors of the United States of America. Making the Star-Spangled Banner and the smaller flag was a cooperative effort. Pickersgill had help from her thirteen-year old daughter, Caroline, and from two nieces, Eliza and Margaret Young. She also probably received the assistance of her mother, Rebecca Flower Young.

It took several weeks to do the measuring, cutting, and sewing of the flags' components. The Star-Spangled Banner's fifteen stars were each about two feet long and the fifteen stripes measured just under two feet in width. The stars were made of cotton; the stripes and the blue canton of English woolen bunting. When the flags were ready to be put together, Pickersgill and company asked and received permission to use the malt house floor of nearby Claggett's Brewery to do the final assembling. They did the work in the evenings after the brewery ceased operations for the day.

"I remember seeing my mother down on the floor, placing the stars," Caroline Pickersgill Purdy wrote in an 1876 letter. "After the completion of the flag, she superintended the topping of it, having it fastened in the most secure manner to prevent its being torn away by [cannon] balls." The flag, she said, contained "four hundred yards of bunting, and my mother worked many nights until twelve o'clock to complete it in the given time."

The flags were delivered on August 19, 1813, to Fort McHenry. The larger flag, the Star-Spangled Banner, weighed about fifty pounds, and it took eleven men to raise it onto a ninety-foot flagpole at the fort. After the 1814 battle, George Armistead was promoted to lieutenant colonel and took possession of the Star-Spangled Banner. The fate of the smaller storm flag, which also flew over Fort McHenry during the Battle of Baltimore, is not known. After George Armistead died on April 25, 1818, his widow, Louisa Hughes Armistead, inherited the Star-Spangled Banner.

During the four decades Louisa Armistead possessed the flag she allowed it to be shown in public only on a few occasions. That included the emotional October 1824 visit to Baltimore by the Marquis de Lafayette, where the flag was displayed at Fort McHenry, and the 1844 Whig Party national convention in that city. Louisa Armistead also made an addition and a deletion to the flag. She cut out one of the stars and gave it to an acquaintance whom her daughter later described as "some official person," and whose identity is not known. And she sewed what appears to be a red chevron—an upside-down V—onto the third white stripe from the bottom of the flag. A small letter "B" is embroidered on one side of the chevron. The other side has an "M" inscribed on it in ink. Historians believe that the chevron was intended to be the capital letter "A" for Armistead. They are not certain what the "B" or "M" were meant to signify, although there has been speculation that they could stand for "Baltimore, Maryland."

After Louisa Armistead's death on October 3, 1861, the Star-Spangled Banner went to her youngest child, Georgiana Armistead Appleton, who was born at Fort McHenry on November 25, 1817. Over the years Louisa and Georgiana Appleton, who lived with her family in Baltimore, allowed veterans of the Battle of Baltimore and others to snip off small pieces of the flag as mementos. This was not an uncommon practice at the time. "Snipping," said Marilyn Zoidis, the Smithsonian Institution's curator of The Star-Spangled Banner Project, "appealed to the mentality of the nineteenth century." Several of the fragments have been acquired by the Smithsonian and are on display today at the National Museum of American History's Star-Spangled Banner exhibit.

By the mid-1870s, as the flag became nationally known and its value increased greatly, the family placed the Star-Spangled Banner in a vault in the New England Historical and Genealogical Society in Boston for safekeeping. Georgiana Appleton gave permission to have some pieces of the flag cut off for the society. It was moved in January 1876 to another vault in the Historical Society of Pennsylvania in Philadelphia with the idea that it would be exhibited at the Philadelphia Centennial Exhibition. But the Exhibition's organizers decided not to display it because of the flag's fragile condition. Later, on June 14, 1877, Georgiana Appleton allowed the Star-Spangled Banner to be exhibited publicly on the centennial celebration of Flag Day at Boston's Old South Meeting House.

Following Georgiana Appleton's death on July 15, 1878, the flag was bequeathed to her son, Eben Appleton, who also cut pieces from it as special favors. He soon thereafter placed the flag in a safe deposit box in New York City. Despite many requests to do so, it was leant out only once, on October 13, 1880, for the dedication of a monument to Eben Appleton's grandfather, George Armistead, in Baltimore as the city celebrated its sesquicentennial. With great pomp and ceremony the Old Defenders, the veterans of the Battle of Baltimore, paraded the flag through the streets of Baltimore.

The Smithsonian estimates that about eight feet of material was missing from the Star-Spangled Banner when Eben Appleton loaned the flag to the nation's museum in 1907. Appleton shipped the flag from New York to Washington, where it was hung outside on the wall of the old Smithsonian building known as the "Castle" for the benefit of newspaper photographers. The flag was then moved indoors and placed in a special exhibit case in the Arts and Industries Building. Five years later, in 1912, Appleton made the loan permanent, stipulating that the Star-Spangled Banner stay in the Smithsonian in perpetuity and giving the museum permission to do whatever was necessary for its preservation.

The flag was not in good condition when the Smithsonian took possession of it. Much of the flag was shredded and split and attached to a canvas backing. That backing had been sewn onto the flag in June of 1873 at the behest of Rear Adm. George Preble, the author of the first well-researched history of the American flag. Preble had convinced Georgiana Appleton to ship the flag to his office in the Boston Navy Yard. There he arranged for the new backing, hung the flag from four windows on the side of a building, and had it photographed for the first time for his book.

In an effort to stabilize the flag, the Smithsonian in 1914 hired a noted flag restorer and embroidery teacher, Amelia Bold Fowler of Boston. She oversaw the replacement of the canvas backing with a new one made of heavy, unbleached Irish linen, which was considerably lighter than the canvas. She was paid $1,243 for the work, including materials. It took ten seamstresses eight weeks, from May to July, to complete the job. In the end, some 1.7 million stitches were used to sew on the new backing.

After the seamstresses sewed the new backing in place, the museum created another specially designed and constructed case for the flag and displayed it near the main entrance of the Smithsonian's Arts and Industries Building. In 1931, it was moved to yet another case, which turned out to be too small for the entire flag, so about half of the banner had to be folded into the bottom of the case. All that was on view to visitors was the canton and the eight stripes next to it. Because of the way the backing was attached, the flag was displayed with the canton of blue stars to the right of the red and white stripes.

For two years during World War II museum officials moved the Star-Spangled Banner as a precautionary measure about 115 miles south to a warehouse in the Shenandoah National Park in the Blue Ridge Mountains near Luray, Virginia. The flag returned to the Arts and Industries Building in November 1944. It was taken out of the case in September 1961 in preparation for its move to a new museum, the National Museum of History and Technology on the other side of the National Mall. Three years later, in 1964, the flag was displayed prominently in the three-story main entrance hall, called Flag Hall, of that newly opened building, which is now known as the National Museum of American History. It hung there for thirty-four years, greeting tens of millions of visitors.

In 1982 Smithsonian conservators cleaned the flag thoroughly. When the banner was rehung, museum officials decided to expose the flag to limited amounts of light and dust. A protective shield made of gray linen painted with nineteenth-century American historical scenes was placed in front of the flag. It dropped down for a minute every half hour to allow for public viewing.

Despite preservation and conservation work done at the Smithsonian over the years, the Star-Spangled Banner in the early 1990s suffered from the effects of nine decades of public display and exposure to light and dust. In December 1998 the flag was taken down to undergo an extensive $18 million conservation treatment. It took eight conservators working with a team of riggers to remove the 1,020-square-foot flag from its display. The riggers were responsible for lowering the flag; the conservators for insuring the safety of the flag and for tilting it into a horizontal position and rolling it onto a 35-foot-long tube.

"We're not trying to restore the flag," Marilyn Zoidis said. "We're conserving it as a historical artifact."

The conservation work is being carried out in public in the museum's Star-Spangled Banner exhibit area in a customized two-thousand-square-foot laboratory behind a fifty-foot-long, floor-to-ceiling glass wall. After the laboratory opened in May 1999, a team of conservators began the enormous job of cleaning and stabilizing the flag. The first order of business was taking off the old linen backing one stitch at a time. Conservators did that painstaking job lying on their stomachs on a specially constructed gantry that hovered four inches above the flag. The job of removing the stitches took nearly a year to complete. When it was done, it marked the first time the covered side of the flag had been visible since 1914.

The conservators today are studying the best manner in which to display the flag permanently once the preservation effort is completed. It has not yet been determined exactly how one of the oldest surviving fifteen-star, fifteen-stripe flags will be displayed, but one thing is certain: the Star-Spangled Banner will not be displayed hanging vertically.

The journey of the Star-Spangled Banner from its beginnings in Mary Pickersgill's house in downtown Baltimore in 1813 to its hallowed place in the Smithsonian Institution today paralleled the changing ways that Americans viewed their flag. When it flew over Fort McHenry, the flag still was closely associated with the American military. Today the flag is viewed by many as the nation's ultimate symbol.

As Pres. Bill Clinton put it in 1998: The Star-Spangled Banner "and all its successors have come to embody our country, what we think of as America. It may not be quite the same for every one of us who looks at it, but in the end we all pretty much come out where the framers did. We know that we have a country founded on the then revolutionary idea that all of us are created equal, and equally entitled to life, liberty, and the pursuit of happiness."

CHAPTER SIX

Additions and a Subtraction

*   *   *

Be it enacted . . . that the flag of the United States be thirteen horizontal stripes, alternate red and white: that the union be twenty stars,
white in a blue field. And be it further enacted, that on the admission
of every new state into the Union, one star be added to the union of
the flag, and that such addition shall take effect on the fourth of July
then next succeeding such admission.

—The third Flag Act, April 4, 1818

WHEN THE FIFTEEN-star, fifteen-striped Star-Spangled Banner flew over Fort McHenry during the Battle of Baltimore, the number of
states had increased to eighteen. Tennessee had joined the Union in June 1,
1796; Ohio on March 1, 1803; and Louisiana on April 30, 1812. Still, no
one in Congress evinced interest in changing the look of the flag to reflect
the new number of states until December 9, 1816. On that day New York
representative Peter Wendover submitted a resolution in the House of
Representatives calling for a committee to be appointed "to inquire into the
expediency of altering the flag of the United States."

Peter Hercules Wendover was born in New York City August 1, 1768.
He spent most of his adult life in politics, holding several local and state offices, including serving as a member of the New York State Assembly in
1804. Wendover was elected as a Republican to the U.S. Congress from
New York City in 1814 and served three terms in the House. After leaving
Congress, Wendover served as sheriff of New York County from 1822 to
1825. He died in New York City on September 24, 1834.

On December 12, 1816, two days after Indiana became the nineteenth
state in the Union, the House took Wendover's advice and set up a panel
to determine the future makeup of the Stars and Stripes. The committee

consisted of Wendover, Burwell Bassett of Virginia, Henry Middleton of South Carolina, Artemas Ward Jr. of Massachusetts, and James Brown Mason of Rhode Island.

In his motion asking for the committee to be appointed, Wendover made it clear that he did not intend to make any "essential alteration" to the flag, something he hoped "no man in the House would consent to." He simply wanted, Wendover said, to make "an unessential variation" reflecting the fact that since the Second Flag Resolution of 1794 four new states had entered the Union.

Republican representative John W. Taylor of New York agreed that a change was needed, but for a different reason: for naval identification purposes. Taylor "had been informed," he said, "by naval gentlemen that our flag could be seen and recognized on the ocean at a greater distance than that of any other nation." If the number of stars and stripes were to be increased, Taylor said, "the flag would become less distinct to distant observation," something he "was desirous to prevent." Taylor therefore recommended permanently "restoring the flag to its original character" of thirteen stars and thirteen stripes.

Wendover's committee made its report to the House on January 2, 1817. The committee said that it had not considered changing the "general form" of the flag nor the "distribution of its parts." To do so, the report said, "would be unacceptable to" Congress "and to the people, as it would be incongenial with the views of the committee" because the stars and stripes "were truly emblematical of our origin and existence as an independent nation."

That said, the committee made its case for "a change in the arrangement of the flag" to reflect changes in the number of states in the Union. Looking ahead to the addition of future states, the committee said it would be "highly inexpedient to increase the number of stripes" every time a new state joined the Union. For one thing, a new, many-striped flag would be unwieldy and would "decrease [the stripes's] magnitude, and render them proportionally less distinct to distant observation." Since the flag, the committee said, was so widely used "by vessels of almost every description," it was also important not to make "great or expensive alterations."

A way to accomplish this would be to reduce the number of stripes to the original thirteen, the committee said, and to increase the number of stars "to correspond with the number of States now in the Union." For the future, the solution would be to "add one star to the flag whenever a new State shall be fully admitted."

The matter rested there for nearly a year, until December 16, 1817—six days after Mississippi had become the twentieth state. On that day Wendover asked the House to appoint a second flag alteration committee because the matter had been pushed aside due to "the pressure of business deemed more important." Again Wendover said that the flag "would be essentially injured" if new stars and stripes were added every time a new state joined the Union. He included a new argument, as well, complaining about "flags in general use" that greatly varied from each other. As examples Wendover pointed to the flags flying on Capitol Hill and in the Washington Navy Yard, "one of which contained nine stripes, the other eighteen, and neither of them in [conformance] to the law."

The House agreed to his motion and appointed a second flag committee that day. It was made up of Wendover, Mason, Thomas Newton Jr. of Virginia, John Ross of Pennsylvania, and George Poindexter of Mississippi. That committee reported a bill based on its predecessor's recommendations — calling for the flag to contain thirteen stripes and twenty stars and adding a star for each new state — to the House on January 6, 1818.

The American flag, the committee's report said, "was truly emblematical of our origin and existence as a nation" and therefore "having met the approbation and received the support of the citizens of the union . . . ought to undergo no change that would decrease its conspicuity, or tend to deprive it of its representative character." The report reiterated Wendover's complaint of December 16, decrying the "great want of uniformity" in flags, "particularly when used on small private vessels."

The matter came up for debate on the House floor on March 24. Wendover began with a long, flowery speech that again made his case for the slight alterations. "The importance attached to the national flag, both in its literal and figurative use, is so universal and of such ancient origin, that we seldom inquire into the meaning of their various figures as adopted by other nations and are in some danger of forgetting the symbolical application of those composing that of our own," Wendover said. "Suitable symbols were devised by those who laid the foundation of the Republic, and I hope their children will ever feel themselves in honor precluded from changing these, except so far as necessity may dictate, and with a direct view of expressing by them their original design."

The flag was adopted in 1777, he said, "as appropriate to and emblematical of" the first thirteen states, "contending for the rights of man and the rich boon of an independent government." The same principles, he said, were "retained and applied" in the second Flag Resolution. But continuing to add stars and stripes for each new state, he argued, would be "improper and inconvenient."

The proposed alteration with thirteen stripes and a star for each state,

Wendover said, "will direct the view to two striking facts in our national history," the number of original states and the current number of states. The arrangement also would honor those who fought in the Revolution, Wendover said. "In their memory, and to their honor, let us restore substantially the flag under which they conquered, and at the same time engraft into its figure the after-fruits of their toil."

Veterans of the Revolutionary War, he said, "have been preserved to see [the flag] acquire a renown which I trust will never fade; have lived to witness in their sons that heroic spirit, which assures them that their privations and their arduous struggle in defense of liberty have not been in vain." No disgrace, he said, "has attached to your 'Star Spangled Banner.' It has been the signal of victor on the land, of successful valor on the lakes, and waved triumphantly on the ocean."

He concluded: "The subject is plain and well understood. And though not of a character to be classed with those of the highest national importance, it still [is] proper to be acted on and worthy of the attention of the Representatives of a people whose flag will never be insulted for want of protectors, and which, I hope and believe, will never be struck to an inferior or equal force."

The bills, as reported, did not contain language addressing the arrangement of the stars. Wendover suggested adopting the committee recommendation that the stars be arranged in one of two ways: either "in the form of one great luminary," or, using the words of the 1777 Flag Resolution, in an unspecified arrangement that represented "a new constellation." He also noted that neither of the first two Flag Resolutions specified the direction of the stripes. The committee, therefore, he said, "deemed it advisable to direct that the stripes be horizontal." Words to that effect were contained in the resolution.

Gen. Samuel Smith, the commander of American forces at the Battle of Baltimore who was a congressman from Maryland, made a motion to table the bill before it could come to a vote. The House voted that motion down unanimously. At that point a flag—presumably one with twenty stars and thirteen stripes—was hoisted on the House floor. Poindexter then introduced an amendment calling for the number of stars to be reduced to seven to honor the seven states that had entered the Union after independence and to reduce the stripes to thirteen to honor the original states. Walter Folger Jr. of Massachusetts asked for an amendment to have the number of stars permanently set at thirteen. The House rejected those two proposed amendments with little debate.

The House went on to pass the nation's Third Flag Resolution that day with only a handful of negative votes. The Senate unanimously concurred a week later, on March 31. Pres. James Monroe signed the bill into law on April 4. A new twenty-star, thirteen-striped flag—with the stars shaped into one large star—arrived by mail on Capitol Hill on April 13. Even though the new law stipulated that it would not be official until July 4, that flag was promptly hoisted on the flagstaff of the House of Representatives.

"I am pleased with its form and proportions," Wendover wrote that day, "and have no doubt it will satisfy the public mind."

Peter Hercules Wendover is given credit for crafting the artful compromise that retained the stars and stripes of the 1777 Flag Resolution, and at the same time honored the thirteen original states with the stripes and each of the existing and new states with a star. He did not act alone, however. Shortly after his first flag committee submitted its report to the House in

U.S. Navy Captain Samuel Chester Reid, working with Congressman Peter Wendover of New York, drew up the guidelines for the third, and last, Flag Resolution that Congress passed in 1818. That measure set the number of stripes at thirteen and called for adding a new star for each new state. Reid is shown in an 1815 portrait by the artist John Wesley Jarvis. *U.S. Naval Academy Museum*

January 1817, Wendover sought out the advice of navy captain Samuel Chester Reid, a hero of the War of 1812 who was living in Washington. Samuel Reid deserves as much credit as Wendover does for coming up with the guidelines that have shaped the American flag from 1818 to today.

Reid was born August 24, 1783, in Norwich, Connecticut. He joined the U.S. Navy at age seventeen and was the commanding officer of the privateer *General Armstrong* during the War of 1812. On September 25, 1814, while docked in the neutral Portuguese port of Fayal in the Azores, three British warships attacked Reid's privateer. Although vastly outnumbered and outgunned, Reid and his men put up a strong fight in a vicious battle that included hand-to-hand fighting aboard the *General Armstrong*.

The British forced the Americans to abandon their ship, and Reid and his crew took refuge in an old castle on shore where they awaited a British attack. The British commander, though, who had suffered nearly two hundred casualties in the fight, chose not to engage the Americans. One of his ships was completely out of commission and the other two transported more than one hundred wounded sailors and marines to British bases.

Reid's actions are credited with delaying the British ships, which were en route to the Gulf of Mexico, for more than a month. That gave Gen. Andrew Jackson crucial time to organize the defense of New Orleans and helped him defeat the British in the bloody Battle of New Orleans, which began in December of 1814. Reid was honored for his wartime heroics during a triumphal journey from Savannah, Georgia, to New York in the spring of 1815. When he reached New York on April 7 the state legislature presented him a ceremonial sword.

Two years later, in January of 1817, Reid worked hand in hand with Wendover to shape the future of the American flag. According to his own account of the matter, Reid was "a principal actor" in the decision to scale back the number of stripes to thirteen and to add a new star for each new state. Wendover, Reid said in a February 17, 1850, letter to his son, "call'd on me" and "was in a dilema (*sic*) as to how the change should be made and requested that I would help him out of it & give him my views."

Reid then went to work and sketched not one, but three, flags. The first, which he called "the People's Flag," was the concept that Wendover and his committee settled on, including Reid's recommendation (which did not appear in the final resolution) that the stars should be "formed into one great star as forming one great Nation." That flag, Reid said, would be used by all merchant ships and by "the Nation in general." He also proposed a "Government Flag" to be used by navy warships and "all other government vessels,

Forts, castles, & all gov't. Stations." That flag would have thirteen stripes with an eagle, rather than stars, in the canton.

Reid called his third flag the "Standard of the union" or "the great National Standard." It would be used, he said, on "gala days, to wave over the National Halls, to be hoisted at the installation of our Presidents, goveanors (*sic*), &c." That flag would be divided into four equal parts, containing the "great luminary" star made up of other stars in the upper left, the Great Seal below it, the stripes to its right, and the Goddess of Liberty in the upper right.

While Samuel Reid no doubt was a principal actor in the new design of the flag that was adopted in 1818, Wendover's committee never seriously considered his proposed eagle-bedecked Government Flag nor his busy National Standard.

★   ★   ★

In 1818 the flag was used primarily for government and military purposes. So it is not surprising that the first official order dealing with the arrangement of stars on the new flag following passage of the Flag Resolution came from the Navy Commissioners' Office. On May 18 the office issued a directive setting the size of American flags for U.S. Navy ships and naval installations—fourteen by twenty-four feet. It also stipulated that that the union (the canton) be one third the length of the flag, with six stripes next to the union and seven longer stripes below. That order also provided a sketch of the arrangement of the stars: four rows of five in a staggered pattern.

The commissioners slightly amended the pattern four months later, on September 18, at the behest of Pres. James Monroe. The new lineup of stars contained the same four rows of five, but the rows were aligned symmetrically. The circular also ordered naval commanders to fire a twenty-gun salute when the flag was first hoisted each day.

The U.S. Army didn't get around to adopting the Stars and Stripes as its official garrison flag until 1834. The directive came in the form of a general regulation that applied only to artillery troops. Infantry regiments received that order seven years later in 1841. Unlike the navy, the army did not describe the arrangement of the stars in the canton. The regulation said that the canton, or union, should contain one star for each state in the Union and that the canton should be in the upper left quarter, extending one-third the length of the flag. The regulation did not prescribe any dimensions for the flag nor did it set out the size or shape of the stars.

⋆   ⋆   ⋆

Despite the 1818 law—and because it was not specific about several key points, including the arrangement of the stars—American flags, which flag makers made by hand one at a time, varied widely in size, shape, and design in the decades following the measure's passage. Making the situation more complicated was the fact that the number of states grew from twenty in 1818 to thirty-four when the Civil War started in 1861. Each new state required one more star in the flag, and with no guidelines, flags contained many different arrangements of stars. The stars themselves often differed in size and style. Some flags had stars shaped into a larger star, or a diamond or a circle or into fanciful images such as an anchor. Emblems such as eagles often were sewed into the canton.

"Before the Civil War especially," Whitney Smith said, "flags were made to taste by each individuals since hand-stitching was then the common mode of manufacture."

Thirteen-star flags remained popular throughout the nineteenth century. Small boats in the U.S. Navy, for example, used the thirteen-star flag as their ensign from 1797 until at least 1916. Thirteen-star flags also were commonly displayed during holidays and other special commemorative events, and in fact continue to be used today on those occasions. That was true in 1826 when the nation celebrated its Jubilee, and in 1832 when the nation marked George Washington's hundredth birthday and at other patriotic occasions such as annual Fourth of July celebrations.

⋆   ⋆   ⋆

U.S. Navy lieutenant Charles Wilkes, flying under a twenty-six-star flag, led the first American expedition that explored Antarctica. That flag became official on July 4, 1837, following Michigan's entry into the Union. Wilkes commanded four naval vessels on an exploring and surveying expedition authorized by Congress that began in 1838. The pioneering Wilkes Expedition reached Antarctica in February 1839. During the next year, his ships sailed along fifteen hundred miles of Antarctica's ice pack, proving for the first time that Antarctica was a continental land mass.

The twenty-six-star flag that the Wilkes Expedition ultimately flew around the world was replaced by the twenty-seven-star flag on July 4, 1845. That followed Florida's entry into the Union on March 3 of that year.

One year later, on July 4, 1846, came the twenty-eight-star flag, recognizing Texas's entry into the Union on December 29, 1845.

Ten years earlier Texas had broken away from Mexico and formed an independent nation, the Republic of Texas. It had two official national flags: the first, a blue banner with a yellow star, was superseded on January 25, 1839, by the three-part, red, white, and blue "Lone Star" flag that remains the state flag today.

In January of 1846 the explorer and mapmaker John C. Frémont, on his third trip to the west for the U.S. Army's Topographical Engineers, carried with him a one-of-a-kind American flag. His wife, Jessie Benton Frémont, the daughter of Missouri senator Thomas Hart Benton, designed and made the flag, which featured the standard thirteen red and white stripes. She painted an eagle clutching a peace pipe and nine arrows in its claws in the white canton. Twenty-six five-pointed stars surrounded the eagle — thirteen above it and thirteen below. Frémont flew that flag from a fortified position atop Galivan Mountain in defiance of the Mexican military commander, who ordered him to leave the Salinas Valley in California.

Five months later Frémont received his commission as a U.S. Army major and joined forces with American settlers fighting for independence from Mexico. The conflict is sometimes known as the "Bear Flag Revolt" in honor of the banner flown by the rebels in their June–July 1846 war of independence in the Sacramento Valley. That white flag contained a grizzly bear standing on all fours facing a red star and featured the words "California Republic." After more American troops entered the fray, the California Republic dissolved and the Stars and Stripes replaced the bear flag.

Texas's entry into the Union in December 1845 precipitated the Mexican War, which began in April 1846 and ended less than two years later with the signing of the Treaty of Guadeloupe Hidalgo on February 2, 1848. In that war the United States defeated Mexico and took control of more than five hundred thousand square miles of territory that contained nearly all of what would become the states of New Mexico, Utah, Nevada, Arizona, and California, as well as most of western Colorado.

That conflict is significant in the history of the American flag because it was the first war in which American troops carried the Stars and Stripes into battle. It is not clear if the flag was flown in the skirmish that opened hostilities on April 25, 1846, in an area between the Rio Grande and Nueces Rivers that both nations claimed. That fight took place two days after Mexican president Mariano Paredes announced that a state of "defensive war" existed between the two countries. In the war's first major battle, a four-hour fight on May 8 in Palo Alto near Brownsville, U.S. Army general Zachary Taylor, the future president, flew the twenty-eight-star flag as his men defeated the Mexican army of the North.

The Mexican War also marked a milestone in the public perception of the American flag. In countless newspaper articles and personal accounts in books describing the war, the flag was depicted as the symbol of the American cause: a symbol of valor, patriotism, and victory. U.S. Army captain W. S. Henry, for example, in his account of the war published in 1848, referred to the Stars and Stripes as the "most beautiful of all flags, dyed in the blood of our fore-fathers, and redyed in that of their sons upon the fierce battle-field . . . an emblem of American possession to the Sierra Madre!"

The Mexican War, although costly in terms of lives lost (some ten thousand) and expenditures (some one hundred million dollars), was a popular one. As a result of the victory, the Stars and Stripes stretched from the Atlantic to the Pacific. It flew briefly in conquest in Mexico as well. On September 14, 1847, Gen. Winfield Scott and his men rode into Mexico City's main plaza flying the flag and stormed the Castillo de Chapultepec, the fabled residence of the nation's rulers, also known as the Halls of Montezuma.

Another indication of the jump in the flag's popularity occurred in 1847. Annin & Co., today the nation's oldest and largest flag manufacturer, began making American flags that year in a sail loft in New York City. The company had been producing signal flags for sailing ships since the 1820s. It incorporated in 1847. Two years later, when Zachary Taylor was sworn in as president, a flag made by Annin waved in Washington. An Annin & Co. flag has flown at every presidential inauguration since then.

The flag, while still primarily used by the government and the military, became in the pre–Civil War period more popular among the public in decorative arts and in early forms of advertising and promotion, as well as in political campaigns. The flag's image, primarily but not exclusively depicted as being flown on ships, also found its way onto consumer items such as hatboxes, wallpaper, and toys. In the 1830s the flag was used, for example, in the design of a game of Parcheesi, the backgammonlike board game, and on the covers of some needle books designed to teach young girls how to sew. In the 1840s hotels around the nation for the first time began flying American flags emblazoned with the hotel's name from their roofs and doorways.

The flag's image became part of a national political campaign for the first time in the presidential election of 1840, which pitted the Whig Party nominee William Henry Harrison, who was born in Virginia, and his running mate John Tyler against incumbent president Martin Van Buren, a New York Democrat. Van Buren, who was born in 1782, has the distinction of being the first American president born as an American citizen and under the Stars and Stripes.

Harrison had gained fame for his military exploits, especially his role in putting down a Shawnee Indian uprising at the Battle of Tippecanoe on November 7, 1811, in Indiana, and his leadership in the victorious War of 1812 Battle of the Thames in Ontario. Harrison's campaign dealt with few national issues and instead concentrated on building the candidate's image as a war hero and a man of the people. It featured political songs and slogans, including the famous "Tippecanoe and Tyler, too." And it featured the widespread distribution of miniature log cabins and jugs of hard cider.

The flag became part of a national political campaign for the first time in 1840 when William Henry Harrision and John Tyler used it on banners and broadsides, along with two other symbols of "Tippicanoe and Tyler Too," the log cabin and the jug of hard cider. *The Library of Congress, Prints and Photographs Division*

The log cabin logo was pasted on campaign banners, bandannas, ribbons, and broadsides. A Star-Spangled Banner flew prominently alongside some of the cabins—at a time when it was almost unheard of for private individuals to fly the flag. The campaign also employed Stars and Stripes banners with Harrison's name inscribed on them. Most had thirteen-star cantons. Some had his portrait in the center of the flag.

One campaign ribbon contained an image of Harrison, an eagle, and a display of battle flags. The ribbon's inscription read: " 'Tis the Star-Spangled Banner! / O'Long May it Wave / O'er the Land of the Free and the Home of the Brave / Conquer We must—Our cause is just."

Harrison defeated Van Buren to become the nation's ninth president. His use of the flag in the campaign proved to be an important factor in that

victory. More significantly, the campaign's use of the flag's image was a precursor of things to come in future presidential and other political campaigns.

The next presidential election, in 1844, saw the first widespread use of
political parade banners. Both candidates—the winning Democrat, James
K. Polk of Tennessee, and his Whig opponent, Henry Clay of Virginia—
used the colorful banners. Polk and Clay also used flag banners in their political advertisements. Most commonly, the names of the candidates and
their running mates—George M. Dallas, the Democrat, and the Whig
Theodore Frelinghuysen—were emblazoned on the campaign flags. Sometimes the names were stitched in the canton with the stars removed; other
times they were written across the stripes.

"Each new election [after 1844] brought some interesting variations,"
the historian Scot Guenter observed, "but the practice of advertising candidates on the American flag went unquestioned when it was introduced and
it quickly became accepted as common procedure."

★　　★　　★

Another party that made an impact on the national political scene during
the 1840s and 1850s, the Know-Nothings, used the American flag as one of
its primary symbols. The Know-Nothings, the first anti-immigrant nativist
movement in the United States, gained adherents following the large number of primarily Irish and German Catholics who came to this country beginning in the mid-1840s. The Know-Nothing movement began in New
York City in 1849 with the founding of the Order of the Star-Spangled
Banner and used that emblem liberally in its publications.

The group, which quickly gained adherents in the early 1850s, limited its
membership to Protestant adults who pledged their belief in God and their
willingness to abide by the order's rules. The order had its own members-
only passwords, signs, and phrases of recognition. Its avowed purpose was
"to place in all offices of honor, trust, or profit, in the gift of the people, or by
appointment, none but native-born Protestant citizens."

When asked by established political leaders about their organizations,
the members of the Order of the Star-Spangled Banner and the other
groups had orders to say they "knew nothing." That led the noted newspa-
perman Horace Greeley to christen the movement the "Know-Nothings" in
his *New York Tribune* in November 1853.

The flag-waving Know-Nothing parties went public under the banner of
the American Party in the early 1850s. At its peak in 1853, the American

The anti-immigrant Know-Nothing Party, which made an impact on the national political scene during the 1840s and 1850s, used the American flag as one of its primary symbols. This illustrated sheet music cover, produced in May 1844, uses the flag to glorify the
party's nativist cause. *The Library of Congress, Prints and Photographs Division*

Party had some one million members in thirty-one states. The party reached
its height of influence in 1854 when it elected more than two dozen candidates to the House of Representatives. Despite the movement's election success, however, none of its stringent anti-immigrant policies became law. In
1856, when party members deeply split over the issue of slavery, the American Party and Know-Nothing movement collapsed.

CHAPTER SEVEN

A House Divided
Against Itself

★　　★　　★

War! Young men your country calls, 'Tis duty to obey! All who are
ready to volunteer, to serve their country, now in its hour of danger, to
march in defence of the Government, and to protect our Glorious
Flag, the Star Spangled Banner.

— Recruiting Poster, 104th Pennsylvania Infantry Regiment,
August 1861

THE ISSUE OF SLAVERY and the broader issue of states' rights
brought the United States into the Civil War in 1861, a cataclysmic event in
the nation's young history—and an event that marked a sea change in the
evolution of the cultural importance of the American flag. As soon as Americans began killing Americans on American soil, Americans from every
strata of society in the North for the first time embraced the flag as a symbol of American patriotism. In short order the Stars and Stripes became a
beloved, cherished icon in the North, a widely held symbol of the Union
and the fight to keep it whole.

The bitterly contested, bloody Civil War dragged on for four long years
and cost the lives of at least six hundred thousand Americans—almost as
many as the number who died in all American wars combined. The magnitude of that national tragedy is reflected in the fact that never again would
Americans, in the North or in the South, look upon the flag in the same
manner.

The Civil War, Whitney Smith said, "became a fight for the flag, and it
was expressed in those terms. The flag was everywhere. Every school flew
a flag and prior to that there is only one known instance—in 1817—of a
school flying an American flag. Union soldiers even carried miniature flags

called Bible flags, small enough to fit in the Bible they would take with them to the battlefield. The start of the Civil War was the beginning of the sense we have today of the American flag as an everyday object and of something that belongs to everyone."

A hint of the flag's important role in the Civil War on both sides of the conflict may be found in the long, impassioned speech that Jefferson Davis made on the U.S. Senate floor on January 10, 1861. Davis, then a senator from Mississippi, would on February 18 be inaugurated as the first president of the Confederate States of America. A hero of the Mexican War, Davis had also served in the U.S. House of Representatives and was secretary of war under Pres. Franklin Pierce.

In his January 10 speech, which came the day after Mississippi seceded from the Union and the day that Florida seceded, Davis gave his assessment of the "state of the country." His main theme was a strong defense of states' rights, including his adamant belief that states had the right to withdraw from the Union. Davis spoke passionately about his wish to avoid armed conflict between the states. But he repeatedly warned that war would be inevitable if president-elect Abraham Lincoln and his Republican Party—whom he called "feeble hands" and "drivelers"—continued to act illegally and aggressively against the Southern states.

Davis peppered the speech with references to American history and the American flag. The last book Davis had checked out from the Library of Congress in December of 1860, in fact, was the then-standard work on the Stars and Stripes, Schuyler Hamilton's *History of the American Flag.* Early on in the speech Davis spoke of the "rich inheritance" given the nation by our Founding Fathers. He went on to invoke Fort McHenry, "memorable in our history as the place where, under bombardment, the Star-Spangled Banner floated though the darkness of night, the point which was consecrated by our national song."

In making his case for federal troops to withdraw from Fort Sumter in Charleston, South Carolina, Davis again invoked the flag. South Carolina had been the first state to secede from the Union on December 20, 1860. Five days later, U.S. Army major Robert Anderson moved federal troops into the fort. The next day, with great ceremony, he raised an enormous twenty- by thirty-six-foot, thirty-three-star American flag over the fort. As the flag was unfurled, Anderson wrote four days later, his troops presented arms and his band played "The Star-Spangled Banner," after which "three cheers were given for the flag and three for the Union," which Anderson called "a solemn, and to all, a most interesting ceremony."

Davis had heard, he said in his Senate speech, that the "greatest objection" to having the federal troops withdraw from Fort Sumter "was an unwillingness to lower the flag." He derided that argument, claiming that Southerners and Northerners had equally strong feelings about the Stars and Stripes. Southerners, he said, "are your brethren; and they have shed as much glory upon that flag as any equal number of men in the Union."

Davis spoke passionately about the Revolutionary War battle that took place near Fort Sumter in Charleston harbor on June 28, 1776, at what was then called Fort Sullivan. In that engagement colonial forces under William Moultrie fought off an attacking British Fleet in a nine-hour battle. The victory saved Charleston from British occupation and became a significant morale booster in the colonies, coming just six days before the Continental Congress adopted the Declaration of Independence on July 4.

Davis said that the defenders of Fort Sullivan (later renamed Fort Moultrie) "are the men, and that is the location where the first Union flag was unfurled," an event he said that had occurred in October 1775. (The consensus of historical opinion, however, is that the first Union flag, the Continental Colors, was unfurled by George Washington on New Year's Day of 1776 near Boston.) In the June 28 fight, Davis said, the "fort was assailed by the British fleet, and bombarded until the old logs, clinging with stern tenacity to the enemy that assailed them, were filled with balls, the flag still floated there . . ."

He then ridiculed the idea that there was any kind of shame in removing the American flag from Fort Sumter in 1861. "Can there be a point of pride," Davis asked rhetorically, "against laying upon that sacred soil today the flag for which our fathers died?" His pride, Davis said, "is that the flag shall not set between contending brothers." If the worst happened and war broke out, and the Stars and Stripes would no longer "be the common flag of the country," Davis recommended that the American flag be "folded up and laid away like a vesture [an article of clothing] no longer used; that it shall be kept as a sacred memento of the past, to which each of us can make a pilgrimage, and remember the glorious days in which we were born."

Later in the speech he returned to the Revolutionary War, referring to the flag as "the constellation," using the words of the 1777 Flag Resolution. Davis inserted his states' rights interpretation into his version of what the flag stood for. The flag, he said, "was set in the political firmament as a sign of the unity and confederation and community independence, coexistent with confederate strength." It "has served to bless our people," Davis said, and its "regenerative power will outlive, perhaps, the Government as a sign for which it was set."

He described his pride serving under the flag in the Mexican War and then lamented the fact that he would be turning away from "the flag of the Union." Davis spoke, too, of his "deep sorrow" as he contemplated "taking a last leave of that object of early affection and proud association, feeling that henceforth it is not to be the banner which, by day and by night, I am ready to follow, to hail with the rising and bless with the setting sun."

In his farewell speech to the Senate eleven days later, on January 21, Davis did not mention the American flag.

On January 11, 1861, the day after Davis's flag-heavy Senate speech, Alabama seceded from the Union. Georgia followed suit on January 19 and Louisiana on January 26. On January 29, Kansas joined the Union and on the Fourth of July 1861, the thirty-four-star flag became official. This was notwithstanding the fact that Texas, Virginia, Arkansas, Tennessee, and North Carolina had seceded in the interim, and that eleven of the thirty-four states did not consider themselves a part of the "constellation" any longer.

In the North, some people cut eleven stars out of their personal flags in protest. After the war began there was sentiment in Congress to remove the stars officially. Abraham Lincoln, however, stood steadfastly against removing stars from the flag because of his belief that the rebellious Southern states remained part of the national government.

The official national flag at the outset of the Civil War, therefore, contained thirty-four stars. On July 4, 1863, during the war, the flag gained another star in honor of West Virginia's entry into the Union on June 20. Nevada became the thirty-sixth state during the war, in October 1864. The thirty-six-star flag, which became official on July 4, 1865, typically contained five rows of stars. The first, third, and fifth rows held eight stars each; the second and four rows had six each.

                    ★   ★   ★

Jefferson Davis was not the only prominent American who spoke out about the flag in the months before the Civil War began. Samuel F. B. Morse, the inventor of the telegraph, devoted considerable energy trying to stop the outbreak of war. In doing so, Morse came up with the idea of a secession or peace flag. Morse, who was sixty-nine years old and in his retirement in 1860, suggested that the states come together in a new national convention to try to iron out their differences. If that failed, he proposed two separate, allied nations, each with half of the United States flag.

Morse envisioned a Northern flag that would have the top six and a half stripes and half the canton divided diagonally with the corresponding number of stars. The Southern flag would have the six and a half stripes on the bottom and half the canton. If war with a foreign nation came, Morse said, "under our treaty of offence and defence the two separate flags, by national affinity, would clasp fittingly together, and the glorious old flag of the Union, in its entirety, would again be hoisted, once more embracing all the sister States."

Not surprisingly, the odd idea of secession or peace flags did not catch on. A few were raised in the North, but proved not to be very popular. In April, after the war had begun, a man who flew the secession flag in East Fairhaven, Massachusetts, was tarred and feathered by a mob, made to give three cheers for the Stars and Stripes, swear allegiance to the Constitution, and promise never to fly any flag other than the intact Stars and Stripes.

In the months prior to Fort Sumter, as it appeared that war was imminent, there were signs that the flag was becoming increasingly important as an everyday patriotic symbol in the North. Before a huge crowd outside Independence Hall in Philadelphia on February 22, 1861, for example, president-elect Abraham Lincoln, en route to Washington from Illinois, personally raised a Stars and Stripes flag that had been flown by American troops in the Mexican War. That act was greeted by a wave of intense emotion from the huge crowd that had gathered to hear him speak.

"I could not help hoping that there was, in the entire success of that beautiful ceremony, at least something of an omen of what is to come," Lincoln said later that night in Harrisburg. "I think the flag of our country may yet be kept flaunting gloriously."

On that same day in New Orleans, one of the last American flags flew in the South before the war began. The flag, inscribed "United We Stand, Divided We Fall," featured two clasped hands. A battle almost erupted between Southern patriots and the Northern sympathizers who unfurled the flag. It was averted when a group of armed men protected the flag throughout the day and then took it down voluntarily.

At Fort Sumter itself, Major Anderson received letters of support from friends and strangers, letters that typically mentioned the defense of the American flag. A Baltimore bricklayer wrote, for example, that he would be happy to come to Anderson's aid with other workingmen "who would not hesitate to lay the trowel if it became necessary and help to defend their country's flag."

*   *   *

On February 4, 1861, the Provisional Confederate Congress held its opening session in the Capitol Building in Montgomery, Alabama. The delegates' first orders of business were creating a Constitution for the breakaway Confederate States of America, electing a president and vice president, and choosing a flag and seal. Christopher Memminger of South Carolina presented the first proposed flag to the body on February 9—a banner, he reported, whose design came from "the ladies of South Carolina."

The Congress that day set up a select committee to choose a flag. That panel, the Committee on Flag and Seal, received scores of additional design suggestions from citizens from across the South during the next several weeks. A large percentage of the suggested flags were red, white, and blue. Many contained stars and stripes. Many envisioned the American flag's canton-and-stripes theme. Many had arrangements of seven stars, representing the seven Confederate states at the time. Several replaced the canton and inserted differing arrangements of stars on, above, below, or surrounded by red and white stripes.

A large percentage of the proposed flags were variations on the Stars and Stripes. But the Confederate Congress quickly dismissed a resolution by Walter Brooke of Mississippi on February 13, to instruct the flag committee "to adopt and report a flag as similar as possible to the flag of the United States." Brooke's proposal was met with derision in the Congress, and he withdrew the recommendation.

On March 4 Pres. Abraham Lincoln took the oath of office on the East Portico of the U.S. Capitol in Washington, D.C. On that same day in the Southern capital, Montgomery, William Porcher Miles, the chairman of the flag committee, presented the panel's recommendation to the Congress. Miles, who had argued heatedly against Brooke's proposal, reiterated his opposition to it in his report. First, there would be "practical difficulties" in a flag similar to the Stars and Stripes, Miles said. Second, there would be "no propriety in retaining the ensign of a government which, in the opinion of the States composing this Confederacy, had become so oppressive and injurious to their interests as to require their separation from it. It is idle to talk of 'keeping' the flag of the United States when we have voluntarily seceded from them."

Miles went on to lambaste those who spoke of the "glories of the old flag." He reminded those present that the battles of the Revolution, "about which our fondest and proudest memories cluster," were not fought under the Stars and Stripes. He spoke of Southerners' contributions to the War of 1812 and the Mexican War, but then derided any strong association with their service in that war and the American flag, which he called "a mere piece of striped bunting." He compared the Confederacy to the breakaway colonies who "did not desire to retain the British flag or anything similar to it." We "think it good to imitate [the colonies] in this comparatively little manner," he said.

Miles went on to mock two countries, Liberia and the Sandwich Islands, for choosing flags similar to the Stars and Stripes, saying they "had been pilfered and appropriated by a free Negro community and a race of savages." He said, though, that it would be appropriate for the Confederacy to "retain at least a suggestion of the old Stars and Stripes." Then Miles offered the committee's proposed flag, which the Congress adopted—the flag that has since become known as the Stars and Bars. It consists of three horizontal stripes, one white and two red, and a canton of blue containing a circle of seven white stars.

"If adopted," Miles said, "long may it wave over a brave, a free, and a virtuous people. May the career of the Confederacy, whose duty it will then be to support and defend it, be such as to endear it to our children's children, as the flag of a loved . . . a just and benign government, and the cherished symbol of its valor, purity, and truth."

The Confederate Congress approved the flag that day. The following day the Stars and Bars flew over the Capitol Building in Montgomery. The flag, however, so resembled the Stars and Stripes that Confederate commanders early on in the war stopped using it on the field of battle. By the end of the year, the Southern troops began displaying a different banner, the Confederate Battle Flag, known as the Southern Cross.

That came about as a direct result of the difficulty of distinguishing the Stars and Bars from the Stars and Stripes at the war's initial large engagment, the First Battle of Bull Run in Manassas, Virginia, on July 21, 1861. In that bloody and smoky fight the Confederates under Generals P. G. T. Beauregard and Joseph E. Johnston defeated the Union army under Gen. Irvin McDowell.

Because the Confederate troops had trouble seeing the colors through the heavy gun smoke at First Manassas, the Confederacy adopted an entirely new battlefield flag. Beauregard, Johnston, and Miles worked with

the Confederate War Department to design the Battle Flag, which was presented formally in ceremonies to the troops in December. The red, white,
and blue Battle Flag, consisting of a blue cross of St. Andrew containing
thirteen white stars, with narrow white edges on the cross—sometimes
known as the "Southern Cross"—became the Confederate war banner for
the duration of the war.

A third flag, known as the Stainless Banner, was used mainly by the Confederate navy and maritime fleet. It consisted of the Battle Flag in the canton
and a completely white field. The Confederate Congress adopted that banner
as the official Confederate national flag on May 1, 1863. Near the end of
the war, on March 4, 1965, it was modified with the addition of a wide red
vertical stripe because it was reported that on windless days only the field
showed, making the flag appear as if it were a white flag of surrender.

★   ★   ★

The event that launched the Civil War—the Confederate attack on Fort
Sumter in South Carolina—also precipitated an unprecedented explosion
of devotion to the Stars and Stripes that swept over the North when the
flag was lowered in defeat in Charleston harbor. The bombardment of the
fort on that man-made island of seashells and granite at the entrance to
Charleston began at 4:30 in the morning of April 12. By that time the Confederacy had taken possession of all American military forts and arsenals in
the seven-state South, with the exception of Fort Pickens on Santa Rosa Island on Pensacola Bay in Florida and Fort Sumter.

Fort Pickens, despite repeated attacks, never did fall to the Confederate
army. But that was not the case at Sumter, a solidly built, five-sided ediface
with fifty-foot-high walls as thick as twelve feet. Lincoln did not give in to
the Confederate demand to evacuate the fort after he took office in March.
Instead, he made plans to resupply Anderson's small garrison there in early
April. That news was greeted by commanding Confederate general Beauregard's demand for the fort's immediate evacuation and surrender. When
Lincoln refused, Beauregard received an order by telegraph from Secretary of War Leroy Pope Walker in Montgomery ordering the bombardment of the fort. Two days later, after thirty-four hours of being hit by some
four thousand shells, Anderson surrendered.

Anderson, a Kentucky-born professional soldier, West Point class of
1825, and his men had put up a valiant fight. They raised the white flag of
surrender at 2:00 in the afternoon on April 13, after Confederate guns had

set the fort's barracks on fire, completely destroying the building, as well as the main gate, and seriously damaging some of the fort's walls and with the fort's food stores severely depleted. Anderson asked as part of the surrender terms that the Confederates allow him to give a one-hundred-gun salute as he lowered the fort's American flag.

Beauregard had agreed to that condition in his initial demand to Anderson to surrender. "The flag which you have upheld so long and with so much fortitude, under the most trying circumstances, may be saluted by you on taking it down," he said. "In recognition of the gallantry exhibited by the garrison," Beauregard said in his after-action report to President Davis, "I cheerfully agreed that on surrendering the fort the commanding officer might salute the flag."

Sumter's garrison flag had flown over the fort from December 26, 1860, until the first shots rang out at dawn on April 12. After high winds tore it in half, the flag was replaced by a smaller storm flag, which received the surrender salute. Ironically, it was during that salute—which began at two o'clock in the afternoon on April 14—that the first and only soldier on either side of the conflict was killed in action. During the loading of the forty-seventh salute cannon, an errant cartridge set off a pile of other shells that hit Pvt. Daniel Hough, who died instantly. Pvt. Edward Gallway, who was severely wounded, died three days later. Four other men were seriously wounded.

Anderson cut short the salute at fifty shots. At four o'clock, he and Capt. Abner Doubleday—who is sometimes credited with having invented the game of baseball—gathered the men on the parade ground. The Union troops then lowered the flag, and marched out of the fort as the small Union band played "Yankee Doodle Dandy." They boarded the steamer *Isobel*, which took them to the transport *Baltic*, upon which they sailed to New York, arriving on April 16. As he led his men out of Fort Sumter, Anderson had the garrison flag folded and tucked under his arm.

"At that hour," Beauregard reported, "the place having been evacuated by the United States garrison, our troops occupied it, and the Confederate flag was hoisted on the ramparts of Sumter with a salute from the various batteries."

Or, as the *New York Times* put it in the second paragraph of its front-page April 15, 1861, article headlined "FORT SUMPTER FALLEN": "The American flag has given place to the Palmetto of South Carolina."

Watching this unfold from the USS *Pawnee*, anchored outside the harbor, navy commander S. C. Rowan gave his version of events starting at

8:00 that morning: "Appearances of great rejoicing in Charleston Harbor. Smoke still rising from Fort Sumter. At 1 P.M. observed the American flag flying over Fort Sumter. At 2, a salute of fifty guns was fired and the flag was hauled down. At 4 P.M., the so-called Confederate flag . . . was hoisted on Fort Sumter amid a general fire from all the [surrounding] forts batteries."

★   ★   ★

Jefferson Davis had bitterly derisive—and only partially correct—words for those in the North who framed the fight at Fort Sumter in terms of an attack on the American flag, calling such sentiments the "disingenuous rant of demagogues." Davis, however, was completely correct in his assessment that the fall of Fort Sumter "was seized upon to inflame the mind of the Northern people."

A large part of that inflammation centered on feelings about the flag. "When the stars and stripes went down at Sumter, they went up in every town and county in the loyal states," Admiral Preble wrote in 1871. "Every city, town, and village suddenly blossomed with banners." What happened at Fort Sumter, he said, "created great enthusiasm throughout the loyal States, for the flag had come to have a new and strange significance. The heart of the nation swelled to avenge the insult cast by traitors on its glorious flag. It is said that even laborers wept in the streets for the degradation of their country. One cry was raised, drowning all other voices—'War! War to restore the Union! War to avenge the flag!'"

While Preble was not exactly an unbiased observer—a career officer, he served in various capacities with the U.S. Navy during the Civil War—his assessment of the "new and strange" role of the flag in the North following Fort Sumter is accurate. What happened at Sumter aroused bitterly strong feelings in the North and served as a unifying force for the war that was to come. A significant portion of the emotional component of the Union's war fever involved the flag.

"Romantic flag-waving rhetoric," in the words of the eminent Civil War historian James M. McPherson, swept through the North and South when the war began, as it does in virtually all societies during times of intense national strife. One example among many in the North: a letter written by James Welsh to his brother John shortly after the Stars and Stripes came down at Fort Sumter. The Welsh brothers grew up in Virginia, but John Welsh moved to Ohio in 1853 and was incensed by his brother's support of the Confederate cause. He never dreamed his brother would "raise a hand to tear down the glorious Stars and Stripes," James Welsh wrote, "a flag that we have been taught from our cradle to look on with pride. . . . I would strike down my own brother if he would dare raise a hand to destroy that flag."

Newspapers and magazines in the North ran red-hot flag-oriented editorials in the wake of the fall of Fort Sumter. An editorial in *Harper's Weekly*, the widely read news magazine published in New York, for example, vehemently condemned the Southern states for leaving the Union, partly framing the entire Civil War issue in terms of an assault on what the American flag stood for. The "rebels know," the magazine said, "that, as surely as the sun rises, the honor of the country's flag will presently be vindicated." The flag, the editorial announced, "is the symbol of the Government which secures and protects [the Southerner] in all his rights and interests; and when he excuses the crime [of warring against the Union], he invites anarchy and the universal destruction not only of all property, but of all the guarantees of civil society."

The editorial went on to express disgust that Southerners, who "have grown and prospered under [the flag] more than any nation in the world" would "strike their hands at the flag and their fangs at the peaceful and happy system which it symbolizes." It accused the Confederates of being "totally devoid of love of country," a feeling that "indicates the values" of "a moral monster," and "a lump of inhuman selfishness."

The *New York Times* offered an equally defiant, flag-waving editorial on May 6. "If anyone goes around among our soldiers now and asks the reason for their enlistment, they will very probably say, 'It was the insult to the old Flag at Sumter,' or 'It is for the Stars and Stripes,'" the newspaper said. Now "is the time of its peril, when the shot of traitors have pierced it, when it is discarded and outcast by those who have so long used it to protect their inequities, the feeling of the people springs towards it like a passion." The Stars and Stripes, the editorial predicted, "shall yet wave over Richmond and Charleston, and Mobile and New Orleans."

The editorial concluded with a plea to Northerners to fly the flag everywhere and for Union soldiers to pledge themselves to the flag. Let "the glorious banner flaunt from every housetop, from window and chimney, from monument and church—for no place is too sacred for it. In this time of its danger, we will wear it over our breasts, and bear it on our persons; and you who go forth to defend the Flag, remember that nothing can dishonor it but treachery and cowardice! Bear the old Stars and Stripes, as the emblem of your country, before you in battle, count it honor enough that you have been able to bleed and suffer for it, and a sweet and glorious thing if for that Flag you can die."

As Preble reported, all across the North citizens spontaneously began flying the flag from their homes and their businesses. The flag flew at public schools, colleges and universities, and in front of churches. Women wore small flags on their hats; men pinned small flags to their lapels and hat bands. Flags were tucked into horses' headstalls and wrapped around dogs.

"The patchwork of red, white, and blue, what had flaunted in their faces for generations without exciting much emotion, in a single day stirred the pulses of the people to battle," Preble wrote (breathlessly if not inaccurately), and "became the inspiration of national effort."

On April 12, the day the attack on Sumter had begun, a flag-bedecked rally took place in the city of Troy, New York, on the Hudson River north of Albany. "Will you permit that flag to be desecrated and trampled in the dust by traitors now?" one of the town's prominent citizens asked the crowd. "That flag must be lifted up from the dust into which it has been trampled, placed in the proper position and again set floating in triumph to the breeze."

In Boston flags "blossomed everywhere," according to Mary A. Livermore, who went on to serve as a Union nurse. The Stars and Stripes, she said, "floated from the roofs of the houses, were flung to the breeze from chambers of commerce and boards of trade, spanned the surging streets, decorated the private parlor, glorified the school-room, [and] festooned the church walls and pulpit."

On April 16, Livermore described the scene at Boston's Faneuil Hall where a large crowd of men had come to sign up for the Union cause. "I saw the dear banner of my country, rising high and high to the top of the flagstaff, fling out fold after fold . . . , and float proudly over the hallowed edifice," she wrote in her autobiography. "Oh, the roar that rang out from ten thousand throats! Old men, with white hair and tearful faces, lifted their hats to the national ensign, and reverently saluted it. Young men greeted it with fierce and wild hurrahs, talking the while in terse Saxon of the traitors of the Confederate States, who had dragged in the dirt this flag of their country, never before dishonored."

Maj. Robert Anderson and his men were greeted with an enormous display of American flags when they arrived in New York City by ship from Fort Sumter. The flag, one observer said, "flew out to the wind from every housetop" as "wildly excited crowds marched the streets demanding that the suspected or lukewarm should show the symbol of nationality as a committal to the country's cause." Tens of thousands of American flags flew throughout New York City that day. The city's artists joined in, immediately turning out engravings and lithographs prominently featuring the flag and other patriotic symbols. What the *New York World* on April 20 called "flag mania" soon gripped the city.

On April 19 Anderson had the Fort Sumter flag hung from a flagpole of a building on Broadway during a sendoff ceremony he took part in for New York's Seventh Regiment. The famed political cartoonist Thomas Nast memorialized that event in an oil painting, *Seventh Regiment Departing for the War*, which depicts the tattered Fort Sumter flag along with scores of Stars and Stripes being waved on the street.

The next day, April 20, a crowd of some one hundred thousand rallied in New York's Union Square where both Anderson and the Sumter flag made appearances. The center of attention was Henry K. Brown's large *Washington on Horseback* bronze sculpture. The tattered Fort Sumter flag was attached to a flagstaff allegedly taken from the fort and placed in George Washington's hands. "The national banners waving from ten thousand windows in your city today proclaim your affection and reverence for the Union," Republican U.S. senator Edward Dickinson Baker told the throng. Another speaker urged the crowd to "rally to the Star-Spangled Banner so long as a single stripe can be discovered, or a single star shall shimmer from the surrounding darkness."

Also in New York City a homemade thirty-foot flag flew on April 24 at a store on Maiden Lane. It was sewed by four generations of women of the Newcomb family. Also seen on the streets of New York: a flag over a sign painter's door with the words that eerily echo bumper stickers that appeared after the September 11, 2001, terrorist attacks: "*Colors* warranted not to run."

On April 25 U.S. senator Stephen Douglas of Illinois gave what has since come to be known as his "Preserve the Flag" speech to a joint session of the Legislature of Illinois in the Old Capitol Building in Springfield. Douglas and Lincoln were political enemies who had squared off in a historic series of debates during the 1858 Illinois Senate race over the issue of slavery. In his April 25 speech, however, Douglas urged Northerners to set aside their differences and unite under the flag against the Confederacy.

"For the first time since the adoption of the Federal Constitution, a widespread conspiracy exists to destroy the best government the sun of heaven ever shed its rays upon," Douglas told cheering state legislators.

"Hostile armies are now marching on the Federal Capitol, with a view of planting a revolutionary flag upon its dome," he said. "When all propositions of peace fail, and a war of aggression is proclaimed, there is but one course left to the patriot, and that is to rally under the flag which has waved over the Capitol from the days of Washington, and around the government established by Washington, Madison, Hamilton, and their compeers."

That was Douglas's last speech. He died on June 3, 1861, in Chicago. After his death, Americans in both the North and South took Douglas's admonition to "rally under the flag" to heart.

CHAPTER EIGHT

Flagmania

★   ★   ★

Yes, we'll rally round the flag, boys / Rally once again. . . .

— *"The Battle Cry of Freedom,"* George F. Root, 1862

TWO DAYS AFTER Douglas's farewell speech, Edward Everett —
the former Massachusetts governor, ambassador to England, president of
Harvard, and secretary of state in the Fillmore administration — gave a
rousing speech at a flag-raising ceremony in Boston. "Why is it," Everett
asked rhetorically, "that the flag of the country, always honored, always
beloved, is now at once worshipped, I may say, with passionate homage of
this whole people? Why does it float, as never before, not merely from ar-
senal and masthead, but from tower and steeple, from the public edifices,
the temples of science, the private dwellings, in magnificent display of
miniature presentiment?"

Everett answered his own question with two words: "Fort Sumter."

When word of the flag under siege at Sumter reached the Northern
states, Everett said, "One deep, unanimous, spontaneous feeling shot with
the tidings through the breasts of twenty millions of freemen, that its outraged honor must be vindicated."

Everett's oratory stood as a shining, if hyperbolic, example of what the
New Orleans Picayune called the "flagmania" that swept both the Northern
and Southern states in the weeks and months after the Confederate flag replaced the Stars and Stripes at Fort Sumter. In the South, the Confederate

flag flew conspicuously in front of homes and businesses, much as the Stars and Stripes did in the North. Many women wore clothes embroidered with the Confederate flag or displayed small flags on their dresses.

"I wear one pinned to my bosom," twenty-year-old Sarah Morgan Dawson of Baton Rouge, Louisiana, wrote in her diary in 1862. "The man who says take it off will have to pull it off for himself; the man who dares attempt it—well! A pistol in my pocket fills the gap. I am capable too."

At send-off ceremonies in small and large towns and cities across the South, troops heading off to war were almost always presented with the Stars and Bars—and later the Southern Cross—most often by women who had sewn the flags themselves. Local politicians and clergymen often attended these events and made emotional speeches that were heavily covered in local newspapers. The Confederate soldiers went to war with florid, patriotic words ringing in their ears not to surrender the flag or, as a last resort, to destroy the banner rather than surrender it to the Yankees.

Send-offs were similar in the North. Milton Scott Lytle, a private in the 125th Pennsylvania Volunteers, described his unit's leave taking before a huge crowd of men, women, and children at the courthouse in Huntingdon County, Pennsylvania, as a flag-drenched, superpatriotic occasion. The second minister to speak, the Reverend. G. W. Zahnizer of the Presbyterian Church, Lytle said, "pointed to the American flag, and appealed to" the men "to return only when the dishonor heaped upon it shall be wiped out, and it again floats in triumph in every section of our country." Methodist minister S. L. M. Couser then "seized" the flag, Lytle said, and waved it over his head, declaring "his readiness to shoulder his musket in defense of the glorious emblem of liberty." The shouts that went up after he spoke those words "were deafening," Lytle said.

As the men marched to the train depot, the crowd followed along. "The scene there baffles description," Lytle wrote. "Mothers, wives and sisters weeping over their friends who thus willingly offer to lay down their lives in defense of their flag."

The Stars and Stripes began to appear on stationery and envelopes within weeks after the Confederate takeover of Fort Sumter. One of the first such images was a full-color American flag that covered the outside of an entire envelope. Printers in the South soon came up with a flag envelope of their own, using the Stars and Bars. The white stripe in the middle made a convenient place for the address. Envelopes and stationery in the North also featured patriotic slogans along with the flags. They included "Liberty and Union," "The Flag of the Free," and "Forever Float That Standard Sheet."

Other envelopes were adorned with flags and portraits of Abraham Lincoln and prominent military men such as John Frémont and Winfield Scott. Another popular envelope featured the flag and the words "I shall wave again over Sumter."

The actual Fort Sumter garrison flag itself became almost a holy relic in the North. Soon after it flew over Union Square, the flag was placed in a vault in New York City's Metropolitan Bank. It was loaned periodically during the war to the U.S. Sanitary Commission, a civilian group made up primarily of women set up by the Union government in June of 1861 to perform nursing and other medical and social work at field hospitals, soldiers' homes, and other venues. The commission, headed by the celebrated landscape architect Frederick Law Olmstead, used the flag as an effective fund-raising tool. The flag made a tour of cities around the country, where it was put up for "auction." The highest bidder then turned the money—and the flag—over to the commission.

As the war progressed, the flag became a visible and integral part of rallies and patriotic celebrations throughout the Union. The Fourth of July celebration in San Francisco in 1864, for example, turned out to be an especially flag-drenched affair. Mark Twain, then a reporter for the *San Francisco Daily Morning Call*, called the city's commemoration of the Fourth that year "the most remarkable day San Francisco has ever seen" in terms of "magnificence, enthusiasm, crowds, noise, wind and dust."

The "whole city," Twain reported, "was swathed in a waving drapery of flags—scarcely a house could be found which lacked this kind of decoration. The effect was exceedingly lively and beautiful." Montgomery Street, he said, "was no longer a street of compactly built houses, but simply a quivering cloud of gaudy red and white stripes, which shut out from view almost everything but itself. Some houses were broken out all over with flags, like small-pox patients; among these were Brannan's Building, the Occidental Hotel and the Lick House, which displayed flags at every window."

Poetry, stories, and songs about the flag became increasingly popular after the war began. Bands played "The Star-Spangled Banner" at patriotic rallies throughout the North, although Julia Ward Howe's "The Battle Hymn of the Republic," which first published in February 1862, became the Union army's de facto official anthem during the war. In July 1862, in a burst of patriotic spirit, the composer and lyricist George F. Root wrote "The Battle Cry of Freedom," which begins with the memorable words that later became a catch phrase: "Yes, we'll rally round the flag, boys / rally once again."

Root wrote the song following President Lincoln's July 2, 1862, call for three hundred thousand Union army volunteers. The song was performed for the first time on July 24. "The Battle Cry of Freedom" became an immediate hit and was performed at countless war rallies and other patriotic occasions. By war's end, more than a half million copies of the sheet music had been sold in the North.

Among the other songs published in 1861 extolling the American flag were "Defend the Stars and Stripes" by Gustave A. Scott; "The American Flag" by the Reverend J. D. Dickson; "The Red, White & Blue of '61", and

The start of the Civil War in 1861 precipitated an unprecedented explosion of devotion to the Stars and Stripes throughout the North. Its image was used extensively throughout the war, including in this patriotic 1862 Unionist sheet music illustration. *The Library of Congress, Prints and Photographs Division*

"Our Country's Flag" by G. Gumpert; "The Stars and Stripes" by James T. Field and O. B. Brown; "The Starry Flag" by John Savage; and "The Stripes and the Stars" by George A. Mietike.

These words from the Field-Brown "The Stars and Stripes" embody the tenor of those songs:

> *Let the Traitors brag;*
> *Gallant lads, fire away!*
> *And fight for the flag.*
>
> *Their flag is but a rag*
> *Ours is the true one*
> *Up with the Stars and Stripes!*
> *Down with the new one!*

With passions running so strong in the North and South, the flag inevitably became involved in violent, sometimes deadly, incidents. Southern sympathizers in the North risked mob violence if they displayed the Confederate flag publicly. The same was true with Northern patriots in the South. In some cases mobs in the North carried out attacks against individuals and businesses that failed to fly the Stars and Stripes.

A few days after the surrender of Fort Sumter, for example, an unruly throng in Philadelphia descended on the offices of the *Palmetto Flag*, a secessionist newspaper named for the state flag of South Carolina. The crowd dispersed only after the newspaper's employees displayed an American flag. Philadelphia's mayor Alexander Henry expressed the day's strong feelings for the flag but also cautioned the city's residents against violence. "By the grace of God, treason shall never rear its head or have foothold in Philadelphia. I call upon you, as American citizens, to stand by your flag and protect it all hazards," Henry told the crowd. "But in doing so, remember the rights due your fellow citizens and their private property."

In the South Union sympathizers who dared display the Stars and Stripes could be prosecuted under the Alien Enemies Act, which the Confederate Congress passed in August of 1861. That act ordered the departure of all Northerners and authorized the arrest of those considered to be hostile to the Confederate government. Private citizens in the South made their own anti-American flag sentiments known throughout the war. After Virginia seceded from the Union on April 17, for example, a crowd burned an American flag in the public square of Liberty, Mississippi. On April 21, a crowd cheered the public burial of an American flag in Memphis, Tennessee. On May 7, a riot broke out in Knoxville, Tennessee, after an American flag was hoisted; one man was killed in the ensuing melee.

What is believed to be the first fatal incident during a Civil War engagement involving a flag took place on May 24, 1861, the day that federal troops captured the city of Alexandria, Virginia, across the Potomac River from Washington, D.C. The commander of the New York Fire Zouave's First Regiment, twenty-four-year-old Col. Elmer Ellsworth, a close friend of Abraham Lincoln, was among the troops in the city that day. As they marched down one of Alexandria's main streets, Ellsworth and his men noticed that the Marshall House, an inn, displayed a large, sixteen-by thirty-foot Confederate Stars and Bars. Ellsworth entered the establishment to cut the flag down. After doing so, he was shot and killed by the innkeeper, James W. Jackson, with one close-in blast of his double-barreled shotgun. One of Ellsworth's men, Private Francis E. Brownell, then killed Jackson.

Lincoln was devastated by the news of his friend's death—the first union officer to die in the war. After recovering from the shock, Lincoln found some comfort in what occurred after the killings. "There is one fact that has reached me which is a great consolation to my heart and quite a relief after this melancholy affair," Lincoln told a group of White House visitors, including a reporter from the *New York Herald*. "I learn from several persons that when the Stars and Stripes were raised again in Alexandria, many of the people of the town actually wept for joy, and manifested the liveliest gratification at seeing this familiar and loved emblem once more floating about them."

Lincoln ordered that Ellsworth lay in state in the East Room of the White House where thousands attended his funeral. As the news of what became known as "The Marshall House Incident" spread—mainly through an illustrated, cover story in the June 15, 1861, issue of *Harper's Weekly*—Ellsworth was mourned throughout the North and became the Union's first Civil War martyr. Several regiments adopted the Zouave name in his honor, including the 44th New York Volunteer Infantry, which became known as "Ellsworth's Avengers," and Union troops took up the battle cry, "Avenge Ellsworth." Ellsworth's image appeared on stationery, sheet music, and in memorial lithographs. One envelope pictured Ellsworth attired in an idealized Zouave uniform holding a rifle and a large American flag. Above him were the words, "To Richmond," and below the words, "Remember Ellsworth."

The bloody Confederate flag that Ellsworth clutched in his hands was conveyed to the White House where Mary Todd Lincoln hid it away in a drawer. Tad Lincoln, the president's young son, enjoyed playing with the flag and sometimes displayed it during official occasions.

"When the President was reviewing some troops from the portico of the White House, Tad sneaked this flag out and waved it back of the President, who stood with a flag in his hands," Julia Taft Bayne, a playmate of Tad's, remembered. "The sight of a rebel flag on such an occasion caused some commotion, and when the President saw what was happening he pinioned his bad boy and the flag in his strong arms and handed them together to an orderly, who carried the offenders within."

When the captain of a U.S. Treasury Department revenue cutter ship, the *McClelland* in New Orleans, refused to obey orders from Washington in January of 1861, Buchanan administration treasury secretary John A. Dix telegraphed what would become a famous order to his agent in that city. In it Dix—a former U.S. senator and postmaster of the United States who later became a Civil War general—authorized the takeover of the *McClelland* and gave orders to treat those who disobeyed as mutineers.

"If any one attempts to haul down the American flag," Dix said on January 21, "shoot him on the spot." That order was not carried out, but Dix's words became something of a catch phrase among Union soldiers during the war. Not long after the war began, Dix's words appeared on stationery and envelopes, accompanied by images of the American flag.

New Orleans was the scene in 1862 of more threats of violence involving the flag, as well as the hanging of a Confederate supporter for the crime of taking the American flag down from the U.S. Mint. On April 25 Flag Officer David G. Farragut led his eighteen-vessel naval force to a decisive victory over the Confederate Mississippi River Squadron. After that battle some seven hundred of Farragut's troops landed to take over the city, the largest in the Confederacy. Farragut, who went on to compile a string of other naval Civil War victories, was born in Tennessee and raised in Virginia. He nevertheless was dedicated to the Union and ordered the city's mayor, John T. Monroe, to surrender the city.

Farragut also ordered, in Monroe's words, "the hoisting of the United States flag on the Customhouse, Post office, and Mint" and that "the Louisiana flag should be hauled down from City Hall." Monroe replied that Confederate general Mansfield Lovell controlled the city, and that as mayor he therefore didn't have the authority to raise the Stars and Stripes. Monroe also gave Farragut an "unqualified refusal" on his demand to lower the Louisiana flag from city hall.

Monroe was forced to concede defeat when Lovell pulled his disorganized troops out of the city. But the mayor vehemently and emotionally vowed that he would not replace the Confederate and Louisiana flags with the Stars and Stripes. "The man lives not in our midst whose hand and heart would not be palsied at the mere thought of such an act," Monroe replied to Farragut. "Nor could I find in my entire constituency so wretched and desperate a renegade as would dare to profane with his hand the sacred emblem of our aspirations."

From his flagship, the *Hartford*, Farragut again demanded the "unqualified" surrender of the city. And he again ordered that the American flag, "the emblem of the sovereignty of the United States," be hoisted over city hall, the Mint, and the Custom House. He also ordered that all flags, "or other emblems of sovereignty, other than those of the United States, shall be removed from all public buildings" by noon of the following day.

Farragut also expressed his concerns about New Orleans's citizens who taunted and threatened the Union troops in the city and about reports of attacks upon civilians who saluted the American flag. "I shall speedily and severely punish any person or persons who shall commit such outrages as were witnessed yesterday—armed men firing upon helpless men, women and children for giving expression to their pleasure at witnessing the old flag."

After the city's formal surrender on April twenty-eighth, Farragut sent a team of men to raise the flag at the Customs House and the Mint, ordering them not to fire unless fired upon. Citizens harassed the troops, but the military men refrained from firing their weapons. Upon hearing of the incident, Farragut fired off a dispatch to Mayor Monroe. His men, Farragut told the mayor, "have been insulted in the grossest manner and the flag which had been hoisted by my orders on the Mint was pulled down and dragged through the streets." If that continued, he warned, "the fire of this fleet may be drawn upon the city at any moment."

The mayor dared Farragut to fire at the defenseless city. Farragut replied on April 29 with the demand, again, that the city "haul down and suppress every symbol of government, whether State or Confederate, except that of the United States." The mayor finally capitulated. At noon that day a contingent of heavily armed marines went to city hall, removed the Louisiana flag, and replaced it with the Stars and Stripes. In the end Farragut did not order his fleet to fire on the city, but his threat to do so ranks among the strongest reactions to threats to desecrate the American flag.

On May 1 Gen. Benjamin Franklin Butler's fourteen-hundred-man army landed and occupied New Orleans. Butler, a brigadier general in the

Massachusetts militia who was appointed a major general in the Union army by President Lincoln on May 16, 1861, was vilified in New Orleans for what were considered his draconian measures as military governor. That—and a birth defect that caused one eye to be permanently twisted—earned him the nickname "the Beast." Reacting to constant harassment of his troops, Butler issued General Order No. 28 on May 15, 1862, ordering that any woman who insulted a Union soldier would "be treated as a woman of the town plying her avocation," that is, a prostitute.

That caused a furor. But what cemented Butler's nefarious legacy among the citizens of New Orleans—and throughout the South—was his insistence on court-martialing a man who pulled down the Stars and Stripes from the Mint and then desecrated the flag. Butler's troops arrested the man, twenty-one-year-old William Mumford. He was tried and sentenced to death. Butler had it in his power to stay the execution but chose not to do so.

Instead, Butler issued Special Order 10 on June 5. Mumford, the order said, having been "convicted before a military commission of treason, and an overt act thereof in tearing down the United States flag from a public building of the United States, for the purpose of inciting other evil-minded persons to further resistance to the laws and arms of the United States," would be executed. Mumford was summarily hanged. "His hanging of Mumford for hauling down the flag," according to a *New York Times* editorial, "effectually made the flag feared and respected from that time on."

Jefferson Davis reacted by issuing a death sentence for Butler. President Lincoln reacted on December 16, 1862, by relieving Butler of his command.

"The name of Mumford," Admiral Preble noted, "if we may believe the Confederate newspapers, was immediately added to their roll of martyrs to the cause of liberty."

*   *   *

Perhaps the most famous incident—which did not end in violence—involving a civilian and the American flag during the Civil War is the story of Barbara Frietschie of Frederick, Maryland. The famed American poet and ardent abolitionist, John Greenleaf Whittier, immortalized the story in his poem, "Barbara Frietchie," which the *Atlantic Monthly* published in its October 1863 issue. In it Whittier described how the townspeople of Frederick had taken down their American flags just before Robert E. Lee's

Army of Northern Virginia marched through that western Maryland city on September 10, 1862, two weeks prior to the bloody Battle of Antietam. The patriotic Frietschie, then ninety-five years old, according to Whittier, bravely defied the Confederates by brazenly flying the flag from her window.

"She took up the flag the men hauled down," Whittier wrote. "In her attic window the staff she set / To show that one heart was loyal yet."

When Confederate general Thomas J. Stonewall Jackson rode by her house, he saw the flag and ordered his men to shoot it down, which they did. The determined Barbara Frietschie took that fallen flag, "leaned far out on the window-sill," Whittier wrote, and "shook it forth with a royal will."

"'Shoot, if you must, this old gray head, but spare your country's flag,' she said."

Her outspokenness shamed Jackson, who then told his men: "'Who touches a hair of yon gray head / Dies like a dog! March on!' he said."

Barbara Frietschie proudly kept her lone flag flying.

"All day long through Frederick Street," Whittier wrote, "sounded the tread of marching feet. All day long that free flag tost / over the heads of the rebel host."

Mainly due to the popularity of that poem, the Barbara Frietschie story gained wide currency throughout the country during the decades after the Civil War and remains popular today. The story spawned a play, *Barbara Frietschie*, by the playwright Clyde Fitch (who was born in 1865), which had eighty-three performances on Broadway in 1899 and 1900. *My Maryland*, a musical based on the play, became a popular Broadway attraction in 1927 and 1928. Two silent Hollywood movies based on Fitch's play—both called *Barbara Frietschie*—came out in 1915 and 1924. The 1924 version featured twenty-nine-year-old Florence Vidor in the title role.

The 1922 book, *Poems of American Patriotism*, edited by Brander Mathews, contains the Whittier poem illustrated with a painting by the renowned illustrator N. C. Wyeth. It shows the gray-haired Frietschie leaning out a dormer with broken windows and a smashed flagpole, clutching a tattered Stars and Stripes in her right hand, her mouth open, shouting down to the street in defiance. Another Wyeth illustration in that book, *The Old Continentals*, depicts two Revolutionary War soldiers, with one unfurling the thirteen-star "Betsy Ross" flag—a banner that was never flown by the American fighters in that war.

Certainly no one doubted that Barbara Frietschie—born Barbara Hauer, the daughter of German immigrants eleven years before the First Flag Resolution of 1777 in Lancaster, Pennsylvania—was a very patriotic, strong-willed woman. But questions about the flag-waving episode arose soon after Whittier's poem was published. Critics claimed that Whittier's story was highly exaggerated at best. Historians now believe it is a myth.

They point to the fact, first, that there were no eyewitnesses to the scene, including the poet. Whittier learned the story from the popular sentimental novelist Emma Dorothy Eliza Nevitte Southworth, known as Mrs. E.d.e.n. Southworth, who lived in Washington, D.C., and had read newspaper accounts about it. So his information was third hand at best. It was soon determined, moreover, that Stonewall Jackson did not ride past the Frietschie house, which was razed during the Civil War but reconstructed in 1926 and today is known as the Barbara Frietschie House and Museum.

Historians now believe it is possible that Frietschie may have waved a small American flag from her porch or from a second-floor window and that that action morphed into the fanciful "shoot if you must this old gray head" story. There is stronger evidence, however, that the story evolved from an incident that day involving another Frederick woman who made a show of flying the American flag. The woman in question, Mary A. Quantrill, was the sister-in-law of the infamous Confederate captain William Clarke Quantrill, who led Quantrill's Raiders in guerrilla attacks against Union sympathizers in Missouri and Kansas during the Civil War.

Mary Quantrill, though, was a Union supporter who lived in Frederick. She and her daughter sat in front of her house on September 10, 1862, as Lee's men wended their way through town. They waved the Confederate flag and tied American flags to their horses' tails, Quantrill wrote in 1869, "as a warning to Unionists of what might occur thereafter." Quantrill heard a Confederate officer insult the American flag, shouting, "G_ d_ the stars and stripes to the dust, with all who advocate them." That, Quantrill said, was "too much." She took a "flaglet" from her daughter and "held it firmly" in her hand as the Confederate troops marched past.

Another officer rode up and ordered Quantrill to turn over the flag. She refused, he rode off, and she attached the small flag to the railing on her porch. Another Confederate soldier chopped it off with his bayonet and tore "the flag into pieces and [stomped] them in the dust." A neighbor, Mary Hopwood, produced a second small flag and they mounted it on the porch. It, too, was cut down by the same Confederate soldier.

Historians believe Quantrill's tale. Barbara Frietschie did not live to tell hers. She died in Frederick on December 18, 1862, two weeks after her ninety-sixth birthday.

Whittier's popular poem, however, immortalized Barbara Frietschie.

The tale of a frail old woman bravely defying the Confederates by flaunting her devotion to the American flag struck a nerve among Northerners. The story became an inspiration to millions during the Civil War, and for more than a century afterward. Whittier's work — perhaps the best-known American verse dealing with the American flag — provides a strong example of the powerful hold the Stars and Stripes has in the American psyche.

★   ★   ★

The other famed flag-defying tale that took place during the Civil War involves William Driver, a sea captain born in Salem, Massachusetts, in 1803. The story begins with a present that Driver received on his twenty-first birthday from his mother in 1824: a homemade twenty-four-star flag. When he first hoisted the flag and it unfurled in the wind, Driver was moved to name it "Old Glory." He proudly displayed that flag on board his small whaler, the *Charles Doggett,* as he sailed throughout the world. That ship's most notable voyage came in August and September 1831 when Driver and his crew transported sixty-five descendants of the survivors of the famed 1789 mutiny on the British ship the *Bounty* from Tahiti to their homes on Pitcairn Island in the South Pacific.

William Driver gave up the sea and moved to Nashville following the death of his first wife in 1837. He took his cherished flag with him to Tennessee, where he worked in a store owned by his brother, remarried, and had nine children, in addition to the three from his first marriage. Driver flew the flag on three occasions every year: Washington's Birthday, St. Patrick's Day (his own birthday), and the Fourth of July. He flew Old Glory on those days, "rain or shine," his daughter Mary Jane Driver Roland wrote in her privately published memoir, "on a rope suspended from the attic window [of his house] and stretching across the street, connecting with a pulley on a locust tree."

In 1860 Driver's wife and daughters repaired the tattered flag, removed the old stars, and sewed thirty-four new ones onto it. According to his daughter, Driver "supplemented our labor with the anchor, which he sewed on." That small white anchor still adorns Old Glory in the lower right corner of the canton.

After Tennessee seceded on May 7, 1861, the Driver family hid the flag away, sewing it inside a quilt used as a bed comforter. Twice during the war Confederate partisans came to the Driver house and demanded that he surrender the flag. He adamantly refused. "If you want my flag," Driver told the second group (according to his daughter), "you'll have to take it over my dead body."

Old Glory made its first public appearance after the war began on February 25, 1862, when federal troops occupied Nashville. Driver celebrated that event by liberating Old Glory from inside the quilt, taking it with an escort of troops from the Sixth Ohio Regiment to the Tennessee State Capitol Building and hoisting it from the Capitol's dome. The event was greeted with "frantic cheering and uproarious demonstrations by soldiers and a sprinkling of civilians," Mary Driver Roland, an eyewitness to the scene, said. That event also popularized the name "Old Glory" as a nickname for the American flag.

It received more publicity when James Whitcomb Riley's poem, "The Name of Old Glory," came out in the *North American Review* in December 1898. The poem by Riley—the prolific and popular Indiana poet known as "the poet of the common people"—is an ode to the flag and a rumination on the answer to the question: "Who gave you the name of Old Glory?" Riley did not mention William Driver in his ode. He concluded in the poem's fourth and final stanza that the fluttering of the flag itself provided "an audible answer" to his question.

> *And it spake, with a shake of the voice, and it said:*
> *By the driven snow-white and the living blood-red*
> *Of my bars, and their heaven of stars overhead*
> *By the symbol conjoined of them all, skyward cast,*
> *As I float from the steeple, or flap at the mast,*
> *Or droop o'er the sod where the long grasses nod,*
> *My name is as old as the glory of God.*
> *. . . So I came by the name of Old Glory.*

The Driver family took Old Glory home the day after flying it over the Tennessee Capitol. They kept it out of sight again until the two-day Battle of Nashville in December 1864, when Confederate general John Bell Hood tried to retake the city and the Union troops under Gen. George H. Thomas fought back the attack. "The morning of the battle, December 15," Mary Roland wrote, "my father hung Old Glory out of the third-story window, in plain sight." Before he left the house to help defend the city at nearby Fort Negly, the sixty-one-year-old Driver "called together the entire household and said, 'If Old Glory is not in sight, I'll blow the house out of sight, too.'"

Captain Driver died on March 3, 1886, and was buried in Nashville's

City Cemetery. Although his grave is not one of the places authorized by Congress where the flag may be flown twenty-four hours a day, the care-takers of Driver's grave fly the flag there night and day in honor of the man who came up with the storied nickname of Old Glory.

Thirteen years before his death, on July 10, 1873, William Driver had given Old Glory to his daughter Mary. "This is my ship-flag Old Glory," he said as he turned the flag over, according to Mary Roland's recollection of the event. "I love it as a mother loves her child; take it and cherish it as I have always cherished it; for it has been my steadfast friend and protector in all parts of the world—savage, heathen and civilized."

Old Glory remained in Mary Roland's possession until December of 1922, when she donated it to Pres. Warren Harding, who turned it over to the Smithsonian. The museum did not put the flag on exhibit, however, be-cause of its fragile condition, its large size—about ten feet by seventeen feet—and because of the Smithsonian's limited conservation budget. After a series of articles on the state of Old Glory appeared in the Nashville *Ten-nessean* newspaper in 1980, four Tennessee American Legion posts and the Tennessee Society of the Daughters of the American Revolution undertook a fund-raising effort for the flag's preservation.

After the money was raised, a team of Smithsonian textile conservators went to work on Old Glory in June 1981. The flag was spread out on a large table and photographed, and a technical analysis was undertaken of the fabric. Then the conservators vacuumed the flag, steamed it to smooth out wrinkles, and removed the backing material. They covered the flag with crepeline, a loosely woven, almost invisible type of silk imported from France that is often used as a backing support for fragile textiles. Old Glory went on public display in a custom-made exhibit case on December 10, 1982, in the Smithsonian's National Museum of American History in Washington where it remains today.

*   *   *

Barbara Frietschie and William Driver made names for themselves during the war for their devotion to the flag. But countless numbers of Union and Confederate soldiers whose names were barely known outside their units risked their lives—and in some cases were killed or wounded—symbolically or physically defending the flag. Many were flag bearers, assigned to carry the American flag and the regimental colors into battle.

All Union infantry regiments had color companies or color guards. The colors were an integral part of the regiments since they were used in battle to mark positions and to serve as morale boosters and rallying points for the troops. Bearing the national colors into battle was considered an honor, and members of the color guards were chosen based on their courage under fire.

Courage was necessary because those who carried the Stars and Stripes — known as color sergeants — went into battle unarmed. Color corporals, who did carry weapons, nominally protected the flag bearers. The corporals had orders, however, not to fire unless the flag itself came under attack. Losing the flag in battle was considered catastrophic. Capturing the enemy's flag was a high honor. On many occasions, more than one color sergeant was killed or wounded in the war's larger engagements. Two Fifth New Hampshire Regiment color sergeants, for example, were

This *Harper's Weekly* cover in 1862 featuring a Thomas Nast drawing of a gallant Union Army color-bearer illustrates how the flag was used in the North to bolster the Civil War effort. *The Library of Congress, Prints and Photographs Division*

severely wounded at the Battle of Fredericksburg, on December 11–13, 1862, and a third sergeant gave up his weapon to fly the flag for the rest of that bloody engagement in which the Union suffered thirteen thousand casualties.

The same was true with Confederate color bearers. On July 1, 1863, for example, on the first day of the Battle of Gettysburg, F. W. Faucette, the color bearer of the Thirteenth North Carolina Regiment, was shot in the right arm during a charge. That arm, "with which he bore the colors, was shivered and almost torn from its socket," said Maj. Gen. John B. Gordon in his war memoir. "Without halting or hesitating, he seized the falling flag in his left hand, and, with his blood spouting from the severed arteries and his right arm dangling in shreds at his side, he still rushed to the front, shouting to his comrades: 'Forward, forward!'"

Union prisoners of war also regularly rallied around the flag. On July 4, 1864, for example, at the Confederate prison camp in Macon, Georgia, a captain from the Eighth New Jersey Volunteers unfurled a small American flag he had hidden in his hat. The other prisoners cheered its appearance and broke into "The Star-Spangled Banner" and "The Battle Cry of Freedom." The American flag, historian Scot Guenter observed, "was a vital symbol for the prisoners, and the telling of such incidents in the North only further contributed to its importance at home."

★   ★   ★

The American flag also had a significant impact among African Americans, both in the North and South, during the Civil War. After 1863, when Lincoln allowed blacks to fight in the Union army, flags became "every bit as central to the wartime experience of African Americans as they were to other Civil War participants," noted the historian Robert E. Bonner. "Despite unequal treatment, black troops entered Union service as citizen-soldiers and as full participants in the flag culture of the Union cause." There were flag presentation ceremonies for the free blacks in the North as they went off to war, just as there were for whites in the North and South. Black women typically presented homemade flags to the departing soldiers just as their white counterparts did.

In South Carolina thousands of former slaves flocked for protection to the Union troops that landed on the island town of Beaufort in late 1861 to anchor the blockade of the ports of Charleston and Savannah, Georgia. A year later black volunteers were accepted in the Union army and formed the First Regiment of South Carolina Volunteers, the first black unit to serve in the war. Their commander, Col. Thomas Higginson, a Harvard-educated Unitarian minister and ardent abolitionist, was white.

Higginson's troops took part in flag-waving rallies late that year and early in 1863. During one such occasion, on December 6, 1862, Cpl. Price Lambkin "brought out one of the few really impressive appeals for the American flag that I have heard," Higginson wrote in his journal. He quoted Lambkin in black dialect speaking of how Southern slave owners who lived under the flag, "got dere wealth under it," and used their slaves to enrich themselves. But as soon as Southerners thought that the flag "mean freedom for we colored people, dey pull it right down and run up de rag ob dere own." Lambkin concluded with a plea to his men never to "desert de ole flag, boys, neber; we had lib under it for eighteen hundred sixty-two years, and we'll die for it now."

During a rally on New Year's Day 1863 — the day that President Lincoln's September 22, 1862, Emancipation Proclamation took effect — Higginson picked up an American flag, "which now for the first time meant anything to these poor people," he said, and began waving it. "There followed," he wrote, "an incident so simple, so touching, so utterly unexpected & startling that I can scarcely believe it when I recall it, though it gave the keynote to the whole day." As Higginson waved the flag, he said, "there suddenly arose, close beside the platform, a strong male voice (but rather cracked and elderly), into which two women's voices instantly blended, singing." The song they sang began with the words: "My country 'tis of thee / Sweet land of Liberty."

The crowd sang along, and Higginson said, "I never saw anything so electric; it made all other words cheap; it seemed the choked voice of a race, at last unloosed." The event marked, he said, "the first flag they had ever seen which promised anything to their people."

The actions of Sgt. William Carney of the Fifty-fourth Massachusetts Colored Regiment at the assault on Fort Wagner, South Carolina, on July 18, 1863, are perhaps the best-known example of an African-American Union soldier's devotion to the flag. During that bloody assault — which is depicted in the 1989 Hollywood film, *Glory* — the unit's flag bearer was wounded, and the twenty-three-year-old Carney dropped his rifle and grabbed the Stars and Stripes before it hit the ground. Carney then was shot in the leg. Despite his wounds, he carried the flag and led the advance on the fort. He hoisted the flag over Fort Wagner and suffered another wound before the battle ended.

On May 25, 1900, William Carney was awarded the Medal of Honor, the military's highest award for valor for "most distinguished gallantry in action." He was the first African American to receive the award. The official citation reads: "When the color sergeant was shot down, this soldier grasped the flag, led the way to the parapet and planted the colors thereon. When the troops fell back, he brought off the flag, under a fierce fire in which he was twice severely wounded."

★   ★   ★

When Robert E. Lee surrendered to Ulysses S. Grant on April 9, 1865, at Appomattox Courthouse in Virginia, the Confederate troops, in addition to their weapons, had orders to surrender their battle flags. The "torn and tattered battle-flags were either leaned against the stacks [of weapons] or laid upon the ground," said Maj. Gen. John B. Gordon, who had risen through the ranks to command the Confederate Second Corps. "Some of the men who had carried and followed those ragged standards through the four long years of strife rushed, regardless of all discipline, from the ranks, bent about their old flags, and pressed them to their lips." Others tore their flags from their staffs, Gordon—who later became Georgia's governor and a U.S. senator—said, "and hid them in their bosoms, as they wet them with burning tears." They "loved those flags," he said, "and will love them forever, as mementos of the unparalleled struggle."

Union Brevet Maj. Gen. Joshua Lawrence Chamberlain of Maine, a veteran of twenty-four battles and a recipient of the Medal of Honor, received the formal surrender. Chamberlain described the scene in similar words. The Confederate soldiers, Chamberlain said, came forward at the end of the surrender ceremonies "reluctantly, with agony of expression." They "tenderly fold their flags, battle-worn and torn, blood-stained, heart-holding colors, and lay them down; some frenziedly rushing from the ranks, kneeling over them, clinging to them, pressing them to their lips with burning tears. And only the Flag of the Union greets the sky!"

★   ★   ★

Five days after the Confederate surrender, on April 14, 1865, Robert Anderson, the commanding officer at Fort Sumter in 1861 who had been promoted to major general, came out of retirement for one reason: to reraise his flag at the South Carolina fort where the war began. Sumter had been under intermittent attack by Union forces from July 1863 to February 1865, when it was retaken. On February 18, 1865, Union troops raised an American flag at the fort, which had suffered extensive damage and had been nearly reduced to rubble.

Edwin M. Stanton, the U.S. Secretary of War, issued an order in Washington on March 27 directing that at twelve noon on April 14, 1865, Anderson "will raise and plant upon the ruins of Fort Sumter, in Charleston Harbor, the same United States flag that floated over the battlements of that fort during the rebel assault" exactly four years before. The order also called for a one-hundred-gun salute and "a national salute from every fort and rebel battery that fired upon Fort Sumter."

On April 14, which happened to be Good Friday, Stanton's orders were carried out. A fleet of U.S. Navy vessels, each decked out in full dress colors, sat in Charleston harbor. A large crowd assembled around the flagstaff at the fort. They sang "Victory at Last" and "The Battle Cry of Freedom." Prayers were read. Then the old flag, Admiral Preble wrote, "was attached to the halyards, when General Anderson, after a brief and touching address, hoisted it to the head of the flag-staff amid loud huzzas, which were followed by singing 'The Star-Spangled Banner.' "

The guns then blazed in salute on land and on the sea. The ceremony ended with an address by Henry Ward Beecher, the prominent Congregational minister who had been an outspoken abolitionist and was one of the nation's most popular orators of the day.

John G. Nicolay, President Lincoln's private secretary who had just been appointed U.S. Consul General to France, was among a large group that had sailed from New York to be among the crowd at Sumter that day. When Nicolay returned to New York, he learned that at about 10:15 p.m. on the day that Anderson's flag was reraised at Sumter Abraham Lincoln had been shot and killed during a performance of the play *Our American Cousin* in his flag-bedecked box at Ford's Theatre.

The box was decorated with two American flags on staffs on each end and two American flags draped as bunting over the box's railings. The regimental flag of the U.S. Treasury Guards hung from a staff attached to the box's center pillar. The Treasury flag played a role in the escape and eventual capture of Lincoln's assassin, John Wilkes Booth.

After Booth shot Lincoln, Union army major Henry Rathbone—a guest of the Lincolns that evening with his fiancée Clara Harris—grappled with Booth. As the actor attempted to jump over the railing toward the stage, he caught the spur of his boot heel on the fringe of the Treasury flag, which came tumbling down. Booth lost his balance and fell nearly twelve feet onto the stage, breaking his left leg in the process.

The end of the Civil War marked another significant step in the evolution of the meaning of the American flag. Although animosities remained in the North and South, the nation once more united under one banner, the Stars and Stripes. In the years that followed, as American unity was slowly re-established, the American flag played an important role in that achievement.

CHAPTER NINE

A Band of Brothers

★　　★　　★

. . . patriotic groups like the Union veterans who formed the Grand Army of the Republic dedicated themselves to gaining mass and official support for everything from anthems to holidays, but most important, they promoted enshrinement of the flag as the nation's most sacred symbol.

— Cecelia Elizabeth O'Leary

ON MARCH 2, 1865, during the waning days of the Civil War, Congress passed and President Lincoln signed into law a measure requiring that the federal government purchase bunting—the lightweight, loosely woven woolen fabric used to make flags—only from American manufacturers. Until then virtually all the bunting that went into flags in this country was imported from England. That law led to the creation of what some called "the first American flag," meaning that it was the first (or among the first) flags made in this country entirely with American-made wool bunting.

That flag was produced by the newly founded United States Bunting Company in Lowell, Massachusetts. Its founder, U.S. army general Benjamin Franklin Butler, is the same General Butler who ordered the execution in 1862 of a man in New Orleans for desecrating the American flag. Butler had been a very prosperous businessman in Lowell before the war. Among other interests, he had purchased the Middlesex Company, a large woolen manufacturer, in 1859. Butler founded U.S. Bunting in 1865 after he played a leading role in lobbying Congress to enact the law requiring American flags used by the government to be made exclusively of domestically produced bunting.

Butler, who was still in the Union army, presented that twelve-by-six-foot first flag, which had thirty-seven stars (in anticipation of the Nebraska Territory's entry into the Union), to President Lincoln on April 11, 1865, two days after Lee's surrender at Appomattox, and four days before Lincoln's death. The stars were arranged in a centered diamond of twenty-seven flanked on both sides by vertical rows of five stars. On February 2, 1866, a large thirty-six-star flag manufactured by U.S. Bunting made of all American materials flew over the Capitol Building in Washington, D.C.

U.S. Bunting was the first factory in this country to develop a process to dye blue bunting successfully. Before 1865, flags were made by sewing strips of red, white, and blue bunting together and then stitching the white stars onto the blue field. DeWitt C. Farrington, the manager and one of Butler's partners at U.S. Bunting, helped develop a new process, known as clamp dyeing. In it, the bunting "is first woven like the old, but in dyeing the stripes, stars, or other designs are colored in the piece so that no sewing is necessary," a *Scientific American* magazine article reported in 1869. In that year, the magazine said, nearly all American flag makers used American-made bunting and the new method of flag making, and "no less than three thousand yards per day are now made at the works of the company."

That was a very good thing, the magazine said. When all of America's flags were made of English bunting, "our national banner was a humiliating witness to our dependence upon the industry of other nations." American genius, the magazine said, had "triumphed over the disabilities which involved such a necessity. Now the American flag may be made of American wool by American labor, and 'long may it wave' over a land independent in deed as well as in name."

In December 1865, nine months after the law requiring all government flags to be made of all-American materials, U.S. Bunting signed a contract with the government to be its sole manufacturer of flags. The company retained that contract until the 1920s, long after Butler died in 1893. "Wherever the flag of the United States flies over government property, either in this country or in the farthest reaches of the world, there the name of the [U.S.] Bunting Company is represented," a 1930 history of Massachusetts industries proclaimed, "inasmuch as the concern makes all the bunting for the United States government which is fashioned into the flags used by the nation."

The Reconstruction period after the Civil War was an era of often bitter antagonism between many white Southerners and the Northerners (known as carpetbaggers), Southern blacks and cooperating Southern whites who administered the state governments of the former Confederacy. But that bitterness did not, in general, spill over to feelings about the American flag. While it was by no means universal, a large majority of Southerners, including veterans of the Confederate army, figuratively pledged their allegiance to the Stars and Stripes after the Civil War ended. Some, echoing the feelings expressed by Jefferson Davis in 1861, played down the fact that the flag had been the emblem of the Confederacy's enemy during the Civil War and concentrated on the flag as a symbol of the Revolutionary War. Some white political leaders took a pragmatic route, embracing the American flag in an effort to try to secure a place for themselves at the table in national affairs.

Many acts of reconciliation involving the flag took place in the months and years after the war. Sometimes the respect came grudgingly. On May 16,1865, for example, when the Stars and Stripes was officially raised in Atlanta to honor President Lincoln, it was immediately lowered. At other times the respect was fulsomely displayed. At the annual Charleston, South Carolina, fire department parade on April 27, 1867, for example, the city's fire chief noticed that the American flag was conspicuously absent among the many banners on display. He stopped the parade, found a flag, and displayed it prominently. "Every person in the column readily and cheerfully saluted it by lifting his hat or cap in passing," Admiral Preble reported.

⋆   ⋆   ⋆

One of the clearest examples of the widespread respect for the Stars and Stripes in the South took place beginning in January 1868 when Union veteran Gilbert H. Bates, acting on a bet, undertook a now almost-forgotten, amazing, four-month, fourteen-hundred-mile trek on foot through the old Confederacy carrying an American flag. Bates, a former sergeant in the First Wisconsin Heavy Artillery, was a shopkeeper in Edgerton, Wisconsin. He believed that such a journey would be met with a warm reception. Fellow Civil War veterans thought otherwise, claiming that Southerners felt nothing but antipathy for the American flag and would attack anyone— especially a former Union soldier—who dared to display it.

Bates undertook what some called his "star-spangled march" to try to prove them wrong. "Bates is to carry the flag unfurled," the marching orders he and his fellow veterans drew up, said, "except at night, during storms, or when eating but is not to pass through cities or collections of people with it furled. He is to travel only during the day time; to be always unarmed, to go on foot; not to employ anybody to protect him; may employ one person as a guide when necessary; if any parties choose voluntarily to escort him, they are at liberty to do so."

Bates went South without a dime in his pocket, wearing old farmer's clothes. He said he would sell photographs of himself for twenty-five cents along his route and would turn the proceeds over to a fund for Civil War widows and orphans of soldiers from both sides of the conflict. Telegraph operators reported his progress to newspapers across the country.

Mark Twain, the great American humorist and writer, made light of Bates's endeavor. Bates, Twain predicted late in January, "will get more black eyes down there among those unconstructed rebels than he can ever carry along with him without breaking his back." Twain said he expected to see Bates "coming into Washington some day on one leg and with one eye out and an arm gone. He won't amount to more than an interesting relic by the time he gets here and then he will have to hire out for a sign for the Anatomical Museum." Southerners, Twain, said, "have no sentiment in them. They won't buy his picture. They will be more likely to take his scalp."

Whether Twain was being satirical or not, his prediction was completely wrong. At the thirty-year-old Bates's first stop, in war-ravaged Vicksburg, Mississippi, he received a warm welcome from the mayor and the town's leading citizens. A group of women made him an American flag, which replaced the tattered regimental Stars and Stripes Bates had brought with him from Wisconsin. As Bates began his march out of Vicksburg, the mayor and the town councilmen escorted him on horseback, along with a brass band, and townspeople along the route cheered him heartily.

Bates met similarly warm receptions throughout his trek, in small towns and large cities. "Joyful multitudes everywhere hail his advance as though it were the advance of an Emperor," a *New York Times* editorial said. People invited Bates into their homes and offered food and shelter. Strangers gave him warm clothing to fight off the cold weather. Bates received a hero's reception in Jackson, Mississippi, where he gave a speech and waved his flag from the balcony of the state capitol. In Meridian, Mississippi, he was paraded through the streets. Bates received a welcoming reception as he marched through Alabama and even when he waved the Stars and Stripes in Montgomery, Alabama, the first capital of the Confederacy.

The story was the same as the Union veteran made his way through Georgia, South and North Carolina, and Virginia, receiving nothing but an outpouring of Southern hospitality from women, children, and former Confederate soldiers all along his route. Welcoming cannon fire and five hundred people greeted him at the end of his Southern sojourn when Bates arrived in Virginia's capital, Richmond, on April 8. After checking into a hotel, Bates jogged to the State Capitol Building, where the Confederate Congress once met—and which Thomas Jefferson designed—and waved his American flag to the cheers of a large crowd that had gathered in an adjoining park.

Bates again received a hero's welcome when he arrived in Washington, D.C., on April 14, three years after the Stars and Stripes had been reraised at Fort Sumter. A large crowd and a brass band ushered him to the White House where Pres. Andrew Johnson greeted Bates on the front steps and took him into the East Room. When Johnson and Bates came out of the White House, the band broke into a rendition of "The Star-Spangled Banner."

Bates intended next to plant his flag on the Capitol dome. When he arrived on Capitol Hill with a crowd of followers, however, police officers would not permit him to enter the building because he didn't have the proper authorization from the House of Representatives' Sergeant-at-Arms. Bates and his followers then decided to plant the flag at the Washington Monument, but were thwarted again when, after arriving on the Monument grounds, they couldn't find a halyard. So they took his flag to his hotel, the Metropolitan, where it was placed on public exhibit.

Bates's American flag journey was more than a footnote to history. It proved that the Stars and Stripes could be a healing, all-American symbol during the difficult days of Reconstruction. As the *New York Times* put it, if those who were skeptical of Bates's reception "would start out a-marching with their waving flags, as the Sergeant has done, they would render their country a better service than by staying at home and growling at the rebels."

After his Southern tour, Gilbert Bates tried to make a living out of displaying the national colors. But he was less than successful in turning his goodwill triumph into a paying profession. During the summer of 1868, Bates charged admission for flag-waving personal appearances at venues such as the Holiday Street Theatre in Baltimore, a Civil War veterans' convention, and at the New York Democratic Party Convention. At the latter event Bates met "no recognition whatever on the part of the delegates," one observer said, "and after hiding a few moments behind the rostrum celebrities, he groped his way unattended and unnoticed out of the hall."

Bates did have personal—if not financial—success in a second flag-bearing pilgrimage in 1872. That year, probably as the result of another bet, Bates went overseas, where he set out on another star-spangled walking tour, this time from Gretna Green in Scotland to London. He had the same goal: to show that the British people harbored no ill will against the

reunited United States since the English ruling class had strongly sympa-
thized with the South during the Civil War. His reception in Scotland and
England mirrored what he had found four years earlier in the old Confederacy; adoring crowds and spontaneous celebrations greeted him wherever he went.

When Bates arrived in London, "the populace of England were wild in
their demonstrations," a *Philadelphia Times* reporter said. As he "stood up in
a magnificent carriage drawn by six beautiful dapple gray horses, the
turnout elegantly festooned with American and British flags, he was the
lion of the day, and all London turned to gaze upon the eccentric American
soldier . . . So enthusiastic and excited were the populace of London, that
when Bates appeared upon the scene they seemed to lose all control over
themselves."

In 1878 Bates conceived of a second Southern trip for the summer of
1880 — one it appears he did not undertake — to carry an American flag
containing the names of all the Republican candidates throughout the
South. In the summer of 1881, a reporter tracked Bates down in the central
Illinois town of Saybrook. Bates, who appeared to be drinking heavily,
lived in a "miserable, tumble-down looking sort of a house," the reporter
said. "He was a lantern-jawed and sallow-faced, hungry looking sort of a
fellow" who wore "an old pair of dilapidated boots, which were, like the
wearer, run down at the heel." He "continually dwells on the flag business,
and he never seems to tire of talking of his trips through the South and
England."

Sergeant Bates seemingly pulled himself out of that stupor a few years
later. In 1883 Buffalo Bill Cody hired Bates to appear in his Stars-and-
Stripes-bedecked Wild West Show. Not surprisingly, Buffalo Bill hired
Bates to be the flamboyant show's flag bearer.

★   ★   ★

Another act in the postwar period that might be considered in the reconciliation category was the issuance in 1869 of the first American postage stamp
containing an image of the American flag. It was a thirty-cent stamp with a
ferocious-looking eagle perched atop a shield, flanked on both sides by the
Stars and Stripes. Other U.S. postage stamps issued that year contained images of Benjamin Franklin, George Washington, Abraham Lincoln, Christopher Columbus, the signing of the Declaration of Independence, and the
Pony Express.

★   ★   ★

Union veterans of the Civil War, who began to organize on an unprecedented scale almost immediately after the shooting stopped in the spring of
1865, turned into a social force that propelled the movement known as the
"cult of the flag" into full flower by the end of the nineteenth century. These
groups had several functions. They started as social and fraternal organizations. They then began helping needy veterans and their families and lobbying the federal and state governments for veterans' programs. By the
1890s, the veterans' groups had become potent political entities, focusing
on veterans issues and flag-waving patriotism.

The nation's first veterans' organization, the Order of Cincinnati, also
known as the Society of the Cincinnati, was formed in 1783 and was made
up of officers who fought in the Revolution. Two veterans' groups formed
after the War of 1812 mainly to lobby for pensions. The Aztec Club of 1847,
a group of Mexican War officers, was primarily a social organization.

The American veterans' movement came into its own following the Civil
War. The two-day, flag-bedecked Grand Review of Union troops victory
parade in Washington, D.C., on May 23 and 24, 1865, was a precursor of
sorts of the soon-to-be powerful movement. Some 150,000 soldiers from
Gen. George Meade's Army of the Potomac and Gen. William Tecumseh
Sherman's Army of Georgia and the Army of the Tennessee marched
through the nation's capital on those two days.

The marches ended at a presidential reviewing stand in front of the
White House bedecked with Stars-and-Stripes bunting and over which
flew a huge American flag. The city, still mourning President Lincoln's as-
sassination, did not go all out during those two days in the flag-display department however. Some citizens did display flags, floral arches, banners,
and bunting; but many buildings were still draped with black crepe. In a
matter of days following the march the two huge armies disbanded.

Soon after, the first Civil War veterans' groups were born. They included the Union Veteran Legion, the Veteran Brotherhood, the Veterans'
Rights Union, the Society of the Army of the Cumberland, and the Society
of the Army of Ohio. Gen. John A. Logan of Illinois organized the Society
of the Army of the Tennessee in August 1865. A veteran of the Mexican
War, a lawyer, and a member of Congress, Logan had become one of the
top Union generals in the Civil War, serving under Gen. U. S. Grant at
Vicksburg. In 1866 Logan, a Democrat before the war, was elected as a

Republican to Congress. That year he also helped found by far the largest and most influential Civil War veterans' group, the Grand Army of the Republic, an organization that spearheaded the movement to spread the cult of the flag across the country.

The GAR was open to all honorably discharged veterans—officers and enlisted men—who served in the Union army between April 12, 1861, and April 9, 1865. Logan served as the GAR's commander in chief for four terms beginning 1868. The first of what would become thousands of local GAR posts formed on April 6, 1866, in Decatur, Illinois.

The GAR soon far eclipsed all the other veterans' groups. Within three months, thirty-nine posts formed in Illinois alone. Then the GAR went nationwide rapidly. Ten states and the District of Columbia sent delegations to its first national convention—called an encampment because many members bedded down in tents—in Indianapolis on November 20. The flag-bedecked encampments took place annually beginning in 1867 on the state and national levels.

The Grand Army of the Republic's motto was "Fraternity, Charity and Loyalty." Its posts offered fraternity among fellow Union veterans; charity for needy veterans, widows, and orphans of veterans; and steadfast loyalty to the United States in the form of ardent, flag-waving patriotism. Working on the local level, GAR posts helped found veterans' homes and lobbied for veterans' issues. The group soon became a powerful social and political force in the country. GAR posts helped build memorials to Union veterans across the country and helped preserve Civil War sites and artifacts, including regimental and national flags. GAR state departments and the national organization led the late-nineteenth-century movement to have flags flown at all the nation's schools and to teach schoolchildren to venerate and respect the flag. GAR members also worked to have the Stars and Stripes displayed in the nation's churches.

The GAR was primarily responsible for creating an American institution of which the American flag is an integral part, Memorial Day. Springtime cemetery ceremonies honoring those who died in the Civil War had taken place in the South during the war. In 1866, the year after the war ended, such ceremonies also took place in cities in the North and the South. On April 25, 1866, in Columbus, Mississippi, for example, a group of local women placed flowers on the Friendship Cemetery graves of Confederate and Union soldiers who had perished at the nearby 1862 Battle of Shiloh. The Ladies Memorial Association of Petersburg, Virginia, which was formed on May 6 of that year, set aside June 9—the anniversary of the 1864 Siege of

Petersburg—as an annual Memorial Day to honor the men of the Petersburg militia. On May 5 the citizens of Waterloo, New York, honored their Civil War dead with a city-wide commemoration in which businesses closed for one hour, flags flew at half staff, and townspeople decorated the graves of Union soldiers with flowers, wreaths, and crosses.

Similar ceremonies took place throughout the spring of 1866 in Macon and Columbus, Georgia; Richmond, Virginia; Boalsburg, Pennsylvania; and Carbondale, Illinois. After Mary Simmerson Cunningham Logan, the wife of John Logan, had visited Petersburg in March 1868 and learned of the annual observance there, General Logan issued a general order on May 5 to all GAR chapters. The order instructed the chapters to set aside May 30, 1868, as Decoration Day, a day to remember the Union dead by placing flowers on their graves. Historians believe that Logan chose May 30 because flowers generally are in bloom throughout the country at that time.

"The 30th of May, 1868," General Order No. 11 said, "is designated for the purpose of strewing with flowers, or otherwise decorating the graves of comrades who died in defense of their country during the late rebellion, and whose bodies now lie in almost every city, village and hamlet churchyard in the land." The order prescribed no specific ceremony, advising local GAR posts "in their own way, [to] arrange such fitting services and testimonial of respect as circumstances may permit."

Along with garlanding graves with "choicest flowers of springtime," the order also said: "let us raise above them the dear old flag they saved."

"The most notable act of [Logan's] administration, indeed of any [GAR] administration was the order . . . designating May 30 as Memorial Day," Maj. George S. Merrill, GAR commander in chief from 1881 to 1882, said in 1890. "To the bright offerings of springtime the Grand Army has very generally added the flag in miniature. . . . Through the months of summer the tiny flag is kissed by the breezes as it marks the resting place of one of the nation's dead."

The first formal, official observance of Decoration Day took place on May 30, 1868, at the National Cemetery in Arlington, Virginia. General and Mrs. U. S. Grant and other officials, including congressman James A. Garfield, opened the ceremonies with speeches from the verandah of Robert E. Lee's former house overlooking the cemetery. GAR members then decorated graves, both Union and Confederate, with flowers.

In subsequent years Decoration Day was commemorated in many different ways. In some communities ceremonies were held at schools featuring visits by war veterans who wore their uniforms and told war stories.

Many cities held parades in which flag-waving veterans led marches to local cemeteries where they decorated graves and photographs were taken of the soldiers posing with American flags. In some communities flags and military insignia were placed at soldiers' graves along with flowers.

"Patriotic color," the historian Robert E. Bonner noted, "was a centerpiece of commemorative [Memorial Day] activities" after the Civil War. Bonner and others have argued that the use of flags at Memorial Day commemorations paved the way for the outpouring of American flags following national tragedies such as the September 11, 2001, terrorist acts. Memorial Day flag rituals "perpetuated what would become an instinctive reliance on flags to give solace during times of national tragedy," Bonner said.

In 1873, New York became the first state to make Decoration Day a holiday; many other states soon followed suit. The GAR lobbied successfully in 1882 to have the holiday renamed Memorial Day, although many continued to call it Decoration Day because of the occasion's grave-decoration origins. After World War I the commemoration was broadened to honor those who perished in all American wars. Since 1971 it has been celebrated on the last Monday in May.

The nation's official Memorial Day ceremony takes place at Arlington National Cemetery across the Potomac River from Washington, D.C. It features speeches, veterans' organization color guards, and the laying of a wreath at the Tomb of the Unknowns. Beginning in the late 1950s, the American flag has played a prominent role in the Arlington National Cemetery Memorial Day commemoration. In the early morning hours of the Friday before Memorial Day, the twelve hundred soldiers of "the Old Guard," the Third U.S. Infantry Regiment that guards the Tomb of the Unknowns, place small American flags on every one of the more than 280,000 gravestones at the nation's largest cemetery, a task that takes about three hours to complete. The Old Guard then mounts a twenty-four-hour guard for the balance of the Memorial Day weekend to make sure the flags remain in place.

CHAPTER TEN

The Hundredth
Anniversary

★   ★   ★

you, mottled Flag I love

— Walt Whitman, *Leaves of Grass*, 1891–92

THE AMERICAN FLAG played a prominent role in the Centennial year of 1876 as Americans celebrated the nation's evolution into a world power and looked back with pride on one hundred years of independence. Individual flag makers around the nation used the occasion to create a wide variety of unique celebratory flags, many of which included the dates "1776" or "1786." One popular flag had both dates spelled out with stars in the canton. Others contained the word "Centennial," typically nestled among the strips. Some Centennial flags had thirteen stars to commemorate the original states. Most had thirty-seven stars, the official number, arrayed in various patterns.

Some businesses used the occasion of the Centennial to create advertisements incorporating the flag. The Baltimore & Ohio (B&O) Railroad, for example, produced an ad that consisted of a waving thirty-eight star flag. The words "Go to the Centennial via the Baltimore and Ohio R.R. and Washington City" were printed in blue capital letters on the white stripes. In addition to a fanciful arrangement of the stars, the canton contained the date "1876" in gold, along with a golden wreath and red ribbon.

Many flags celebrated Colorado's entry into the Union on August 1, 1876, by adding a thirty-eighth star. Others contained thirty-nine stars in the mistaken belief that two states would be added that year. As it turned out, there never was an official thirty-nine-star flag. That's because four states—North and South Dakota, Montana, and Washington—came into the Union in 1889 and Idaho became a state on July 3, 1890. So the official flag changed from thirty-eight stars on July 4, 1877, to forty-three stars on July 4, 1890.

Officials made plans all across the country to usher in 1876 with lavish ceremonies that prominently featured the Stars and Stripes. In San Francisco, for example, Mayor A. J. Bryant issued a proclamation calling for the flag to be "displayed on all public buildings, places of amusement and business, and on the shipping in the harbor, from sunrise to sunset" on New Year's morning. The city of Philadelphia put on an elaborate celebration on New Year's Eve. At the stroke of midnight Mayor William S. Stokley ushered in the New Year by raising the Continental Colors over the old State Capitol Building. The city then erupted with the ringing of church bells, the firing of cannons, and a massive fireworks display.

The City of Brotherly Love played host later that year to the mammoth Centennial Exhibition, a world's fair officially known as the International Exhibition of Arts, Manufactures and Products of the Soil and Mine. It opened on May 10 at Fairmount Park. Before it closed six months later some nine million people had entered the turnstiles to take in the fair. The American flag was one of the most prominent features of the Centennial Exhibition. Hundreds were displayed on the exhibition's buildings, including four eleven-by-eighteen-foot flags at the main entrance of the enormous Main Exhibition Hall, which covered twenty acres and was the largest building in the world in 1876. Popular souvenir items included paper hand fans decorated with American flags. "No one," the noted writer and critic William Dean Howells said, "can see the fair without a thrill of patriotic pride."

Thirty-seven nations took part in the exhibition, which showcased American culture and the emergence of the United States as a thriving industrial world power. The *Philadelphia Public Ledger* called the May 10 opening-day ceremonies "the grandest ever witnessed in America." Whether or not it was the grandest, the ceremonies certainly were impressive. Pres. U. S. Grant presided, addressing a huge, boisterous crowd. At the end of his welcoming speech, Grant declared the exhibition officially open, and as he did, hundreds of flags were unfurled throughout the grounds and an orchestra and a thousand-voice choir performed the "Hallelujah Chorus."

The city of Philadelphia decked itself out in American flags and red, white, and blue bunting for the fair's opening. "All the public buildings, many stores, and private residences had the American colors floating from the house-tops or windows, and some were profusely decorated with small flags," the *New York Times* reported on May 11. "Broadway looked as though it had been prepared for the entry of a triumphal procession. The City Hall, the shipping in the harbor, and all the ferry-boats were gayly decorated with bunting."

The Trans-Continental Hotel, near the fairgrounds, a *Philadelphia Public Ledger* reporter wrote, "is brightened up by numbers of flags, which hang from its many windows and flutter in the breeze." The nearby Globe Hotel also was "decorated with the National colors," the newspaper reported. Restaurants and small hotels also flew "banners and flags in profusion," as did the Pennsylvania Railroad depot.

Inside the fair grounds one of the most popular attractions was an enormous "Origin of Our Flag" exhibit in the U.S. Government Building. That exhibit traced the history of the American flag using an elaborate display of some two dozen historic banners, including the Union Jack, early colonial flags, and the Continental Colors. The building itself was decorated with American flags and bunting inside and out.

* * *

In the celebratory and patriotic climate of the year 1876, several specious stories dealing with the American flag were promulgated and widely accepted. Some persist to this day. That year saw the publication, for example, of *Washington: A Drama in Five Acts*, a drama in verse by the popular English poet Martin Farquhar Tupper. In it Benjamin Franklin proclaims that the design of the Stars and Stripes was based on the coat of arms of George Washington. "We, and not he—it was unknown to him," Franklin says, "took up his coat of arms, and multiplied and magnified it every way to this, our glorious national banner."

The play was widely performed, and its false message resonated with the American public. The story was repeated many times, including regularly in the popular children's magazine *St. Nicholas*. In 1882, for example, the magazine published "The Origin of the Stars and Stripes," an article by Edward W. Tuffley, which was later reproduced in booklet form. In the article and booklet, Tuffley described his visit in the 1860s to the church in Brington, in Northhamptonshire, England, where George Washington's forefathers worshipped.

"On passing down the middle aisle of the church the parish clerk called our attention to the memorial brass plate of the Washingtons,'" Tuffley wrote, pointing out that the plate "bears the arms of the family—the Stars and Stripes."

"Do you mean to say," Tuffley quoted himself as responding, "that the family arms of the Washingtons were the Stars and Stripes?"

"Certainly they were," the clerk replied. He went on to tell Tuffley that a monument to a Washington family member "has the Stars and Stripes on, too."

While the Washington family coat of arms has two horizontal stripes and three red stars, there is no evidence whatsoever that it was the basis for the flag's design. Nevertheless, Tupper's apocryphal tale set in motion a myth that still is reported as the truth today.

Another flag falsehood that gained widespread currency in the Centennial period centered around a twelve-star flag that was billed as the banner that flew on John Paul Jones's *Bonhomme Richard*. That flag, which was shot down during the famed "I have not yet begun to fight" battle in September 1779 was said to have been saved from the sea by the daring act of James Bayard Stafford, a seaman on the ship. Stafford's family claimed that Congress's Maritime Committee had bestowed the flag on him in 1784 as a reward for his meritorious service.

The flag surfaced during the Civil War when Stafford's daughter, Sarah Smith Stafford, allowed it to be used at U.S. Sanitary Commission fundraising events. She later cut off a piece of the flag and presented it to President Lincoln. The flag was displayed at the Philadelphia Centennial Exhibition in 1876 and described as John Paul Jones's flag from the *Bonhomme Richard*. After Sarah Stafford's death in 1880, her brother Samuel Bayard Stafford and his wife inherited it. They took the flag to the 1887 national encampment of the Grand Army of the Republic where it was billed as "the first Stars and Stripes ever made."

The family donated the flag to Pres. William McKinley, who turned it over to the Smithsonian Institution in Washington. Although some flag experts and historians expressed doubts about the flag's authenticity, the Smithsonian exhibited it as John Paul Jones's flag until the 1930s. That's when Georgetown University history professor George Tansill examined the flag, determined it was a fraud and the museum withdrew it from public display.

Another widely viewed object exhibited at the Centennial Exhibition in Philadelphia also presented a false picture of the American flag: Ohio artist

Archibald M. Willard's *The Spirit of '76*, originally titled *Yankee Doodle*. Willard, whose grandfather had served with the Green Mountain Boys in the Revolutionary War, was a color bearer in the Civil War with the Eighty-sixth Ohio Regiment. Before the war he had worked in a wagon and carriage shop in Wellington, Ohio, painting peddlers' wagons with landscapes and images of animal heads.

After the war Willard turned to canvas and created several paintings of Civil War scenes. The artist began what his business partner James F. Ryder called his "greatest achievement and his crowning success" in 1875 at his studio in Cleveland specifically for the Centennial Exhibition. Willard "was deeply stirred by the impulse to do something to mark the great event," Ryder said. "He wished to express in a painting for publication the highest sense of patriotic fervor."

Willard gave a somewhat different account of the painting's genesis. "The centennial year was approaching and Mr. Ryder and I agreed that that year ought to be made memorable and financially profitable by a humorous picture," Willard said in a 1912 interview. "The title 'Yankee Doodle' suggested itself and I set to work to make a picture to fit the title." After he began the painting, however, Willard changed his mind about the humorous nature of the work. Something "of self-condemnation came over me that I had ever treated this theme as a humorous one," he explained.

The inspiration for the oil painting came from patriotic parades Willard had witnessed growing up in small Ohio towns. "I had boyhood memories of a country Fourth of July celebration, in which the local musicians bore their conspicuous share," he said. "There was a 'three-fingered Dick'; who tossed the drumsticks. . . . I made him the central figure."

The Spirit of '76 depicts three heroic figures: a drummer boy in a tricorner hat; a hatless older man—the central figure—with a drum who slightly resembles George Washington but was based on Willard's father; and a fife player with a white headband. They are resolutely marching in step, clouds of smoke from a battle hovering over them, as they pass a wounded soldier raising himself on his elbow in salute.

Behind them is a Continental Army flag bearer. He is flying the "Betsy Ross" flag, with thirteen stars arrayed in a circle in the canton. "The man who had carried the Stars and Stripes," Ryder said, "marching under the same thrilling tune, put his heart into the picture."

Ryder first exhibited the painting in the window of his Cleveland art gallery. It caused an immediate sensation. "The crowds which gathered about it blockaded the entrance to the gallery and obstructed the sidewalk" so much, Ryder said, that he was forced to move the painting to the back of the store, where it was on view for several days. During that time, he said, "all business in the store was discontinued on account of the crowds, which filled the place."

Ryder and Willard then took the painting to Philadelphia, where it was displayed prominently at Memorial Hall, the Centennial Exhibition's art gallery, and the only significant building from the 1876 fair that still stands today. "It was a life-size canvas, and hung on the line and crowds thronged it day after day," Willard said. Ryder created chromolithographs of the painting to promote the exhibit. He sold hundreds of thousands of them. After the fair ended, the painting was exhibited for several weeks at the Old South Meeting House in Boston. It then went on to Washington, Chicago, San Francisco, and other cities, "so great was the desire of the public to see the painting, which had such welcome in the hearts of patriotic people," as Ryder put it. *The Spirit of '76*, he said, "stirred the heart of a nation."

The fact that the Continental Army, as we have noted, did not fly the Stars and Stripes had seemingly no effect on the extremely positive public reaction to the painting. The continuing widespread popularity of *The Spirit of '76* to the present day has had the unintended side effect of contributing to the commonly held misconception that Washington's army defeated the British under the Stars and Stripes.

The Centennial era, too, saw the widespread acceptance of the Betsy Ross myth, which began in 1870 with the speech by her grandson William Canby at the Historical Society of Pennsylvania. The story was in widespread circulation as Betsy Ross's popularity zoomed in the 1880s and 1890s, as we noted in chapter 3.

★ ★ ★

Americans celebrated the centennial Fourth of July with particularly profuse displays of the Stars and Stripes. New York City, for example, was ablaze in American flags and bunting. The Bowery's "exhibition of patriotism is of the most effusive sort," the *New York Times* reported. "There is not an undecorated building it its entire length." On Canal Street, "nearly every one of [the] large furniture warehouses is crowded to its utmost capacity with emblems of various kinds." In Los Angeles, bunting and flags "were liberally used" throughout the city that day, "a triple arch adorned Main Street; statues of national heroes and pictures of Washington bedecked the town, and . . . a truly typical American Fourth of July procession of the Victorian epoch paraded through the streets. . . ."

Fifteen thousand men, including five thousand Union veterans marching with the Grand Army of the Republic, paraded through Philadelphia's streets in a nighttime Independence Day celebration. "The streets over which the procession passed were crowded with spectators, and at many points hearty applause was bestowed," the *Philadelphia Public Ledger* reported. The American flag was very much in evidence, as were old battle flags, proudly carried by GAR members from posts in Pennsylvania, New Jersey, and other states. One of the oldest was the Eutaw flag, a rough-hewn banner of crimson cloth that William Washington flew at the Revolutionary War battles of Cowpens and Eutaw Springs.

A group of those veterans that day founded a new organization, the Centennial Legion of Historical Military Commands. Its founders, Maj. George W. McLean of New York and Capt. Robert C. Gilchrist of South Carolina, fought on opposite sides in the Civil War. Their new organization, which still exists today, was formed to keep alive the memory of the military organizations that served in the Revolutionary War. Part of its mission was fostering patriotism; one of its primary objectives was teaching respect for the American flag.

A patriotic group called the Sons of Revolutionary Sires also was organized on the Centennial Fourth of July in San Francisco. That group became the first state society of the organization that came to be known as the National Society of the Sons of the American Revolution, which incorporated fourteen years later, in 1890, in Connecticut. The SAR, which remains active today, formed to honor the memory of those who fought in the Revolutionary War. Membership is open only to descendants of those who served in the American military in that war or otherwise fought the British during the conflict.

The seeds for the name of Flagstaff, Arizona, were sowed on July 4, 1876, when Thomas F. McMillan and a group of settlers from Boston raised the Stars and Stripes in that northern Arizona town at the base of the San Francisco Peaks. The town had been named Agassiz by a group of settlers from Boston, known as the First Boston Party, when they had laid out the town's plan three months earlier. Local lore holds that those men had raised an American flag on a flagpole they had fashioned by stripping the branches off a pine tree growing near their camp.

The Tennessee-born McMillan, known as the father of Flagstaff, had started a sheep ranch at about the same time in Antelope Valley just north of the city. His cabin there was the first structure built in the town. On the Fourth of July, 1876, McMillan and the Bostonians who camped out in his corral, known as the Second Boston Party, decided to do something special to celebrate the nation's one-hundredth birthday. So they reputedly cut down a pine tree, stripped off its limbs and bark, mounted it on the cabin, and attached an American flag to it. McMillan's spread thereafter became known as Flag Staff Ranch. In 1881, the town officially changed its name to Flagstaff.

As many as twenty thousand people turned out for the Fourth of July parade on Gay Street in Knoxville, Tennessee, on July 4, 1876. One of the highlights of that big celebration was the ride by some two hundred horsemen across the Tennessee River where they displayed a silk American flag with the words "South America"—the nickname for the South Knoxville section of the city—embroidered on it. In Portland, Oregon, a Mexican War veteran named Thomas S. Mountain unfurled a huge, forty-foot by eighty-foot American flag that day on a two-hundred-foot flagpole. Mountain, a former gold miner, paid $365 for the enormous flag.

★   ★   ★

The nation did not go all-out to celebrate the one-hundredth anniversary of the First Flag Resolution of June 14, 1777. Congress took note of the occasion and asked that the flag be flown on all public buildings that day, and remembrances took place in several cities. The biggest celebration took place in Boston. The "flag," Admiral Preble wrote, "was displayed from all the public buildings, from the shipping in the harbor, and numerous private buildings were ornamented with bunting and miniature flags." A celebratory cannon was fired at noon at Boston Common.

A well-attended rally took place that evening at the historic Old South Meeting House, where the Boston Tea Party began, presided over by Boston mayor Frederick O. Prince. The original Star-Spangled Banner made a rare public appearance and "The Star-Spangled Banner" was performed with "the audience joining in the chorus," Preble said.

That event was not named but it is now viewed as the first Flag Day celebration held in this country. Flag Day would not be officially recognized by Congress and the president until 1949.

CHAPTER ELEVEN

The Golden Age of Fraternity

★   ★   ★

The American people "regard the flag as a symbol of their country's power and prestige, and will be impatient if any open disrespect is shown towards it."

—**U.S. Supreme Court justice John Harlan, 1907**

S OMETIMES REFERRED TO as the "Golden Age of Fraternity," the 1880s and early 1890s saw the emergence of scores of patriotic, veterans, hereditary, and fraternal organizations, many of which took a keen interest in promoting the American flag. Most of the groups established national organizations, augmented with affiliated groups in the states.

The Grand Army of the Republic underwent a remarkable rebirth during those two decades, both in numbers of members and in its influence on patriotic matters, including encouraging veneration of the American flag. GAR membership had dropped during the 1870s to some twenty-seven thousand adherents nationwide. By 1890, however, membership soared to a peak of more than four hundred thousand in some seven thousand local posts in small and large towns and cities.

GAR posts were set up in all the states that remained loyal to the Union, in the states that came into the Union after the war, and even in most of the former states of the Confederacy. Virtually every prominent Union veteran of the Civil War joined the Grand Army of the Republic. That included five U.S. presidents: U. S. Grant, Rutherford B. Hayes, James Garfield, Benjamin Harrison, and William McKinley.

Former GAR commander in chief George S. Merrill characterized the rapid growth of the organization in the 1880s and 1890s as "the most con-spicuous and convincing monument of patriotism which American pos-sesses." Merrill called GAR members "the survivors of the grandest army the word has ever seen," who were "animated alone by a sprit of loyalty to liberty and a devotion to the flag." In addition to its work memorializing the war effort and its charitable acts, the GAR, Merrill said, "inculcates lessons of gratitude and awakens the sweet sympathies and patriotic impulses of the whole people."

The GAR's devotion to the Stars and Stripes was most visible at parades and at the state and national encampments. Old and new flags were promi-nently and profusely displayed at the encampments, where veterans rever-ently saluted them. During the Twenty-sixth National GAR Encampment in Washington, D.C., in September 1892, for example, the nation's capital was "dressed in flags from the dome of the Capitol, where four great banners float under the feet of the Goddess of Liberty, to the humblest negro cabin, with its tiny cotton streamers," according to one newspaper account.

GAR parades also were flag-saturated occasions. "American flags flut-tered everywhere" during the Thirty-seventh National GAR Encampment parade in August 1903 in San Francisco, a newspaper in that city noted, "from hundreds of street poles, from tops of buildings, from innumerable windows, and from tens of thousands of right hands raised in tribute" to the marching Union veterans.

In 1897 one observer estimated that some 5.4 million Americans belonged to secret, fraternal orders—about one in eight adult males. That did not in-clude the 400,000-plus members of the GAR and other veterans and military groups. The newly formed organizations included patriotic groups that worked to foster an appreciation of the nation's history by supporting historic preservation, love of country, and respect for and adoration of the American flag. The most active were hereditary societies that looked to the American Revolution for inspiration: the Sons of the Revolution, the Colonial Dames of America, the Society of Colonial Wars, the Sons of the American Revolution (SAR), and the Daughters of the American Revolution (DAR).

The General Society of the Sons of the Revolution (SR), which first came together in Washington, D.C., in 1876, incorporated in New York in 1884, and began organizing state societies in the early 1890s. A women's group, the National Society of the Colonial Dames of America, was established in 1891 in Philadelphia. The American Society of Colonial Wars, which organized in 1892, became the General Society of Colonial Wars in 1893. The National So-ciety of the Sons of the American Revolution (SAR, which was not affiliated with the SR) was formally established on April 30, 1889, the one hundredth anniversary of George Washington's first inauguration. The National Society received a charter from Congress on June 6, 1906 signed by Pres. Theodore Roosevelt, himself an SAR member.

The SAR, which had allowed women to join, changed its policy in 1890 and admitted only men. That led to the founding on October 11, 1890, of the women-only Daughters of the American Revolution. The DAR offered membership to women who were directly descended from someone who fought in the Revolutionary War. The organization grew steadily in power and influence in the 1890s and received a congressional charter on December 2, 1896. By the turn of the twentieth century, the DAR had more than thirty thousand members and some five hundred local chapters. The DAR's mission included working for the establishment of patriotic holidays and for "the enshrinement of the flag as the nation's most sacred symbol," as the historian Cecilia Elizabeth O'Leary put it.

The Grand Army of the Republic had several affiliated groups. The largest and most influential was the Woman's Relief Corps, which formed in July 1883. The Woman's Relief Corps still exists and has as its mission to perpetuate the GAR's memory and to promote patriotism, which includes, as the organization puts it, "the love and honor of our flag."

★   ★   ★

The patriotic and veterans groups threw their support, beginning in the late 1880s, behind the movement to make June 14 a national holiday in honor of the first Flag Resolution of 1777, which became law that day. The first call for what would become known as Flag Day had come in 1861. On June 8, less than two months after the Civil War began, Charles Dudley Warner, the editor of the *Hartford Evening Press*, wrote an editorial calling for two new American holidays, Constitution Day on September 17, and Flag Day on June 14. Flags flew in Connecticut on June 14, 1861, and there was a flurry of media interest in the North. Warner's idea did not take hold in the North or nationwide after the Civil War, but the custom of displaying flags on June 14 continued for several years throughout the city of Hartford.

"The day was a beautiful one," the *Hartford Courant* noted on June 14, 1870, in an editorial lamenting the fact the city no longer celebrated Flag Day. "Our streets were decked with the colors, flags waved from every conspicuous point; in city and country the windows were gay with the bright show, and life, for a day, took on a festive air."

On the hundredth anniversary of the first Flag Resolution, June 14, 1877, the *New York Times* called for "a general display of the American flag throughout the country," but stopped short of recommending a national holiday. "There will not be any very general celebration of this peculiar anniversary," a *Times* editorial said, "but every citizen may signify anew his love for 'the old flag' by hoisting its folds to the breeze today."

Several notable Flag Day ceremonies did take place around the nation. In Boston, the original Star-Spangled Banner was displayed at the city's official celebration hosted by Mayor Frederick O. Prince at the Old South Meeting House. "I wish that every citizen of our great republic could gaze upon this very flag we are so fortunate as to have here tonight," Nathan Appleton, a cousin by marriage of the flag's inheritor, Georgiana Appleton, said in his speech. "Let us all take it with us in thought at least, as we travel through these United States." The New York City Teachers' Association held a large Flag Day commemoration that day at the Academy of Music.

The idea for a national Flag Day was revived in 1885 by Bernard John (B.J.) Cigrand, a nineteen-year-old, forty-dollar-a-month teacher at the one-room Stony Hill Schoolhouse in Waubeka, Wisconsin. Cigrand, the son of immigrants from Luxembourg, was a very patriotic man who kept a small American flag in his classroom. On June 14, 1885, he asked his students to write an essay about what the flag meant to them. The exercises he held that day in the classroom in Waubeka—which is about midway between Chicago and Green Bay—are generally recognized as the nation's first Flag Day observance.

Organizing the Flag Day exercises set Cigrand on a long quest to lobby for the creation of a national Flag Day holiday, which he initially called Flag Birthday. "He was a historian and he loved the flag," Barbara Trayer Michael, Cigrand's great granddaughter, said in 2002. "His parents came over from Luxembourg and they loved the country. They instilled that love of the country in him and really took it to the pinnacle." The patriotic Cigrand, who joined the navy in his forties to fight in World War I, was—like Francis Hopkinson and other flag aficionados—an expert on seals and heraldry. He designed several official seals, including those of the city of Chicago and Cook County, Illinois.

Beginning with "The Fourteenth of June," an article he wrote in June 1886 in the Chicago newspaper *Argus*, Cigrand penned countless pro–Flag Day newspaper and magazine articles and pamphlets, along with several books. He also made hundreds of speeches espousing his Flag Day cause. Soon after his first Flag Day commemoration, B. J. Cigrand left teaching to attend dental school. Although he practiced dentistry in Aurora, Illinois, and taught at the Dental College of the University of Illinois, lobbying on behalf of Flag Day remained Cigrand's passion throughout his life.

Soon after he had graduated from dental school, Cigrand made a flag speech before the Chicago branch—called a "camp"—of the Patriotic Order Sons of America, which had been formed in 1847 in Pennsylvania and was part of the anti-immigrant Know-Nothing movement. Soon thereafter Cigrand began editing a new patriotic magazine, The *American Standard*, published by the Order. He wrote many articles in the magazine on his favorite cause, calling attention to the American flag and the date of the first Flag Resolution. The Order made securing a law making Flag Day a national holiday one of its highest priorities.

Beginning in the early 1890s, Cigrand's flag celebration idea took hold in many cities and towns. Flags flew from public and private buildings, ceremonies took place at city halls and other municipal venues, streetcars in big cities were decked out with flags and bunting, and flag commemorations took place in public schools. A Flag Day ceremony was held at the Betsy Ross House in Philadelphia on June 14, 1891. In 1894 Cigrand's missionary work on behalf of Flag Day—which included helping found the Illinois Flag Day Association and the American Flag Day Association with William T. Kerr of Pittsburgh—resulted in its first big success in Chicago. On June 14 some three hundred thousand schoolchildren took part in citywide Flag Day activities held in five parks, the first public school celebration of its kind.

That same year New York Gov. Roswell P. Flower signed an order directing that all public buildings in the Empire State display the flag on June 14. The following year, 1895, Charles R. Skinner, a former member of Congress who was then superintendent of the New York State Department of Public Instruction, recommended that all schools in New York hold "appropriate" Flag Day "exercises" on June 14. "I would specially recommend that the flag be raised on each school building at precisely 9 o'clock, and that, if locality and weather permit, a part of the morning programme take place in the open air, in connection with the raising of the flag," New York City public school superintendent John Jasper wrote to the principals of that city's schools in 1896.

Veterans and patriotic groups played a large part in lobbying for Cigrand's cause and helped spread the Flag Day concept around the nation. In 1890, the Connecticut SAR Society proposed that that state set aside June 14 as Flag Day and promoted the idea of flying the flag every day at all public buildings, in courtrooms and in post offices. The idea caught on the following year when thousands of flags were displayed widely on Flag Day throughout New England and in New York City, Philadelphia, Baltimore, Chicago, and Washington, D.C.

The Pennsylvania Society of Colonial Dames, along with the Pennsylvania SR branch, lobbied successfully to have the city of Philadelphia display the flag on June 14 on all public buildings in 1893. That same year Flag Day exercises took place in Philadelphia's Independence Square for the city's schoolchildren. In March 1895 the Massachusetts SAR Society petitioned the Boston city government to enact an ordinance mandating that American flags be flown on all public buildings and grounds on June 14. It was passed and signed into law by Mayor Edwin Curtis at the end of the year. On June 14, 1895, Boston held its first official Flag Day commemoration, which included special exercises in the city schools.

The GAR initially rebuffed attempts to support a June 14 Flag Day holiday. The leadership believed that the date was too close to Memorial Day and the Fourth of July. But sentiment for Flag Day grew within the organization and in its sister group, the Woman's Relief Corps, which signed on in support of the work of Cigrand's American Flag Day Association. In 1892, the Iowa GAR called for a Flag Day holiday—but chose February 22 in honor of George Washington's birthday.

The flag and Flag Day played a prominent role in the 1896 presidential election campaign between Ohio's Republican governor William McKinley and the Democrat and Populist Party nominee, William Jennings Bryan of Nebraska. Flags had been used by virtually every presidential candidate in all the post–Civil War presidential elections. McKinley's campaign manager, the industrialist Mark Hanna, however, linked his candidate to the flag in a new and unprecedented manner in a campaign that cost a record $3.5 million. Hanna figuratively wrapped McKinley, a Civil War veteran, in the American flag.

During the campaign the Republicans handed out hundreds of thousands of flags at rallies across the country. Hanna devised a campaign button that contained the image of the American flag. He also created what he called the Patriotic Heroes' Battalion, which was made up primarily of revered Civil War generals. The Battalion undertook an extensive train tour throughout the Midwest and West under banners that read "1896 is as Vitally Important as 1861." The train was bedecked with oceans of flag bunting. Two thirty-foot collapsible flagpoles sat atop one of the train's flat cars, and a campaign worker unfurled the Stars and Stripes at countless stops.

At a rally on September 4 in New York City, American flags and banners emblazoned with the names of McKinley and running mate Garret A. Hobart flew in profusion along a six-block-long stretch of Broadway. "There was a dazzling display" of flags from Seventeenth Street to Twenty-third Street, the *New York Times* reported the next day. "A half dozen large banners and hundreds of small ones were flung to the breeze at 5 o'clock." Enormous flags, "some of them thirty-six feet long, were unfurled, and at the same time the smaller flags were waved furiously. It presented a beautiful and impressive sight. Most of the banners were the National colors, having at the end a strip bearing the names of McKinley and Hobart."

A military band playing "The Star-Spangled Banner" led a procession of "several thousand business men" marching up Broadway, according to the *Times*. "The procession halted at every block, and as it paused, more banners were unfurled. There was a large crowd along the line of march, which cheered lustily whenever another group of banners was displayed."

On October 26, Hanna declared October 31, 1896, national Flag Day. He called on Republican state central committees throughout the nation to "make a special effort" that day to "assemble in the cities, villages, and hamlets nearest their homes and show their patriotism, devotion to country and the flag, and their intention to support the [Republican Party] by having patriotic speeches and such other exercises as will be appropriate for the occasion and tend to make the day a general holiday as far as possible."

Republicans heeded Hannah's call by holding Flag Day events across the country that day, just three days before the election. Large events took place in cities such as Washington, D.C., Chicago, San Francisco, and New York. They featured mass displays of flags and appearances by former Union generals. The message was that the Republican Party of McKinley saved the nation under the flag by prevailing in the Civil War and that voting Republican was the proper patriotic thing to do.

"The flag was everywhere" at the enormous New York City Flag Day demonstration, the *New York Tribune* reported. "It flaunted from every window; it waved from every portico; it flew from every roof; it floated over almost every street, and many times in every block. The marching thousands trampled between walls of human faces that were almost entirely folded in the stripes and dotted with the stars, while every man in the whole vast line carried a flag of his own."

A *New York Times* editorial that day expressed the view that the display of flags was more than a political strategy. Showing the flag "is not merely a proclamation of the politics of him who displays it," the editorial said, "but it is the celebration in advance of a victory. Confidence in that victory is simply trust in the American people and belief in their capacity for self-government." Those who flew the flag proclaimed "their fealty to the Republic and their defiance of its enemies, and to celebrate in advance the victory it will win" on Election Day, the editorial said.

But that is not the way Democrats and Populists saw it. Some reacted indignantly to the ploy and tore down flags at McKinley rallies that day. In Sedalia, Missouri, according to a report the next day in the *New York Times,* Bryan supporters seized a flag from a young boy and burned it, along with a pile of McKinley campaign literature. Most Democrats, however, responded with flag-waving ceremonies of their own that day.

The red, white, and blue display by the Democrats in Washington, D.C., that day had an impact on Mabel Hubbard Bell, Alexander Graham Bell's wife. A staunch Republican, she nevertheless had had qualms about flying the flag on October 31 from their house on Connecticut Avenue in Washington. But Mabel Bell wound up displaying "a lot of flags," she said in a letter to her husband. "A whole lot of houses on Connecticut Ave. were decorated and Penna. Ave. and F Street were very gay with flags," she reported. "At first, I did not approve for I did not believe in the bringing of our national emblem in party strife." Mabel Bell changed her mind, she said, after she saw the flags displayed at the Democratic headquarters and remembered that Bryan had endorsed Hanna's suggestion.

"I didn't see why I shouldn't show my interest in the election, why in fact it wasn't meritorious," she said, "so I stopped at a flag store and got some."

Mabel Hubbard Bell's cautionary note about bringing the flag into "party strife" was prescient. She realized that she was taking part in something unprecedented. Even though the Democrats and Populists also celebrated Flag Day and tried to make the point that the flag was not the property of one party, their effort came too late, and the Republicans succeeded in tying their candidate to the flag and the patriotic feelings that went along with it.

"Although members of both parties demonstrated their patriotism by flying the flag that day," Scot Guenter noted, "the attempt to appropriate it for one partisan ideology by creating a special Flag Day illustrated the power political strategists recognized in the symbol."

★　　★　　★

Flag Day celebrations picked up steam following McKinley's election. A large, city-wide celebration took place, for example, on June 14, 1897, in

New York, sponsored by the Empire State Society of the Sons of the American Revolution. "On all of the Federal and municipal buildings the flags were hoisted at sunrise, as they were also on the Liberty Pole at the Battery and at the old fort in Central Park." The *New York Times* reported the following day. "As the city awakened, the rainbow effect was extended till it reached the entire length of Broadway and of the avenues, through the cross streets, and along the water front, on piers and on shipping." The Stars and Stripes also was "displayed from every schoolhouse" and "draped in the assembly rooms, and in many of the up-town schools the children were provided with small flags, which they waved in time with the singing of the National airs."

Beginning at the turn of the twentieth century, many states and localities officially celebrated Flag Day. In Michigan, for example, the legislature approved a Flag Day resolution in 1901. The state's governor, Aaron T. Bliss, then issued a proclamation designating June 14, 1902, as Flag Day in the Wolverine state.

"The breezes stealing in from the Great Lakes and the rising sun should find Old Glory waving from every home, from every schoolhouse, from every church and every public building," the governor proclaimed. "Every flag staff should bear aloft the banner which has never known a stain. There should be appropriate exercises in every school" and "each child should have for his own a flag to be treasured and revered through the passing years."

On May 30, 1916, as it became increasingly likely that American troops would soon be fighting a world war, Pres. Woodrow Wilson established a national Flag Day through a presidential proclamation. Wilson made a Flag Day speech on June 14 that year near the Washington Monument after having led a flag-saturated Preparedness Parade in which some sixty-six thousand marchers took part from the Capitol along Pennsylvania Avenue to the White House. Wilson himself carried the Stars and Stripes at the head of the parade.

"I regard this day as a day of rededication to all the ideals of the United States," Wilson said. "As I see the winds lovingly unfold the beautiful lines of our great flag, I shall seem to see a hand point the way of duty, no matter how hard, no matter how long, which we shall tread while we vindicate the glory and honor of the United States."

In 1918, responding to a plea by the National Security League, a private organization made up primarily of bankers and industrialists, nationwide Flag Day celebrations took place in an effort to boost patriotism after

Before the United States entered World War I, flag-bedecked Preparedness Parades took place throughout the country, including this one in Washington on June 14, 1916, in which marchers passed before a reviewing stand in front of the White House. *The Library of Congress, Prints and Photographs Division*

President Woodrow Wilson led the parade, leading some 66,000 marchers from Capitol Hill to the White House, carrying the Stars and Stripes. *The Library of Congress, Prints and Photographs Division*

America entered World War I. In many states audiences in movie theaters sang "The Star Spangled Banner" and one other patriotic song that day and special celebrations, proposed by the federal government's Bureau of Education, took place in factories. They included the raising of the flag accompanied by a bugle call, a recitation of the Pledge of Allegiance, and singing patriotic songs.

Despite the popularity of Flag Day celebrations, President Wilson did not make Flag Day a legal public holiday. Nor has any president done so since then. Only Pennsylvania, which took action in 1937, has chosen to make June 14 a legal state holiday. Even though it is not an official national holiday, Flag Day observances have taken place every year since Wilson's proclamation. On August 3, 1949, Pres. Harry Truman signed into law a resolution passed by Congress designating June 14th of each year National Flag Day. That measure calls upon the president to issue an annual proclamation calling for a Flag Day observance and for the display of the flag on all federal government buildings. In 1966 Congress passed a Joint Resolution asking the president to issue an annual National Flag Week proclamation as well, and to call on American citizens to display the flag during the entire week in which June 14 falls.

Every year since then our presidents have issued Flag Day and Flag Week Proclamations, directing U.S. government officials to fly the flag on all government buildings and asking all Americans, as Pres. Ronald Reagan put it in his 1981 Flag Day Proclamation, to fly the flag "from their porches, windows and storefronts."

★   ★   ★

The veterans and patriotic organizations—led by the Grand Army of the Republic and by the Sons and Daughters of the American Revolution—played the leading role in what became known as the flag protection movement, which grew up in the late 1880s. The movement came about as a result of what many saw as the out-of-control commercialization of the use of the flag.

In the absence of laws governing the use of the flag's image or any accepted rules of flag etiquette, marketers and advertisers routinely printed the Stars and Stripes directly on their products and on advertisements for them and had no qualms whatsoever about printing their messages directly on American flags. A 1878 advertisement for McFerran's Magnolia Hams, for example, had Uncle Sam pointing to a ham sitting in front of a flag with the words "The Magnolia Ham is an American Institution" printed across the stripes.

Politicians also took liberties with the American flag, including inserting candidates' names and messages across the stripes and nestled among the stars. The practice dated to before the Civil War. A flag made for the 1860 Abraham Lincoln–Hannibal Hamlin Republican Party presidential ticket, for example, had a likeness of Lincoln in the canton surrounded by twenty-nine small stars in a circle and four larger stars in the canton's corners. Four white stripes contained the words: "For President, Abram Lincoln. For Vice President, Hannibal Hamlin." The stripes of a flag produced for the Republican ticket in the 1884 presidential campaign included the slogan, "For President James G. Blaine. For Vice President John A. Logan 1884." The canton contained the requisite thirty-eight stars, as well as likenesses of

By 1860, it had become common practice for politicians to use American flags as campaign posters. This flag promotes the candidacy of Abraham Lincoln and his vice presidential running mate that year, Hannibal Hamlin. *The Library of Congress, Prints and Photographs Division*

Blaine and Logan, who had been the GAR commander in chief from 1868 to 1871.

As the nation rapidly industrialized in the last third of the century, color printing developed on a large scale. Low-cost color postcards proliferated in the 1880s and 1890s; many of them featured red, white, and blue American flags. Flag business cards also were popular, and the flag was a common letterhead theme embossed on private and commercial stationery. Advertising in newspapers and magazines and on billboards and signs also flourished in this period.

Images of the flag found their way into an astonishing number of advertisements for scores of different types of products. The long, long list includes baking powder, bicycles, beer, cigarettes, corned beef, toilet paper, tobacco products, window shades, and whiskey barrels. As one late-nineteenth-century reference book for advertisers put it, flags "are admirably adapted to all purposes of heraldic display and their rich, glowing colors appeal to feel-

The first laws enacted by the states and the U.S. Congress against flag desecration came in the early 1890s in reaction to the rampant use of the Stars and Stripes in advertising, including this late 19th century ad for Young America hams and breakfast bacon. *The Library of Congress, Prints and Photographs Division*

ings of patriotism and win purchasers of the merchandise to which they are affixed."

The rampant use of the flag for commercial purposes did not sit well with the veterans' and patriotic organizations nor with some members of Congress. The first attempt to legislate against misuse of the flag in advertising and political campaigns was a bill introduced in the House of Representatives in 1878 by Congressman Samuel Sullivan Cox of Ohio. Cox's measure called for criminal penalties for anyone who "shall disfigure the national flag, either by printing on said flag, or attaching to the same, or otherwise, any advertisement for public display." That bill died in committee.

So did a similar measure introduced in 1880 by Congressman Hiram Barber Jr. of Illinois. Barber's bill was designed to "protect the national flag from desecration" by banning the flag's image for "advertisement of merchandise or other property or of any person's trade, occupation or business." Cox and Barber's measures failed mainly because they were ahead of their time. Significant sentiment in favor of enacting a federal law outlawing flag desecration did not manifest itself in Washington until the early 1890s.

That sentiment was much stronger in the House of Representatives than in the Senate. In 1890 the House for the first time passed a flag-desecration bill, which was introduced by Congressman John Alexander Caldwell of Ohio. That measure made it a misdemeanor punishable by a fifty-dollar fine or thirty days in jail to use the flag in any way in "advertisements for public display or private gain." The Senate did not take action on the measure, however, and it did not become law.

Beginning in the mid-1890s the patriotic and veterans' groups launched a strong nationwide campaign to lobby the state and federal governments to enact flag protection laws. The first shot in the campaign was fired in 1895 by U.S. Army captain Philip H. Reade, an amateur historian who served as a historian for the Society of Colonial Wars (whose Illinois branch he headed) and the Sons of the American Revolution. Reade (1844–1919), who claimed that he was descended from two dozen colonial ancestors, had graduated from West Point, served in the Union army in the Civil War, and went on to fight in the Indian wars and in the Spanish-American War.

In 1895 Reade—whom the political scientist Robert Justin Goldstein called the "Johnny Appleflag" of the flag protection movement—helped shape a Society of Colonial Wars resolution that called on Congress to enact legislation reining in the commercial use of the flag. In that same year he set up a society committee headed by Charles Kingsbury Miller that compiled a list of the names and addresses of companies and organizations that used the flag for commercial purposes. The committee published a pamphlet called "Misuse of the National Flag," which described advertising excesses using the flag and distributed it widely to politicians, colleges, clergy, and newspaper editors, as well as to patriotic and veterans groups.

Reade heavily lobbied other patriotic and veterans organizations to join the movement to protect the flag with legal sanctions. He traveled extensively speaking to many organizations, urging them to support desecration legislation. And he achieved great success, winning support from many state branches and from the national organizations of the leading groups, including the SAR, SR, DAR, GAR, and the Loyal Legion. From 1897 to 1899, those groups established committees to work for flag protection legislation and later formed the American Flag Association to coordinate the effort.

Another of the movement's most effective leaders was Frances Saunders Kempster of the Milwaukee DAR chapter. Her lobbying on behalf of flag protection legislation bore fruit in 1897 when the DAR National Convention endorsed the idea and she was named the head of a new DAR National Flag Committee. A third important player in the movement, Col. Ralph E. Prime, a Civil War veteran and the former deputy attorney general of New York, headed the national SAR Flag Committee.

In February 1898, Prime brought representatives of the flag committees of the other patriotic and veterans' organizations together in New York's City Hall. That meeting resulted in the founding on February 12 of the American Flag Association, which was made up of representatives of thirty state and national flag committees. The group included national and state SAR and DAR flag committees, along with representatives of several other veterans and patriotic groups. The association soon attracted many more groups, including eight states and the national GAR Flag Committee. Prime became the Flag Association's founding president, serving in that position until 1908 and leading the effort to foster "public sentiment in favor of honoring the flag of our country and preserving it from desecration, and of initiating and forwarding legal efforts to prevent such desecration."

The association and the many national flag committees worked hard to convince Congress to enact legislation. Despite decades of lobbying, however, no legislation would be passed on Capitol Hill until 1968. Crucial roadblocks came from the powerful Republican chairmen of the Senate and House Judiciary Committees throughout most of the 1890s, Sen. George F. Hoar of Massachusetts and Rep. David B. Henderson of Iowa. Hoar objected to flag desecration legislation for several reasons, including the possibility of lawsuits from firms that had registered their commercial flag images with the United States Patent and Trademark Office. Hoar, who said he initially favored flag desecration legislation, also believed that politicians would strongly object if they were no longer permitted to put their images on campaign posters featuring the flag.

Henderson, who also served as Speaker of the House from 1899 to 1903, said that prohibiting the use of the flag on commercial products would not be good for business. Henderson, a colleague said, "hoped the American people would continue to wrap hams in the flag, not to teach patriotism, but to teach ham eaters to eat American hams."

With legislation for a national law solidly bottled up in Congress, the advocates for flag desecration legislation turned their attention to the states. In 1897, Pennsylvania, Illinois, and South Dakota enacted flag protection laws; by Flag Day of 1905 thirty-two states and the Arizona and New Mexico Territories had followed suit.

There were other successes, as well. U.S. Army inspector general Joseph C. Breckinridge, a member of the American Flag Association's executive committee, in 1899 ended the long-standing military practice of inscribing flags with unit names and the battles they took part in. Four years later, the U.S. Commissioner of Patents and Trademarks ruled that his office no longer would register any trademarks on commercial products that made use of the flag. Congress in 1905 codified that ruling into law.

On March 4, 1907, the U.S. Supreme Court, in the case of *Halter v. Nebraska,* upheld state flag protection laws when it ruled that a 1903 Nebraska flag protection measure did not violate the Constitution. That law, among other things, made it a misdemeanor, punishable by a fine or imprisonment, to "sell, expose for sale, or have in possession for sale" any merchandise "upon which shall have been printed or placed, for purposes of advertisement" the image of the American flag. This marked the first time the nation's highest court offered its views on flag protection laws.

Justice John M. Harlan, delivering the opinion, ruled against the appeal of a Nebraska company that had been convicted and fined fifty dollars for painting the American flag on beer bottles for advertising purposes. "It would seem difficult," Harlan said, "to hold that the statute of Nebraska, in forbidding the use of the flag of the United States for purposes of mere advertisement, infringes any right protected by the Constitution of the United States."

In his opinion Harlan gave a short history of the American flag and noted that every "true American has not simply an appreciation, but a deep affection" for the flag. "No American, nor any foreign-born person who enjoys the privileges of American citizenship, ever looks upon it without taking pride in the fact that he lives under this free government."

States, he said, have the power "to strengthen the bonds of the Union, and therefore, to that end, may encourage patriotism and love of country among its people." A state, he said, would be ignoring "the well-being of its people if it ignores the fact that they regard the flag as a symbol of their country's power and prestige, and will be impatient if any open disrespect is shown towards it." He characterized using the flag in advertising as "a purpose wholly foreign to that for which it was provided by the nation."

Such use, he said, "tends to degrade and cheapen the flag in the estimation of the people, as well as to defeat the object of maintaining it as an emblem of national power and national honor." The court, he said, could not hold that "any privilege of American citizenship or that any right of personal liberty is violated by a state enactment forbidding the flag to be used as an advertisement on a bottle of beer."

★   ★   ★

In the middle of the first decade of the twentieth century, amid the veterans' and patriotic groups' clamor for flag protection, the American flag played a leading role in two of Broadway's most popular stage musicals, *Little Johnny Jones* and *George Washington, Jr.* Both of those smashingly successful shows were written and produced by Broadway's first superstar, George M. Cohan, who also starred in the productions. *Little Johnny Jones*, which opened on November 7, 1904, at the Liberty Theater, went on the road and ran for two more years. It is the story of an American horse jockey, played by Cohan, trying to win the English Derby. It was Cohan's third Broadway show and the one that made his reputation. Its songs were wildly popular, especially "Give My Regards to Broadway" and "Yankee Doodle Dandy," which Cohan performed surrounded by an American flag-waving retinue.

George Washington, Jr. opened in 1906. Cohan wrote the script, coproduced the show, starred in it, and wrote the words and music to all the songs, including the show stopper, "You're a Grand Old Flag." Cohan, playing the title character, a senator's son who out of patriotism refuses to marry a British nobleman's daughter, belted out that tune with a large American flag in hand marching back and forth across the stage. The song was a huge success; it became the first tune from a musical to sell more than a million copies of sheet music.

Cohan had written the song after a chance meeting with a Civil War veteran of the Battle of Gettysburg. They were sitting next to each other at a funeral when Cohan noticed that the veteran had an old American flag folded in his lap. In the ensuing conversation, the man referred to the tattered flag as "a grand old rag." That inspired Cohan to write the song he called "You're a Grand Old Rag," which is how the song was performed when *George Washington, Jr.* opened. Cohan soon changed the words after complaints from critics, veterans, and patriotic and veterans' groups.

The word change satisfied those who took offense, and *George Washington, Jr.* and Cohan's succeeding shows became huge hits. Still, he was not immune from criticism for his use of the flag. The drama critic James Metcalfe, for example, lambasted *George Washington, Jr.* for its "mawkish appeals to the cheapest kind of patriotism." If Cohan "can bring himself to coin the American flag and national heroes into box-office receipts," Metcalfe said, "it is not his blame but our shame." That criticism did not stop Cohan from repeating his flag-waving routine in subsequent shows.

One composer who received not a whit of criticism for his use of the flag in his music was John Philip Sousa. The man known as "the March King" composed 136 military marches, including "The Stars and Stripes Forever," which became the nation's official march by an act of Congress in 1987. Sousa led the U.S. Marine Band from 1880 to 1892 and was resoundingly popular in this country and Europe for the next four decades as he presented countless concerts with his own band. Sousa wrote "The Stars and Stripes Forever" in December 1896; it became a national sensation within a year. Sousa's band typically played the song at the end of its concerts, at which point audiences rose in tribute to the song and the flag. It remains a popular, stirring patriotic tune that is widely performed today.

*   *   *

The United States went to war with Spain in April of 1898, and handily defeated the Spanish in Cuba and the Philippines by the end of the year. The Spanish-American War is significant in the evolution of the American flag for several reasons. First, and most important, it was the first war fought by the entire nation under the Stars and Stripes since the Mexican War ended fifty years earlier. Americans from the states that fought each other under the Confederate flag and the Stars and Stripes during the Civil War came together under the forty-five-star American flag to fight in Cuba and the Philippines against the Spanish in 1898. Former Confederate general John Brown Gordon, expressing a common sentiment as the war began, pledged that southerners would fight in the Spanish-American War "wrapped in the folds of the American flag."

The "greatest good" the Spanish-American War did, then New York governor Theodore Roosevelt said in August 1899, "was that beneath the same banner marched the sons of the blue and the gray. The nation is now united in deed as well as well as in name. After being the son of a man who wore the blue, the next best thing is to be a son of a man who wore the gray. We are now all Americans, proud of our forefathers and their bravery on both sides."

That conflict, the nation's first declared war fought entirely overseas, also stirred up tremendous patriotic fervor in the United States following the sinking of the USS *Maine* in Havana harbor on February 15. That fervor often was expressed using the American flag. After the United States declared war on Spain on April 25, Americans put on a "great display of flag flying, flag waving, and flag saluting," Scot Guenter noted.

"The demand for bunting within the last ten days is in excess of the supply," the *Wall Street Journal* reported on May 2. "The demand is such that orders have been taken for delivery from three to four months ahead." The demand for bunting and flags led to price increases of fifty cents for bunting and twenty-five cents for flags, the *Journal* reported.

When the American Fifth Army Corps under Gen. William Shafter took Santiago de Cuba on July 17 after three weeks of bloody fighting, forcing Spain to sue for peace, the American flag flew in triumph over the Governor's Palace. "The ceremony of hoisting the Stars and Stripes was worth all the blood and treasure it cost," the *New York Times* opined the next day. "A vast concourse of ten thousand people witnessed the stirring and thrilling scene that will live forever in the minds of all the Americans present."

The Spanish-American War also saw the display of a spate of extraordinarily large flags. That included the 120-foot by 43-foot Stars and Stripes raised in Havana on January 1, 1899, and the massive 500-foot flag that Comm. George Dewey's flagship, the USS *Olympia*, flew when it steamed home in triumph after the Battle of Manila Bay.

By the turn of the twentieth century, the American flag had secured a strong place in the hearts and minds of the American public. That was due mainly to the influence of veterans' and patriotic groups, the easing of lingering tensions left over from the Civil War, and a national climate that was ready to embrace patriotism and its symbols. The next important step in the flag's history took root during this period as well: the birth, growth, and nationwide acceptance of the idea of schoolchildren making a daily vow to pledge their allegiance to the flag and what it stands for.

CHAPTER TWELVE

One Nation Indivisible

*   *   *

I pledge allegiance to my flag and the Republic for which it stands;
one nation indivisible, with liberty and Justice for all.

—The Youth's Companion, September 8, 1892

T*HE YOUTH'S COMPANION* began publishing in Boston in 1827.
By 1890, it had become one of the most popular magazines in the nation,
with a circulation of nearly five hundred thousand. Its content initially was
geared toward children, but in 1857 the weekly magazine also began to appeal to adults. It attracted some of the best writers of the day, including
Ralph Waldo Emerson, Harriet Beecher Stowe, John Greenleaf Whittier,
William Dean Howells, Jack London, and Emily Dickinson. The magazine's owner from 1867 to 1899, Daniel Sharp Ford, filled the Boston-based
The Youth's Companion with essays and articles on diverse subjects, along
with poetry, humorous stories, and fiction.

The Youth's Companion also was a highly commercial operation. Advertisements filled its pages and the Premium Department gave flags and other
items as incentives to new and renewing subscribers. In 1886, Ford appointed his nephew James B. Upham to head that department, as well as a
subsidiary called the Perry Mason Company. Soon thereafter, Upham, who
was born in New Hampshire in 1845, spearheaded a mission known as the
school flag movement or schoolhouse flag movement. It was designed to
put American flags in all of the schools in the country—flags that, it was
hoped, would be purchased from *The Youth's Companion.*

"At that time," said John W. Baer, the author of a history of the Pledge of Allegiance, "a flag was considered an unnecessary expense, especially for one-room schoolhouses. A flag pole and a flag amounted to expenses school committees didn't want."

The Grand Army of the Republic and its auxiliary organization, the Woman's Relief Corps, joined the movement to bring American flags to the public schools beginning in 1889. The Rochester, New York, GAR Post that year presented flags to all of that city's public schools to mark George Washington's birthday. At the national encampment in Milwaukee that year the GAR voted to ask each post to provide a flag to every public school that did not have one. "Let the eight million boys and girls in our elementary schools be thus imbued with a reverence for the flag and all it represents," GAR commander in chief William Warner, a former Missouri U.S. congressman, said in 1892. "Then the future of the Republic is assured and that flag shall forever wave."

Patriotic ceremonies revolving around the flag took place in New York City public schools beginning in early 1888. They were introduced by Col. DeWitt C. Ward, a New York City school trustee. George T. Balch, the Board of Education's auditor, embraced the idea and publicized it and other patriotic school endeavors in his 1889 book, *Methods of Teaching Patriotism in the Public Schools*. Balch worked closely with Margaret Pascal, who taught primarily immigrant children. Pascal fostered patriotism among her students by, among other things, encouraging girls to sew flags and boys to make flagstaffs. Balch, who also was a teacher and a Civil War veteran, called for schools to display the flag and to institute flag ceremonies that included what he called "The American Patriotic Salute." The historian Scot Guenter calls Balch's idea "the first known organized [flag] salute designed for use in American public schools."

Balch's salute began with students touching their foreheads and then their hearts and saying: "We give our Heads!—and our Hearts!—to God! and our Country!" The students then extended their right arms, palms down, and said, "One Country! One Language! One Flag!" By 1893 some six thousand students—many of them the children of immigrants—who attended New York City's twenty-one Children's Aid Society schools recited Balch's salute every morning. Teachers in the U.S. government's Indian schools in the West also adopted the salute. The GAR and the Women's Relief Committee enthusiastically endorsed Balch's school flag salute concept.

The Youth's Companion magazine offered for sale many sizes of flags, including small pocket-sized versions with carrying cases. It sold six-foot-long flags, "just right for a 'little country school,'" an advertisement in the magazine said, for $3.50 and nine-foot-long flags for $5.35. "At these prices," the ad said, "we pay postage. The boys can cut the flag-staff." Staffs were favored over flagpoles because poles were deemed too expensive and because, outside of military bases, they were rarely used to display the Stars and Stripes at the time.

The magazine also offered free "flag certificates" to schools to sell as a way to raise money to purchase flags. "By the sale of these Flag Certificates for ten cents each to the friends of the pupils," the ad said, "your school can raise money for its Flag in one day." The certificates read: "This Certificate entitles the holder thereof to one share in the patriotic influence of a Flag over the schoolhouse."

The magazine promoted the endeavor heavily, pitching it as a way to foster love of country, especially among foreign-born children and the children of immigrants who came to this country primarily from southern and eastern Europe by the millions in the 1880s and 1890s. The "school house flag," Upham wrote in *The Youth's Companion*, "seen so often so constantly present in the pupil's thoughts, has a marked influence, as several teachers report, upon foreign born children and the children of foreign born parents."

In 1890, the magazine ran an essay contest on the theme, "The Patriotic Influence of the American Flag When Raised over the Public Schools." The prize for the winner in each state was a nine-by-fifteen-foot American flag. The magazine sold some 25,000 flags to schools by mid-1892. Upham in 1891 had formed the Lyceum League of America, a patriotic and debating society made up primarily of high school students, to help the cause. And the magazine prominently featured the flag in graphics and illustrations in many flag-inspired articles and stories. That included "George Washington II," the story of a brave, patriotic boy, which appeared in 1891; "The Story of a War Song," a history of the song "The Battle Cry of Freedom" by George Root, which appeared in the August 25, 1892, issue; and "His Day for the Flag," the story of children who raise money to purchase a flag for their school, which also ran in 1892.

The magazine also heavily promoted state laws mandating that school boards provide flagstaffs and flags for the schools in their jurisdictions. That campaign was successful. In 1895, Massachusetts—the home of the magazine—became the first state to mandate compulsory flags and flagstaffs in its public schools. Wisconsin followed suit in 1889. By 1905, nearly two dozen states, all of them in the North and West, had laws making school flags compulsory.

In 1891, Ford had hired a new assistant editor, thirty-six-year-old Francis Bellamy, who was a close friend, a Baptist minister, and—along with Edward Bellamy, his famous cousin—an adherent of Christian socialism.

The year before, James Upham had come up with the idea of what he called a Public School Celebration, a patriotic commemoration of Columbus Day 1892. In 1891 Upham presented the organizers of the Columbian Exposition (also known as the Chicago World's Fair of 1893) with a plan for the event, which he renamed the National School Celebration. It was designed to take place at the same time as the fair's proposed groundbreaking on October 21, 1892, marking the four-hundredth anniversary of Christopher Columbus's voyage of discovery to America. Upham's plan, which the Exposition accepted in January 1892, was to have all the nation's schoolchildren take part in a flag-raising and flag-saluting ceremony that day. The National Education Association (NEA) and William Harris, the U.S. Commissioner of Education, endorsed the idea. The NEA formed a committee to promote the celebration; Francis Bellamy was chosen to be its chairman.

Former president Grover Cleveland, the Democratic nominee for president in 1892, also endorsed the National School Celebration. After intense lobbying from Bellamy, Congress passed a resolution on June 29 calling for the nation to observe Discovery Day on October 21 with "public demonstrations" and "suitable exercises in the schools and other places of assembly." October 21 was chosen because changes that were made in the calendar in the sixteenth century moved the date of Columbus's landing from October 12 to 21. Bellamy had been lobbying Pres. Benjamin Harrison to sign on to the idea, as well. As part of that campaign Bellamy wrote a letter to the president, urging Harrison to support a nationwide observance of Columbus Day in the schools.

"I am very much pleased with the idea," Harrison replied in a letter he wrote to Bellamy from the White House on May 23. "Properly conducted, such exercises will be very instructive to the pupils and will excite in every village in the land an interest in this great anniversary."

On July 21, Harrison issued a presidential proclamation making October 21 a "general holiday," and calling on schools to take part in the National Columbian Public School Celebration. *The Youth's Companion* published Harrison's proclamation in its September 8 issue. "Let the National Flag," the president proclaimed, "float over every schoolhouse in the country, and the exercises be such as shall impress upon our youth the patriotic duties of American citizenship."

The magazine promoted the upcoming celebration heavily. And it used it as an opportunity to sell flags. An advertisement for flags offered to send the celebration's official program—written by Francis Bellamy—to teachers for free. "Your school," the ad said, "will not let itself be left out of the Celebration. It must have a Flag."

One aspect of *The Youth's Companion* campaign to promote the celebration called for students across the land to ask their teachers and school boards to set up committees to organize local celebrations. Bellamy wrote many press releases and other materials, distributing them to thousands of newspapers and magazines pushing the idea. The Grand Army of the Republic signed on to help promote the event. "It is an immense thing," the GAR commander in chief John Palmer wrote to Bellamy. "It is the best thing the public school has ever thought of doing. It will impress all these pupils that they've got a country and it will make our people understand what a thing our free public school system is for America."

Bellamy also won the support of many members of Congress and other prominent national figures, including Theodore Roosevelt, who was then a U.S. Civil Service commissioner and a big supporter of the Lyceum League. "The part the Flag is to play appeals to me tremendously," Roosevelt wrote to Bellamy. "We are all descendants of immigrants, but we want to hasten that day, by every possible means when we shall be fused together. . . . Consequently, by all means in our power we ought to inculcate, among the children of this country, the most fervent loyalty to the Flag."

Public schools and the flag, Roosevelt continued, "stand together as the arch-typical of American civilization." The flag, he said, "represents not only those principles of equality, fraternity and liberty, but also the great pulsing nation with all its hopes, and all its past, and all its moral power. So it is eminently fitting that the Common School and the Flag should stand together on Columbus Day."

★   ★   ★

The "Official Programme for the National Columbia Public School Celebration of October 21, 1892," which Francis Bellamy wrote under Upham's direction, appeared in a page-and-a-half spread in the September 8 issue of *The Youth's Companion*. The program called for a flag raising by a group of veterans, a prayer, a Columbus Day song, and several speeches. It also included a "Salute to the Flag." Bellamy, John Baer said, built the program "around a flag ceremony and they built the flag ceremony around this new Pledge of Allegiance."

The salute contained twenty-two words: "I pledge allegiance to my Flag and the Republic for which it stands, one nation, indivisible, with liberty and justice for all." Bellamy looked for inspiration in choosing those words, he later wrote, in the Declaration of Independence and "the salient points of our national history," including "the meaning of the Civil War."

The "true reason" for allegiance to the flag, Bellamy said, "is the 're-public for which it stands.'" Bellamy said he considered "the republic" to be "the concise political word for the Nation—the One Nation which the Civil War was fought to prove. To make that One Nation idea clear, we must specify that it is indivisible, as Webster and Lincoln used to repeat in their great speeches." As for "liberty and justice for all," Bellamy said he was inspired by "Liberty, Equality, and Fraternity," the "historic slogan of the French Revolution which meant so much to Jefferson and his friends."

Bellamy drew up specific instructions for the entire ceremony, including what later was dubbed "the Bellamy salute." "At a signal from the Princi-pal, the pupils, in ordered ranks, hands to the side, face the Flag. Another signal is given; every pupil gives the military salute: right hand lifted, palm downward, to a line with the forehead and close to it. Standing thus, all re-peat together slowly [the Pledge]. At the words 'to my Flag,' the right hand is extended gracefully, palm upwards, toward the Flag, and remains in this gesture till the end of the affirmation; whereupon all hands immediately drop to the side. Then, still standing, as the instruments strike a chord, all will sing AMERICA—'My Country, 'tis of Thee.'"

The pledge was first recited at New York City's ceremony on October 12, when some thirty-five-thousand schoolchildren took part in the first of three days of Columbus Day celebrations. The rest of the nation celebrated on October 21, which was believed to be Christopher Columbus's true birthday. Millions of children all across the country took part. After Bel-lamy heard thousands of students in Boston recite the Pledge that day he added a twenty-third word, changing the Pledge slightly to read "I pledge allegiance to my Flag and *to* the Republic . . ."

All forty thousand public school students took part in Bellamy's special Columbus Day activities at their schools in Washington, D.C. The Pledge also was recited that day at a pomp-filled ceremony at the end of a three-day celebration in Chicago dedicating the Manufactures and Liberal Arts Building of the World's Columbian Exposition. Some 140,000 people, in-cluding many foreign visitors, attended. Two days earlier Chicago's schoolchildren had taken part in large-scale gatherings to pledge allegiance to the flag.

A National Liberty Pole and Flag Raising Ceremony held at the Navesink Atlantic Highlands Light Station in New Jersey, on April 25, 1893, featured the first massive adult Pledge recitation. The ceremony was the brainchild of William McDowell, one of the founders of the Sons and the Daughters of the American Revolution. Upham and Bellamy attended the ceremony, which took place several days before the Chicago World's Fair's opening. The site was chosen because it was one of the highest points on the eastern seaboard. A large flagpole was erected for the occasion. The Lyceum League donated the flags for the event.

At the ceremony a DAR member raised a flag, and it received a salute from U.S. Navy ships at anchor offshore. The attendees then saluted the flag with their right arms outstretched. Bellamy, with Upham beside him, led the recitation of the Pledge. In Upham's address he spoke about the importance of training patriotic young Americans to help America "fulfill her divine mission."

The World's Columbian Exposition, popularly known as the Chicago World's Fair of 1893, opened in the Windy City on May 1 that year. As was the case with the 1876 Centennial celebration in Philadelphia, the Chicago World's Fair celebrated the Industrial Age's progress in science, industry, and culture. The Ferris wheel was unveiled for the first time in America at the fair, as were the ice cream cone, Aunt Jemima pancakes, and the popcorn concoction known as Cracker Jack.

Pres. Grover Cleveland opened the fair by pushing an ivory-and-gold "electric button" that turned on the electric power for the exposition. Cleveland's action instantly illuminated a hundred thousand incandescent light bulbs and removed the shroud covering a statue of the *Republic* in the fair's main fountain. It also unfurled a large American flag. "The first tangible sign of the accomplishment of a conception which took 15,000 men and $33,000,000 three years to accomplish was then breaking loose at the top of the tapering mast in front of the grand stand of the Stars and Stripes as the sailor at the front pulled the halyards," the *New York Times* reported. "The glorious emblem threw its folds wide to the breeze, and cheer rose on cheer from 600,000 throats." From "every flagstaff along the upper edges of the buildings and on the towers and pinnacles, 2,000 flags and banners and pennants were unfurled. In the lagoons the steam launches blew their whistles, and a cloud of white vapor rose to the sky."

The act that marked the official closing of the fair on October 30: the lowering of the American flag.

★   ★   ★

Five years later, in 1898, New York became the first state to mandate that students recite the Pledge of Allegiance in public schools at the beginning of each school day. In 1916, the New York State Department of Education produced a textbook, *The Citizen Syllabus*, which was used in night school for adult immigrants nationwide. The forty-eight-page book contains a section on the American flag that includes the Pledge of Allegiance. By 1918, Rhode Island, Arizona, Kansas, and Maryland had enacted mandatory Pledge laws.

Delegates to the National Flag Conference in Washington, D.C., in 1923

The Pledge of Allegiance, which Francis Bellamy wrote in 1892, did not become officially recognized until 1942 when Congress included it in the U.S. Flag Code. New York City public school students are shown saluting the flag in January 1943. *The Library of Congress, Prints and Photographs Division*

and 1924 made two changes to the wording of the Pledge. At the behest of representatives from the American Legion and the Daughters of the American Revolution, the words "my Flag" were replaced with, first, "to the Flag of the United States," and, then later "to the flag of the United States of America."

On June 22, 1942, Congress officially recognized the Pledge of Allegiance by including it in the U.S. Flag Code, which also abolished the "Bellamy salute" because it resembled the salute used by the Nazis in Hitler's Germany. In October of that year the DAR's National Committee on the Correct Use of the Flag sponsored nationwide ceremonies marking the Pledge's fiftieth anniversary.

Section 4 of the Code states that the Pledge "should be rendered by standing at attention facing the flag with the right hand over the heart." Those not wearing a military uniform "should remove their headdress with their right hand and hold it at the left shoulder, the hand being over the heart." Those in uniform "should remain silent, face the flag, and render the military salute." The code also mandates that all future changes in the Pledge's wording—as well as any other flag "rule or custom"—may be made by the president, acting as commander in chief of the armed forces, "whenever he deems it to be appropriate or desirable; and any such alteration or additional rule shall be set forth in a proclamation."

Two years earlier, on June 3, 1940, the U.S. Supreme Court had ruled that a Pennsylvania law making it mandatory for teachers and students to salute the flag as part of daily school exercises was constitutional. That case, *Minersville School District v. Gobitis,* involved two children, Lillian and William Gobitis, who were expelled from school after refusing to salute the flag because their religion, Jehovah's Witnesses, considers the American flag an icon and follows the biblical injunction not to "bow down to graven images."

On January 9, 1942, the West Virginia Board of Education instituted a new policy in that state, ordering that the Pledge Allegiance become "a regular part of the program of activities in the public schools" and requiring that teachers and pupils "participate in the salute honoring the nation represented by the flag." Those who refused to salute the flag would be expelled and not permitted to return to school unless they agreed to take part in the daily Pledge of Allegiance.

That action prompted another legal challenge from Jehovah's Witnesses after several children were expelled from West Virginia public schools for refusing to recite the Pledge. This time the Supreme Court reversed its earlier ruling. By a 6–3 vote, the court voted to overturn the *Gobitis* decision. On Flag Day, June 14, 1943, the court, in *West Virginia State Board of Education v. Barnette,* ruled that schoolchildren could not be compelled to recite the Pledge.

Civil libertarians see that ruling as a precedent-making freedom of speech decision—and one that used the American flag to make its point. The historian Arthur M. Schlesinger Jr., for example, said the decision "clarified the meaning of the flag as the symbol of patriotism." The decision showed, Schlesinger said, that saluting the flag and pledging allegiance to the flag are "forms of speech," and that requiring "people to do these things violated their constitutional rights to freedom of speech."

Supreme Court justice Robert H. Jackson, in fact, prominently cited the First Amendment in writing the majority's decision. "If there is any fixed star in our constitutional constellation, it is that no official, high or petty, can prescribe what shall be orthodox in politics, nationalism, religion, or other matters of opinion, or force citizens to confess by word or act their faith therein," Jackson said. "If there are any circumstances which permit an exception, they do not now occur to us. The action of the local authorities in compelling the flag salute and pledge transcends constitutional limitations on their power, and invades the sphere of intellect and spirit which it is the purpose of the First Amendment to our Constitution to reserve from all official control."

Although the court had ruled on the unconstitutionality of mandatory pledge laws, state legislators nevertheless have enacted many such laws since the 1943 ruling. In 1970, for example, the Maryland General Assembly and the Massachusetts Legislature passed mandatory Pledge bills. Gov. Francis W. Sargent of Massachusetts vetoed the legislation in his state, and a Maryland Circuit Court overturned the Maryland law.

In the wake of the September 11, 2001, terrorist attacks, state legislatures across the country took a new interest in mandatory pledge laws. In the 2002 and 2003 legislative sessions, seventeen states enacted new pledge laws or amended existing Pledge of Allegiance policies. That brought the total number of states with some form of mandatory Pledge laws to thirty-five. The laws either required school districts to have teachers lead the Pledge or to have students to recite it. Nearly all of the state laws, because of the 1942 Supreme Court decision, contained language making the Pledge optional for students who objected to saying it on religious or other grounds.

Pennsylvania's 2003 law, which required the parents of students who refused to say the Pledge give written notification to that effect, was struck down by U.S. District Court judge Robert F. Kelly on July 15, 2003. Kelly ruled that the parental notification abridged students' First Amendment rights because it could put coercive pressure on their decision whether or not to recite the Pledge. The Pennsylvania statute, one of the most stringent Pledge laws in the nation, required public and private school students in the state, from preschool through high school, to face the flag and recite the Pledge or sing the National Anthem at the beginning of each school day. Kelly had blocked implementation of the law on February 6, 2003, after public and private school students challenged its constitutionality. The state of Pennsylvania appealed the case to the United States Court of Appeals for the Third Circuit, which heard arguments on March 9, 2004, and upheld the ruling on August 19, 2004.

*   *   *

The third change in the Pledge's wording came in 1954 when, prodded by a national campaign led by Luke E. Hart, the Supreme Knight of the Knights of Columbus, the Catholic men's fraternal benefit society, Pres. Dwight D. Eisenhower added the words "under God" after "one nation indivisible."

Congressman Louis C. Rabaut, a Michigan Democrat, had introduced a resolution in the House of Representatives the previous year calling for the addition of the words "under God" in the Pledge. But no action was taken on Capitol Hill on the matter until February of 1954. The catalyst for congressional action was a sermon given by Rev. Dr. George M. Docherty on February 7, 1954, at the New York Avenue Presbyterian Church in Washington, D.C. There was "something missing" in the Pledge of Allegiance, Reverend Docherty said. "Apart from the mention of the phrase, 'the United States of America,' this could be a pledge of any republic. In fact, I could hear little Muscovites repeat a similar pledge to their hammer-and-sickle flag in Moscow with equal solemnity."

Among the parishioners in church that day was President Eisenhower. Within days after the sermon, seventeen resolutions were introduced in the House and Senate to add "under God" to the Pledge. Both houses approved the resolutions in June. "At this moment in our history the principles underlying our American government and the American way of life are under attack by a system that does not believe in God," Congressman Charles Wolverton, a New Jersey Republican, said during the House floor debate on June 7. "The inclusion of God in our Pledge of Allegiance rightly and most appropriately acknowledges the dependence of our people and our government upon that divinity that rules over the destinies of nations as well as individuals."

President Eisenhower signed the measure into law on Flag Day, June 14, 1954. "From this day forward," he said, "millions of our schoolchildren will daily proclaim in every city and town, every village and rural school house, the dedication of our nation and our people to the Almighty. To anyone who truly loves America, nothing could be more inspiring than to contemplate this rededication of our youth, on each school morning, to our country's true meaning."

Including the words "under God," Eisenhower said, reaffirmed "the transcendence of religious faith in America's heritage and future. In this way we shall constantly strengthen those spiritual weapons which forever will be our country's most powerful resource, in peace or in war."

The inclusion of "under God" came during the Cold War with the Soviet Union. Two years later, in 1956, the words "In God We Trust," which first appeared on the two-cent coin in 1864, became the nation's national motto. "Since the Soviet Union was avowedly atheistic, many believed that the United States needed vigorously to support religion—specifically Christianity—in order to be successful in the titanic struggle," Whitney Smith of the Flag Research Center said.

The decision to include "under God" in the Pledge was not controversial in 1954. It, however, soon was challenged by parents, teachers, students, and others who argued that those two words violated the concept of separation of church and state. In 1964, the U.S. Supreme Court refused to review a New York state court's 1960 decision that upheld the use of the words "under God" as constitutional. In June 2002, the United States Court of Appeals Ninth Circuit, however, ruled in favor of Michael A. Newdow, an atheist, who sued the public school district in California where his daughter attended classes, arguing that the mandatory recitation of the Pledge with the words "under God" in schools violated the Establishment Clause of the First Amendment to the Constitution.

The U.S. Supreme Court agreed to hear the case on October 14, 2003, and heard arguments on March 24, 2004. On Flag Day, June 14, 2004, the court issued its decision in the case, unanimously reversing the Court of Appeals for the Ninth Circuit's ruling. The court, however, did not base its ruling on the constitutional question. Instead, it ruled that Michael Newdow—who was not married to his daughter's mother but shared custody of the ten-year-old—lacked the legal standing to sue on behalf of his daughter.

The Vikings likely flew this raven flag on their ships that landed in Newfoundland a thousand years ago. If so, this banner was the first flag to fly in North America. *Xande Anderer*

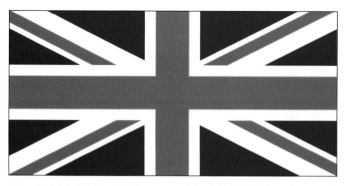

The British Union Jack, created in 1606 by King James I, is an amalgam of the crosses and the red, white and blue colors of St. George (England) and St. Andrew (Scotland). *Xande Anderer*

The Gadsden Flag, created by Colonel Christopher Gadsden in 1775, was the first of several "Don't Tread on Me" flags flown by American military units during the Revolutionary War. *Xande Anderer*

Pine Tree flags were popular during the Revolution in New England. Col. William Prescott's militiamen fought under this banner at the Battle of Bunker Hill on June 17, 1775. *Xande Anderer*

Liberty flags date from the summer of 1765 and the secret anti-British group, the Sons of Liberty. These flags typically were solid colored, usually white, with the word "liberty" spelled out in large capital letters. *Xande Anderer*

George Washington unveiled the Continental Colors on New Year's Day 1776 near Boston. The Continental Army and Navy flew this flag—not the Stars and Stripes—during the Revolutionary War. *Xande Anderer*

On December 3, 1775, U.S. Navy hero John Paul Jones likely raised the Continental Colors for the first time on an American fighting vessel, the *Alfred*, as depicted in this 1942 painting by N.C. Wyeth for a John Morrell & Co. calendar. *U.S. Naval Academy Museum*

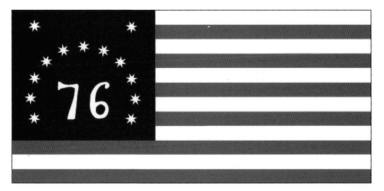

The Bennington Flag, one of several militia flags with thirteen stars and thirteen stripes, is thought to have been flown by the Green Mountain Boys at the August 16, 1777, Battle of Bennington in Vermont. *Xande Anderer*

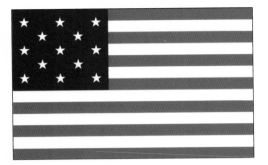

This thirteen-star flag, designed by Francis Hopkinson, likely was the first Stars and Stripes produced after the June 14, 1777, Flag Resolution set forth the design of the American flag. *Xande Anderer*

The so-called "Betsy Ross" flag with thirteen stars arrayed in a circle. This flag was not used by the American military during the Revolutionary War, as has often been portrayed in paintings such as "Washington Crossing the Delaware." *Xande Anderer*

Charles H. Weisgerber created his fanciful painting, "Birth of Our Nation's Flag," in 1892. The image of Betsy Ross sewing the first American flag at George Washington's behest has since then been popularly accepted as the true story of the creation of the flag. Because no portrait of Betsy Ross existed, Weisgerber based his Betsy Ross on miniatures of her two daughters.
State Museum of Pennsylvania Historical and Museum Commission

...*we here highly resolve that these dead shall not have died in vain*...

REMEMBER DEC. 7th!

One of the first posters issued by the government's Office of War Information after Pearl Harbor was this painting by the artist Allen Saalburg of a tattered American flag flying at half-staff. *The Library of Virginia*

1943 Women's Army Corps recruiting poster. *The Library of Congress, Prints and Photographs Division*

Are you a girl with a Star-Spangled heart?

JOIN THE **WAC** NOW!

THOUSANDS OF ARMY JOBS NEED FILLING!

Women's Army Corps United States Army

Many government-produced World War II home front posters featured heroic images of the American flag, such as this 1944 poster for U.S. war bonds. . . . *The Library of Congress, Prints and Photographs Division*

. . . and this U.S. Navy recruiting poster. *The Library of Congress, Prints and Photographs Division*

Associated Press photographer Joe Rosenthal's famed Iwo Jima photo inspired Felix de Weldon's Marine Corps War Memorial, which was dedicated near Arlington National Cemetery in 1954. *National Park Service*

The image of astronaut Buzz Aldrin planting a three-by-five-foot nylon American flag on the moon's surface on July 20, 1969, has become the iconic moment of *Apollo 11*'s historic voyage into outer space. *National Aeronautics and Space Administration*

In the wake of the events of September 11, 2001, the flag became an instant and widely used symbol of a nation united against terrorism as millions of Americans proudly and defiantly unfurled the Stars and Stripes in every corner of the country. That included these newspaper boxes in California. . . . *Michael Pretzer*

. . . and this house in Washington, D.C. *Michael Pretzer*

The Flag Day 2004 Supreme Court ruling, U.S. attorney general John Ashcroft said in a prepared statement, "insures that schoolchildren in every corner of America can start their day by voluntarily reciting the Pledge of Allegiance."

The ruling, though, left open the question of whether the words "under God" made the Pledge unconstitutional. Observers expected that more litigation would follow to force the courts to rule on that issue. "The justices ducked this constitutional issue today," the Reverend Barry W. Lynn, executive director of Americans United for Separation of Church and State, said on June 14, 2004, "but it is certain to come back in the future."

★   ★   ★

When *The Youth's Companion* published the original Pledge no credit was given for its authorship. An article in the magazine in December 1917 claimed that James Upham wrote the Pledge. For many years, until his death in 1931, Francis Bellamy spoke out strongly, claiming that he was the Pledge's author. The matter was settled in 1939 when the United States Flag Association, an organization formed in 1924 to promote the proper use and display of the flag, appointed a committee of distinguished historians to look into the matter. The committee weighed all the evidence and unanimously agreed on May 16, 1939, that Bellamy wrote the Pledge. A seventeen-month study undertaken by the Library of Congress in 1957 came to the same conclusion.

In 1985, President Reagan signed a law recognizing the pause for the Pledge of Allegiance, encouraging all Americans to recite the Pledge on Flag Day. In 1988, the Pledge became an issue in the presidential campaign between Republican George H. W. Bush and Democrat Michael Dukakis. Bush criticized Dukakis for vetoing a bill that would have required the Pledge to be recited in Massachusetts's public schools when Dukakis was the governor of that state in 1977. Dukakis, Bush said, "isn't willing to let the teachers lead the kids in the Pledge of Allegiance." Dukakis responded that he vetoed the legislation after being advised by the Supreme Judicial Court of Massachusetts and his state attorney general Francis X. Bellotti that a mandatory pledge law was unconstitutional and unenforceable.

During the height of the campaign, on September 13, 1988, the Pledge was recited on the floor of the House of Representatives for the first time. Republican members of the House, who were in the minority, offered a resolution to that effect; and Speaker of the House Jim Wright, a Texas Demo-

crat, accepted it. Congressman G. V. Sonny Montgomery, the chairman
of the House Committee on Veterans' Affairs, a Mississippi Democrat, recited the Pledge that day. Speaker Wright ruled that from that day forward
the Pledge would be recited at the start of business each day the House of
Representatives was in session.

The U.S. Senate did not adopt the daily recital of the Pledge until June
24, 1999. Republican senator Strom Thurmond of South Carolina recited
the Pledge that day for the first time in that legislative body after the Senate
unanimously adopted a resolution offered by Sen. Bob Smith, an Independent from New Hampshire. It went into effect the same day that the House
of Representatives had voted to adopt an amendment to the Constitution to
ban flag desecration.

"The U.S. Senate started reciting the Pledge in 1999; the House in 1988.
Essentially, it's moved from a children's procedure to one that adults use,"
noted John Baer. "Local governments and state legislatures now recite the
Pledge. You have a fascinating phenomenon there."

That phenomenon also includes the fact the United States is the only
nation in the world that has codified the use of a pledge of allegiance to its
national flag. As Baer put it: "The verbal flag salute is unique and has something to do with the fact that we are a republic. It's right up there with the
Declaration of Independence and the Gettysburg Address."

CHAPTER THIRTEEN

The Great War

★   ★   ★

As I see the winds lovingly unfold the beautiful lines of our great flag,
I shall seem to see a hand pointing the way of duty, no matter how
hard, no matter how long, which we shall tread while we vindicate the
glory and honor of the United States.

—Pres. Woodrow Wilson, Flag Day, June 14, 1916

HAVE NAILED THE STARS and Stripes to the Pole." Those
were the words of a telegram sent from the Smoky Tickle telegraph station
at Indian harbor in Labrador on September 6, 1909, by U.S. Navy rear admiral Robert Edwin Peary to his wife, Josephine, at their summer home on
Eagle Island in Casco Bay off the Maine coast. The pole the veteran polar
adventurer referred to was the North Pole, which he and his associate and
fellow explorer Matthew Henson and their four Inuit guides had reached
five months earlier, on April 6—the first humans to do so.

The American flag "had a certain sacred symbolism to" Peary, his daughter Marie Peary Stafford explained. "In a sense, the flag *was* the country,
and flags had always played an important and thrilling part in his explo-
ration work."

In 1898 Josephine Peary made a large, gold-fringed, taffeta, forty-five-
star American flag for her husband as he was about to embark on a four-
year expedition into the Arctic. That silklike homemade flag, his daughter
said, "meant more to him than all the replicas in the world. He carried it with
him always when in the field, wrapped around his body underneath his fur
clothing because he did not wish to trust it to a sledge," which might break
through the ice. Peary cut out five pieces of the flag to leave as markers at

noteworthy places "whenever he had attained one of his objectives," as his daughter put it, in northern Greenland and northern Ellesemere Island in Canada in 1900 and 1906. The "Stars and Stripes" that the Peary party planted at the North Pole actually was the sixth piece of Josephine Peary's flag, a four-inch-wide diagonal strip of that flag cut diagonally to include both stars and stripes.

That act captured the popular imagination in this country. Even though the flag placed at or near the North Pole (probably by Henson) was but a fragment of an entire flag, the image of an intact Old Glory flying on a pole at the top of the world became instantly accepted when the news of Peary's feat reached the American populace. That image has resonated with the American public since then. Newspaper and magazine accounts helped spread the idea. That included the newspaper columnist and poet Leigh Mitchell Hodges's ode to Perry and Henson's achievement, "The Flag That Tops the World." It contained the stanza:

> You may sing a song of banners that are brave against the breeze,
> Of flags that ne'er in time of need are furl'd;
> You may boast the battle ensigns that have swept the seven seas,
> But I toast the starry flag that tops the world!

Had Peary's flag been official and up to date, it would have had forty-six stars, in recognition of Oklahoma's entry into the Union in 1907. A government study undertaken when Oklahoma became a state found that federal agencies were flying sixty-six different-sized and proportioned American flags. That situation prompted the federal government to set up a special panel to consider the look of the forty-six-star flag. The panel was put together by the War Department—the predecessor of the Department of Defense—and consisted of army and navy officers. Eighty-year-old admiral of the navy George Dewey, who was then serving as the president of the General Board of the Navy, headed up the effort. Dewey's panel recommended a flag with six rows of stars in the canton: four rows of eight and two rows of seven.

The Territories of New Mexico (on January 6) and Arizona (on February 14) became the nation's forty-seventh and forty-eighth states in 1912. That prompted another session of Dewey's panel to consider the arrangement of the forty-eight-star flag, which would become official on July 4, 1912. The committee recommended a flag with the stars arranged in six horizontal even rows of eight stars each, with one point of each star facing upward.

On June 24, 1912, Pres. William Howard Taft accepted the Dewey committee's recommendation and signed a groundbreaking executive order setting out the star arrangement for the forty-eight-star flag. That executive order marked the first time since the Stars and Stripes was born in 1777 that a president officially clarified exactly what the American flag should look like and what dimensions the government would accept for its flags. Taft's order cut the number of official government flag sizes to twelve and used the Dewey panel's recommended forty-eight-star arrangement.

Taft's executive order applied only to government flags, but it also served to curtail the number of creatively designed flags by private individuals. One exception was the Whipple flag of 1912, the creation of Wayne Whipple, a Germantown, Pennsylvania, author who had written a hagiographic history, *The Story of the American Flag,* for children in 1910. Whipple designed a flag in a heraldry contest and had high hopes that it would become the official forty-eight-star flag. He took his flag to President Taft. The president, Whipple said, "went into ecstasies over it," and recommended it to the War and Navy Departments. Whipple also lobbied veterans' and patriotic groups across the nation on behalf of his creation.

In his flag thirteen stars were arrayed midcanton in the shape of a six-sided star; twenty-five stars circled that star, with ten additional stars sitting in an outer circle. The thirteen stars symbolized the original states; the twenty-five stars stood for the states that entered the Union in the nation's first one hundred years; the ten stars represented the states that joined after 1876. Whipple referred to his creation, which was not chosen as the nation's official banner, as the "Peace Flag."

World peace, however, was shattered in Europe in 1914 with the outbreak of World War I, the mammoth "war to end all wars" that forever altered the world's political landscape and caused unprecedented loss of life and carnage in western Europe and Russia. The Great War, as it was called—along with the 1918 influenza pandemic—resulted in the deaths of some 8.5 million combatants and some 13 million civilians, in addition to some 21 million wounded and 7.7 million missing or imprisoned. The United States entered the war in April 1917.

Shortly after war broke out in Europe in August 1914, former president Theodore Roosevelt and U.S. Army chief of staff Gen. Leonard Wood, among others, formed the preparedness movement. The idea was to lobby the Wilson administration and to convince the American public of the need to get the nation ready for war. The movement called for compulsory military training for all able-bodied young men. In conjunction with organizations such as the National Security League, the American Defense Society, and the League to Enforce Peace, it organized a series of preparedness parades around the nation to publicize the cause. These parades prominently featured the Stars and Stripes.

The first preparedness parades took place in 1914. For the next three years, until the United States entered the war in April 1917, similar parades were put on all over the country, mostly in cities, from Buffalo to San Francisco. Preparedness parades reached a peak in 1916 as it became clear that this country would be sending troops to Europe to fight in the war.

Some seven thousand people marched in Baltimore's preparedness parade on May 17, 1916, and more than one hundred thousand flag-waving spectators cheered them on. On Saturday, June 3, 1916, more than fifty-two thousand men and women took part in a massive, flag-waving, seven-hour preparedness parade in Providence, Rhode Island. That same day some thirty-five thousand men marched in New Orleans's preparedness parade. Only two banners were permitted in that parade: the Stars and Stripes and the Stars and Bars held aloft by Confederate veterans.

An even larger preparedness parade had taken place in New York City on May 13, 1916. The eleven-hour parade began at City Hall Park and moved up Broadway and Fifth Avenue. It featured some 125,000 marching civilians and dozens of brass bands and drum corps. An estimated crowd of a million people lined the march. The parade was led by an enormous, ninety-five-foot by fifty-foot American flag that had been made by the Amoskeag Manufacturing Company in Manchester, New Hampshire, in 1914.

That huge flag was far from the only one flying that day. "Almost every marcher carried an American flag," the *New York Times* reported. "Almost every building along the line of march was covered with the red, white and blue bunting of the national colors. Every spectator wore 'Old Glory' or carried a tiny flag. The effect was a sea of red, white and blue that billowed and moved. Probably never before in history has there been such a showing of the flag and its colors."

The profusion of flags in the city and at the parade proved to be an inspiration to Childe Hassam, the nation's leading Impressionist painter. Soon after the May 1916 New York parade, the prolific and influential Hassam began a series of paintings that featured the streets of New York decorated with American flags. "I painted the flag series after we went into the war," Hassam told an interviewer in 1927. "There was that Preparedness Day, and I looked up the avenue and saw these wonderful flags waving, and I painted the series of flag pictures after that."

Hassam, whose studio was on West Fifty-seventh Street near Sixth Avenue, turned out thirty flag paintings during the next three years, inspired by that first preparedness parade and the many patriotic parades held in the city thereafter during the war. The paintings featured flags mounted on buildings along Fifth Avenue between Thirty-third and Fifty-seventh Streets and other nearby New York streets. The subjects included the Waldorf-Astoria Hotel, the Union League Club, the Friar's Club, and St. Patrick's Cathedral.

Hassam executed "Allies Day, May 1917" following the visit of the French and British war commissioners to this country the month after the United States entered the war. It showed a grouping of the British Union Jack, the French Tricolor, and the Stars and Stripes, which likely was the first time those three flags had been displayed together in public. Hassam's goal was to keep the flag paintings together as a tribute to the American war effort, but they were sold individually. Today the paintings are in private collections and art museums, including the National Gallery of Art in Washington and the White House.

Childe Hassam was not the only American artist who used the flag in his work during World War I. A group of artists, led by the famed illustrator Charles Dana Gibson, in April 1917 organized the Division of Pictorial Publicity for the federal government's Committee on Public Information. In the next eighteen months Dana and many other artists turned out 700 posters, 287 cartoons, and 432 newspaper advertisements. All were designed to build public support for the war effort. The Stars and Stripes was used widely in those works. "The American flag," the art critic Ilene Susan Fort noted, "was an extremely potent symbol of unity and liberty and often appeared [in the Pictorial Publicity works] in conjunction with other stock subjects," such as the Statue of Liberty.

One of the committee's contributors, the serendipitously named James Montgomery Flagg, had created one of the nation's most famous and enduring posters for the cover of the July 6, 1916, *Leslie's Weekly*. Titled "What Are You Doing for Preparedness?" the poster shows a scowling "Uncle Sam," replete with a red- white- and blue-starred hatband, pointing an accusatory finger at the viewer. More than four million copies of that poster with the inscription "I Want You for U.S. Army" underneath were printed by 1918. The poster went on to become an icon of American culture.

The figure of Uncle Sam, usually clad in striped pants and a white jacket festooned with stars, dates from the War of 1812. Historians believe

The aptly named James Montgomery Flagg created one of the nation's most famous and enduring posters for the cover of the July 6, 1916, *Leslie's Weekly.* More than four million copies of that poster with the inscription "I Want You For U.S. Army" underneath were printed by 1918. The image soon became an icon of American culture. *The Library of Congress, Prints and Photographs Division*

he was based on Samuel Wilson, a patriotic meat packer in Troy, New York. Wilson supplied food to the U.S. military, stamping his shipments with the letters "U.S." for the United States government. Wilson soon became known as "Uncle Sam" Wilson. Thomas Nast and other political cartoonists made frequent use of a stylized, stars-and-stripes-clad figure of Uncle Sam throughout the nineteenth century as a symbol representing the United States and patriotism.

The flag also was a prominent feature on many other World War I home-front posters, including military recruiting posters and those produced by civic groups such as the YMCA and the Red Cross, the United War Work Campaign, the U.S. Department of Labor, and the U.S. Food

Administration. "Rally 'Round the Flag with United States Marines," said a Marine Corps recruiting poster that featured an image of marines storming a beach with a large American flag waving overhead. A 1918 Red Cross poster by Harrison Fisher depicts a beautiful young woman volunteer clasping a large American flag to her bosom with the U.S. Capitol in the background. Her mouth is open and the words "I summon you to Comradeship in the Red Cross" are emblazoned on the poster.

The flag was a prominent feature on many World War I home-front posters, including military recruiting posters and those produced by civic groups such as the YMCA and the Red Cross. *The Library of Congress, Prints and Photographs Division*

In many ways the outpouring of affection for the flag prior to and during World War I resembled the outburst of flag waving in the North that began at the start of the Civil War in 1861 and lasted until the fighting ended four years later. Within hours after World War I was declared on April 6, 1917, flags were displayed from public and private buildings all across America. "Though the city has been besprinkled with flags in the last weeks, a veritable flood of bunting broke forth yesterday" in New York City, the *New York Times* reported April 7. "Now is the time above all others that citizens should show their country's colors," the *Los Angeles Times* editorialized on April 6. "The Stars and Stripes should wave from every business, house and residence in the city."

In Washington, D.C., in response to a nationwide public outcry, American flags began flying twenty-four hours a day over the east and west fronts of the U.S. Capitol. Flag-waving patriotic pageants, with names such as "Building of the Flag, or Liberty Triumphant" and "A Pageant of the Stars and Stripes," took place in communities and schools throughout the nation.

A joint resolution Congress passed on May 8, 1914, authorizing the president to designate the second Sunday in May as Mother's Day contained language calling for the American flag to be displayed that day "upon all Government buildings," as well as for "the people of the United States to display the flag at their homes or other suitable places" as "a public expression of our love and reverence for the mothers of our country." President Wilson issued the first Mother's Day holiday proclamation the next day. Two years later he established June 14 as national Flag Day through a presidential proclamation.

Not long after the United States entered the war in April 1917, the New York commissioner of education, Henry Sterling Chapin, organized a nation-wide contest to choose a national creed, what Chapin envisioned as "the best summary of the political faith of America." Some three thousand entries were submitted. Baltimore's mayor, James H. Preston, offered a one thousand dollar prize. The winning entry was the work of William Tyler Page of Chevy Chase, Maryland, a descendant of U.S. president John Tyler. Page worked in the U.S. House of Representatives and in 1919 became the Clerk of the House.

Page's winning entry, now known as the American's Creed, was published in the *Congressional Record* on April 3, 1918, the day Page was awarded his one-thousand-dollar prize on Capitol Hill by Mayor Preston. The federal government has never accepted the creed officially; but many patriotic groups, including the Daughters of the American Revolution, have adopted it. The creed contains words and phrases borrowed from Lincoln's Gettysburg Address, the Declaration of Independence, and the Preamble to the Constitution. It ends with a pledge of allegiance to the nation and its flag: "I believe it is my duty to my country to love it, to support its Constitution, to obey its laws, to respect its flag, and to defend it against all enemies."

World War I created an "unprecedented demand and runaway market" for American flags, the Federal Trade Commission reported in July 1917. Sales of flags reached an all-time high during the war. Businesses, including Wanamaker's Department Store in Philadelphia and Marshall Field & Company in Chicago, produced and distributed written materials promoting the flag. Marshall Field's sixteen-page pamphlet, *Laws and Customs Regulating the Use of the Flag of the United States*, was written by B. J. Cigrand, the Chicago dentist and national Flag Day proponent.

"In presenting to the public this booklet for distribution, it is with the hope that it may prove to service in making readily available such information as will tend to increase the evidences of public respect for our national emblem," Cigrand wrote in his introduction.

National Geographic magazine devoted an entire special issue in October 1917 to flags, concentrating on the history of the American flag. The navy's top flag expert, Lt. Cmdr. Byron McCandless, an aide to the chief of naval operations William S. Benson and to the secretary of the navy Josephus Daniels, edited the issue. It contained a sixteen-page history of the American flag with illustrations and photographs, including one of the Star Spangled Banner being restored by "expert needlewomen" at the Smithsonian. Another photo, with the caption, "The French Army's First Salute to the Stars and Stripes on French Soil," showed a flag ceremony on the French front in June 1917 with members of the American Ambulance Corps and the French army. Five thousand copies of the issue were distributed free of charge to American troops on their way over to France.

Men went off to war with flag-inspired patriotic words ringing in their ears. "The American flag and the many things that it stands for should be their constant thought," former senator J. C. Pritchard of North Carolina, then a judge of the U.S. Court of Appeals, Fourth Circuit, told a patriotic gathering of citizens in Raleigh on September 23, 1917. "Let them cherish this glorious emblem of our liberty."

African Americans, the overwhelming majority of whom supported the war effort, also exhibited affection for the American flag. Some 350,000 black Americans served in World War I in segregated units. Although most of the black units were support troops, several fought in the trenches in France. "True Sons of Freedom," a 1918 poster by Charles Gustrine, depicts black American fighting men in hand-to-hand combat with German soldiers. The American flag waves prominently in the background, with Abraham Lincoln looking down benignly on the scene. The words "Liberty and Freedom Shall Not Perish" are inscribed under Lincoln's visage. The poster also contains the words: "COLORED MEN: The First Americans Who Planted Our Flag on the Firing Line."

At home, many black women were active in efforts to support the war. The thinking among most black Americans was that patriotically taking part in the war effort would lead to more freedom at home after the fighting ended. On June 14, 1918, large numbers of African Americans marched in several flag-saturated parades in honor of Flag Day, including a large parade in Wilmington, Delaware. "Material manifestation of the patriotism of the Negroes of Wilmington was given," the *Cleveland Advocate* reported, "when in honor of the Flag Day—the anniversary of the Stars and Stripes—5,000 local members of the race, men women and children, gave a decidedly credible parade, which was applauded by thousands of white persons who lined the streets over which it passed."

The startling success of a fund-raising event for Liberty Bonds (U.S. government war bonds) in New York City in 1918 featuring an American flag flown in battle in Europe offers a good illustration of the unfettered veneration Americans held for the flag during the war. The flag in question actually consisted of two streamers cut from an American flag and flown on the struts of a British Royal Flying Corps (RFC) plane by the first American air ace of the war, Frederick Libby, an all-but-forgotten American military hero.

Libby grew up on a ranch in Sterling, Colorado. As a young man he became one of the last of a dying breed, a true American cowboy who made his living roping, punching cattle, and taming horses in Arizona, New Mexico, and in his home state. Libby found himself in Calgary, Alberta, Canada, when the war broke out in 1914. He promptly joined the Canadian army and went to France where he signed up as an aerial observer/machine gunner with the RFC, immediately taking to the air in a wooden two-seater FE 2b biplane.

In May 1916, Libby moved to the pilot's seat, where he took part in some of the world's first aerial battles, going head to head with, among others, the legendary German ace Manfred von Richthofen. Libby survived his showdown with the Red Baron and went on to shoot down fourteen enemy aircraft before transferring to the U.S. Air Service in September 1917.

At Buckingham Palace in November 1916 King George V awarded Libby the British Military Cross for conspicuous gallantry in action. In 1917, Libby took the streamers from an American flag and hooked them onto the struts of the plane he flew in battle. An English RFC major "suggested that I use [the flag] as a streamer or streamers just to show the Hun

that America had a flyer in action," Libby said in his memoir. "This I did—
from May 28 until my return to America" in October. "During this period,
there were always one or two streamers of an American flag over the German lines." It was not done "with any idea of a stunt to be first with anything," Libby said. "It was done in the line of duty and at the suggestion of
my squadron commander."

Libby came back to this country in October 1917 and brought the
streamers to New York City, where he donated them to the Aero Club of
America to auction off at a Carnegie Hall fund-raiser for Liberty Bonds.
"The action wasn't intended by me as a stunt for publicity," Libby said. "In
fact, I had a feeling of embarrassment, as these streamers had been a part of
my plane for many, many hours of combat service."

When Libby took the Carnegie Hall stage at the October 17, 1918, fund-
raiser, the crowd "rolled forward in tumult of noise, men and women with
welcome in their voices and tears in their eyes," the *New York Tribune* reported. "Then a girl reached out and over the crowd, caught hold of the tattered thing, held it hard and with swimming eyes raised it to her lips. The
voices stopped and the air was silent as a prayer." Then the crowd "sought to
grasp the precious stripes" of the flag and to shake Libby's hand. "And so
the procession passed along," the article said. "Some touched it lightly, some
shook it as if it were a paw. The women kissed it, the soldiers saluted it."

The enthusiastic reception given Libby's American flag streamers was
reminiscent of the situation in the North during the Civil War when Major
Anderson's Fort Sumter Stars and Stripes was used as a highly effective
fund-raising tool at auctions supporting the war effort. Libby's streamers
outdid the Fort Sumter flag, however. The streamers were auctioned at
Carnegie Hall following the bidding on a French Legion of Honor cordon.
As the bidding on Libby's streamers began, someone in the audience
shouted, "If the cordon of the French Legion of Honor is worth a million
dollars, how much is Old Glory worth?" The answer was provided by the
National Bank of Commerce, which bought Libby's tattered streamers for
$3,250,000—the equivalent of more than $40 million today. The winning
bid contained the proviso that Captain Libby would be allowed to keep the
streamers.

The American flag also was popular in Canada, England, France, and
Belgium and elsewhere outside of Germany in western Europe after the
United States entered the war. On April 6, 1917, the day the United States
declared war on Germany, the American flag flew for the first time ever
alongside the Union Jack on the Canadian Parliament Building in Ottawa.

The Stars and Stripes also was raised over Ottawa's city hall and many other public buildings that day. The citizens of England expressed their gratitude to this country in the days after the United States declared war with an unprecedented display of the American flag. That included, for the first time in history, the flying of a foreign flag next to the Union Jack outside of Parliament.

"The Stars and Stripes almost instantaneously broke out on private dwellings, shops, hotels, and theatres" in London when the United States declared war on Germany, one observer wrote. "Street hucksters did a thriving business selling rosettes of the American colours, which even the most stodgy Englishmen did not disdain to wear in their buttonholes; wherever there was a band or an orchestra, the Star Spangled Banner acquired a sudden popularity."

U.S. ambassador Walter H. Page organized what he called "an American Dedicatory Service" at St. Paul's Cathedral in London in April. The royal family attended, as did British government officials, members of Parliament, the ambassador corps, and a hundred wounded Americans serving in the Canadian army. My "Navy and Army staff went in full uniform," Page said in a May 3, 1917, letter, "the Stars and Stripes hung before the altar, a double brass band played the Star Spangled Banner and the Battle Hymn of the Republic, and an American bishop preached a red-hot American sermon, the Archbishop of Canterbury delivered the benediction; and a foreign flag flew over the Houses of Parliament."

The situation was similar in France. When the United States entered the war, the American flag flew at the French National Assembly at the Palais Bourbon in Paris next to the French Tricolor and along the streets of Paris and other French cities. On April 11, Raymond Poincaré, the president of the French Republic, joined with many other government officials, French military officers, and others in ceremonies commemorating the American entry into the war. "Great crowds surrounded the building" where the ceremonies were held, the *Washington Post* reported. "There were many tiny American flags, and vendors had a lively traffic in postcards of Uncle Sam and President Wilson and rosettes of French and American flags entwined." That same day the Lafayette Flying Squadron (or Escadrille), a group of Americans fighter pilots serving with the French, received orders to don American uniforms and thereby became the first American unit to take the Stars and Stripes into battle in World War I.

By the summer of 1918, the American flag was a common sight in the streets of the French capital. "In Paris, the red, white and blue of France is so blended with the red, white and blue of America that it is difficult to tell at a glance where one flag begins and the other ends," *New York Times* correspondent Charles A. Seldon reported on July 3. Sheldon described the American flag flying at several of Paris's famed landmarks, including the Louvre, the Place de la Concorde, and the Hotel de Cluny. He found the flag as well "in regions where English will never be spoken" and "in obscure little streets that were streets long before America was discovered, in streets of old Paris, of the Franks and the Romans."

★   ★   ★

Not long after the United States entered the war, the U.S. Department of Justice let it be known that Germans and other aliens who were discovered "abusing or desecrating" the American flag "in any way" would be subject to "summary arrest and confinement" as a "danger to the public peace or safety" during the duration of the war. In 1918 Congress passed and President Wilson signed into law an addition to the June 1917 Espionage Act, called the Sedition Act. That measure, among other things, made it illegal to "willfully utter, print, write or publish any disloyal, profane, scurrilous, or abusive language" about the Constitution, the government, or the American flag. The Sedition Act also banned the willful display of the flag "of any foreign enemy." Those acts were punishable by a fine of not more than ten thousand dollars or twenty years in jail. The law also mandated that any U.S. government employee or official who, "in an abusive and violent manner criticizes the Army or Navy or the flag of the United States shall be at once dismissed from the service."

During World War I several states strengthened the language and increased the penalties of their flag protection laws—which originally had been designed mainly to cut down on the commercial use of the flag. And Congress, on February 8, 1917, approved a bill making it a misdemeanor punishable by a one-hundred-dollar fine or thirty days in jail for manufacturing, selling, or advertising items decorated with the American flag in the District of Columbia. That included canned goods, post cards, and sheet music, as well as stores' show-window decorations.

Kansas enacted a law in 1915 making it a misdemeanor to "publicly mutilate, deface, defile, or defy, trample upon, or cast contempt, either by words or act upon any" American flag. Three years later Frederick Shumaker Jr. of Wetmore, Kansas, was convicted under the statute for making "a very vulgar and indecent use of the flag." He was accused of using language in a blacksmith's shop so foul that the court would not spell it out because the words would become part of the official record. Shumaker apparently had referred to the flag as "a rag." He appealed his case to the Kansas Supreme Court and lost.

Texas's Disloyalty Act, which became law on March 11, 1918, made flag desecration punishable by up to twenty-five years in jail. The law imposed that strict penalty on those convicted of using "any language" in public or private that "cast contempt" on the American flag.

Montana enacted a similarly worded law in February 1918. Six months later a man named E. V. Starr was arrested, tried, and convicted in Montana for the words he said after a mob tried to force him to kiss an American flag. "What is this thing anyway, nothing but a piece of cotton with a little paint on it and some other marks in the corner there," Starr said. "I will not kiss that thing. It might be covered with microbes."

It is unclear from court records and newspaper accounts if the mob turned on Starr for political reasons. What is clear is that federal and state officials enforced flag protection laws during the war primarily against those who spoke out against the war effort—most often labor activists, pacifists, socialists, anarchists, and communists—as well as German immigrants, German-Americans, and those who expressed sympathy for the German cause. A New York City woman was arrested and sent to jail for six months in March 1918, for example, for displaying a German flag and for taking down an American flag put in her window and then saying the words: "To hell with the American flag. I want my own flag."

Outside of the law, citizens took measures against German-Americans and others who spoke out against the war effort. Vigilante actions of this sort typically involved forcing a suspected unpatriotic person to salute the flag, to recite the Pledge of Allegiance, or to kiss the flag. The self-appointed flag defenders may have taken their cue from the stern words of President Wilson in his April 2, 1917, war message to a special session of Congress. Speaking about Americans "of German birth and native sympathy who live among us," Wilson warned what would happen if they were not loyal during the upcoming war. "If there should be disloyalty," he said, "it will be dealt with with a firm hand of stern repression."

Shortly after the war began in April 1917, a man thought to have insulted a flag in Santa Cruz, California, was forced to kneel on the sidewalk and kiss it. At around the same time, a mob of angry citizens attacked a socialist and two suffragists who would not rise for the playing of "The Star-Spangled Banner" at a New York City supper club. On April 12, 1918, in Collinsville, Oklahoma, a mob forced a German-American, Henry Rheimer, to kiss an American flag and then tried, unsuccessfully, to hang him with an electrical cord.

The day the war ended, November 11, 1918, five carloads of men drove eleven miles outside of Burrton, Kansas, and ransacked the house and farm of John Schrag, a German-speaking Mennonite who had immigrated to this country when he was thirteen years old in 1874. The men took Schrag into town where he faced a larger mob, unhappy over the fact that he had refused to buy Liberty bonds. Schrag offered, instead, to donate money to the Red Cross or Salvation Army. The mob then demanded that Schrag salute the American flag and parade it through town. He refused.

When a flag that was forced on him dropped to the ground, the crowd set upon Schrag, covered him with yellow paint, and attempted to hang him. He was saved by the head of the local Anti-Horse-Thief Association. Schrag escaped with his life but was arrested for violating the Espionage Act because he allegedly desecrated the American flag. He was tried in federal court in Wichita and found not guilty.

The most egregious incident involving the flag and a German-American's supposed criticism of the war occurred near St. Louis in April 1918. Robert Paul Prager, a thirty-year-old German-American, was taken from his home in nearby Collinsville, Illinois, by a mob of some three hundred people — members, the *Chicago Daily Tribune* said, "of the local loyalist committee." Prager was forced to march down the street barefoot carrying two small American flags. He was wrapped in a large American flag and made to kiss the flag as he walked. An unemployed miner, Prager had given a speech earlier in the evening at a socialist meeting in which he allegedly made disloyal remarks.

Collinsville police placed him in custody for his own safety. Outside the jail, the mayor of Collinsville talked the mob into dispersing. But the group reformed, broke into the jail, and hanged Prager to death from a tree just after midnight on April 5. At his funeral on April 10, a large American flag was draped over Prager's coffin. Police arrested eleven men and charged them with Prager's murder. A jury found them not guilty in Edwardsville, Illinois, on June 8.

As the Prager case showed only too well, the American flag evoked exceptionally strong emotions during World War I. When the war ended in 1918, most Americans continued to feel very strongly about the flag and what it stood for. Those strong feelings continued unabated in the 1920s, pushed along in large part by veterans of the Great War who banded together to form the powerful veterans' service organization, the American Legion.

CHAPTER FOURTEEN

One Hundred Percent Americanism

★   ★   ★

The Flag of the United States—a beautiful, artistic, inspiring emblem, standing for our National sovereignty, ideals, traditions, and institutions; a sacred symbol of our political faith, appealing so strongly to every American—affords, indeed, an ideal rallying point for the citizens of the Republic—rich and poor, high and low—to assemble and join hands in working together for lofty Americanism, sturdy patriotism, and good citizenship which shall make stronger and more secure the foundations on which this Government is built.

—**United States Flag Association, 1924**

WORLD WAR I ended with the armistice on November 11, 1918, thanks in no small measure to the battlefield contributions of the two-million-strong American Expeditionary Force under U.S. Army general John Joseph "Black Jack" Pershing. Not long after hostilities ended, state legislatures began enacting laws declaring November 11 Armistice Day to remember the sacrifices of those who served in Europe. Twenty-seven states had made November 11 a legal holiday by 1926.

On June 4 of that year Congress passed a resolution asking the president to issue an annual proclamation for a federal Armistice Day holiday. The resolution called for the American flag to be displayed on all government buildings that day and urged all Americans to observe the day "in schools and churches, or other suitable places, with appropriate ceremonies of friendly relations with all other peoples." On May 13, 1938, Congress approved legislation that made November 11 an annual legal holiday.

When World War I ended, American troops helped occupy Germany and remained in Europe throughout the first half of 1919. On March 15, 1919, at the behest of U.S. Army lieutenant colonel Theodore Roosevelt Jr., the son of the nation's twenty-sixth president, a group of army officers and enlisted men met at the Cirque de Paris, a large building bedecked with American flags and red, white, and blue bunting for the occasion. This was the Paris caucus at which Roosevelt and company founded the American Legion, a veterans' service organization that became the spiritual successor of the Grand Army of the Republic, which by the 1920s was rapidly declining in membership and influence.

The American Legion was born at the end of that three-day caucus in Paris and immediately began attracting large numbers of World War I veterans. A thousand delegates showed up at the Legion's first American caucus on May 8 in St. Louis, where the organization pledged itself to work for "God and Country." When Congress granted the Legion its national charter of incorporation on September 16, there already were 5,670 local posts in every state in the Union and in Europe. By 1920, some 840,000 World War I veterans had joined, about a fifth of those eligible for membership. Within a year after the Paris caucus met "the Legion established itself . . . as the most powerful veterans organization in American history," as the historians John Lax and William Pencak put it.

Today the American Legion has nearly three million members in some fifteen thousand local posts, making it the largest veterans' organization in the world. The Legion's posts are organized into fifty-five departments in the fifty states, the District of Columbia, Puerto Rico, France, Mexico, and the Philippines. The Legion's national headquarters is in Indianapolis, and it maintains a large additional office in Washington, D.C.

From the beginning the American Legion, as was the case with its spiritual predecessor the GAR, had several agendas. At its heart the organization was an advocacy group working on behalf of disabled veterans and their families. It was also a fraternal organization that offered fellowship and companionship at local posts across the country. But the American Legion also was a political organization. Its constitution pledged that the Legion would be "absolutely nonpolitical" and not be used "for the dissemination of partisan principles" or to endorse political candidates. However, the constitution also said that the Legion would work to "maintain law and order; to foster and perpetuate a one hundred percent Americanism," and to "combat the autocracy of both the classes and the masses."

The Legion's 100 percent Americanism agenda came about in reaction to the 1914 communist revolution in Russia and to the leftist social and political movements related to Bolshevism and Marxism in the United States that had gained many adherents by 1919. The Legion's political agenda included a heavy attachment to the flag, a deep involvement in promoting respect for the flag, and teaching proper flag etiquette. In one of its first actions, in January of 1921, the Legion successfully lobbied the Massachusetts Boxing Commission to issue a ruling prohibiting boxers from wearing the American flag in the ring during state-sanctioned boxing matches.

A political cartoon that appeared in the Memphis *Commercial Appeal* in 1919 clearly illustrates the importance of the American flag to the American Legion. Titled "The New National Figure," the cartoon by James P. Alley depicts a giant of a man attired in a World War I army hat and britches, his face resolute, his well-muscled arms crossed at his chest, and the words "American Legion" on his shirt. Behind him a large American flag is unfurled. At his feet are small, shiftless human figures labeled "Anarchy," "Lawlessness," "Class Autocracy," and "Petty Politics."

This was a time of severe social conflict in the United States that included anarchist bombings, extreme labor unrest, race riots, and lynchings of African Americans in the South and elsewhere. Many believed Communists were behind the unrest. What was called the Red Scare—a fear of communists, socialists, anarchists, labor radicals, and a xenophobic reaction against immigrants—spread throughout the nation. That fear often was expressed as an assault on the American flag by political cartoonists in the nation's top newspapers. A Fred Morgan cartoon in 1919 in The *Philadelphia Inquirer*, for example, consisted of a large American flag (with only thirty-six stars) being attacked by a bearded, evil-looking man clutching a large knife with the word "Bolshevism" on it and a flaming torch labeled "Anarchy."

A 1919 Raymond O. Evans cartoon in the Baltimore *American* showed an anarchist tossing a bomb that was blocked by a large American flag and sent on its way back to blow him up. A John H. Cassel cartoon in the New York *Evening World* in 1920 depicted an evil Karl Marx–like figure holding an emasculated American flag that consisted only of the red stripes—red being the color of communism.

The flag itself often was used as a symbol in the fight against the Red Scare. That was the case, for example, during a three-day strike by local unions that nearly shut down the city of Seattle in February 1919. Mayor Ole Hanson, calling the strikers anarchists and comparing them to Bolsheviks, threatened to impose martial law to end the strike. To boost his cause, the mayor draped a large American flag over his car as he led a detachment of U.S. Army troops from nearby Fort Lewis to confront the strikers.

The world's largest American flag of its day, measuring 71 feet by 37 feet and weighing 90 pounds, hung from the interior courtyard of the old U.S. Post Office Building in Washington, D.C., in the summer of 1922. *The Library of Congress, Prints and Photographs Division*

One of the first orders of business for the American Legion in 1919 was setting up its Americanism Committee, which later became the National Americanism Commission. The committee's goal was to promote what it termed "100 percent Americanism" by fighting what it believed were anti-American activities, by teaching immigrants and American citizens the principles of Americanism, and by spreading the word on Americanism in the nation's schools. The American flag was the primary symbol of the Legion's Americanism effort. Other groups, including the American Protective League and the Ku Klux Klan, used similar Americanism tactics as a way to counteract the influence of political radicals.

In 1917, the National Conference of Commissioners on Uniform State Laws—an organization that since the early 1890s had been drawing up suggested model laws for state legislatures—approved a Uniform Flag Law. It was almost identical to New York's flag protection law, which that state had adopted in 1905. That measure provided that "No person shall publicly mutilate, deface, defile, defy, trample upon, or by word or act cast contempt upon any such flag, standard, color, ensign or shield." Even though the conference approved the proposed law, it was adopted by only a handful of states.

Garland W. Powell, a World War I veteran and former Maryland state senator who had a strong interest in the American flag, became the American Legion's National Director of Americanism in 1919. In his book, *Service for God and Country,* Powell offered a treatise on Americanism, including advice about flag etiquette. Powell contacted other groups interested in the flag, proposing that they meet in a national conference to put together a uniform national code of flag etiquette.

Even though President Taft's 1912 executive order had cut down drastically on free-lance American flag designing, "there were a lot of flags being used during and directly after World War I," Whitney Smith said. "A lot of people thought [the flag] was being used improperly. The Army and Navy had regulations regarding the flag because they have regulations regarding everything. Various veterans' organization had their own ideas. So . . . they all decided to get their act together."

Powell's organizing efforts came to fruition on June 14, 1923, when the Legion's Americanism Committee convened the first National Flag Conference. It took place at Memorial Continental Hall, located in the DAR's national headquarters complex near the Washington Monument and the White House in Washington, D.C. In addition to the Legion and the DAR, sixty-six other groups took part in the gathering. The U.S. Army and Navy sent representatives. Samuel Gompers, the president of the American Federation of Labor, attended, as did representatives from groups such as the DAR, the Sons of the American Revolution, the Boy Scouts of America, the National Congress of Mothers and Parent-Teachers Associations, the United Daughters of the Confederacy, and the Ku Klux Klan.

"I hope you will succeed in forming a code that will be welcomed by all Americans," Pres. Warren G. Harding said during his forty-minute speech at the opening ceremonies, "and that every patriotic and educational society in the republic will commit itself for the endorsement and observance and purposes of that code." American Legion national commander Alvin Owsley, in a statement issued from the organization's Indianapolis headquarters, said the conference "will develop a definite code of rules so that every man, woman and child in this country may know how to honor and revere the American flag. Let us not be ashamed to demonstrate our loyalty and affection for the flag. May we take pride in revealing this sentiment before our fellow countrymen, for it is a worthy and manly emotion."

The conferees did, indeed, agree on the nation's first Flag Code. They based it heavily on a War Department *Flag Circular* that had been published earlier in the year. Much of what the code contained was apolitical and had to do with practical matters, such as the proper ways, times, positions, and occasions to display the flag. The code also included the Pledge of Allegiance and the proper ways to render it, as well as a section on the proper ways to respect the flag. The conference agreed to replace the words "my Flag" in the Pledge of Allegiance with "to the Flag of the United States." The Second National Flag Conference on May 15, 1924, amended that language slightly to read: "to the flag of the United States of America."

There was, however, an antisocialist, anticommunist political dimension to the conference. Harding administration secretary of labor James J. Davis expressed the gist of that feeling when he warned the conference that "disrespect for the flag" was one of the "first steps" toward communist revolution.

The Flag Code that the conference came up with became big news. In the weeks after the 1923 conference, virtually all of the nation's large newspapers published the new code. Other newspapers followed suit on the Fourth of July. The American Legion and the other organizations that took part in the conference published their own booklets explaining the new code and distributed them by the millions. Fifty-one additional patriotic, hereditary, and veterans organizations took part in the Second National Flag Conference in Washington in 1924. That gathering, however, made only minor revisions to the work done the year earlier.

The Flag Code did not become the law of the land until 1942 during World War II. On June 22 of that year, Congress passed a resolution, which Pres. Franklin D. Roosevelt signed into law, adopting the code with several small changes as part of Title 36 of the United States Code. The code was slightly amended in December 1942 and several other times in subsequent years. It remains in effect today. Although the Flag Code is a national public law, it does not call for penalties for violations of its provisions.

"It is a set of guidelines for proper flag usage, but it is not illegal to display the flag in contravention of the Code," Whitney Smith noted. "Military and civil branches of the government have their own regulations, but in the private sector it is appropriate that the freedom symbolized by the flag itself should be reflected in the way citizens display it."

★   ★   ★

When the white supremacist Ku Klux Klan—which formed late in 1865 and had been virtually dormant since the early 1870s—was revitalized in the 1920s the group soon took a strong interest in promoting the American flag. Klansmen dressed in white robes, hoods, and sheets decorated with Klan symbols and, later, the American flag. The group had disbanded in 1869 as Klan violence veered out of control but was reborn with a vengeance in the fall of 1915 under Col. William Joseph Simmons. The former preacher led a group of men flying the American flag to the top of Stone Mountain, Georgia, where they set a pine cross on fire and proclaimed the Klan's rebirth. The KKK gained hundreds of thousands and then millions of adherents, primarily in the South, Midwest, and West, by the early 1920s.

The Klan crusaded against Catholics, Jews, immigrants, African Americans, political corruption, labor unions, and immorality, and pushed for prohibition and traditional family values. Violence and physical intimidation sometimes were used. But the Klan of the 1920s also often worked openly. It staged parades, marches, conventions, and social events that included the prominent display of the American flag and the organization used the flag as one of its primary symbols. Members, for instance, were required to swear allegiance to the flag and to the U.S. Constitution.

Local Klan groups, known as klaverns, typically gave flags—and Bibles—to Protestant churches and schools. The KKK "stands for the two greatest gifts that Heaven has bestowed, namely the Holy Bible" and "the American flag handed down by our forefathers who fought and died to keep it clean and spotless." Those words were contained in a letter presented to the minister of the Methodist Church in Prescott, a small town in southwest Arkansas, by a group of ten white-robed Klansmen who made an appearance during Sunday services there in the fall of 1922. Another example of many: At the April 1923 dedication of the Riverside Church of Christ in Wichita, Kansas, the local KKK chapter presented the congregation with a large American flag and a flagstaff.

The Klan lobbied for legislation requiring schools to fly the flag. It endorsed the Flag Code and required its Junior League members to learn proper flag etiquette. Local Klan groups took part in Flag Day parades, often on horseback, always with the American flag flying prominently. At Klan rallies members flew American flags from their cars and Klanswomen wore dresses made from American flags. A KKK meeting in Sidney, Ohio, in August 1923 ended with a display of cross burnings and "the American flag in fireworks," according to an account in the *Sidney Daily News*. In Oregon and other states robed Klansmen nailed American flags to the doors of Catholic schools.

The Klan featured the American flag prominently on its paraphernalia. A KKK poster of the era, entitled "We are all Loyal Klansmen," depicts a stars-and-stripes-clad Uncle Sam holding a large American flag with five white-hooded-and-robed Klansmen standing behind him. A 1920s KKK pewter commemorative coin featured a night rider on one side and an American flag and a fiery cross on the other, along with the words "America First" and "Preserve Racial Purity." A 1920s Klan bronze belt buckle shows a Klansman holding a Bible and carrying an American flag in front of a burning cross on a hillside.

The KKK used distortions and outright lies about the flag to deliver its message. A report in the May 31, 1924, Klan publication, *The Fiery Cross*, for example, made up stories about clashes with University of Notre Dame students that supposedly took place at a May 17 KKK parade in South Bend, Indiana. Under the headline, "Roman Students of Notre Dame Trample Flag," an article reported that the Catholic students had stoned a flag that flew over the Klan headquarters building, insulted and ridiculed Klan women, and assaulted an elderly Klan couple.

The Klan's power and influence began to wane significantly in the late 1920s. The organization won few supporters during the Depression and disbanded in 1944. There was a second rebirth during the mid-1960s in reaction to the Civil Rights Act of 1964. The KKK still exists today with comparatively few members in several separate and competing groups. At its public gatherings, KKK members continue to fly the American flag, often alongside the Confederate battle flag and the flag of Nazi Germany.

*   *   *

On April 24, 1924, retired U.S. Army colonel James A. Moss, a West Point graduate and a veteran of the Spanish-American War and World War I, founded the United States Flag Association in Washington, D.C. Moss headed the foundation until his death in 1941. His association soon became an influential national voice that focused on promoting flag etiquette and patriotism based on veneration for the flag and what it symbolized. The association also worked to counteract the spread of communism, crime, and anarchy.

When asked why there was a need for the association, Col. Thomas Denny, the governor of the Society of Mayflower Descendants and an officer of the association's New York State board, said: "Growing influences and forces which are detrimental to the ideals, traditions, institutions and principles on which the Republic is founded and which are symbolized by the flag of the United States."

The association had a national council of forty-eight members, one from each state. Moss recruited thirteen prominent men and women—"typifying the 13 stripes of the flag," he noted—to be the organization's titular sponsors. The group included former Supreme Court justice (and future chief justice) Charles Evans Hughes, then serving as U.S. Secretary of State; Wilson administration vice president Thomas R. Marshall; Card. William Henry O'Connell of Boston; Rabbi Abram Simon of Washington Hebrew Congregation; Bishop James E. Freeman of the Washington Cathedral; union leader Samuel Gompers; and New York governor Alfred E. Smith. Pres. Calvin Coolidge agreed to be the association's honorary president; Pres. Herbert Hoover followed suit in 1929; and Franklin D. Roosevelt did so in 1933.

Moss also named Elihu Root, the 1912 Nobel Peace Prize recipient who had been William McKinley's Secretary of War and Theodore Roosevelt's Secretary of State, the organization's "active president." The presidents and the sponsors, though, did little more than lend their names to the United States Flag Association. "The Association was mostly a one-man effort that Moss ran as director-general," Scot Guenter said. "Financial support came mostly from Washington politicians whose aid Moss procured. The Association's main activity was the production and distribution of pamphlets and books that Moss wrote on proper flag etiquette."

The association also lobbied for Congress to enact flag protection legislation. In December 1924, the association linked that message to a call for the American public not to buy Japanese-made American flags. "Flags made in Japan," the association said, "are of such cheap material that, when they become wet, the colors run and the result is something that looks more like the red flag of Bolshevik Russia than the flag of the United States." The statement noted that the association issued the public appeal because Congress had "refused to enact a national law prohibiting the improper use of the flag."

One of the association's first publications, *Today's Flag Day, June 14th*, was a combination brochure and membership application published in 1924. The brochure painted an unabashedly positive picture of the American flag's history and meaning, showering accolades on the flag in flowery, ultrapatriotic prose.

On its front page the brochure repeated the Betsy Ross myth as if it were fact. Under a drawing of Betsy Ross with the flag on her lap was the caption: "George Washington, Colonel Ross, and Robert Morris, committee appointed by Congress 'designate a suitable flag for the Nation,' commissioning Betsy Ross to make the first Flag." The caption under an accompanying drawing of a thirteen-star "Betsy Ross" flag contained the completely fanciful statement that the arrangement of the stars "in a circle typifies that the Union shall be without end."

The brochure also set out Moss's vision of what his organization would do to promote the flag. The flag, he said, "should be brought into greater consideration and more appreciative regard by the citizenry of the Republic." Schoolchildren, he said, "should be taught what the Flag stands for" and "they should be taught to pay it proper respect and reverence." The association's "aims and purposes," Moss said, were "in the interest of lofty Americanism, sturdy patriotism, and good citizenship: To bring into greater consideration and higher appreciative regard by the citizenry of the Republic the Flag of the United States as the visible, symbolic representation of our National sovereignty, ideals, traditions, and institutions."

Life membership in the association, which Moss referred to as a "great American patriotic society," was open only to American citizens. The membership fee was one dollar for adults and twenty-five cents for children. All members signed on to the association's pledge: "I pledge myself to assist in carrying out the aims and purposes of The United States Flag Association, encouraging the paying of reverence to the Flag and helping to prevent it from being subjected to disrespect or improper use."

In the 1930s the association became more involved in crime fighting and fighting communism in the United States. Moss set up what he called the Steering Committee of the National Council of '76 to work on the effort. The committee sponsored a National Anti-crime Conference in 1933. It focused on "helping to create and galvanize into action public sentiment for the enforcement of law and the defeat of communism in the United States," as Patrick J. Hurley, the former secretary of war, put it at an association program held on July 4, 1935.

In 1938 Moss began a campaign to have the second week of June celebrated as Flag Week. He called for a week-long commemoration of the flag and what it stands for with rallies at schools and patriotic, civic, and social clubs, along with parades and community celebrations. By 1941, thirty of the forty-eight governors had proclaimed National Flag Week, along with some 650 mayors.

James Moss died in an automobile accident in New York City on April 23, 1941. A little more than a year later the U.S. Flag Association ceased to exist. Its mantle was taken up, however, by several other organizations, including the American Flag Movement and the United States Flag Foundation, which was established in December 1942. The latter organization was the predecessor of the National Flag Foundation, the Pittsburgh-based nonprofit group that was founded in 1968 and today is, in many ways, the twenty-first-century equivalent of Moss's United States Flag Association.

The National Flag Foundation bills itself as "America's flag authority" and "the voice of patriotic education." George F. Cahill, a patriotic World War II veteran who headed the Boy Scouts of America's regional council in Pittsburgh, founded the foundation. The nonprofit group promotes the display of the flag, as well as "love of country, respect for the flag and civic responsibility to all Americans." It maintains a Flags of America art collection at its headquarters in Pittsburgh's Flag Plaza, and sells prints of flag artwork.

The foundation aims its main programs at schoolchildren. That includes its Young Patriots educational program, which provides teachers with videos, Web sites, and teachers' guides that contain the flag's history, teach respect for the flag, and encourage students to recite the Pledge of Allegiance.

The foundation's Flags Across America program promotes establishing flag plazas in cities and towns across the land. The main feature of each plaza is an enormous thirty-foot-by-sixty-foot American flag and its 120-foot flagpole. The first such site, in Johnstown, Pennsylvania, was dedicated in 1989 to commemorate the one-hundredth anniversary of the devastating Johnstown flood. The purpose of the program, the foundation says, "is to boost patriotism, unite citizens, and build greater respect for our national symbol." Several dozen plazas have been dedicated and many more are in the planning stages.

The Veterans of Foreign Wars of the United States (VFW), which was formed when several Spanish-American War veterans' organizations merged in 1913, also heavily promotes reverence for the American flag and proper flag etiquette through its flag-oriented Americanism Program. The VFW, which today has some 1.8 million members in some nine thousand local posts around the world, is open to veterans who have served overseas in war zones or other hazardous duty areas around the world. The VFW's

Americanism Program grew out of the VFW's Americanization Committee's drive to "Americanize America" in the 1920s by promoting the use of
the English language among immigrants, encouraging immigrants to become American citizens, instituting a nationwide "Buy American" campaign, and working to take "un-American" textbooks out of the nation's
schools.

"The fact that our population is becoming more varied as immigration
continues presents [a] problem," Herman R. La Tourette, Patriotic Director for the VFW's Department of New York, told a crowd of some five
thousand on June 14, 1926, at the fifth annual Americanization rally in
Prospect Park in Brooklyn. "We repudiate all who profess even the smallest
degree of loyalty to any other nation. We assert that no man is an American
who bears in his heart the slightest allegiance to any flag except the Stars
and Stripes, and we mean not only the flags of foreign powers, but the red
flag of anarchy and the black flag of international socialism."

The VWF's Americanization Committee produced a booklet, "Etiquette
of the Stars and Stripes," which it distributed widely to schools, local VFW
posts, and to other organizations. The VWF also was a leader in the movement to have "The Star-Spangled Banner" declared the National Anthem.

Today flags and flag education remain important elements of the VFW's
Americanism Department's Citizenship Education Program, which promotes the teaching of citizenship in the nation's schools. The VFW's School
Flag Education Program brings members of the organization into the nation's schools to teach respect for the flag and flag etiquette. Color guards
from local posts take part in flag presentation ceremonies at many events,
including get-out-the-vote drives and Veterans Day, Pearl Harbor Day,
Memorial Day, Fourth of July, and other commemorations. The VFW's
Emblem and Supply Department sells flag patches, flag information booklets, as well as some 250,000 flags each year.

CHAPTER FIFTEEN

United We Stand

* ★ ★ ★

Take every other normal precaution for the protection of Army headquarters, but let's keep the flag flying.

**—Dispatch from Gen. Douglas MacArthur, December 15, 1941,
U.S. Army Far Eastern Forces Headquarters, Manila**

T HE AMERICAN FLAG, Pres. Herbert Hoover said in his Flag
Day 1932 message, "stands for all that has been accomplished by our people in the century and a half of this nation's existence. That accomplishment
was based on and made possible by faith, fortitude, resolution, courage,
and character." Hoover went on to make a plea to the American people to
"renew" that faith and to resolve "that we will hand on to the next generation, unimpaired by the passing emotions of temporary distress, these national traits and the American system which they have built."

The "temporary distress" Hoover referred to was the Great Depression,
which had begun in 1929 and would turn out not to be temporary. By the
end of 1932, the year Hoover uttered those words, manufacturing output in
the United States had dropped to more than half of what it was in 1929,
and the nation's unemployment rate reached nearly 30 percent. Economic
and social conditions did not improve until the late 1930s. America's entry
into World War II in December 1941 ended the Great Depression, the
longest and most severe economic downturn in American history.

The American flag was an important symbol of the war effort for American troops on the fields of battle in Europe, Africa, Asia, and the Pacific, as
well as on the home front. On December 8, 1941, the day the United States

declared war on Japan following the December 7 attack on Pearl Harbor, Americans used the flag as they did at the outbreak of World War I and of the Civil War: to show solidarity in time of national crisis.

"As if by magic, Fifth Avenue and other thoroughfares [in New York City] showed a spontaneous display of American flags" on December 8, the *New York Times* reported that day. Loudspeakers broadcast President Roosevelt's "a date which will live in infamy" radio address that afternoon to outdoor crowds. "Men removed their hats when 'The Star-Spangled Banner' was played," following the speech, the newspaper said, "in restaurants and offices, every one stood up."

John Cashmore, the borough president of Brooklyn, issued a proclamation on December 11 urging all Brooklynites to fly the flag every day during the war. Flying the flag, the proclamation said, would be "visible evidence of the determination of the people of America to remain steadfast in their resolve that this nation under God will stamp out the treacherous forces of tyranny and aggression which are now attempting to enslave the world."

Soon after Pearl Harbor, dry cleaners across the country announced that they would clean American flags without charge. The first cleaning establishment that offered that patriotic service was the C. G. Howes Company of Boston, which had begun free flag cleaning in August 1940. Upon doing so, the company was deluged with more than a thousand flags a week from churches, schools, American Legion posts, and businesses. "If there was ever a time in the history of the Nation when the Stars and Stripes should be universally displayed, it is in these crucial days," the United States Flag Association wrote to Howes's general manager. "We wish to commend you for your patriotic efforts to encourage and stimulate the display of our Country's Flag."

Citizens everywhere flew flags as a sign of support for the war effort. The residents of one block in New York City's South Bronx—158th Street between Melrose and Courtlandt Avenues—displayed 146 large American flags on gleaming white poles every day during the war in honor of the men from the street who were serving in the armed forces. On Memorial Days the residents—nearly all of them of Irish, Italian, Polish, and German ancestry—added four more flags suspended from ropes across their street.

As it did during World War I, the flag also resonated with America's allies in the war against Germany and Japan. On New Year's Day 1942 the American flag flew alongside the British Union Jack at Westminster Abbey in London in observance of a special day of prayer. Eight days later

Royal Air Force planes dropped nearly two million propaganda leaflets over German-occupied Paris and its environs and the city of Lille in France. The leaflets, printed in French, contained a photograph of the Statue of Liberty—a gift to the United States from France—and of the American flag. In December 1941 the official Tass news agency in the Soviet Union produced large anti-German posters prominently featuring images of the American, British, and Soviet flags and distributed them throughout that nation.

"Until recently," Walter B. Kerr, the *New York Tribune* foreign correspondent reported from Moscow, "the American flag seldom has been seen in this country, except over the American Embassy at Moscow and the consulate at Vladivostok."

Pres. Franklin D. Roosevelt, on June 22, 1942, approved the U.S. Flag Code that had been passed by Congress. On February 19, 1944, Roosevelt issued a presidential proclamation allowing the use of the flag's image on items exported to American allies, exempting those items from the portion of the code that prohibited placing images of the flag on commercial products. Roosevelt's decree authorized use of the flag on labels, packages, cartons, and containers intended for export as Lend-Lease Aid, as relief and rehabilitation aid and as emergency supplies for American territories and possessions. Such use, his proclamation said, "shall be considered a proper use of the flag of the United States and consistent with the honor and respect due the flag."

Roosevelt took that step, he said, after five U.S. senators had made a battle-front tour in 1943 and reported that British firms put the image of the Union Jack on food items sent to the Allies. American companies had been hesitant to take the step because they were afraid some flag-embossed food containers would inadvertently be distributed in the United States, thereby violating the Flag Code. The flag, Roosevelt said in his proclamation, is "universally representative of the principles of the justice, liberty, and democracy enjoyed by the people of the United States." People "all over the world recognize," the Stars and Stripes, he noted, "as symbolic of the United States."

Allowing the image of the American flag to be used on products shipped to our Allies, Roosevelt said, would foster "a proper understanding by the people of other countries of the material assistance being given by the government of the United States." Not to mention help with the "effective prosecution of the war."

Back at home, in San Francisco, the city Park Commission ordered that the Japanese Tea Garden in Golden Gate Park fly the American flag for the first time. The commission also changed the Tea Garden's restaurant's bill of fare from tea served by young women in kimonos to coffee and donuts served by women in "American garb." In Los Angeles, the city council enacted an ordinance on March 11, 1942, making it illegal to sell American flags and other "patriotic emblems" that were not endorsed by the city's Social Service Commission. The action was taken after City Councilman Carl Rasmussen had purchased a small American flag from a street vendor and then noticed that it was made in Japan.

Americans at home did not tolerate the few recorded instances of disrespect to the flag during the war. Five days after Pearl Harbor, for example, two factory workers at the Hatfield Wire & Cable Co. in Hillside, New Jersey, were fired for refusing to salute the flag at a lunch-hour flag raising. The dismissals of the unidentified workers, the *New York Times* reported on December 12, "were demanded by other employees who said they would not return to work if the two were retained by the company." The plant's United Electrical Radio and Machine Workers Union affiliate approved the action. A New York magistrate fined Dietrich Meyer, a naturalized German citizen, fifty dollars in May 1945 for displaying an upside-down American flag in his delicatessen in the Bronx. The charge was disorderly conduct.

In the nation's capital, the outbreak of war changed the custom of lowering the American flag at the White House when the president was not in residence. Instead, the White House staff, in an effort not to make President Roosevelt's itinerary public, raised the flag in the morning and lowered it at sundown every day. The practice of flying two flags twenty-four hours a day at the Capitol Building, which began during World War I, continued with one change. The flags no longer were illuminated at night because of blackout regulations.

Some patriotic observers felt that Americans did not display the flag in sufficient numbers in the first months after the United States entered World War II. "Everybody flew the flag during the last war, but this time people have hardly realized yet that we are at war," W. A. Mandelberg, the manager of the soon-to-be disbanded United States Flag Association's New York City office, said in January 1942. "Look out my office window. You can see . . . four flags on a dozen flagstaffs." That, he said, was "not enough. In wartime, every building ought to fly the flag."

Two weeks after war was declared, the demand for flags was heavy, but not at World War I levels. Flag sales "are now showing increases of between 15% and 25%," the *Wall Street Journal* reported on December 17, 1941, "as compared with a 100% increase when this country entered World War I." In Chicago, on the other hand, flag dealers sold out their entire inventories a day after war was declared. That came despite the fact that the dealers had stocked up on flags during the spring and summer of 1941. A survey of flag manufacturers and dealers in New York City the next summer found "an industry besieged with orders, from both civilians and the government," the *New York Times* reported August 2, 1942, "most companies reporting a demand that was either 'terrific' or 'very high.'"

President Roosevelt issued a proclamation on May 10, 1942, directing the federal government and asking state and local governments and individual Americans to fly the Stars and Stripes on Flag Day, June 14, in honor of "the nation's mothers and their valiant sons in the service." He also took the unprecedented step of encouraging Americans "where feasible" to fly the twenty-six flags of the nation's World War II allies that day.

As was the case in World War I, scores of colorful, patriotic posters urging Americans at home to back the war effort featured a flag motif. Artists working for the government, patriotic groups, and private industries produced the posters. One of the first issued by the Office of War Information after it was created to serve as the federal government's main wartime propaganda agency was a painting by the artist Allen Saalburg of a tattered American flag flying at half-mast. The poster featured the famous phrase from Lincoln's Gettysburg Address: ". . . we here highly resolve that these dead shall not have died in vain . . ." at the top and "REMEMBER DEC. 7th!" in red capital letters on the bottom.

Large corporations pitched in by commissioning posters designed to build morale, increase industrial production, and conserve materials needed for the war effort. Those posters were distributed to the military, to government offices, and to defense plants. One such poster, produced by the General Cable Corporation, consisted of Uncle Sam's accusatory finger bursting through the stripes of an American flag with the words: "Are YOU doing all you can?"

Military recruiting and government war bond posters, not surprisingly, also featured the flag. That included the women's branches of the armed services. "Are you a girl with a Star-Spangled heart?" asked a Women's Army Corps (WAC) poster. Below those words a large American flag flew behind the image of a beautiful, resolute-looking Army WAC. A Navy WAVE poster had a similar design: a young, attractive woman in uniform staring purposefully, with a large Stars and Stripes making up the poster's background.

"Follow the Flag" were the words on a navy recruiting poster that contained the image of an athletically built, determined male sailor planting a
large American flag on a faraway island. "Let's Go Get 'Em!" topped a U.S.
Marine Corps recruiting poster, which depicted two marines in battle with
the Stars and Stripes and the Marine Corps flag waving behind them. A war
bond poster contained the image of an American soldier grasping a large
Stars and Stripes with the caption, "To Have and to Hold!" Another depicted
the Statue of Liberty, an American flag, and a city skyline along with the
words, "Keep Old Glory Forever Free. Buy More Bonds for Victory."

Magazine advertisements often bore patriotic messages and the image
of the American flag. An ad for Camel cigarettes that appeared in *Life* magazine in 1943, for example, focused on a Pan American Airways employee,
Patricia Garner, who worked as a ground traffic controller. She was pictured waving her guiding flags in front of a Pan Am aircraft with the American flag painted on its fuselage. "Behind those flags in her hands there's a
flag in her heart," the ad says, "the Stars and Stripes she's serving while
working at a war job. A man's job!—but she's the *real* All-American girl,
1942 model."

★   ★   ★

The most extensive home front display of the American flag during the war
came in July 1942, seven months after Pearl Harbor. That month more
than four hundred magazines put versions of the Stars and Stripes on their
covers in a coordinated effort called "United We Stand." The name came
from a line in "The Liberty Song," a 1768 tune written by the Pennsylvania
patriot and statesman John Dickinson. The song, which was popular during the American Revolution, contained the words:

> *Then join in hand, brave Americans all!*
> *By uniting we stand, by dividing we fall.*

Paul MacNamara, a Hearst Corporation publicist, conceived the 1942
"United We Stand" campaign. He envisioned it as a way of selling more
magazines and boosting home-front morale during a time when the U.S.
war effort had yet to produce much positive news. Roosevelt administration treasury secretary Henry Morgenthau Jr. supported the endeavor,
seeing it as an opportunity to sell war bonds. The Treasury Department un-
derwrote special displays for the magazines in some twelve hundred stores

nationwide. Walter Winchell, whose blunt-talking gossip column appeared in some eight hundred newspapers across the nation, backed the campaign by warning magazine publishers of the consequences if they didn't get on board.

Hundreds of publishers, large and small, did get on board. That included all the popular magazines, such as the *Saturday Evening Post, National Geographic, Life, Look, Time, Vogue, Esquire, Harper's Bazaar, The New Yorker, Popular Mechanics, Business Week, Family Circle, Gourmet,* and *Ladies Home Journal.* The covers of children's comic books depicted superheroes clutching American flags. Specialty magazines such as *Steel* and *The Lutheran* also joined in. *The Ring* magazine's cover had a photograph of heavyweight boxing champion Joe Louis and his challenger Billy Conn in army uniforms, saluting, with an American flag in the background. *Screenland,* the movie magazine, offered a photograph of the sultry movie star Veronica Lake in a red-and-white bathing suit, alongside an American flag. The cover of *Poultry Tribune* showed a young boy saluting a phalanx of eggs aligned in platoon formation with the lead egg flying a small American flag. Many magazines also used the words "United We Stand" on their covers and urged readers to buy war bonds.

The United States Flag Association, then in its last year of existence, supported the "United We Stand" magazine campaign by sponsoring a contest to reward the best covers. A panel of judges, including the photographers Margaret Bourke-White and Edward Steichen and the artist Norman Rockwell, chose *House & Garden*'s cover as the overall winner. It consisted of an image by Allen Saalburg of a large American flag folded back at one corner with Mount Vernon, George Washington's home, in the background.

The 1942 "United We Stand" campaign used the American flag to enforce the message that the home front was a crucial part of the war effort. "The flag was a rallying point," said Paul Kreitler, a retired Episcopal priest who owns a collection of about 325 of the magazines. "People saw in the red, white, and blue certain meanings: White represented purity, blue loyalty, red the blood that generations before us shed to preserve our freedoms. The flag became identified with the fact that we might lose these freedoms if we all don't participate."

During the war singing "The Star-Spangled Banner" became a standard feature at movie theaters across the country. Theater owners and the Hollywood studios cooperated in that patriotic endeavor. In addition to producing a steady stream of war films idealizing the American effort, the

studios also produced National Anthem trailers designed to be shown before the feature films started. The trailers depicted patriotic images including the American flag, or simply the image of a waving flag. The Fox
Movietone News version, sung by Merrill Miller, included a crawl with the
words to the song. When the trailer came on the screen, audiences stood,
placed their right hands over their hearts and sang along. Some theaters repeated the ritual after the feature film ended.

One of the most popular movies released during World War II was
1942's *Yankee Doodle Dandy*. That ultra-flag-waving musical told the story of
the life of George M. Cohan, who had made his reputation with a series of
flag-waving hits on Broadway four decades earlier. James Cagney starred
as Cohan in a film that featured lavish, flag-drenched production numbers
of the title song and of "You're a Grand Old Flag."

Audiences also sang the National Anthem before performances by sym-
phony orchestras around the country, as well as before Broadway shows.
"They did it in every Broadway theater. If it was a musical, the orchestra
would play and everyone in the audience would stand and sing along," a
New York City woman said. "If there wasn't an orchestra, someone would
come on stage and lead the audience in singing."

★   ★   ★

More than sixteen million American men and women served virtually everywhere around the globe during the Second World War. Nearly everywhere
they went, American troops displayed the Stars and Stripes. Paratroopers of
the U.S. Army's 82nd Airborne Brigade and 101st Airborne Division, for example, wore red, white, and blue American flags on their jump suit sleeves
when they parachuted behind enemy lines on D day, June 6, 1944. "They
wore American flags on their right shoulder to identify themselves to French
citizens in occupied areas who had never seen an American soldier, but
would recognize the Stars and Stripes," said Dale Dye, the former marine
who is Hollywood's leading military technical adviser. "They generally kept
the flag on their uniforms until later in the hedgerow fighting when some removed the patch to assist in camouflage efforts."

Within a day after the D day invasion, U.S. troops had anchored American flags on the Normandy cliffs. As they took French towns from the
Germans in the ensuing days, the troops often displayed American flags;
some were the same flags the troops had raised in triumph as they fought
their way up the Italian peninsula in 1943 and 1944.

American troops taken prisoner by the Japanese when they captured the Philippine island of Mindanao in 1942 managed to bring the canton of an American flag with them to their prison camp in Japan. They kept it hidden for three years. Then, in 1945, using materials that had been dropped by parachute from American planes, the prisoners fashioned a complete Stars and Stripes. That flag now is on exhibit in the Admiral Nimitz Museum and Historical Center in Fredericksburg, Texas. The flag "exemplifies all that they struggled for," said Helen McDonald, the center's curator. "Had they been found with those stars, as prisoners of war, they would have been punished, or even executed."

American pilots and crews carried small American flags with the words "I am an American" printed on them in Russian on bombing raids over eastern Germany near the end of the war. "They gave us small American flags to put in one of the zippered pockets of our flight suits," said Harry A. Dooley, who served as a B-17 navigator in the Eighth Air Force's Ninety-first Bombardment Group. "If you [were shot down and] thought you might be in friendly territory, but weren't sure because of the language barrier, you'd show them the flag, and they'd understand you weren't Russian or English. That flag was your universal I.D. There aren't too many people who don't recognize the American flag."

The Stars and Stripes flew in triumph in cities across Europe as the American forces defeated the German army in Italy and moved into Germany in the spring of 1945. U.S. troops also unfurled American flags in the war against Japan in the Pacific. In his World War II memoir, the historian William Manchester described the American flag that a fellow marine hung and flew during the fierce August 1942 battle of Tanambogo Island during the first part of the Guadalcanal Campaign against the Japanese. American flags were planted as U.S. forces landed and took over other Japanese-occupied islands in the South Pacific.

That included the seven-mile-long island of Iwo Jima, located in the Bonin volcano group in the Western Pacific. That small island of volcanic rock dominated by an extinct volcano, the 556-foot Mount Suribachi, held strategic significance. It contained an airfield that the Japanese used as a base for fighter aircraft—and which the Americans planned to use to launch bombing raids over Japan. Some twenty-one thousand Japanese troops defended the island from an elaborate system of tunnels and caves.

On the morning of February 19, 1945, the first wave of Fourth and Fifth Marine Division troops landed on Iwo Jima. The fighting went on for thirty-six days and Iwo Jima became one of the bloodiest battles of World War II. When it was over, of the more than 71,000 marines who had landed on the island, 5,910 were killed in action and 17,372 wounded. Only 216 Japanese troops were taken prisoner; the rest perished. The Medal of Honor, the nation's highest award for courage under fire, went to twenty-two marines, four navy corpsmen, and a navy landing craft commander for their actions on Iwo Jima. Nearly half were awarded posthumously.

As brutal and as strategically significant as the fighting was on Iwo Jima, the island's name will forever be associated in American history with the American flag and the actions of five marines and one sailor on February 23, 1945, four days after the initial landing. That's when marines Ira Hayes, Franklin Sousley, Harlon Block, Michael Strank, Rene Gagnon, and navy corpsman (medic) John Bradley raised a large American flag on a long drainage pipe left behind by the Japanese atop Mount Suribachi.

The most reproduced image of the American flag is Associated Press photographer Joe Rosenthal's Pulitzer Prize–winning photograph of U.S. Marines raising the Stars and Stripes atop Mount Suribachi on February 23, 1945, at the bloody Battle of Iwo Jima. *AP World Wide Photos*

Associated Press photographer Joe Rosenthal, on assignment with the military's Still Picture Pool, caught them in the act. "People ask, 'Was the picture posed?'" Rosenthal said in a 1950 interview. "No, it wasn't. I went into the beach on a [landing craft]. I heard the boys were going to plant the flag, so when we landed I dashed right up the hill. I had a couple of minutes to get set while they were getting the flag ready, but they didn't pose. I just caught them in a candid shot. The light and the wind were with me. It was a million-to-one lucky break."

Rosenthal did not know that at the time however. After shooting the marines atop Mount Suribachi, Rosenthal put his exposed film on a military transport and it was flown to Guam that night. The film was developed, and prints sent by radio signal to the Associated Press headquarters in New York. The photo appeared in hundreds of newspapers on February 25. It caused an immediate sensation. Responding to demands from readers, newspapers across the nation published special editions that contained only the image of the stirring photo. It became the most recognized image of the war, won the Pulitzer Prize and other top photojournalism awards, and became one of the most reproduced images of the twentieth century.

"People would always remember where they were the moment they saw the photo," said James Bradley, John Bradley's son, in his book *Flags of Our Fathers*. "The flag-raising photograph signaled victory and hope, a counterpoint to the photos of sinking ships at Pearl Harbor that had signaled defeat and fear four years earlier."

The Iwo Jima flag raising also served to bolster the morale of the marines on the island. "It meant we secured the island and that we were going home soon and in thirty-plus days we did," former marine Bernard Dobbins of Lebanon, Connecticut, said in 2004. "We had just happened to look at the mountain and it was in all its glory."

Only three of the men—Bradley, Hayes, and Gagnon—survived the fighting on Iwo Jima. President Roosevelt issued an order for them to come to Washington, where they were greeted as national heroes. Roosevelt recruited the men to be the centerpiece of the Seventh Bond Tour. The Treasury Department commissioned a color poster of the photo by the artist C. C. Beall. Some 3.5 million copies of the poster were distributed to about a million retail stores around the nation. The poster also was displayed in tens of thousands of theaters, banks, factories, railroad stations, billboards, and other public venues.

The Seventh Bond Tour was a rousing success, raising millions of dollars for the war effort. Bradley, Hayes, and Gagnon met newly installed

Pres. Harry Truman at the White House on April 20, 1945, eight days after Roosevelt's death, to kick off the tour. On May 9, their Iwo Jima flag, which had been badly damaged during the fighting, was hoisted over the U.S. Capitol dome in ceremonies attended by a thousand people. Two days later, at the Bond Tour event in New York City, the three Iwo Jima survivors raised the flag over a fifty-five-foot statue based on the Rosenthal photo at ceremonies in Times Square and on Wall Street before a huge, roaring crowd estimated at 1.4 million. The tour went on to similarly enthusiastic receptions in Chicago, Boston, Indianapolis, Detroit, Cleveland, Phoenix, Los Angeles, and several other cities.

The statue was the work of Austrian-born sculptor Felix de Weldon, who served as a U.S. Navy aviation artist in Virginia. De Weldon, one of the first to see the photo, was immediately captivated by it. De Weldon was so taken by the image that, on his own, he worked virtually nonstop for three days to create a three-foot-high model, using a mixture of floor and ceiling wax because modeling clay was not available. De Weldon's work made an impression on Defense Department officials.

"When it was sent to Washington, the navy had it," de Weldon said in 1998. "The two-star admiral at the time had four Navy captains escort it to the other end of the Navy Annex to show it to the Commandant of the Marine Corps with the instructions to 'make sure it comes back.' When it got there [Marine Corps Commandant] General Alexander Vandegrift pointed to it and said, 'This statue better stay right here.'"

De Weldon was then commissioned to create a nine-foot version of the model in plaster, which the government sent across the nation on the war-bond fund-raising tour. The three survivors posed for that statue and de Weldon used Rosenthal's Iwo Jima photo and other photographs for the likenesses of the marines who were killed. After the war, Congress, prodded by lobbying from military and government officials, passed a joint resolution commissioning de Weldon to create an outdoor memorial to the Marine Corps with his statue based on Rosenthal's photograph as the centerpiece.

It took more than nine years for de Weldon and his team to complete the bronze statue. The casting alone lasted three years. The one-hundred-ton, forty-eight-foot-high statute was finished in 1954 and dedicated as the Marine Corps War Memorial on a hillside near Arlington National Cemetery by President Eisenhower on November 10, the 179th anniversary of the Marine Corps. No public funds were used to cover the $850,000 cost of the statute and memorial site. Individuals, including many marines and former marines, donated the money.

The memorial, which is under the purview of the National Park Service, is dedicated to all marines who have lost their lives in action since 1775. In 1961, Congress passed a joint resolution and President Kennedy signed a proclamation giving official sanction to flying the American flag twenty-four hours a day from the statue's one-hundred-foot-high flagpole. The "raising of the American flag during that battle," Kennedy said, "symbolizes the courage and valor of the American fighting forces in World War II." The flag flown from Mount Suribachi is in the Marine Corps Museum in Washington. Felix de Weldon died on June 3, 2003, at age ninety-six.

When the war ended with Japan's surrender on August 14, 1945, tens of millions of Americans took to the streets and joined in loud, sustained, wild celebrations. In New York City an estimated two million people jammed into Times Square by ten o'clock that night. They shouted, cheered, danced, paraded, sang, and cried. Servicemen kissed civilian women. Cars blew their horns. Office workers showered the streets with paper, confetti, and streamers. Effigies of Japan's emperor Hirohito burned in the streets. And the American flag was very much in evidence.

A young girl dressed in an American flag dress raised the morale of celebrating GI's at Camp Patrick Henry in Virginia on June 22, 1945. *The Library of Virginia*

"Thousands of pedestrians" in New York "carried small American flags" that day, "and there was hardly a vehicle that did not display the Stars and Stripes," the *New York Times* reported.

Also on that day the American flag that had been lowered from the U.S. Embassy in Tokyo on December 7, 1941—the day Japan bombed Pearl Harbor—was raised over the Ontario County Courthouse in Canandaigua, New York. H. Merrill Benninghoff, an embassy employee, had brought the flag home from Japan in 1942, and county officials decided to wait for an auspicious day to display it. They chose August 14, 1945, the day the emperor of Japan announced his nation's surrender and the end of World War II.

CHAPTER SIXTEEN

The Cold War

★   ★   ★

I never set out to design the flag of the nation. I just wanted to keep from getting a bad grade in history.

—Bob Heft, the designer of the fifty-star flag

W HEN WORLD WAR II ENDED, the United States and its allies entered into the Cold War against the Soviet Union and its allies. The Cold War heated up with undeclared shooting wars in Korea and in Vietnam before Soviet communism began to collapse in 1989. During the Cold War the American flag symbolized a nation that had become the acknowledged No. 1 superpower in what was then known as the "free world."

The flag played a symbolic but important role in the post–World War II decision to station American troops in the U.S.-controlled zone of Berlin, located deep inside Soviet-occupied communist East Germany. In 1945, Berlin was divided into four zones, controlled by Britain, France, the United States, and the Soviet Union. Walter H. Judd, a former congressman from Minnesota and U.S. delegate to the United Nations, for one, believed that the American flag helped dissuade the Soviet Union from a military takeover there.

"They can take Berlin any weekend," Judd said in 1970 when the city was still divided. "We haven't got enough troops there to stop them. Why don't they do it? Because we do have one regiment in Berlin—and the American flag." The flag, he said, is "a symbol of American power and interest. If we take everything out of Berlin, that gives them the green light to come in. So we keep American forces in Berlin—and the flag."

The Stars and Stripes was displayed prominently at many civic and cultural events during the Cold War, including the 1951 Shenandoah Apple Blossom Festival in Winchester, Virginia, in 1951. *The Library of Virginia*

On June 24, 1948, the Soviet Union blockaded Berlin's three western-controlled zones by suspending ground travel into and out of the city. Within days the English, French, and Americans inaugurated a massive airlift to circumvent the blockade and keep their sectors supplied with the necessities of life. The Soviet Union did not end the blockade until May 12, 1949; the Berlin airlift ended on September 30. The flag played a role in the American decision to join the airlift, according to Edloe Donnan, an aide to U.S. Army general Lucius D. Clay, the military governor of Germany at the time.

General Clay "made up his mind . . . with [President] Truman that the American flag was going to stay flying in Berlin," Donnan said in 1995. Clay said, "We are going to keep that flag flying in Berlin and we're going to keep the Berlin people in coal, fuel and what have you."

President Truman's speech at Flag Day ceremonies in San Francisco on June 14, 1948, contained veiled references to the American flag's Cold War role. "That flag has significance now, and has had always a significance that no other flag in the world ever had," Truman said in his remarks at Golden Gate Park. The Stars and Stripes, he said, is "the most beautiful flag in the world, and a flag that stands for everything that is sacred on this continent, and stands for everything the world should strive for as a whole." A year later, on August 3, 1949, Truman signed into law legislation that Congress passed designating June 14th of each year as Flag Day.

Students from John Handley High School in Winchester, Virginia, displayed an enormous American flag at that city's 1951 Shenandoah Apple Blossom Festival during the early years of the Cold War. *The Library of Virginia*

In July 1953, with the Cold War in full swing, Truman's successor, Pres. Dwight D. Eisenhower, signed legislation to amend the U.S. Flag Code. The new language prohibited "the display of flags of international organizations or other nations in equal or superior prominence or honor to the flag of the United States except under specified circumstances, and for other purposes." The measure was intended to set out rules for displaying the American flag in this country when flown with the United Nations flag or with any other national or international flag. It became law despite international flag usage regulations that forbid displaying one nation's flag above another nation's during peacetime. The following year, President Eisenhower signed legislation that added the words "under God" to the Pledge of Allegiance—a move that was widely seen as a response to the officially atheist Soviet Union.

The Korean War began when seven communist North Korean infantry divisions crossed the thirty-eighth parallel and invaded South Korea on June 25, 1950. That brutal, bloody, bitter war lasted until a cease-fire went into effect in July 1953. The United States, which came to South Korea's defense along with fifteen other nations under the umbrella of the United Nations, paid a steep price. More than 33,600 Americans were killed in action fighting the North Koreans and their communist Chinese allies. Some 20,600 Americans died in accidents and from other noncombat causes, and more than 103,000 Americans were wounded. Nearly 226,000 South Korean troops died on the battlefield. The war consisted of ground, air, and naval operations that led to what amounted to a stalemate. When the cease-fire took effect in 1953, the Korean peninsula still was divided at the thirty-eighth parallel.

American troops displayed the Stars and Stripes in Korea. Within a half hour after the first U.S. Marine battalion landed on Wolmi-do Island during the Inchon landing on September 15, 1950, for example, the troops raised an American flag on the island's high ground. But the Korean War produced no widespread displays of the Stars and Stripes after the Americans took back the territory that the North Koreans and Chinese captured in South Korea, either among the troops or among the South Korean people, as was the case in World War II in England and France. Nor was there an iconic flag moment such as the flag raising at Iwo Jima. Because the Korean War sputtered to an inconclusive end, no flag-flying victory celebrations took place at home after the fighting ended.

★   ★   ★

The biggest flag developments during the 1950s involved the pending statehood of Hawaii and Alaska. Hawaii had been a United States territory since 1898. Alaska, which the United States purchased from Russia in 1867, became an official territory in 1912. The first Alaska statehood bill came before Congress in 1916; the first bill for Hawaii statehood was introduced in 1919. Statehood legislation for Hawaii and Alaska came up virtually every year after that, but serious consideration did not take place until after the Korean War ended.

Congress voted to make Alaska the forty-ninth state on July 7, 1958. Since the flag resolutions of 1777, 1794, and 1818 provided no guidance, the questions of the exact arrangement of the stars and who would choose the forty-nine-star design had been debated for several years. In 1953, Congress proposed that a joint congressional committee recommend the official forty-nine-star design, but that panel never was set up. During the 1950s, as statehood legislation seemed to be making progress in Congress, American citizens, schoolchildren, flag manufacturers, and patriotic groups sent hundreds of unsolicited proposed designs to Capitol Hill, to various branches of the federal government, and to the White House. All of them wound up at the Research and Engineering Division of the Pentagon's office of the Quartermaster General, Heraldic Branch, which provides heraldic services to federal government agencies.

On September 27, 1958, President Eisenhower named three members of his cabinet—Secretary of State John Foster Dulles, Secretary of the Treasury Robert B. Anderson, and Secretary of Defense Neil H. McElroy—and the chairman of the Commission on Fine Arts David E. Finley to a commission to recommend the official forty-nine-star flag design. The committee asked the Quartermaster Corps' Heraldic Branch to do the staff work for the proposed new design. Corps officers, including Quartermaster General Maj. Gen. Andrew T. McNamara, sifted through some nineteen hundred proposed designs and came up with several prototype forty-nine-star designs and flags.

The suggested flag designs included many with doves, crosses, shields, eagles, and other symbols, and others with words such as "Peace," "In God We Trust," and "Freedom." Suggested star arrangements included circles, five-pointed stars, and an arrangement forming the letters "U.S.A." The commission presented several options to President Eisenhower on November 18, 1958. "From all these suggestions and from a study of the history and traditions of the flag, it finally was decided to recommend [the] arrangement of the forty-nine stars in seven staggered rows," according to an official Pentagon publication.

The proclamation that the president signed on January 3, 1959, admitting Alaska to the Union contained the design Eisenhower chose that day for the new forty-nine-star American flag, which would be effective on July 4. The forty-eight-star flag, which had become official on July 4, 1912, had the distinction of being the longest official American flag in use since the first Flag Resolution of 1777. It was the nation's official flag for forty-seven years.

On August 21, 1959, President Eisenhower signed a proclamation admitting Hawaii to the Union. At the ceremonies he unfurled the new fifty-star flag, which would become official on the Fourth of July, 1960. That flag, the nation's twenty-seventh, has nine rows of stars, alternating between six and five stars per row. If no other states are admitted to the Union, the fifty-star flag will become the nation's longest-serving flag on July 4, 2007.

The name of the designer of the forty-nine-star flag has not surfaced. But the person who designed the fifty-star flag is a matter of public record: Robert G. (Bob) Heft, a retired high school teacher and former seven-term mayor of Napoleon, Ohio, who today is the education manager for the Saganaw County, Michigan, Junior Achievement program. How Bob Heft's design became the official flag is one of the more intriguing stories in the history of the Stars and Stripes. That's because Bob Heft designed the flag when he was a seventeen-year-old junior at Lancaster High School near Columbus, Ohio, in 1958. He came up with the design as part of an American history project—a history project for which he received a B minus.

"I was the only one in the class who decided to pick a flag for that project," Heft said. "I studied flags as a kid. I was always fascinated with the Betsy Ross story. I was also very interested in politics." At the time it appeared as though Alaska, and not Hawaii, would gain statehood. But Heft believed that President Eisenhower, a Republican, would push to have Hawaii admitted soon after Alaska came into the Union because Alaska was heavily dominated by the Democratic Party and Hawaii was predominantly Republican.

"So I played a hunch," Heft said. "While the professional flag makers were working on the forty-nine-star flag, I decided to make a fifty-star flag."

Heft used his mother's old foot-operated sewing machine to make his flag. "I had never sewn before and since sewing the flag together myself, I've never sewn since then," he said. "I took a 48-star flag that we had in the closet and unsewed the area that separated the blue field from the red and white stripes, and then sewed in a blank blue field." He then cut out a hundred white stars, using a cardboard pattern from the stars on the old flag.

"I took a razor blade and cut [the pattern] real accurately," Heft said. "Then I took a real sharp pencil and I sketched out a hundred stars on the fabric. Then I took a pair of scissors and cut them out. I took a piece of chalk and put a dot on the top of each star. I laid it out with a yardstick and proportionately divided it on the blue field. Then I took the stars and touched them with a hot iron so they would be even and symmetrical. Then I took the hot iron and pressed them on."

The work took about twelve hours to complete over three days. Heft's history teacher, Stanley Pratt, was impressed, but not overly so. "The teacher said, 'Where did you get your crystal ball to make a fifty-star flag?' He gave me a B minus and that was the first time I ever challenged a teacher. He said, 'It's got too many stars on it. You get good grades in here, and you don't even know how many states there are. You've got too many.'" Pratt then told Heft that if Congress accepted the design, he would change the grade to an A.

That turned out to be an incentive for Heft. "If he would have given me an A, I probably would have taken that flag home and put it away," Heft said. "I never set out to design the flag of the nation. I just wanted to keep from getting a bad grade in history. I thought I would do something to prove the teacher wrong."

So Heft sent his fifty-star flag to Ohio's governor, Mike DiSalle, the former mayor of Toledo. "I did it just to verify that the flag was in existence long before it became official," Heft said. He was soon notified, though, that DiSalle had put the flag on display in the Ohio State Capitol Building and later at the Governor's Mansion. After retrieving his flag from the governor, Heft took it to his congressman, Walter Henry Moeller, who lived in Lancaster.

"I put the flag in a box and a letter in the box and I got on my bicycle and rode clear across town. He happened to be back in the district," Heft said. "He came to the door and he was chewing on a chicken leg and said, 'What can I do for you, sonny?'" Heft stammered out his homemade fifty-star-flag story and asked Moeller to take it to Washington.

"I said he could put it in a file cabinet or closet or whatever and if there was ever a need for a fifty-star flag, if there was a contest—I didn't know how they went about it then—this was my concept of what it should look like."

President Eisenhower went back to his four-member committee for a recommendation for the design of the fifty-star flag after Alaska entered the Union and Hawaii was on the way in. "They were charged with the responsibility of taking all of the designs and filtering them through and selecting their top five choices," Heft said, "and the President would select from those five."

The president selected Heft's design, which Congressman Moeller had brought to the design committee for consideration. Heft received a call from the White House with the good news in August 1959, then came to Washington to meet the president and receive accolades for his gift to the nation. Heft stood beside President Eisenhower on July 4, 1960, when the first official fifty-star flag was raised in Washington.

The flag that Heft made for his history project has traveled all over the world. It has flown over the White House, at every state capitol building, and at dozens of American embassies. Bob Heft still has that flag, although he no longer displays it.

"It cost me $2.87 to make," Heft said in 2004. "I had decided never to part with it. I just recently turned down an offer for half a million dollars for it from a museum."

On September 20, 2003, the Ohio Historical Society dedicated an Ohio Historical Marker titled "50 Star American Flag" in front of Lancaster High School. The marker reads, in part: "A national symbol for more than 40 years, the design for the 50-star flag was born at Lancaster High School in 1958. Constructed of an old 48-star flag and some blue and white cloth, student Robert Heft designed the flag for a history project. . . . President Eisenhower made the flag official in 1960. It is the only flag in American history to have flown over the White House under five administrations."

CHAPTER SEVENTEEN

The Generation Gap

★   ★   ★

Millions and millions of Americans regard [the flag] with an almost mystical reverence regardless of what sort of social, political, or philosophical beliefs they may have.

—Chief Justice William Rehnquist, June 21, 1989

THE YEAR THAT the fifty-star flag made its debut, 1960, the United States had fewer than a thousand military advisers in South Vietnam. They were working with that nation, officially known as the Republic of Vietnam, in its fight against indigenous communist guerrillas, the Vietcong, and their communist allies in the Democratic Republic of (North) Vietnam. The direct American military commitment to South Vietnam had begun in 1954, following North Vietnam's victory over France, Indochina's former colonial ruler.

In the next several years Presidents Eisenhower, Kennedy, and Johnson sent increasing numbers of troops to South Vietnam. President Johnson greatly escalated the war in August 1964 following congressional passage of the Tonkin Gulf Resolution, giving the president the authority to take "all necessary measures to repel any armed attacks against the forces of the United States and to prevent further aggression" in Vietnam.

By 1968, at the height of American involvement, more than 536,000 U.S. Army, Navy, Marine, Air Force, and Coast Guard personnel were on the ground in South Vietnam and its territorial waters. More than 58,000 Americans died in the Vietnam War and some 304,000 were wounded in a conflict that became the nation's longest war. The United States withdrew its combat forces in January 1973; the war ended two years later with the communist takeover of South Vietnam.

The Vietnam War was the most controversial overseas war in American history. Beginning with the rapid troop escalation in 1965, the nation became increasingly split over the question of whether the war should have been fought. The Americans who supported the war (hawks) tended to be older and politically conservative. Those who opposed it (the doves) mainly were of the younger Baby Boom generation (born after 1945); they were college aged and politically liberal. A deep cultural divide—sometimes called the Generation Gap—grew between the hawks and doves.

The American flag became an important symbol for both hawks and doves. Unlike all of the other wars fought by the United States, in which flying the American flag symbolized commitment to the war effort, the flag's role during the Vietnam War was vastly different. By the end of the 1960s what the political scientist Robert Justin Goldstein called "a cultural war using the flag as a primary symbol" had broken out in the nation. The flag, Burt Neuborne of the American Civil Liberties Union said in 1970, "has become a partisan symbol. The pro-war people have adopted the flag as the symbol of their side. The antiwar people would like to have the flag symbolizing their activities as well."

Hawks displayed the flag as the primary emblem of their support for the war, as well as their anticommunism and their disdain for those who spoke out against the war, expressed in phrases such as "Love it or leave it" and "My country right or wrong." Barry Goldwater, the conservative Republican senator from Arizona who ran against Pres. Lyndon Johnson in 1964, for example, began his campaign rallies with a recitation of the Pledge of Allegiance. And he received thunderous applause from campaign audiences when he pledged—as he did at a rally in Los Angeles in March—that he would not tolerate the Stars and Stripes being "torn down, spat upon and burned around the world."

Doves flew the flag as well, but the message they conveyed was not support for the war. To the contrary, doves displayed the flag upside down as a sign of distress; they created posters with the stars arrayed in the peace sign and other forms of protest; they wore American flag shirts and bandannas; or they simply displayed the Betsy Ross and fifty-star flags. The most radical elements of the antiwar movement defiantly displayed the Vietcong flag. Some antiwar protesters burned the Stars and Stripes to protest the American war in Vietnam.

★   ★   ★

Many of those who protested against the Vietnam War used the American flag as a symbol of their cause, including these members of Vietnam Veterans Against the War shown in a 1971 antiwar demonstration in Washington. *Bernard Edelman*

In February 1969, *Reader's Digest* magazine distributed eighteen million flag decals nationwide with the advice to "Fly This Flag—Proudly." Gulf Oil Company soon followed suit, distributing twenty million flag decals of its own. Banks, gas stations, and other businesses across the country offered flag decals as a part of sales promotions. Other organizations, including veterans' and patriotic groups and civic groups such as the Benevolent & Protective Order of Elks, distributed them. The Elks flag decal included the phrase "Love it or Leave." The decals were instantly popular among those who supported the war.

William J. Windecker, who in 1969 chaired the Elks's Americanism

Committee, said that his organization's American flag decal originally was intended as a message to Cuban refugees in Miami. "We had a few resenters about the slogan who thought it was too rough, and we had no right to tell people about this, but we figured the opposition would die out," Windecker said. "There is so much confusion in the country today with antagonistic groups trying to overthrow the government. It's time we stand up and be counted."

Flag decals "have become a fixture on fire trucks, police cars, and motorcycles throughout the country," *Life* magazine reported in an article examining what it called "decalcomania." "Cab drivers and truck drivers are particularly addicted to them. . . . Old Glory, it seems, is putting out a signal of its own and to many it reads, 'My Country, Right or Wrong.'"

★   ★   ★

Towns and cities across the country began requiring police officers to display American flag decals on their patrol cars and to wear flag shoulder patches on their uniforms. After Macon, Georgia, police began wearing flag patches "not a single police officer has been assaulted in the line of duty, and it has also led the officer to do a better job," Mayor Ronnie Thompson said. The reason, he said, had to do with the patriotism "all Americans have and recognition that the policemen and his shield are direct representatives of the flag."

Some Americans were troubled by decalcomania. That included the outspoken Major League baseball player, Jim Bouton, whose iconoclastic book, *Ball Four*, was published in 1970. Bouton, in his journal of the 1969 season, said he and others who were against the war in Vietnam were "troubled by the stiff-minded emphasis on the flag that grips much of the country these days." A flag, he said, "after all, is still only a cloth symbol. You don't show patriotism by showing blank-eyed love for a piece of cloth. And you can be deeply patriotic without covering your car with flag decals."

The folk music singer/songwriter John Prine satirized decalcomania with the antiwar song "Your Flag Decal Won't Get You into Heaven Anymore." The chorus goes:

> *But your flag decal won't get you*
> *Into heaven any more.*
> *They're already overcrowded*
> *From your dirty little war.*

Now Jesus don't like killin'
No matter what the reason's for,
And your flag decal won't get you
Into heaven any more.

TIME magazine, in its January 5, 1970, issue that named "Middle Americans" as its 1969 "Person of the Year," singled out the importance of the flag in that choice. "Everywhere they flew the colors of assertive patriots," the magazine noted. "Their car windows were plastered with American-flag decals, their ideological totems. In the bumper-sticker dialogue of the freeways, they answered Make Love Not War with Honor America. . . ."

President Nixon spoke out during the war in praise of Middle Americans and others who flew the flag, saying they made up the "Great Silent Majority" who patriotically supported the nation and the war effort in Vietnam. "I don't believe that I have ever seen in any American city, either here or anyplace else, more American flags than I saw today," Nixon said on May 25, 1971, as he arrived for a visit to Birmingham, Alabama. "I know what that flag means to you. It means that you love your country, that you want your country to be strong, that you want your country to work for the great cause of peace in the world, as well as peace for America—that cause we are dedicated to and that we are going to bring."

An incident involving the American flag sparked the ensuing bloody riot in the streets of Chicago during the Democratic National Convention in August 1968. On Wednesday, August 28, two days after the convention opened, some ten thousand demonstrators gathered at the band shell in Chicago's Grant Park for an antiwar rally. During the rally a young man wearing an army helmet started to climb a flagpole near the band shell to lower the American flag. When police moved in to arrest him, a group of men surrounded the flagpole, lowered the flag, and replaced it with a red T-shirt. The police then charged the crowd, beating and arresting protesters. That set in motion the events of that night and the next two days during which twelve thousand police officers used clubs, dogs, and tear gas to attack and arrest hundreds of protesters.

Police officials later said that disrespect for the flag was the primary reason that they took physical action against the antiwar demonstrators. The "profanity and spitting" by the demonstrators "did not have the same effect on the police that incidents involving the flag did," a Chicago police official later testified. "Abuse or misuse of the flag deeply affected the police."

Jasper Johns, one of the nation's leading artists, had used the American flag in his work—usually classified as Pop Art—since the mid-1950s. Johns's paintings of white flags, flags on orange backgrounds, flags with sixty-four stars, flags in superimposed triplicate, and other flag images were nonpolitical, the artist and the art establishment agreed.

In 1969, however, the Leo Castelli Gallery in New York, which had represented Johns since 1957, asked him to design a poster for the planned nationwide series of antiwar demonstrations held October 15, 1969, known as Moratorium Day. The colors of the fifty-star flag in Johns's poster, titled "Moratorium," make a subtle antiwar statement. The stars and six stripes are black; seven stripes are done in a green camouflage pattern. The canton's field is painted orange. The word "Moratorium" is stenciled underneath.

"Johns's print successfully became a symbol of protest," the artist Debora Wood wrote, "because he changed his approach. The image is immediately recognizable as a symbol for America, but there is obviously something wrong because the colors are distorted. A single word 'Moratorium' requires no complex analysis."

The popular rock musical *Hair*, which opened on Broadway in April 1968, contained a scene that some Americans—including William F. Buckley Jr., in his review in the *National Review*—believed desecrated the flag. During the musical number "Don't Put It Down" the characters, a group of hippies, hold a satiric flag-folding ceremony during which one of them is wrapped in a flag and then cradled and rocked in it.

When a road version of *Hair* previewed in Boston in February 1970, Suffolk County district attorney Garret Byrne and Boston's Licensing Bureau head Dick Sinnott vehemently objected to the musical's use of obscenities and nudity, as well as its flag scene. "Most sickening was the manner in which the American flag was degraded and used as some sort of symbolic dust rag," Sinnott said. In a speech to a veterans' group in April, Sinnott offered his opinion that anyone "who abuses the American flag should be horsewhipped in public on Boston Common."

The show's producers closed the Boston production on April 10 rather than comply with the district attorney's order to cut out the nude scenes. Legal wrangling over that order wound up in the U.S. Supreme Court where the justices upheld a U.S. District Court ruling that held that the district attorney acted unconstitutionally in ordering the play to cut out the nude scenes and the flag-folding scene.

Two American astronauts, James A. Lovell Jr., and John L. Swigert Jr., walked out on a Broadway performance of *Hair* in June 1970 because the flag scene offended them. "I don't like what you're doing to the flag," Swigert said outside the theater. "I don't like the way they wrapped the flag around that guy."

★   ★   ★

A flag that demonstrators burned at one of the first large antiwar rallies, a gathering of some two hundred thousand people on April 15, 1967, in Central Park in New York City, led to congressional passage in 1968 of the nation's first federal flag desecration law. Several other politically motivated flag burnings and other acts of flag desecration had taken place around the nation since 1965. In Cordele, Georgia, for example, Rufus Hinton was convicted of flag desecration on May 6, 1966, for helping to haul down an American flag and a Georgia state flag at the Crisp County Courthouse during a civil rights demonstration in March of that year. In Seattle, Floyd Turner was convicted in July 1967, for his role in helping burn a flag at a party.

Although flag desecration laws were on the books in every state, the spate of flag burnings and other similar incidents in the mid-sixties led to lobbying by patriotic and veterans' groups, and editorializing by some newspapers, in favor of a federal flag desecration law. "The flag belongs to all the American people and thusly should be protected by national legislation," Veterans of Foreign Wars national Commander in Chief Andy Borg said in 1966. Borg declared that he was "sick and tired of the American flag being burned, stomped upon, torn apart and vilified by communist-inspired peaceniks and others."

Many members of Congress agreed. "Which is the greater contribution to the security of freedom," Republican congressman Dan Kuykendall of Tennessee asked on the House floor. "The inspiring photo of the Marines at Iwo Jima or the shameful pictures of unshaven beatniks burning that same flag in Central Park?" Charles Wiggins, a California Republican, among others, tied flag desecration directly to the war effort. "The public act of desecration of our flag tends to undermine the morale of American troops," he said. "That this finding is true can be attested by many Members who have received correspondence from servicemen expressing their shock and disgust of such conduct."

After a series of hearings in May and June, the House and Senate passed the first federal flag desecration legislation. President Johnson signed the bill into law on July 4, 1968. It provided fines of up to one thousand dollars and one year in jail for anyone who "knowingly" cast "contempt" upon "any flag of the United States by publicly mutilating, defacing, defiling, burning, or trampling upon it."

As was the case during World War I, several states revised their flag desecration laws during the Vietnam War to stiffen penalties. In Alabama, Indiana, Oklahoma, and Illinois the newly revised laws increased the sentences for those convicted of flag desecration from a maximum of thirty days in jail and a hundred-dollar fine to a maximum of between two and five years in jail and fines of three thousand to ten thousand dollars. Virtually all the state flag laws contained language adopted during the first two decades of the century making it illegal to put marks or pictures on the flag, to use the flag commercially, or to burn or otherwise desecrate the flag.

Hundreds of flag desecration prosecutions took place during the Vietnam War. Nearly all of them were "used against 'peace' demonstrations," Robert Justin Goldstein found after studying sixty flag desecration cases adjudicated between 1966 and 1976. Goldstein concluded that officials enforced the state flag protection laws extremely arbitrarily. " 'Establishment' and 'patriotic' elements who wore flag pins in their lapels (including President Nixon and the White House staff and the police departments of Boston and New York City) or flag patches on their shoulders and placed flag decals on their windows and cars by the tens of millions, often in technical violation of the flag desecration statutes, invariably were unhindered," Goldstein said.

On October 3, 1968, three months after Congress passed the first national flag desecration law, Abbie Hoffman, a flamboyant leader of the radical Youth International Party (known as the Yippies), became the first person arrested for violating the new federal statute. That afternoon Hoffman was taking part in a protest demonstration against a House Committee on Un-American Activities hearing outside the Cannon House Office Building on Capitol Hill in Washington. For the occasion he wore a red, white, and blue American flag shirt and buttons that read "Wallace for President: Stand Up for America" and "Vote Pig in Sixty-Eight, Yippie."

As they took Hoffman into custody, District of Columbia police tore off the shirt, which he had purchased in a store. He was held overnight in jail. Hoffman was convicted of flag desecration on November 21 in the Washington, D.C., Court of General Sessions, and sentenced to thirty days in jail.

Hoffman testified that he wore the shirt "to dress symbolically to express the way we felt" in "the tradition of the founding fathers." After his conviction, Hoffman told the court: "I consider this decision ridiculous.

Everyone who wears an Uncle Sam suit is just as guilty." He appealed the verdict. During the appeals process, in the spring of 1969, Hoffman appeared as a guest on Merv Griffin's popular CBS television talk show. Hoffman arrived on the set wearing a jacket, which he took off after the show started to reveal that he was wearing another American flag shirt. When the taped show was broadcast, a blue screen blocked his image.

A federal appeals court in Washington overturned Hoffman's 1968 conviction on March 29, 1971. The three-judge panel ruled that his shirt did not defile or desecrate the flag.

Supreme Court rulings in 1969, 1972, and 1974 found that sections of flag desecration laws in New York, Massachusetts, and Washington violated First Amendment provisions of free speech and were therefore unconstitutional. That led the legislatures in some twenty states to narrow the scope of their flag desecration laws in the next decade. Most of the changes adopted the 1968 federal law's provisions by focusing on flag mutilation and other forms of physical desecration rather than on verbal abuse or commercial or political misuse of the flag.

Fourteen years after the end of the Vietnam War, in a landmark decision, the Supreme Court on June 21, 1989, in *Texas v. Johnson,* ruled 5–4 that burning the flag is a form of symbolic speech protected by the First Amendment. In the case under review, Gregory Lee "Joey" Johnson, a member of the Revolutionary Communist Party, had burned an American flag while participating in a political demonstration during the 1984 Republican National Convention in Dallas. He was convicted of violating Texas's flag desecration law, fined two thousand dollars, and sentenced to a year in jail. The Texas Court of Criminal Appeals overturned the conviction, ruling that Johnson was exercising his First Amendment right of freedom of speech. Prosecutors asked the U.S. Supreme Court to review the decision.

"Johnson burned an American flag as part—indeed, as the culmination— of a political demonstration that coincided with the convening of the Republican Party and its re-nomination of Ronald Reagan for President. The expressive, overtly political nature of this conduct was both intentional and overwhelmingly apparent," Justice William Brennan said in his majority opinion. "Johnson was not, we add, prosecuted for the expression of just any idea; he was prosecuted for his expression of dissatisfaction with the policies of this country, expression situated at the core of our First Amendment values."

Forbidding "criminal punishment for conduct such as Johnson's will not endanger the special role played by our flag or the feelings it inspires,"

Brennan said. "To paraphrase Justice [Oliver Wendell] Holmes, we submit that nobody can suppose that this one gesture of an unknown man will change our Nation's attitude towards its flag." The "flag's deservedly cherished place in our community will be strengthened, not weakened, by our holding today," Brennan said. "Our decision is a reaffirmation of the principles of freedom and inclusiveness that the flag best reflects, and of the conviction that our toleration of criticism such as Johnson's is a sign and source of our strength."

In his dissenting opinion, Chief Justice William Rehnquist offered a brief history of the American flag that included the words to "The Star Spangled Banner" and John Greenleaf Whittier's poem "Barbara Frietschie." For "more than 200 years of our history," Rehnquest said, the American flag "has come to be the visible symbol embodying our Nation." No "other American symbol has been as universally honored as the flag," he said, pointing out Congress's adoption in 1931 of "The Star-Spangled Banner" as the National Anthem, the 1919 establishment of Flag Day, the 1987 adoption of John Philip Sousa's "The Stars and Stripes Forever" as the national march, the Pledge of Allegiance's inclusion in the U.S. Flag Code, and the fact that the flag "has appeared as the principal symbol on approximately 33 United States postal stamps and in the design of at least 43 more, more times than any other symbol."

The flag, Rehnquist said, "does not represent the views of any particular political party, and it does not represent any particular political philosophy. . . . Millions and millions of Americans regard it with an almost mystical reverence regardless of what sort of social, political, or philosophical beliefs they may have. I cannot agree that the First Amendment invalidates the Act of Congress, and the laws of 48 of the 50 states, which make criminal the public burning of the flag." Since 1777, he said, "the American flag has occupied a unique position as the symbol of our Nation, a uniqueness that justifies a governmental prohibition against flag burning. . . ."

The Supreme Court's decision invalidated the 1968 national flag desecration law, as well as the flag desecration laws on the books in forty-eight states (all except Wyoming and Alaska). In response, Congress passed and Pres. George H. W. Bush signed into law the Flag Protection Act of 1989, which went into effect on October 28, 1989. The next few days saw "perhaps the largest single wave of [flag-burning] incidents in American history," Robert Justin Goldstein noted. Groups of protesters challenging the new law burned American flags in about a dozen cities. Two groups were arrested for doing so in Washington, D.C., and Seattle. Their cases wound up in the Supreme Court, which ruled 5–4 on June 11, 1990, that the 1989 law unconstitutionally violated the protesters' free-speech rights by making it illegal to burn a flag in a public protest.

The 1989 and 1990 Supreme Court decisions overturning the nation's flag desecration laws led to a national movement to bypass the legislative process and amend the U.S. Constitution to make flag desecration illegal. "Congress tried to protect [the flag] by legislation. That legislation did not stand up," Pres. George H. W. Bush said on June 12, 1990, the day after the second Supreme Court ruling. "When it was knocked down by the [Supreme] Court, I feel there's no other way to go but this Constitutional Amendment." In 1989 Bush had termed such an amendment a way "to protect that unique symbol of America's honor." The flag, he said, "is too sacred to be abused."

"I believe," Bush had said at a June 27, 1989, White House news conference, "that the flag of the United States should never be the object of desecration. Flag burning is wrong. Protection of the flag, a unique national symbol, will in no way limit the opportunity nor the breadth of protest available in the exercise of free-speech rights." As president, Bush said, "I will uphold our precious right to dissent, but burning the flag goes too far, and I want to see that matter remedied."

Since 1994, the leading voice in the effort to adopt a flag desecration Constitutional Amendment has been the Citizens Flag Alliance, which was founded in June of that year by the American Legion. The alliance is "engaged in a war to recapture Old Glory," its chairman, retired U.S. Army general Patrick H. Brady, said in 2000. "Our primary task is to capture the constitutional arguments and convince the members of Congress, through common sense and through the people, that the Supreme Court made a mistake and we have an obligation, even a sacred duty, to correct it."

Brady, testifying in favor of a proposed flag protection Constitutional Amendment on Capitol Hill in 2004, said that the 1989 Supreme Court decision "took away a fundamental right of the American people, a right we possessed since our birth as a nation, the right to protect the flag." The decision, Brady said, "was an egregious error and distorted our Constitution. We do not believe the freedom to burn the American flag is a legacy of the freedoms bestowed on us by" the Founding Fathers. "To distort the work of these great men unable to defend themselves, to put flag burning side by side with pornography as protected speech, is outrageous."

The American Legion had begun a lobbying campaign in 1990 to induce the state legislatures to pass memorializing resolutions calling upon Congress to adopt a flag protection constitutional amendment. The Texas Legislature had been the first to do so on July 10, 1989, nineteen days after the *Johnson* decision. By the end of 1993, thirty-five state legislatures had adopted the nonbinding resolutions. In January 2002, Vermont became the fiftieth state to approve a memorializing resolution. The Vermont Legislature ended nearly a decade of often-emotional debate by approving the resolution by a 113–23 vote in the House and a 22–6 vote in the Senate.

Opponents of the resolution in Vermont framed their arguments on First Amendment grounds, as the majority in the Supreme Court had done in 1989 and 1990. "I can't support legislation that would encourage the abridgment of the right of free speech as contained in the First Amendment to the U.S. Constitution," said state representative Betty Nuovo. "Abridging this freedom is desecration of the flag." Supporters of the resolution pointed to the fact that the overwhelming majority of Americans supported flag protection legislation. "Let there be no doubt. The people's House is on record for a Constitutional Amendment to correct the error of the U.S. Supreme Court," said Vermont State representative Duncan Kilmartin.

The first proposed flag desecration Constitutional Amendment—specifying that "the Congress and the States have the power to prohibit the physical desecration of the flag of the United States"—was introduced in the U.S. Congress in the summer of 1990 immediately after the second Supreme Court ruling. It received majority votes in the House and Senate, but not the two-thirds majorities required for constitutional amendments. The amendment has come up in every Congress since, but has failed to gain the needed two-thirds majority votes in both the House and Senate.

★   ★   ★

During the Vietnam War at least one very public display of the American flag was cheered by hawks and doves: the planting of the Stars and Stripes on the Moon on July 20, 1969. At 10:56 p.m. Eastern Daylight Saving Time that day, American astronaut Neil Armstrong became the first human being to set foot on the Moon. Soon thereafter—four days, fourteen hours, and nine minutes into the mission—Armstrong and his fellow Apollo 11 astronaut Buzz Aldrin planted an American flag on the Moon's surface, an event that was broadcast live and beamed back to Earth on television.

The decision to plant the Stars and Stripes on the Moon did not come lightly. The United Nations had adopted a treaty in 1967 denying any nation the right to claim sovereignty over any object in space. Planting an American flag, it was believed, could be construed as an act of taking possession of the Moon.

"There were people at the time, and have been people since then, who thought that planting any flag up there was a bad idea," Chief Historian Roger Launius of the National Aeronautics and Space Administration (NASA) said in 2000. "After the fifteenth century when Europe was pushing outward, the Europeans were planting flags all over the place and claiming the territory for their home countries. They thought that set a bad precedent."

The astronauts themselves had no qualms about planting the flag. "I certainly felt that the American flag is what belonged there," Aldrin said in 1999. "It's a characteristic of previous explorations, to plant a symbol upon arriving at a new shore. And it indeed was a philosophical moment of achievement. It was also a technical challenge."

NASA had set up a Committee on Symbolic Activities for the First Lunar Landing in February 1969 to look into the efficacy of planting a flag on the Moon, given the United Nations' dictum. The committee, after considering options such as leaving miniature flags of all nations or some type of commemorative marker on the Moon, decided that the astronauts would plant only one large American flag. To show that the United States was not trying to take possession of the Moon, the committee also decided that the astronauts would mount an explanatory plaque on the lower half of the lunar module that they left behind on the Moon's surface. The plaque, which contained an image of the American flag, said: "Here men from the planet Earth first set foot upon the Moon July 1969, AD. We came in peace for all mankind."

NASA engineers decided to use a three-by-five-foot nylon flag (purchased commercially for $5.50—accounts differ as to where) and a ten-pound collapsible flagpole with a telescoping horizontal arm designed to keep the flag extended and perpendicular. The folded flag and the pole were placed inside a heat resistant tube attached to the left side of the ladder on the Lunar Landing Module. The flag and its pole survived the Moon landing intact, but the astronauts had trouble planting the flag on the moon's surface.

First, the telescoped rod did not work and was discarded, which is why the flag appears to be rippling in the wind in the photographs beamed back to Earth. Then the astronauts' bulky space suits hindered Armstrong and Aldrin's efforts to plant the flag deeply into the Moon's hard surface. "The flag didn't exactly perform as we put it together," Aldrin remembered thirty years later. "It didn't stick in the ground exactly the way we thought it would." Aldrin and Armstrong persevered though, and left the Stars and Stripes standing on the Moon when they rocketed back to Earth.

"Even though the event took only 10 minutes of the 2½ hour [lunar extravehicular activity], for many people around the world the flag-raising was one of the most memorable parts of the Apollo 11 lunar landing," a NASA report said. "There were no formal protests from other nations that the flag-raising constituted an illegal attempt to claim the moon. Buzz Aldrin, in an article written for *Life* magazine, stated that as he looked at the flag, he sensed an 'almost mystical unification of all people in the world at that moment.'"

American astronauts left five additional Stars and Stripes on the Moon during subsequent lunar missions. Because the first flag was not anchored deeply into the Moon's surface and because of exposure to ultraviolet and solar radiation on the Moon, it is likely that the six Stars and Stripes on the Moon have seriously deteriorated. "My guess is the flags themselves, because they're nylon, the UV rays have probably made them very brittle. Maybe [they] fell off into the dust," Apollo 12 astronaut Alan Bean said in 2001. "I'm sure they've faded to white, but the poles are still there."

*   *   *

The most vivid example of the ability of the flag to evoke deep emotions at home during the Vietnam War came on Friday, May 8, 1970, in New York City. Just before noon, some two hundred construction workers—many of whom wore hard hats embossed with American flags—marched through the streets of lower Manhattan carrying large American flags. They converged from four directions on an antiwar rally on Wall Street where they confronted a large group of young demonstrators. Most were college students from New York University and Hunter College. The workers—dubbed "hard hats"— chased and beat dozens of demonstrators with lead pipes and crowbars.

"We came here to express our sympathy for those killed at Kent State and they attacked us with lead pipes wrapped in American flags," Drew Lynch, a nineteen-year-old New York City employee, said.

The workers pushed their way through the demonstrators to Wall Street's Federal Hall National Memorial, the U.S. Subtreasury Building, where George Washington was inaugurated as the nation's first president in 1789. The workers placed American flags on the statue of George Washington that stands on the building's steps. From there, they forced their way into New York's City Hall a few blocks away. A postal worker raised the American flag on the building's roof to full staff. New York City mayor John Lindsay had ordered the flag to be flown at half-staff in mourning for four students who had been shot and killed by National Guard troops during an antiwar demonstration at Kent State University on May 4.

When an aide to Mayor Lindsay lowered the flag to half-staff again, he ignited a small riot outside City Hall. "The mob reacted in fury," the *New York Times* reported. "Workers vaulted the police barricades, surged across the tops of parked cars and past half a dozen mounted policemen. Fists flailing, they stormed through the policemen guarding the barred front doors. Uncertain whether they could contain the mob, the police asked city officials to raise the flag. Deputy Mayor Richard R. Aurelio, in charge during the absence of Mayor Lindsay . . . ordered the flag back to full staff." As the flag went up, "the workers began singing 'The Star-Spangled Banner.'"

Construction workers held other flag-rich rallies in New York's financial district during the next several weeks. At one such event, on May 12, another confrontation took place between construction workers and antiwar demonstrators in the same area of lower Manhattan. With a heavy police presence, this time little violence occurred. That was because, one worker said, "there was no provocation; no one spit on the flag."

The flag and what it stood for was a recurring theme among those who took part in the May 8 and subsequent hard hat rallies. "Outside of God, [the flag] is the most important thing I know," John Nash, a World War II veteran who marched at a May 20 parade in support of the Nixon administration's Vietnam War policies in downtown New York, said. "I know a lot of good friends died under this. It stands for America."

Eighty percent of the American people "are behind America and the flag," said Robert Geary, whose son was killed in Vietnam. The flag, Geary said, "is me. It's part of me. I fought for it myself two or three years in the Second World War." The United States "is the greatest country in the world. All they [antiwar demonstrators] have to do is move out."

Morty Grutman, an electrician who took part in the May 8 hard hat events, said that the antiwar demonstrators' lack of respect for the flag was a prime reason for the construction workers' counterdemonstrations. "A lot of us are World War II vets and fathers and purple hearts," Grutman said. "We're from a generation that believes in the flag over everything."

For a time after the May 8 incident, the hard hat adorned with an American flag decal became a symbol for those who supported the war.

On May 14, at a Conservative Party rally in New York, for example, the event's promoters showed up wearing hard hats decorated with American flags. On May 26 Peter J. Brennan, the president of the Building and Construction Trades Council of Greater New York, and twenty-two other union leaders were guests of President Nixon at the White House. At the end of the meeting Brennan presented the president with a hard hat and placed an American flag pin on his lapel.

Other antiwar demonstrations in the days after the Kent State killings—mainly at more than four hundred colleges and universities across the nation—included emotionally charged, sometimes violent conflicts over the flag. At the University of New Mexico students physically fought over whether the American flag should be lowered to half-staff. Three antiwar students suffered knife wounds.

At Northwestern University—which, like many other colleges, had been shut down due to antiwar unrest—there was a tussle over a flag that protesting students waved upside-down. "A hefty man in work clothes tried to grab the flag, shouting: 'That's my flag! I fought for it! You have no right to it!'" *TIME* magazine reported. "The students began arguing with him. 'To hell with your movement,' the man responded. 'There are millions of people like me. We're fed up with your movement. You're forcing us into it. We'll have to kill you. All I can see is a lot of kids blowing a chance I never had.'"

Philip Caputo, the author and former Vietnam War Marine Corps lieutenant, covered that event as a Chicago journalist. "Flying an upside-down American flag alongside the black flags of the anarchists and the red banners of revolution, the demonstrators mounted makeshift barricades to shout epithets at the police, antiwar chants to whomever would listen," Caputo later recalled. "A stocky, dark-haired man in his early fifties waded into the crowd and seized the U.S. flag, declaring in a voice quavering with rage that he was an electrician and a former marine who had fought for that flag on Iwo Jima, seen it raised on Mount Suribachi, and he was damned if he would allow a mob of long-haired, pot-smoking hippies to desecrate it."

Several demonstrators, Caputo reported, "cried out that the man should be allowed to have his say, but the rest shouted them down, and then the cops waded in with nightsticks."

The Stars and Stripes was a very visible presence at the July 4, 1970, Honor America Day rally held at the Lincoln Memorial and the Washington Monument grounds in the nation's capital. Billed as a nonpartisan celebration, the event was organized by politically conservative supporters of the Nixon administration. The day featured hawkish speeches and ultrapatriotic comments as well as an antiwar demonstration against the rally that turned violent.

More than 250,000 people attended the rally, which was organized by the head of the Marriott Corporation, J. Willard Marriott, at the behest of President Nixon and by Hobart Lewis, the publisher and editor of *Reader's Digest*. Bob Hope cohosted the day's activities, with the Reverend Billy Graham. The list of performers included politically conservative show business figures Red Skelton, James Stewart, Andy Williams, Kate Smith, Pat Boone, Dinah Shore, and Jack Benny.

In his speech from the steps of the Lincoln Memorial bedecked with American flags, Graham denounced "extremist elements" who had "desecrated our flag, disrupted our educational system, laughed at our religious heritage and threatened to burn down our cities." Newspapers reported that many of those who attended the event displayed the American flag and many others brought along American flag blankets and wore articles of clothing containing images of the flag.

In Vietnam American troops flew the flag as their fathers had done in Korea and in Europe and Japan during World War II and as their grandfathers had done in the trenches in World War I. The flag flew over American bases, remote outposts, and landing zones. Some troops carried small flags into battle, especially during the war's early years before it became controversial at home. During the bloody November 1965 Battle of the Ia Drang Valley, for example, at least one American infantryman displayed a small American flag on his backpack. After the first part of that battle was over, the soldier flew the flag on a tree branch.

"When I saw that [flag] I felt very proud. It's something that always stuck with me," one GI said. It was "just like Iwo Jima, another battle we had won for the United States." That small Stars and Stripes, noted Gen. Hal Moore, who commanded the First Cavalry Division Battalion that fought in that battle, "flew over Landing Zone X-Ray for the rest of the fight, raising all our spirits."

That flag was attached to "a shattered tree . . . about ten feet off the ground," said J. D. Coleman, a former First Cav officer who was on the scene. "True, it was a cliché camera shot from every war movie ever made, but there on LZ X-Ray, in the midst of death, destruction, and unbelievable heroism, its impact transcended the stereotype."

The American flag proved to be an unequivocally positive symbol during the Vietnam War to the men held as prisoners of war in Hanoi. The

U.S. Navy pilot Michael Christian, who was shot down in North Vietnam
and taken prisoner on April 24, 1967, was perhaps the most devoted to the
flag. When he was held in the infamous Hanoi Hilton prison camp, Christian fashioned an American flag out of a few ragged bits of red and white
cloth that he sewed into the inside of his prison-issue blue pajamas with a
bamboo needle.

"Every afternoon we would hang Mike's shirt on the wall of our cell and
say the Pledge of Allegiance," said U.S. Sen. John McCain, a former navy
pilot who was held with Christian. "For those men in that stark prison cell,
it was indeed the most important and meaningful event of our day." When
prison guards discovered the flag in 1971, they beat Christian mercilessly,
battering his face and breaking his ribs. While recovering from his wounds,
Christian secretly made a replacement flag.

A few days after the beating, "Mike approached me. He said: 'Major,
they got the flag, but they didn't get the needle I made it with. If you agree,
I'm making another flag,'" said air force colonel George "Bud" Day, a
Medal of Honor recipient held at the Hanoi Hilton from 1967 to 1973. "My
answer was, 'Do it.'"

It took Christian "several weeks" to make that second flag, Day said.
After he finished it, "there was never a day from that day forward that the
Stars and Stripes did not fly in my room, with forty American pilots
proudly saluting."

Al Kroboth, a U.S. Marine Corps A-6 navigator, was shot down July 7,
1972, over South Vietnam. Severely wounded, he was forced to march to
the Hanoi Hilton where he was held until March 27, 1973, when the North
Vietnamese released him and the other American POWs. When he saw the
U.S. Air Force transport plane land in Hanoi to pick up the POWs that
day, Kroboth said, he did not feel emotional until he noticed the large
American flag painted on the airplane's tail.

"That flag," he told the novelist Pat Conroy, a college classmate. "It had
the biggest American flag on it I ever saw. To this day, I cry when I think of
it. Seeing that flag, I started crying. I couldn't see the plane; I just saw the
flag. All the guys started cheering. But that flag . . . that flag."

CHAPTER EIGHTEEN

United We Stand Again

★ ★ ★

I always get a chill up and down my spine when I say that Pledge of Allegiance.

— Pres. Ronald Reagan, June 14, 1985

OUR LONG NATIONAL NIGHTMARE is over," Gerald Ford said on August 9, 1974, when he was sworn in as president of the United States. Ford was referring to the political and constitutional turmoil that rocked the nation during the Watergate scandal, which had caused Pres. Nixon to resign. But Ford's words easily could have applied to the war in Vietnam, which wound down that summer and would end in April 1975 with the communist takeover of all of South Vietnam.

When the "nightmare" ended for the United States in Vietnam, the antiwar movement, which had been losing strength and adherents since 1971, all but ceased to exist. By the end of the war, too, the American flag all but ceased to be the divisive symbol it was in the late 1960s and early 1970s.

During the late 1970s, things were quiet, too, on the flag desecration front. One notable, widely publicized flag-burning incident did occur though during that period. It took place on April 25, 1976, during a Major League baseball game at Dodger Stadium in Los Angeles. In the bottom of the fourth inning, two men bolted from the stands and ran into the outfield, where they placed an American flag on the ground, doused it with lighter fluid and tried to light it on fire with a match. Before they could do so,

Chicago Cubs center fielder Rick Monday ran over to the men, grabbed the flag, and spirited it to safety.

"To this day, I don't know what I was thinking, except bowl them over," Monday said in 1998. "What they were doing was extremely wrong as far as I was concerned."

Monday received an ovation from the crowd in the stands that day and similar accolades at stadiums around the country during the rest of the 1976 season. Tommy Lasorda, the Los Angeles Dodgers's third-base coach that year who was on the field during the incident, called Monday's actions "One of the most heroic acts ever to take place on the field during a Major League baseball game."

Unlike the Centennial year of 1876, there was no single Bicentennial exhibition celebrating the nation's two-hundredth birthday in 1976. Instead, Americans marked the occasion throughout the year with tens of thousands of flag-rich local special events and celebrations. That included the Bicentennial's first official event, a flag-raising ceremony by National Guard troops at sunrise, 4:31 a.m. on July 4, 1976, at Mars Hill Mountain in Maine. Throughout the year Americans painted the Stars and Stripes on fire hydrants and on locomotives. The American flag appeared on countless T-shirts, ties, jackets, sweaters, and other items of apparel, as well as on dishes, coffee mugs, and countless other consumer products. Network television ran mini–history lessons called *Bicentennial Minutes*, and many schools and colleges offered new or expanded American history courses.

The American Revolution Bicentennial Commission coordinated the state celebrations, as well as the massive event held July 4, 1976, on the Mall in Washington, D.C. Millions attended that and other big Fourth of July 1976 festivities in Philadelphia and in New York City, where thousands of flag-bedecked ships, large and small, converged in New York harbor and the city put on a mammoth fireworks display. The Associated Press called the New York harbor event the "greatest maritime spectacle in American history." The vessels on hand included hundreds of small pleasure craft, a small armada of historic "tall ships," the American aircraft carrier *Forrestall*, and more than fifty warships from twenty-two countries. All of the ships, American and foreign, that day flew the Stars and Stripes. On that day also a record 10,471 American flags flew over the U.S. Capitol, and the Battle of Baltimore—complete with a Star-Spangled Banner withstanding British "bombs" bursting in air—was reenacted at Fort McHenry.

During the eight years that Ronald Reagan was president, from 1981 to 1989, the national mood seemed to reflect the president's conservative, patriotic sensibilities. That included an often-stated reverence for the American flag. The Stars and Stripes, Reagan said on Flag Day, June 14, 1983, for example, stands "for freedom and the forces of good. We apologize to no one for our ideals or our principles, nor the prosperity that we've made for ourselves and shared with the world. Let this grand flag forever be a symbol of the potential before us that free men and women can soar as high as their dreams and energy and ambitions will take them."

The "grand flag" Reagan referred to was a seven-ton Stars and Stripes called the Great American Flag that was displayed on the national Mall in Washington. Billed as the largest American flag ever made, it was more than four-hundred-feet long and 200-feet wide. Each of the fifty stars measured thirteen feet across. The nylon and polyester flag had been manufactured by an Evansville, Indiana, tent manufacturer, Anchor Industries, in 1980, and an organization called the Great American Flag Fund presented it that day to the government.

"I always get a chill up and down my spine when I say that Pledge of Allegiance," Reagan said at the June 14, 1985, Flag Day ceremonies held at Fort McHenry in Baltimore, marking the hundredth anniversary of the first organized Flag Day commemoration in Boston. "From the mountains of Kentucky to the shores of California to the Sea of Tranquillity on the Moon, our pioneers carried our flag before them, a symbol of the indomitable spirit of a free people. And let us never forget that in honoring our flag, we honor the American men and women who have courageously fought and died for it over the last 200 years—patriots who set an ideal above any consideration of self and who suffered for it the greatest hardships. Our flag flies free today because of their sacrifice."

Flag sales rose significantly during the Reagan years. Flag waving reached its zenith during the Reagan administration at the 1984 Summer Olympics in Los Angeles. The United States dominated those games when the Soviet Union and thirteen of its communist allies boycotted the event in retaliation for the American boycott of the 1980 games in protest over the Soviet invasion of Afghanistan.

The Olympic emphasis on the flag began at the White House in Washington on Flag Day, June 14, 1984, when President Reagan presented the Stars and Stripes that would be carried in the opening and closing ceremonies to William Simon, the president of the United States Olympic Committee. "The team, walking behind the banner, our flag, in the opening ceremonies will truly be our team, America's team," the president said. "And I can't help believing that on that day, July 28th, the members of our team will feel all of us there with them—all of us behind them. They'll feel our pride in them, and they'll feel the unity, the patriotism, and the deep love we share for America, for our land of the free."

American athletes took home an unprecedented 174 medals at the Los Angeles Olympics, including 83 first-place gold medals. American fans cheered on those victories with displays of waving American flags that appeared prominently in ABC Television's extensive coverage of the games and in newspaper accounts for sixteen days, beginning with the July 28 opening ceremonies. Winning American athletes waved large and small flags and posed for victory celebrations in front of giant Stars and Stripes. Perhaps the games' most publicized image was track star Carl Lewis, who won four gold medals, taking a large American flag from a spectator in the stands after one of his victories and waving it triumphantly over his head as he took a long, slow victory lap around the Los Angeles Coliseum track.

Since the mid-nineteenth century, virtually every major party presidential candidate had used the Stars and Stripes in advertising and as a prop at campaign stops. Ronald Reagan, though, put the flag to extraordinarily wide use during his successful 1984 reelection campaign against Democratic nominee Walter Mondale. It was not uncommon for the President and Mrs. Reagan to appear at campaign rallies in 1984 holding small American flags with a gigantic Stars and Stripes serving as a backdrop. A widely used campaign ad pictured the president's visage atop the White House with an American flag arrayed behind him and the words "REAGAN FOR PRESIDENT: Let's make America great again."

On May 12, 1986, President Reagan issued a proclamation, following congressional passage of a joint resolution asking him to do so, proclaiming 1986 the Year of the Flag. "There is no greater, more beautiful, and instantly recognizable symbol of our nation and its ideals, traditions and values than the flag of the United States," the president said. "Let [1986] be the year we as a people commemorate our flag as the proud banner that the winds of freedom lovingly caress, for which generations of patriots have fought and died—the sign and symbol of a people ruled by a Constitution that protects all and enshrines our hopes and our history."

★   ★   ★

The flag played a significant role in the 1988 George H. W. Bush–Michael Dukakis presidential election campaign. Vice President Bush and his supporters—including his vice presidential running mate Sen. Dan Quayle of Indiana, Education secretary William Bennett, and Pres. Ronald

Reagan—made former Massachusetts governor Dukakis's 1977 veto of a bill that would have required the Pledge of Allegiance to be recited in Massachusetts's public schools into one of the main issues of his campaign. Congressman Newt Gingrich of Georgia raised the issue for the first time in Washington on May 19, when he circulated a copy of Dukakis's eleven-year-old veto message. "I would just love to see him explain on national television for three or four minutes why a bill requiring the Pledge of Allegiance at the beginning of the school day is unconstitutional," Gingrich, who later became Speaker of the House, said. "When the country realizes that the lawyers who advised him to veto that bill are the people he'd put on the Supreme Court, we've won the South."

Bush kept the issue alive in speeches throughout the summer. In his acceptance speech at the Republican National Convention in New Orleans in August Bush asked rhetorically: "Should public school teachers be required to lead our children in the Pledge of Allegiance? My opponent says no—I say yes." Bush ended that speech by leading delegates in the Pledge. He went on to recite it regularly at campaign rallies, where Bush also continued to condemn the 1977 veto. "What is it about the Pledge of Allegiance that upsets him so much," Bush said at an August 24 rally in Los Angeles with Pres. Ronald Reagan at his side. "It is very hard for me to imagine that the Founding Fathers—Samuel Adams and John Hancock and John Adams—would have objected to teachers leading students in the Pledge of Allegiance to the flag of the United States."

Bush highlighted his attachment to the flag by paying a campaign visit in September to the Annin and Co. flag factory in Bloomfield, New Jersey, and making an appearance at the Flag City Festival in Findlay, Ohio. That northwest Ohio city had been designated "Flag City USA" by a U.S. House of Representatives Joint Resolution in 1974 in honor of the fact that since the mid-1960s city residents displayed some fourteen thousand flags every year on Flag Day.

During the campaign, a Bush ally, Republican senator Steve Symms of Idaho, accused—falsely, as it turned out—Dukakis's wife Kitty of burning an American flag at an antiwar demonstration in the 1960s, a charge that he later withdrew. Speaking at the Veterans of Foreign Wars annual convention on August 22 in Chicago, Bush made a reference to flag burning in his heated response to allegations that Senator Quayle had avoided service in the Vietnam War by joining the National Guard. "He did not go to Canada," Bush said of Quayle. "He did not burn his draft card and he damn sure did not burn the American flag."

Quayle brought the flag into the October 5 nationally broadcast vice presidential debate with Dukakis's running mate, Sen. Lloyd Benson of Texas. In his closing statement Quayle contrasted the two presidential nominees. Dukakis, Quayle said, stood for "bigger government, higher taxes" and "cuts in national defense." Bush, he said, stood for "an America second to none, with visions of greatness, economic expansion, tough laws, tough judges, strong values, respect for the flag and our institutions."

George Bush denied that he used the flag for partisan political purposes during the election campaign. "I don't view that as partisanship," he said at a June 27, 1989, White House news conference. "I think respect for the flag transcends political party. It isn't Republican or Democrat; it isn't liberal or conservative. And I just feel very, very strongly about it." During the campaign, he said, "I didn't put it on the basis that Republicans are for the flag and Democrats not."

Bush's patriotic embrace of the flag resonated with many voters. "I like Bush's attitude," a voter in Modesto, California, said during the campaign. "It's the patriotism thing, the flag—you know, the Pledge of Allegiance and all that. I'm not sure he'll be able to do much about the deficit, which worries me a lot, but he's patriotic, so I'm sure that he'll try."

★   ★   ★

In February 1989, a month after George Bush had taken the presidential oath of office—and as the *Johnson* case was pending before the U.S. Supreme Court—an exhibit featuring the American flag at the School of the Art Institute of Chicago stirred up a great deal of outraged protest. The work in question, an installation called "What is the Proper Way to Display a U.S. Flag?" was created by a student at the school, Scott Tyler, who used the name Dread Scott. The three-part installation consisted of a photomontage of South Korean students burning American flags and six American flag-draped coffins in a military transport plane hanging on the wall. Below it was a blank-paged book and pens on a shelf. A three-foot-by-five-foot American flag sat on the floor in front of the book and montage. The artist asked visitors to write their responses to the installation's titular question in the book. While doing so, they could choose to stand on the American flag.

The school began having second thoughts about Scott's artwork before the show opened on February 17. Officials asked Scott to substitute another work, but he declined to do so. Several veterans' groups, including the Veterans of Foreign Wars, the American Legion, and VietNow, filed suit in

Cook County Circuit Court to close the show. A judge dismissed the suit. Newly installed President Bush spoke out on the issue, calling the show "disgraceful." Congress in March added an amendment to the 1968 federal Flag Protection Act making it illegal to place a flag on the floor. Bob Dole, the Senate Minority Leader, said the amendment would apply to "the so-called 'artist' who has invited the trampling on the flag."

The Illinois and Indiana Legislatures and the Chicago City Council passed resolutions condemning the exhibition. The Illinois Legislature also cut the Art Institute School's state funding from seventy thousand to one dollar. Some five thousand people mounted a protest demonstration on March 12, and smaller protests took place every day the exhibit was open to the public.

For its part the Art Institute school maintained that Scott's installation, no matter how provocative, did not desecrate the flag. "We are trying to defend the notion that all art, provocative art, can be displayed," said James McManus, chairman of the school's Liberal Arts Department.

The artist has exhibited the installation thirteen times since 1989. He maintains it is a political work that is designed to prompt debate about the meaning of the Stars and Stripes. "My intent with the work was to open up discussion about America, U.S. patriotism, and the U.S. flag," Scott said in 2003. "My intent was neither to desecrate, nor not to desecrate the flag." Scott, who describes himself as a "revolutionary," said that he "has no love for this flag" because "America has committed towering crimes" under it and the nation "is profoundly unjust." As for the installation, he characterized it as "a participatory work" that "in some respects doesn't reflect—and has little to do with—my personal view of America or its flag."

Scott said he "had no idea, and nobody else did either, that this work by an unknown artist would become the center of a national controversy." When he designed the installation in 1988, Scott said, "the first George Bush was campaigning for president and stopping in all these flag factories." By "placing the flag on the ground and enabling people to walk on it and including pictures of South Korean students burning flags, the work enables those who are oppressed by America to know that their thoughts and ideas are welcome within the context of the work. Normally these voices are silenced in any discussion of the flag. This art brings these voices into the debate within the broad range of people who interact with the work."

Although his intent "was not to desecrate the flag," Scott said, the work "welcomes the sentiments of those who would and encourages many to think about why some may want to do so."

*   *   *

The first Persian Gulf War, the fighting portion of which was known as Operation Desert Storm, began in the early morning hours of January 17, 1991. It ended on March 3, after coalition forces, led by the United States, pushed Iraqi president Saddam Hussein's troops out of Kuwait. That conflict, the first large-scale war fought by the United States since the Vietnam War, liberated Kuwait with minimal American casualties. Fewer than three hundred American military personnel died in Desert Storm and fewer than five hundred were wounded.

Americans, partly in reaction to the negative reception given to Vietnam War veterans by many doves and even by some hawks, rallied around the troops who fought in Operation Desert Storm. While there was some criticism of the efficacy of the war, there was near unanimity in the outpouring of support for the American men and women who fought in Kuwait and Iraq in 1991. A good portion of that support was expressed using the American flag.

As was the case with the Civil War in the North and World War I throughout the nation, Americans of all walks of life displayed the Stars and Stripes at the outset of the 1991 Persian Gulf War. "Our pride in the skill and professionalism of our troops has stirred a renewed sense of patriotism throughout our country and is reflected in the tremendous number of American flags that now fly daily over homes and businesses," Congressman C. W. "Bill" Young, a Florida Republican, said on the floor of the House of Representatives on June 19, 1991. "We will forever remember the site of the Kuwaiti people rejoicing as American troops, flying the American flag, triumphantly entered a newly liberated Kuwait City and hoisted the flag over the American Embassy."

At home, sports teams at every level showed their patriotism and their support for the troops during the Persian Gulf War by adding American flags to their uniforms and showcasing the Stars and Stripes at athletic events. "There is hardly a pro or college team in the land that hasn't made some symbolic gesture in support of the U.S. forces," *Sports Illustrated* reported on February 25. "Flag decals and patches are everywhere, from the helmets of NFL players to the backboards of NBA arenas, from the shoe of a high school wrestler to the jersey of Waad Hirmez, the Iraqi-born soccer star of the San Diego Sockers."

Crowds of families and friends, many waving American flags, emotionally and enthusiastically welcomed the 467,000 American troops who served in the Persian Gulf when their units returned home in the spring of 1991. Later the troops took part in flag-rich welcome-home parades across the nation, including the nationally televised "Operation Welcome Home" ticker tape parade in New York City on June 10 and the National Victory Celebration in Washington, D.C., on June 8.

The Wm. Wrigley Jr. Company of Chicago commissioned a massive, eight-story-high, four-story-wide American flag to display at that city's welcome home parade for Operation Desert Storm veterans on May 10. Wrigley, the world's largest chewing gum manufacturer, had the flag made by Flags Unlimited of Saint Charles, Illinois. The enormous flag consisted of seventy different pieces of material sewed together with more than a mile of thread. It was suspended by cables and hung from the Wrigley Building on North Michigan Avenue.

★   ★   ★

For a decade after the end of Operation Desert Storm, the United States was at peace. The flag did not come up as a political issue in the 1992, 1996, or 2000 presidential elections. There were no flag controversies or changes in the flag during the eight years, 1993–2001, during which Bill Clinton served as president. The most memorable flag-related event of the Clinton presidency came on July 13, 1998, when he gave a speech at the Smithsonian Institution's National Museum of American History at ceremonies marking the start of the restoration of the Star-Spangled Banner.

"You can neither honor the past, nor imagine the future, nor achieve it without the kind of citizenship embodied by all of our memories of the flag," Clinton said that day. "So as you see this flag and leave this place, promise yourself that when your great-grandchildren are here, they'll not only be able to see the Star Spangled Banner, it will mean just as much to them then as it does to you today."

★   ★   ★

In the wake of the events of September 11, 2001, the American flag became an instant and widely used symbol of a nation united against terrorism. Within days after the attacks in New York, Washington, and Pennsylvania, millions of Americans proudly and defiantly unfurled American flags in every corner of the country. Flags appeared on cars and trucks, on front lawns, and hung from living room windows, office buildings, and in commercial establishments of every stripe. People stuck small flags into their hats and taped them to their computers at work and at home. Police departments, departments of corrections, and other state and local agencies directed employees to wear American flag patches on their uniforms.

Flags flown at the World Trade Center and the Pentagon became instant and widely seen symbols of American patriotism, defiance, and resolve in the face of the attacks. Those attacks took the lives of more than three thousand civilians and rescue workers—more than the number of Americans who died in the War of 1812, the Spanish-American War, or in the first Persian Gulf War.

The day after the attacks, firefighters at the Pentagon unfurled a twenty-by-thirty-eight-foot Stars and Stripes—a garrison flag that had been used by the U.S. Army Band as a concert backdrop—from the roof of the building's western wall. That was where the Al Qaeda terrorists had crashed an American Airlines jet, killing 189 people in the plane and in the building. The flag hung on the Pentagon until October 11. Pentagon officials then turned it over to the U.S. Army Center of Military History and displayed it at the Smithsonian Institution's National Museum of American History in Washington in the same spot where the Star-Spangled Banner had hung from 1964 to 1998.

A tattered flag, the only one flying outside the World Trade Center when the terrorist attacks took place, was rescued from the buildings' rubble three days later. The flag was given to the Port Authority Police and displayed at funerals and memorial services for the thirty-seven Port Authority Police officers who perished September 11 at the World Trade Center. The flag flew over Yankee Stadium during the three games of the 2001 World Series in October. "We wanted a place America could see this flag," said Port Authority sergeant Antonio Scannella, who escorted the flag to Yankee Stadium. "So they could see the rips in it, but it still flies."

The flag was then displayed at the New York City Veterans Day Parade, the Macy's Thanksgiving Day Parade, during the singing of the National Anthem at the Super Bowl in New Orleans on February 2, 2002, and at the NCAA college championship basketball game in Atlanta on April 1. Eight athletes, escorted by a phalanx of New York City firefighters and police officers, carried the flag into Rice-Eccles Stadium on February 8 during the opening ceremonies of the 2002 Winter Olympics in Salt Lake City.

"It was pretty emotional," said army sergeant Kristina Sabasteanski, one of the eight Olympians who carried the flag that day. "This is the World Trade

Center flag and it represents the power of America that we can come back. Then you're thinking this flag was what was left of three thousand lives. One second you'd be inspired, elated, and the next you're choking back tears."

Another flag recovered in the World Trade Center debris—along with a Marine Corps flag from the Pentagon, an American flag donated by the state of Pennsylvania and six thousand small American flags—was taken aboard the shuttle *Endeavour* on its December 5, 2001, mission to the International Space Station. Soon after the Russian and American astronauts returned to Earth on December 17 NASA distributed the small flags to families of the September 11 victims.

On October 2, 2001, the U.S. Postal Service (USPS) unveiled a new thirty-four-cent stamp with an image of a waving red, white, and blue American flag and the words "United We Stand." Hundreds of millions of those stamps were soon in post offices around the nation. "It is fitting that the U.S. Postal Service—which has served the people of this nation since the dawn of our republic—is planning to issue the 'United We Stand' postage stamp," Robert F. Rider, the chairman of the USPS Board of Governors, said October 2. "For our primary job has always been 'to bind the nation together.' Today, more than ever, the people of America are united in their purpose, their pride, and their determination. This postage stamp is graphic representation of that unity."

On October 9, U.S. secretary of education Rod Paige sent a letter to more than hundred thousand public and high school principals across the nation encouraging them to be a part of an event that was similar to the National Columbian Public School Celebration of October 21, 1892. Paige asked the schools to take part in a "Pledge Across America" program by participating in a synchronized Pledge of Allegiance at two o'clock in the afternoon Eastern time on Columbus Day, October 12. The secretary also contacted governors, state legislators, mayors, and state education heads, asking them to join the event, which Celebration USA, a California-based patriotic group, organized.

Teachers nationwide, Paige said in his October 9 letter, "have been working with students to help them understand what happened on September 11, and to overcome their fears and concerns. They have also worked to teach them more about our proud and rich national history and the foundations of our free society. Today, I ask students, teachers, parents, and other proud Americans across the country to join me in showing our patriotism by reciting the Pledge of Allegiance at a single time and with a unified voice. . . . Together, we can send a loud and powerful message that will be heard around the world: America is 'one nation, under God, indivisible, with liberty and justice for all.'"

In the months following September 11, 2001, several states adopted new laws mandating or encouraging the use of the American flag. The Mississippi State Legislature, for example, enacted a law in 2002 requiring that the Stars and Stripes be displayed in all public school classrooms at all times while schools were in session. The same law required Mississippi school districts to provide instruction to students on flag etiquette and to recite the Pledge of Allegiance daily at the beginning of class.

Many Americans followed the lead of Pres. George W. Bush, who—along with the White House staff and many administration leaders and members of Congress—began wearing American-flag-shaped lapel pins on their suit jackets after September 11. Television news reporters and anchors, including the entire staff of *FOX News*, also sported the small but very visible flag lapel pins. When *ABC News* barred its journalists from wearing the flag pins on the air in the name of objectivity, *FOX News* correspondent Brit Hume criticized the network on the air for doing so.

At the same time, the television evangelist Rev. Jerry Falwell offered free Pray for America flag lapel pins to those who pledged to pray for the nation and its leaders. A Gallup survey taken four days after the attacks reported that 82 percent of those polled said they had flown or planned to fly the American flag in response to the attacks.

Not surprisingly, sales of flags soared, and flag manufacturers across the nation were inundated with orders. Many retail outlets sold out of American flags within days after the terrorist attacks. Wal-Mart, the nation's largest retailer, reported that it sold some 450,000 American flags in the three days after September 11. In the next twelve months, Wal-Mart stores sold more than 7.8 million American flags.

In the summer of 2002, the nation's top flag manufacturer, Annin & Co., reported that its factory in Coshocton, Ohio, was turning out more than 250,000 flags a week—flags the company supplied to large retailers such as Wal-Mart. The plant produced flags ranging in size from four-by-six inches to four-by-six feet; the most popular was the three-by-five-foot flag most often displayed from front porches. "We've been running two ten-hour shifts six days a week to keep up with the demand," said plant manager Richard Merrell.

Aside from millions of small, medium, and large-size flags, a spate of gigantic American flags made appearances around the nation in the days, weeks, and months after September 11. In Fayetteville, North Carolina, for example, more than a dozen volunteers helped paint a forty-six-foot-wide, eighty-six-foot-long flag on the roof of a barn on Joe Gillis's farm. "We were just trying to say, 'Hey, we're right here, nobody's going to tread on us,'" Gillis said. "We couldn't pick up a rifle and go yonder, but we wanted everybody to know we were supporting them."

In October 2001, Ricoh Corporation, the office machine company, and Tahari Fashions cosponsored the display of the largest American flag ever flown in New York City, a five-story, one-hundred-fifty-foot-long, fifty-two-foot-high Stars and Stripes that was draped over the office building the two companies shared at Fifth Avenue and Forty-third Street. The flag was made of see-through mesh material. The company's president and CEO said the huge flag was meant to be "another way to show the [human] spirit" that was alive in the city after September 11.

The Adera Corporation of Las Vegas produced dozens of enormous American flags in the weeks after September 11. The largest, commissioned by Siebel Systems of San Mateo, California, measured twenty thousand square feet—one hundred feet high and two hundred feet wide. The flag was produced with a special wide-format ink-jet printer on perforated window vinyl. It was installed at a Siebel office building close to Interstate 80 in Emeryville, near San Francisco, and was visible to some 293,000 freeway drivers every weekday.

On Flag Day, June 14, 2002, Duck Tape brand duct tape showed off the world's largest American flag made of the familiar gray-colored adhesive in New York City's Union Square Park. The fifty-by-ninety-five-foot flag, produced by the duct tape artist Todd Scott, consisted of 1,120 rolls of duct tape—some thirteen miles of it—and weighed more than five hundred pounds. On Friday, May 23, 2003, the start of Memorial Day weekend, Marshall Field's department store flew a fifty-by-one-hundred-foot American flag from the seventh floor of its store on State Street in Chicago. The massive Stars and Stripes, billed as the largest American flag ever displayed in a department store, flowed down to the first floor. It revived a tradition dating to World War I. "Marshall Field's is proud to resurrect a tradition that began at the State Street store in 1916 when the first fifty-by-one-hundred-foot American flag was hoisted in honor of this holiday," said Ralph Hughes, the store's regional director.

A 940-pound, football-field-size flag, measuring 255 by 505 feet, which had been displayed at events such as the Super Bowl and the World Series and at the Washington Monument and Hoover Dam, made an appearance in Ocean City, Maryland, on Sunday, May 25, 2003. Some five hundred volunteers displayed the flag on the beach, a first for that gigantic Stars and Stripes, which cannot be unfurled in winds of over twenty-five miles per hour.

The large flags were not confined to large cities and metropolitan areas. On September 21, 2002, more than thirteen hundred people holding red, white, and blue pieces of paper formed a human American flag at Nara Park in Acton, Massachusetts, west of Boston. The event, part of the annual Acton Day festivities, was recognized as the "largest human national flag" by the Guinness organization until September 10, 2003, when 10,371 spectators at a European Championship soccer match in Dortmond, Germany formed the black, red, and gold German flag.

A thirty-by-sixty-foot American flag was raised on Flag Day 2003 at Wylie Park outside of Aberdeen, South Dakota. Local schoolchildren raised the funds to purchase the flag in conjunction with the National Flag Foundation's Flags Across America program. After September 11, Elizabeth Barnes of Norfolk, Virginia, conceived of a giant cross-stitched American flag, made up of squares containing the names of Americans killed in terrorist incidents since 1971. With the help of many volunteers, Barnes completed the flag, measuring thirty-five by sixty feet, in 2002. Since then, it has been displayed in Jacksonville, North Carolina, and Chambersburg, Pennsylvania, among other places.

"Originally, I was going to make little flags for victims of the Pentagon," Barnes said, "but then I decided to do one flag remembering the victims of September 11. It snowballed into this huge flag."

On June 2, 2003, a thirty-by-sixty-foot American flag, billed as the largest in the state of Wisconsin, was raised near Interstate 43 in Sheboygan on a one-hundred-fifty-foot flagpole, the tallest in the state. ACUITY, a regional insurance company, sponsored the flag and flagpole, which received a twenty-one-gun salute from an Army Reserve Rifle Team and a flyby from four F-16 Wisconsin Air National Guard jets. The company announced it would replace the flag every month and that sixteen one-thousand-watt spotlights would illuminate it at night.

The American Legion's Americanism Division in Indianapolis was inundated with questions about flag usage in the days after the September 11 attacks, according to Michael Buss, the division's assistant director. "I normally answer twenty-five to thirty questions, at most, about the flag by email or telephone each week," Buss said. "After 9/11 for a good month, we were averaging two or three hundred questions a week. I couldn't get off the phone quick enough with reporters wanting to know this and that."

Most of the questions from the media and the public, Buss said, involved displaying the flag. "Right after 9/11, the President issued a proclamation to display the flag at half staff, so people wanted to know how long it was to be and how to do it, especially with the house set, a flag on a pole attached to the porch. The physical make-up of that type of display pretty much prohibits it being placed at half staff." There were also questions about displaying the flag at night, and the propriety of wearing a flag patch.

Soon the Legion was fielding questions about the proper way to dispose of flags that had been torn or tattered. "We point them in the direction of the American Legion headquarters in their state and they can try and get them in contact with a post that does that service," Buss said.

Section 3 of the U.S. Flag Code prohibits the manufacture, sale, or exposure for sale (or to public view) of any article of merchandise "upon which shall have been printed, painted, attached or otherwise placed a representation" of the flag. In the wake of the September 11 events, though, that stricture (which, as is the case with the entire code, is not enforceable) was widely disregarded amid the explosion of American flag images that adorned products of virtually every description. That included countless items of apparel, led by the ubiquitous American flag T-shirt.

The list of post–September 11, 2001, flag-adorned consumer items also included:

- American flag contact lenses from CooperVision, with net proceeds temporarily going to the United Way September 11 fund.

- Tootsie Rolls in Stars and Stripes wrappers sent to American troops in Afghanistan in February 2002.

- Little Patriot disposal diapers in red, white, and blue from Paragon Trade Brands, with 10 percent of the proceeds going to the Red Cross.

- A Luciano Barbera cashmere American flag blanket, retail price: $1,995.

- Hallmark greeting cards adorned with the flag and other patriotic symbols.

- A special edition "American Patriots" Hummel figurine of two boys marching side by side, one playing a drum, the other holding a waving American flag.

Very few Americans objected to the fact that these and other consumer items violated the U.S. Flag Code. Traditionally patriotic segments of society wholeheartedly embraced the American flag. That included country music performers such as Alan Jackson, Toby Keith, Darryl Worley, and the duo of Brooks & Dunn, all of whom featured large American flags, patriotic songs, and flag-waving montages in their music videos and stage acts. Keith's song, "Courtesy of the Red, White, and Blue (The Angry American)," written a week after the September 11 terrorist attacks, became a huge hit the following year and was the centerpiece of Keith's popular concert shows. Keith strummed an American flag–embossed acoustic guitar at his live performances, which also featured a rendition of "The Star-Spangled Banner" by his guitarist and explosions of red, white, and blue confetti.

Politically liberal Americans—many of whom a generation earlier had used the American flag to voice their dissatisfaction with the Vietnam War—also embraced the Stars and Stripes after the terrorist attacks. "September 11 made it safe for liberals to be patriots," the critic George Packer wrote in late September. American academics, many of whom are politically liberal, are "not noted for [their] public display of patriotic sentiments," Walter Berns, a resident scholar at the conservative American Enterprise Institute, said after September 11. "So I was pleasantly surprised by the public response to 9/11, particularly the extent to which the flag was displayed." As Berns indicated, many politically liberal Americans changed their thinking about the meaning of the flag in the wake of the terrorist attacks and flew the Stars and Stripes out of respect to those who lost their lives and in resolve to back the nation's future fight against terrorism.

Not all former flag-flying disdainers felt that way, however. Katha Pollitt, a columnist for the liberal magazine *The Nation*, objected when her high-school-aged daughter suggested flying the flag from their living room window in New York City. "Definitely not, I say: The flag stands for jingoism and vengeance and war," Pollitt wrote. "There are no symbolic representations right now for the things the world really needs—equality and justice and humanity and solidarity and intelligence."

*   *   *

When the United States began military operations against Iraq in March 2003, the American people again reacted with a large showing of the American flag in support of the troops. Flag sales increased markedly, flags were displayed nationwide in abundance, and there was another spike in the popularity of flag-embossed clothing and other consumer items. Some Americans, though, in actions similar to what happened during the Vietnam War, used the flag to protest the preemptive military strike into Iraq designed to oust the nation's repressive leader Saddam Hussein and to seize his regime's weapons of mass destruction.

Antiwar activists lowered flags to half-staff or flew them upside down in protest. At a U.S. Army and Marine Corps recruiting station in a Lansing, New York, shopping mall, protesters splattered human blood onto an American flag. Some, including Arizona State University students at a rally in Tempe on March 20, burned the Stars and Stripes in protest. The war also sparked some Americans to speak out about ubiquitous flag waving.

"The flag's been hijacked and turned into a logo, the trademark of a monopoly on patriotism," Bill Moyers, the PBS TV commentator, said several weeks before the war began, on the February 23, 2003, edition of *NOW With Bill Moyers*. "On those Sunday morning talk shows, official chests appear adorned with the flag as if it is the *Good Housekeeping* Seal of Approval.... When I see flags sprouting on official lapels, I think of the time in China when I saw Mao's little red book on every official's desk, omnipresent and unread."

Moyers, who wore a flag pin on his lapel on the program, said he did so "as a modest riposte to men with flags in their lapels who shoot missiles from the safety of Washington think tanks, or argue that sacrifice is good as long as they don't have to make it [and] to remind myself that not every patriot thinks we should do to the people of Baghdad what Bin Laden did to us." The flag, Moyers said, "belongs to the country, not to the government. And it reminds me that it is not un-American to think that war—except in self-defense—is a failure of moral imagination, political nerve and diplomacy."

Retired U.S. Army general Wesley K. Clark, a candidate for the 2004 Democratic Party presidential nomination, spoke out strongly in the fall and winter of 2003 against politicians who figuratively wrapped themselves in the American flag for political purposes in the wake of the Iraq war. In late November Clark began integrating what journalists called a "grasp the flag and talk" segment into his campaign speeches.

"That's the flag I served under. That's the flag I fought for," Clark said, for example, at a December 5 campaign stop in McMinnville, Tennessee, as he held an American flag. "It's going to be about the Republicans trying to take away our flag and patriotism and our faith from us. With me as your candidate, I'm not going to let them do that."

The American flag, Clark said later that month in a speech at Phillips Exeter Academy in New Hampshire, "doesn't belong to the Republican

Party." As he had done earlier, Clark had stopped his speech, turned from the lectern, and grabbed a Stars and Stripes displayed at the back of the stage. Clark then asked veterans in the audience to stand. "That's our flag," he said. "We saluted that flag. We served under it. We fought for it. We watched brave men and women buried under it. And no [Republican House Majority Leader] Tom Delay or [U.S. Attorney General] John Ashcroft or George W. Bush is going to take this flag away from us."

The political essayist and social critic Barbara Ehrenreich spoke in February 2003 of a "virus-like proliferation of American flags." The flag, she said, "has, through sheer repetition, been reduced to the equivalent of wallpaper: flag sweaters, flag pins, flag earrings, flag Christmas lights, flag bathing suits, flag sweatshirts, flag underwear. Inevitably, this results in flag burning, since almost any random mound of garbage you ignite is bound to contain some flag or flag-like representation."

A collegiate basketball player, Toni Smith of Manhattanville College in New York, created a mini national stir when she began turning her back to the American flag during the playing of the National Anthem before her team's games in February. "A lot of people blindly stand up and salute the flag, but I feel that blindly facing the flag hurts more people," Smith said. "There are a lot of inequities in this country and these are issues that need to be acknowledged. The rich are getting richer and our priorities are elsewhere." Veterans and others criticized Smith's actions, but she was allowed to continue her silent protests. "It is not about the flag to us," Richard A. Berman, the president of Manhattanville College, said. "We support our troops, but I think it is healthy to have kids on college campuses expressing their views. That's where the energy comes from."

In Iraq itself, American troops, whose uniforms contained an American flag patch on the right sleeve, were—for perhaps the first time since the military began flying the national flag in the War of 1812—under orders not to fly the Stars and Stripes. The reason: not to give the impression that the Americans were leading an invasion of Iraq. "It's imposing enough that we're coming into another society," said U.S. Army captain Frank Stanco, a 101st Airborne Division artillery unit commander. "I tell our soldiers we want to maintain our professionalism. We could be making history. I call it being quiet professionals."

The non–flag-flying directive was not strictly followed. Some American troops defiantly carried the Stars and Stripes with them into Iraq. That included Cpl. Edward Chin of the U.S. Marine Corps's First Tank Battalion. On April 2, Chin and another marine climbed to the top of a large statue of

Saddam Hussein in Firdos Square in Baghdad as a crowd tried to dismantle it. Chin covered the statue's face with an American flag just before the statue came down. The flag was only on the statue for a few minutes before it was replaced by an Iraqi flag, but Abu Dhabi Television broadcast the image live.

"You can understand these Marines who have put their lives on the line, sweated with blood and guts for the past three weeks wanting to show the Stars and Stripes in this moment of glory," *FOX News* television anchor David Asman said of Chin's actions. "It is understandable, but no doubt [the Arab television network] Al-Jazeera and others will make hay with that."

Two weeks later, when a group of marines unfurled an American flag as they took over a regional governor's office in Mosul, Iraqis began a violent street protest over the flying of the Stars and Stripes. In the ensuing fire-fight at least seven Iraqis were killed. "You must respect the flag," an Iraqi said. "They say to us they want to leave our country soon. How can we believe them if they put up the American flag?"

The Pentagon continued its policy of not showing the flag in Iraq following the June 28, 2004, transfer of sovereignty to an interim Iraqi government. That policy included a special order issued on July 4 at the First Cavalry Division's Forward Operating Base (FOB) Eagle near Sadr City. The words "You cannot display an American flag outside the FOB" were written in red marker on a message board outside one platoon's barracks. Inside the compound the American troops celebrated the Fourth with modest displays of the flag, including a card table–size cake depicting the Stars and Stripes.

On the day that the transfer of sovereignty was official, June 30, U.S. Marines raised an American flag at the new U.S. Embassy in Baghdad—the first time the Stars and Stripes had flown there since the start of the first Persian Gulf War in 1991. The new U.S. Embassy was housed temporarily in a former palace of the ousted Iraqi leader Saddam Hussein in the heavily fortified area known as the Green Zone.

When the war began, the U.S. military brought a supply of American flags to Iraq for the grim purpose of covering the caskets of Americans killed there. The custom of using a flag as a pall to cover the body or the coffin of a fallen soldier dates from the time of the Romans. "We believe that the original form of the pall was a Roman soldier's cloak that was draped over his body as it was carried in procession to the grave," said Jon N. Austin, the director of the Museum of Funeral Customs in Illinois. "The cloak gave way to a rectangular piece of cloth emblazoned with the arms of the deceased or parish guild prior to the general use of a coffin or burial container."

In a sense, Austin said, "the use of the American flag probably has ancient military origins in which the deceased veteran is figuratively wrapped
in his country's colors in recognition of service to his country."

Historians believe that the custom of draping military caskets with national flags began during the Napoleonic Wars in the late-eighteenth and
early-nineteenth century. In this country the tradition likely began during
the Civil War. "It was simply a matter that there was a shortage of caskets,
predominately in the North, and flags were used to cover the bodies," said
Tom Sherlock, the historian at Arlington National Cemetery.

American military funeral flags are provided to family members by the
branch of service of those who are killed on active duty. The U.S. Department of Veterans Affairs provides the flags for other veterans' funerals.
When the flag is draped over a casket in a military funeral, it is placed so
that the canton is at the head and over the left shoulder. The flag, which is
not allowed to touch the ground, is not placed in the grave. It is folded thirteen times into the shape of a triangle and presented to the next of kin at the
end of the funeral.

The origin of the custom of folding the American flag into the shape of
a triangle at the end of military funerals and on other occasions is unknown. Some have postulated that it is a tribute to the tricornered hats
wore by patriots during the American Revolution. "There is no meaning to
the triangle," according to Whitney Smith. "It's simply a matter of conve-
nience that [the] military came up with."

Historians believe the flag-folding ceremony probably originated during World War I, a period of time when the flag was heartily embraced as
the nation's symbol. There is a reference to the custom in James A. Moss's
1930 book, *The Flag of the United States: Its History and Symbolism*. Widely
promulgated flag-folding ceremonies developed by the American Legion
and the National Flag Foundation, which give a meaning for each of the
thirteen folds, are not based on any provisions of the U.S. Flag Code nor on
any official government flag etiquette edict.

The American flag has been used in a much more positive manner during the Iraq war—to greet troops as they return home. Individuals and
"Support Our Troops" groups across the nation organized the flag-waving,
welcome-home celebrations. Members of those groups and others also have
waved flags and displayed patriotic signs near military installations. Scores
of "Support Our Troops" rallies featuring American flags took place nationwide after the fighting began in March 2003. That included a large flag-
waving rally held March 22 at Cathedral Square in Milwaukee. On April 5,

2003, a crowd of some two hundred, many waving American flags, gathered in the parking lot of the La Mesa, California, American Legion post to sing patriotic songs and hear speeches in support of the war effort. Most of the more than two hundred people who marched in a Support Our Troops rally on April 13 in Grand Island, Nebraska, wore red, white, and blue clothing and many carried American flags.

★   ★   ★

It's difficult to believe that the members of the Continental Congress who resolved on June 14, 1777, that "the flag of the United States be thirteen stripes, alternate red and white: that the union be thirteen stars, white in a blue field representing a new constellation" envisioned that the emblem they created would become the most revered symbol of the nation they created and would play a pivotal role in the nation's political and cultural history into the twenty-first century. Old Glory, in its unparalleled position as *the* symbol of the United States, has become one of the lasting legacies created by our Founding Fathers—even though we are not certain exactly which of those fathers (or mothers) conceived of the design.

The flag's design is at once simple and meaningful. The constellation of stars representing the states has more than stood the test of time as it grew from thirteen to fifty. For whatever reason, as the nation has grown from a feisty group of thirteen colonies into the world's most powerful nation during the last 227 years hundreds of millions of American have found special meaning in the red, white, and blue colors and the stars-and-stripes motif. They have risked their lives to defend it and clung to it with emotional white heat in times of national crisis.

Why did this flag—which began almost as an afterthought, and which was used almost exclusively as a military and government banner from 1777 to the start of the Civil War—take on such powerful meaning to millions of Americans beginning in 1861?

There is no definitive answer, probably because the underlying reasons are psychological, social, spiritual, and political. People, whatever nation they live in, have an emotional need to attach themselves to a unifying symbol. But that doesn't explain why Americans have a unique, special feeling for our national flag and why that situation continues as strong as ever in the first decade of the twenty-first century.

One important part of the answer has to do with the fact that the United States is a nation of immigrants. As the nation grew, state by state, and as the stars on the flag grew accordingly, the continuous updating of the nation's banner helped create a lasting, emotional attachment to the flag among those in the new and existing states, and particularly among the new arrivals to these shores, tens of millions of whom ventured here to live under the freedom and democracy that the Stars and Stripes stands for.

"An immigrant comes to the country, moves to a territory that becomes a state, and then becomes part of that flag," said Jeffrey Kohn. "I don't know of any other national flag that's that way."

The children of those immigrants who came to this country beginning in the early 1890s were the first to pledge allegiance to the flag. One of the Pledge of Allegiance's goals, in fact, was to help Americanize the newcomers to these shores. The Pledge itself certainly has been an important factor in promoting devotion to the American flag. The Pledge has evolved from a schoolchildren's ritual to a mantra that is recited by adults today throughout the nation in state and local legislative bodies, the U.S. House and Senate, and at meetings of veterans' and patriotic groups.

The Stars and Stripes has had special meaning for another group of immigrants, slaves. Some slaves fought under the flag for the North in the Civil War; virtually every slave viewed the banner as a symbol of the freedom that would come with the end of slavery. Civil Rights advocates displayed the red, white, and blue at rallies and demonstrations in the mid-twentieth century, again to symbolize the promises of freedom Old Glory stands for.

The simple fact is that—despite its changing meaning over the years—since 1777 the American flag has symbolized the values and ideals upon which this nation was built. Those who display the flag today do so, in nearly every instance, to call attention to those admirable qualities. Others fly the flag to associate themselves or their commercial products with the nation's most important symbol. Others show the flag to demonstrate their belief that the nation is not living up to what the flag symbolizes.

The American flag—whether it is an enormous banner stretched across a football field, a head-to-toe Uncle Sam suit, or a huge Stars and Stripes flying over a used car lot, the U.S. Capitol, or at a demonstration or political rally—represents the American nation's great experiment in democracy.

Appendix:
Stars and Stripes

THE NATION'S THIRD AND FINAL FLAG ACT, which became law on April 4, 1818, mandated that one star be added to the American flag "on the admission of every new state into the Union," and that the addition of the star would take effect "on the fourth of July then next succeeding such admission." What follows is a list of the dates that the stars were added to the flag, as well as the dates that the individual states were admitted to the Union.

13 Stars — June 14, 1777
15 Stars — January 13, 1795
20 Stars — July 4, 1818
21 Stars — July 4, 1819
23 Stars — July 4, 1820
24 Stars — July 4, 1822
25 Stars — July 4, 1836
26 Stars — July 4, 1837
27 Stars — July 4, 1845

28 Stars — July 4, 1846
29 Stars — July 4, 1847

30 Stars—July 4, 1848
31 Stars—July 4, 1851
32 Stars—July 4, 1858
33 Stars—July 4, 1859
34 Stars—July 4, 1861
35 Stars—July 4, 1863
36 Stars—July 4, 1865

37 Stars—July 4, 1867
38 Stars—July 4, 1877
43 Stars—July 4, 1890
44 Stars—July 4, 1891
45 Stars—July 4, 1896
46 Stars—July 4, 1908
48 Stars—July 4, 1912
49 Stars—July 4, 1959
50 Stars—July 4, 1960

1. Delaware—December 7, 1787
2. Pennsylvania—December 12, 1787
3. New Jersey—December 18, 1787
4. Georgia—January 2, 1788
5. Connecticut—January 9, 1788
6. Massachusetts—February 6, 1788
7. Maryland—April 28, 1788
8. South Carolina—May 23, 1788
9. New Hampshire—June 21, 1788
10. Virginia—June 25, 1788

11. New York—July 26, 1788
12. North Carolina—November 21, 1789
13. Rhode Island—May 29, 1790
14. Vermont—March 4, 1791
15. Kentucky—June 1, 1792
16. Tennessee—June 1, 1796
17. Ohio—March 1, 1803
18. Louisiana—April 30, 1812
19. Indiana—December 11, 1816
20. Mississippi—December 10, 1817

21. Illinois—December 3, 1818
22. Alabama—December 14, 1819
23. Maine—March 15, 1820
24. Missouri—August 10, 1821
25. Arkansas—June 15, 1836
26. Michigan—January 26, 1837
27. Florida—March 3, 1845
28. Texas—December 29, 1845
29. Iowa—December 28, 1846
30. Wisconsin—Mary 19, 1948

31. California—September 9, 1850
32. Minnesota—May 11, 1858
33. Oregon—February 14, 1859
34. Kansas—January 29, 1861
35. West Virginia—June 29, 1863
36. Nevada—October 31, 1864
37. Nebraska—March 1, 1867
38. Colorado—August 1, 1876
39. North Dakota—November 2, 1889

40. South Dakota—November 2, 1889
41. Montana—November 8, 1889
42. Washington—November 11, 1889
43. Idaho—July 3, 1890
44. Wyoming—July 10, 1890
45. Utah—January 4, 1896
46. Oklahoma—November 15, 1907
47. New Mexico—January 6, 1912
48. Arizona—February 14, 1912
49. Alaska—January 3, 1959
50. Hawaii—August 21, 1959

Notes

THIS WORK IS INTENDED for a general audience, not a scholarly one. That is why there are no footnotes in the text. However, I have tried to be as thorough as possible in researching the vast amount of primary and secondary material dealing with the history of the American flag. This book, therefore, builds upon the work of historians, vexillologists (flag experts), journalists, and others who have gone before me. It also is based on interviews I conducted in 2003 and 2004 with historians, researchers, and other American flag specialists.

For the first seven chapters, I learned a great deal from the work of the nation's—and perhaps the world's—top vexillologist, Whitney Smith, in his *The Flag Book of the United States* (Morrow, 1975). Smith, a former Boston University political science professor, has run the Flag Research Center in Winchester, Massachusetts, since 1970. He is the author of many other books and pamphlets on the American and other flags and has advised organizations such as the United Nations, the Smithsonian National Museum of American History, national Olympic committees, and the U.S. Department of Defense on matters of "vexillology," a word he invented. Among his other accomplishments, Smith designed the national flag of the nation of Guyana.

For the chapters on the history of the flag through the Civil War, I also made extensive use of the first fully researched history of the American flag, Rear Adm. George Henry Preble's *Origin and History of the American Flag* (Nicholas L. Brown, 1917), Vol. I., first published in 1871. Admiral Preble, the nephew of Commo. Edward Preble, commander of the U.S. naval forces during the 1803-4 Battle of Tripoli, conducted an exhaustive study of the American flag, including its origins, during his retirement.

There is also excellent material on flags flown during the colonial period and in the nation's early years through the Civil War in *Standards and Colors of the American Revolution* (University of Pennsylvania Press, 1982) by Edward W. Richardson, an encyclopedic reference book focusing on the various designs of the early flags, and in *So Proudly We Hail: The History of the United States Flag* (Smithsonian Institution Press, 1981) by Rear Adm. William Rea Furlong, Commo. Byron McCandless, and Harold D. Langley, which also is encyclopedic in its detailed descriptions of eighteenth-century American flags.

Boleslaw and Marie-Louise D'Otrange Mastai's *The Stars and the Stripes: The American Flag as Art and as History from the Birth of the Republic to the Present* (Knopf, 1973), also contains a great deal of information about the origins of the flag and its early history, along with many illustrations from the late authors' extensive collection of historic American flags. Scot Guenter's *The American Flag, 1777–1924: Cultural Shifts from Creation to Codification* (Fairleigh Dickinson University Press, 1990) is a thoroughly researched history of the American flag that stands as the best reference work on the changing uses, customs, and meaning of the flag from the beginnings to 1924.

One: Antecedents

7.   The flag of today represents: Frederic J. Haskin, *Flags of the United States* (National Capital Press, 1941), p. 2.

7.   It is believed that the ancient Chinese: See Ralph D. Sawyer, translator, *Sun-tzu: The Art of War* (MetroBooks, 1994); D. C. Lau and Roger T. Ames, *Sun Pin and the Art of Warfare* (Ballantine, 1996).

10.   It is believed that the *Mayflower* flew: See Hugh F. Rankin, "The Naval Flag of the American Revolution," *The William and Mary Quarterly* (July 1954): pp. 339–53.

12. Gadsden appointed Esek Hopkins of Rhode Island: For data on Continental navy ships, see the nine-volume *Dictionary of American Naval Fighting Ships*, U.S. Naval Historical Center, 1959–91.

14. "Certainly Trumbull, like many artists": Smith, p. 47.

17. An English ship in the harbor reported: A detailed accounting of the Saint Eustatius naval saluting, based on contemporary records, is contained in "Where our Flag Was First Saluted," William Elliot Griffis, *The New England Monthly* (July 1893), pp. 576–85.

17. "it is expected that you contend warmly": Marine Committee to Nicholas Biddle, February 15, 1777, in Charles Oscar Paullin, ed., *Out-Letters of the Continental Marine Committee and Board of Admiralty* I (1914), p. 76.

18. In his January 1776 report: "A British Spy in Philadelphia," *Pennsylvania Magazine of History and Biography* (January 1961), p. 22. See also, David McCullough, *John Adams* (Simon & Schuster, 2001), pp. 96–97.

Two: The Birth of a Symbol

22. Three weeks earlier, on Saturday, June 14, 1777: See Smith, pp. 42–68; Scott M. Guenter, *The American Flag, 1777–1924* (Fairleigh Dickenson University Press, 1992), pp. 15–24; and Preble, pp. 259–89.

23. "The American flag as a sovereign flag": Henry Moeller, author interview, June 9, 2003. See also Moeller's book, *Shattering an American Myth: Unfurling the History of the Stars and Stripes* (Amereon House, 1995). Moeller, a member of the North American Vexillogical Association, is professor emeritus of marine biology at Dowling College in Oakdale, New York. He has studied the origins of the American flag for more than twenty-five years.

25. "The most powerful motive . . . I had or have": Library of Congress, *Thomas Jefferson Papers*, Series 1, General Correspondence, 1651–1827, John Trumbull to Thomas Jefferson, June 11, 1789.

27. Historians believe though that it dates from the War of 1812: See Furlong, et al., p. 113.

28. However an investigation of the flag: See Furlong, et al., pp. 133–34. "The problem with Maryland's 'Cowpens Flag'": Letter

dated March 23, 1984, from Gregory C. Stiverson to Robert P. Kelm, State of Maryland, Department of General Services, Hall of Records.

28.   "As for the Colours": *George Washington Papers at the Library of Congress, 1741–99*, Series 4, General Correspondence. 1697–1799, Continental Congress War Board to George Washington, May 10, 1779.

29.   However a significant clue as to who designed: See Richard S. Patterson and Richardson Dougall, *The Eagle and the Shield: A History of the Great Seal of the United States* (U.S. Department of State, 1978).

33.   "Accept my thanks": Library of Congress, *Thomas Jefferson Papers*, Series 1, General Correspondence, 1651–1827, Thomas Jefferson to Francis Hopkinson, March 13, 1789.

33.   "Francis Hopkinson . . . designed the flag": Whitney Smith quoted in Michael Corcoran, *For Which It Stands: An Anecdotal Biography of the American Flag* (Simon & Schuster, 2002), p. 34. For an in-depth examination of Francis Hopkinson's role in designing the Stars and Stripes, see Earl P. Williams Jr., "The 'Fancy Work' of Francis Hopkinson: Did He Design the Stars and Stripes?" in *Prologue: Quarterly of the National Archives*, Spring 1988, and George E. Hastings, *The Life and Works of Francis Hopkinson* (University of Chicago Press, 1926), pp. 240–54.

Three: Mother of Invention

37.   Betsy Ross sewed the first American flag: The Betsy Ross Homepage Web site, www.ushistory.org/betsy/index.html

37.   There is no substantiation for the legend: Milo M. Quaife, et. al., *The History of the United States Flag* (Harper & Row, 1961), p. 98. William C. Kashatus's "Seamstress for a Revolution" in the August 2002 issue of *American History*, pp. 20–26, contains excellent biographical information on Betsy Ross.

40.   When college students were asked: Michael Frisch, "American History and the Structures of Collective Memory: A Modest Exercise in Empirical Iconography," *The Journal of American History* (March 1939), p. 1,144. Frisch interviewed more than one thousand students at the State University of Buffalo in the study.

41. "The next and last resort then of the historian": The text of William Canby's paper may be found at www.ushistory.org/ betsy/more/canby.htm; Canby's argument is spelled out in more detail in *The Evolution of the American Flag* (Ferris and Leach, 1909), written by William Canby's brother George Canby and Lloyd Balderson. Letters Canby wrote to Admiral Preble elaborating on the story on March 29, 1870, and November 9, 1871, may be found in Preble, pp. 266–67.

43. Betsy Ross "became America's founding mother": quoted by Valerie Reitman in "Tale of Betsy Ross It Seems Was Made Out of Whole Cloth," the *Wall Street Journal*, June 12, 1992.

43. "The flaglets were made by": Jeffrey Kohn, author interview, September 4, 2003.

44. The "construction of the first national standard of the United States": H. K. W. Wilcox, "National Standards and Emblems," *Harper's New Monthly Magazine* (July 1873): p. 181.

45. That painting "is the primary reason that the circle of stars": Edward W. Richardson, *Standards and Colors of the American Revolution* (University of Pennsylvania, 1982), p. 269.

45. Weisgerber's inspiration . . . according to family lore: See interview with Charles H. Weisgerber Jr. in the *Philadelphia Inquirer,* September 27, 1997.

46. The *Philadelphia Ledger* reported that the city's two councils: Reprinted in the *New York Times,* December 15, 1895.

46. . . . as his promotional literature put it: Betsy Ross Memorial Association, Library of Congress, Printed Ephemera Collection; Portfolio 160, Folder 45.

46. The *New York Times* in 1908 called six-year-old Vexil Weisgerber: The *New York Times,* July 5, 1908.

47. . . . Kent, who led a fund-raising effort: Atwater Kent, an inventor, industrialist, and philanthropist, in 1938 bought a nearby building on Seventh Street, the original home of the Franklin Institute, and donated it to the city of Philadelphia. Today it is the Atwater Kent Museum, which tells Philadelphia's cultural and industrial history.

47. "When I first learned of the condition of the Betsy Ross House": Quoted in the *New York Times,* February 14, 1937.

48. "Birth of Our Nation's Flag," is "important": Stevens and Weisgerber quoted in Amy Worden, "Betsy Ross Painting Finds New

Home in Pennsylvania's State Museum," Knight Ridder/Tribune News Service, December 27, 2001.

49.   . . . Canby's Betsy Ross story "a fake of the first water": Quoted in the *New York Times,* June 19, 1908.

49.   "So, of course, she's saying, 'I made the flag'": Lisa Moulder, author interview, January 28, 2004.

49.   The brochure notes: "The Betsy Ross House," brochure published by the American Flag House & Betsy Ross Memorial, 2003.

50.   "There are elements of the Betsy Ross story": Richardson, pp. 272–73.

50.   On the other hand, Smith said: Smith, p. 68.

51.   . . . an exhaustive study undertaken by Henry Moeller: "A List of Pennsylvania Flag Makers, 1775–1777," paper presented at the Sixth Annual Flag Symposium, March, 28–29, 2003, Harrisburg, Pennsylvania.

51.   Margaret Manny, who began making jacks: Ernest C. Rogers, *Connecticut's Naval Office at New London During the American Revolution* (New London Historical Society, 1933), pp. 130–31.

51.   "Everyone knows about Betsy Ross": Barbara Tuchman, *The First Salute: A View of the American Revolution* (Knopf, 1988), p. 47.

52.   "Would that it were true": A search done by Mark Benbow, the historian at the Woodrow Wilson House in Washington, D.C., of the sixty-volume *Papers of Woodrow Wilson,* Wilson's Flag Day speeches of 1916 and 1917, his books on the Revolutionary War, and other sources came up with no evidence that Wilson made the remark.

Four: First Additions

53.   "At this time we had no national colors": Preble, p. 264.

54.   A letter dated October 9, 1778, from Benjamin Franklin and John Adams: Library of Congress, U.S. Congressional Documents and Debates, 1774–1875, "The Revolutionary War Diplomatic Correspondence, Vol. II—Franklin and Adams to the Ambassador of Naples."

54.   Some flags had emblems sewn into them: Preble, pp. 288–89.

54.   A twenty-four-year-old American, Elkanah Watson: Watson's journal and an 1836 magazine article about it are discussed in "The First American Flag Hoisted in Old England" by Jane Carson in *The William and Mary Quarterly* (July 1954), pp. 434–40.

55.   It was "the first vessel": Preble, p. 291.

56.   The House of Representatives took up: The debate over the Second Flag Act may be found in the *Annals of Congress*, House of Representatives, 3rd Congress, 1st Session, pp. 164–66.

57.   The fight was waged by a heavily outnumbered force: See Joseph Wheelan, *Jefferson's War: America's First War on Terror, 1801–1805* (Carroll & Graf, 2003), pp. 282–85.

57.   . . . supported by three U.S. Navy ships, the *Argus*, the *Hornet*, and the *Nautilus:* The *Argus* went on to become one of the most successful American ships that confiscated British merchant ships in the English Channel during the War of 1812. See Ira Dye, *The Fatal Cruise of the* Argus: *Two Captains in the War of 1812* (Naval Institute Press, 1994).

Five: Our Flag Was Still There

59.   And it was true with the War of 1812: A comprehensive, well-written, well-documented history of the Star-Spangled Banner, the flag, is contained in Lonn Taylor's *The Star-Spangled Banner: The Flag That Inspired the National Anthem* (National Museum of American History/Harry N. Abrams, 2000). Taylor is a historian in the Division of Social History at the Smithsonian Institution's National Museum of American History where the Star-Spangled Banner is preserved. Other good sources are Scott S. Sheads, *The Rockets' Red Glare: The Maritime Defense of Baltimore, 1814* (Tidewater, 1986) and Walter Lord, *The Dawn's Early Light* (Norton, 1992). Sheads is a historian and park ranger at the Fort McHenry National Monument and Historical Shrine.

62.   " . . . hoisted a splendid and superb ensign": Robert J. Barrett, "Naval Recollections of the Late American War," *United Service Journal* (April 1841): p. 460. See also Taylor, p. 21.

64.   "The following beautiful and animating effusion": Photostat of *Baltimore Patriot and Evening Advertiser,* September 20, 1814, part

of uncatalogued clippings and photostats relating to the Star Spangled Banner, Music Division, Library of Congress.

64. The article indicated that the song was meant: For an overview of the history of the song, see Irwin Molotsky, *The Flag, The Poet and the Song* (Dutton, 2001). The National Anthem contains four verses, but the last three are rarely sung in public. The entire song's words are:

Oh, say can you see by the dawn's early light
What so proudly we hailed at the twilight's last gleaming?
Whose broad stripes and bright stars through the perilous fight,
O'er the ramparts we watched were so gallantly streaming?
And the rocket's red glare, the bombs bursting in air,
Gave proof through the night that our flag was still there.
Oh, say does that Star-Spangled Banner yet wave
O'er the land of the free and the home of the brave?

On the shore, dimly seen through the mists of the deep,
Where the foe's haughty host in dread silence reposes,
What is that which the breeze, o'er the towering steep,
As it fitfully blows, half conceals, half discloses?
Now it catches the gleam of the morning's first beam,
In full glory reflected now shines in the stream:
'Tis the Star-Spangled banner! Oh long may it wave
O'er the land of the free and the home of the brave.

And where is that band who so vauntingly swore
That the havoc of war and the battle's confusion,
A home and a country should leave us no more!
Their blood has washed out of of their foul footsteps' pollution.
No refuge could save the hireling and slave
From the terror of flight and the gloom of the grave:
And the Star-Spangled banner in triumph doth wave
O'er the land of the free and the home of the brave.

Oh! thus be it ever, when freemen shall stand
Between their loved home and the war's desolation!
Blest with victory and peace, may the heav'n rescued land

Praise the Power that hath made and preserved us a nation.
Then conquer we must, when our cause it is just,
And this be our motto: "In God is our trust."
And the Star-Spangled banner in triumph shall wave
O'er the land of the free and the home of the brave.

66. In 1917 the army and navy officially named: See George J. Svejda, *History of the Star-Spangled Banner from 1814 to the Present* (U.S. Department of the Interior, 1969), and Taylor, pp. 37–38.

67. Rep. Jefferson Levy, a New York: For a comprehensive post-Jefferson history of Monticello, see Marc Leepson, *Saving Monticello: The Levy Family's Epic Quest to Rescue the House That Jefferson Built* (Free Press, 2001; University of Virginia Press, 2003).

67. "'The Star-Spangled Banner' suggests that patriotism": Quoted in Molotsky, p. 157.

67. The VWF had been on record as early as 1917: At its 1917 national convention in New York City, the VWF sent a letter of complaint to the Cathedral of Saint John after its bishop had forbidden the playing of "The Star-Spangled Banner" because he believed it "created an enthusiasm for war." See "Say Bishop Barred Anthem: Veterans of Foreign Wars Ask Why Star-Spangled Banner Was Stopped," the *New York Times*, August 29, 1917, p. 8.

67. "There is a powerful and well-financed propaganda emanating from pacifist sources": Quoted in the *New York Times*, December 28, 1926.

68. . . . "to refute," the *New York Times* said: the *New York Times*, February 1, 1930, p. 1.

68. "She sewed the Star Spangled Banner flag": Sally Johnston, author interview, May 27, 2003.

70. Mary Pickersgill was born on February 12, 1776: For a brief biography of Mary Young Pickersgill, see her entry in the Maryland Archives "Maryland Women's Hall of Fame" series, Maryland Commission for Women, 2002.

70. "All kinds of colours, for the Army": A copy of the ad is reproduced in Furlong, p. 136.

72. "Snipping," said Marilyn Zoidis: Marilyn Zoidis, author interview, June 14, 2003.

73.   With great pomp and ceremony the Old Defenders . . . paraded
           the flag through the streets of Baltimore: On the first anniversary
           of the Battle of Baltimore, September 12, 1815, the city cele-
           brated that day with a parade, called the Defender's Day Caval-
           cade, which then became an annual event. In the late-nineteenth
           century tens of thousands took part in that patriotic celebration
           as municipal employees and schoolchildren were given the day
           off. But interest waned in the twentieth century and today the
           celebration is muted, although the 2003 celebration included a
           reenactment and fireworks display at Fort McHenry.

74.   . . . one of the oldest surviving fifteen-star, fifteen-stripe flags:
           The Fort Niagara Flag, which was made in 1809 and is housed
           today at the Old Fort Niagara Historic Site in Youngstown,
           New York, is believed to be the oldest surviving fifteen-star,
           fifteen-stripe flag. George Armistead, the commanding officer
           of Fort McHenry, served at Fort Niagara before and during the
           War of 1812, prior to taking over Fort McHenry in 1813.

75.   As Pres. Bill Clinton put it in 1998: Speaking at the National
           Museum of American History, July 13, 1998.

Six: Additions and a Subtraction

77.   . . . Wendover submitted a resolution in the House: *House Journal*
           (Monday, December 9, 1816).

78.   In his motion asking for the committee: *Annals of Congress*, House
           of Representatives, 14th Congress, 2nd Session, December 12,
           1816, p. 268.

82.   According to his own account of the matter: Reid offered his ver-
           sion of his role in creating the flag in a letter he wrote on February
           17, 1850, to his son Sam. It may be found in the Library of Con-
           gress Manuscript Division and on line at www.loc.gov/exhibits/
           treasures/trmo98.html

83.   On May 18 the office issued: Navy Commissioner's Office circu-
           lar, dated May 18, 1818. See Preble, p. 349.

84.   "Before the Civil War especially": Smith, p. 75.

84.   Small boats in the U.S. Navy: See Grace Rogers Cooper, *Thirteen-
           Star Flags: Keys to Identification* (Smithsonian Institution Press,
           1973), p. 1.

86.   ... the "most beautiful of all flags": W. S. Henry, *Campaign Sketches of the War with Mexico* (Harper & Brothers, 1848), p. 215. See also Cecilia Elizabeth O'Leary, *To Die For: The Paradox of American Patriotism* (Princeton University Press, 2000), p. 22.

86.   The flag, while still primarily used: See Guenter, pp. 49–65.

87.   One campaign ribbon contained: See Roger A. Fisher and Edmund B. Sullivan, *American Political Ribbons and Ribbon Badges: 1825–1981* (Quaterman, 1985), pp. 55–56 and O'Leary, p. 21.

88.   "Each new election [after 1844]": Guenter, p. 52.

88.   ... used the American flag as one of its primary symbols: For a history of the Know-Nothing party, see Ray Allen Billington, *The Protestant Crusade, 1800–1860: A Study in the Origins of American Nativism* (Macmillan, 1938); Carleton Beals, *Brass-Knuckle Crusade: The Great Know-Nothing Conspiracy, 1820–1860* (Hastings House, 1960); Mark Voss-Hubbard, *Beyond Party: Cultures of Antipartisanship in Northern Politics Before the Civil War* (Johns Hopkins University Press, 2002), and David Harry Bennett, *The Party of Fear: From Nativist Movements to the New Right in American History* (University of North Carolina Press, 1988).

88.   Its avowed purpose: Quoted in Nelson Manfred Blake, *A History of American Life and Thought* (McGraw-Hill, 1963), p. 174.

Seven: A House Divided Against Itself

91.   In short order, the Stars and Stripes became: Robert E. Bonner's detailed, inclusive look at the Confederate flag, *Colors and Blood: Flag Passions of the Confederate South* (Princeton University Press, 2002), also has a good deal of information about flag matters in the North during the Civil War. I used this excellent book as a road map for this chapter.

91.   The Civil War, Whitney Smith said: Quoted in Corcoran, p. 77.

92.   In his January 10 speech: The *Congressional Globe*, 36th Congress, 2nd Session, January 10, 1861, pp. 306–12.

92.   As the flag was unfurled, Anderson wrote: Anderson letter of December 30, 1860, quoted in Preble, p. 421.

92.   The last book Davis had checked out: Bonner, p. 8.

95.   If war with a foreign nation came: Quoted in Preble, p. 404.

95.   "I could not help hoping that there was": Preble, p. 411.

95.   On that same day in New Orleans: Mastai, p. 124.

95.   At Fort Sumter itself: Quoted in Bruce Caton, *The Coming Fury, The Centennial History of the Civil War* (Doubleday, 1961), pp. 174–75.

96.   . . . quickly dismissed a resolution: *Journal of the Confederate Congress* (February 13, 1861).

98.   Anderson, a Kentucky-born professional soldier: For more details on the fighting at Fort Sumter, see Caton, *The Coming Fury;* Robert Hendrickson, *Fort Sumter: The First Day of the Civil War* (Scarborough House, 1990); and Maury Klein, *Days of Defiance: Sumter, Succession, and Coming of the Civil War* (Knopf, 1997).

99.   Watching this unfold from the USS *Pawnee*: U.S Naval War Records Office, *Official Records of the Union and Confederate Navies of the Rebellion,* Series I, *Operations on the Atlantic Coast, January 1, 1861 to June 7, 1861,* p. 255.

100.   Jefferson Davis had bitterly derisive . . . words: Jefferson Davis, *The Rise and Fall of the Confederate Government* (Da Capo Press, 1990), p. 252. The book was originally published in 1881.

100.   "When the stars and stripes went down at Sumter": Preble, p. 453.

100.   "Romantic flag-waving rhetoric": James M. McPherson, *What They Fought For: 1861–1865* (Anchor, 1995), p. 42.

101.   He never dreamed his brother would "raise a hand": Quoted in James McPherson: *For Cause and Comrades: Why Men Fought in the Civil War* (Oxford University Press, 1998), p. 15.

101.   The "rebels know," the magazine said: *Harper's Weekly* (May 4, 1861).

102.   On April 12, the day the attack on Sumter had begun: Quoted in the *New York Times,* April 17, 1861.

102.   In Boston flags "blossomed everywhere": Mary A. Livermore, *My Story of the War* (Arno Press, 1972), p. 90. The book was first published in 1889. See also Guenter, p. 69.

102.   The flag, one observer said, "flew out to the wind from every housetop": Quoted in Jacob D. Cox, "War Preparation in the North" in Robert Underwood Johnson and Clarence Clough Buel., eds., *Battles and Leaders of the Civil War* (Castle Publishing, 1991), p. 84. See also Harold Holzer, "New Glory for Old Glory: A Lincoln-Era Tradition Reborn," *White House Studies,* Spring 2002.

103.   "The national banners waving from ten thousand windows":
         Quoted in Preble, p. 457. Six months later, on October 21,
         1861, Baker, serving as a major general in the Pennsylvania
         Volunteers, was killed at the Battle of Balls Bluff near Leesburg
         in northern Virginia.

103.   Another speaker urged the crowd to: Quoted in Mark E. Neely
         Jr., and Harold Holzer, *The Union Image: Popular Prints of the
         Civil War North* (University of North Carolina Press, 2000), p. 4.

Eight: Flagmania

105.   . . . what the *New Orleans Picayune*: April 17, 1861. See also,
         Bonner, p. 59.

106.   "I wear one pinned to my bosom": Sarah Morgan Dawson, *A
         Confederate Girl's Diary* (Houghton Mifflin, 1913), p. 24.

106.   Send-offs were similar in the North: Milton S. Lytle, *History of
         Huntingdon County in the State of Pennsylvania From the Earliest
         Times to the Centennial Anniversary of American Independence*
         (W. H. Roy, 1876), pp. 190–91.

106.   The Stars and Stripes began to appear on stationery: See James
         Parton, "Caricature in the United States," *Harper's New Monthly*
         (December 1878), p. 39.

107.   Mark Twain, then a reporter: Writing in the *San Francisco Daily
         Morning Call*, July 6, 1864. See also: Edgar M. Branch, *Clemens
         of the 'Call': Mark Twain in San Francisco* (University of California
         Press, 1969).

108.   Among the other songs published: The Public Domain Music
         Web site, www.pdmusic.org, created by Benjamin Robert
         Tubb, contains a comprehensive list of Civil War songs, based
         on original sheet music sources.

110.   The commander of the New York Fire Zouave's First Regiment:
         "The Murder of Colonel Ellsworth," *Harper's Weekly* (June 15,
         1861). Ellsworth had gained national fame in 1859–60 as the
         founder and leader of United States Zouave Cadets, a group of
         young men recruited from the Illinois State Militia that special-
         ized in close-order drills. They wore flamboyant uniforms that
         Ellsworth designed featuring fezzes, balloon pants, and red vests,
         and performed in front of large, adoring crowds. The name came

from a regiment of the French colonial army made up of fierce warriors from the Kabyli tribe that lived in the hills of Algeria and Morocco. The French Zouaves made their reputation during the Crimean War of 1854–56.

110.   One of Ellsworth's men, Private Francis E. Brownell: For his actions that day, Pvt. Brownell was awarded the Medal of Honor, the first given in the Civil War. See the *New York Times*, March 16, 1894.

111.   "When the President was reviewing some troops": Julia Taft Bayner and Mary A. Decredico, *Tad Lincoln's Father* (University of Nebraska Press, 2001), pp. 39–40. A fragment of that flag is on exhibit at the Fort Ward Museum in Alexandria, Va.

111.   "If anyone attempts to haul down the American flag": Quoted in Robert Underwood Johnson and Clarence Clough Buel, eds., *Battles and Leaders of the Civil War* II (Castle Books, 1985), p. 147.

111.   Farragut also ordered, in Monroe's words: New Orleans Public Library, City Archives and Louisiana Division Special Collections, *Correspondence between the Mayor and Federal Authorities relative to the Occupation of New Orleans together with the Proceedings of the Common Council, 1862*, p. 6. For a complete account of New Orleans's fall to Farragut, see Chester G. Hearn, *The Capture of New Orleans, 1862* (Louisiana State University Press, 1995).

113.   "His hanging of Mumford for hauling down the flag": "The Redemption of New-Oreans," editorial, the *New York Times*, December 7, 1862, p. 4.

113.   "The name of Mumford": Preble, pp. 473–74.

115.   They waved the Confederate flag: In a letter to the *Washington Star*, February 9, 1869. See Preble, pp. 489–90.

116.   He flew Old Glory on those days: Mary J. Driver Roland, *Old Glory: The True Story* (privately printed), 1918, p. 27. A copy of this book may be found in the Library of Congress in Washington, D.C.

118.   Although his grave is not one of the places: There are only eight sites in this country where the flag is flown twenty-four hours a day under specific legal authority; that is, by law or by presidential proclamation. They are: Fort McHenry National Monument in Baltimore: (Presidential Proclamation No. 2795, July 2, 1948); Flag House Square (Mary Pickersgill's "Star Spangled"

House) in Baltimore (Public Law 83-319, March 26, 1954); the U.S. Marine Corps Memorial (Iwo Jima) in Arlington, Virginia (Presidential Proclamation No. 3418, June 12, 1961); on the Green of the town of Lexington, Massachusetts (Public Law 89-335, November 8, 1965); The White House (Presidential Proclamation No. 4000, September 4, 1970); the Washington Monument (Presidential Proclamation No. 4064, July 10, 1971); U.S. Customs Ports of Entry (Presidential Proclamation No. 4131, May 5, 1972); and Valley Forge, Pennsylvania (Public Law 94-53, July 4, 1975). The flag also is flown at many other sites day and night, including the U.S. Capitol and at William Driver's grave, without the benefit of legal sanction. See John R. Luckey, "The United States Flag: Federal Law Relating to Display and Associated Questions," Congressional Research Service, Library of Congress, June 14, 2000, p. 9.

120.   That arm, "with which he bore the colors": John Brown Gordon, *Reminiscences of the Civil War* (Scribner's, 1904), p. 114. Electronic Edition, Academic Affairs Library, University of North Carolina at Chapel Hill, http://docsouth.unc.edu/gordon/gordon.html

120.   On July 4, 1864, for example: Preble, p. 491.

120.   The American flag, historian Scot Guenter observed: Guenter, p. 77.

120.   After 1863, when Lincoln allowed blacks to fight: Bonner, pp. 145, 147.

121.   During one such occasion: Thomas Wentworth Higginson, *Army Life in a Black Regiment* (Norton, 1984), p. 46. Higginson originally published his Civil War memoir in 1869. See also: Christopher Looby, ed., *The Complete Civil War Journal and Selected Letters of Thomas Wentworth Higginson* (University of Chicago Press, 1999).

122.   The "torn and tattered battle-flags": Gordon, p. 444.

122.   The Confederate soldiers, Chamberlain said: Joshua Lawrence Chamberlain, *The Passing of the Armies: An Account of the Final Campaign of the Army of the Potomac, Based Upon Personal Reminiscences of the Fifth Army Corps* (Bantam, 1993), p. 196. Chamberlain's memoirs were first published in 1915.

123.   Then the old flag, Admiral Preble wrote: Preble, p. 452.

Nine: A Band of Brothers

125.   . . . patriotic groups like the Union veterans: Cecilia Elizabeth
            O'Leary, "The Radicalism of Patriotism, 1865–1918," in John
            Bodnar, ed., *Bonds of Affection: Americans Define Their Patriotism*
            (Princeton University Press, 1996), p. 61.

125.   That flag was produced by the newly founded: That flag was
            auctioned on October 11, 2001, for $58,250 by Sotheby's in
            New York. The buyer was Ames Stevens, a great great grand-
            son of General Butler. Stevens donated it to the American Tex-
            tile Museum in Lowell, Massachusetts. General Butler resigned
            from the army in November of 1865 and went into politics. He
            was elected to the U.S. Congress, serving from 1867 to 1875
            and 1877 to 1879. A Radical Republican, he was a leader in the
            impeachment trial of Pres. Andrew Johnson. Butler later be-
            came a Democrat and was elected governor of Massachusetts in
            1882. The business records of the United States Bunting Com-
            pany are in the files of the American Textile Museum in Lowell,
            Massachusetts.

126.   In it the bunting: *Scientific American*, October 2, 1869, p. 218.

126.   "Wherever the flag of the United States": Orra L. Stone, *His-
            tory of Massachusetts Industries: Their Inception, Growth and Success*
            (S. J. Clarke, 1930), p. 748.

127.   "Every person in the column": Preble, p. 591.

127.   One of the clearest examples: See Irwin Ross, "The Most Sen-
            sational Walk in American History," *The Old Farmer's Almanac*,
            1974.

127.   "Bates is to carry the flag unfurled": Quoted in the *New York
            Times*, March 5, 1868.

128.   Mark Twain, the great American humorist and writer: Writing
            in the *Virginia City Territorial Enterprise*, February 27, 1868. The
            article was dated January 30 and was written from Washing-
            ton, D.C.

129.   At the latter event Bates met: the *New York Times*, July 8, 1868.

130.   When Bates arrived in London: Reprinted in the *Washington
            Post*, July 14, 1881.

130.   Bates, who appeared to be drinking heavily: Ibid.

131.   . . . the Order of Cincinnati, also known as the Society of the
            Cincinnati: The last full member of the group died in New York

in 1854. The society has been active continuously since then as a hereditary organization based in Washington, D.C. It supports educational, cultural, and literary activities that, in the society's words, "promote the ideals of liberty and constitutional government." See Wallace Evan Davies, *Patriotism on Parade: The Story of Veterans' and Hereditary Organizations in America, 1783–1900* (Harvard University Press, 1955).

132.   That year he also helped found: For a concise history of the Grand Army of the Republic, see: "The Grand Army of the Republic and Kindred Societies," Library of Congress, Bibliographies and Guides, compiled by Albert E. Smith Jr., Humanities and Social Sciences Division, 2001. See also O'Leary, pp. 35–48.

133.   "The most notable act of [Logan's] administration": George S. Merrill, "The Grand Army of the Republic," *The New England Magazine*, August, 1890, p. 614.

134.   "Patriotic color," the historian Robert E. Bonner noted: Robert E. Bonner, "Star-spangled Sentiment," www.common-place.org, January 2003.

Ten: The Hundredth Anniversary

136.   Thirty-seven nations took part: See Robert W. Rydell, *World of Fairs: The Century-of-Progress Expositions* (University of Chicago Press, 1993).

136.   The city of Philadelphia decked itself out in American flags: *Philadelphia Public Ledger*, May 11, 1876.

138.   Another flag falsehood: See Preble, pp. 280–82, Quaife, pp. 100–101, and Guenter, pp. 99–101.

139.   Before the war he had worked: See James F. Ryder, "The Painter of 'Yankee Doodle,'" *The New England Magazine* (December 1895): pp. 483–94.

139.   "The centennial year was approaching": Quoted in the *Washington Post*, July 21, 1912.

140.   The Bowery's "exhibition of patriotism is of the most effusive sort": the *New York Times*, July 3, 1876, p. 8.

140.   In Los Angeles, bunting and flags "were liberally used" throughout the city that day: "Celebrations of Old-Time Days Recited," *Los Angeles Times*, July 3, 1927, p. G1.

142.   In Portland, Oregon: See Joseph P. Gaston, *Portland, Oregon: Its History and Builders* (S. J. Clarke, 1891), p. 369.

142.   The "flag," Admiral Preble wrote: Preble, p. 600.

Eleven: The Golden Age of Fraternity

143.   Sometimes referred to as the "Golden Age of Fraternity": The term was first used by W. S. Harwood in his article, "Secret Societies in America," which appeared in *The North American Review*, April 1897, p. 623.

143.   . . . the rapid growth of the organization in the 1880s and 1890s: Merrill, p. 620. The GAR, which restricted its membership to Civil War veterans, held its final encampment in Indianapolis in 1949. When its last member, Albert Woolson, died in 1956, the GAR dissolved.

144.   During the Twenty-sixth National GAR Encampment: the *Washington, D.C. News*, September 23, 1892.

144.   "American flags fluttered everywhere": "Keep Step to Memories of Days of Sixty-One," *San Francisco Chronicle*, August 20, 1903, p. 1. See also O'Leary, p. 58.

144.   In 1897 one observer estimated: Harwood, p. 617.

145.   The DAR's mission included: O'Leary, p. 79.

146.   "I wish that every citizen of our great republic": Quoted in the *New York Times*, June 15, 1877.

146.   The idea for a national Flag Day was revived in 1885: See Gregory Presto, "The Stars and Stripes Forever," *Northwestern Alumni News*, Summer 2003; Ernest Hooper, "Flag Day Memories," *St. Petersburg Times*, June 18, 2002; and the National Flag Day Foundation Web site, www.flagday.org

146.   . . . at the one-room Stony Hill Schoolhouse: The last class was held at the schoolhouse in 1916. The building stood empty for many years until it was restored in 1952. Today it resembles the structure in which B. J. Cigrand held the first Flag Day observance in 1885. Every year a special commemorative program is held there on the Sunday before June 14.

147.   . . . American Flag Day Association with William T. Kerr of Pittsburgh: Kerr, who worked for the Pennsylvania Railroad, was president of the association from 1898 to 1950. He lobbied during that time for a national Flag Day celebration.

147.   "I would specially recommend that the flag be raised on each
           school building": Quoted in the *New York Times*, June 14, 1896.

149.   He called on Republican state central committees throughout
           the nation: Quoted in the *New York Times*, October 27, 1896.

150.   "A whole lot of houses on Connecticut Ave: Letter from Mabel
           Hubbard Bell to Alexander Graham Bell, November 1, 1896,
           The Alexander Graham Bell Family Papers, Library of Con-
           gress, Mabel Hubbard Bell, Family Correspondence, Novem-
           ber 1–17, 1896.

150.   "Although members of both parties": Guenter, p. 135.

151.   "I regard this day as a day of rededication": "A Flag Day Ad-
           dress," June 14, 1916, in Arthur R. Link, ed., *The Papers of
           Woodrow Wilson, Vol. 37, May 9–August 7, 1916* (Princeton Univer-
           sity Press, 1981), pp. 224–25.

155.   As one late-nineteenth-century reference book for advertisers:
           See Robert Justin Goldstein, *Saving "Old Glory": The History of
           the American Flag Desecration Controversy* (Westview Press, 1995),
           p. 9, and Guenter, pp. 138–39.

156.   The first attempt to legislate against: Guenter, p. 140.

156.   Beginning in the mid-1895s: See Davies, p. 221.

156.   In 1895 Reade: Goldstein, p. 31. Goldstein is a professor of po-
           litical science at Oakland University in Rochester, Michigan,
           who has specialized in the flag protection movement. In addi-
           tion to *Saving "Old Glory,"* his books on that subject include *Flag
           Burning and Free Speech: The Case of* Texas v. Johnson (University
           Press of Kansas, 2000), *Burning the Flag: The Great 1989–1990
           American Flag Desecration Controversy* (Kent State University
           Press, 1998), and *Desecrating the American Flag: Key Documents of
           the Controversy from the Civil War to 1995* (Syracuse University
           Press, 1996).

157.   Prime became the Flag Association's founding president: Gold-
           stein, *Saving "Old Glory":* p. 35.

158.   Henderson, a colleague said: See Guenter, p. 143.

158.   On March 4, 1907, the U.S. Supreme Court: U.S. Supreme
           Court: *Halter v. Nebraska,* 205 U.S. 34, 1907.

160.   The song was a huge success: See John McCabe, *George M. Co-
           han: The Man Who Owned Broadway* (Doubleday, 1973), p. 72 and
           Guenter, pp. 156–57.

160.   . . . which became the nation's official march: U.S. Code, Title
           36, Section 10, Paragraph 188.

161.   Former Confederate general John Brown Gordon: Quoted in Bonner, *Colors and Blood*, p. 165.

161.   The "greatest good" the Spanish-American War did: Roosevelt was the guest of honor at a flag-waving National Army Day celebration in Chautauqua, New York. His speech was quoted in the *Chautauqua Assembly Herald*, August 19, 1899.

161.   . . . a spate of extraordinarily large flags: See Mastai, p. 226.

Twelve: One Nation Indivisible

164.   "At that time," said John W. Baer: Author interview, May 12, 2003. Baer, a retired university professor, is the author of the well-researched, detailed account of the history of the Pledge of Allegiance, *The Pledge of Allegiance: A Centennial History, 1892–1992*. Several chapters of the book are available online at: http://history.vineyard.net//pdgecho.htm; another excellent source of information on the pledge is Margarette S. Miller's *Twenty-Three Words* (Printcraft Press, 1976). The book is written in the first person from Francis Bellamy's point of view. It contains many primary source materials, including newspaper articles and many of Bellamy's letters and speeches. Bellamy's family papers are in the Rare Books, Special Collections and Preservation Department at the University of Rochester's Rush Rees Library.

164.   The Grand Army of the Republic . . . joined the movement. See Guenter, p. 105.

164.   Balch, who also was a teacher: Guenter, p. 117.

164.   By 1893 some six thousand students: See O'Leary, p. 154.

164.   It sold six-foot-long flags: Premium offer in *The Youth's Companion*, September 29, 1892.

165.   That campaign was successful: See John Baer, *The Pledge of Allegiance: A Short History* (1992).

166.   October 21 was chosen: Colorado in 1907 was the first state to adopt October 12 as a state holiday. New York followed in 1909. Columbus Day has been a federal holiday since 1971; it is celebrated on the second Monday in October.

166.   "I am very much pleased with the idea": The letter is reproduced in Miller, p. 102.

167. The GAR commander in chief; Miller, p. 96.

168. Bellamy looked for inspiration in choosing those words: Quoted by Baer, *The Pledge of Allegiance: A Short History*.

169. The World's Columbian Exposition: See Donald L. Miller, "The White City," *American Heritage* (July–August 1993) and Stanley Appelbaum, *The Chicago World's Fair of 1893* (Dover Publications), 1980.

170. The forty-eight-page book contains a section on the American flag: "Citizenship Syllabus Now Being Distributed," the *New York Times*, April 2, 1916.

172. The historian Arthur M. Schlesinger Jr., for example: Arthur M. Schlesinger Jr., "The Flag: Who Owns Old Glory?" *Rolling Stone*, May 15, 2003.

172. . . . justice Robert H. Jackson, in fact, prominently cited the First Amendment: *West Virginia State Board of Education v. Barnette*, 319 U.S. 624 (1943).

172. In the 2002 and 2003 legislative sessions, seven states: Jennifer Piscatelli, "Pledge of Allegiance," *StateNotes*, Education Commission of the States, August. 2003.

173. "At this moment in our history the principles": U.S. Congress, House of Representatives, *Congressional Record*, 83rd Congress, 2nd Session, June 7, 1954, p. 7,763.

174. "Since the Soviet Union was avowedly atheistic": In an April 13, 2001, lecture at the 27th National Convention of American Atheists. Reprinted in "One Nation Under God: The Crusade to Capture the American Flag," *American Atheist* (Summer 2001), p. 18.

175. "The justices ducked this constitutional issue today": Quoted in the *Washington Post*, June 15, 2004.

175. Dukakis, Bush said, his opponent "isn't willing to let the teachers lead the kids": Quoted in the *Los Angeles Times*, September 3, 1988.

176. "The U.S. Senate started reciting": Baer, author interview, May 12, 2003.

Thirteen: The Great War

177. The American flag "had a certain sacred symbolism": Marie Peary Stafford, "The Peary Flag Comes to Rest," *National Geographic*, October 1954, p. 519.

178. The "Stars and Stripes" that the Peary party planted: Peary gave his flag, minus the six pieces he had cut out, to his wife, Josephine, after he returned from the North Pole. The family permitted the flag to be exhibited at the Smithsonian Institution in Washington, and in 1954 turned it over to the National Geographic Society in the nation's capital.

178. That act captured the public imagination: Mastai, p. 226. See also Wally Herbert, *The Noose of Laurels: Robert E. Peary and the Race to the North Pole* (Atheneum, 1989) and Robert M. Bryce, *Cook and Peary: The Polar Controversy Resolved* (Stackpole, 1997).

178. A government study undertaken: See Quaife, et al., p. 109.

179. Taft's order cut the number of official government flag sizes to: The sizes and proportions were slightly modified in a second Taft executive order on October 29, 1912, and a third by President Wilson on May 29, 1916. See Furlong, et al., p. 212.

179. He took his flag to President Taft: Quoted in the *Washington Post*, May 10, 1914, p. M3.

180. The parade was led by: See *National Geographic* (October 1917).

180. The profusion of flags in the city: See Ilene Susan Fort, *The Flag Paintings of Childe Hassam* (Los Angeles County Museum of Art/Harry N. Abrams, 1988).

181. "The American flag," the art critic Ilene Susan Fort noted: Fort, p. 11. See also Lynn Dumenil, "American Women and the Great War," *OAH Magazine of History*, October 2002.

184. The creed contains words and phrases: The American's Creed, in its entirety, reads:

> I believe in the United States of America as a Government of the people, by the people, for the people, whose just powers are derived from the consent of the governed; a democracy in a Republic; a sovereign Nation of many sovereign States; a perfect Union, one and inseparable; established upon those principles of freedom, equality, justice, and humanity for which American patriots sacrificed their lives and fortunes.
>
> I therefore believe it is my duty to my Country to love it; to support its Constitution; to obey its laws; to respect its flag, and to defend it against all enemies.

185.   World War I created an "unprecedented demand: See *Prices of American Flags*, a report to the U.S. Senate, 65th Congress, 1st Session, July 26, 1917. See also Guenter, p. 163.

185.   Businesses, including Wanamaker's Department Store: See Guenter, pp. 162–63.

185.   Men went off to war with: Reprinted in the *Congressional Record*, September 6, 1917.

186.   "Material manifestation of the patriotism of the Negroes": "5000 Delaware Colored People Honor 'Flag Day,'" *Cleveland Advocate*, June 22, 1918.

186.   Libby grew up on a ranch: See Frederick Libby's memoir, *Horses Don't Fly: A Memoir of World War I* (Arcade, 2000).

186.   An English RFC major "suggested that I use [the flag] as a streamer": Libby, p. 216.

187.   When Libby took the Carnegie Hall stage at the October 17, 1918, fund-raiser: Libby, pp. 260–61.

187.   As the bidding . . . began, someone in the audience shouted: See the *New York Times*, October 18, 1918.

188.   "The Stars and Stripes almost instantaneously broke out": Burton J. Hendrick, *The Life and Letters of Walter H. Page* (Doubleday, 1923).

189.   In 1918 Congress passed and President Wilson signed: *Statutes at Large*, Washington, D.C., 1918, p. 553.

189.   Three years later Frederick Shumaker Jr.: See Guenter, p. 168 and O'Leary, p. 235.

190.   Texas's Disloyalty Act, which became law on March 11, 1918: See Goldstein, *Saving "Old Glory,"* p. 80 and O'Leary, pp. 234–35.

191.   The day the war ended, November 11, 1918: See "Showdown in Burrton, Kansas" by James C. Juhnke in John E. Sharp, *Gathering at the Hearth: Stories Mennonites Tell* (Herald Press, 2001) and James C. Juhnke, "John Schrag Espionage Case," *Mennonite Life* (July 1967): pp. 121–22.

191.   The most egregious incident involving the flag: "Illinoisan Lynched for Disloyalty," *Chicago Daily Tribune*, April 5, 1918. See also: "German Enemy of U.S. Hanged by Mob," *St. Louis Globe-Democrat*, April 5, 1918, and "German Is Lynched by an Illinois Mob," the *New York Times*, April 5, 1918.

Fourteen: One Hundred Percent Americanism

193.   Not long after hostilities ended: Nine years after the end of
            World War II, in 1954, President Eisenhower signed a bill that
            changed the name of Armistice Day to Veterans Day to honor
            all of the nation's veterans. As part of the Uniform Holiday Bill
            in 1968, Congress moved the national commemoration of Veter-
            ans Day to the fourth Monday in October effective in 1971. But
            many states kept the traditional November 11 date. So in 1975
            President Ford signed legislation restoring Veterans Day to
            November 11 beginning in 1978. The official national Veterans
            Day commemoration takes place at the amphitheater of the
            Tomb of the Unknowns at Arlington National Cemetery. It fea-
            tures a flag ceremony with a color guard and the laying of a
            presidential wreath.

194.   . . . a group of army officers and enlisted men: See Anne Cipri-
            ano Venzon, ed., *The United States in the First World War: An Ency-
            clopedia* (Garland, 1999), pp. 29–30.

194.   . . . the spiritual successor of the Grand Army of the Republic:
            The GAR limited its membership to Union veterans of the Civil
            War, thus ensuring its own demise as an organization. Its last na-
            tional encampment took place in 1949. Six of its remaining six-
            teen members attended. The last GAR member died in 1956.
            The American Legion originally was open only to World War I
            veterans, but changed its charter to admit veterans of World War
            II in 1942, and again during the Korean and Vietnam Wars and
            the conflicts in the 1990s, including the Persian Gulf War.

194.   Within a year after the Paris caucus met "the Legion established
            itself": John Lax and William Pencak, "Creating the American
            Legion," *The South Atlantic Quarterly* (Winter, 1982): p. 44.

195.   Mayor Ole Hanson, calling the strikers anarchists: See Lynn
            Dumenil and Eric Foner, eds., *The Modern Temper: American Cul-
            ture and Society in the 1920s* (Hill and Wang, 1995), p. 219.

196.   . . . was setting up its Americanism Committee: The American
            Legion's National Americanism Commission today is made up
            of thirty-two volunteer members from around the nation. The
            commission provides guidance to the Legion's Americanism,
            Children and Youth Division staff at the group's national head-
            quarters in Indianapolis.

197.   Even though President Taft's 1912 executive order: Quoted in
            Corcoran, p. 139.

197.   American Legion national commander Alvin Owsley: Quoted
            in the *New York Times*, June 15, 1923.

198.   Harding administration secretary of labor James J. Davis:
            Quoted in the *New York Times*, June 15, 1923. See also Gold-
            stein, p. 86.

198.   In the weeks after the 1923 conference: See Guenter, pp.
            177–78.

198.   Although the Flag Code is a national public law: The American
            Legion's National Americanism Commission's booklet, *Let's Be
            Right on Flag Etiquette* (January 2002), provides a clear explana-
            tion of the many facets of the U.S. Flag Code.

198.   "It is a set of guidelines": Whitney Smith, *Honor the Flag! The
            United States Code Annotated and Indexed* (Flag Research Center,
            1998), p. 5.

199.   Those words were contained in a letter presented to: The *Nevada
            News*, November 2, 1922.

200.   . . . according to an account in the *Sidney Daily News*: August 16,
            1923. See also David M. Chalmers, *Hooded Americanism: The First
            Century of the Ku Klux Klan, 1865–1965* (Franklin Watts, 1965).

200.   A report in the May 31, 1924, Klan publication: See Arthur J.
            Hope, *Notre Dame — One Hundred Years* (University of Notre
            Dame Press, 1999).

200.   The KKK still exists today: The flag remains an important part
            of the Ku Klux Klan today, as evidenced by the following state-
            ment that appears on the Web site (http://www.unitedknights
            .org/Our Flag.html) of the United Knights of the Ku Klux
            Klan:

> One of the very finest things about the Klan is that its
> every act and throughout its every ritual it inculcates an
> abiding love for country and flag. No communist can be
> a true Klansman for from the first time he enters a Klav-
> ern till the last time he is around the Klan he is con-
> fronted with the flag and required to salute it. It means
> so much to us — it typifies the finest country in all the
> world. . . . There's something within that majestic em-
> blem which causes the heart of every Klansman to swell

with conscious pride when the flag of our country is unfurled and takes its rightful place at the head of our
parading legions. My, it's great to be a Klansman! IT's
great to serve our country! IT's great to own such a
flag—our flag—America's flag.

201.   When asked why there was a need for the association: Quoted
in the *New York Times*, April 20, 1925.

201.   "The Association was mostly a one-man effort": Guenter,
pp. 179–180.

201.   "Flags made in Japan," the statement said: Quoted in the *New
York Times*, December 21, 1924.

202.   It focused on "helping to create and galvanize": Reprinted in
the *Congressional Record*, 74th Congress, 1st Session, July 10,
1935.

203.   The National Flag Foundation bills itself: National Flag Foundation brochure, "Pledge Allegiance to the Flag! Join the National Flag Foundation," 2003.

203.   The Veterans of Foreign Wars: The VFW's origins date to 1899
with the founding of the Veterans of the Spanish-American War
and the Philippine Insurrection and their affiliated organization, the American Veterans of Foreign Service. That group in
1913 joined forces with the Colorado Society and the Army of
the Philippines and adopted the name, the Veterans of Foreign
Wars of the United States.

204.   "The fact that our population is becoming more varied as immigration continues": Quoted in the *New York Times*, June 14,
1926.

Fifteen: United We Stand

206.   "If there was ever a time in the history of the Nation": Quoted
in the *Christian Science Monitor*, February 24, 1942, p. 4.

207.   Walter B. Kerr, the *New York Tribune* foreign correspondent:
"War Posters Bring U.S. Flag to Russia Again," *Washington Post*,
December 8, 1941.

207.   Pres. Franklin D. Roosevelt, on June 22, 1942: Proclamation
No. 2605, "Flag of the United States," February 18, 1944.

208. The action was taken after City Councilman: See the *Los Angeles Times*, March 12, 1942, p. 1.

208. "Everybody flew the flag during the last war": Quoted in the *New York Times*, January 25, 1942.

211. "People saw in the red, white, and blue": Quoted in Emily Gold Boutilier, "The Symbol: What One Man's Obsession Reveals About the Stars and Stripes," *Brown Alumni Magazine* (May/June 2002). Rev. Kreitler loaned about a hundred magazines from his collection to the Smithsonian Institution's National Museum of American History for its exhibit, "July 1942: United We Stand," which ran from March to October 2002. See also, Fred L. Schultz, "United We Stood," *Naval History* (August 2002).

212. "They did it in every Broadway theater": Sally Sherman, author interview, November 12, 2003.

212. "They wore American flags on their right shoulder": Dale Dye, author interview, November 15, 2003. Dye served twenty years in the U.S. Marine Corps, was the editor of *Soldier of Fortune* magazine, and in 1986 reinvented the concept of cinematic military technical advising when he worked with Oliver Stone on his acclaimed Vietnam War film, *Platoon*. Among many other films, Dye was in charge of the military details on Stephen Spielberg's *Saving Private Ryan* (1998). That includes the opening scene, the D day landing, which is widely considered the most realistic depiction of that event on film.

213. The flag "exemplifies all that they struggled for": Quoted by Stacy Barnwell, "The Admiral Nimitz Museum and Historical Center," *American History*, June 2000, p. 14.

213. "They gave us small American flags to put in one of the zippered pockets": Quoted in Corcoran, p. 174.

213. In his World War II memoir: William Manchester, *Goodbye, Darkness: A Memoir of the Pacific War* (Little Brown, 1980), p. 173.

214. When it was over: Statistics from John Whiteclay Chambers II, ed., *The Oxford Companion to American Military History* (Oxford University Press, 1999), p. 344. See also: Eric Bergerud, *Touched with Fire: The Land War in the South Pacific* (Penguin Books, 1997).

214.   That's when marines Ira Hayes, Franklin Sousley, Harlon
            Block, Michael Strank, Rene Gagnon, and . . . John Bradley:
            The Stars and Stripes the 5 marines and 1 navy corpsman
            raised actually was the second American flag displayed on the
            mountain that day. The first one, which was raised by marines
            who secured the crest of Mount Suribachi under the com-
            mand of First Lt. Harold G. Schrier of Company E., Second
            Battalion, Twenty-eighth Marines, was too small to be recog-
            nized at a distance. The second, larger flag came from the
            navy landing craft, *LST-779*. The craft's communications offi-
            cer, Lt. J. G. Alan Wood, gave the flag to a marine who "was
            dirty and looked tired and had several day's growth of beard
            on his face," Wood later said. When Wood asked the marine
            why he needed the flag, he replied: "Don't worry. You won't
            regret it." See R. C. House, "Iwo Jima: Its Heroes and Flag,"
            World War II magazine (January 2000).

215.   "People ask, 'Was the picture posed?'": Quoted in the *Christian
            Science Monitor,* September 6, 1950, p. 9.

215.   "People would always remember where they were": James
            Bradley with Ron Powers, *Flags of Our Fathers* (Bantam Books,
            2000), p. 220.

215.   "It meant we secured the island": Quoted in the *New Britain Her-
            ald,* February 23, 2004.

216.   "When it was sent to Washington": Speaking at a June 19,
            1998, Marine Corps ceremony honoring him in Arlington, Vir-
            ginia. Quoted in Fred Carr, "Marine Corps War Memorial
            Sculptor Honored at Sunset Parade," *Henderson Hall News,* June
            12, 1998.

Sixteen: The Cold War

219.   "They can take Berlin any weekend": Oral History Interview,
            April 13, 1970, Truman Presidential Museum and Library.

220.   General Clay "made up his mind . . . with [President] Truman":
            Oral History Interview, November 26, 1995, National Security
            Archive.

222.   Within a half hour after the first U.S. Marine battalion landed
            on Wolmi-do Island: See Roy E. Appleman, *United States Army in*

the Korean War: South to the Naktog, North to the Yalu (June–November 1950), U.S. Army Center of Military History, 1961, p. 506.

223.   "From all these suggestions and from a study": John D. Martz Jr., "The Story Behind a New Star for the Flag," *Army Information Digest* (July 1959).

224.   . . . the new fifty-star flag, which would become official: Section 1 of the U.S. Flag Code still contains the words used when it was codified in 1942: "The flag of the United States shall be thirteen horizontal stripes, alternate red and white; and the union of the flag shall be forty-eight stars, white in a blue field." The president of the United States, however, has the power, under Section 10 to change "any rule or custom" in the code. See Whitney Smith, *Honor the Flag! The United States Flag Code Annotated and Indexed* (Flag Research Center, 1998), p. 7.

224.   "I was the only one in the class who decided to pick a flag": Robert Heft, author interview, May 8, 2003.

226.   "It cost me $2.87 to make": Quoted in the Newark, Ohio, *Advocate*, June 2, 2004.

Seventeen: The Generation Gap

227.   The year that the fifty-star flag made its debut: See the following Vietnam War reference books: Harry G. Summers Jr., *Vietnam War Almanac* (Facts on File, 1985); Marc Leepson, ed., *The Webster's New World Dictionary of the Vietnam War* (Macmillan, 1998); and Spencer C. Tucker, ed., *Encyclopedia of the Vietnam War: A Political, Social, and Military History* (ABC-CLIO, 1998).

228.   . . . "a cultural war using the flag as a primary symbol": Goldstein, *Saving "Old Glory,"* p. 148.

228.   The flag, Burt Neuborne of the American Civil Liberties Union said in 1970: Quoted in the *Wall Street Journal*, June 12, 1970.

228.   . . . he received thunderous applause from campaign audiences: Quoted in the *New York Times*, March 23, 1964.

230.   Flag decals "have become a fixture on fire trucks": "Decalcomania over the American Flag," *Life* (July 18, 1969): p. 32.

230.   . . . Mayor Ronnie Thompson said: Thompson and Windecker quoted in the *New York Times*, July 4, 1969.

230.   . . . "troubled by the stiff-minded emphasis on the flag": Jim
             Bouton, *Ball Four* (Wiley, 1990), p. 59.

230.   . . . "Your Flag Decal Won't Get You": copyright John Prine,
             lyrics used by permission of Oh Boy Records, Inc.

231.   President Nixon spoke out during the war: Nixon mentioned
             the "great silent majority" for the first time in a November 3,
             1969, televised address to the nation on his Vietnam War policy
             during a period of intense antiwar activity. "Tonight, to you, the
             great silent majority of Americans, I ask for your support," the
             president said near the end of his speech. "I pledged in my cam-
             paign for the Presidency to end the war in a way that we could
             win the peace. I have initiated a plan of action which will enable
             me to keep that pledge. The more support I can have from the
             American people, the sooner that pledge can be redeemed. For
             the more divided we are at home, the less likely the enemy is to
             negotiate. . . . "

231.   During the rally a young man . . . started . . . to lower the
             American flag: See Terry H. Anderson, *The Movement and the
             Sixties* (Oxford University Press, 1996), p. 223.

231.   The "profanity and spitting" by the demonstrators: See Charles
             Kaiser, *1968 in America: Music, Politics, Chaos, Counterculture, and the
             Shaping of a Generation* (Weidenfeld & Nicolson, 1988), p. 240.

232.   "Johns's print successfully became a symbol of protest": Deb-
             ora Wood, "Art and Transformation," 1998, online at http://
             users.rcn.com/erebora/debora/transform.html

232.   "Most sickening was the manner in which the American flag
             was degraded": Quoted in *Variety*, February 25, 1970.

233.   "I don't like what you're doing to the flag": Quoted in the *New
             York Times*, June 6, 1970.

233.   "The flag belongs to all the American people": See Goldstein,
             Saving "Old Glory," p. 119.

233.   "Which is the greater contribution to the security of freedom":
             Kuykendall was speaking during a House debate on June 20,
             1967, *Congressional Record*, 113th Congress, p. 16,446; Wiggins
             remarks, p. 16,459.

234.   Nearly all of them were "used against 'peace' demonstrations":
             Goldstein, p. 153.

234.   . . . he wore a red, white, and blue American flag shirt: See
             Jonah Raskin, *For the Hell of It: The Life and Times of Abbie Hoff-
             man* (University of California Press, 1996), pp. 178–79.

235.   "Johnson burned an American flag as part": Supreme Court of
                the United States, *Texas v. Johnson, 38–155,* argued March 21,
                1989; decided June 21, 1989.

236.   . . . "perhaps the largest single wave of [flag-burning] inci-
                dents": Goldstein, *Saving "Old Glory,"* p. 215.

237.   Their cases wound up in the Supreme Court: Supreme Court of
                the United States, *United States v. Eichman, 89–1433* and *United
                States v. Haggerty, 89–1434,* decided June 11, 1990. The votes on
                the *Johnson* and *Eichman* cases were identical. In both cases Jus-
                tice William Brennan delivered the majority opinion, joined by
                Justices Thurgood Marshall, Harry Blackmun, Antonin Scalia,
                and Anthony Kennedy. Chief Justice William Rehnquist John
                Paul Stevens, Byron White, and Sandra Day O'Connor dis-
                sented.

237.   "Congress tried to protect [the flag] by legislation": In an ex-
                change with reporters in the White House's Rose Garden, fol-
                lowing his remarks after receiving a replica of the Marine
                Corps (Iwo Jima) Memorial.

237.   In 1989 Bush had termed such an amendment: In his remarks
                to the American Legion Annual Convention in Baltimore, Sep-
                tember 7, 1989.

237.   The alliance is "engaged in a war to recapture Old Glory": Citi-
                zens Flag Alliance, "Let the People Decide," 2000, pp. 1–2. The
                Citizens Flag Alliance was chartered in May 1994 by the Amer-
                ican Legion to promote a Flag Desecration Constitutional
                Amendment and to foster flag education.

237.   . . . "took away a fundamental right of the American people":
                Testifying March 10, 2004, before the Senate Judiciary Com-
                mittee.

238.   . . . two-thirds majority required for constitutional amend-
                ments: Once passed by two-thirds majorities in the House and
                Senate a proposed amendment to the Constitution does not be-
                come effective until it is ratified by the legislatures of three-
                fourths of the states within seven years after it is submitted for
                ratification.

239.   "There were people at the time, and have been people since
                then": Quoted in Steven Siceloff, "Stars and Stripes in Space,"
                Florida Today, July 4, 2001, n.p.

239.   "I certainly felt that the American flag is what belonged there":
        Appearing on *NewsHour with Jim Lehrer*, PBS-TV, July 20, 1999.

240.   "Even though the event took only 10 minutes": Anne Platoff,
        "Where No Flag Has Gone Before: Political and Technical As-
        pects of Placing a Flag on the Moon," NASA Contractor Re-
        port 188251, August 1993.

240.   "My guess is the flags themselves, because they're nylon":
        Quoted in *Florida Today*, July 4, 2001.

240.   "We came here to express our sympathy for those killed at Kent
        State": Quoted in the *Wall Street Journal*, May 11, 1970.

241.   That was because, one worker said: Quoted in the *Wall Street
        Journal*, May 13, 1970.

241.   "Outside of God, [the flag] is the most important thing I know":
        Quoted in the *New York Times*, May 21, 1970.

241.   "A lot of us are World War II vets and fathers": Quoted in the
        New York Post, May 9, 1970.

242.   At the end of the meeting Brennan: See Fred J. Cook, "Hard-
        Hats: The Rampaging Patriots," *The Nation* (June 15, 1970).

242.   At the University of New Mexico: See "At War with War,"
        TIME (May 18, 1970): n.p.

242.   Philip Caputo, the author: In a lecture given at the U.S. Air
        Force Academy, April 27, 2000. See U.S. Air Force Academy,
        War, Literature & the Arts (Spring–Summer 2000), p. 25.

243.   It was "just like Iwo Jima": Quoted in Harold G. Moore and
        Joseph L. Galloway, *We Were Soldiers Once and Young* (Random
        House, 1992), p. 169.

243.   That flag was attached to "a shattered tree": J. D. Coleman,
        Pleiku: The Dawn of Helicopter Warfare in Vietnam (St. Martin's,
        1988), p. 226.

244.   "Every afternoon we would hang Mike's shirt": Senator McCain
        first told the story of Mike Christian at the 1988 Republican
        National Convention. A copy of that speech is on his "Straight
        Talk America" Web site: www.straighttalkamerica.com

244.   A few days after the beating: From a letter written by Colonel
        Day, submitted in testimony on the flag protection Constitutional
        Amendment before the U.S. Senate Judiciary Committee. See
        Citizens Flag Alliance undated booklet, *Let the People Decide*.

244.   "That flag," he told the novelist Pat Conroy, a college classmate:
        Quoted in Pat Conroy, *My Losing Season* (Bantam, 2002), p. 371.

Eighteen: United We Stand Again

246.   "To this day, I don't know what I was thinking": Quoted in the Everett, Washington, *Herald,* June 14, 1998.

246.   . . . "one of the most heroic acts ever to take place": Testifying before the U.S. Senate Judiciary Committee, July 8, 1998, in favor of a flag desecration Constitutional Amendment.

246.   On that day also a record 10,471 American flags flew over the U.S. Capitol: Americans may purchase flags that have been flown over the U.S. Capitol through the offices of individual members of Congress. Every day, three sizes of cotton and nylon flags—three-by-five feet, four-by-six feet, and five-by-eight feet—are run up a Capitol Building flagpole on the House side for less than a minute by staffers in the office of the Architect of the Capitol. The practice began in 1937. Today some 350 flags a day are raised over the Capitol and sold for less than twenty dollars apiece. Each flag comes with a certificate noting that if flew over the U.S. Capitol and the date that it was flown. At a "Salute to Heroes Night" charity auction in Washington, D.C., on March 4, 2004, a flag that flew over the Capitol on September 11, 2002, in honor of those who perished in the September 11, 2001, terrorist attacks sold for more than five thousand dollars.

249.   "I would just love to see him explain on national television": Quoted in the *New York Times,* May 20, 1988.

249.   In his acceptance speech at the Republican National Convention: Quoted in the *Washington Post,* August 24, 1988.

249.   "What is it about the Pledge of Allegiance": Quoted in the *New York Times,* August 24, 1988.

249.   During the campaign, a Bush ally, Republican Senator Steve Symms: See John L. Sullivan, Amy Fried, and Mary G. Dietz, "Patriotism, Politics and the Presidential Election of 1988," *American Journal of Political Science* (February 1991): pp. 200–234.

250.   "I like Bush's attitude.": Quoted in the *New York Times,* October 30, 1988.

251.   "We are trying to defend the notion that all art": Quoted in "Flag-on-the-Floor Furor," *TIME* (March 13, 1989): p. 27. Scott's installation also was met by vehement protests from veterans and others when it was part of eighty-one works of art

that made up a show called "Old Glory: The American Flag in Contemporary Art" at the Phoenix Art Museum in March and April 1996. Veterans' groups led peaceful protests when the installation was included in a show called "Vexillology: The American Symbol in Art" at the Nassau County Community College's Firehouse Art Gallery in Garden City, Long Island, New York, in September and October 2003.

251.   "My intent with the work was to open up discussion about America": Dread Scott, author interview, December 5, 2003.

251.   When he designed the installation in 1988: Quoted in *Newsday*, September 16, 2003.

252.   "There is hardly a pro or college team in the land: Steve Wulf, "Old Glory and New Wounds: The True Meaning of the Flag is Lost in the World of Sports," *Sports Illustrated*, February 25, 1991, p. 7.

254.   "We wanted a place America could see this flag": Quoted in the *Albuquerque Journal*, November 23, 2001.

254.   "It was pretty emotional": Quoted in Brian Lepley, "Soldier Carries WTC Flag at Olympic Opener," Armed Forces Press Service, February 11, 2002.

256.   A Gallup survey taken four days after the attacks: Quoted in Lisa Sanders, et al., "All-American Ads," *Advertising Age*, September 24, 2001.

256.   "We've been running two ten-hour shifts six days a week": Quoted in the *Akron Beacon-Journal*, July 3, 2002.

257.   "We were just trying to say": Quoted in the *Fayetteville Observer*, November 30, 2003.

257.   The company's president and CEO said: Kirk Yoshida, quoted in Business Wire, October 18, 2001, p. 2,352.

257.   "Marshall Field's is proud to resurrect a tradition": Quoted in the *Chicago Sun-Times*, May 24, 2003.

258.   "Originally, I was going to make little flags": Quoted in the Waynesboro and Greencastle (Pennsylvania) *Record Herald*, June 24, 2003.

258.   "I normally answer twenty-five to thirty questions, at most": Michael Buss, author interview, July 12, 2003.

259.   " . . . the President issued a proclamation to display the flag at half staff": According to W. G. Perrin in his book, *British Flags* (Cambridge University Press, 1922), flying a flag at half-staff

(also known as "half-mast") to honor the death of an individual dates from 1612 when a British sailing master was murdered by Eskimos in present-day Canada and the captain of his ship flew his flag halfway down on the mast as a sign of mourning. Many nations honor their dead in this fashion today, including the United States.

The U.S. Flag Code provides specific, detailed instructions on flying the flag at half-staff.

The Code authorizes the president of the United States to order that the flag be flown at half-staff "upon the death of principal figures" of the federal and state governments and for the deaths of notable private citizens. The flag is flown at half-staff for thirty days from the day of death of the president or a former president; for ten days on the death of the vice president, the chief justice, a retired Supreme Court chief justice, or the speaker of the House of Representatives; from the day of death until the burial of an associate justice of the Supreme Court, a member of the cabinet, a former vice president, the president pro tempore of the Senate, the majority and minority leaders of the Senate, or the majority and minority leaders of the House; and on the day of death and the next day for a senator, representative, territorial delegate, or resident commissioner.

The Code does not prohibit private individuals from displaying a flag at half-staff.

As far as flags that are permanently attached on a pole, two black ribbons may be tied on the flagpole—not on the flag—because the flags cannot be physically flown at half-staff, according to the National Flag Foundation.

"The flag, when flown at half-staff, should be hoisted to the peak for an instant, then lowered to the half-staff position," half the distance between the top and bottom of the staff, the Code notes. "The flag should be again raised to the peak before it is lowered for the day."

260.   "September 11 made it safe for liberals to be patriots": George Packer, "Recapturing the Flag," the *New York Times Magazine*, September 30, 2001, p. 15.

260. "So I was pleasantly surprised:" Quoted in "Patriot Practitioner," *American Enterprise,* September 2002.

260. "Definitely not, I say": Katha Pollitt, "Put Out No Flags," *The Nation,* October 8, 2001.

261. "That's the flag I served under": Quoted in The *Tennessean,* December 6, 2003.

262. "That's our flag," he said: Quoted in the *Washington Post,* December 22, 2003.

262. The flag, she said, "has, through sheer repetition, been reduced": Barbara Ehrenreich, "Citizen Curmudgeon," *Progressive,* February 2003.

262. "A lot of people blindly stand up and salute the flag": Quoted in the *New York Times,* February 26, 2003.

262. . . . whose uniforms contained an American flag patch on the right sleeve: Those patches show the flag with the canton on the right, in the "reversed field" position. That is because the flag is on the uniform's right sleeve and is intended to look as though it is blowing in the wind as the person who wears the flag walks forward. Flag patches worn on the left sleeve should have the canton on the left. Reversed field flags also appear on the right side of vehicles and planes, including Air Force One.

262. "It's imposing enough that we're coming into another society": Quoted in the *New York Times,* March 20, 2003.

263. "You can understand these Marines who have put their lives on the line": Quoted in the *New York Times,* April 3, 2003.

263. "You must respect the flag": Quoted by Reuters News, April 23, 2003.

263. . . . "You cannot display an American flag outside the FOB": Quoted in the *Washington Post,* July 5, 2004.

263. "We believe that the original form of the pall": Jon Austin, author interview, May 13, 2003.

264. "It was simply a matter that there was a shortage of caskets": Tom Sherlock, author interview, May 6, 2003.

264. It is folded . . . and presented to the next of kin at the end of the funeral: See "Flag Facts: Folding the United States Flag," National Flag Foundation, 2001.

264.   "There is no meaning to the triangle": Quoted in Corcoran, p. 143.

266.   "An immigrant comes to the country, moves to a territory": Jeffrey Kohn, author interview, September 4, 2003.

Bibliography

Books

Adams, Gridley, *So Proudly We Hail*, United States Flag Foundation, 1953.

Anderson, Terry H., *The Movement and the Sixties: Protest in America from Greensboro to Wounded Knee*, Oxford University Press, 1995.

Appleton, Nathan, *The Star-Spangled Banner*, Lockwood, Brooks, 1877.

Balch, George T., *Methods of Teaching Patriotism in the Public Schools*, D. Van Nostrand, 1890.

Barry, John W., *Masonry and the Flag*, The Masonic Service Association, 1924.

Beath, Robert Burns, *History of the Grand Army of the Republic*, Bryan, Taylor & Co. 1888.

Bennett, Mabel R., *So Gallantly Streaming*, Drake, 1974.

Berns, Walter, *Making Patriots*, University of Chicago Press, 2001.

Blumenthal, Sidney, *Pledging Allegiance: The Last Campaign of the Cold War*, HarperCollins, 1990.

Bodnar, John, ed., *Bonds of Affection: Americans Define Their Patriotism*, Princeton University Press, 1996.

Boime, Albert, *The Unveiling of National Icons: A Plea for Patriotic Iconoclasm in a Nationalist Era*, Cambridge University Press, 1998.

Bonner, Robert E., *Colors and Blood: Flag Passions of the Confederate South*, Princeton University Press, 2002.

Bradley, James, *Flags of Our Fathers*, Bantam, 2000.

Canby, George and Lloyd Balderston, *The Evolution of the American Flag*, Ferris & Leach, 1909.

Cooper, Grace Rogers, *Thirteen-Star Flags: Keys to Identification*, Smithsonian Institution Press, 1973.

Corcoran, Michael, *For Which It Stands: An Anecdotal Biography of the American Flag*, Simon & Schuster, 2002.

Cortwright, Edgar M., *Apollo Expeditions to the Moon*, U.S. Government Printing Office, 1975.

Crouthers, David D., *Flags of American History*, Hammond & Co. 1962.

Curtis, Michael Kent, ed., *The Constitution and the Flag*, Garland, 1993.

Davies, Wallace Evan, *Patriotism on Parade: The Story of Veterans' and Hereditary Organizations in America, 1783–1900*, Harvard University Press, 1955.

Dearing, Mary R., *Veterans in Politics: The Story of the G.A.R.*, Louisiana State University Press, 1952.

Delaplaine, Edward S., *Francis Scott Key: Life and Times*, Willow Bend Books, 2001.

Detzer, David, *Allegiance: Fort Sumter, Charleston, and the Beginning of the Civil War*, Harcourt, 2001.

Drake, Joseph Rodman, *The American Flag*, James G. Gregory, 1861.

Druckman, Nancy, and Jeffrey Kenneth Kohn, *American Flags: Designs for a Young Nation*, Abrams, 2003.

Eggenberger, David, *Flags of the U.S.A.*, Crowell, 1964.

Elliott, Peter, *Home Front: American Flags from Across the United States*, University of Chicago Press, 2003.

Fischer, David Hackett, *Washington's Crossing*, Oxford University Press, 2004.

Fisher, Leonard Everett, *Stars & Stripes: Our National Flag*, Holiday House, 1993.

Foner, Eric, *The Story of American Freedom*, W. W. Norton, 1998.

Fort, Ilene Susan, *The Flag Paintings of Childe Hassam*, Horizon Books, 1990.

Fow, John H., *The True Story of the American Flag*, William J. Campbell, 1908.

Freeman, Mae Blacker, *Stars and Stripes: The Story of the American Flag*, Random House, 1964.

Furlong, William Rea and Byron McCandless, *So Proudly We Hail: The History of the United States Flag*, Smithsonian Institution Press, 1981.

Goldstein, Robert Justin, *Burning the Flag: The Great 1989–1990 American Flag Desecration Controversy*, Kent State University Press, 1998.

Goldstein, Robert Justin, ed., *Desecrating the American Flag: Key Documents of the Controversy from the Civil War to 1995*, Syracuse University Press, 1996.

Goldstein, Robert Justin, *Flag Burning and Free Speech: The Case of Texas v. Johnson*, University Press of Kansas, 2000.

Goldstein, Robert Justin, *Saving Old Glory: The History of the American Flag Desecration Controversy*, Westview Press, 1995.

Gordon, John B., *Reminiscences of the Civil War*, Charles Scribner's Sons, 1904.

Guenter, Scot M., *The American Flag, 1777–1924: Cultural Shifts from Creation to Codification*, Associated University Press, 1990.

Hannings, Bud, *The Story of the American Flag*, Seniram, 2001.

Hastings, George E., *The Life and Works of Francis Hopkinson*, University of Chicago Press, 1926.

Healy, Nick, *The American Flag*, Lake Street Publishers, 2003.

Hendrickson, Robert, *Fort Sumter: The First Day of the Civil War*, Scarborough House, 1990.

Hickey, Donald R., *War of 1812: A Forgotten Conflict*, University of Illinois Press, 1989.

Higham, John, *Strangers in the Land: Patterns of American Nativism, 1860–1925*, 2nd ed., Rutgers University Press, 1988.

Hinrichs, Kit, and Delphine Hirasuna, *Long May She Wave: A Graphic History of the American Flag*, Ten Speed Press, 2001.

Hobswam, Eric, *Nations and Nationalism Since 1780: Programme, Myth, Reality*, Cambridge University Press, 1990.

Horner, Harlan Hoyt, *The American Flag*, State of New York Education Department, 1910.

Johannsen, Robert W., *To the Halls of Montezuma: The Mexican War in the American Imagination*, Oxford University Press, 1985.

Johnson, Willis Fletcher, *The National Flag: A History*, Houghton Mifflin, 1930.

Jones, Richard Seely, *A History of the American Legion*, Bobbs-Merrill, 1946.

Kazin, Michael, *The Populist Persuasion: An American History*, rev. ed., Cornell University Press, 1998.

Kohn, Hans, *American Nationalism: An Interpretive Essay*, Macmillan, 1957.

Kreitler, Peter Gwillim, *United We Stand: Flying the American Flag*, Chronicle Books, 2002.

Krythe, Maymie R., *What So Proudly We Hail: All About Our American Flag, Monuments, and Symbols*, Harper & Row, 1968.

Lord, Walter, *By the Dawn's Early Light*, W. W. Norton, 1972.

Lorenz, Lincoln, *John Paul Jones: Fighter for Freedom and Glory*, U.S. Naval Institute, 1943.

Manwaring, David Roger, *Render unto Caesar: The Flag Salute Controversy*, University of Chicago Press, 1962.

Marling Karal Ann, *Old Glory: Unfurling History*, Bunker Hill, 2004.

Marvin, Caroline and David W. Ingle, *Blood Sacrifice and the Nation: Totem Rituals and the American Flag*, Cambridge University Press, 1999.

Mayer, Jane, *Betsy Ross and the Flag*, Random House, 1952.

Mastai, Boleslaw and Marie-Louise D. Mastai, *The Stars and Stripes: The American Flag as Art and as History from the Birth of the Republic to the Present*, Alfred A. Knopf, 1973.

McCabe, John, *George M. Cohan: The Man Who Owned Broadway*, Doubleday, 1973.

McPherson, James M., *For Cause and Comrades: Why Men Fought in the Civil War*, Oxford University Press, 1998.

McPherson, James M., *What They Fought For: 1861–1865*, Anchor, 1995.

Miller, Margarette S., *Twenty-Three Words, A Biography of Francis Bellamy: Author of the Pledge of Allegiance*, Printcraft Press, 1976.

Moeller, Henry, *Shattering an American Myth: Unfurling the History of the Stars and Stripes*, Amereon House, 1992.

Molotsky, Irwin, *The Flag, The Poet, and the Song: The Story of the Star-Spangled Banner*, Dutton, 2001.

Morison, Samuel Eliot, *John Paul Jones: A Sailor's Biography*, Little, Brown, 1959.

Morris, Robert, *The Truth About the Betsy Ross Story*, Wynnehaven, 1982.

Moss, James A., *The Flag of Our United States: Its History and Symbolism*, Rand McNally & Co., 1940.

Moss, James A., *Our Country's Flag: The Symbol of All We Are — All We Hope to Be*, United States Flag Association, 1937.

Muller, Charles G., *The Darkest Day: 1814*, Lippincott, 1963.

O'Leary, Cecilia E., *To Die For: The Paradox of American Patriotism*, Princeton University Press, 2000.

Parrish, Thomas, *The American Flag: The Symbol of Our Nation Throughout Its History*, Simon & Schuster, 1973.

Parry, Edwin S., *Betsy Ross: Quaker Rebel*, John C. Winston Company, 1930.

Patterson, Richard S. and Richardson Dougall, *The Eagle and the Shield: A History of the Great Seal of the United States*, United States Department of State, 1976.

Pencak, William, *For God and Country: The American Legion, 1919–1941*, Northeastern University Press, 1989.

Perrin, W. G., *British Flags*, Cambridge University Press, 1922.

Pitch, Anthony, *The Burning of Washington: The British Invasion of 1814*, Naval Institute Press, 2004.

Preble, George Henry, *Origin and History of the American Flag*, 2 vols., Nicholas L. Brown, 1917.

———. *The History of the Flag of the United States*, A. Williams and Co., 1880.

Quaife, Milo M., Melvin J. Weig, and Roy E. Appleman, *The History of the American Flag; From the Revolution to the Present, Including a Guide to Its Use and Display*, Harper and Row, 1961.

Randall, Ruther Painter, *Colonel Elmer Ellsworth: A Biography of Lincoln's Friend and First Hero of the Civil War*, Little, Brown, 1960.

Richardson, Edward W., *Standards and Colors of the American Revolution*, University of Pennsylvania, 1982.

Robinson, Marlyn and Christopher Simoni, eds., *The Flag and the Law: A Documentary History of the Treatment of the American Flag by the Supreme Court and Congress*, vols. 1–4, William Hein & Co, 1992.

Roland, Mary J. Driver, *Old Glory: The True Story*, self-published, 1918.

Rowan, Bob, *Old Glory and Friends*, Unique Printing Services, 2002.

Rubin, David S., ed., *Old Glory: The American Flag in Contemporary Art*, Cleveland Center for Contemporary Art, 1994.

Schneider, Dick, *Stars & Stripes Forever: The History, Stories, and Memories of Our American Flag*, Morrow, 2003.

Sedeen, Margaret, *Star-Spangled Banner: Our Nation and its Flag*, National Geographic Society, 1993.

Skinner, Peter, ed., *God Bless America: The American Flag Book: 120 Stories, Poems and Quotations About the American Flag*, Megapolis, 2002.

Smith, Whitney, *The Flag Book of the United States*, Morrow, 1975.

———. *Flags and Arms Across the World*, McGraw-Hill, 1980.

———. *Flags Through the Ages and Across the World*, McGraw-Hill, 1975.

———. *Honor the Flag: The United States Flag Code Annotated and Indexed*, Flag Research Center, 1998.

Sollod, Celeste, ed., *The American Flag*, Friedman / Fairfax, 2001.

Sonneck, Oscar George Theodore, *Report on "the Star-Spangled Banner" "Hail Columbia" "America" "Yankee Doodle,"* Dover, 1972.

Stewart, Charles W., *Stars and Stripes: A History of the United States Flag*, Boylston Publishing Co., 1915.

Taylor, Lonn, *The Spangled Banner: The Flag That Inspired the National Anthem*, Harry N. Abrams, 2000.

Tuchman, Barbara W., *The First Salute: A View of the American Revolution*, Alfred A. Knopf, 1988.

Virga, Vincent, *Eyes of the Nation: A Visual History of the United States*, Alfred A. Knopf, 1997.

Waldstreicher, David, *In the Midst of Perpetual Fetes: The Making of American Nationalism, 1776–1820*, University of North Carolina Press, 1997.

Whipple, Wayne, *The Story of the American Flag*, Henry Altemus, 1910.

Williams, Earl P. Jr., *What You Should Know About the American Flag*, Maryland Historical Press, 1987.

Zaroulis, Nancy and Gerald Sullivan, *Who Spoke Up? American Protest Against the War in Vietnam, 1963–1975*, Doubleday, 1984.

Articles, Reports, and Studies

American Vexillum magazine, selected issues.

Baer, John, *The Pledge of Allegiance: A Centennial History*, 1992, published online at http://history.vineyard.net/pdgecho.htm

Bonner, Robert E., "Flag Culture and the Consolidation of Confederate Nationalism," *Journal of Southern History*, May 2002.

Boutilier, Emily Gold, "What One Man's Obsession Reveals About the Stars and Stripes," *Brown Alumni Magazine*, May/June 2002.

Brandt, Nat, "To the Flag," *American Heritage*, June 1971.

Carr, Fred, "Marine Corps War Memorial Sculptor Honored at Sunset Parade, *Henderson Hall News*, June 12, 1998.

Carlson, Sarah-Eva H., "Preparing for War: Ellsworth, the Militias, and the Zouaves," *Illinois History*, February 1996.

Carson, Jane, "The First American Flag Hoisted in Old England," *The William and Mary Quarterly*, July 1954.

Clausen, Christopher, "Pledge of Allegiance," *The American Scholar*, Winter 2003.

Conniff, Ruth, "Patriot Games," *The Progressive*, January 2002.

Conover, Kirsten A., "Fluent in the Language of Flags: Every Year Is a Banner Year for Whitney Smith," *Christian Science Monitor*, July 2, 1990.

"Decalomania Over the American Flag," *Life*, July 18, 1969.

Dougherty, Steven, "When the World Runs Something New Up the Flagpole, Scholar Whitney Smith Is the First to Salute," *People Weekly*, June 17, 1985.

Fawcett, Charles, "The Striped Flag of the East India Company and Its Connection with the American 'Stars and Stripes,'" *The Journal of The Society for Nautical Research*, October 1937.

Fetto, John, "Patriot Games," *American Demographics*, July 2000.

Flag Bulletin, The, selected issues.

"Flag Facts," National Flag Foundation, 2001.

"The Fort Sumter Flags: A Study in Documentation and Authentication," U.S. Department of the Interior, National Park Service, Harpers Ferry Center 1981.

Gelb, Norman, "Reluctant Patriot," *Smithsonian*, September 2004.

Gitlin, Todd, "Patriotism Is Sticky," *The American Scholar*, summer 2003.

Goldstein, Robert Justin, "The Great 1989–90 Flag Flap: An Historical, Political and Legal Analysis, *University of Miami Law Review*, vol. 45, September 1990.

Goldstein, Robert Justin, "The Vietnam War Flag Flap," *The Flag Bulletin*, vol. 153, August 1993.

"The Great Seal of the United States," U.S. Department of State, Bureau of Public Affairs, July 2003.

Griffis, William Elliot, "Where Our Flag Was First Saluted," *The New England Magazine*, July 1893.

Grossman, Lloyd, "Why We Love the Flag and the Frontier," *New Statesman*, December 17, 2001.

Haskin, Frederic, J., "Flags of the United States," National Capital Press, 1941.

Hayes, Stephen F., "Fly the Flag—Or Else," *Reason*, April 2001.

Holzer, Harold, "New Glory for Old Glory: A Lincoln-Era Tradition Reborn," *White House Studies*, spring 2002.

House, R. C., "Iwo Jima: Its Heroes and Flag," *World War II*, January 2000.

Jones, Jeffrey Owen, "The Pledge's Creator," *Smithsonian*, November 2003.

Jost, Kenneth, "Patriotism in America," *CQ Researcher*, June 25, 1999.

Kashatus, William C., "Seamstress for a Revolution: An Intriguing Controversy Surrounds Betsy Ross and the Making of the First American Flag," *American History*, August 2002.

Kaufmann, Bill, "The Bellamy Boys Pledge Allegiance," *The American Enterprise*, October–November 2002.

Kazin, Michael, "A Patriotic Left," *Dissent*, fall 2002.

Kernan, Michael, "Saving the Nation's Flag," *Smithsonian*, October 1998.

Kohn, Jeffrey Kenneth, "Stars & Stripes: Star-Spangled Style Has Inspired Artisans and Advertisers Alike," *Country Living*, July 2002.

Lax, John and William Pencak, "Creating the American Legion," *The South Atlantic Quarterly*, winter 1982.

"Let's Be Right on Flag Etiquette," National Americanism Commission, The American Legion, January 2002.

"Let the People Decide," The Citizens Flag Alliance, 2000.

Luckey, John, "Flag Protection: A Brief History and Summary of Recent Supreme Court Decisions and Proposed Constitutional Amendments," Congressional Research Service, Library of Congress, January 27, 2003.

Luckey, John, "The United States Flag: Federal Law Relating to Display and Associated Questions," Congressional Research Service, Library of Congress, June 14, 2000.

Marling, Karal Ann, "The Stars and Stripes, American Chameleon," *The Chronicle of Higher Education*, October 16, 2001.

Martz, John D. Jr., "The Story Behind a New Star for the Flag," *Army Information Digest*, July 1959.

"The Middle Americans: Person of the Year," *TIME*, January 5, 1970.

"Old Glory: A Beloved National Symbol Woven into the Fabric of American Life," U.S. Postal Service, 2003.

Old Glory News, Citizens Flag Alliance, selected issues.

"Old Glory's Strength," *The Economist*, July 3, 1999.

Packer, George, "Recapturing the Flag," *The New York Times Magazine*, September 30, 2001.

Park, Edwards, "Our Flag Was Still There," *Smithsonian*, July 2000.

Paul, Marilyn H., "I Pledge Allegiance . . . ," *Prologue: Quarterly of the National Archives*, winter 1992.

Platoff, Anne, "Where No Flag Has Gone Before: Political and Technical Aspects of Placing a Flag on the Moon," NASA Contractor Report 188251, August 1993.

Presto, Gregory, "The Stars and Stripes Forever," *Northwestern*, summer 2003.

Rankin, H. F., "The Naval Flags of the American Revolution," *William and Mary Quarterly*, vol. XI, July 1954.

Rogers, John, "New Wave," *Landscape Architecture*, July 2003.

Ruffin, Edmund, "The First Shot at Fort Sumter," *William and Mary Quarterly Historical Magazine*, October 1911.

Ryder, James F., "The Painter of 'Yankee Doodle,'" *The New England Magazine*, December 1895.

Sanders, Lisa, *et al.*, "All-American Ads: Marketers Rally Around Flag but Try Not to Push Patriotism, Too," *Advertising Age*, September 24, 2001.

Schlesinger, Arthur M. Jr., "The Flag: Who Owns Old Glory?" *Rolling Stone*, May 15, 2003.

Schultz, Fred L., "United We Stood, 1942," *Naval History Magazine*, August, 2002.

Smith, Whitney, "One Nation Under God: The Crusade to Capture the American Flag," *American Atheist*, summer 2001.

Solis-Cohen, Lisa, "More Flags at Sotheby's," *Maine Antique Digest*, October 2002.

Southgate, M. Therese, "Allies Day, May 1917," *Journal of the American Medical Association*, May 24–31, 2000.

Stafford, Marie Peary, "The Peary Flag Comes to Rest," *National Geographic*, October 1954.

"Stars and Hypes," *Forbes Magazine*, December 24, 2001.

"The Story of the American Flag," *National Geographic*, October 1917.

Sullivan, John L., Amy Fried, Mary G. Dietz, "Patriotism, Politics and the Presidential Election of 1988," *American Journal of Political Science*, February 1992.

Svejda, George J., "History of the Star-Spangled Banner from 1814 to the Present," U.S. Department of the Interior, 1969.

Timmons, Carlin and Sandy Pusey, "Fort Sumter National Monument's New Facility at Liberty Square," *Cultural Resource Management*, National Park Service, vol. 25, No. 4, 2002.

Wellner, Alison Stein, "The Perils of Patriotism," *American Demographics*, September 2002.

Whiteside, Rob, "Through the Perilous Fight: When Americans Suit Up in the Flag, *Harper's Magazine*, July 2002.

Williams, Earl P., Jr. "The 'Fancy Work' of Francis Hopkinson: Did He Design the Stars and Stripes?" *Prologue: Quarterly of the National Archives*, spring 1988.

Wilson, Jim, "Defending the Flag: Conservators Work to Preserve and Restore the Original American Flag," *Popular Mechanics*, July 2000.

Wolkomir, Richard, "Near and Far, We're Waving the Banner for Flags," *Smithsonian*, June 1997.

Wu, Corinna, "Old Glory, New Glory: The Star-Spangled Banner Gets Some Tender Loving Care," *Science News,* June 26, 1999.

Wulf, Steve, "Old Glory and New Wounds: The True Meaning of the Flag Is Lost in the World of Sports," *Sports Illustrated,* February 25, 1991.

Index